P9-DHF-783

William Shakespeare was born in Stratford-upon-Avon in April 1564, and his birth is traditionally celebrated on April 23. The facts of his life, known from surviving documents, are sparse. He was one of eight children born to John Shakespeare, a merchant of some standing in his community. William probably went to the King's New School in Stratford, but he had no university education. In November 1582, at the age of eighteen, he married Anne Hathaway, eight years his senior, who was pregnant with their first child, Susanna. She was born on May 26, 1583. Twins, a boy, Hamnet (who would die at age eleven), and a girl, Judith, were born in 1585. By 1592 Shakespeare had gone to London, working as an actor and already known as a playwright. A rival dramatist, Robert Greene, referred to him as "an upstart crow, beautified with our feathers." Shakespeare became a principal shareholder and playwright of the successful acting troupe, the Lord Chamberlain's Men (later, under James I, called the King's Men). In 1599 the Lord Chamberlain's Men built and occupied the Globe Theatre in Southwark near the Thames River. Here many of Shakespeare's plays were performed by the most famous actors of his time, including Richard Burbage, Will Kempe, and Robert Armin. In addition to his 37 plays, Shakespeare had a hand in others, including *Sir Thomas More* and *The Two Noble Kinsmen*, and he wrote poems, including *Venus and Adonis* and *The Rape of Lucrece*. His 154 sonnets were published, probably without his authorization, in 1609. In 1611 or 1612 he gave up his lodgings in London and devoted more and more of his time to retirement in Stratford, though he continued writing such plays as *The Tempest* and *Henry VIII* until about 1613. He died on April 23, 1616, and was buried in Holy Trinity Church, Stratford. No collected edition of his plays was published during his lifetime, but in 1623 two members of his acting company, John Heminges and Henry Condell, put together the great collection now called the First Folio.

William Shakespeare

MEASURE FOR MEASURE
ALL'S WELL THAT ENDS WELL
TROILUS AND CRESSIDA

Edited by
David Bevington
and
David Scott Kastan

BANTAM CLASSIC

MEASURE FOR MEASURE
ALL'S WELL THAT ENDS WELL
TROILUS AND CRESSIDA
A Bantam Book / published by arrangement with Pearson Education, Inc.

PUBLISHING HISTORY
Scott, Foresman edition published January 1980
Bantam edition, with newly edited text and substantially revised, edited, and
amplified notes, introduction, and other materials / February 1988
Bantam reissue with updated notes, introduction,
and other materials / March 2006

Published by Bantam Dell
A Division of Random House, Inc.
New York, New York

All rights reserved
Copyright © 2004 by Pearson Education, Inc.
Volume introduction copyright © 1988, 2006 by David Bevington
Cover art copyright © 1988 by Mark English
This edition copyright © 2006 by Bantam Books
Revisions and annotations to Shakespeare texts and their footnotes
and textual notes, Shakespeare's Sources essays and notes for the source,
and the individual play introductions © 1988, 2006 by David Bevington
The Playhouse text © 1988 by David Bevington
Measure for Measure, All's Well That Ends Well, and *Troilus and Cressida,* on Stage
and on Screen, © 1988, 2006 by David Bevington and David Scott Kastan
Memorable Lines © 1988, 2006 by Bantam Books
Annotated bibliographies © 1988, 2006 by David Scott Kastan
and James Shapiro

Valuable advice on staging matters has been provided by Richard Hosley
Collations checked by Eric Rasmussen
Additional editorial assistance by Claire McEachern

Book design by Virginia Norey

Library of Congress Catalog Card Number: 87-19539

If you purchased this book without a cover, you should be aware that this book
is stolen property. It was reported as "unsold and destroyed" to the publisher,
and neither the author nor the publisher has received any payment for this
"stripped book."

Bantam Books and the rooster colophon are registered trademarks of
Random House, Inc.

ISBN-10: 0-553-21287-7
ISBN-13: 978-0-553-21287-7

Printed in the United States of America
Published simultaneously in Canada
OPM   9 8 7 6

CONTENTS

❧

SHAKESPEARE'S PROBLEM PLAYS

❧

The three plays in this volume are pivotal in Shakespeare's development as an artist. Written between 1601 and 1604, they are later than most of the romantic comedies, such as *A Midsummer Night's Dream* (c. 1594–1595), *Much Ado About Nothing* (c. 1598–1599), *As You Like It* (c. 1598–1600), and *Twelfth Night* (1600–1602). They are instead contemporaneous with several of Shakespeare's greatest tragedies, including *Hamlet* (c. 1599–1601), *Othello* (c. 1603–1604), and *King Lear* (c. 1605). Two of these dark plays, *All's Well That Ends Well* and *Measure for Measure*, are comedies in that they end in forgiveness and marriage; yet their resolutions are so perilously achieved that we remain troubled by the image of a dark world of human failing in which the comic spirit must struggle to survive. The third play in this group, *Troilus and Cressida*, cannot be said to be a comedy at all, though it is not a true tragedy either: in it, the love affair between Troilus and Cressida ends dismally, but without the death of either lover, while the Trojan War produces nothing more conclusive than a stalemate and the unchivalric slaughter of Hector by Achilles. The uncertainty we feel about the genre of *Troilus and Cressida* seems appropriate for this period in Shakespeare's career, when he was turning from romantic comedy and English historical drama to tragedy.

These three plays are sometimes grouped together under the generic label of "problem plays." The label is, to be sure, a convenience of modern literary criticism and one that can be challenged. The first complete edition of Shakespeare's plays, the First Folio (1623), simply includes *All's Well* and *Measure for Measure* among Shakespeare's comedies; of the three, only *Troilus and Cressida* appears as an anomaly, inserted late in the printing process between the histories and comedies. Not until the late nineteenth century was the term "problem play" applied by F. S. Boas to these plays (referring both to the difficulty of categorizing them and to the problematic nature of evil and of love presented in them), and the exact definition of the group remains in dispute. Boas himself included *Hamlet* (as did E. M. W. Tillyard), while other scholars, such as Ernst Schanzer and Peter Ure, have applied the term to *Julius Caesar, Antony and Cleopatra,* and *Timon of Athens.* One can argue, moreover, that the problematic nature of evil intrudes into Shakespearean comedy well before 1601: in Shylock's murderous threat against Antonio (*The Merchant of Venice*), in Don John's slander of Hero (*Much Ado About Nothing*), or even in old Egeon's rendezvous with public execution for violating the laws of Ephesus (*The Comedy of Errors*). In fact, Shakespearean comedy regularly delivers its long-suffering and deserving protagonists from the perils of exile, separation, and character assassination, as well as the prospect or illusion of death.

Despite all these qualifications, which in fact point to the remarkable continuity of Shakespeare's artistic development, a strong case can be made for there being a cohesiveness among the three plays included in this volume. To begin with, the fictional worlds of these plays are generally darker than those of the earlier romantic comedies; Shakespeare presents us with a whole world in conflict with itself. The mood of *All's Well* is elegiac; many of its most attractive figures, such as the Countess and Lafew, are old (a surprising thing in a comedy), while the young, particularly Bertram and Parolles, are apt to be callow. Repeatedly this play expresses a longing for a better world now seemingly vanished, one that is appreciated only when it is no longer present to be enjoyed: "That's good that's gone" (5.3.61). The world of Vienna in *Measure for Measure* is morally corrupt at every level; much of the joking is about venereal disease, copulation, police incompetence, and the roguish attempts of pimps and bawds to stay one step ahead of the law. War is the pervasive fact of life in *Troilus and Cressida,* and an especially unglamorous war at that, one for which "all the argument is a whore and a cuckold" (2.3.71–2). Again the acerbic humor tends to center on diseases, lechery, and infidelity. Small wonder that the lovers in these surroundings find themselves threatened by a sense of universal human failure of which their own inadequacy is an inescapable part.

A significant corollary of this sense of universal malaise is that the lovers of the problem plays find themselves confronted with problems not external to themselves but within themselves. Unlike the young lovers of A Midsummer Night's Dream, who must find a way to circumvent stern parental edicts and the harsh Athenian law, or the revelers of Twelfth Night, who must do battle with Malvolio as a mirthless defender of propriety, the young people of the problem plays must examine their own affections. A chief difficulty in All's Well is that Bertram cannot bring himself to accept the love of a young woman who, though below him in social station, is regarded by all observers as worthy and virtuous. Helena, for her part, adds to the problem by being aggressive in her pursuit of Bertram and all too ready to assume that love is something she can deserve. The French King, in his gratitude and admiration for what Helena has done to cure him, is perhaps obtuse in his insistence that Bertram marry according to the King's choice. Love is, in any event, a problem. Angelo, in Measure for Measure, discovers to his horror that he is by no means free of the lecherous impulse that runs rampant in Vienna; his appetite for self-destructive lust shows itself to be limitless and vile when, seemingly, no one is in authority over him. The lovers in Troilus and Cressida are separated by an external obstacle, the war, and yet their failures too are ultimately internal: though Troilus protests his undying devotion to Cressida, a misplaced idealism prompts him to agree that she be returned to the Greeks, whereupon she despairingly surrenders to the faithless role expected of her by Troilus and by all the men she meets.

To say, however, that love is deeply problematic in these three plays is not to criticize them as defective comedies. Shakespeare seems to have turned away consciously from the protective situations of his earlier romantic comedies in which the young women are so unthreatening and even at first so unsexual (frequently taking the disguise of young men), or of his history plays in which women seldom appear as romantic partners for the men. With the problem plays we enter a complex world, not unlike that of *Hamlet* or *Othello*, in which women can be threatening indeed, in good part because men's need to possess and use women leaves men deeply vulnerable to the fear (usually illusory) of being betrayed. Women occupy a dependent status in such a world, but they have the power to deny what men seem to need most, the sense of superiority and proprietorship. In this potentially tragic configuration Shakespeare discovers a source of dramatic conflict only hinted at in earlier comedies, such as *Much Ado About Nothing*. It is a conflict that tests the very generic limits of comedy and makes problematic the achievement of comic resolution, but it does so with a candor about human sexuality that greatly enlarges the consequences of erotic passion.

The failure of young men to deal with threatening sexuality is particularly vivid in *All's Well* and *Measure for Measure*. Gone from these plays are the friendly encounters of Orlando and Rosalind in *As You Like It*, or of Orsino and Viola in *Twelfth Night*, enabling men to ease gracefully into the role of wooer. Instead, Bertram, in *All's Well*, finds himself pursued by an attractive and importunate young woman, Helena, and so chooses to go off to war with his male friends instead. Bertram refuses to be one who, in Parolles's words, "hugs his kicky-wicky here at home, / Spending his manly marrow in her arms" (2.3.281–2). Bertram is all too ready to seduce another young woman whom he thinks he can possess and then discard, but the demands of a serious commitment unnerve him and challenge his sense of masculinity. Angelo in *Measure for Measure* suffers from a similarly bifurcated view of women: he thinks himself above erotic entanglement, only to discover that he lusts after a young woman, Isabella, who is on the verge of entering a convent. Feminine modesty can more easily betray Angelo's sensual nature than immodesty; Isabella's very purity inspires in Angelo a perverse desire to "raze the sanctuary" (2.2.176–8). Angelo and Bertram are so frightened by the claims of mature sexuality that they must be tricked into the adult role they are so unwilling to embrace. An ethically dubious "bed trick" is necessary in both cases to trap the erring male into fulfilling the heterosexual role that he physically craves but irresponsibly abuses; he must be taught that sexual pleasure and the mature responsibilities of marriage go hand in hand.

Troilus and Cressida depicts Troilus in much the same immature and callow terms as Bertram and Angelo; though not inconstant in love, he is possessive, demanding, insecure. The main difference in this play, and perhaps a chief reason that the play moves further toward tragic engagement, is that Cressida fails to be constant in a way that Helena, Isabella, and Mariana do not. Bereft of the steadying presence of such heroines, who, whatever their own failings, make comedy at least problematically possible in their respective plays, *Troilus and Cressida* can end only in disillusionment and surrender to the encroaching spirit of appetite, that "universal wolf" (1.3.121). The portrayal of Cressida is thus a major new step in Shakespeare's developing exploration of tragic dilemma. What is to save the erring and irresponsible male, so unwilling to face the demands of maturity, if the female is unable to nurture him or is repulsed finally by his way of using her? What if the woman is vulnerable, hurt, groping for sustenance from men despite her wariness of them, unable finally to be charitable or loyal in the light of her own embittered experience? The frightening answer, glanced at also in the "Dark Lady" sonnets, written perhaps at about the same time or shortly before these plays, does much to inform the generic uncertainty with which Shakespeare's problem plays (and especially *Troilus and Cressida*) hover between satiric comedy and tragedy.

UTRECHT UNIVERSITY LIBRARY

This early copy of a drawing by Johannes de Witt of the Swan Theatre in London (c. 1596), made by his friend Arend van Buchell, is the only surviving contemporary sketch of the interior of a public theater in the 1590s.

THE PLAYHOUSE

❧

From other contemporary evidence, including the stage directions and dialogue of Elizabethan plays, we can surmise that the various public theaters where Shakespeare's plays were produced (the Theatre, the Curtain, the Globe) resembled the Swan in many important particulars, though there must have been some variations as well. The public playhouses were essentially round, or polygonal, and open to the sky, forming an acting arena approximately 70 feet in diameter; they did not have a large curtain with which to open and close a scene, such as we see today in opera and some traditional theater. A platform measuring approximately 43 feet across and 27 feet deep, referred to in the de Witt drawing as the *proscaenium*, projected into the yard, *planities sive arena*. The roof, *tectum*, above the stage and supported by two pillars, could contain machinery for ascents and descents, as were required in several of Shakespeare's late plays. Above this roof was a hut, shown in the drawing with a flag flying atop it and a trumpeter at its door announcing the performance of a play. The underside of the stage roof, called the heavens, was usually richly decorated with symbolic figures of the sun, the moon, and the constellations. The platform stage stood at a height of 5½ feet or so above the yard, providing room under the stage for underworldly effects. A trapdoor, which is not visible in this drawing, gave access to the space below.

The structure at the back of the platform (labeled *mimorum aedes*), known as the tiring-house because it was the actors' attiring (dressing) space, featured at least two doors, as shown here. Some theaters seem to have also had a discovery space, or curtained recessed alcove, perhaps between the two doors—in which Falstaff could have hidden from the sheriff (*1 Henry IV,*

2.4) or Polonius could have eavesdropped on Hamlet and his mother (*Hamlet*, 3.4). This discovery space probably gave the actors a means of access to and from the tiring-house. Curtains may also have been hung in front of the stage doors on occasion. The de Witt drawing shows a gallery above the doors that extends across the back and evidently contains spectators. On occasions when action "above" demanded the use of this space, as when Juliet appears at her "window" (*Romeo and Juliet*, 2.2 and 3.5), the gallery seems to have been used by the actors, but large scenes there were impractical.

The three-tiered auditorium is perhaps best described by Thomas Platter, a visitor to London in 1599 who saw on that occasion Shakespeare's *Julius Caesar* performed at the Globe:

> The playhouses are so constructed that they play on a raised platform, so that everyone has a good view. There are different galleries and places [*orchestra, sedilia, porticus*], however, where the seating is better and more comfortable and therefore more expensive. For whoever cares to stand below only pays one English penny, but if he wishes to sit, he enters by another door [*ingressus*] and pays another penny, while if he desires to sit in the most comfortable seats, which are cushioned, where he not only sees everything well but can also be seen, then he pays yet another English penny at another door. And during the performance food and drink are carried round the audience, so that for what one cares to pay one may also have refreshment.

Scenery was not used, though the theater building itself was handsome enough to invoke a feeling of order and hierarchy that lent itself to the splendor and pageantry on stage. Portable properties, such as thrones, stools, tables, and beds, could be carried or thrust on as needed. In the scene pictured here by de Witt, a lady on a bench, attended perhaps by her waiting-gentlewoman, receives the address of a male figure. If Shakespeare had written *Twelfth Night* by 1596 for performance at the Swan, we could imagine Malvolio appearing like this as he bows before the Countess Olivia and her gentlewoman, Maria.

MEASURE
FOR MEASURE

INTRODUCTION

◆◆◆

"A play Caled Mesur for Mesur" by "Shaxberd" was performed at court, for the new King James I, by "his Maiesties plaiers" on December 26, 1604. Probably it had been composed that same year or in late 1603. The play dates from the very height of Shakespeare's tragic period, three years or so after *Hamlet*, contemporary with *Othello*, shortly before *King Lear* and *Macbeth*. This period includes very little comedy of any sort, and what there is differs markedly from the festive comedy of the 1590s. *Troilus and Cressida* (c. 1601–1602), hovering between satire and tragedy, bleakly portrays a hopeless love affair caught in the toils of a pointless and stalemated war. *All's Well That Ends Well* (c. 1601–1604) resembles *Measure for Measure* in its portrayal of an undeserving protagonist who must be deceived into marriage by the ethically ambiguous trick of substituting one woman for another in the protagonist's bed. *Measure for Measure*, perhaps the last such comedy from the tragic period, illustrates most clearly of all what critics usually mean by "problem comedy" or "problem play."

Its chief concern is not with the triumphs of love, as in the happy comedies, but with moral and social problems: "filthy vices" arising from sexual desire and the abuses of judicial authority. Images of disease abound in this play. We see corruption in Vienna "boil and bubble / Till it o'errun the stew" (5.1.326–7). The protagonist, Angelo, is for most of the play a deeply torn character, abhorring his own perverse sinfulness, compulsively driven to an attempted murder in order to cover up his lust for the heroine, Isabella. His soliloquies are introspective, tortured, focused on the psychological horror of an intelligent mind succumbing to criminal desire. The disguised Duke Vincentio, witnessing this fall into depravity and despair, can offer Angelo's intended victims no better philosophical counsel than Christian renunciation of the world and all its vain hopes. Tragedy is averted only by providential intervention and by the harsh trickery of "Craft against vice" (3.2.270), in which the Duke becomes involved as chief manipulator and stage manager. Of the concluding marriages, two are foisted on the bridegrooms (Angelo and Lucio) against their wills, whereas that of the Duke and Isabella jars oddly with his stoical teachings and with her previous determination to be a nun. The ending thus seems arbitrary; both justice and romantic happiness are so perilously achieved in this play that they seem inconsistent with the injustice and lechery that have prevailed until the last.

Yet the very improbability of the ending and the sense of tragedy narrowly averted are perhaps intentional. These features are appropriate, not only for problem comedy, but also for tragicomedy or comedy of forgiveness, overlapping genres toward which Shakespeare gravitated in his late romances. Angelo is, like Leontes in *The Winter's Tale* (or like Bertram in *All's Well That Ends Well* and Claudio in *Much Ado About Nothing*), an erring protagonist forgiven in excess of his deserving, spared by a benign, overseeing providence from destroying that which is most precious to him.

That providence is partly ascribed to divine intervention, as when the disguised Duke, at a loss for a means of saving Claudio from imminent death, and learning that a prisoner named Ragozine has just died and is enough like Claudio physically that his head can be substituted for that of Claudio as proof that an execution has taken place, exclaims, "Oh, 'tis an accident that heaven provides!" (4.3.77). Yet most of the "providential" oversight in this play is essentially theatrical and humanly devised. It is engineered by "the old fantastical Duke of dark corners" (4.3.156–7), the resourceful Vincentio. Indeed, this mysterious Duke becomes a kind of embodiment of the manipulations and sleights of hand through which this dark comedy achieves its improbable ends.

The play's title, *Measure for Measure*, introduces a paradox of human justice which this "problem" play cannot wholly resolve.

How are fallible humans to judge the sins of their fellow mortals and still obey Christ's injunction of the Sermon on the Mount: "Judge not that ye be not judged"? Three positions emerge from the debate: absolute justice at one extreme, mercy at the other, and equity as a middle ground. Isabella speaks for mercy, and her words ring with biblical authority. Since all humanity would be condemned to eternal darkness were God not merciful as well as just, should not humans also be merciful? The difficulty, however, is that Vienna shows all too clearly the effects of leniency under the indulgent Duke. Vice is rampant; stern measures are needed. Though he has not wished to crack the whip himself, the Duke firmly endorses "strict statutes and most biting laws, / The needful bits and curbs to headstrong steeds" (1.3.19–20). To carry out necessary reform, the Duke has chosen Angelo, spokesman for absolute justice, to represent him. Angelo's position is cold but consistent. Only by a literal and impartial administering of the statutes, he maintains, can the law deter potential offenders. If the judge is found guilty, he must pay the penalty as well. One difficulty here, however, is that literal enforcement of the statute on fornication seems ironically to catch the wrong culprits. Claudio and Juliet, who are about to be married and are already joined by a "true contract" of betrothal, are sentenced to the severest limit of the law, whereas the pimps and whores of Vienna's suburbs manage at first to evade punishment entirely. Angelo's deputy, Escalus, can only shake his head in dismay at this unjust result of strict justice. Angelo has not remembered fully the terms of his commission from the Duke: to practice both "Mortality and mercy" in Vienna, to "enforce or qualify the laws / As to your soul seems good." The attributes of a ruler, like those of God, must include "terror" but also "love" (1.1.20–67).

Escalus's compassionate and pragmatic approach to law illustrates equity or the flexible application of the law to particular cases. Because Claudio is only technically guilty (though still guilty), Escalus would pronounce for him a light sentence. Pompey and Mistress Overdone, on the other hand, require vigorous prosecution. The problem of policing vice is compounded by the law's inefficiency, as well as by erring human nature, which will never be wholly tamed. Constable Elbow, like Dogberry in *Much Ado*, is a pompous user of malapropisms, less clever by far than the criminals he would arrest. His evidence against Pompey is so absurdly circumstantial that Escalus is first obliged to let off this engaging pimp with a stern warning. Yet Escalus patiently and tenaciously attends to such proceedings, unlike Angelo, whose interest in the law is too theoretical. Escalus deals with day-to-day problems effectively. He orders reforms of the system by which constables are selected, instructs Elbow in the rudiments of his office, and so proceeds, ultimately, to an effective arrest. Vice is not eliminated; as Pompey defiantly points out, unless someone plans to "geld and splay all the youth of the city," they "will to't then" (2.1.229–33). Still, vice is held in check. Law can shape the outer person and hope for some inner reform. Even Pompey is taught a trade, albeit a grisly one, as an apprentice hangman. The law must use both "correction" and "instruction."

The solutions arrived at in the comic subplot do not fit the case of Angelo, for he is powerful enough to be above the Viennese law. Indeed, he tries finally to brazen it out, pitting his authority against that of the seemingly friendless Isabella, much like the biblical Elders when justly accused of immorality by the innocent Susannah. Society is on Angelo's side—even the well-meaning Escalus; only a seeming providence can rescue the defenseless. The Duke of Vienna, hovering in the background and seeing all that happens, intervenes just at those points when tragedy threatens to become irreversible. Moreover, the Duke is testing those he observes. As he says to Friar Thomas, explaining why he has delegated his power to Angelo: "Hence shall we see, / If power change purpose, what our seemers be" (1.3.53–4). The Duke obviously expects Angelo to fall. Indeed, he has known all along that Angelo had dishonorably repudiated his solemn contract to Mariana when her marriage dowry disappeared at sea (3.1.215–25). Like an all-seeing deity who keeps a reckoning of humanity's good and evil deeds, the Duke has found out Angelo's great weakness. As Angelo confesses, "I perceive Your Grace, like power divine, / Hath looked upon my passes" (5.1.377–8). Paradoxically, this seemingly tragic story of temptation and fall yields precious benefits of remorse and humility. Angelo is rescued from his self-made nightmare of seduction, murder, and tyranny. Knowing now that he is prone like other mortals to fleshly weakness, he knows also that he needs spiritual assistance and that, as judge, he ought to use mercy. Seen in retrospect, his panic, despair, and humiliation are curative.

The Duke is no less a problematic character than Angelo, Isabella, and the rest. Vienna's deep corruption is, in part, the result of his unwillingness to bear down on vice, and yet, rather than undertake to remedy the failure himself, this strange monarch elects to leave the business to one he suspects will make matters worse. The Duke has a great deal to learn about his own dislike of crowds, his complacent tolerance of human weakness, and his naive supposition that all his subjects speak well of him. He is a highly manipulative character, the one most responsible in the play for the ethically dubious solutions through which craft must be employed against vice. The comforting words of spiritual counsel he offers Claudio, Juliet, and the rest are spoken by a secular ruler fraudulently disguised as a friar. Certainly, the Duke is no allegorized god-figure, for all his omniscience and final role as both punisher and forgiver. As deus ex machina of this problem comedy, the Duke is human, frail, and vulnerable—as indeed he ought to be in a play that explores with such rich complexity the ironic distance between divine and human justice.

Yet, for all his manifest and even comic weaknesses, the Duke is finally the authority figure who must attempt to bring order to the imperfect world of Vienna. The devices he employs, including the bed trick, seem morally questionable and yet are palpable comic fictions that unmistakably notify us what genre we are watching. If the Duke's role is more that of artist than ruler or diety, his being so is appropriate to the artistically contrived and theatrical world that Shakespeare presents to us. Within the world of this play, the disguised Duke's chief function is to test the other characters and to mislead them intentionally into expecting the worst, in order to try their resolve. On a comic level, he exposes the amiable but loose-tongued Lucio as a slanderer against the Duke himself and devises for Lucio a suitably satirical exposure and witty punishment. More seriously, as confessor to Juliet, he assures her that her beloved Claudio must die on the morrow. As she ought, she penitentially accepts "shame with joy" and so is cleansed (2.3.37). Because the Duke is not really a friar, he does not have the spiritual authority to do this, and the ruse strikes us as theatrical, employing devices of illusion that actors and dramatists use. Even so, it provides real comfort for Juliet. The very theatricality of the illusion, by reminding us that we are in the theater, enables us to see the Duke as a kind of morally persuasive playwright who can change the lives of his characters for the better.

Similarly, the counsel of Christian renunciation offered to Claudio by the bogus friar (3.1) is at once illusory and comforting. The Duke's poignant reflection on the vanity of human striving is made ironic but not invalid by our awareness that we are viewing a deception with a seemingly benign purpose—that of persuading Claudio to see matters in their true perspective. The Duke characterizes life as a breath, a dreamlike "after-dinner's sleep," a fever of inconstancy in which timorous humans long fretfully for what they do not have and spurn those things they have. Claudio responds as he ought, resolving to "find life" by "seeking death" (3.1.5–43). He achieves this calm, however, in the face of certain execution; ironically, what he must then learn to overmaster is the desperate hope of living by means of his sister's dishonor. Claudio is broken by this test and perversely begs for a few years of guilty life at the cost of eternal shame for himself and Isabella. From this harrowing experience, he emerges at length with a better understanding of his own weakness and a greater compassion toward the weakness of others.

The searing encounter between Claudio and Isabella puts her to the test as well, and her response seems hysterical and no doubt prudish to modern audiences. She has much to learn about the complexities of human behavior. Although she is sincere in protesting that she would lay down her life for her brother and is correct, in the play's terms, to prefer virtue to mere existence, her tone is too strident. Like other major characters, she must be humbled before she can rise. She and Claudio must heed the Duke's essential admonition: "Do not satisfy your resolution with hopes that are fallible" (3.1.170–1). Only then, paradoxically, can Isabella and Claudio go on to achieve earthly happiness.

Isabella and Angelo are paradoxically alike. Both have retreated from the world of carnal pleasure into havens they regard as safe but that turn out not to work in the way they had hoped. Isabella longs for the restraints of the sisterhood into which she is about to enter. Her suspicions about human frailty can be seen in her testing of her brother; she fears he will fail her by begging life at the cost of her eternal shame, and when he does just that, she reacts with shrill condemnation and even hatred. This is a dark moment for Isabella, and she needs the spiritual counsel of the disguised Duke to enable her to forgive not only her brother but also herself. Angelo, meanwhile, has attempted to put down the rebellion of the flesh by suppressing and denying all such feeling in himself. We see him at first as the workaholic official who is not hesitant to condemn in others what he believes he is free of personally. He cherishes restraint as much as Isabella does, and that is why he is so terrified when the apparent absence of his only superior, the Duke, opens up to him the abyss of his own licentiousness. Once his word is law, Angelo perceives that he can play the tyrant and seducer without check. He is horrified to discover not only that he has ungovernable sexual longings within him but also that they perversely direct themselves toward a woman who is virginal and saintly. Why does he yearn to "raze the sanctuary" thus (2.2.178)? The revelation to him of his own innate evil is virtually tragic in the intensity of his self-loathing, and yet, in this strange comedy, this revelation is a first step toward coming to terms with his reprobate self. Until Angelo acknowledges the carnal within, he cannot begin looking for a way to understand

and accept this frailty. The Duke's test provides the means of self-discovery that Angelo cannot fashion on his own.

In her final testing, Isabella shows greatness of spirit. Here, Shakespeare significantly alters his chief sources, George Whetstone's *Promos and Cassandra* (1578), Giovanni Baptista Giraldi Cinthio's *Hecatommithi*, and Whetstone's *Heptameron of Civil Discourses*. In all these versions, the character corresponding to Angelo does actually ravish the heroine, and in the *Hecatommithi* he also murders her brother. Shakespeare, by withholding these irreversible acts, not only gives to Angelo a technical innocence, but also allows the Duke, as deus ex machina, to practice virtuous deception on Isabella one more time. Can she forgive the supposed murderer of her brother? Her affirmative answer confutes the Old Testament ethic of "An Angelo for Claudio, death for death" whereby "Like doth quit like, and measure still for measure" (5.1.417–19). Although Angelo concedes that he deserves to die for what he intended, the forfeit need not be paid so long as humanity can reveal itself capable of Isabella's godlike mercy.

With its apparently unsuitable marriages and its improbable plotting, *Measure for Measure* does end by dealing directly with the problems of human nature confronted in the earlier scenes. The bed trick (switching Mariana for Isabella) may seem a legalistic and contrived way to bring Angelo to terms with his own carnality, but it is instructive not only to him but also to Isabella; she, like Angelo, must learn to accept the realities of the human condition. By helping Mariana to achieve her legitimate desire to couple and marry, Isabella sees into her own need. Her begging for Angelo's life is not merely an act of forgiveness to an enemy; it is a gift of continued marriage to Mariana. This realization helps to prepare Isabella herself for a marriage that, although dramatically surprising on stage (and even rejected by her in some modern productions), may be intended to demonstrate her having given up the cloistered life for all that marriage signifies. *Measure for Measure* is thus essentially comic (unlike *Troilus and Cressida*), despite its harrowing scenes of conflict and its awareness of vice everywhere in human nature. The play celebrates the *felix culpa* of human nature, the fall from grace that is an integral part of humanity's rise to happiness and self-knowledge. Throughout, in the play's finest scenes, poignancy is tempered by a wit and humor that are ultimately gracious. The formal and substantive emphasis on marriage stresses not just the benefits of remorse and humility but also the real possibility of psychic and spiritual growth: Isabella can acknowledge that she is a woman, Angelo can be genuinely freed from repression, and Claudio can value life more intensely because he has confronted death. All these recognitions affirm the acceptance and proper use of the physical and sexual side of human nature, and yet they are achieved only through charity and forgiveness. Humanity can learn, however slowly and painfully, that the talents entrusted to it by providence are to be used wisely.

The guardedly hopeful reading of the play offered here is, to be sure, not the only way in which it can be understood. The history of *Measure for Measure* on stage and screen highlights much that is problematic and troubling about it. For virtually all of the seventeenth, eighteenth, and nineteenth centuries, after its initial production, the play disappeared from the theater, other than in a heavily rewritten adaptation of the Restoration period and an even more radically recast nineteenth-century operatic version by Richard Wagner called *Das Liebesverbot* ("Forbidden Love"). The play was, it seems, too disagreeable for audiences in those centuries, too given over to vice and moral ambiguity. Readers were sometimes warned away from it. The twentieth and twenty-first centuries, conversely, have found in *Measure for Measure* a persuasive and even devastating dramatization of human imperfection. In an age that has learned to distrust authority figures, Duke Vincentio can come across as officious and sadistic in his manipulation of human lives, rather than ultimately benign. Then, too, the marriages with which the play ends are often held up to skeptical scrutiny. Is Angelo chastised by his searing experience into resolving to be a good husband to Mariana, or does he snarl at her when he is led off with her to be married? Most significantly, perhaps, does Isabella accept the surprising offer of marriage from the Duke who has protected her but also deceived her into believing that her brother was dead? Today, beginning with Estelle Kohler in John Barton's production at Stratford-upon-Avon in 1970, actresses and directors get to choose; since Isabella is given no lines indicating her acceptance, the actress may simply be bewildered or may decide, with a gesture of defiance or indifference, to have nothing to do with men. The range of options is extraordinary, and helps demonstrate the way in which Shakespeare provides such an unsettling challenge to actors, directors, and audiences alike. See stage and screen histories, below, for detailed history and analysis.

MEASURE FOR MEASURE
ON STAGE

❧

Measure for Measure has been a controversial and sometimes neglected play through much of its stage history. With an ethically dubious bed trick, impersonations of religious authority, a whimsical presentation of civil authority, and a detailed exploration of the world of vice in Vienna, the play has had to wait for the twentieth century to find audiences that could be amused and challenged by the work as Shakespeare wrote it. As with the other problem plays, *All's Well That Ends Well* and *Troilus and Cressida*, Shakespeare seems to have written a play that was centuries ahead of its time.

A performance of "Mesur for Mesur" by "Shaxberd" and acted by the King's Men took place, according to the Revels Accounts, at the palace at Whitehall on December 26, 1604. No other performance is known to have occurred until the Restoration, when, on February 18, 1662, diarist Samuel Pepys saw the Duke's company at the theater in Lincoln's Inn Fields, London, in *The Law against Lovers*. Pepys thought it "a good play and well performed, especially the little girl's (whom I never saw act before) dancing and singing." The remarkable innovations introduced by William Davenant as he adapted Shakespeare's play suggest the extent to which *Measure for Measure* was thought to be in need of "improvement." The "little girl" so much admired by Pepys is Viola (from *Twelfth Night*), now a younger sister of Beatrice, who, along with Benedick, is imported from *Much Ado About Nothing*. Benedick is made a brother to Angelo, while Beatrice is Angelo's ward. Benedick and Beatrice are soon involved in a plot to liberate Claudio (the Claudio of *Measure for Measure*) and his lover Juliet from jail.

Juliet is Beatrice's cousin (Hero is nowhere to be seen), in a much augmented role. It is she, not Claudio, who begs Isabella to save Claudio's life at the expense of her chastity, in reply to which Isabella proposes that Juliet instead take her place in Angelo's bed. Juliet thus plays a part like that of Mariana in Shakespeare's play. Angelo turns out not to be the villain Shakespeare made him after all; he has long loved Isabella and tempts her only to test her virtue. Angelo is punished by the Duke for what he has done but is then permitted to marry Isabella. The low comedy is expunged, and even Lucio becomes nearly respectable. Pepys's little girl, Viola, sings a song, is then joined in a chorus ("Our Ruler has got the Vertigo of State") by Benedick, Beatrice, Escalus, and Lucio, and dances a saraband with castanets. The language of almost the whole play, said one observer, was "borrowed from Shakespeare, yet, where the language is rough or obsolete, our author has taken care to polish it."

Charles Gildon was the next to "improve" the play in his *Measure for Measure, or Beauty the Best Advocate*, acted at Lincoln's Inn Fields in 1699–1700 by Thomas Betterton (Angelo) and Anne Bracegirdle (Isabella) some five years after they and some other actors had seceded from the Theatre Royal in Drury Lane. Gildon did away with the additions from *Much Ado*, but otherwise his production shows again the preference of the age for avoiding moral blemishes and unpleasantness. The lowlife characters—Froth, Pompey, Mistress Overdone, Abhorson, Barnardine—all disappear, and Lucio is limited to the first scene. Because Angelo and Mariana have married in secret, the bed trick poses no problem of morality. Claudio too is clandestinely married to Juliet, and his speech to his sister on the horrors of death (a speech that also offended Davenant) is excused on the grounds that he is really asking that Juliet be looked after when he is dead. The characters are all redeemable, even noble, and marital propriety is never offended. The Duke does not marry Isabella. Gildon also flatters the taste of the age by adding to the music that Davenant had included. In fact the piece becomes nearly operatic. Escalus undertakes to honor

Angelo's birthday with a four-part masque. Musical episodes unfold as the play proceeds, providing a grand entry at the end of each act based on the fable of Dido and Aeneas and employing elaborate machinery to create the effects of storms, ships, witches, dancing furies, Phoebus and Venus in their chariots, Nereides and Tritons rising out of the sea, nymphs, morris dancers, and still more.

James Quin produced the play in 1720 at Lincoln's Inn Fields, with Quin as the Duke and Anna Seymour as Isabella, in a version that made some effort to restore Shakespeare's text to the stage. Quin revived the play the following year, and he chose it for his benefit performance in 1737 at Drury Lane in which Susannah Cibber appeared as Isabella. She then chose the play for her benefit the following year. Quin and Cibber acted the play at the Theatre Royal, Covent Garden, in the 1742–1743 season and again in 1746–1747. After Quin retired, Cibber regularly played Isabella opposite Henry Mossop.

The play was popular throughout the eighteenth century, having had the support of strong actors: in addition to Quin and Mossop as the Duke, William Smith successfully acted the role; Lacy Ryan acted Claudio; Charles Macklin, Lucio; and a succession of fine actresses, in addition to Susannah Cibber, played Isabella, including Peg Woffington, Hannah Pritchard, George Anne Bellamy, Mary Ann Yates, and above all Sarah Siddons (in 1779 and the following years). David Garrick staged the play at Drury Lane but never took a part himself. Sarah Siddons's brother, John Philip Kemble, had success with the play around the turn of the century, first taking the part of the Duke in 1794 at Drury Lane. Even in this era of relative success, however, the play was egregiously bowdlerized. John Bell's acting edition of 1773 suggests what audiences did and did not see. Mistress Overdone almost entirely disappears, along with the bawdy talk among Lucio and the gentlemen in scene 2. The trial of Pompey and Froth before Escalus is retained but with the excision of some seven pages of "absolute ribaldry." Pompey is kept mainly for his clowning in the prison scenes.

The nineteenth century evidently found even this remainder

of a play too much, and it was seldom performed. Kemble revived the play in 1803 at Covent Garden, and in 1811, in her last year on stage, Sarah Siddons performed the play eight times, despite the fact that she was now so weak with age that she needed the Duke's aid to rise after kneeling before him in the final scene. Eliza O'Neill successfully played Isabella at Covent Garden, in 1816, with Harriet Faucit (Helen Faucit's mother) as Mariana. William Charles Macready played the Duke for three performances at Drury Lane in 1824; and Samuel Phelps produced the play in 1846 at the Sadler's Wells Theatre. Adelaide Neilson was notable as Isabella at the Haymarket Theatre in 1876 and 1878, but the play did not appear again in London until 1893 when William Poel produced the play in the Royalty Theatre. Taking the role of Angelo, Poel converted the Royalty Theatre into a near replica of the Fortune playhouse (built in 1600) in order that he might present "an Elizabethan play under the conditions it was written to fulfill." In 1888 Helena Modjeska acted Isabella in the United States at the Hollis Street Theatre in New York. Oscar Asche revived the play in 1906 at London's Adelphi Theatre, playing Angelo, with Lily Brayton as Isabella.

Still, *Measure for Measure* did not seem an appropriate vehicle for the prosperous actor-managers such as Henry Irving and Herbert Beerbohm Tree. The play as Shakespeare wrote it seemed unnecessarily unpleasant and disreputable. When Richard Wagner wrote an operatic version called *Das Liebesverbot* (first performed in 1842), he converted Angelo into a romantic hero who has long been in love with Isabella, much as William Davenant had done in 1662. In 1906, when Shakespeare's play was put on by the Oxford University Dramatic Society, residents complained of its obscenity. Even the theater historian George Odell, writing in 1920, declared the play to be "exceedingly offensive" on stage and wondered if it should ever be acted.

In spite of a successful production at the Old Vic in 1933, directed by Tyrone Guthrie and starring Charles Laughton, the play continued to outrage public decency. In 1936 *The Scotsman* protested a production of the play in Edinburgh, and in the following year the inclusion of a production by Tyrone Guthrie in the Buxton Theatre Festival led Canon Charles Scott-Moncrieff to attack the festival organizers for allowing a play so obviously "disfigured" by its sexual preoccupations. This prudery seems no doubt quaint to modern audiences familiar with women's liberation and the sexual revolution. By 1950, Peter Brook could successfully direct John Gielgud (as Angelo) at Stratford-upon-Avon in an austere production in which the sordid and the sacred uncomfortably coexisted.

Today, the play perhaps demands an even tougher sensibility, and it is not uncommon to see Isabella refuse the surprising offer of marriage made by the Duke in act 5. Estelle Kohler, in John Barton's production in 1970 at Stratford-upon-Avon, was obviously shocked by the Duke's proposal and was left alone on stage as the Duke went off bewildered by her reaction. In a fine production at Stratford, Ontario, in 1975, Martha Henry, directed by Robin Phillips, expressed the resentment and pent-up fury of a woman thoroughly wronged by men and sharing with Mariana a sense of victimization. On the male side, the play's painful candor about sexuality has prompted searing performances of the roles of Angelo and Claudio. At Stratford-upon-Avon in 1962, Marius Goring played Angelo as a sado-masochistic Puritan whose public arrogance was countered by his private indulgence in flagellation. Jonathan Pryce, in Barry Kyle's 1978 production at Stratford-upon-Avon, appeared "trapped between duty and desire," repelled by his own actions but unable to resist Isabella. On the modern stage the Duke has also become a complex character, no longer a benign agent of an active Providence but an enigmatic meddler in the lives of others. Directors have not always taken kindly to him as an authority figure, and his management of affairs is apt to suggest a capricious universe in which all authority is lacking or flawed by self-indulgence. Perhaps the most extreme example of this tendency was Barrie Ingham's Duke in Keith Hack's 1974 production at Stratford-upon-Avon. Ingham's Duke was deeply implicated in the corruption of Vienna. His manipulations were transparently hypocritical, and he was obviously resented by those whose lives he undertook to manage. In the final act, he descended from the flies (the space over the stage where equipment and scenery are hung), literalizing his chosen role as a deus ex machina. In modern productions, Lucio has also come into his own as an ingratiating rake, no doubt overly licentious and loose-tongued but endearing and vivacious, as in Lenny Baker's performance in John Pasquin's 1976 production for the New York Shakespeare Festival at the Delacorte Theatre (starring Meryl Streep as Isabella and Sam Waterston as the Duke).

The comic figures thrive as well. Michael Bogdanov's *Measure for Measure* at Stratford, Ontario, in 1985 showed how far performances of this play have come from the sheltered days of Victorian England. Bogdanov's company positively reveled in decadence. For thirty minutes or so before showtime the theater became a cabaret with bar and barstools, actors who chatted with theatergoers in the lobby or lounged about talking inaudibly among themselves, a sleazy master of ceremonies announcing that gentlemen might not remove their trousers but that ladies could remove anything they wished, transvestite dancers, headline items about nightclub raids and drug charges, and the like. In the play itself Bogdanov added to rather than subtracted from the bawdy exchanges of Pompey and Lucio by some invented dialogue and some borrowings from the bordello scene in *Pericles*. Added business in Mistress Overdone's club provided at various times an entourage of soldiers and other customers, quantities of black leather, strobe lighting, the wail of sirens, and a raid in which policemen checked the aisles. For her scene at the Moated Grange, Mariana wore a "Walkman" radio and listened to rock music. Isabella (Barbara March) was a modern nun in black skirt and sweater, Angelo (Nicholas Pennell) an administrator in a business suit, the Provost an official in a blazer. The Duke (Alan Scarfe) made his reappearance in act 5 carrying his car keys, while off stage were heard the sounds of traffic, a helicopter, and television coverage.

It has not proven necessary, however, so literally to insist on the play's contemporaneousness in order to let this troubling play make its case to our own troubled world. In various ways, in various settings, modern productions have found ways to tap different aspects of the play to make gripping theater. In 1987, for the Royal Shakespeare Company in Stratford, Nicholas Hytner found a local habitation and a name for the play's focus on the tensions between private morality and public order in Weimar Germany, in its striking confrontation of social decadence and Nazi repression. In 1991, Trevor Nunn, at London's intimate Other Place, focused more on the play's psychological realities. Nunn set the play in late-nineteenth-century Vienna, seemingly to invoke the cultural world of Freud, who provided much of this production's subtext as well as the source for many of its physical details. Philip Madoc's bearded and bespectacled Duke was primarily interested in the psychopathology of Angelo's everyday life, while Nunn seemed primarily interested in the psychopathology of the Duke. All of the Duke's rule seemed an elaborate laboratory experiment; he watched the reunion of Isabella (Clare Skinner) and Claudio (Jason Durr) with the clinical interest of a scientist, and even his proposal to Isabella seemed motivated more by scientific curiosity about her response than by his own desire. Her silence and eventual acceptance seemed to gratify him mainly for confirming his hypothesis about how she would respond. In this production it was the Duke who was at the center of interest, a Duke who was capable of brilliant insights into everyone's motives but his own. The following year, in Stratford, Ontario, Michael Langham set the play in about the same time frame but in some less specific geographical locale. Stanley Silverman's atonal score set the tone of this discordant production, in which male sexual desire overwhelmed the hope for any genuinely reassuring human connections. Elizabeth Marvel's Isabella was, like Clare Skinner's in Nunn's production, unusually young and vulnerable, and when she was not terrified she was bewildered by the emotions she occasioned. Even the joyful reunion of Claudio and Isabella was undermined by the untimely proposal of the Duke, and the play ended with the sharp snapping off of the lights before she could respond to his outstretched hand.

In the fall of 1994, the Royal Shakespeare Company again

staged the play, this time directed by Stephen Pimlott. Pimlott offered a taut, moody production that was recognizably if indistinctly modern in its setting. Michael Feast's Duke was troubled and intense, bordering on the psychotic. He more than Angelo was the disturbing character in this production, voyeuristic and sadistic, leaving people and relationships damaged wherever he interfered. Alex Jennings's Angelo was precise and efficient, and if unappealing, hardly the danger the Duke, in his need to control, revealed himself to be. In 1998, Michael Boyd's production for the RSC similarly focused mainly on the Duke, but here less as the play's most disturbing character than as its most disturbed. Robert Glenister's Duke was first seen drinking alone in a dark room, trying to read his opening speech into a recording machine but fleeing in some advanced stage of alcoholic breakdown and leaving the appointment of Angelo (Stephen Boxer) to be heard in his absence. The sense was that disappointments and frustrations had driven the Duke both to drink and then to depart, leaving control to the cold and contemptuous Angelo. It was the contrasts and similarities of the two men that were at the center of this production, and pointedly the Duke regained his psychic composure only when he was once again fully in control.

London in 2004 saw two radically contrasting versions of the play in both production style and focus, and yet both offered eloquent testimony to the play's theatrical power. At the National Theatre, Simon McBurney directed a bleak, distressing *Measure for Measure*, in which Paul Rhys's Angelo was more a monster of self-loathing than a monster to be loathed, while David Traughton's enigmatic Duke was revealed as the greatest "seemer" of the play, withholding his power in order to trap his victims and revealing himself only at the end as the commanding figure he had always been. In the last moments of the play, a curtain in the back went up, obscenely revealing a double bed with a red rose on the pillow, somehow suggesting that all that had happened was part of his plan to get Isabella, half his age (and half his size), into bed with him. Though Naomi Frederick's Isabella was sexy and self-possessed, nothing had prepared her for this, and she stared out at the audience, stunned and gasping for words that would not come.

No more than a mile further down the south bank of the Thames, at the reconstructed Globe Theatre, Shakespeare's play appeared in a very different mode. Modern dress gave way to Jacobean costumes, a jarring contemporary sound design was replaced by the gentle tones of early instruments, and indeed the brutality of McBurney's production in which Isabella's inflexible chastity was the play's most appealing moral position found an answer in the Globe's gentler version dominated by Mark Rylance's Duke, who oversaw the action with a hesitant, bumbling charm. While never losing sight of the hypocrisy and vice of the play's Vienna, the Globe production treated it as venial rather than venal, remediable through the Duke's hopeful ministrations. If it had taken him some time to see the world clearly, by the end his actions had assured that all had worked out as well as it ever can in a fallen world; and even his awkward proposal to Isabella, as a mark of this production's difference from that at the National, though initially greeted with a distressed silence, was finally accepted, as she reached for his hand to join together in the company dance that generally ends Globe productions. Though the two London productions of 2004 could hardly be any more different, their mutual success testifies to the rich concentration of theatrical possibilities in this dense and difficult play and to the powerful imaginations of the theater professionals who continue to explore and expose unexpected aspects of it.

MEASURE FOR MEASURE
ON SCREEN

❧

For a play that ranks among Shakespeare's finest, *Measure for Measure* has received scant treatment in film or video. Indeed, the only production of note is that of the BBC in its television series the Shakespeare Plays. Produced by Cedric Messina and directed by Desmond Davis, this version has been widely regarded as easily the best of the series' first year, 1978–1979. As with *All's Well That Ends Well*, televised some two years later, this production capitalizes on television's ability to display lush interiors inspired by Dutch painters like Vermeer and Rembrandt, with closeups of characters interacting in a tense drama of sexual blackmail and attempted murder. The lighting and sets have won warm accolades. Tim Pigott-Smith, as Angelo, is a tortured, guilty man unable to resist the temptation to abuse the awesome power of the state unexpectedly put into his grasp; Kate Nelligan is convincing as an immensely serious young religious novice made painfully aware that she is the unwilling target of Angelo's lust and that her beauty has set him on. Especially in the searing encounters between these two, television is at its best in small-scale intensity of focus on emotionally charged confrontations. John McEnery, familiar to some viewers as Mercutio in Zeffirelli's 1968 *Romeo and Juliet*, takes the part of the engaging rascal Lucio. Kenneth Colley is an image-conscious and enigmatic Duke Vincentio. The courtroom scenes and large finale are less successful than the fine intimate scenes of moral conflict.

Measure for Measure
Filmography

1. 1942—*Dente per Dente*
Atlas Films
Giuseppe Gallia and Yorick Gentile, producers
Marco Elter, director

 Duke—Alfredo Varelli
 Angelo—Carlo Tamberlani
 Isabella—Caterina Boratto

2. 1979
BBC/Time-Life Television
Cedric Messina, producer
Desmond Davis, director

 Duke—Kenneth Colley
 Angelo—Tim Pigott-Smith
 Isabella—Kate Nelligan
 Claudio—Christopher Strauli
 Lucio—John McEnery
 Pompey—Frank Middlemass

3. 1994
BBC
Peter Cregeen, producer
David Thacker, director

 Duke—Tom Wilkinson
 Angelo—Corin Redgrave
 Isabella—Juliet Aubrey
 Claudio—Ben Miles

MEASURE
FOR MEASURE

The Names of All the Actors

VINCENTIO, *the Duke*
ANGELO, *the deputy*
ESCALUS, *an ancient lord*
CLAUDIO, *a young gentleman*
LUCIO, *a fantastic*
Two other like GENTLEMEN
PROVOST
THOMAS,
PETER, } *two friars*
[A JUSTICE]
[VARRIUS, *a friend of the Duke*]

ELBOW, *a simple constable*
FROTH, *a foolish gentleman*
CLOWN [Pompey, *a servant to Mistress Overdone*]
ABHORSON, *an executioner*
BARNARDINE, *a dissolute prisoner*

ISABELLA, *sister to Claudio*
MARIANA, *betrothed to Angelo*
JULIET, *beloved of Claudio*
FRANCISCA, *a nun*
MISTRESS OVERDONE, *a bawd*

[A SERVANT *of Angelo*
BOY *singer*
A MESSENGER *from Angelo*

Lords, Officers, Citizens, Servants, and other Attendants]

THE SCENE: *Vienna*

1.1 ❧ *Enter Duke, Escalus, lords, [and attendants].*

DUKE   Escalus.

ESCALUS   My lord.

DUKE

Of government the properties to unfold   3
Would seem in me t'affect speech and discourse,   4
Since I am put to know that your own science   5
Exceeds, in that, the lists of all advice   6
My strength can give you. Then no more remains   7
But that to your sufficiency   8
. . . . as your worth is able, 9
And let them work. The nature of our people,
Our city's institutions, and the terms   11
For common justice, you're as pregnant in   12
As art and practice hath enrichèd any   13
That we remember. There is our commission,

                              [*giving a paper*]

From which we would not have you warp.—Call
   hither,   15
I say, bid come before us Angelo.   [*Exit one.*]
What figure of us think you he will bear?   17

1.1 *Location: Vienna. The court of Duke Vincentio.*
3–4 Of . . . discourse For me to deliver an oration on the qualities
needed in governing well would make me seem enamored of my
own pomposity   **5 put to know** obliged to admit.   **science**
knowledge   **6 that** i.e., properties of government (line 3).
lists limits   **7 strength** power of mind   **8–9 But . . . able**
(The passage appears in the Folio as a single line. Several attempts
at emendation have been made, but the most plausible explanation
is that something has been deleted or inadvertently omitted.)
11 terms terms of court; or, modes of procedure   **12 pregnant**
well-informed   **13 art** learning, theory   **15 warp** deviate.
17 What . . . bear? i.e., How do you think he will do as my
substitute?

For you must know, we have with special soul   18
Elected him our absence to supply,   19
Lent him our terror, dressed him with our love,   20
And given his deputation all the organs   21
Of our own power. What think you of it?

ESCALUS
If any in Vienna be of worth
To undergo such ample grace and honor,   24
It is Lord Angelo.

      Enter Angelo.

DUKE   Look where he comes.

ANGELO
Always obedient to Your Grace's will,
I come to know your pleasure.

DUKE   Angelo,
There is a kind of character in thy life
That to th'observer doth thy history
Fully unfold. Thyself and thy belongings   30
Are not thine own so proper as to waste   31
Thyself upon thy virtues, they on thee.   32
Heaven doth with us as we with torches do,   33
Not light them for themselves; for if our virtues
Did not go forth of us, 'twere all alike   35

---

18 **special soul** all the powers of the mind; whole heart
19 **Elected** chosen.   **supply** fill, make up for   20 **terror**
power to inspire awe and fear   21 **his deputation** him as
deputy.   **organs** instruments   24 **undergo** bear the weight of
30 **belongings** attributes, endowments   31 **proper** exclusively
31–2 **as to . . . thee** that you can expend all your efforts
developing your own talents or use them solely for your own
advantage.   33 **torches** (Compare Jesus' command that we not
hide our light under a bushel, Matthew 5:14–16.)   35 **forth of
us** out of us and into the world.   **'twere all alike** it would be
exactly the same

As if we had them not. Spirits are not finely touched   36
But to fine issues, nor Nature never lends   37
The smallest scruple of her excellence   38
But, like a thrifty goddess, she determines   39
Herself the glory of a creditor,   40
Both thanks and use. But I do bend my speech   41
To one that can my part in him advertise.   42
Hold, therefore, Angelo:
In our remove be thou at full ourself.   44
Mortality and mercy in Vienna   45
Live in thy tongue and heart. Old Escalus,
Though first in question, is thy secondary.   47
Take thy commission.   [*He gives a paper.*]

ANGELO   Now, good my lord,
Let there be some more test made of my mettle   49
Before so noble and so great a figure
Be stamped upon it.

DUKE   No more evasion.
We have with a leavened and preparèd choice   52
Proceeded to you; therefore take your honors.

36–7 Spirits . . . issues Souls are not deeply moved unless for
noble purposes   **38 scruple** bit. (Literally, a small weight.)
39–41 But . . . use unless, like a thrifty goddess, she gathers to
herself the glory due to a creditor, gaining both thanks from her
debtor and interest on the loan.   **41 bend** direct   **42 that . . .
advertise** who can instruct my role as duke now vested in him,
i.e., who knows already more about governing in my absence than
I can tell him.   **44 In . . . ourself** During my absence be in every
respect my deputy. (The royal plural.)   **45 Mortality** The full
rigor of the law, the death sentence   **47 first in question** senior
and first appointed   **49 mettle** substance, quality. (With play on
"metal," a common variant spelling, continued in the coining
imagery of lines 50–1.)   **52 leavened** i.e., carefully considered
(just as yeast is given time to leaven dough)

Our haste from hence is of so quick condition   54
That it prefers itself and leaves unquestioned   55
Matters of needful value. We shall write to you,
As time and our concernings shall importune,   57
How it goes with us, and do look to know   58
What doth befall you here. So, fare you well.
To th' hopeful execution do I leave you   60
Of your commissions.

ANGELO   Yet give leave, my lord,   61
That we may bring you something on the way.   62

DUKE   My haste may not admit it;   63
Nor need you, on mine honor, have to do   64
With any scruple. Your scope is as mine own,   65
So to enforce or qualify the laws
As to your soul seems good. Give me your hand.
I'll privily away. I love the people   68
But do not like to stage me to their eyes;   69
Though it do well, I do not relish well   70
Their loud applause and "aves" vehement,   71
Nor do I think the man of safe discretion   72
That does affect it. Once more, fare you well.   73

ANGELO
The heavens give safety to your purposes!

54–5 **Our . . . itself** The cause for my hasty departure is so urgent
that it takes precedence over all other matters
55 **unquestioned** not yet considered   57 **concernings** affairs.
importune urge   58 **look to know** expect to be informed
60 **th' hopeful** exciting hopes of success.   **execution** carrying
out   61 **leave** permission   62 **bring you something**
accompany you for a short distance   63 **admit** permit
64–5 **have . . . scruple** have the least doubt or hesitation about
what is to be done.   68 **I'll privily away** I'll go away secretly.
69 **stage me** make a show of myself   70 **do well** i.e., serves a
political purpose   71 **aves** hails of acclamation   72 **safe** sound
73 **affect** desire, court

ESCALUS
　　Lead forth and bring you back in happiness!   75

DUKE   I thank you. Fare you well.   *Exit.*

ESCALUS
　　I shall desire you, sir, to give me leave
　　To have free speech with you; and it concerns me   78
　　To look into the bottom of my place.   79
　　A power I have, but of what strength and nature
　　I am not yet instructed.

ANGELO
　　'Tis so with me. Let us withdraw together,
　　And we may soon our satisfaction have
　　Touching that point.

ESCALUS   I'll wait upon Your Honor.

　　　　　　　　　　　　　　　　　　　　　　　Exeunt.

1.2 ☙ *Enter Lucio and two other Gentlemen.*

LUCIO   If the Duke with the other dukes come not to
　　composition with the King of Hungary, why then all   2
　　the dukes fall upon the King.   3

FIRST GENTLEMAN   Heaven grant us its peace, but not
　　the King of Hungary's!

SECOND GENTLEMAN   Amen.

LUCIO   Thou conclud'st like the sanctimonious pirate
　　that went to sea with the Ten Commandments but
　　scraped one out of the table.   9

SECOND GENTLEMAN   "Thou shalt not steal"?

75 **Lead** May the heavens conduct you   78 **free** frank   79 **the
bottom of my place** the extent of my commission.

1.2 *Location: A public place.*
2 **composition** agreement   3 **fall upon** attack   9 **table**
tablet.

LUCIO   Ay, that he razed.   11

FIRST GENTLEMAN   Why, 'twas a commandment to
command the captain and all the rest from their function; they put forth to steal. There's not a soldier of   14
us all that, in the thanksgiving before meat, do relish   15
the petition well that prays for peace.

SECOND GENTLEMAN   I never heard any soldier dislike it.

LUCIO   I believe thee, for I think thou never wast where
grace was said.

SECOND GENTLEMAN   No? A dozen times at least.

FIRST GENTLEMAN   What, in meter?

LUCIO   In any proportion or in any language.   22

FIRST GENTLEMAN   I think, or in any religion.

LUCIO   Ay, why not? Grace is grace, despite of all   24
controversy; as, for example, thou thyself art a wicked   25
villain, despite of all grace.

FIRST GENTLEMAN   Well, there went but a pair of shears   27
between us.   28

LUCIO   I grant; as there may between the lists and the   29
velvet. Thou art the list.   30

FIRST GENTLEMAN   And thou the velvet. Thou art good

---

11 **razed** scraped out. (The word may also suggest *rased*, "erased.")
14 **put forth** set out to sea   15 **thanksgiving before meat**
saying of grace before a meal. (As in line 19.)   22 **proportion**
form   24–5 **Grace . . . controversy** (Refers to the Catholic-
Protestant *controversy*, line 25, as to whether humanity can be saved
by works or by grace alone; with punning on *grace* as "thanks for a
meal," line 19, and "gracefulness" or "becomingness," line 26.)
27–8 **there . . . between us** i.e., we're cut from the same cloth.
29–30 **as . . . list** (Lucio jokes that the shears might also cut
between, i.e., distinguish between, the mere *lists* or selvages, edges
of a woven fabric, and the *velvet* betokening a true gentleman.
Lucio wittily asserts himself to be a true gentleman; the other
speaker, not.)

velvet; thou'rt a three-piled piece, I warrant thee. I had 32
as lief be a list of an English kersey as be piled, as thou 33
art piled, for a French velvet. Do I speak feelingly now? 34

LUCIO   I think thou dost, and indeed with most painful
feeling of thy speech. I will, out of thine own confession, learn to begin thy health, but, whilst I live, forget 37
to drink after thee. 38

FIRST GENTLEMAN   I think I have done myself wrong, 39
have I not?

SECOND GENTLEMAN   Yes, that thou hast, whether
thou art tainted or free. 42

Enter bawd [Mistress Overdone].

LUCIO   Behold, behold, where Madam Mitigation 43
comes! I have purchased as many diseases under her
roof as come to—

SECOND GENTLEMAN   To what, I pray?

LUCIO   Judge. 47

---

32 **three-piled** having a threefold pile or nap, the best grade.
(Velvet patches might be used to conceal syphilitic sores or scars.)
33 **as lief** as soon, rather.   **kersey** a coarse woolen fabric. (The
First Gentleman turns the joke on Lucio by saying he would rather
be a plain, homespun Englishman than a Frenchified velvet
gentleman in decay and threadbare. *Velvet* suggests prostitutes and
venereal disease, as in the following notes.)   **be piled** (1) have a
cloth nap (2) suffer from hemorrhoids (3) be pulled or peeled, i.e.,
hairless, bald, as a result of mercury treatment for syphilis (known
as the "French disease"; see *French velvet* in the next line and *French
crown*, line 50)   34 **feelingly** to the purpose, so as to hit home.
(But Lucio's reply quibbles on "painfully," meaning the
Gentleman's mouth is affected by the French disease; hence, Lucio
will not drink from the same cup after him.)   37 **begin thy
health** drink to your health   37–8 **forget . . . thee** take care not
to drink from your cup.   39 **done myself wrong** i.e., asked for
that   42 **tainted** infected   43 **Mitigation** (So called because
her function is to relieve desire.)   47 **Judge** Guess.

SECOND GENTLEMAN   To three thousand dolors a year.   48

FIRST GENTLEMAN   Ay, and more.

LUCIO   A French crown more.   50

FIRST GENTLEMAN   Thou art always figuring diseases in   51
me, but thou art full of error. I am sound.

LUCIO   Nay, not, as one would say, healthy, but so
sound as things that are hollow. Thy bones are   54
hollow; impiety has made a feast of thee.   55

FIRST GENTLEMAN   [to Mistress Overdone] How now,
which of your hips has the most profound sciatica?   57

MISTRESS OVERDONE   Well, well; there's one yonder
arrested and carried to prison was worth five thousand of you all.

SECOND GENTLEMAN   Who's that, I pray thee?

MISTRESS OVERDONE   Marry, sir, that's Claudio, Signor   62
Claudio.

FIRST GENTLEMAN   Claudio to prison? 'Tis not so.

MISTRESS OVERDONE   Nay, but I know 'tis so. I saw him
arrested, saw him carried away; and, which is more,   66
within these three days his head to be chopped off.

LUCIO   But, after all this fooling, I would not have it so.   68
Art thou sure of this?

MISTRESS OVERDONE   I am too sure of it; and it is for
getting Madam Julietta with child.

LUCIO   Believe me, this may be. He promised to meet

---

48 **dolors** (Quibbling on *dollars;* spelled "Dollours" in the Folio.)
50 **French crown** (1) gold coin (2) bald head incurred through
syphilis, the "French disease"   51 **figuring** (1) imagining
(2) reckoning. (Recalling the monetary puns of lines 48 and 50.)
54 **sound** (1) healthy (2) resounding (because of hollow bones
caused by syphilis)   55 **impiety** wickedness   57 **sciatica** a
disease affecting the sciatic nerve in the hip and thigh, thought to
be a symptom of syphilis.   62 **Marry** i.e., By the Virgin Mary
66 **which** what   68 **after** notwithstanding

me two hours since, and he was ever precise in   73
promise-keeping.

SECOND GENTLEMAN   Besides, you know, it draws   75
something near to the speech we had to such a   76
purpose.   77

FIRST GENTLEMAN   But most of all agreeing with the
proclamation.

LUCIO   Away! Let's go learn the truth of it.

                          Exit [Lucio with the Gentlemen].

MISTRESS OVERDONE   Thus, what with the war, what
with the sweat, what with the gallows, and what with   82
poverty, I am custom-shrunk.   83

           Enter Clown [Pompey].

How now, what's the news with you?

POMPEY   Yonder man is carried to prison.

MISTRESS OVERDONE   Well, what has he done?   86

POMPEY   A woman.

MISTRESS OVERDONE   But what's his offense?

POMPEY   Groping for trouts in a peculiar river.   89

MISTRESS OVERDONE   What? Is there a maid with child
by him?

POMPEY   No, but there's a woman with maid by him.   92
You have not heard of the proclamation, have you?

MISTRESS OVERDONE   What proclamation, man?

---

73 **ever** always   75–6 **draws . . . near to** approaches, sounds
somewhat like   76–7 **to . . . purpose** on that topic.
82 **sweat** sweating sickness (often fatal), or the plague; also, the
sweating tub, a treatment for syphilis   83 **custom-shrunk**
having fewer customers.   86 **done** (Pompey quibbles in line 87
on a sexual sense of the word, present also in Mistress Overdone's
name.)   89 **peculiar** privately owned. (With bawdy suggestion.)
92 **woman with maid** (Pompey playfully corrects Mistress
Overdone's use of the word "maid," joking that a pregnant woman
cannot be a virgin [*maid*] though the child she carries is one.)

POMPEY All houses in the suburbs of Vienna must be 95
plucked down.

MISTRESS OVERDONE And what shall become of those
in the city?

POMPEY They shall stand for seed. They had gone 99
down too, but that a wise burgher put in for them. 100

MISTRESS OVERDONE But shall all our houses of resort
in the suburbs be pulled down?

POMPEY To the ground, mistress.

MISTRESS OVERDONE Why, here's a change indeed in
the commonwealth! What shall become of me?

POMPEY Come, fear not you. Good counselors lack no 106
clients. Though you change your place, you need not 107
change your trade; I'll be your tapster still. Courage! 108
There will be pity taken on you. You that have worn 109
your eyes almost out in the service, you will be con- 110
sidered.

MISTRESS OVERDONE What's to do here, Thomas Tapster? Let's withdraw.

POMPEY Here comes Signor Claudio, led by the Pro- 114
vost to prison; and there's Madam Juliet.   *Exeunt.* 115

        Enter Provost, Claudio, Juliet, Officers; Lucio
        and two Gentlemen [follow].

95 houses i.e., brothels.   **suburbs** (Location of the brothels in
Shakespeare's London, as in other walled cities.)   **99 for seed** to
preserve the species. (With ribald pun.)   **100 burgher** citizen.
put . . . them interceded on their behalf, offered to acquire them.
106–7 Good . . . clients Good lawyers (and, by implication, pimps
and bawds) are never at a loss for clients.   **108 tapster** one who
draws beer in an alehouse   **109–10 worn . . . out** i.e., worked so
hard. (Perhaps with an ironic reference to the traditional image of
the blind Cupid, often depicted on signs hung at the doors of
brothels.)   **114–15 Provost** officer charged with apprehension,
custody, and punishment of offenders

CLAUDIO [*to the Provost*]
    Fellow, why dost thou show me thus to the world?
    Bear me to prison, where I am committed.

PROVOST
    I do it not in evil disposition,
    But from Lord Angelo by special charge.

CLAUDIO
    Thus can the demigod Authority
    Make us pay down for our offense, by weight,   121
    The words of heaven. On whom it will, it will;   122
    On whom it will not, so; yet still 'tis just.   123

LUCIO
    Why, how now, Claudio? Whence comes this
        restraint?

CLAUDIO
    From too much liberty, my Lucio, liberty.
    As surfeit is the father of much fast,   126
    So every scope, by the immoderate use,   127
    Turns to restraint. Our natures do pursue,
    Like rats that ravin down their proper bane,   129
    A thirsty evil, and when we drink we die.

LUCIO   If I could speak so wisely under an arrest, I   131
would send for certain of my creditors. And yet, to say   132
the truth, I had as lief have the foppery of freedom as   133
the morality of imprisonment. What's thy offense,
Claudio?

121–2 **Make . . . heaven** make us pay the full penalty for our
offenses called for in the Bible.   122–3 **On whom . . . 'tis just**
(Compare Romans 9:18: "Therefore hath he [God] mercy on
whom he will have mercy, and whom he will he hardeneth.")
126 **As . . . fast** Just as excessive indulgence inevitably leads to
revulsion and abstinence   127 **scope** liberty, license
129 **ravin . . . bane** greedily devour what is poisonous to them
131–2 **If . . . creditors** If imprisonment would gain me such
wisdom, I would send for those to whom I owe money and thus be
arrested for debt.   133 **lief** willingly.   **foppery** folly

CLAUDIO
What but to speak of would offend again.

LUCIO
What, is't murder?

CLAUDIO   No.

LUCIO   Lechery?

CLAUDIO
Call it so.

PROVOST   Away, sir, you must go.

CLAUDIO
One word, good friend.—Lucio, a word with you.

LUCIO
A hundred, if they'll do you any good.
Is lechery so looked after?   141

CLAUDIO
Thus stands it with me: upon a true contract   142
I got possession of Julietta's bed.
You know the lady; she is fast my wife,   144
Save that we do the denunciation lack   145
Of outward order. This we came not to,   146
Only for propagation of a dower   147
Remaining in the coffer of her friends,   148
From whom we thought it meet to hide our love 149
Till time had made them for us. But it chances 150

141 **looked after** kept under observation.   142 **a true contract**
i.e., one made in the presence of witnesses, though without a
religious ceremony. (Such a precontract was binding but, in the
eyes of the Church, did not confer the right of sexual
consummation before the nuptials.)   144 **fast my wife** i.e.,
firmly bound by precontract   145 **denunciation** formal
declaration   146 **outward order** public ceremony.
147 **propagation** increase, begetting   148 **friends** relatives
149 **meet** fitting, necessary   150 **made . . . us** disposed them in
our favor.

The stealth of our most mutual entertainment
With character too gross is writ on Juliet.   152

LUCIO
With child, perhaps?

CLAUDIO   Unhappily, even so.
And the new deputy now for the Duke—
Whether it be the fault and glimpse of newness,   155
Or whether that the body public be
A horse whereon the governor doth ride,
Who, newly in the seat, that it may know
He can command, lets it straight feel the spur;   159
Whether the tyranny be in his place,   160
Or in his eminence that fills it up,   161
I stagger in—but this new governor   162
Awakes me all the enrollèd penalties   163
Which have, like unscoured armor, hung by the wall
So long that nineteen zodiacs have gone round   165
And none of them been worn; and for a name   166
Now puts the drowsy and neglected act
Freshly on me. 'Tis surely for a name.

LUCIO   I warrant it is, and thy head stands so tickle on 169
thy shoulders that a milkmaid, if she be in love, may
sigh it off. Send after the Duke and appeal to him.

CLAUDIO
I have done so, but he's not to be found.
I prithee, Lucio, do me this kind service:
This day my sister should the cloister enter   174

---

152 **character too gross** writing too evident   155 **the fault . . .
newness** the faulty flashiness of novelty   159 **straight** at once
160 **in his place** inherent in the office   161 **his eminence** the
eminence of him   162 **I stagger in** I am uncertain
163 **Awakes me** i.e., awakes, activates. (*Me* is used colloquially.)
enrollèd written on a roll or deed   165 **zodiacs** i.e., years
166 **for a name** for reputation's sake   169 **tickle** uncertain,
unstable   174 **cloister** i.e., convent

And there receive her approbation.   175
Acquaint her with the danger of my state;
Implore her, in my voice, that she make friends
To the strict deputy; bid herself assay him.   178
I have great hope in that, for in her youth
There is a prone and speechless dialect   180
Such as move men; beside, she hath prosperous art   181
When she will play with reason and discourse,
And well she can persuade.

LUCIO   I pray she may, as well for the encouragement of   184
the like, which else would stand under grievous impo-   185
sition, as for the enjoying of thy life, who I would   186
be sorry should be thus foolishly lost at a game of tick-   187
tack. I'll to her.   188

CLAUDIO   I thank you, good friend Lucio.

LUCIO   Within two hours.

CLAUDIO   Come, officer, away!   *Exeunt.*

1.[3] ᧬ *Enter Duke and Friar Thomas.*

DUKE
No, holy Father, throw away that thought;
Believe not that the dribbling dart of love   2
Can pierce a complete bosom. Why I desire thee   3
To give me secret harbor hath a purpose   4

175 **approbation** novitiate, period of probation.   178 **To** with.
assay try, test   180 **prone** eager, apt, supplicating.   **dialect**
language   181 **prosperous art** skill or ability to gain favorable
results   184–6 **as well . . . life** both for the encouragement of
similar sexual activity, which otherwise would be subject to grave
charges or accusations, and for you to continue to live
187–8 **tick-tack** a form of backgammon in which pegs were fitted
into holes. (Here applied bawdily.)

1.3 Location: A friary.
2 **dribbling** falling short or wide of the mark   3 **complete**
perfect, whole, strong   4 **harbor** shelter

More grave and wrinkled than the aims and ends   5
Of burning youth.

FRIAR THOMAS   May Your Grace speak of it?

DUKE
My holy sir, none better knows than you
How I have ever loved the life removed   8
And held in idle price to haunt assemblies   9
Where youth and cost witless bravery keeps.   10
I have delivered to Lord Angelo,
A man of stricture and firm abstinence,   12
My absolute power and place here in Vienna,
And he supposes me traveled to Poland;
For so I have strewed it in the common ear,
And so it is received. Now, pious sir,
You will demand of me why I do this.

FRIAR THOMAS   Gladly, my lord.

DUKE
We have strict statutes and most biting laws,
The needful bits and curbs to headstrong steeds,   20
Which for this fourteen years we have let slip,   21
Even like an o'ergrown lion in a cave   22
That goes not out to prey. Now, as fond fathers,   23
Having bound up the threat'ning twigs of birch
Only to stick it in their children's sight
For terror, not to use, in time the rod
Becomes more mocked than feared, so our decrees,
Dead to infliction, to themselves are dead;   28

---

5 **wrinkled** i.e., mature   8 **removed** retired   9 **in idle price**
as little worth. *Idle* means "unprofitable."   10 **Where . . . keeps**
where youth and costly expenditure put themselves foolishly on
display.   12 **stricture** strictness   20 **steeds** (The Folio reading,
"weedes," is possible in the sense of "lawless and uncontrolled
impulses.")   21 **fourteen** (Claudio mentions nineteen years at
1.2.165; possibly the compositor confused *xiv* and *xix*.)
22 **o'ergrown** too old and large   23 **fond** doting   28 **Dead to
infliction** dead in that they are not executed

And liberty plucks justice by the nose,   29
The baby beats the nurse, and quite athwart   30
Goes all decorum.

FRIAR THOMAS   It rested in Your Grace   31
To unloose this tied-up justice when you pleased;
And it in you more dreadful would have seemed
Than in Lord Angelo.

DUKE   I do fear, too dreadful.
Sith 'twas my fault to give the people scope,   35
'Twould be my tyranny to strike and gall them   36
For what I bid them do; for we bid this be done   37
When evil deeds have their permissive pass   38
And not the punishment. Therefore indeed, my father,
I have on Angelo imposed the office,   40
Who may in th'ambush of my name strike home,   41
And yet my nature never in the fight   42
To do in slander. And to behold his sway   43
I will, as 'twere a brother of your order,
Visit both prince and people. Therefore, I prithee,
Supply me with the habit, and instruct me   46
How I may formally in person bear   47
Like a true friar. More reasons for this action
At our more leisure shall I render you.   49
Only this one: Lord Angelo is precise,   50
Stands at a guard with envy, scarce confesses   51

---

29 **liberty** license   30 **athwart** wrongly, awry   31 **decorum**
social order.   **It rested . . . Grace** It lay in your ducal authority,
was incumbent on you   35 **Sith** Since   36 **gall** chafe, injure
37 **we . . . done** i.e., we virtually order a crime to be committed
38 **pass** sanction   40 **office** duty   41 **Who . . . home** who
may, under cover of my ducal authority, strike to the heart of the
matter   42 **nature** i.e., personal identity (as distinguished from
official capacity)   43 **do in slander** act so as to invite slander
(for being too repressive).   **sway** rule   46 **habit** garment (of a
friar)   47 **formally** in outward appearance.   **bear** bear myself
49 **more** greater   50 **precise** strict, puritanical   51 **Stands . . .**
envy guards himself severely against calumny

That his blood flows or that his appetite   52
Is more to bread than stone. Hence shall we see,   53
If power change purpose, what our seemers be.

                                        Exeunt.

1.[4]   ❧ *Enter Isabella and Francisca, a nun.*

ISABELLA
  And have you nuns no farther privileges?

FRANCISCA   Are not these large enough?

ISABELLA
  Yes, truly. I speak not as desiring more,
  But rather wishing a more strict restraint
  Upon the sisterhood, the votarists of Saint Clare.   5

LUCIO (*within*)
  Ho! Peace be in this place!

ISABELLA   Who's that which calls?

FRANCISCA
  It is a man's voice. Gentle Isabella,
  Turn you the key, and know his business of him.
  You may, I may not; you are yet unsworn.   9
  When you have vowed, you must not speak with men
  But in the presence of the prioress;
  Then if you speak you must not show your face,
  Or if you show your face you must not speak.
  He calls again. I pray you, answer him.   [*Exit.*]

52–3 **or . . . stone** or that he has an appetite for bread (i.e., food or physical pleasure) any more than if it were stone. (See Matthew 4.3, where the devil tempts Jesus to turn stone into bread.)

1.4 *Location: A convent.*
5 **votarists of Saint Clare** An order founded in 1212 by Saint Francis of Assisi and Saint Clare; its members were enjoined to a life of poverty, service, and contemplation.   9 **you . . . unsworn** i.e., you have not yet taken your formal vows to enter the convent.

ISABELLA
    Peace and prosperity! Who is 't that calls?

    [*She opens the door. Enter Lucio.*]

LUCIO
    Hail, virgin, if you be, as those cheek roses   16
    Proclaim you are no less. Can you so stead me   17
    As bring me to the sight of Isabella,   18
    A novice of this place, and the fair sister
    To her unhappy brother Claudio?   20

ISABELLA
    Why "her unhappy brother"? Let me ask,
    The rather for I now must make you know   22
    I am that Isabella, and his sister.

LUCIO
    Gentle and fair, your brother kindly greets you.
    Not to be weary with you, he's in prison.   25

ISABELLA   Woe me! For what?

LUCIO
    For that which, if myself might be his judge,
    He should receive his punishment in thanks:
    He hath got his friend with child.

ISABELLA
    Sir, make me not your story.

LUCIO   'Tis true.   30
    I would not—though 'tis my familiar sin   31
    With maids to seem the lapwing, and to jest,   32
    Tongue far from heart—play with all virgins so.

---

16 **cheek roses** i.e., blushes   17 **stead** help   18 **As** as to
20 **unhappy** unfortunate   22 **The rather for** the more so
because   25 **weary** wearisome   30 **story** subject for mirth.
31 **familiar** customary   32 **lapwing** peewit or plover. (The
lapwing runs away from its nest in order to draw away enemies
from its young, much as Lucio throws up smokescreens in his
seductive talk with young women.)

I hold you as a thing enskied and sainted   34
By your renouncement, an immortal spirit
And to be talked with in sincerity
As with a saint.

ISABELLA

You do blaspheme the good in mocking me.   38

LUCIO

Do not believe it. Fewness and truth, 'tis thus: 39
Your brother and his lover have embraced.
As those that feed grow full, as blossoming time   41
That from the seedness the bare fallow brings   42
To teeming foison, even so her plenteous womb   43
Expresseth his full tilth and husbandry.   44

ISABELLA

Someone with child by him? My cousin Juliet?

LUCIO   Is she your cousin?

ISABELLA

Adoptedly, as schoolmaids change their names   47
By vain though apt affection.

LUCIO   She it is.   48

ISABELLA

Oh, let him marry her.

LUCIO   This is the point.
The Duke is very strangely gone from hence;

---

34 **enskied** placed in heaven   38 **You . . . me** You blaspheme goodness itself when you mockingly praise me, unworthy as I am, for saintliness.   39 **it** i.e., that I am mocking.   **Fewness and truth** In few words and truly   41–3 **As . . . foison** Just as the season of blossoming brings the sowing of the bare untilled land to teeming fruitfulness   44 **Expresseth . . . husbandry** makes plainly visible Claudio's tilling of the crop, i.e., his plowing and fertilizing Juliet's body.   47 **change** exchange   48 **vain though apt** girlish though natural and suitable

Bore many gentlemen, myself being one,   51
In hand and hope of action; but we do learn,   ,   52
By those that know the very nerves of state,
His givings-out were of an infinite distance   54
From his true-meant design. Upon his place,   55
And with full line of his authority,   56
Governs Lord Angelo, a man whose blood
Is very snow broth; one who never feels   58
The wanton stings and motions of the sense,   59
But doth rebate and blunt his natural edge   60
With profits of the mind, study, and fast.
He—to give fear to use and liberty,   62
Which have for long run by the hideous law
As mice by lions—hath picked out an act,
Under whose heavy sense your brother's life   65
Falls into forfeit. He arrests him on it
And follows close the rigor of the statute
To make him an example. All hope is gone,
Unless you have the grace by your fair prayer
To soften Angelo. And that's my pith of business   70
Twixt you and your poor brother.

ISABELLA   Doth he so
Seek his life?

LUCIO   He's censured him already,   72
And, as I hear, the Provost hath a warrant
For 's execution.

ISABELLA   Alas, what poor
Ability's in me to do him good?

51–2 **Bore . . . action** i.e., he misleadingly kept us in expectation
of some military action   54 **givings-out** public statements
55 **Upon** In   56 **line** extent   58 **snow broth** melted snow
(i.e., ice water)   59 **motions . . . sense** promptings of sexual
desire   60 **But . . . edge** but dulls and blunts the sharp desire of
sexuality   62 **use and liberty** habitual licentiousness
65 **heavy sense** severe interpretation   70 **my pith of business**
the essence of my business   72 **censured** sentenced

LUCIO   Assay the power you have.   76

ISABELLA
  My power? Alas, I doubt.

LUCIO   Our doubts are traitors,
  And makes us lose the good we oft might win,   78
  By fearing to attempt. Go to Lord Angelo,
  And let him learn to know, when maidens sue
  Men give like gods, but when they weep and kneel,
  All their petitions are as freely theirs   82
  As they themselves would owe them.   83

ISABELLA   I'll see what I can do.

LUCIO   But speedily.

ISABELLA   I will about it straight,
  No longer staying but to give the Mother   87
  Notice of my affair. I humbly thank you.
  Commend me to my brother. Soon at night   89
  I'll send him certain word of my success.   90

LUCIO
  I take my leave of you.

ISABELLA   Good sir, adieu.

                              Exeunt [separately].

2.1 ᦸ *Enter Angelo, Escalus, and servants, [a] Justice.*

ANGELO
  We must not make a scarecrow of the law,
  Setting it up to fear the birds of prey,   2

76 **Assay** Try   78 **makes** make   82 **their petitions** i.e., the
things the maidens ask for   83 **As . . . them** as they themselves
would wish to have them.   87 **but** than.   **Mother** Mother
Superior, prioress   89 **Soon at night** Early tonight   90 **my
success** how I have succeeded.

2.1 *Location: A court of justice.*
2 **fear** frighten

And let it keep one shape till custom make it
Their perch and not their terror.

ESCALUS   Ay, but yet
Let us be keen and rather cut a little   5
Than fall and bruise to death. Alas, this gentleman   6
Whom I would save had a most noble father!
Let but Your Honor know,   8
Whom I believe to be most strait in virtue,   9
That, in the working of your own affections,   10
Had time cohered with place, or place with wishing,
Or that the resolute acting of your blood   12
Could have attained th'effect of your own purpose,   13
Whether you had not sometime in your life   14
Erred in this point which now you censure him,   15
And pulled the law upon you.

ANGELO
'Tis one thing to be tempted, Escalus,
Another thing to fall. I not deny
The jury, passing on the prisoner's life,
May in the sworn twelve have a thief or two
Guiltier than him they try. What's open made to
     justice,
That justice seizes. What knows the laws   22
That thieves do pass on thieves? 'Tis very pregnant,   23
The jewel that we find, we stoop and take't
Because we see it; but what we do not see
We tread upon and never think of it.
You may not so extenuate his offense
For I have had such faults; but rather tell me,   28

5 **keen** sharp   6 **fall** let fall heavily.   **bruise** i.e., crush
8 **know** consider   9 **strait** strict   10 **affections** desires
12 **blood** passion   13 **effect** realization   14 **had** would have.
sometime on some occasion   15 **censure him** sentence him
for   22–3 **What . . . on thieves?** Who knows what laws thieves
apply to their fellow thieves?   23 **pregnant** clear   28 **For**
because

When I that censure him do so offend,
Let mine own judgment pattern out my death   30
And nothing come in partial. Sir, he must die.   31

   Enter Provost.

ESCALUS
Be it as your wisdom will.

ANGELO   Where is the Provost?

PROVOST
Here, if it like Your Honor.

ANGELO   See that Claudio   33
Be executed by nine tomorrow morning.
Bring him his confessor; let him be prepared.
For that's the utmost of his pilgrimage.   36

        [Exit Provost.]

ESCALUS
Well, heaven forgive him, and forgive us all!
Some rise by sin, and some by virtue fall;
Some run from breaks of ice and answer none,   39
And some condemnèd for a fault alone.   40

  Enter Elbow, Froth, Clown [Pompey], officers.

ELBOW Come, bring them away. If these be good   41
people in a commonweal that do nothing but use their   42
abuses in common houses, I know no law. Bring them   43
away.

30–1 **Let . . . partial** let the sentence I have imposed serve as a
model in sentencing me if I commit a crime, no partiality or
extenuating circumstances being admitted. 33 **like** please
36 **that's . . . pilgrimage** that's the furthest point of his life's
journey. 39 **Some . . . none** some break the ice repeatedly (i.e.,
commit serious infractions of the law) and yet escape punishment.
(A famous crux; the Folio reads "brakes of Ice.") 40 **a fault
alone** one single infraction. 41 **away** onward. 42–3 **use . . .
houses** practice their vices in bawdy houses

ANGELO   How now, sir, what's your name? And what's
the matter?

ELBOW   If it please Your Honor, I am the poor Duke's   47
constable, and my name is Elbow. I do lean upon   48
justice, sir, and do bring in here before Your good Honor
two notorious benefactors.

ANGELO   Benefactors? Well, what benefactors are they?
Are they not malefactors?

ELBOW   If it please Your Honor, I know not well what
they are; but precise villains they are, that I am sure of,   54
and void of all profanation in the world that good   55
Christians ought to have.

ESCALUS [to Angelo]   This comes off well. Here's a
wise officer.

ANGELO   Go to. What quality are they of?—Elbow is   59
your name? Why dost thou not speak, Elbow?

POMPEY   He cannot, sir; he's out at elbow.   61

ANGELO   What are you, sir?

ELBOW   He, sir? A tapster, sir, parcel-bawd, one that   63
serves a bad woman, whose house, sir, was, as they
say, plucked down in the suburbs; and now she

---

47 poor Duke's i.e., Duke's poor   **48 lean upon** rely on, appeal
to. (With an unintended comic reference to the idea of leaning on
one's elbow.)   **54 precise** complete. (Or perhaps a blunder for
"precious." *Precise* unintentionally recalls the description of Angelo
as *precise,* i.e., strict or puritanical, at 1.3.50.)   **55 profanation** (A
blunder for "profession," or a word meaning "irreverence" where
Elbow intends "reverence." Elbow already has used several
malapropisms, including *lean upon, benefactors,* and *precise.*)
59 Go to An expression of impatience or reproof.   **quality**
social standing, occupation   **61 out at elbow** (1) impoverished,
threadbare, hence without any ideas (2) missing his cue, i.e., at a
loss for words after being called by his name.   **63 parcel-bawd**
part-time bawd (and part-time tapster)

professes a hothouse, which I think is a very ill house   66
too.

ESCALUS   How know you that?

ELBOW   My wife, sir, whom I detest before heaven and   69
Your Honor—

ESCALUS   How? Thy wife?

ELBOW   Ay, sir; whom I thank heaven is an honest
woman—

ESCALUS   Dost thou detest her therefore?

ELBOW   I say, sir, I will detest myself also, as well as
she, that this house, if it be not a bawd's house, it is
pity of her life, for it is a naughty house.   77

ESCALUS   How dost thou know that, Constable?

ELBOW   Marry, sir, by my wife, who, if she had been a
woman cardinally given, might have been accused in   80
fornication, adultery, and all uncleanliness there.

ESCALUS   By the woman's means?

ELBOW   Ay, sir, by Mistress Overdone's means; but as
she spit in his face, so she defied him.   84

POMPEY   Sir, if it please Your Honor, this is not so.

ELBOW   Prove it before these varlets here, thou honor-   86
able man, prove it.   87

ESCALUS [to Angelo]   Do you hear how he misplaces?

POMPEY   Sir, she came in great with child, and longing,
saving Your Honor's reverence, for stewed prunes. Sir,   90

66 **professes a hothouse** professes to run a bathhouse
69 **detest** (For "protest.")   77 **pity of her life** a great pity.
naughty wicked   80 **cardinally** (For "carnally.")   **given**
inclined   84 **she spit . . . face** Elbow's wife spat in the face of
Pompey (who, as pimp, was acting as Mistress Overdone's *means,*
line 83).   86–7 **varlets . . . honorable** (Elbow reverses or *misplaces*
these epithets.)   90 **saving . . . reverence** i.e., begging your
pardon for what I'm about to say.   **stewed prunes** (Commonly
served in houses of prostitution, or *stews,* and therefore suggesting
prostitutes. The dialogue throughout is sexually suggestive.)

we had but two in the house, which at that very
distant time stood, as it were, in a fruit dish, a   92
dish of some threepence. Your Honors have seen such
dishes; they are not China dishes, but very good
dishes—

ESCALUS   Go to, go to. No matter for the dish, sir.

POMPEY   No, indeed, sir, not of a pin; you are therein   97
in the right. But to the point. As I say, this Mistress
Elbow, being, as I say, with child, and being great-
bellied, and longing, as I said, for prunes; and having
but two in the dish, as I said, Master Froth here, this
very man, having eaten the rest, as I said, and, as I
say, paying for them very honestly—for, as you
know, Master Froth, I could not give you threepence
again.   105

FROTH   No, indeed.

POMPEY   Very well. You being then, if you be
remembered, cracking the stones of the foresaid   108
prunes—

FROTH   Ay, so I did indeed.

POMPEY   Why, very well; I telling you then, if you be
remembered, that such a one and such a one were
past cure of the thing you wot of, unless they kept   113
very good diet, as I told you—   114

FROTH   All this is true.

POMPEY   Why, very well, then—

ESCALUS   Come, you are a tedious fool. To the purpose.

---

92 **distant** (Blunder for "instant"?)   97 **a pin** i.e., an insignificant
trifle   105 **again** back.   108 **stones** pits. (With suggestion also
of "testicles.")   113 **the thing . . . of** you know what I mean
(i.e., venereal disease)   114 **diet** strict regimen prescribed for
medical treatment

What was done to Elbow's wife, that he hath cause to
complain of? Come me to what was done to her.   119

POMPEY Sir, Your Honor cannot come to that yet.

ESCALUS No, sir, nor I mean it not.

POMPEY Sir, but you shall come to it, by Your Honor's
leave. And, I beseech you, look into Master Froth here,
sir, a man of fourscore pound a year, whose father   124
died at Hallowmas.—Was 't not at Hallowmas, Mas-   125
ter Froth?

FROTH All-hallond eve.   127

POMPEY Why, very well. I hope here be truths. He, sir,
sitting, as I say, in a lower chair, sir—'twas in the   129
Bunch of Grapes, where indeed you have a delight to   130
sit, have you not?

FROTH I have so, because it is an open room and good   132
for winter.

POMPEY Why, very well, then. I hope here be truths.

ANGELO
This will last out a night in Russia,
When nights are longest there. I'll take my leave
And leave you to the hearing of the cause,   137
Hoping you'll find good cause to whip them all.

ESCALUS
I think no less. Good morrow to Your Lordship.   139
                                        Exit [Angelo].

---

119 **Come me** i.e., Come. (*Me* is used colloquially. Pompey makes
a vulgar joke on the words *come* and *done;* see note at line 140.)
124 **of . . . year** i.e., well off   125 **Hallowmas** All Saints' Day,
November 1   127 **All-hallond eve** Halloween, October 31.
129 **a lower chair** i.e., an easy chair (?)   130 **Bunch of Grapes**
(It was not uncommon to designate particular rooms in inns by
such names.)   132 **open** public   137 **cause** case. (With word
play on *cause,* "reason," in the next line. See also the play on *leave* in
136–7.)   139 **I . . . less** I think so, too.

Now, sir, come on. What was done to Elbow's wife,   140
once more?

POMPEY   Once, sir? There was nothing done to her
once.   143

ELBOW   I beseech you, sir, ask him what this man did
to my wife.

POMPEY   I beseech Your Honor, ask me.

ESCALUS   Well, sir, what did this gentleman to her?

POMPEY   I beseech you, sir, look in this gentleman's
face. Good Master Froth, look upon His Honor; 'tis for
a good purpose. Doth Your Honor mark his face?   150

ESCALUS   Ay, sir, very well.

POMPEY   Nay, I beseech you, mark it well.

ESCALUS   Well, I do so.

POMPEY   Doth Your Honor see any harm in his face?

ESCALUS   Why, no.

POMPEY   I'll be supposed upon a book, his face is the   156
worst thing about him. Good, then; if his face be the
worst thing about him, how could Master Froth do the
Constable's wife any harm? I would know that of Your
Honor.

ESCALUS   He's in the right, Constable. What say you
to it?

ELBOW   First, an it like you, the house is a respected   163
house; next, this is a respected fellow; and his mistress
is a respected woman.

POMPEY   By this hand, sir, his wife is a more respected
person than any of us all.

---

140 **done** (Pompey, in his answer, uses *done* in a sexual sense.)
143 **once** only once. (Pompey replies wittily to Escalus's *once more*
in 141, meaning "once again.")   150 **mark** observe
156 **supposed** (A malapropism for "deposed," i.e., sworn.)
book i.e., Bible   163 **an it like** if it please.   **respected** (For
"suspected.")

ELBOW   Varlet, thou liest! Thou liest, wicked varlet! The time is yet to come that she was ever respected with man, woman, or child.

POMPEY   Sir, she was respected with him before he married with her.

ESCALUS   Which is the wiser here, Justice or Iniquity?— 173
Is this true?

ELBOW   O thou caitiff! O thou varlet! O thou wicked 175
Hannibal! I respected with her before I was married to 176
her?—If ever I was respected with her, or she with me, let not Your Worship think me the poor Duke's officer.—Prove this, thou wicked Hannibal, or I'll have mine action of battery on thee. 180

ESCALUS   If he took you a box o'th'ear, you might have 181
your action of slander too.

ELBOW   Marry, I thank Your good Worship for it. What is't Your Worship's pleasure I shall do with this wicked caitiff?

ESCALUS   Truly, officer, because he hath some offenses in him that thou wouldst discover if thou couldst, let 187
him continue in his courses till thou know'st what 188
they are.

ELBOW   Marry, I thank Your Worship for it.—Thou see'st, thou wicked varlet, now, what's come upon thee: thou art to continue now, thou varlet, thou art to continue. 192

ESCALUS [to Froth]   Where were you born, friend?

FROTH   Here in Vienna, sir.

173 **Justice or Iniquity** (Personified characters in a morality play.)
175 **caitiff** knave, villain.   176 **Hannibal** (A blunder for "cannibal," perhaps also suggested by the fact that Hannibal and Pompey were both famous generals in the classical world.)
180 **battery** (An error for "slander," as Escalus amusedly points out.)   181 **took** gave.   **o'** on   187 **discover** (1) detect (2) reveal   188 **courses** courses of action   192 **continue** (Elbow may confuse the word with its opposite.)

ESCALUS   Are you of fourscore pounds a year?   195

FROTH   Yes, an't please you, sir.

ESCALUS   So. [*To Pompey*] What trade are you of, sir?

POMPEY   A tapster, a poor widow's tapster.

ESCALUS   Your mistress' name?

POMPEY   Mistress Overdone.

ESCALUS   Hath she had any more than one husband?

POMPEY   Nine, sir. Overdone by the last.   202

ESCALUS   Nine?—Come hither to me, Master Froth.
Master Froth, I would not have you acquainted with
tapsters. They will draw you, Master Froth, and you   205
will hang them. Get you gone, and let me hear no   206
more of you.

FROTH   I thank Your Worship. For mine own part, I
never come into any room in a taphouse but I am   209
drawn in.   210

ESCALUS   Well, no more of it, Master Froth. Farewell.
                                        [*Exit Froth.*]
Come you hither to me, Master Tapster. What's your
name, Master Tapster?

POMPEY   Pompey.

ESCALUS   What else?

POMPEY   Bum, sir.

ESCALUS   Troth, and your bum is the greatest thing
about you; so that in the beastliest sense you are Pompey the Great. Pompey, you are partly a bawd, Pom-

195 **of** possessed of   202 **Overdone . . . last** (1) Her name,
Overdone, was given her by her last husband (2) She has been
worn out (*overdone*) by the last one.   205 **draw** (1) cheat, take in
(2) empty, deplete. (With a pun on the tapster's trade of drawing
liquor from a barrel, and on Froth's name.) (3) disembowel, or
drag to execution   206 **will hang them** will be the cause of
their hanging.   209 **taphouse** alehouse   210 **drawn in**
enticed. (Still another meaning of *draw*, line 205.)

pey, howsoever you color it in being a tapster, are you   220
not? Come, tell me true. It shall be the better for you.

POMPEY   Truly, sir, I am a poor fellow that would live.

ESCALUS   How would you live, Pompey? By being a   223
bawd? What do you think of the trade, Pompey? Is it
a lawful trade?

POMPEY   If the law would allow it, sir.

ESCALUS   But the law will not allow it, Pompey; nor it
shall not be allowed in Vienna.

POMPEY   Does Your Worship mean to geld and splay all   229
the youth of the city?

ESCALUS   No, Pompey.

POMPEY   Truly, sir, in my poor opinion they will to't
then. If Your Worship will take order for the drabs and   233
the knaves, you need not to fear the bawds.

ESCALUS   There is pretty orders beginning, I can tell
you. It is but heading and hanging.   236

POMPEY   If you head and hang all that offend that way
but for ten year together, you'll be glad to give out a   238
commission for more heads. If this law hold in Vienna   239
ten year, I'll rent the fairest house in it after threepence   240
a bay. If you live to see this come to pass, say Pompey   241
told you so.

ESCALUS   Thank you, good Pompey. And, in requital of   243
your prophecy, hark you: I advise you let me not find
you before me again upon any complaint whatsoever;
no, not for dwelling where you do. If I do, Pompey, I

---

220 **color** disguise   223 **live** make a living   229 **splay** spay
233 **take order** take measures.   **drabs** prostitutes   236 **It . . .
hanging** Beheading and hanging are the order of the day.
238 **year together** years at a stretch   239 **commission** order.
hold remain in force   240 **after** at the rate of   241 **bay**
division of a house included under one gable.   243 **requital of**
return for

shall beat you to your tent and prove a shrewd Caesar   247
to you; in plain dealing, Pompey, I shall have you
whipped. So for this time, Pompey, fare you well.

POMPEY   I thank Your Worship for your good counsel.
[*Aside*] But I shall follow it as the flesh and fortune
shall better determine.
Whip me? No, no, let carman whip his jade.   253
The valiant heart's not whipped out of his trade.

                                                Exit.

ESCALUS   Come hither to me, Master Elbow; come
hither, Master Constable. How long have you been in
this place of constable?

ELBOW   Seven year and a half, sir.

ESCALUS   I thought, by the readiness in the office, you   259
had continued in it some time. You say, seven years
together?

ELBOW   And a half, sir.

ESCALUS   Alas, it hath been great pains to you. They do
you wrong to put you so oft upon't. Are there not
men in your ward sufficient to serve it?   265

ELBOW   Faith, sir, few of any wit in such matters. As
they are chosen, they are glad to choose me for them.   267
I do it for some piece of money and go through with   268
all.   269

ESCALUS   Look you bring me in the names of some six   270
or seven, the most sufficient of your parish.

ELBOW   To Your Worship's house, sir?

---

247 **shrewd** harsh, severe.   **Caesar** (Julius Caesar defeated
Pompey at Pharsalia in 48 B.C.)   253 **carman** cart driver.
jade broken-down horse.   259 **readiness** proficiency, alacrity
265 **sufficient** able   267 **for them** i.e., to take their place.
268–9 **go . . . all** i.e., perform my duties thoroughly.   270 **Look**
See to it that

ESCALUS   To my house. Fare you well.   [*Exit Elbow.*]
  What's o'clock, think you?

JUSTICE   Eleven, sir.

ESCALUS
  I pray you home to dinner with me.   276

JUSTICE   I humbly thank you.

ESCALUS
  It grieves me for the death of Claudio;
  But there's no remedy.

JUSTICE   Lord Angelo is severe.

ESCALUS   It is but needful.
  Mercy is not itself, that oft looks so;   281
  Pardon is still the nurse of second woe.   282
  But yet—poor Claudio! There is no remedy.
  Come, sir.   *Exeunt.*

2.2 ❧ *Enter Provost [and a] Servant.*

SERVANT
  He's hearing of a cause; he will come straight.   1
  I'll tell him of you.

PROVOST   Pray you, do.   [*Exit Servant.*]
                              I'll know
  His pleasure; maybe he will relent. Alas,
  He hath but as offended in a dream!   4

276 **dinner** (Dinner was customarily eaten just before midday.)
281 **Mercy . . . so** i.e., What seems merciful may not really be so
(since it may encourage crime and hence lead to more
punishment)   282 **Pardon . . . woe** i.e., pardon continually
nurtures and encourages a repetition of offenses and hence of
punishment.

**2.2 Location: Adjacent to the court of justice, perhaps at
Angelo's official residence.**
1 **hearing . . . cause** listening to a case.   **straight** immediately.
4 **He . . . dream** offended only as if in a dream.

All sects, all ages smack of this vice—and he   5
To die for't!

    Enter Angelo.

ANGELO   Now, what's the matter, Provost?

PROVOST
Is it your will Claudio shall die tomorrow?

ANGELO
Did not I tell thee yea? Hadst thou not order?
Why dost thou ask again?

PROVOST   Lest I might be too rash.
Under your good correction, I have seen   11
When, after execution, judgment hath
Repented o'er his doom.   13

ANGELO   Go to; let that be mine.   14
Do you your office, or give up your place,
And you shall well be spared.   16

PROVOST   I crave Your Honor's pardon.
What shall be done, sir, with the groaning Juliet?   18
She's very near her hour.

ANGELO   Dispose of her   19
To some more fitter place, and that with speed.

    [Enter a Servant.]

SERVANT
Here is the sister of the man condemned
Desires access to you.

ANGELO   Hath he a sister?   22

PROVOST
Ay, my good lord, a very virtuous maid,

5 **All sects . . . smack** All classes of people of all ages (and in all past history) partake   11 **Under . . . correction** i.e., Allow me to say   13 **doom** sentence.   14 **mine** my business.   16 **well be spared** easily be done without.   18 **groaning** (with labor pains)   19 **hour** time of delivery.   22 **Desires** who desires

And to be shortly of a sisterhood,
If not already.

ANGELO   Well, let her be admitted.

                              [*Exit Servant.*]

See you the fornicatress be removed.
Let her have needful but not lavish means.
There shall be order for't.

        Enter Lucio and Isabella.

PROVOST   Save Your Honor!   28

ANGELO [*to Provost*]
   Stay a little while. [*To Isabella*] You're welcome.
      What's your will?

ISABELLA
   I am a woeful suitor to Your Honor,
   Please but Your Honor hear me.

ANGELO   Well, what's your suit?   31

ISABELLA
   There is a vice that most I do abhor,
   And most desire should meet the blow of justice,
   For which I would not plead, but that I must;
   For which I must not plead, but that I am
   At war twixt will and will not.

ANGELO   Well, the matter?

ISABELLA
   I have a brother is condemned to die.
   I do beseech you, let it be his fault,   38
   And not my brother.

PROVOST [*aside*]   Heaven give thee moving graces!

ANGELO
   Condemn the fault, and not the actor of it?

---

28 **Save** May God save   31 **Please . . . me** if Your Honor will
please hear me.   38 **let . . . fault** i.e., let the fault die, be
condemned

Why, every fault's condemned ere it be done.
Mine were the very cipher of a function,
To fine the faults, whose fine stands in record,   43
And let go by the actor.

ISABELLA   Oh, just but severe law!
I had a brother, then. Heaven keep your honor!

LUCIO [aside to Isabella]
Give't not o'er so. To him again, entreat him!   47
Kneel down before him; hang upon his gown.
You are too cold. If you should need a pin,   49
You could not with more tame a tongue desire it.
To him, I say!

ISABELLA [to Angelo]
Must he needs die?

ANGELO   Maiden, no remedy.

ISABELLA
Yes, I do think that you might pardon him,
And neither heaven nor man grieve at the mercy.

ANGELO
I will not do't.

ISABELLA   But can you, if you would?

ANGELO
Look what I will not, that I cannot do.   56

ISABELLA
But might you do't, and do the world no wrong,
If so your heart were touched with that remorse   58
As mine is to him?

ANGELO   He's sentenced. 'Tis too late.

LUCIO [aside to Isabella]   You are too cold.

---

43 **To fine . . . record** to punish only the faults, for which the
penalty stands in the statute books   47 **Give't . . . so** Don't give
up so soon.   49 **need a pin** i.e., ask for the smallest trifle
56 **Look what** Whatever   58 **remorse** pity

ISABELLA

    Too late? Why, no; I that do speak a word
    May call it back again. Well, believe this:
    No ceremony that to great ones 'longs,   64
    Not the king's crown, nor the deputed sword,   65
    The marshal's truncheon, nor the judge's robe   66
    Become them with one half so good a grace
    As mercy does.
    If he had been as you, and you as he,
    You would have slipped like him; but he, like you,   70
    Would not have been so stern.

ANGELO   Pray you, begone.

ISABELLA

    I would to heaven I had your potency,
    And you were Isabel. Should it then be thus?
    No, I would tell what 'twere to be a judge   74
    And what a prisoner.

LUCIO [aside to Isabella]   Ay, touch him; there's the vein.   75

ANGELO

    Your brother is a forfeit of the law,   76
    And you but waste your words.

ISABELLA   Alas, alas!

    Why, all the souls that were were forfeit once,   78
    And He that might the vantage best have took   79
    Found out the remedy. How would you be,   80

---

64 'longs is fitting, belongs   **65 deputed sword** sword of
justice entrusted to the ruler   **66 truncheon** staff borne by
military officers   **70 like you** in your situation   **74 tell** make
known   **75 there's the vein** i.e., that's the right approach. (*Vein*
means "lode to be profitably mined," or perhaps "vein for
bloodletting.")   **76 a forfeit** one who must incur the penalty
78–80 Why . . . remedy (A reference to God's redemption of
sinful humanity when He would have been justified in destroying
humankind.)

If He, which is the top of judgment, should   81
But judge you as you are? Oh, think on that,
And mercy then will breathe within your lips,
Like man new-made.

ANGELO   Be you content, fair maid.   84
It is the law, not I, condemn your brother.
Were he my kinsman, brother, or my son,
It should be thus with him. He must die tomorrow.

ISABELLA
Tomorrow! Oh, that's sudden! Spare him, spare him!
He's not prepared for death. Even for our kitchens
We kill the fowl of season. Shall we serve heaven   90
With less respect than we do minister
To our gross selves? Good, good my lord, bethink
     you:
Who is it that hath died for this offense?
There's many have committed it.

LUCIO [aside to Isabella]   Ay, well said.

ANGELO
The law hath not been dead, though it hath slept.
Those many had not dared to do that evil
If the first that did th'edict infringe
Had answered for his deed. Now 'tis awake,
Takes note of what is done, and like a prophet
Looks in a glass that shows what future evils,   100
Either now, or by remissness new-conceived   101
And so in progress to be hatched and born,   102

---

81 **top of judgment** supreme judge   84 **new-made** i.e., created
new by salvation, born again.   90 **of season** that is in season
and properly mature.   100 **glass** magic crystal   101 **Either . . .
new-conceived** i.e., both evils already hatched and those that
would be encouraged by continued laxity of enforcement
102 **in progress** in the course of time

Are now to have no successive degrees,   103
But ere they live, to end.

ISABELLA   Yet show some pity.   104

ANGELO
I show it most of all when I show justice;
For then I pity those I do not know,
Which a dismissed offense would after gall,   107
And do him right that, answering one foul wrong,   108
Lives not to act another. Be satisfied;
Your brother dies tomorrow. Be content.

ISABELLA
So you must be the first that gives this sentence,
And he that suffers. Oh, it is excellent
To have a giant's strength, but it is tyrannous
To use it like a giant.

LUCIO [aside to Isabella]   That's well said.

ISABELLA   Could great men thunder
As Jove himself does, Jove would never be quiet,   116
For every pelting, petty officer   117
Would use his heaven for thunder,
Nothing but thunder. Merciful heaven,
Thou rather with thy sharp and sulfurous bolt   120
Splits the unwedgeable and gnarlèd oak   121
Than the soft myrtle; but man, proud man,
Dressed in a little brief authority,

---

103 **successive degrees** successors or future stages. (Future evils
are to be aborted before they are born and propagate.)   104 **ere
they live** i.e., before they can be committed   107 **Which . . .
gall** whom a forgiven offense would give trouble to later on
108 **do . . . answering** do justice to that person who, by paying
the penalty for   116 **be quiet** (1) have any quiet; or (2) cease
thundering   117 **pelting** paltry   120 **bolt** thunderbolt
121 **unwedgeable** unsplittable

Most ignorant of what he's most assured,   124
His glassy essence, like an angry ape   125
Plays such fantastic tricks before high heaven
As makes the angels weep; who, with our spleens,   127
Would all themselves laugh mortal.   128

LUCIO [aside to Isabella]
Oh, to him, to him, wench! He will relent.
He's coming, I perceive't.

PROVOST [aside]   Pray heaven she win him!   130

ISABELLA
We cannot weigh our brother with ourself.   131
Great men may jest with saints; 'tis wit in them,   132
But in the less, foul profanation.   133

LUCIO [aside to Isabella]
Thou'rt i'th' right, girl. More o' that.

ISABELLA
That in the captain's but a choleric word   135
Which in the soldier is flat blasphemy.

LUCIO [aside to Isabella]   Art advised o' that? More on't.   137

ANGELO
Why do you put these sayings upon me?   138

124–5 **Most . . . essence** i.e., most ignorant of what religion teaches
him to know, his spiritual nature; or, of that which is most certain, his
natural frailty.   125 **angry ape** i.e., ludicrous buffoon
127–8 **who . . . mortal** who, if they had the organs of laughter that
we have, would laugh themselves mortal, becoming like us. (The
spleen was thought to be the seat of laughter.)   130 **coming** coming
around   131–3 **We . . . profanation** We cannot judge our fellow
mortals by the same standards we use in judging ourselves. Persons of
great authority are allowed liberties that in lesser persons would be
condemned as blasphemies. (Lines 135–6 make much the same point.)
135 **That . . . word** i.e., We treat the abusive language a commanding
officer uses in anger merely as an outburst; we are indulgent toward
the failings of *great men*. (As in lines 131–3, Isabella's point seems to be
that our judgments are biased by our inordinate regard for authority.)
137 **advised** informed, aware.   **on't** of it.   138 **put . . . me** apply
these sayings to me.

ISABELLA

Because authority, though it err like others,   139
Hath yet a kind of medicine in itself   140
That skins the vice o'th' top. Go to your bosom;   141
Knock there, and ask your heart what it doth know
That's like my brother's fault. If it confess
A natural guiltiness such as is his,
Let it not sound a thought upon your tongue
Against my brother's life.

ANGELO [aside]   She speaks, and 'tis such sense   147
That my sense breeds with it.—Fare you well.   148

                                   [He starts to go.]

ISABELLA   Gentle my lord, turn back.   149

ANGELO

I will bethink me. Come again tomorrow.   150

ISABELLA

Hark how I'll bribe you. Good my lord, turn back.

ANGELO   How? Bribe me?

ISABELLA

Ay, with such gifts that heaven shall share with you.   153

LUCIO [aside to Isabella]   You had marred all else.   154

ISABELLA

Not with fond sicles of the tested gold,   155
Or stones whose rate are either rich or poor   156
As fancy values them, but with true prayers   157
That shall be up at heaven and enter there

139–41 **Because . . . top** Because authority, though prone to
sinfulness like all of humankind, has a way of seeming to heal
itself by covering over the boil with a film of skin, leaving the sore
unhealed.   147–8 **sense . . . sense** import . . . sensuality
149 **Gentle my lord** My noble lord   150 **bethink me** think it
over.   153 **that** as   154 **else** otherwise.   155 **Not . . . gold**
Not with foolishly valued shekels of pure gold. (*Shekels* are
Hebrew coins.)   156–7 **Or . . . them** or jewels the value of
which is merely subjective and transitory

Ere sunrise—prayers from preservèd souls,   159
From fasting maids whose minds are dedicate   160
To nothing temporal.

ANGELO   Well, come to me tomorrow.

LUCIO [*aside to Isabella*]   Go to, 'tis well. Away!

ISABELLA
Heaven keep Your Honor safe!

ANGELO [*aside*]   Amen!
For I am that way going to temptation,
Where prayers cross.

ISABELLA   At what hour tomorrow   165
Shall I attend Your Lordship?

ANGELO   At any time 'fore noon.

ISABELLA   Save Your Honor!   168

                    [*Exeunt Isabella, Lucio, and Provost.*]

ANGELO   From thee, even from thy virtue!
What's this, what's this? Is this her fault or mine?
The tempter or the tempted, who sins most, ha?
Not she, nor doth she tempt; but it is I
That, lying by the violet in the sun,
Do, as the carrion does, not as the flower,   174
Corrupt with virtuous season. Can it be   175
That modesty may more betray our sense   176
Than woman's lightness? Having waste ground
    enough,   177
Shall we desire to raze the sanctuary

159 **preservèd souls** devout religious who have withdrawn from
the world   160 **fasting maids** i.e., nuns.   **dedicate** dedicated
165 **cross** are at cross purposes.   168 **Save** May God save
174 **carrion** decaying flesh   175 **Corrupt . . . season**
i.e., putrefy while all else flourishes. (The warmth of flowering
time causes the violet, Isabella, to blossom but causes the carrion
lying beside it, Angelo, to rot.)   176 **modesty** virtue, chastity.
sense sensual nature   177 **lightness** immodesty, lust.

And pitch our evils there? Oh, fie, fie, fie!   179
What dost thou, or what art thou, Angelo?
Dost thou desire her foully for those things
That make her good? Oh, let her brother live!
Thieves for their robbery have authority
When judges steal themselves. What, do I love her,
That I desire to hear her speak again
And feast upon her eyes? What is't I dream on?
Oh, cunning enemy that, to catch a saint,   187
With saints dost bait thy hook! Most dangerous
Is that temptation that doth goad us on
To sin in loving virtue. Never could the strumpet,
With all her double vigor—art and nature—   191
Once stir my temper; but this virtuous maid   192
Subdues me quite. Ever till now,
When men were fond, I smiled and wondered how.   194

                                                    Exit.

2.3 ⮜ *Enter, [meeting,] Duke [disguised as a friar]*
       and Provost.

DUKE
   Hail to you, Provost—so I think you are.

PROVOST
   I am the Provost. What's your will, good Friar?

DUKE
   Bound by my charity and my blest order,
   I come to visit the afflicted spirits

179 **pitch our evils there** i.e., erect a privy, not on *waste ground*
(line 177), but on sanctified ground. (*Evils* also has the more
common meaning of "wickedness.")   187 **enemy** i.e., Satan
191 **double . . . nature** twofold power (of alluring men) through
artifice and a sensuous nature   192 **temper** temperament
194 **fond** foolishly in love

2.3 *Location: A prison.*

Here in the prison. Do me the common right   5
To let me see them and to make me know
The nature of their crimes, that I may minister
To them accordingly.

PROVOST
I would do more than that, if more were needful.

     Enter Juliet.

Look, here comes one: a gentlewoman of mine,
Who, falling in the flaws of her own youth,   11
Hath blistered her report. She is with child,   12
And he that got it, sentenced—a young man   13
More fit to do another such offense
Than die for this.

DUKE
When must he die?

PROVOST   As I do think, tomorrow.
[*To Juliet*] I have provided for you. Stay awhile,   17
And you shall be conducted.   18

DUKE
Repent you, fair one, of the sin you carry?

JULIET
I do, and bear the shame most patiently.

DUKE
I'll teach you how you shall arraign your conscience,   21
And try your penitence, if it be sound   22
Or hollowly put on.   23

JULIET   I'll gladly learn.

DUKE   Love you the man that wronged you?

JULIET
Yes, as I love the woman that wronged him.

---

5 **common right** i.e., right of all clerics   11 **flaws** (1) weaknesses,
fissures (2) sudden gusts (of passion)   12 **blistered her report**
marred her reputation.   13 **got** begot   17 **provided** provided
a place to stay   18 **conducted** taken there.   21 **arraign**
accuse   22 **try** test   23 **hollowly** falsely

DUKE

> So then it seems your most offenseful act
> Was mutually committed?

JULIET   Mutually.

DUKE

> Then was your sin of heavier kind than his.

JULIET

> I do confess it and repent it, Father.

DUKE

> 'Tis meet so, daughter. But lest you do repent   31
> As that the sin hath brought you to this shame,   32
> Which sorrow is always toward ourselves, not heaven,   33
> Showing we would not spare heaven as we love it,   34
> But as we stand in fear—

JULIET

> I do repent me as it is an evil,
> And take the shame with joy.

DUKE   There rest.   37

> Your partner, as I hear, must die tomorrow,
> And I am going with instruction to him.
> Grace go with you. *Benedicite!*   *Exit.*   40

JULIET

> Must die tomorrow? O injurious love,   41
> That respites me a life whose very comfort   42
> Is still a dying horror!

31 **'Tis meet so** It is fitting that you do so   32 **As that** merely
because   33 **toward ourselves** i.e., narrowly self-concerned
rather than loving virtue for its own sake   34 **Showing . . . it**
showing that we wish to avoid offending heaven not out of sheer
love of goodness   37 **There rest.** Hold fast to that truth.
40 *Benedicite!* Blessings on you!   41–3 **O . . . horror!** i.e.,
O sinful pregnancy, that prolongs a life whose greatest comfort
will always be a deadly horror! (Pregnancy could save a woman
from being executed. However, *love* is sometimes emended to *law*.)

PROVOST   'Tis pity of him.   *Exeunt.*   43

2.4 ❧ *Enter Angelo.*

ANGELO
When I would pray and think, I think and pray
To several subjects. Heaven hath my empty words,   2
Whilst my invention, hearing not my tongue,   3
Anchors on Isabel; Heaven in my mouth,
As if I did but only chew His name,   5
And in my heart the strong and swelling evil
Of my conception. The state, whereon I studied,   7
Is like a good thing, being often read,
Grown sere and tedious. Yea, my gravity,   9
Wherein—let no man hear me—I take pride,
Could I with boot change for an idle plume,   11
Which the air beats for vain. O place, O form,   12
How often dost thou with thy case, thy habit,   13
Wrench awe from fools and tie the wiser souls   14
To thy false seeming! Blood, thou art blood.   15

43 **pity of** a pity about

2.4 *Location: Angelo's official residence.*
2 **several** separate   3 **invention** imagination   5 **His** i.e.,
Heaven's, God's   7 **conception** thought.   **The state** Statecraft
9 **sere** withered, old   11–12 **Could . . . vain** I could willingly
exchange (my gravity) for the frivolity of a pleasure-loving gallant,
sporting a feather that seems to beat the air in its vanity (or, perhaps,
is beaten by the air in reproof of its vanity).   12 **O place,
O form** O authority of high position, O ceremonial dignity of office
13 **thy case . . . habit** your mere outward appearance and garb
14–15 **Wrench . . . seeming** intimidate ordinary foolish men and
subjugate even the wise to the seeming virtue of authority.
15 **Blood . . . blood** i.e., No position of authority or birth, no matter
how lofty, can protect a person from his own lustful appetites.

Let's write "good angel" on the devil's horn,   16
'Tis not the devil's crest.

      Enter Servant.

                      How now? Who's there?   17

SERVANT
One Isabel, a sister, desires access to you.

ANGELO   Teach her the way.   [*Exit Servant.*]
                        Oh, heavens!   19
Why does my blood thus muster to my heart,   20
Making both it unable for itself   21
And dispossessing all my other parts
Of necessary fitness?
So play the foolish throngs with one that swoons,   24
Come all to help him, and so stop the air
By which he should revive; and even so
The general subject to a well-wished king   27
Quit their own part and in obsequious fondness   28
Crowd to his presence, where their untaught love   29
Must needs appear offense.

      Enter Isabella.

                    How now, fair maid?   30

ISABELLA   I am come to know your pleasure.

16–17 **Let's . . . crest** i.e., No matter how hard we try to disguise
evil under the semblance of good, it remains recognizably evil still.
(In heraldic terms, the devil is known by his baleful horns; the
heraldic crest on his coat of arms does not alter his true identity.)
19 **Teach** Show   20 **muster to** assemble like soldiers in
21 **unable** ineffectual   24 **play** behave   27 **general subject**
i.e., commoners, subjects.   **well-wished** attended by good
wishes   28 **Quit . . . part** abandon their proper function and
(politely distant) place   29 **untaught** ignorant, unmannerly
30 **Must needs** will necessarily

ANGELO
    That you might know it would much better please me   32
    Than to demand what 'tis. Your brother cannot live.   33

ISABELLA
    Even so. Heaven keep Your Honor!   34

                                        [*She turns to leave.*]

ANGELO
    Yet may he live awhile; and, it may be,
    As long as you or I. Yet he must die.

ISABELLA   Under your sentence?

ANGELO   Yea.

ISABELLA
    When, I beseech you? That in his reprieve,
    Longer or shorter, he may be so fitted   40
    That his soul sicken not.

ANGELO
    Ha? Fie, these filthy vices! It were as good   42
    To pardon him that hath from nature stolen   43
    A man already made, as to remit   44
    Their saucy sweetness that do coin heaven's image   45
    In stamps that are forbid. 'Tis all as easy   46
    Falsely to take away a life true made
    As to put metal in restrainèd means   48
    To make a false one.

32–3 **That . . . 'tis** i.e., I wish you could know the nature of my
desire without your asking and my having to be explicit. (*Know*
suggests carnal knowledge.)   34 **Even so** So be it.   40 **fitted**
prepared   42–6 **It were . . . forbid** One might as well pardon
the murderer of a man already alive as pardon the wanton
pleasures of those persons who produce illegitimate offspring, like
counterfeit coiners. (*Heaven's image* is humankind, made in God's
likeness; Genesis 1:27.)   48 **metal** i.e., the metal used in coining
(lines 45–6), with a play on *mettle,* natural vigor or spirit.
restrainèd prohibited, illicit (both in counterfeiting coinage and in
begetting illegitimate children)

ISABELLA
    'Tis set down so in heaven, but not in earth.   50

ANGELO
    Say you so? Then I shall pose you quickly: 51
    Which had you rather, that the most just law
    Now took your brother's life, or, to redeem him,
    Give up your body to such sweet uncleanness
    As she that he hath stained?

ISABELLA   Sir, believe this,
    I had rather give my body than my soul.   56

ANGELO
    I talk not of your soul. Our compelled sins   57
    Stand more for number than for account.

ISABELLA   How say you?   58

ANGELO
    Nay, I'll not warrant that, for I can speak   59
    Against the thing I say. Answer to this:
    I, now the voice of the recorded law,
    Pronounce a sentence on your brother's life;
    Might there not be a charity in sin
    To save this brother's life?

ISABELLA   Please you to do't,   64
    I'll take it as a peril to my soul;   65
    It is no sin at all, but charity.

50 'Tis . . . earth i.e., Equating murder and bastardizing accords
with divine law but not with human law, according to which
murder is more heinous.   51 pose you put a perplexing
question to you   56 give i.e., give to death or punishment.
(Isabella avoids or does not understand the drift of the question.)
57–8 Our . . . account Our sins committed under compulsion are
recorded but not charged to our spiritual account.   59 I'll . . .
that i.e., I'm not necessarily endorsing the view I just expressed
64 Please you If you please   65 take accept

ANGELO

Pleased you to do't at peril of your soul   67
Were equal poise of sin and charity.   68

ISABELLA

That I do beg his life, if it be sin,
Heaven let me bear it! You granting of my suit,
If that be sin, I'll make it my morn prayer
To have it added to the faults of mine,
And nothing of your answer.

ANGELO   Nay, but hear me.   73
Your sense pursues not mine. Either you are ignorant
Or seem so craftily; and that's not good.

ISABELLA

Let me be ignorant, and in nothing good,
But graciously to know I am no better.   77

ANGELO

Thus wisdom wishes to appear most bright
When it doth tax itself, as these black masks   79
Proclaim an enshield beauty ten times louder   80
Than beauty could, displayed. But mark me.
To be receivèd plain, I'll speak more gross: 82
Your brother is to die.

ISABELLA   So.

ANGELO

And his offense is so, as it appears,
Accountant to the law upon that pain.   86

ISABELLA   True.

67 **Pleased** If it pleased   68 **Were equal poise** there would be
equal balance   73 **of your answer** to which you will have to
answer.   77 **graciously** through divine grace   79 **tax itself**
accuse itself (of ignorance).   **these** (Generically referring to
any.)   80 **enshield** shielded, protected from view behind the
black masks   82 **receivèd plain** plainly understood.   **gross**
(1) openly (2) offensively   86 **Accountant** accountable.   **pain**
penalty.

ANGELO
    Admit no other way to save his life—   88
    As I subscribe not that, nor any other,   89
    But in the loss of question—that you, his sister,   90
    Finding yourself desired of such a person   91
    Whose credit with the judge, or own great place,
    Could fetch your brother from the manacles
    Of the all-binding law; and that there were
    No earthly means to save him, but that either
    You must lay down the treasures of your body
    To this supposed, or else to let him suffer.   97
    What would you do?

ISABELLA
    As much for my poor brother as myself:
    That is, were I under the terms of death,   100
    Th'impression of keen whips I'd wear as rubies,
    And strip myself to death as to a bed
    That longing have been sick for, ere I'd yield   103
    My body up to shame.

ANGELO   Then must your brother die.

ISABELLA   And 'twere the cheaper way.
    Better it were a brother died at once   107
    Than that a sister, by redeeming him,
    Should die forever.

ANGELO
    Were not you then as cruel as the sentence
    That you have slandered so?

88 **Admit** Suppose   89–90 **As . . . question** since I will admit
no alternative possibility in our discussion. (*Loss of question* means
"forfeiting the terms of our debate.")   91 **of** by   97 **supposed**
hypothetical person.   **him** i.e., Claudio   100 **terms** sentence
103 **That . . . for** i.e., that I have been sick with longing for.
(Isabella's images are of love, death, and flagellation.)   107 **died
at once** should die once for all, rather than *die forever* (line 109) in
the death of the soul through sin

ISABELLA

Ignomy in ransom and free pardon   112
Are of two houses. Lawful mercy   113
Is nothing kin to foul redemption.   114

ANGELO

You seemed of late to make the law a tyrant,
And rather proved the sliding of your brother   116
A merriment than a vice.

ISABELLA

Oh, pardon me, my lord. It oft falls out,
To have what we would have, we speak not what
    we mean.
I something do excuse the thing I hate   120
For his advantage that I dearly love.

ANGELO

We are all frail.

ISABELLA   Else let my brother die,
If not a fedary but only he   123
Owe and succeed thy weakness.   124

ANGELO   Nay, women are frail too.

ISABELLA

Ay, as the glasses where they view themselves,   126
Which are as easy broke as they make forms.   127

112–14 **Ignomy . . . redemption** Being ransomed under
ignominious circumstances and being released without conditions
are two entirely different things. Mercy under law bears no relation
to being spared under foul stipulations.   116 **proved** argued
120 **something** to some extent   123 **fedary** confederate,
companion who is equally guilty   124 **Owe . . . weakness**
possess and inherit the weakness you speak of, or the weakness to
which all men as a class are prone. (Isabella argues that Claudio
should die only if he is the only man who is frail.)   126 **glasses**
mirrors   127 **forms** (1) images (2) copies of themselves, i.e.,
children

Women? Help, heaven! Men their creation mar   128
In profiting by them. Nay, call us ten times frail,   129
For we are soft as our complexions are,   130
And credulous to false prints.

ANGELO   I think it well.   131
And from this testimony of your own sex—   132
Since I suppose we are made to be no stronger   133
Than faults may shake our frames—let me be bold.   134
I do arrest your words. Be that you are,   135
That is, a woman; if you be more, you're none.   136
If you be one, as you are well expressed   137
By all external warrants, show it now   138
By putting on the destined livery.   139

ISABELLA
I have no tongue but one. Gentle my lord,   140
Let me entreat you speak the former language.   141

ANGELO   Plainly conceive, I love you.

ISABELLA   My brother did love Juliet,
And you tell me that he shall die for't.

ANGELO
He shall not, Isabel, if you give me love.

128–9 **Men . . . them** Men mar their creation in God's likeness by
taking advantage of women.   130 **complexions** constitutions,
appearance   131 **credulous . . . prints** susceptible to false
impressions. (The metaphor is from the stamping of coins and
other metal.)   132 **of** about   133 **we** i.e., men and women
134 **Than** than that   135 **arrest your words** take what you
have said and hold you to it.   **that** what   136 **if . . . none** i.e.,
if you insist on remaining a virgin and free of fleshly desire, you
are no woman as we have defined the term—that is, frail and
susceptible.   137–8 **expressed . . . warrants** shown to be by
your physical beauty   139 **putting . . . livery** i.e., assuming the
characteristic frailty that all women possess.   140 **tongue**
language   141 **speak . . . language** speak to be understood, in
the language I understand.

ISABELLA
  I know your virtue hath a license in't,   146
  Which seems a little fouler than it is   147
  To pluck on others.

ANGELO   Believe me, on mine honor,   148
  My words express my purpose.

ISABELLA
  Ha! Little honor to be much believed,
  And most pernicious purpose! Seeming, seeming!
  I will proclaim thee, Angelo, look for't!
  Sign me a present pardon for my brother,   153
  Or with an outstretched throat I'll tell the world
      aloud
  What man thou art.

ANGELO   Who will believe thee, Isabel?
  My unsoiled name, th'austereness of my life,
  My vouch against you, and my place i'th' state   157
  Will so your accusation overweigh
  That you shall stifle in your own report
  And smell of calumny. I have begun,   160
  And now I give my sensual race the rein.   161
  Fit thy consent to my sharp appetite;
  Lay by all nicety and prolixious blushes   163
  That banish what they sue for. Redeem thy brother   164
  By yielding up thy body to my will,
  Or else he must not only die the death,   166
  But thy unkindness shall his death draw out

146–8 **I know . . . others** i.e., I am sure that you, out of virtuous
motives, are speaking licentiously (and with the license of
authority) in order to put me to the test.   153 **present**
immediate   157 **vouch** allegation   160 **calumny** slander.
161 **I give . . . rein** I give free rein to my sensual desires to gallop
as they please.   163–4 **Lay . . . sue for** Set aside all the coyness
and time-wasting blushes that make a pretense of repulsing the
embrace they actually beg for.   166 **die the death** be put to
death

To ling'ring sufferance. Answer me tomorrow,   168
Or, by the affection that now guides me most,   169
I'll prove a tyrant to him. As for you,
Say what you can, my false o'erweighs your true.

Exit.

ISABELLA

To whom should I complain? Did I tell this,   172
Who would believe me? O perilous mouths,   173
That bear in them one and the selfsame tongue,   174
Either of condemnation or approof,   175
Bidding the law make curtsy to their will,   176
Hooking both right and wrong to th'appetite,   177
To follow as it draws! I'll to my brother.   178
Though he hath fall'n by prompture of the blood,   179
Yet hath he in him such a mind of honor
That, had he twenty heads to tender down   181
On twenty bloody blocks, he'd yield them up
Before his sister should her body stoop
To such abhorred pollution.
Then, Isabel, live chaste, and, brother, die;
More than our brother is our chastity.
I'll tell him yet of Angelo's request,
And fit his mind to death, for his soul's rest.   *Exit.*

168 **sufferance** torture.   169 **affection** passion   172 **Did I
tell** If I told   173–8 **O perilous . . . draws!** O dangerous voices
of authority, able with one tongue either to condemn or approve,
forcing both right and wrong to obey the willful appetite!
179 **prompture** prompting, suggestion   181 **tender down** lay
down in payment

3.1 ❧ *Enter Duke [disguised as before], Claudio, and*
Provost.

DUKE
So then you hope of pardon from Lord Angelo?

CLAUDIO
The miserable have no other medicine
But only hope.
I have hope to live and am prepared to die.

DUKE
Be absolute for death. Either death or life
Shall thereby be the sweeter. Reason thus with life:
If I do lose thee, I do lose a thing
That none but fools would keep. A breath thou art,
Servile to all the skyey influences   9
That dost this habitation where thou keep'st   10
Hourly afflict. Merely, thou art death's fool,   11
For him thou labor'st by thy flight to shun,
And yet run'st toward him still. Thou art not noble,   13
For all th'accommodations that thou bear'st   14
Are nursed by baseness. Thou'rt by no means valiant,   15
For thou dost fear the soft and tender fork   16
Of a poor worm. Thy best of rest is sleep,   17
And that thou oft provok'st, yet grossly fear'st   18
Thy death, which is no more. Thou art not thyself,
For thou exists on many a thousand grains
That issue out of dust. Happy thou art not,

3.1 *Location: The prison.*
9 skyey influences influence of the stars   **10 this habitation**
i.e., the earth (and the body as well).   **keep'st** dwell
11 Merely Utterly, only   **13 still** always.   **14 accommodations**
conveniences, civilized comforts   **15 nursed by baseness**
nurtured by ignoble means.   **16 fork** forked tongue
17 worm (1) snake (2) grave worm.   **18 thou oft provok'st** you
often invoke, summon

For what thou hast not, still thou striv'st to get,
And what thou hast, forget'st. Thou art not certain,   23
For thy complexion shifts to strange effects,   24
After the moon. If thou art rich, thou'rt poor,   25
For, like an ass whose back with ingots bows,
Thou bear'st thy heavy riches but a journey,
And death unloads thee. Friend hast thou none,
For thine own bowels which do call thee sire,   29
The mere effusion of thy proper loins,   30
Do curse the gout, serpigo, and the rheum   31
For ending thee no sooner. Thou hast nor youth
    nor age,   32
But as it were an after-dinner's sleep   33
Dreaming on both, for all thy blessèd youth   34
Becomes as agèd and doth beg the alms   35
Of palsied eld; and, when thou art old and rich,   36
Thou hast neither heat, affection, limb, nor beauty   37
To make thy riches pleasant. What's yet in this
That bears the name of life? Yet in this life
Lie hid more thousand deaths; yet death we fear,
That makes these odds all even.

CLAUDIO   I humbly thank you.   41
To sue to live, I find I seek to die,   42
And, seeking death, find life. Let it come on.

    Enter Isabella.

---

23 **certain** steadfast   24 **complexion** constitution.   **strange effects** new appearances, manifestations   25 **After** in obedience to, under the influence of   29 **bowels** i.e., offspring   30 **mere** very.   **proper** own   31 **serpigo** a skin eruption.   **rheum** catarrh   32 **nor youth** neither youth   33 **after-dinner's** i.e., afternoon's   34–6 **all . . . eld** your happy youth must decline all too soon into old age and become like a beggar, pleading for the little comfort that palsied infirmity can provide. (Youth is penniless and dependent on the aged, whereas the old lack the physical capacity of youth.)   37 **heat, affection** vigor, passion   41 **makes . . . even** makes all equal.   42 **To sue** Suing, petitioning

ISABELLA

    What, ho! Peace here; grace and good company!   44

PROVOST

    Who's there? Come in. The wish deserves a welcome.

                    [*He goes to greet her.*]

DUKE [*to Claudio*]

    Dear sir, ere long I'll visit you again.

CLAUDIO   Most holy sir, I thank you.

ISABELLA

    My business is a word or two with Claudio.

PROVOST

    And very welcome.—Look, signor, here's your sister.

DUKE [*aside to the Provost*]   Provost, a word with you.

PROVOST   As many as you please.

DUKE

    Bring me to hear them speak, where I may be

    Concealed.   [*The Duke and the Provost withdraw.*]

CLAUDIO   Now, sister, what's the comfort?

ISABELLA   Why,

    As all comforts are: most good, most good indeed.

    Lord Angelo, having affairs to heaven,

    Intends you for his swift ambassador,

    Where you shall be an everlasting leiger.   57

    Therefore your best appointment make with speed;   58

    Tomorrow you set on.

CLAUDIO   Is there no remedy?   59

ISABELLA

    None but such remedy as, to save a head,

    To cleave a heart in twain.

---

44 **grace** God's grace   57 **leiger** resident ambassador.
58 **appointment** preparation   59 **set on** set forward.

CLAUDIO   But is there any?

ISABELLA   Yes, brother, you may live.
There is a devilish mercy in the judge,
If you'll implore it, that will free your life
But fetter you till death.

CLAUDIO   Perpetual durance?   66

ISABELLA
Ay, just; perpetual durance, a restraint,   67
Though all the world's vastidity you had,   68
To a determined scope.

CLAUDIO   But in what nature?   69

ISABELLA
In such a one as, you consenting to't,
Would bark your honor from that trunk you bear   71
And leave you naked.

CLAUDIO   Let me know the point.

ISABELLA
Oh, I do fear thee, Claudio, and I quake   73
Lest thou a feverous life shouldst entertain,   74
And six or seven winters more respect   75
Than a perpetual honor. Dar'st thou die?
The sense of death is most in apprehension,   77
And the poor beetle that we tread upon
In corporal sufferance finds a pang as great
As when a giant dies.

66 **durance** imprisonment.   67 **just** just so   67–9 **a restraint . . .
scope** a confinement to fixed limits or bounds (i.e., to inescapable
guilt and perpetual remorse for the sinful bargain you had struck),
even if you had the entire vastness of the world to wander in.
71 **bark** strip off (as one strips bark from a tree *trunk*)   73 **fear**
fear for   74 **feverous** feverish.   **entertain** maintain, desire
75 **respect** value   77 **apprehension** anticipation

CLAUDIO   Why give you me this shame?
    Think you I can a resolution fetch   82
    From flow'ry tenderness? If I must die,   83
    I will encounter darkness as a bride
    And hug it in mine arms.

ISABELLA
    There spake my brother! There my father's grave
    Did utter forth a voice. Yes, thou must die.
    Thou art too noble to conserve a life
    In base appliances. This outward-sainted deputy,   89
    Whose settled visage and deliberate word   90
    Nips youth i'th' head, and follies doth enew   91
    As falcon doth the fowl, is yet a devil;   92
    His filth within being cast, he would appear   93
    A pond as deep as hell.

CLAUDIO   The prenzie Angelo?   94

ISABELLA
    Oh, 'tis the cunning livery of hell,   95
    The damned'st body to invest and cover   96
    In prenzie guards! Dost thou think, Claudio: 97
    If I would yield him my virginity,
    Thou mightst be freed!

CLAUDIO   Oh, heavens, it cannot be.

82–3 Think . . . tenderness? Do you think I can find the courage
to face death in flowery figures of speech?   **89 In base
appliances** by means of ignoble devices, remedies.
89–92 This . . . fowl This outwardly holy deputy, who with
composed features and judiciously chosen words swoops down on
youth like a falcon and drives his prey into covert. (To *enew* is to
drive prey down into the water or into hiding.)   **93 cast** dug out;
diagnosed; sounded; vomited (?)   **94, 97 prenzie** (A word
unknown elsewhere, perhaps meaning "princely" or "precise.")
95–7 'tis . . . guards it is the cunning ruse of the devil to clothe
and conceal the wickedest man imaginable in decorously proper
trimmings.   **97 Dost thou think** i.e., Would you believe

ISABELLA
   Yes, he would give't thee, from this rank offense,   100
   So to offend him still. This night's the time   101
   That I should do what I abhor to name,
   Or else thou diest tomorrow.

CLAUDIO   Thou shalt not do't.

ISABELLA   Oh, were it but my life,
   I'd throw it down for your deliverance
   As frankly as a pin.

CLAUDIO   Thanks, dear Isabel.   107

ISABELLA
   Be ready, Claudio, for your death tomorrow.

CLAUDIO
   Yes. Has he affections in him,   109
   That thus can make him bite the law by th' nose   110
   When he would force it? Sure it is no sin,   111
   Or of the deadly seven it is the least.

ISABELLA   Which is the least?

CLAUDIO
   If it were damnable, he being so wise,
   Why would he for the momentary trick   115
   Be perdurably fined? Oh, Isabel!   116

ISABELLA
   What says my brother?

CLAUDIO   Death is a fearful thing.

ISABELLA   And shamèd life a hateful.

100–1 **he would . . . still** he would grant you license, in return for
the committing of this foul crime, to continue with your
fornication.   107 **frankly** freely   109 **affections** passions
110 **bite . . . nose** i.e., flout the law   111 **force** enforce. (Claudio
wonders that lust can drive Angelo to make a mockery of the law
even while purporting to enforce it.)   115 **trick** trifle
116 **perdurably fined** everlastingly punished.

CLAUDIO
    Ay, but to die, and go we know not where,
    To lie in cold obstruction and to rot,   120
    This sensible warm motion to become   121
    A kneaded clod, and the delighted spirit   122
    To bathe in fiery floods, or to reside
    In thrilling region of thick-ribbèd ice;   124
    To be imprisoned in the viewless winds   125
    And blown with restless violence round about
    The pendent world; or to be worse than worst 127
    Of those that lawless and incertain thought   128
    Imagine howling—'tis too horrible!
    The weariest and most loathèd worldly life
    That age, ache, penury, and imprisonment
    Can lay on nature is a paradise
    To what we fear of death.   133

ISABELLA   Alas, alas!

CLAUDIO   Sweet sister, let me live.
    What sin you do to save a brother's life,
    Nature dispenses with the deed so far   137
    That it becomes a virtue.

ISABELLA   Oh, you beast!
    Oh, faithless coward! Oh, dishonest wretch!   139
    Wilt thou be made a man out of my vice?
    Is't not a kind of incest, to take life
    From thine own sister's shame? What should I think?
    Heaven shield my mother played my father fair! 143

---

120 **obstruction** cessation of vital functions   121 **sensible** endowed
with feeling.   **motion** organism   122 **kneaded clod** shapeless
lump of earth.   **delighted spirit** spirit that is now attended with
delight, or capable of being so   124 **thrilling** piercingly cold
125 **viewless** invisible   127 **pendent** hanging in space. (A Ptolemaic
concept.)   128 **lawless . . . thought** i.e., wild conjecture   133 **To**
compared to   137 **dispenses with** grants a dispensation for, excuses
139 **dishonest** dishonorable   143 **Heaven . . . fair!** God forbid that
my mother was being faithful to my father when you were sired!

For such a warpèd slip of wilderness   144
Ne'er issued from his blood. Take my defiance,
Die, perish! Might but my bending down   146
Reprieve thee from thy fate, it should proceed.
I'll pray a thousand prayers for thy death,
No word to save thee.

CLAUDIO
Nay, hear me, Isabel.

ISABELLA   Oh, fie, fie, fie!
Thy sin's not accidental, but a trade.   151
Mercy to thee would prove itself a bawd;   152
'Tis best that thou diest quickly.

CLAUDIO   Oh, hear me, Isabella!

[*The Duke comes forward.*]

DUKE
Vouchsafe a word, young sister, but one word.   155

ISABELLA   What is your will?

DUKE   Might you dispense with your leisure, I would
by and by have some speech with you. The satisfaction I would require is likewise your own benefit.   159

ISABELLA   I have no superfluous leisure—my stay
must be stolen out of other affairs—but I will attend 161
you awhile.   [*She walks apart.*]

DUKE   Son, I have overheard what hath passed between
you and your sister. Angelo had never the purpose to
corrupt her; only he hath made an assay of her virtue 165
to practice his judgment with the disposition of na-   166
tures. She, having the truth of honor in her, hath made 167

144 **warpèd . . . wilderness** perverse, licentious scion, one that
reverts to the original wild stock   146 **but** merely
151 **accidental** casual.   **trade** established habit.   152 **prove . . .
bawd** i.e., provide opportunity for sexual license   155 **Vouchsafe**
Allow   159 **require** ask   161 **attend** await; listen to   165 **only
he hath** he has only.   **assay** test   166–7 **his judgment . . .
natures** his ability to judge people's characters.

him that gracious denial which he is most glad to re-   168
ceive. I am confessor to Angelo, and I know this to be
true; therefore prepare yourself to death. Do not satisfy
your resolution with hopes that are fallible. Tomorrow
you must die. Go to your knees and make ready.

CLAUDIO   Let me ask my sister pardon. I am so out of
love with life that I will sue to be rid of it.

DUKE   Hold you there. Farewell.   [Claudio retires.]   175
Provost, a word with you.

    [The Provost comes forward.]

PROVOST   What's your will, Father?

DUKE   That now you are come, you will be gone. Leave
me awhile with the maid. My mind promises with my   179
habit no loss shall touch her by my company.   180

PROVOST   In good time.   Exit [Provost with Claudio].   181

    [Isabella comes forward.]

DUKE   The hand that hath made you fair hath made you
good. The goodness that is cheap in beauty makes   183
beauty brief in goodness; but grace, being the soul of   184
your complexion, shall keep the body of it ever fair.   185
The assault that Angelo hath made to you, fortune
hath conveyed to my understanding; and, but that   187
frailty hath examples for his falling, I should wonder   188
at Angelo. How will you do to content this substitute   189
and to save your brother?

168 **gracious** virtuous   175 **Hold you there** Hold fast to that
resolution.   179–80 **with my habit** as well as my priestly garb
(that)   181 **In good time** i.e., Very well.   183–84 **The
goodness . . . in goodness** i.e., The physical attractions that
come easily with beauty make beauty soon cease to be morally
good   185 **complexion** character and appearance   187 **but
that** were it not that   188 **examples** precedents   189 **this
substitute** i.e., the deputy, Angelo

ISABELLA   I am now going to resolve him. I had rather 191
my brother die by the law than my son should be
unlawfully born. But, oh, how much is the good Duke
deceived in Angelo! If ever he return and I can speak
to him, I will open my lips in vain, or discover his 195
government. 196

DUKE   That shall not be much amiss. Yet, as the matter
now stands, he will avoid your accusation; he made 198
trial of you only. Therefore fasten your ear on my
advisings. To the love I have in doing good a remedy
presents itself. I do make myself believe that you may
most uprighteously do a poor wronged lady a merited
benefit, redeem your brother from the angry law, do
no stain to your own gracious person, and much
please the absent Duke, if peradventure he shall ever
return to have hearing of this business.

ISABELLA   Let me hear you speak farther. I have spirit 207
to do anything that appears not foul in the truth of my 208
spirit. 209

DUKE   Virtue is bold, and goodness never fearful. Have
you not heard speak of Mariana, the sister of Frederick, the great soldier who miscarried at sea?

ISABELLA   I have heard of the lady, and good words
went with her name.

DUKE   She should this Angelo have married, was 215
affianced to her by oath, and the nuptial appointed;
between which time of the contract and limit of the 217
solemnity her brother Frederick was wrecked at sea, 218

---

191 **resolve him** set his mind at rest.   195–6 **discover his
government** expose Angelo's misconduct.   198 **avoid** evade,
refute.   **he made** i.e., he will say that he made   207 **spirit**
courage   208 **truth** righteousness   209 **spirit** soul.
215 **She . . . married** Angelo was supposed to have married her.
was i.e., he was   217–18 **limit . . . solemnity** date set for the
ceremony

having in that perished vessel the dowry of his sister.
But mark how heavily this befell to the poor gentlewoman. There she lost a noble and renowned brother,
in his love toward her ever most kind and natural;
with him, the portion and sinew of her fortune, her   223
marriage dowry; with both, her combinate husband,   224
this well-seeming Angelo.

ISABELLA Can this be so? Did Angelo so leave her?

DUKE Left her in her tears, and dried not one of them
with his comfort; swallowed his vows whole, pretend-   228
ing in her discoveries of dishonor; in few, bestowed   229
her on her own lamentation, which she yet wears for   230
his sake; and he, a marble to her tears, is washed with 231
them but relents not.

ISABELLA What a merit were it in death to take this
poor maid from the world! What corruption in this
life, that it will let this man live! But how out of this can
she avail?   236

DUKE It is a rupture that you may easily heal, and the
cure of it not only saves your brother but keeps you
from dishonor in doing it.

ISABELLA Show me how, good Father.

DUKE This forenamed maid hath yet in her the continuance of her first affection; his unjust unkindness, that
in all reason should have quenched her love, hath, like
an impediment in the current, made it more violent
and unruly. Go you to Angelo; answer his requiring

---

223 **the portion and sinew** i.e., the mainstay   224 **combinate
husband** i.e., betrothed   228–9 **pretending . . . dishonor**
falsely alleging to have found evidence of unchastity in her
229–30 **in few . . . lamentation** in short, left her to her grief.
(With quibble on *bestowed*, meaning "gave in marriage.")
230 **wears** i.e., carries in her heart   231 **a marble to** i.e.,
unmoved by   236 **avail** benefit.

with a plausible obedience; agree with his demands to 246
the point. Only refer yourself to this advantage: first, 247
that your stay with him may not be long, that the time
may have all shadow and silence in it, and the place 249
answer to convenience. This being granted in
course—and now follows all—we shall advise this
wronged maid to stead up your appointment, go in 252
your place. If the encounter acknowledge itself here- 253
after, it may compel him to her recompense. And here, 254
by this, is your brother saved, your honor untainted,
the poor Mariana advantaged, and the corrupt deputy
scaled. The maid will I frame and make fit for his at- 257
tempt. If you think well to carry this as you may, the
doubleness of the benefit defends the deceit from reproof. What think you of it?

ISABELLA   The image of it gives me content already,
and I trust it will grow to a most prosperous perfection.

DUKE   It lies much in your holding up. Haste you speed- 264
ily to Angelo. If for this night he entreat you to his
bed, give him promise of satisfaction. I will presently
to Saint Luke's; there, at the moated grange, resides 267
this dejected Mariana. At that place call upon me; and
dispatch with Angelo, that it may be quickly. 269

ISABELLA   I thank you for this comfort. Fare you well,
good Father.   *Exit. [The Duke remains.]*

246–7 **to the point** precisely.   247 **refer . . . advantage** obtain
these conditions   249 **shadow** darkness, secrecy   252 **stead . . .**
appointment go in your stead   253–4 **If the . . . hereafter**
i.e., If she should become pregnant   257 **scaled** weighed in
the scales of justice (and found wanting).   **frame** prepare
264 **holding up** ability to carry it off.   267 **moated**
grange country house surrounded by a ditch
269 **dispatch** settle, conclude business

[3.2] ⤙⤚ *Enter [to the Duke] Elbow, Clown [Pompey, and] officers.*

ELBOW Nay, if there be no remedy for it but that you will needs buy and sell men and women like beasts, we shall have all the world drink brown and white bastard.   4

DUKE [*aside*] Oh, heavens, what stuff is here?

POMPEY 'Twas never merry world since, of two usur-   6
ies, the merriest was put down, and the worser al-   7
lowed by order of law a furred gown to keep him   8
warm, and furred with fox on lambskins too, to signify that craft, being richer than innocency, stands   10
for the facing.   11

ELBOW Come your way, sir.—Bless you, good Father Friar.

DUKE And you, good Brother Father. What offense hath   14
this man made you, sir?

ELBOW Marry, sir, he hath offended the law; and, sir, we take him to be a thief too, sir, for we have found upon him, sir, a strange picklock, which we have sent   18
to the deputy.

DUKE [*to Pompey*]
Fie, sirrah, a bawd, a wicked bawd!
The evil that thou causest to be done,

3.2 Location: Scene continues. The Duke remains on stage.
4 bastard sweet Spanish wine. (Used quibblingly.)   **6–7 two
usuries** i.e., moneylending (the *worser*) and procuring for
fornication (the *merriest*), both of which yield increase   **8 furred
gown** (Characteristic attire of usurers.)   **10–11 stands . . .
facing** represents the outer covering. (Fox symbolizes *craft* or
craftiness, lambskin, *innocency*.)   **14 Brother Father** (The
Duke's retort to Elbow's *Father Friar*, i.e., Father Brother.)
18 picklock skeleton key, or perhaps a chastity belt in Pompey's
possession as pimp; it might seem *strange* to the innocent Elbow

That is thy means to live. Do thou but think
What 'tis to cram a maw or clothe a back   23
From such a filthy vice; say to thyself,
From their abominable and beastly touches   25
I drink, I eat, array myself, and live.
Canst thou believe thy living is a life,
So stinkingly depending? Go mend, go mend.   28

POMPEY   Indeed, it does stink in some sort, sir. But yet,
sir, I would prove—   30

DUKE
Nay, if the devil have given thee proofs for sin,   31
Thou wilt prove his.—Take him to prison, officer.   32
Correction and instruction must both work
Ere this rude beast will profit.

ELBOW   He must before the deputy, sir; he has given   35
him warning. The deputy cannot abide a whoremas-
ter. If he be a whoremonger and comes before him, he   37
were as good go a mile on his errand.   38

DUKE
That we were all, as some would seem to be,   39
From our faults, as faults from seeming, free!   40

     Enter Lucio.

ELBOW   His neck will come to your waist—a cord, sir.   41

POMPEY   I spy comfort, I cry bail. Here's a gentleman
and a friend of mine.

23 **cram . . . back** fill a stomach or provide clothing   25 **touches**
sexual encounters   28 **depending** supported.   30 **prove** i.e.,
argue, demonstrate   31 **proofs for** arguments in defense of
32 **prove** turn out to be   35 **must** must go.   **deputy** i.e.,
Angelo. (Though Escalus gave Pompey the warning.)   37–8 **he
were . . . errand** i.e., he will have a hard road to travel.   39 **That**
Would that   40 **From . . . free** i.e., free from faults, and our
faults free from dissembling.   41 **His . . . cord** i.e., He is likely
to hang by a cord like that around your waist. (The Duke is habited
as a friar.)

LUCIO   How now, noble Pompey? What, at the wheels
of Caesar? Art thou led in triumph? What, is there   45
none of Pygmalion's images, newly made woman, to   46
be had now, for putting the hand in the pocket and
extracting it clutched? What reply, ha? What say'st thou   48
to this tune, matter, and method? Is 't not drowned i'th'   49
last rain, ha? What say'st thou, trot? Is the world   50
as it was, man? Which is the way? Is it sad, and few   51
words? Or how? The trick of it?   52

DUKE   Still thus, and thus; still worse!

LUCIO   How doth my dear morsel, thy mistress? Pro-
cures she still, ha?

POMPEY   Troth, sir, she hath eaten up all her beef, and   56
she is herself in the tub.   57

LUCIO   Why, 'tis good. It is the right of it, it must be so.
Ever your fresh whore and your powdered bawd; an   59
unshunned consequence, it must be so. Art going to   60
prison, Pompey?

45 **Caesar** (Who defeated Pompey at Pharsalia and led his sons in
triumph after defeating them at Munda.)   46 **Pygmalion's
images** i.e., prostitutes, so called because they "painted" with
cosmetics like a painted statue. (Pygmalion was a sculptor,
according to legend, whose female statue came to life "newly
made.")   48 **clutched** i.e., with money in it. (But also with
sexual suggestion.)   48–50 **What say'st . . . rain** i.e., What do
you say now to this latest turn of events? Are our prospects a little
dampened?   50 **trot** old bawd.   51–2 **Which . . . words?** i.e.,
What is the latest fashion? Is melancholy now in vogue? (A wry
comment on Pompey's silence.)   52 **trick** fashion   56 **eaten . . .
beef** (1) consumed all her salt beef, which had been prepared in a
powder-tub like that also used to treat venereal disease (2) run
through all her prostitutes   57 **in the tub** being treated for
venereal disease by the sweating-tub treatment (much as beef was
salted down in a tub to preserve it).   59 **Ever . . . bawd** i.e., It is
always thus with young whores and old bawds, *powdered* like beef
in a tub and caked with cosmetics   60 **unshunned** unshunnable,
unavoidable

POMPEY   Yes, faith, sir.

LUCIO   Why, 'tis not amiss, Pompey. Farewell. Go, say
I sent thee thither. For debt, Pompey? Or how?

ELBOW   For being a bawd, for being a bawd.

LUCIO   Well, then, imprison him. If imprisonment be
the due of a bawd, why, 'tis his right. Bawd is he
doubtless, and of antiquity too; bawd-born. Farewell,   68
good Pompey. Commend me to the prison, Pompey.
You will turn good husband now, Pompey; you will   70
keep the house.   71

POMPEY   I hope, sir, Your good Worship will be my bail.

LUCIO   No, indeed, will I not, Pompey; it is not the
wear. I will pray, Pompey, to increase your bondage.   74
If you take it not patiently, why, your mettle is the   75
more. Adieu, trusty Pompey.—Bless you, Friar.   76

DUKE   And you.

LUCIO   Does Bridget paint still, Pompey, ha?   78

ELBOW [to Pompey]   Come your ways, sir, come.   79

POMPEY [to Lucio]   You will not bail me, then, sir?

LUCIO   Then, Pompey, nor now.—What news abroad,   81
Friar? What news?

ELBOW   Come your ways, sir, come.

LUCIO   Go to kennel, Pompey, go.

          [Exeunt Elbow, Pompey, and Officers.]
What news, Friar, of the Duke?

DUKE   I know none. Can you tell me of any?

---

68 **antiquity** long continuance.   **bawd-born** a born bawd and
born of a bawd.   70 **good husband** thrifty manager   71 **keep
the house** stay indoors. (With pun on the pimp's function as
doorkeeper.)   74 **wear** fashion.   75–6 **your . . . more** (1) your
spirit is revealed all the more (2) your shackles will be made
heavier. (Playing on *mettle/metal*.)   78 **paint** use cosmetics
79 **Come your ways** Come along   81 **Then** Neither then.
abroad about town

LUCIO   Some say he is with the Emperor of Russia; other   87
         some, he is in Rome. But where is he, think you?   88

DUKE   I know not where; but wheresoever, I wish him
         well.

LUCIO   It was a mad fantastical trick of him to steal from   91
         the state and usurp the beggary he was never born to.   92
         Lord Angelo dukes it well in his absence; he puts   93
         transgression to't.   94

DUKE   He does well in't.

LUCIO   A little more lenity to lechery would do no harm
         in him. Something too crabbed that way, Friar.   97

DUKE   It is too general a vice, and severity must cure it.

LUCIO   Yes, in good sooth, the vice is of a great kindred;   99
         it is well allied. But it is impossible to extirp it quite, 100
         Friar, till eating and drinking be put down. They say
         this Angelo was not made by man and woman after   102
         this downright way of creation. Is it true, think you? 103

DUKE   How should he be made, then?

LUCIO   Some report a sea maid spawned him; some,   105
         that he was begot between two stockfishes. But it is   106
         certain that when he makes water his urine is con-
         gealed ice; that I know to be true. And he is a motion 108
         ungenerative; that's infallible.   109

87–8 **other some** some others   91 **steal** steal away
92 **beggary** i.e., status of a wanderer or traveler. (With
unconscious ironic appropriateness; Lucio clearly does not see
through the Duke's disguise as a mendicant friar.)   93–4 **puts . . .
to't** puts lawbreaking under severe restraint.   97 **Something
too crabbed** Somewhat too harsh   99 **kindred** i.e., family,
numerous and well connected   100 **extirp** eradicate
102 **after** in accordance with   103 **downright** straightforward,
usual   105 **sea maid** mermaid   106 **stockfishes** dried
codfish.   108–9 **motion ungenerative** masculine puppet,
without sexual potency

DUKE   You are pleasant, sir, and speak apace.   110

LUCIO   Why, what a ruthless thing is this in him, for the
rebellion of a codpiece to take away the life of a man!   112
Would the Duke that is absent have done this? Ere he
would have hanged a man for the getting a hundred
bastards, he would have paid for the nursing a
thousand. He had some feeling of the sport; he knew
the service, and that instructed him to mercy.   117

DUKE   I never heard the absent Duke much detected for   118
women. He was not inclined that way.

LUCIO   Oh, sir, you are deceived.

DUKE   'Tis not possible.

LUCIO   Who, not the Duke? Yes, your beggar of fifty;
and his use was to put a ducat in her clack-dish. The   123
Duke had crotchets in him. He would be drunk too,
that let me inform you.

DUKE   You do him wrong, surely.

LUCIO   Sir, I was an inward of his. A shy fellow was the   127
Duke, and I believe I know the cause of his with-
drawing.

DUKE   What, I prithee, might be the cause?

LUCIO   No, pardon. 'Tis a secret must be locked within
the teeth and the lips. But this I can let you understand:
the greater file of the subject held the Duke to   133
be wise.

DUKE   Wise? Why, no question but he was.

110 **pleasant** jocose.   **apace** fast and idly.   112 **codpiece** an
appendage to the front of close-fitting hose or breeches worn by
men, often ornamented and indelicately conspicuous; hence, slang
for "penis"   117 **the service** i.e., prostitution   118 **detected**
accused   123 **his . . . clack-dish** his custom was to put a coin in
her wooden beggar's bowl, with its lid that was "clacked" to attract
attention. (Lucio hints that the Duke had sex with her.)
127 **inward** intimate   133 **the greater . . . subject** most of his
subjects

LUCIO   A very superficial, ignorant, unweighing fellow.   136

DUKE   Either this is envy in you, folly, or mistaking. The   137
very stream of his life and the business he hath helmed   138
must, upon a warranted need, give him a better proc-   139
lamation. Let him be but testimonied in his own   140
bringings-forth, and he shall appear to the envious a   141
scholar, a statesman, and a soldier. Therefore you
speak unskillfully; or, if your knowledge be more, it is   143
much darkened in your malice.

LUCIO   Sir, I know him, and I love him.

DUKE   Love talks with better knowledge, and knowledge with dearer love.

LUCIO   Come, sir, I know what I know.

DUKE   I can hardly believe that, since you know not
what you speak. But if ever the Duke return, as our
prayers are he may, let me desire you to make your
answer before him. If it be honest you have spoke,
you have courage to maintain it. I am bound to call
upon you; and, I pray you, your name?

LUCIO   Sir, my name is Lucio, well known to the Duke.

DUKE   He shall know you better, sir, if I may live to
report you.

LUCIO   I fear you not.

DUKE   Oh, you hope the Duke will return no more, or
you imagine me too unhurtful an opposite. But indeed   160
I can do you little harm; you'll forswear this again.   161

---

136 **unweighing** injudicious   137 **envy** malice   138 **helmed**
steered   139 **upon . . . need** if a warrant were needed
139–40 **give . . . proclamation** proclaim him better (than you
assert).   140–1 **in . . . bringings-forth** by his own public
actions   141 **to the envious** even to the malicious
143 **unskillfully** in ignorance   160 **too . . . opposite** too
harmless an adversary.   161 **forswear this again** deny another
time what you have said under oath.

LUCIO   I'll be hanged first. Thou art deceived in me,
Friar. But no more of this. Canst thou tell if Claudio
die tomorrow or no?

DUKE   Why should he die, sir?

LUCIO   Why? For filling a bottle with a tundish. I would   166
the Duke we talk of were returned again. This ungen-   167
itured agent will unpeople the province with conti-   168
nency. Sparrows must not build in his house eaves,   169
because they are lecherous. The Duke yet would have
dark deeds darkly answered; he would never bring   171
them to light. Would he were returned! Marry, this
Claudio is condemned for untrussing. Farewell, good   173
Friar. I prithee, pray for me. The Duke, I say to thee
again, would eat mutton on Fridays. He's now past it,   175
yet, and I say to thee, he would mouth with a beggar,   176
though she smelt brown bread and garlic. Say that I   177
said so. Farewell.   *Exit*.

DUKE
No might nor greatness in mortality   179
Can censure scape; back-wounding calumny   180
The whitest virtue strikes. What king so strong   181
Can tie the gall up in the slanderous tongue?
But who comes here?

166 **tundish** funnel. (Here representing the penis.)
167–8 **ungenitured agent** sexless deputy   169 **Sparrows**
(Proverbially lecherous birds.)   171 **darkly** secretly
173 **untrussing** undressing. (Specifically, untying the points used
to fasten hose to doublet.)   175 **eat . . . Fridays** i.e., frequent
loose women in flagrant disregard of the law. (Literally, violate
religious observance by eating meat on fast days.)   **past it**
beyond the age for sex   176 **mouth** kiss   177 **smelt brown
bread** smelled of coarse bran bread   179 **mortality**
humankind; human life   180–1 **Can . . . strikes** can escape
censure; backbiting slander strikes even the purest of virtues.
181 **so** be he never so

Enter Escalus, Provost, and [officers with] bawd
[Mistress Overdone].

ESCALUS   Go, away with her to prison.

MISTRESS OVERDONE   Good my lord, be good to me.
Your Honor is accounted a merciful man. Good my
lord.

ESCALUS   Double and treble admonition, and still forfeit   188
in the same kind! This would make mercy swear and   189
play the tyrant.

PROVOST   A bawd of eleven years' continuance, may it
please Your Honor.

MISTRESS OVERDONE   My lord, this is one Lucio's infor-   193
mation against me. Mistress Kate Keepdown was with   194
child by him in the Duke's time; he promised her marriage. His child is a year and a quarter old, come Philip   196
and Jacob. I have kept it myself; and see how he goes   197
about to abuse me!   198

ESCALUS   That fellow is a fellow of much license. Let
him be called before us. Away with her to prison! Go
to, no more words.   [*Exeunt Officers with Mistress*
                                      Overdone.]

Provost, my brother Angelo will not be al-   202
tered; Claudio must die tomorrow. Let him be furnished with divines and have all charitable   204
preparation. If my brother wrought by my pity, it   205
should not be so with him.

PROVOST   So please you, this friar hath been with him,
and advised him for th'entertainment of death.   208

188–9 **forfeit . . . kind** guilty of the same offense.   189 **mercy**
i.e., even mercy   193–4 **information** accusation
196–7 **Philip and Jacob** the Feast of Saint Philip and Saint James
(*Jacobus* in Latin), May 1.   197–8 **goes about** busies himself
202 **brother** i.e., fellow officer of state   204 **divines** clergymen
205 **wrought . . . pity** acted in accord with my impulses of pity
208 **th'entertainment** the reception, acceptance

ESCALUS Good even, good Father.

DUKE Bliss and goodness on you!

ESCALUS Of whence are you?

DUKE

Not of this country, though my chance is now

To use it for my time. I am a brother   213

Of gracious order, late come from the See   214

In special business from His Holiness.

ESCALUS What news abroad i'th' world?

DUKE None but that there is so great a fever on goodness that the dissolution of it must cure it. Novelty is   218
only in request, and, as it is, as dangerous to be aged   219
in any kind of course as it is virtuous to be constant   220
in any undertaking. There is scarce truth enough alive   221
to make societies secure, but security enough to make   222
fellowships accursed. Much upon this riddle runs the   223
wisdom of the world. This news is old enough, yet it
is every day's news. I pray you, sir, of what disposition was the Duke?

ESCALUS One that, above all other strifes, contended   227
especially to know himself.

DUKE What pleasure was he given to?

213 **To . . . time** to dwell here for my present purposes.
214 **the See** Rome   218 **the dissolution . . . cure it** i.e., only
by dying can goodness be rid of the disease.   218–19 **is only in
request** is the only thing people seek   219–21 **as it . . .
undertaking** as things currently stand, (it is) as dangerous to be
constant in any undertaking as it is virtuous to be thus constant.
221–3 **There . . . accursed** i.e., There is hardly enough integrity
extant to establish secure and trusting associations among men, but
binding contractual obligations enough to be the curse of friendship.
(The Duke thus puns on *security* [1] a sense of trust [2] financial
pledge required to borrow money, and on *fellowship* [1] friendship
[2] corporations formed for trading ventures.)   223 **upon this
riddle** in this riddling fashion   227 **strifes** endeavors

ESCALUS   Rather rejoicing to see another merry than
merry at anything which professed to make him re-   231
joice—a gentleman of all temperance. But leave we
him to his events, with a prayer they may prove pros-   233
perous, and let me desire to know how you find Claudio prepared. I am made to understand that you have
lent him visitation.   236

DUKE   He professes to have received no sinister measure   237
from his judge, but most willingly humbles himself to
the determination of justice; yet had he framed to him-   239
self, by the instruction of his frailty, many deceiving   240
promises of life, which I, by my good leisure, have
discredited to him, and now is he resolved to die.

ESCALUS   You have paid the heavens your function, and
the prisoner the very debt of your calling. I have la-   244
bored for the poor gentleman to the extremest shore of   245
my modesty, but my brother justice have I found so   246
severe that he hath forced me to tell him he is indeed
Justice.

DUKE   If his own life answer the straitness of his   249
proceeding, it shall become him well; wherein if he
chance to fail, he hath sentenced himself.

ESCALUS   I am going to visit the prisoner. Fare you well.

DUKE   Peace be with you!

               [Exeunt Escalus and Provost.]
He who the sword of heaven will bear
Should be as holy as severe;

---

231 **professed** attempted   233 **his events** the outcome of his
affairs   236 **lent him visitation** paid him a visit.   237 **sinister
measure** unfair treatment meted out to him   239–40 **framed
to himself** formulated in his mind   240 **by . . . frailty** at the
prompting of his natural human weakness   244 **the prisoner . . .
calling** what your calling as a friar obliges you to give the prisoner,
i.e., the comforts of spiritual counsel.   245–6 **shore . . .
modesty** limit of propriety   249 **straitness** strictness

Pattern in himself to know, 256
Grace to stand, and virtue go; 257
More nor less to others paying 258
Than by self-offenses weighing. 259
Shame to him whose cruel striking
Kills for faults of his own liking!
Twice treble shame on Angelo,
To weed my vice and let his grow! 263
Oh, what may man within him hide,
Though angel on the outward side!
How may likeness made in crimes, 266
Making practice on the times, 267
To draw with idle spiders' strings 268
Most ponderous and substantial things! 269
Craft against vice I must apply.
With Angelo tonight shall lie
His old betrothèd but despisèd;
So disguise shall, by the disguisèd, 273
Pay with falsehood false exacting 274
And perform an old contracting. *Exit.* 275

256–9 Pattern . . . weighing he must know himself and be a
pattern for others to emulate, with the grace to stand firm and the
virtue to guide himself in the straight path, judging and punishing
others with neither more nor less severity than he applies to his
own offenses.   **263 my vice** i.e., vice in everyone except Angelo.
(The Duke speaks chorically on behalf of everyone generally.)
266–9 How . . . things! How may false seeming of a criminal
sort, practicing deception on the world, make weighty and
substantial matters seem as illusory and unsubstantial as spider
webs!   **273–5 So . . . contracting** so shall disguise, employed by
those in disguise (i.e., Mariana and the Duke himself), use a kind
of (virtuous) falsehood to pay back what was exacted through
deception (by Angelo), and thereby fulfill an old contract.

4.1 ❧ *Enter Mariana, and Boy singing.*

Song.

BOY

    Take, oh, take those lips away,
     That so sweetly were forsworn,
    And those eyes, the break of day,
     Lights that do mislead the morn;   **4**
    But my kisses bring again, bring again, **5**
    Seals of love, but sealed in vain, sealed in vain. **6**

    Enter Duke [disguised as before].

MARIANA
Break off thy song, and haste thee quick away.
Here comes a man of comfort, whose advice
Hath often stilled my brawling discontent. [*Exit Boy.*] **9**
I cry you mercy, sir, and well could wish   **10**
You had not found me here so musical.
Let me excuse me, and believe me so,
My mirth it much displeased, but pleased my woe. **13**

DUKE
'Tis good; though music oft hath such a charm
To make bad good, and good provoke to harm. **15**
I pray you, tell me, hath anybody inquired for me here

4.1 *Location: The moated grange at Saint Luke's.*
4 Lights . . . morn eyes that mislead the morning (the goddess of
dawn, Eos or Aurora) into taking them for the rising sun
5 again back **6 Seals** confirmations, pledges **9 brawling**
clamorous **10 cry you mercy** beg your pardon **13 My . . .
woe** i.e., it suited not a merry but a melancholy mood. **15 bad
good** i.e., bad seem good, attractive. (The Duke, echoing
Renaissance conceptions of the psychological effects of music,
warns that music can sometimes give a pleasing appearance to sin
and lead virtue into harm.)

today? Much upon this time have I promised here   17
to meet.

MARIANA   You have not been inquired after. I have sat
here all day.

Enter Isabella.

DUKE   I do constantly believe you. The time is come   21
even now. I shall crave your forbearance a little. May-   22
be I will call upon you anon, for some advantage to   23
yourself.

MARIANA   I am always bound to you.   *Exit.*

DUKE   Very well met, and welcome.
What is the news from this good deputy?

ISABELLA
He hath a garden circummured with brick,   28
Whose western side is with a vineyard backed;
And to that vineyard is a planchèd gate,   30
That makes his opening with this bigger key.   31
                              [*She shows keys.*]
This other doth command a little door
Which from the vineyard to the garden leads;
There have I made my promise, upon the   34
Heavy middle of the night, to call upon him.

DUKE
But shall you on your knowledge find this way?

ISABELLA
I have ta'en a due and wary note upon't.
With whispering and most guilty diligence,

---

17 **Much upon** Pretty nearly about   21 **constantly** confidently
22 **crave . . . little** i.e., ask you to withdraw briefly.   23 **anon**
presently   28 **circummured** walled about   30 **planchèd**
made of boards, planks   31 **his** its   34 **upon** during, at

In action all of precept, he did show me   39
The way twice o'er.

DUKE   Are there no other tokens
Between you 'greed concerning her observance?   41

ISABELLA
No, none, but only a repair i'th' dark,   42
And that I have possessed him my most stay   43
Can be but brief; for I have made him know
I have a servant comes with me along,
That stays upon me, whose persuasion is   46
I come about my brother.

DUKE   'Tis well borne up.   47
I have not yet made known to Mariana
A word of this.—What, ho, within! Come forth!

     Enter Mariana.

I pray you, be acquainted with this maid;
She comes to do you good.

ISABELLA   I do desire the like.

DUKE
Do you persuade yourself that I respect you?   52

MARIANA
Good Friar, I know you do, and have found it.   53

DUKE
Take then this your companion by the hand,
Who hath a story ready for your ear.
I shall attend your leisure. But make haste;
The vaporous night approaches.

39 **In action . . . precept** i.e., teaching by demonstration
41 **her observance** what she is supposed to do.   42 **repair** act
of going or coming to a place   43 **possessed** informed.
my most stay my stay at the longest   46 **stays upon** waits for.
persuasion belief   47 **borne up** sustained, carried out.
52 **respect you** are concerned for your welfare.   53 **found it**
found it to be true.

MARIANA   Will't please you walk aside?

                                     Exit [with Isabella].

DUKE
O place and greatness! Millions of false eyes
Are stuck upon thee. Volumes of report   60
Run with these false and most contrarious quests   61
Upon thy doings; thousand escapes of wit   62
Make thee the father of their idle dream   63
And rack thee in their fancies.

    Enter Mariana and Isabella.

                          Welcome. How agreed?   64

ISABELLA
She'll take the enterprise upon her, Father,
If you advise it.

DUKE   It is not my consent,   66
But my entreaty too.

ISABELLA   Little have you to say   67
When you depart from him but, soft and low,
"Remember now my brother."

MARIANA   Fear me not.   69

DUKE
Nor, gentle daughter, fear you not at all.
He is your husband on a precontract;   71
To bring you thus together, 'tis no sin,

60 **stuck** fastened   60–2 **Volumes . . . doings** Innumerable
rumors follow a false scent and hunt counter in pursuing your
activities   62 **escapes** sallies   63 **Make . . . dream** credit you
with being the source of their fantasies   64 **rack** stretch as on
the rack, distort   66 **not** not only   67 **Little . . . say** Say little
69 **Fear me not** i.e., Don't worry about my carrying out my part.
71 **precontract** legally binding agreement entered into before any
church ceremony. (Compare Claudio's and Juliet's *true contract* at
1.2.142.)

Sith that the justice of your title to him   73
Doth flourish the deceit. Come, let us go.   74
Our corn's to reap, for yet our tithe's to sow.   *Exeunt.*   75

4.2 ❧ *Enter Provost and Clown [Pompey].*

PROVOST   Come hither, sirrah. Can you cut off a man's
head?

POMPEY   If the man be a bachelor, sir, I can; but if he be
a married man, he's his wife's head, and I can never   4
cut off a woman's head.   5

PROVOST   Come, sir, leave me your snatches, and yield   6
me a direct answer. Tomorrow morning are to die
Claudio and Barnardine. Here is in our prison a com-   8
mon executioner, who in his office lacks a helper. If   9
you will take it on you to assist him, it shall redeem
you from your gyves; if not, you shall have your full   11
time of imprisonment and your deliverance with an
unpitied whipping, for you have been a notorious
bawd.

POMPEY   Sir, I have been an unlawful bawd time out of
mind, but yet I will be content to be a lawful hangman.
I would be glad to receive some instruction from
my fellow partner.

PROVOST[*calling*]   What, ho, Abhorson! Where's Abhorson,
there?

---

73 **Sith that** since   74 **flourish** adorn, make fair   75 **Our
corn's . . . sow** We must first sow grain before we can expect to
reap a harvest; i.e., we must get started.   **tithe** grain sown for
tithe dues; or, an error for "tilth"

4.2 *Location. The prison.*
4 **he's . . . head** (Compare Ephesians 5:23: "The husband is the
head of the wife.")   5 **head** (With wordplay on "maidenhead.")
6 **leave . . . snatches** leave off your quibbles   8–9 **common**
public   11 **gyves** fetters, shackles

Enter Abhorson.

ABHORSON   Do you call, sir?

PROVOST   Sirrah, here's a fellow will help you tomorrow
in your execution. If you think it meet, compound   23
with him by the year, and let him abide here with
you; if not, use him for the present and dismiss him.
He cannot plead his estimation with you; he hath   26
been a bawd.

ABHORSON   A bawd, sir? Fie upon him! He will discredit our mystery.   29

PROVOST   Go to, sir, you weigh equally; a feather will
turn the scale.   *Exit.*

POMPEY   Pray, sir, by your good favor—for surely, sir,   32
a good favor you have, but that you have a hanging   33
look—do you call, sir, your occupation a mystery?   34

ABHORSON   Ay, sir, a mystery.

POMPEY   Painting, sir, I have heard say, is a mystery,   36
and your whores, sir, being members of my occupation, using painting, do prove my occupation a
mystery. But what mystery there should be in hanging, if I should be hanged, I cannot imagine.

ABHORSON   Sir, it is a mystery.

POMPEY   Proof?

---

23 **compound** make an agreement   26 **plead his estimation**
claim any respect on account of his reputation   29 **mystery**
craft, occupation.   32 **favor** leave, permission   33 **favor** face
33–4 **hanging look** (1) downcast look (2) look of a hangman
36 **Painting** (1) Painting of pictures (2) Applying cosmetics

ABHORSON   Every true man's apparel fits your thief. If it   43
be too little for your thief, your true man thinks it big   44
enough; if it be too big for your thief, your thief thinks   45
it little enough. So every true man's apparel fits your   46
thief.   47

Enter Provost.

PROVOST   Are you agreed?

POMPEY   Sir, I will serve him, for I do find your hangman is a more penitent trade than your bawd: he doth   50
oftener ask forgiveness.   51

PROVOST   You, sirrah, provide your block and your ax
tomorrow four o'clock.

ABHORSON   Come on, bawd. I will instruct thee in my
trade. Follow!

POMPEY   I do desire to learn, sir; and I hope, if you have
occasion to use me for your own turn, you shall find   57
me yare. For truly, sir, for your kindness I owe you a   58
good turn.

PROVOST
Call hither Barnardine and Claudio.

                 Exit [Pompey, with Abhorson].
Th'one has my pity; not a jot the other,
Being a murderer, though he were my brother.

Enter Claudio.

43–7 **Every . . . thief** (Abhorson alludes to the custom of giving to
the hangman the garments of the executed criminal. Like a thief, a
hangman takes from all sorts of men; death is the great thief. The
hangman's occupation is to settle all scores.)   44–5 **big enough**
i.e., enough of a loss   46 **little enough** little enough for his
efforts.   50–1 **he doth . . . forgiveness** (The executioner
perfunctorily asked forgiveness of those whose lives he was about
to take.)   57 **for . . . turn** (1) as a pimp to provide for your
sexual needs (2) as your hangman when it is your turn to be
hanged or "turned off" the ladder   58 **yare** ready, alacritous.

Look, here's the warrant, Claudio, for thy death.
'Tis now dead midnight, and by eight tomorrow
Thou must be made immortal. Where's Barnardine?   65

CLAUDIO
As fast locked up in sleep as guiltless labor   66
When it lies starkly in the traveler's bones.   67
He will not wake.

PROVOST   Who can do good on him?
Well, go, prepare yourself. [Knocking within.] But hark,
    what noise?
Heaven give your spirits comfort!   [Exit Claudio.]
                    [calling] By and by.—
I hope it is some pardon or reprieve
For the most gentle Claudio.

    Enter Duke [disguised as before].

                    Welcome, Father.

DUKE
The best and wholesom'st spirits of the night
Envelop you, good Provost! Who called here of late?

PROVOST   None since the curfew rung.

DUKE
Not Isabel?

PROVOST   No.

DUKE   They will, then, ere't be long.

PROVOST   What comfort is for Claudio?

DUKE
There's some in hope.

PROVOST   It is a bitter deputy.

---

65 **made immortal** i.e., executed.   66 **fast** firmly, soundly.
guiltless labor (A personification of the well-earned weariness
that tires the innocent laborer.)   67 **starkly** stiffly.   **traveler's
bones** bones of one who travails or labors or journeys.

DUKE

Not so, not so. His life is paralleled   79
Even with the stroke and line of his great justice.   80
He doth with holy abstinence subdue
That in himself which he spurs on his power   82
To qualify in others. Were he mealed with that   83
Which he corrects, then were he tyrannous;
But this being so, he's just. [*Knocking within.*] Now
     are they come.   [*The Provost goes to the door.*]
This is a gentle provost; seldom when   86
The steelèd jailer is the friend of men.   87

                         [*Knocking within.*]

How now? What noise? That spirit's possessed with
     haste
That wounds th'unsisting postern with these strokes.   89

PROVOST [*speaking at the door*]

There he must stay until the officer
Arise to let him in. He is called up.

                         [*He returns to the Duke.*]

DUKE

Have you no countermand for Claudio yet,
But he must die tomorrow?

PROVOST   None, sir, none.

DUKE

As near the dawning, Provost, as it is,
You shall hear more ere morning.

PROVOST   Happily   95
You something know, yet I believe there comes

79-80 **His . . . justice** His life runs parallel and in exact
conformity with the straight line and precise execution of the
justice he carries out.   82 **spurs on** encourages, urges
83 **qualify** mitigate.   **mealed** spotted, stained   86 **seldom
when** i.e., it is seldom that   87 **steelèd** hardened
89 **unsisting** unyielding, unresting, or unresisting (?).   **postern**
small door   95 **Happily** Haply, perhaps

No countermand. No such example have we;   97
Besides, upon the very siege of justice   98
Lord Angelo hath to the public ear
Professed the contrary.

    Enter a Messenger.

               This is His Lordship's man.

DUKE
  And here comes Claudio's pardon.

MESSENGER [*giving a paper*] My lord hath sent you
  this note, and by me this further charge, that you
  swerve not from the smallest article of it, neither in
  time, matter, or other circumstance. Good morrow;
  for, as I take it, it is almost day.

PROVOST   I shall obey him.   [*Exit Messenger.*]

DUKE [*aside*]
  This is his pardon, purchased by such sin
  For which the pardoner himself is in.   109
  Hence hath offense his quick celerity,   110
  When it is borne in high authority.   111
  When vice makes mercy, mercy's so extended   112
  That for the fault's love is th'offender friended.—   113
  Now, sir, what news?

PROVOST   I told you. Lord Angelo, belike thinking me   115
  remiss in mine office, awakens me with this un-   116
  wonted putting-on—methinks strangely, for he hath   117
  not used it before.

---

97 **example** precedent   98 **siege** seat   109 **in** engaged.
110–11 **Hence . . . authority** Hence it is that criminal behavior in
high places has its (*his*) own quick way of covering its tracks.
112–13 **When . . . friended** When criminality acts to save a life, as
in this case, mercy is so strangely broadened in definition that the
offender (here, Claudio) is spared for the fault committed by the
person in authority.   115 **belike** perchance
116–17 **unwonted putting-on** unaccustomed urging

DUKE   Pray you, let's hear.

PROVOST   [*reads*] *the letter* "Whatsoever you may hear
to the contrary, let Claudio be executed by four of
the clock, and in the afternoon Barnardine. For my
better satisfaction, let me have Claudio's head sent   123
me by five. Let this be duly performed, with a
thought that more depends on it than we must yet
deliver. Thus fail not to do your office, as you will   126
answer it at your peril." What say you to this, sir?

DUKE   What is that Barnardine who is to be executed in
th'afternoon?

PROVOST   A Bohemian born, but here nursed up and   131
bred; one that is a prisoner nine years old.   132

DUKE   How came it that the absent Duke had not either
delivered him to his liberty or executed him? I have
heard it was ever his manner to do so.

PROVOST   His friends still wrought reprieves for him;
and indeed his fact, till now in the government of Lord   137
Angelo, came not to an undoubtful proof.

DUKE   It is now apparent?

PROVOST   Most manifest, and not denied by himself.

DUKE   Hath he borne himself penitently in prison? How
seems he to be touched?   142

PROVOST   A man that apprehends death no more dread-   143
fully but as a drunken sleep—careless, reckless, and   144
fearless of what's past, present, or to come; insensible   145
of mortality, and desperately mortal.   146

---

123 **better satisfaction** greater assurance   126 **deliver** make
known.   131 **here** i.e., in Vienna   132 **a prisoner . . . old**
nine years a prisoner.   137 **fact** crime   142 **touched** affected,
touched by remorse.   143–4 **no more dreadfully but** with no
more dread than   145–6 **insensible . . . mortal** incapable of
comprehending the meaning of death, and incorrigible.

DUKE   He wants advice.   147

PROVOST   He will hear none. He hath evermore had the   148
liberty of the prison; give him leave to escape hence,   149
he would not. Drunk many times a day, if not many
days entirely drunk. We have very oft awaked him, as
if to carry him to execution, and showed him a
seeming warrant for it; it hath not moved him at all.

DUKE   More of him anon. There is written in your brow,
Provost, honesty and constancy; if I read it not truly,
my ancient skill beguiles me, but, in the boldness of   156
my cunning, I will lay myself in hazard. Claudio,   157
whom here you have warrant to execute, is no greater
forfeit to the law than Angelo who hath sentenced him.
To make you understand this in a manifested effect, I   160
crave but four days' respite, for the which you are to
do me both a present and a dangerous courtesy.   162

PROVOST   Pray, sir, in what?

DUKE   In the delaying death.

PROVOST   Alack, how may I do it, having the hour
limited, and an express command, under penalty, to   166
deliver his head in the view of Angelo? I may make
my case as Claudio's, to cross this in the smallest.

DUKE   By the vow of mine order I warrant you, if my
instructions may be your guide. Let this Barnardine
be this morning executed, and his head borne to
Angelo.

PROVOST   Angelo hath seen them both and will discover   173
the favor.   174

---

147 wants advice needs spiritual counsel.   **148 evermore**
constantly   **148–9 the liberty . . . prison** freedom to go
anywhere within the prison   **156–7 in the . . . hazard** confident
in my knowledge (of human character), I will put myself at risk.
160 in . . . effect by means of concrete proof   **162 present**
immediate   **166 limited** fixed, set   **173–4 discover the favor**
recognize the face.

DUKE   Oh, death's a great disguiser, and you may add to
it. Shave the head, and tie the beard, and say it was   176
the desire of the penitent to be so bared before his
death. You know the course is common. If anything   178
fall to you upon this more than thanks and good   179
fortune, by the saint whom I profess, I will plead   180
against it with my life.

PROVOST   Pardon me, good Father, it is against my oath.

DUKE   Were you sworn to the Duke or to the deputy?

PROVOST   To him, and to his substitutes.

DUKE   You will think you have made no offense if the
Duke avouch the justice of your dealing?   186

PROVOST   But what likelihood is in that?

DUKE   Not a resemblance, but a certainty. Yet since I see
you fearful, that neither my coat, integrity, nor
persuasion can with ease attempt you, I will go further 190
than I meant, to pluck all fears out of you. Look you,
sir, here is the hand and seal of the Duke. [*He shows a
letter.*] You know the character, I doubt not, and the   193
signet is not strange to you.   194

PROVOST   I know them both.

DUKE   The contents of this is the return of the Duke.
You shall anon overread it at your pleasure, where
you shall find within these two days he will be here.
This is a thing that Angelo knows not, for he this very
day receives letters of strange tenor, perchance of the
Duke's death, perchance entering into some monas-   201
tery, but by chance nothing of what is writ. Look, th'un- 202

176 **tie** tie up, tidy up   178 **course** practice   179 **fall to** befall
180 **the saint . . . profess** i.e., St. Benedict, whose example I
follow   186 **avouch** confirm   190 **attempt** win, tempt
193 **character** handwriting   194 **strange** unknown
201 **entering** of his entering   202 **writ** i.e., written here.

folding star calls up the shepherd. Put not yourself 203
into amazement how these things should be; all difficulties are but easy when they are known. Call your
executioner, and off with Barnardine's head. I will
give him a present shrift and advise him for a better 207
place. Yet you are amazed, but this shall absolutely 208
resolve you. Come away; it is almost clear dawn. 209

Exit [with Provost].

4.3 ৵ Enter Clown [Pompey].

POMPEY I am as well acquainted here as I was in our 1
house of profession. One would think it were Mistress
Overdone's own house, for here be many of her old
customers. First, here's young Master Rash; he's in for 4
a commodity of brown paper and old ginger, nine- 5
score and seventeen pounds, of which he made five 6
marks, ready money. Marry, then ginger was not 7
much in request, for the old women were all dead. 8

202–3 **unfolding star** i.e., morning star, Venus, which bids the
shepherd lead his sheep from the fold   207 **present shrift**
immediate absolution for sins (after confession)
207–8 **advise . . . place** counsel him on the comforts of heaven.
208 **Yet** Still   209 **resolve you** dispel your uncertainties.

4.3 Location: *The prison.*
1 **well** widely   4 **Rash** (All the names mentioned by Pompey
apparently glance at contemporary social affectations and defects.
Rash means "reckless.")   5–8 **a commodity . . . dead** (To
circumvent the laws against excessive rates of interest, moneylenders
often advanced cheap commodities to gullible borrowers in lieu of
cash. Master Rash, having agreed to a valuation of 197 pounds for
such merchandise, has been able to resell it for only five marks,
each mark worth about two-thirds of a pound, and has been
thrown into prison for debt. The ginger has not fetched a good
price, owing to lack of customers, since the old women who are
proverbially fond of ginger are no longer alive.)

Then is there here one Master Caper, at the suit of   9
Master Three-pile the mercer, for some four suits of   10
peach-colored satin, which now peaches him a beggar.   11
Then have we here young Dizzy, and young   12
Master Deep-vow, and Master Copper-spur, and   13
Master Starve-lackey the rapier and dagger man, and   14
young Drop-heir that killed lusty Pudding, and Mas-   15
ter Forthlight the tilter, and brave Master Shoe-tie the   16
great traveler, and wild Half-can that stabbed Pots,   17
and I think forty more, all great doers in our trade, and
are now "for the Lord's sake."   19

Enter Abhorson.

ABHORSON   Sirrah, bring Barnardine hither.

POMPEY [*calling*]   Master Barnardine! You must rise and
be hanged, Master Barnardine!   22

ABHORSON   What, ho, Barnardine!

---

9 **Caper** (To *caper* was to dance or leap gracefully.)   10 **Three-
pile** the thickest nap and most expensive grade of velvet.
mercer cloth merchant.   **suits** (With a play on *suit,* line 9.)
11 **peaches him** denounces him as. (With a play on *peach.*)
12 **Dizzy** i.e., giddy, foolish   13 **Deep-vow** one who swears
earnestly and often.   **Copper-spur** (Copper was often used
fraudulently to simulate gold.)   14 **Starve-lackey** (Spendthrift
gallants often virtually starved their pages.)   15 **Drop-heir**
(Perhaps referring to those who disinherited or preyed on
unsuspecting heirs; or else *Drop-hair,* losing hair from syphilis.)
lusty vigorous.   **Pudding** i.e., sausage   16 **Forthlight**
(Unexplained; perhaps an error for *Forthright,* referring to a style of
tilting.)   **tilter** jouster.   **brave** showy, splendidly dressed.
Shoe-tie (Evidently a nickname for travelers and others who
affected the foreign fashion of elaborate rosettes on the tie of the
shoe.)   17 **Half-can** i.e., a small drinking tankard.   **Pots** i.e.,
ale pots   19 **"for . . . sake"** (The cry of prisoners from jail
grates to passers-by to give them food or alms.)   22 **be hanged**
(With a play on the imprecation; compare "go to the devil.")

BARNARDINE (*within*) A pox o' your throats! Who
makes that noise there? What are you?

POMPEY Your friends, sir, the hangman. You must be
so good, sir, to rise and be put to death.

BARNARDINE [*within*] Away, you rogue, away! I am
sleepy.

ABHORSON Tell him he must awake, and that quickly,
too.

POMPEY Pray, Master Barnardine, awake till you are executed, and sleep afterwards.

ABHORSON Go in to him, and fetch him out.

POMPEY He is coming, sir, he is coming. I hear his
straw rustle.

    Enter Barnardine.

ABHORSON Is the ax upon the block, sirrah?

POMPEY Very ready, sir.

BARNARDINE How now, Abhorson? What's the news
with you?

ABHORSON Truly, sir, I would desire you to clap into   41
your prayers; for, look you, the warrant's come.

BARNARDINE You rogue, I have been drinking all night.
I am not fitted for't.

POMPEY Oh, the better, sir, for he that drinks all night
and is hanged betimes in the morning may sleep the   46
sounder all the next day.

    Enter Duke [disguised as before].

ABHORSON Look you, sir, here comes your ghostly   48
father. Do we jest now, think you?

41 **clap into** quickly begin   46 **betimes** early   48 **ghostly**
spiritual

DUKE   Sir, induced by my charity, and hearing how
    hastily you are to depart, I am come to advise you,
    comfort you, and pray with you.

BARNARDINE   Friar, not I. I have been drinking hard all
    night, and I will have more time to prepare me, or
    they shall beat out my brains with billets. I will not   55
    consent to die this day, that's certain.

DUKE
    Oh, sir, you must, and therefore I beseech you
    Look forward on the journey you shall go.

BARNARDINE   I swear I will not die today for any man's
    persuasion.

DUKE   But hear you—

BARNARDINE   Not a word. If you have anything to say
    to me, come to my ward, for thence will not I today.   63

                                                    Exit.

        Enter Provost.

DUKE
    Unfit to live or die. Oh, gravel heart!   64
    After him, fellows. Bring him to the block.

                        [Exeunt Abhorson and Pompey.]

PROVOST
    Now, sir, how do you find the prisoner?

DUKE
    A creature unprepared, unmeet for death;   67
    And to transport him in the mind he is   68
    Were damnable.

PROVOST   Here in the prison, Father,
    There died this morning of a cruel fever

---

55 **billets** cudgels, blocks of wood.   63 **ward** cell   64 **gravel**
stony   67 **unmeet** unready, unfit   68 **transport him** i.e.,
send him to his doom.   **he is** he is in

One Ragozine, a most notorious pirate,
A man of Claudio's years, his beard and head
Just of his color. What if we do omit   73
This reprobate till he were well inclined,
And satisfy the deputy with the visage
Of Ragozine, more like to Claudio?

DUKE
Oh, 'tis an accident that heaven provides!
Dispatch it presently; the hour draws on   78
Prefixed by Angelo. See this be done,   79
And sent according to command, whiles I
Persuade this rude wretch willingly to die.   81

PROVOST
This shall be done, good Father, presently.
But Barnardine must die this afternoon.
And how shall we continue Claudio,   84
To save me from the danger that might come
If he were known alive?

DUKE   Let this be done:
Put them in secret holds, both Barnardine and
    Claudio.   87
Ere twice the sun hath made his journal greeting   88
To yond generation, you shall find   89
Your safety manifested.

PROVOST   I am your free dependent.   91

DUKE
Quick, dispatch, and send the head to Angelo.

                                        Exit [*Provost*].

73 **omit** ignore, overlook   78 **presently** immediately. (As also in
line 82.)   79 **Prefixed** appointed beforehand, stipulated
81 **rude** uncivilized   84 **continue** preserve   87 **holds** cells,
dungeons   88 **journal** daily   89 **yond** i.e., beyond these walls,
outside the perpetually dark prison (?). Sometimes it is emended to
th' under, the people of the Antipodes, on the opposite side of the
earth, or, people under the sun, the human race.   91 **free
dependent** willing servant.

Now will I write letters to Varrius—   93
The Provost, he shall bear them—whose contents
Shall witness to him I am near at home,
And that, by great injunctions, I am bound   96
To enter publicly. Him I'll desire
To meet me at the consecrated fount   98
A league below the city; and from thence,   99
By cold gradation and well-balanced form,   100
We shall proceed with Angelo.

    Enter Provost [with Ragozine's head].

PROVOST
  Here is the head. I'll carry it myself.

DUKE
  Convenient is it. Make a swift return,   103
For I would commune with you of such things   104
That want no ear but yours.

PROVOST   I'll make all speed.   *Exit.*   105

ISABELLA (*within*)   Peace, ho, be here!

DUKE
  The tongue of Isabel. She's come to know
If yet her brother's pardon be come hither.
But I will keep her ignorant of her good,

---

93 **to Varrius** (The Folio reads "to Angelo," but see line 99 below
and 4.5.12–14; evidently, the Duke's plan is to meet Varrius "a
league below the city" and then proceed to the rendezvous with
Angelo.)   96 **by great injunctions** by powerful precedent or for
compelling reasons   98 **fount** spring   99 **league** (A measure
of varying length but usually about three miles.)   100 **cold . . .
form** i.e., moving deliberately and with proper observance of all
formalities   103 **Convenient** Timely, fitting   104 **commune**
converse   105 **want** require

To make her heavenly comforts of despair   110
When it is least expected.

    Enter Isabella.

ISABELLA   Ho, by your leave!

DUKE
Good morning to you, fair and gracious daughter.

ISABELLA
The better, given me by so holy a man.
Hath yet the deputy sent my brother's pardon?

DUKE
He hath released him, Isabel, from the world.
His head is off and sent to Angelo.

ISABELLA
Nay, but it is not so!

DUKE   It is no other.
Show your wisdom, daughter, in your close patience.   118

ISABELLA
Oh, I will to him and pluck out his eyes!

DUKE
You shall not be admitted to his sight.

ISABELLA
Unhappy Claudio! Wretched Isabel!
Injurious world! Most damnèd Angelo!

DUKE
This nor hurts him nor profits you a jot.   123
Forbear it therefore; give your cause to heaven.
Mark what I say, which you shall find
By every syllable a faithful verity.   126
The Duke comes home tomorrow. Nay, dry your eyes;

---

110 **of** from, transformed out of   118 **close patience** silent
enduring.   123 **nor hurts** neither hurts   126 **By** with
respect to

One of our convent, and his confessor,
Gives me this instance. Already he hath carried   129
Notice to Escalus and Angelo,
Who do prepare to meet him at the gates,
There to give up their pow'r. If you can, pace your
    wisdom   132
In that good path that I would wish it go,
And you shall have your bosom on this wretch,   134
Grace of the Duke, revenges to your heart,   135
And general honor.

ISABELLA   I am directed by you.

DUKE
This letter, then, to Friar Peter give.

                [He gives her a letter.]

'Tis that he sent me of the Duke's return.   138
Say, by this token, I desire his company
At Mariana's house tonight. Her cause and yours
I'll perfect him withal, and he shall bring you   141
Before the Duke, and to the head of Angelo   142
Accuse him home and home. For my poor self,   143
I am combinèd by a sacred vow,   144
And shall be absent. Wend you with this letter.
Command these fretting waters from your eyes   146
With a light heart. Trust not my holy order
If I pervert your course. Who's here?

    Enter Lucio.

---

129 **instance** proof.   132 **pace** teach to move in response to
your will, as with a horse   134 **bosom** heart's desire
135 **Grace of** manifestation of favor from.   **to your heart** to
your heart's content   138 **that** that which.   **of** concerning
141 **perfect** acquaint completely.   **withal** with   142 **head**
i.e., face   143 **home and home** thoroughly.   144 **combinèd**
bound   146 **fretting** corroding

LUCIO Good even. Friar, where's the Provost?

DUKE Not within, sir.

LUCIO Oh, pretty Isabella, I am pale at mine heart to see 151
thine eyes so red. Thou must be patient. I am fain to 152
dine and sup with water and bran; I dare not for my 153
head fill my belly; one fruitful meal would set me 154
to't. But they say the Duke will be here tomorrow. 155
By my troth, Isabel, I loved thy brother. If the old fantastical Duke of dark corners had been at home, he
had lived.   [Exit Isabella.]

DUKE Sir, the Duke is marvelous little beholding to 159
your reports; but the best is, he lives not in them. 160

LUCIO Friar, thou knowest not the Duke so well as I
do. He's a better woodman than thou tak'st him for. 162

DUKE Well, you'll answer this one day. Fare ye well.

                                            [He starts to go.]

LUCIO Nay, tarry, I'll go along with thee. I can tell thee
pretty tales of the Duke.

DUKE You have told me too many of him already, sir, if
they be true; if not true, none were enough.

LUCIO I was once before him for getting a wench with
child.

DUKE Did you such a thing?

LUCIO Yes, marry, did I, but I was fain to forswear it.
They would else have married me to the rotten medlar. 172

---

151 **pale . . . heart** i.e., pale from sighing (since sighs cost the
heart loss of blood)   152 **fain** compelled. (As also in line 171.)
153–4 **for my head** i.e., on my life   154 **fruitful** abundant
154–5 **set me to't** i.e., awaken my lust and thus place me in danger
of Angelo's edict.   159 **marvelous** marvelously.   **beholding**
beholden   160 **he . . . them** i.e., he is not accurately described
by them.   162 **woodman** i.e., hunter (of women)
172 **medlar** a fruit that was eaten after it had begun to rot; here,
signifying a prostitute.

DUKE Sir, your company is fairer than honest. Rest you
well.

LUCIO By my troth, I'll go with thee to the lane's end.
If bawdy talk offend you, we'll have very little of it.
Nay, Friar, I am a kind of burr; I shall stick.   *Exeunt.*

4.4 ∾ *Enter Angelo and Escalus, [reading letters].*

ESCALUS Every letter he hath writ hath disvouched   1
other.

ANGELO In most uneven and distracted manner. His
actions show much like to madness. Pray heaven his
wisdom be not tainted! And why meet him at the   5
gates and redeliver our authorities there?

ESCALUS I guess not.   7

ANGELO And why should we proclaim it in an hour be-   8
fore his entering, that if any crave redress of injustice,
they should exhibit their petitions in the street?   10

ESCALUS He shows his reason for that: to have a
dispatch of complaints, and to deliver us from devices   12
hereafter, which shall then have no power to stand
against us.

ANGELO Well, I beseech you, let it be proclaimed.
Betimes i'th' morn I'll call you at your house. Give   16
notice to such men of sort and suit as are to meet him.   17

ESCALUS I shall, sir. Fare you well.

___

4.4 Location: In Vienna.
1 **disvouched** contradicted   5 **tainted** diseased.   7 **guess not**
cannot guess.   8 **in an hour** i.e., a full hour   10 **exhibit**
present   12 **dispatch** prompt settlement.   **devices** contrived
complaints   16 **Betimes** Early   17 **men . . . suit** men of rank
with a retinue

ANGELO   Good night.   *Exit [Escalus].*

   This deed unshapes me quite, makes me unpregnant   20
   And dull to all proceedings. A deflowered maid,
   And by an eminent body that enforced   22
   The law against it! But that her tender shame   23
   Will not proclaim against her maiden loss,
   How might she tongue me! Yet reason dares her no,   25
   For my authority bears of a credent bulk   26
   That no particular scandal once can touch
   But it confounds the breather. He should have lived,   28
   Save that his riotous youth, with dangerous sense,   29
   Might in the times to come have ta'en revenge
   By so receiving a dishonored life   31
   With ransom of such shame. Would yet he had lived!
   Alack, when once our grace we have forgot,
   Nothing goes right; we would, and we would not.

                                                  Exit.

4.5 ❧ *Enter Duke [in his own habit] and Friar Peter.*

DUKE

   These letters at fit time deliver me.   *[Giving letters.]*   1
   The Provost knows our purpose and our plot.
   The matter being afoot, keep your instruction,   3
   And hold you ever to our special drift,   4
   Though sometimes you do blench from this to that   5

20 **unpregnant** unapt   22 **body** person   23 **But that** Were it
not that   25 **tongue** i.e., reproach, accuse.   **dares her no** i.e.,
frightens her to say nothing   26 **bears . . . bulk** bears such a
huge credibility   28 **But . . . breather** without its confuting the
person who speaks.   29 **sense** passion, intention   31 **By** for,
because of

4.5 Location: Outside the city.
1 **me** for me   3 **keep** keep to   4 **drift** plot   5 **blench . . .
that** swerve from one expedient to another

 As cause doth minister. Go call at Flavius' house, 6
 And tell him where I stay. Give the like notice
 To Valencius, Rowland, and to Crassus,
 And bid them bring the trumpets to the gate; 9
 But send me Flavius first.

FRIAR PETER It shall be speeded well. [*Exit.*] 11

 Enter Varrius.

DUKE
 I thank thee, Varrius. Thou hast made good haste.
 Come, we will walk. There's other of our friends
 Will greet us here anon. My gentle Varrius! *Exeunt.*

4.6 ☞ *Enter Isabella and Mariana.*

ISABELLA
 To speak so indirectly I am loath.
 I would say the truth, but to accuse him so,
 That is your part. Yet I am advised to do it,
 He says, to veil full purpose.

MARIANA   Be ruled by him. 4

ISABELLA
 Besides, he tells me that if peradventure 5
 He speak against me on the adverse side,
 I should not think it strange, for 'tis a physic 7
 That's bitter to sweet end.

 Enter [Friar] Peter.

6 **minister** prompt, provide occasion. 9 **trumpets** trumpeters
11 **speeded** accomplished, expedited

4.6 *Location: Near the city gate.*
4 **veil full purpose** conceal our full plan. 5 **peradventure**
perhaps 7 **physic** remedy

MARIANA
I would Friar Peter—

ISABELLA   Oh, peace, the Friar is come.

FRIAR PETER
Come, I have found you out a stand most fit,   10
Where you may have such vantage on the Duke
He shall not pass you. Twice have the trumpets
    sounded.
The generous and gravest citizens   13
Have hent the gates, and very near upon   14
The Duke is entering. Therefore hence, away!

                                        Exeunt.

5.1 ⮑ *Enter Duke, Varrius, lords, Angelo, Escalus,*
            Lucio, [Provost, officers, and] citizens at several
            doors.

DUKE
My very worthy cousin, fairly met!   1
Our old and faithful friend, we are glad to see you.   2

ANGELO, ESCALUS
Happy return be to Your Royal Grace!

DUKE
Many and hearty thankings to you both.
We have made inquiry of you, and we hear
Such goodness of your justice that our soul
Cannot but yield you forth to public thanks,   7
Forerunning more requital.   8

10 **stand** place to stand   13 **generous** highborn   14 **hent**
reached, occupied.   **very near upon** almost immediately now

5.1 *Location: The city gate.*
0.2 *several* separate   1 **cousin** fellow nobleman. (Addressed to
Angelo.)   2 **friend** i.e., Escalus   7 **yield . . . to** call you forth
to give you   8 **more requital** further reward.

ANGELO   You make my bonds still greater.   9

DUKE
Oh, your desert speaks loud, and I should wrong it
To lock it in the wards of covert bosom,   11
When it deserves with characters of brass   12
A forted residence 'gainst the tooth of time   13
And razure of oblivion. Give me your hand,   14
And let the subject see, to make them know   15
That outward courtesies would fain proclaim   16
Favors that keep within. Come, Escalus,   17
You must walk by us on our other hand,
And good supporters are you.

Enter [Friar] Peter and Isabella.

FRIAR PETER *[to Isabella]*
Now is your time. Speak loud, and kneel before him.

ISABELLA *[kneeling]*
Justice, O royal Duke! Vail your regard   21
Upon a wronged—I would fain have said a maid.
O worthy prince, dishonor not your eye
By throwing it on any other object
Till you have heard me in my true complaint
And given me justice, justice, justice, justice!

DUKE
Relate your wrongs. In what? By whom? Be brief.
Here is Lord Angelo shall give you justice.   28
Reveal yourself to him.

ISABELLA   O worthy Duke,
You bid me seek redemption of the devil.

9 **bonds** obligations   11 **To lock . . . bosom** i.e., to keep
it locked up in my heart   12 **characters** writing, letters
13 **forted** fortified   14 **razure** effacement   15 **the
subject** those who are subjects   16–17 **That . . . within**
that public ceremonies serve as outward manifestations
of the approval my heart feels for you.   21 **Vail your
regard** Look down   28 **shall** who shall

Hear me yourself; for that which I must speak
Must either punish me, not being believed,   32
Or wring redress from you.
Hear me, oh, hear me, hear!

ANGELO
My lord, her wits, I fear me, are not firm.
She hath been a suitor to me for her brother
Cut off by course of justice.

ISABELLA [*standing*]   By course of justice!

ANGELO
And she will speak most bitterly and strange.   38

ISABELLA
Most strange, but yet most truly, will I speak.
That Angelo's forsworn, is it not strange?
That Angelo's a murderer, is 't not strange?
That Angelo is an adulterous thief,
An hypocrite, a virgin-violator,
Is it not strange, and strange?

DUKE   Nay, it is ten times strange.

ISABELLA
It is not truer he is Angelo
Than this is all as true as it is strange.   47
Nay, it is ten times true, for truth is truth
To th'end of reck'ning.

DUKE   ` Away with her! Poor soul,   49
She speaks this in th'infirmity of sense.   50

ISABELLA
O prince, I conjure thee, as thou believ'st
There is another comfort than this world,
That thou neglect me not with that opinion   53

___

32 **not being** if I am not   38 **strange** strangely.   47 **Than** than
that   49 **To . . . reck'ning** to the end of time and Day of
Judgment, always.   50 **in . . . sense** out of a sick mind, out of the
weakness of passion.   53 **with that opinion** out of a supposition

That I am touched with madness. Make not
   impossible   54
That which but seems unlike. 'Tis not impossible   55
But one, the wicked'st caitiff on the ground,   56
May seem as shy, as grave, as just, as absolute   57
As Angelo; even so may Angelo,
In all his dressings, characts, titles, forms,   59
Be an archvillain. Believe it, royal prince,
If he be less, he's nothing; but he's more,   61
Had I more name for badness.

DUKE   By mine honesty,
If she be mad—as I believe no other—
Her madness hath the oddest frame of sense,   64
Such a dependency of thing on thing,   65
As e'er I heard in madness.

ISABELLA   O gracious Duke,
Harp not on that, nor do not banish reason   67
For inequality, but let your reason serve   68
To make the truth appear where it seems hid,
And hide the false seems true.   70

DUKE   Many that are not mad
Have, sure, more lack of reason. What would
   you say?

ISABELLA
I am the sister of one Claudio,
Condemned upon the act of fornication

54 **Make not** Do not consider as   55 **unlike** unlikely.   56 **But**
but that.   **ground** earth   57 **shy** quietly dignified.   **absolute**
flawless   59 **dressings, characts** ceremonial robes, insignia of
office   61 **If . . . nothing** i.e., even if he were less than an
archvillain, he would be worthless   64 **frame of sense** form of
reason   65 **dependency . . . on thing** coherence   67–8 **do . . .
inequality** i.e., do not assume lack of reason on my part because of
the inconsistency between my story and Angelo's refutation, or
because of the inequality in our reputations   70 **hide** put out of
sight, remove from consideration.   **seems** that seems

To lose his head, condemned by Angelo.
I, in probation of a sisterhood,   76
Was sent to by my brother; one Lucio
As then the messenger—

LUCIO   That's I, an't like Your Grace.   78
I came to her from Claudio and desired her
To try her gracious fortune with Lord Angelo
For her poor brother's pardon.

ISABELLA   That's he indeed.

DUKE [to Lucio]
You were not bid to speak.

LUCIO   No, my good lord,
Nor wished to hold my peace.

DUKE   I wish you now, then.
Pray you, take note of it. And when you have
A business for yourself, pray heaven you then
Be perfect.   86

LUCIO I warrant Your Honor.   87

DUKE
The warrant's for yourself. Take heed to 't.

ISABELLA
This gentleman told somewhat of my tale—

LUCIO Right.

DUKE
It may be right, but you are i'the wrong
To speak before your time.—Proceed.

ISABELLA   I went
To this pernicious caitiff deputy—

76 **in probation** i.e., a novice   78 **As then** being at that time.
an't like if it please   86 **perfect** prepared.   87 **warrant**
assure. (The Duke, however, quibbles in line 88 on the meaning
"judicial writ.")

DUKE

That's somewhat madly spoken.

ISABELLA   Pardon it;

The phrase is to the matter.   95

DUKE   Mended again. The matter; proceed.   96

ISABELLA

In brief, to set the needless process by,   97

How I persuaded, how I prayed and kneeled,

How he refelled me, and how I replied—   99

For this was of much length—the vile conclusion

I now begin with grief and shame to utter.

He would not, but by gift of my chaste body

To his concupiscible intemperate lust,   103

Release my brother; and after much debatement   104

My sisterly remorse confutes mine honor,   105

And I did yield to him. But the next morn betimes,   106

His purpose surfeiting, he sends a warrant   107

For my poor brother's head.

DUKE   This is most likely!

ISABELLA

Oh, that it were as like as it is true!   109

DUKE

By heaven, fond wretch, thou know'st not what thou

    speak'st,   110

Or else thou art suborned against his honor   111

In hateful practice. First, his integrity   112

95 **to the matter** to the purpose.   96 **Mended . . .
proceed** That sets things right. Proceed to the main point.
97 **to set . . . by** not to dwell on unnecessary details in the story
99 **refelled** refuted, repelled   103 **concupiscible** lustful
104 **debatement** argument, debate   105 **remorse**
pity.   **confutes** confounds, silences   106 **betimes** early
107 **surfeiting** being satiated   109 **like** likely   110 **fond**
foolish   111 **suborned** induced to give false testimony
112 **practice** machination, conspiracy.

Stands without blemish. Next, it imports no reason   113
That with such vehemency he should pursue
Faults proper to himself. If he had so offended,   115
He would have weighed thy brother by himself   116
And not have cut him off. Someone hath set you on.
Confess the truth, and say by whose advice
Thou cam'st here to complain.

ISABELLA   And is this all?
Then, O you blessèd ministers above,
Keep me in patience, and with ripened time
Unfold the evil which is here wrapped up   122
In countenance! Heaven shield Your Grace from woe,   123
As I thus wronged hence unbelievèd go!

                    [*She starts to leave.*]

DUKE
I know you'd fain be gone.—An officer!
To prison with her. Shall we thus permit
A blasting and a scandalous breath to fall   127
On him so near us? This needs must be a practice.
Who knew of your intent and coming hither?

ISABELLA
One that I would were here, Friar Lodowick.

DUKE
A ghostly father, belike. Who knows that Lodowick?   131

LUCIO
My lord, I know him; 'tis a meddling friar.
I do not like the man. Had he been lay, my lord,   133

---

113 **imports no reason** i.e., makes no sense   115 **proper to himself** of which he himself is guilty.   116 **weighed** judged
122 **Unfold** disclose   122–3 **wrapped . . . countenance** concealed by the privilege of authority.   127 **blasting** blighting
131 **A ghostly . . . belike** A cleric, apparently.   133 **lay** not a cleric

For certain words he spake against Your Grace
In your retirement, I had swinged him soundly.   135

DUKE
Words against me? This' a good friar, belike!   136
And to set on this wretched woman here
Against our substitute! Let this friar be found.

                [*Exit one or more attendants.*]

LUCIO
But yesternight, my lord, she and that friar,
I saw them at the prison. A saucy friar,
A very scurvy fellow.

FRIAR PETER   Blessed be Your Royal Grace!
I have stood by, my lord, and I have heard
Your royal ear abused. First, hath this woman
Most wrongfully accused your substitute,
Who is as free from touch or soil with her
As she from one ungot.   147

DUKE   We did believe no less.
Know you that Friar Lodowick that she speaks of?

FRIAR PETER
I know him for a man divine and holy,
Not scurvy, nor a temporary meddler,   151
As he's reported by this gentleman;
And, on my trust, a man that never yet
Did, as he vouches, misreport Your Grace.

LUCIO
My lord, most villainously, believe it.

FRIAR PETER
Well, he in time may come to clear himself;
But at this instant he is sick, my lord,

---

135 **In your retirement** during your absence.   **had swinged**
would have beaten   136 **This'** This is   147 **ungot** unbegotten.
151 **temporary meddler** meddler in temporal affairs

Of a strange fever. Upon his mere request,   158
Being come to knowledge that there was complaint   159
Intended 'gainst Lord Angelo, came I hither,
To speak, as from his mouth, what he doth know
Is true and false, and what he with his oath
And all probation will make up full clear,   163
Whensoever he's convented. First, for this woman,   164
To justify this worthy nobleman,
So vulgarly and personally accused,   166
Her shall you hear disprovèd to her eyes,   167
Till she herself confess it.   [Exit Isabella, guarded.]

DUKE   Good Friar, let's hear it.

          [Friar Peter goes to bring in Mariana.]
Do you not smile at this, Lord Angelo?
Oh, heaven, the vanity of wretched fools!   170
Give us some seats.   [Seats are provided.]
          Come, cousin Angelo,
In this I'll be impartial. Be you judge
Of your own cause.   [The Duke and Angelo sit.]

     Enter Mariana, [veiled, with Friar Peter].

               Is this the witness, Friar?
First, let her show her face, and after speak.

MARIANA
Pardon, my lord, I will not show my face
Until my husband bid me.

DUKE   What, are you married?

MARIANA   No, my lord.

---

158 **Upon . . . request** Solely at his request   159 **Being . . .
knowledge** he having learned   163 **probation** proof
164 **convented** summoned.   166 **vulgarly** publicly   167 **to
her eyes** i.e., to her face   168 **s.d. Exit Isabella, guarded**
(Isabella seemingly must leave the stage here or soon afterwards.
She is described as "gone" at line 250, and is summoned at line 278.
The phrase "to her eyes" in line 167 may mean "incontrovertibly.")
170 **vanity** folly

DUKE   Are you a maid?

MARIANA   No, my lord.

DUKE   A widow, then?

MARIANA   Neither, my lord.

DUKE   Why, you are nothing then, neither maid, widow, nor wife?

LUCIO   My lord, she may be a punk, for many of them   185
are neither maid, widow, nor wife.

DUKE
Silence that fellow. I would he had some cause
To prattle for himself.   188

LUCIO   Well, my lord.

MARIANA
My lord, I do confess I ne'er was married,
And I confess besides I am no maid.
I have known my husband, yet my husband   192
Knows not that ever he knew me.

LUCIO   He was drunk then, my lord; it can be no better.

DUKE   For the benefit of silence, would thou wert so too!

LUCIO   Well, my lord.

DUKE
This is no witness for Lord Angelo.

MARIANA   Now I come to 't, my lord.
She that accuses him of fornication
In selfsame manner doth accuse my husband,
And charges him, my lord, with such a time   201
When, I'll depose, I had him in mine arms   202
With all th'effect of love.   203

---

185 **punk** harlot   188 **To . . . himself** to speak in his own
defense. (The Duke hints that there might well be charges pending
against Lucio.)   192 **known** had sexual intercourse with
201 **with . . . time** with doing the deed at just the same time
202 **depose** testify under oath   203 **With . . . love** i.e., with
sexual fulfillment.

ANGELO Charges she more than me?   204

MARIANA   Not that I know.

DUKE   No? You say your husband?

MARIANA

Why, just, my lord, and that is Angelo,   207
Who thinks he knows that he ne'er knew my body,
But knows he thinks that he knows Isabel's.

ANGELO

This is a strange abuse. Let's see thy face.   210

MARIANA

My husband bids me. Now I will unmask.

                              [*She unveils.*]

This is that face, thou cruel Angelo,
Which once thou swor'st was worth the looking on;
This is the hand which, with a vowed contract,
Was fast belocked in thine; this is the body   215
That took away the match from Isabel,   216
And did supply thee at thy garden house
In her imagined person.

DUKE [*to Angelo*]   Know you this woman?

LUCIO   Carnally, she says.

DUKE   Sirrah, no more!

LUCIO   Enough, my lord.

ANGELO

My lord, I must confess I know this woman,
And five years since there was some speech of
      marriage
Betwixt myself and her, which was broke off,
Partly for that her promisèd proportions   226

204 **Charges . . . me?** Does she (Isabella) bring charges against
persons besides myself?   207 **just** just so   210 **abuse**
deception.   215 **fast belocked** firmly locked   216 **match**
assignation   226 **for that** because.   **proportions** dowry

Came short of composition, but in chief   227
For that her reputation was disvalued   228
In levity. Since which time of five years   229
I never spake with her, saw her, nor heard from her,
Upon my faith and honor.

MARIANA [*kneeling*]   Noble prince,
  As there comes light from heaven and words from
      breath,
  As there is sense in truth and truth in virtue,
  I am affianced this man's wife as strongly
  As words could make up vows; and, my good lord,
  But Tuesday night last gone in's garden house
  He knew me as a wife. As this is true,
  Let me in safety raise me from my knees,
  Or else forever be confixèd here,   239
  A marble monument!

ANGELO   I did but smile till now.
  Now, good my lord, give me the scope of justice.   242
  My patience here is touched. I do perceive   243
  These poor informal women are no more   244
  But instruments of some more mightier member   245
  That sets them on. Let me have way, my lord,
  To find this practice out.

DUKE   Ay, with my heart,
  And punish them to your height of pleasure.—
  Thou foolish friar, and thou pernicious woman,
  Compact with her that's gone, think'st thou thy oaths,   250
  Though they would swear down each particular saint,   251
  Were testimonies against his worth and credit

227 **composition** agreement   228–9 **disvalued In levity**
discredited for lightness.   239 **confixèd** firmly fixed
242 **scope** full authority   243 **touched** injured, affected.
244 **informal** rash, distracted   245 **But** than   250 **Compact . . .
gone** i.e., in collusion with Isabella   251 **swear . . . saint** call
down to witness every single saint

That's sealed in approbation?—You, Lord Escalus,   253
Sit with my cousin; lend him your kind pains
To find out this abuse, whence 'tis derived.
There is another friar that set them on;
Let him be sent for.

[The Duke rises; Escalus takes his chair.]

FRIAR PETER
Would he were here, my lord! For he indeed
Hath set the women on to this complaint.
Your Provost knows the place where he abides,
And he may fetch him.

DUKE   Go do it instantly.

[Exit Provost.]

And you, my noble and well-warranted cousin,
Whom it concerns to hear this matter forth,   263
Do with your injuries as seems you best,   264
In any chastisement. I for a while
Will leave you; but stir not you till you have
Well determined upon these slanderers.   267

ESCALUS   My lord, we'll do it throughly.   *Exit [Duke].*   268
Signor Lucio, did not you say you knew that Friar
Lodowick to be a dishonest person?

LUCIO   *Cucullus non facit monachum;* honest in nothing   271
but in his clothes, and one that hath spoke most
villainous speeches of the Duke.

ESCALUS   We shall entreat you to abide here till he come,
and enforce them against him. We shall find this friar   275
a notable fellow.   276

---

253 **sealed in approbation** ratified by proof, like weights and
measures being given a stamp or seal to attest to their genuineness.
263 **forth** through   264 **Do . . . best** respond to the wrongs
done you as seems best to you   267 **determined** reached
judgment   268 **throughly** thoroughly.   271 *Cucullus . . .
monachum* A cowl doesn't make a monk   275 **enforce them**
forcefully urge your charges   276 **notable** notorious

LUCIO   As any in Vienna, on my word.

ESCALUS   Call that same Isabel here once again. I would
speak with her.   [Exit an Attendant.]
Pray you, my lord, give me leave to question. You shall
see how I'll handle her.

LUCIO   Not better than he, by her own report.   282

ESCALUS   Say you?

LUCIO   Marry, sir, I think, if you handled her privately,   284
she would sooner confess; perchance publicly she'll
be ashamed.

ESCALUS   I will go darkly to work with her.   287

LUCIO   That's the way, for women are light at midnight.   288

   *Enter Duke [disguised as a friar], Provost, Isabella,
   [and officers].*

ESCALUS   Come on, mistress. Here's a gentlewoman
denies all that you have said.

LUCIO   My lord, here comes the rascal I spoke of, here
with the Provost.

ESCALUS   In very good time. Speak not you to him till
we call upon you.

LUCIO   Mum.

ESCALUS   Come, sir, did you set these women on to
slander Lord Angelo? They have confessed you did.

DUKE   'Tis false.

ESCALUS   How? Know you where you are?

---

282 **Not . . . report** (Lucio salaciously turns Escalus's *handle her*
into a sexual slur: You, Escalus, will do no better at "handling"
Isabella than did Angelo, according to Isabella's testimony.)
284 **if . . . privately** (Lucio continues his sexual joke about
"handling.")   287 **darkly** subtly, slyly   288 **light** wanton,
unchaste

DUKE

    Respect to your great place! And let the devil   300
    Be sometime honored for his burning throne!   301
    Where is the Duke? 'Tis he should hear me speak.

ESCALUS

    The Duke's in us, and we will hear you speak.
    Look you speak justly.

DUKE

    Boldly, at least. But oh, poor souls,
    Come you to seek the lamb here of the fox?
    Good night to your redress! Is the Duke gone?
    Then is your cause gone too. The Duke's unjust,
    Thus to retort your manifest appeal,   309
    And put your trial in the villain's mouth
    Which here you come to accuse.

LUCIO

    This is the rascal. This is he I spoke of.

ESCALUS

    Why, thou unreverend and unhallowed friar,
    Is't not enough thou hast suborned these women
    To accuse this worthy man, but, in foul mouth
    And in the witness of his proper ear,   316
    To call him villain? And then to glance from him
    To th'Duke himself, to tax him with injustice?—   318
    Take him hence. To th' rack with him!—We'll touse
      you   319
    Joint by joint, but we will know his purpose.   320
    What, "unjust"?

DUKE   Be not so hot. The Duke
    Dare no more stretch this finger of mine than he

300–1 **let . . . throne** i.e., may all authority be respected, even the
devil's. (Said sardonically.)   309 **retort** turn back.   **manifest**
obviously just   316 **in . . . ear** within his own hearing
318 **tax him with** accuse him of   319 **touse** tear   320 **but we
will** i.e., if necessary to; until we

Dare rack his own. His subject am I not,
Nor here provincial. My business in this state   324
Made me a looker-on here in Vienna,
Where I have seen corruption boil and bubble
Till it o'errun the stew; laws for all faults,   327
But faults so countenanced that the strong statutes   328
Stand like the forfeits in a barber's shop,   329
As much in mock as mark.

ESCALUS   Slander to th' state!   330
Away with him to prison.

ANGELO
What can you vouch against him, Signor Lucio?
Is this the man that you did tell us of?

LUCIO   'Tis he, my lord.—Come hither, Goodman   334
Baldpate. Do you know me?   335

DUKE   I remember you, sir, by the sound of your voice.
I met you at the prison, in the absence of the Duke.

LUCIO   Oh, did you so? And do you remember what you
said of the Duke?

DUKE   Most notedly, sir.   340

LUCIO   Do you so, sir? And was the Duke a flesh-
monger, a fool, and a coward, as you then reported him to be?

324 **provincial** subject to the religious authority of this province
or state.   327 **stew** (1) stewpot (2) brothel   328 **countenanced**
tolerated and protected by corrupt authority   329 **forfeits**
cautionary displays, or lists of rules and fines for handling razors,
etc., which barbers (who also acted as dentists and surgeons) hung
in their shops   330 **As . . . mark** as often flouted as observed.
334–5 **Goodman Baldpate** (Lucio refers to the tonsure that he
assumes the Duke must have under his hood, though the Duke is
clearly hooded at this point.)   340 **notedly** particularly

DUKE   You must, sir, change persons with me ere you   344
make that my report. You indeed spoke so of him, and
much more, much worse.

LUCIO   Oh, thou damnable fellow! Did not I pluck thee by
the nose for thy speeches?

DUKE   I protest I love the Duke as I love myself.

ANGELO   Hark how the villain would close now, after   350
his treasonable abuses!

ESCALUS   Such a fellow is not to be talked withal. Away
with him to prison! Where is the Provost? Away with
him to prison! Lay bolts enough upon him. Let him   354
speak no more. Away with those giglots too, and with   355
the other confederate companion!   356

           [The Provost lays hands on the Duke.]

DUKE *[to Provost]*   Stay, sir, stay awhile.

ANGELO   What, resists he? Help him, Lucio.

LUCIO   Come, sir, come, sir, come, sir; foh, sir! Why,
you bald-pated, lying rascal, you must be hooded,
must you? Show your knave's visage, with a pox to
you! Show your sheep-biting face, and be hanged an   362
hour! Will't not off?   363

           *[He pulls off the friar's hood, and discovers
                the Duke. Angelo and Escalus rise.]*

DUKE

Thou art the first knave that e'er mad'st a duke.
First, Provost, let me bail these gentle three.   365
[To Lucio] Sneak not away, sir, for the Friar and you
Must have a word anon.—Lay hold on him.

---

344 **change** exchange   350 **close** come to terms, compromise
354 **bolts** iron fetters   355 **giglots** wanton women
356 **confederate companion** i.e., Friar Peter.   362 **sheep-
biting** knavish. (From the action of wolves or dogs that prey on
sheep.)   362–3 **hanged an hour** (A sardonic way of saying
"hanged.")   365 **gentle three** i.e., Mariana, Isabella, and Friar
Peter.

LUCIO   This may prove worse than hanging.

DUKE [*to Escalus*]
What you have spoke I pardon. Sit you down.
We'll borrow place of him. [*To Angelo*] Sir, by your
    leave.   [*He takes Angelo's seat. Escalus also sits.*]
Hast thou or word, or wit, or impudence,   371
That yet can do thee office? If thou hast,   372
Rely upon it till my tale be heard,
And hold no longer out.

ANGELO [*kneeling*]   O my dread lord,   374
I should be guiltier than my guiltiness
To think I can be undiscernible,
When I perceive Your Grace, like power divine,
Hath looked upon my passes. Then, good prince,   378
No longer session hold upon my shame,
But let my trial be mine own confession.
Immediate sentence then and sequent death   381
Is all the grace I beg.

DUKE   Come hither, Mariana.—
Say, wast thou e'er contracted to this woman?

ANGELO   I was, my lord.

DUKE
Go take her hence and marry her instantly.
Do you the office, Friar, which consummate,   386
Return him here again. Go with him, Provost.

                    Exit [*Angelo, with Mariana, Friar Peter, and
                                                    Provost*].

371 **or word** either word   372 **office** service.   374 **hold . . .
out** then persist no longer.   378 **passes** actions, trespasses.
381 **sequent** subsequent   386 **Do . . . office** Please perform the
service.   **consummate** being completed

ESCALUS

My lord, I am more amazed at his dishonor
Than at the strangeness of it.

DUKE   Come hither, Isabel.
Your friar is now your prince. As I was then
Advertising and holy to your business,   391
Not changing heart with habit, I am still
Attorneyed at your service.

ISABELLA   Oh, give me pardon,   393
That I, your vassal, have employed and pained   394
Your unknown sovereignty!

DUKE   You are pardoned, Isabel.
And now, dear maid, be you as free to us.   396
Your brother's death, I know, sits at your heart;
And you may marvel why I obscured myself,
Laboring to save his life, and would not rather
Make rash remonstrance of my hidden power   400
Than let him so be lost. O most kind maid,
It was the swift celerity of his death,
Which I did think with slower foot came on,
That brained my purpose. But peace be with him!   404
That life is better life past fearing death
Than that which lives to fear. Make it your comfort,
So happy is your brother.

    *Enter Angelo, Mariana, [Friar] Peter, [and]
    Provost.*

ISABELLA   I do, my lord.   407

391 **Advertising and holy** attentive and wholly dedicated (in my
priestly role)   393 **Attorneyed at** serving as agent in
394 **pained** put to trouble   396 **as free to us** i.e., as generous in
pardoning me.   400 **rash remonstrance** sudden manifestation
404 **brained** dashed, defeated   407 **So** thus

DUKE

    For this new-married man approaching here,

    Whose salt imagination yet hath wronged   409

    Your well-defended honor, you must pardon

    For Mariana's sake. But as he adjudged your

      brother—

    Being criminal, in double violation

    Of sacred chastity and of promise-breach   413

    Thereon dependent, for your brother's life—   414

    The very mercy of the law cries out   415

    Most audible, even from his proper tongue,   416

    "An Angelo for Claudio, death for death!"

    Haste still pays haste, and leisure answers leisure;   418

    Like doth quit like, and measure still for measure.   419

    Then, Angelo, thy fault's thus manifested,

    Which, though thou wouldst deny, denies thee

      vantage.   421

    We do condemn thee to the very block

    Where Claudio stooped to death, and with like haste.

    Away with him!

MARIANA   O my most gracious lord,

    I hope you will not mock me with a husband!

DUKE

    It is your husband mocked you with a husband.

    Consenting to the safeguard of your honor,

    I thought your marriage fit; else imputation,   428

    For that he knew you, might reproach your life   429

---

409 **salt** lecherous   413–14 **promise-breach . . . dependent**
i.e., breaking his promise made in return for the yielding up of
chastity   415 **The very . . . law** i.e., even mercy itself
416 **his proper** its own   418 **still** always   419 **quit** requite
421 **though** even if.   **vantage** i.e., any advantage. (Angelo must
suffer the same penalty as Claudio.)   428 **fit** appropriate.
imputation accusation, slander   429 **For that he knew you**
since he knew you sexually

And choke your good to come. For his possessions,   430
Although by confiscation they are ours,
We do instate and widow you withal,   432
To buy you a better husband.

MARIANA   O my dear lord,
I crave no other, nor no better man.

DUKE
Never crave him; we are definitive.   435

MARIANA [kneeling]
Gentle my liege—

DUKE   You do but lose your labor.—
Away with him to death! [To Lucio] Now, sir, to you.

MARIANA
O my good lord!—Sweet Isabel, take my part!
Lend me your knees, and all my life to come
I'll lend you all my life to do you service.

DUKE
Against all sense you do importune her.
Should she kneel down in mercy of this fact,   442
Her brother's ghost his pavèd bed would break,   443
And take her hence in horror.

MARIANA   Isabel,
Sweet Isabel, do yet but kneel by me!
Hold up your hands, say nothing; I'll speak all.
They say best men are molded out of faults,   447
And, for the most, become much more the better   448
For being a little bad. So may my husband.
O Isabel, will you not lend a knee?

---

430 **For** As for   432 **widow** endow with a widow's rights
435 **definitive** firmly resolved.   442 **in . . . fact** pleading mercy
for this crime   443 **pavèd bed** grave covered with a stone slab
447 **best men** even the best of men   448 **most** most part

DUKE
    He dies for Claudio's death.

ISABELLA [*kneeling*]   Most bounteous sir,
    Look, if it please you, on this man condemned
    As if my brother lived. I partly think
    A due sincerity governed his deeds,
    Till he did look on me. Since it is so,
    Let him not die. My brother had but justice,
    In that he did the thing for which he died.
    For Angelo,
    His act did not o'ertake his bad intent,
    And must be buried but as an intent   460
    That perished by the way. Thoughts are no subjects,   461
    Intents but merely thoughts.

MARIANA   Merely, my lord.

DUKE
    Your suit's unprofitable. Stand up, I say.

                                    [*They stand.*]

    I have bethought me of another fault.
    Provost, how came it Claudio was beheaded
    At an unusual hour?

PROVOST   It was commanded so.

DUKE
    Had you a special warrant for the deed?

PROVOST
    No, my good lord, it was by private message.

DUKE
    For which I do discharge you of your office.
    Give up your keys.

PROVOST   Pardon me, noble lord.
    I thought it was a fault, but knew it not,   472

---

460 **buried** i.e., forgotten   461 **no subjects** i.e., not subject to
the state's authority   472 **knew it not** was not sure

Yet did repent me after more advice;   473
For testimony whereof, one in the prison,
That should by private order else have died,
I have reserved alive.

DUKE   What's he?

PROVOST   His name is Barnardine.

DUKE
I would thou hadst done so by Claudio.
Go fetch him hither. Let me look upon him.

                                        [*Exit Provost.*]

ESCALUS
I am sorry one so learnèd and so wise
As you, Lord Angelo, have still appeared,   482
Should slip so grossly, both in the heat of blood
And lack of tempered judgment afterward.

ANGELO
I am sorry that such sorrow I procure,   485
And so deep sticks it in my penitent heart
That I crave death more willingly than mercy.
'Tis my deserving, and I do entreat it.   488

        Enter Barnardine and Provost, Claudio [muffled],
        [and] Juliet.

DUKE
Which is that Barnardine?

PROVOST   This, my lord.

DUKE
There was a friar told me of this man.—
Sirrah, thou art said to have a stubborn soul
That apprehends no further than this world,
And squar'st thy life according. Thou'rt condemned;   493

473 **advice** consideration   482 **still** always   485 **procure**
cause, prompt   488.1 *muffled* wrapped up so as to conceal
identity. (As also in line 497.)   493 **squar'st** regulates

But, for those earthly faults, I quit them all,   494
And pray thee take this mercy to provide
For better times to come.—Friar, advise him;
I leave him to your hand.—What muffled fellow's
    that?

PROVOST
This is another prisoner that I saved,
Who should have died when Claudio lost his head,
As like almost to Claudio as himself.

                  [He unmuffles Claudio.]

DUKE [to Isabella]
If he be like your brother, for his sake
Is he pardoned, and for your lovely sake,
Give me your hand and say you will be mine;
He is my brother too. But fitter time for that.
By this Lord Angelo perceives he's safe;
Methinks I see a quick'ning in his eye.
Well, Angelo, your evil quits you well.   507
Look that you love your wife, her worth worth yours.   508
I find an apt remission in myself;   509
And yet here's one in place I cannot pardon.   510
[To Lucio] You, sirrah, that knew me for a fool, a
    coward,
One all of luxury, an ass, a madman—   512
Wherein have I so deserved of you
That you extol me thus?

LUCIO   Faith, my lord, I spoke it but according to the
trick. If you will hang me for it, you may; but I had   516
rather it would please you I might be whipped.

---

494 **for** as for.   **quit** pardon   507 **quits** rewards, requites
508 **her . . . yours** her worthiness richly deserving your love and
worthy of your estate.   509 **apt remission** readiness to show
mercy   510 **in place** present   512 **luxury** lechery
516 **trick** fashion.

DUKE

    Whipped first, sir, and hanged after.—
    Proclaim it, Provost, round about the city,
    If any woman wronged by this lewd fellow—
    As I have heard him swear himself there's one
    Whom he begot with child—let her appear,
    And he shall marry her. The nuptial finished,
    Let him be whipped and hanged.

LUCIO   I beseech Your Highness, do not marry me to a
whore. Your Highness said even now I made you a   526
duke; good my lord, do not recompense me in making me a cuckold.

DUKE

    Upon mine honor, thou shalt marry her.
    Thy slanders I forgive and therewithal   530
    Remit thy other forfeits.—Take him to prison,   531
    And see our pleasure herein executed.   532

LUCIO   Marrying a punk, my lord, is pressing to death,   533
whipping, and hanging.

DUKE

    Slandering a prince deserves it.

                    [Exeunt officers with Lucio.]
    She, Claudio, that you wronged, look you restore.   536
    Joy to you, Mariana! Love her, Angelo.
    I have confessed her, and I know her virtue.
    Thanks, good friend Escalus, for thy much goodness;

---

526 **even** just   530–1 **and therewithal . . . forfeits** i.e., and in
addition to that I will not have you whipped and hanged.
532 **see . . . executed** i.e., see that my order be carried out that
Lucio marry Kate Keepdown (see 3.2.194–6).   533 **pressing to
death** i.e., by having heavy weights placed on the chest. (A
standard form of executing those who refused to plead to a felony
charge.) Lucio wryly complains that marrying a whore is as bad as
death by torture.   536 **She . . . restore** i.e., See to it that you
marry Juliet.

There's more behind that is more gratulate.   540
Thanks, Provost, for thy care and secrecy;
We shall employ thee in a worthier place.
Forgive him, Angelo, that brought you home
The head of Ragozine for Claudio's;
Th'offense pardons itself. Dear Isabel,
I have a motion much imports your good,   546
Whereto if you'll a willing ear incline,
What's mine is yours, and what is yours is mine.—
So, bring us to our palace, where we'll show   549
What's yet behind, that's meet you all should know.   550

                                                   [*Exeunt.*]

---

540 **behind** in store, to come.   **gratulate** gratifying.
546 **motion** proposal (which)   549 **bring** escort   550 **What's
yet behind** what is still to be told

DATE AND TEXT

Measure for Measure first appeared in the First Folio of 1623. The text was evidently set from scrivener Ralph Crane's copy, possibly of Shakespeare's own draft; the usual inconsistencies of composition have not yet been smoothed away by use in the theater. On the other hand, spellings tend to suggest that Crane was copying a transcript. A recent and controversial hypothesis is that Crane based his copy on a playbook in use after Shakespeare's death, which incorporated some theatrical adaptation by Thomas Middleton and some other reviser, including a song (4.1.1–6) that could have originated in *Rollo, Duke of Normandy* (c. 1617) by John Fletcher and others.

The first recorded performance (according to a Revels account document) was on December 26, 1604, St. Stephen's Night, when "a play Caled Mesur for Mesur" by "Shaxberd" was acted in the banqueting hall at Whitehall "by his Maiesties plaiers." Shakespeare's acting company, previously the Lord Chamberlain's Men, had become the King's Men after the accession to the throne of James I in 1603. Several allusions in the play seem to point to the summer of 1604, when the theaters, having been closed for a year because of the plague, were reopened. A reference to the King of Hungary (1.2.1–5) may reflect anxieties in England over James's negotiations for a settlement with Spain; censorship would forbid a direct mentioning of Spain. Mistress Overdone's complaint about the war, the "sweat" (plague), the "gallows" (public executions), and poverty (1.2.81–3) are all suggestive of events in 1603–1604, when war with Spain and the plague were still very much in evidence. Duke Vincentio's reticent habits have been seen as a flattering reference to James's well-known dislike of crowds. Stylistically, the play is clearly later than *Twelfth Night* (1600–1602), so that a date close to the first recorded performance in 1604 is a necessity, even if we cannot be positive about all the supposed allusions to King James.

TEXTUAL NOTES

❧

These textual notes are not a historical collation, either of the early folios or of more recent editions; they are simply a record of departures in this edition from the copy text. The reading adopted in this edition appears in boldface, followed by the rejected reading from the copy text, i.e., the First Folio. Only major alterations in punctuation are noted. Changes in lineation are not indicated, nor are some minor and obvious typographical errors.

Abbreviations used:
F the First Folio
s.d. stage direction
s.p. speech prefix

Copy text: the First Folio.

The Names of All the Actors [at the end of the play in F]

1.1. 76 s.d. [at line 75 in F]

1.2. 58 [and elsewhere] MISTRESS OVERDONE *Bawd*   **83.1** [after line 84 in F]   **85** [and elsewhere] POMPEY *Clo.*   **115** [F begins "*Scena Tertia*" here]   **134 morality** mortality

1.3. [F labels as "*Scena Quarta*"]   **20 steeds** weedes   **27 Becomes more** More   **48** [and elsewhere] **More** Moe   **54.1** *Exeunt Exit*

1.4. [F labels as "*Scena Quinta*"]   **0.1** [and elsewhere] *Isabella Isabell*
2 [and throughout] FRANCISCA *Nun*   **5 sisterhood** Sisterstood
17 stead steed [also at 3.2. 252]   **54 givings-out** giuing-out
61–2 mind, study, and fast. / He minde: Studie, and fast / He
72 He's Has   **78** [and elsewhere] **lose** loose

2.1. 12 your our   **39 breaks** brakes   **90** [and elsewhere] **prunes** prewyns   **139.1** [at line 138 in F]

2.2. 63 back again againe   **104 ere** here

2.3. 31 [and elsewhere] lest least

2.4. 9 sere feard   **17 s.d.** *Enter Servant* [after line 17 in F]
30 s.d. *Enter Isabella* [after line 30 in F]   **48 metal** mettle   **53 or**
and   **75 craftily** crafty   **76 me be** be   **94 all-binding** all-
building

3.1. 29 thee sire, thee, fire   **31 serpigo** Sapego   **52 me to hear
them** them to heare me   **68 Though** Through   **91 enew** emmew
96 damned'st damnest   **131 penury** periury   **200 advisings.
To . . . good a** aduisings, to . . . good; a   **216 by oath** oath

3.2. 0 [not marked as a new scene in F]   **8 law a** Law; a   **9 on** and
26 eat, array eate away   **48 it clutched** clutch'd   **74–5 bondage.
If . . . patiently, why** bondage if . . . patiently: Why
109 ungenerative generatiue   **147 dearer** deare   **214 See** Sea

4.1. 1 BOY [not in F]   **49.1** [after line 48 in F]   **61 quests** Quest
64 s.d. *Enter . . . Isabella* [after line 64 in F]

4.2. 43–7 If . . . thief [assigned in F to *Clo.*]   **58 yare** y'are
60.1 [at line 59 in F]   **72 s.d.** *Enter Duke* [after line 72 in F]
100 This . . . man [assigned in F to *Duke*]   **Lordship's** Lords
101 DUKE *Pro.*   **120 PROVOST** [not in F]

4.3. 92.1 [at line 91 in F]   **93 Varrius** *Angelo*   **100 well** weale

4.4. 6 redeliver reliuer   **15–16 proclaimed. Betimes** proclaim'd
betimes   **19 s.d.** [at line 18 in F]

4.5. 6 Flavius' *Flauia's*

5.1. 14 me we   **34 hear!** heere.   **173 s.d.** *Enter Mariana* [after
line 173 in F]   **174 her face** your face   **226 promisèd** promis'd
268 s.d. [at line 267 in F]   **288.1** [after line 286 in F]   **407 s.d.**
Mariana Maria   **431 confiscation** confutation   **488.2 Juliet**
Iulietta   **550 that's** that

SHAKESPEARE'S SOURCES

~❧~

Stories about corrupt magistrates are ancient and universal, but Shakespeare's particular story in *Measure for Measure* seems to go back to an actual incident in the sixteenth-century Italian court of Don Ferdinando de Gonzaga. A Hungarian student named Joseph Macarius, writing from Vienna, tells about an Italian citizen accused of murder whose wife submitted to the embraces of the magistrate in hopes of saving her husband. When the magistrate executed her husband despite her having fulfilled her bargain, she appealed to the Duke, who ordered the magistrate to give her a dowry and marry her. Thereafter the Duke ordered the magistrate to be executed. This incident seems to have inspired a Senecan drama by Claude Rouillet called *Philanira* (1556), a French translation of this play (1563), a novella in the *Hecatommithi* of G. B. Giraldi Cinthio (1565), and a play by Cinthio called *Epitia* (posthumously published in 1583). Shakespeare may have known both the prose and the dramatic versions by Cinthio.

In Cinthio's story, the wise Emperor Maximian appoints his friend Juriste to govern Innsbruck, warning him to rule justly or expect no mercy from the Emperor. Juriste rules long and well, to the satisfaction of his master and the people of Innsbruck. When a young man named Vico is brought before him for ravishing a virgin, Juriste assigns the mandatory sentence of death. Vico's sister, Epitia, an extraordinarily beautiful virgin of eighteen, pleads for Vico's life, urging that his deed was one of passion and that he stands ready to marry the girl he forced. The judge, secretly inflamed with lust for Epitia, promises to consider the matter carefully. She reports this seemingly encouraging news to Vico, who urges her to persevere. When, however, the judge proposes to take her chastity in return for her brother's life, Epitia is mortified and refuses unless Juriste will marry her. During another interim in these negotiations, Vico begs his sister to save his life at any cost. She then submits to Juriste on the condition that he will both marry her and spare Vico. Next morning, however, the jailer brings her the body of her decapitated brother. She lays her complaint before the Emperor, who confronts Juriste with his guilt. Conscience-stricken, Juriste confesses and begs for mercy. At first Epitia demands strict justice, but when the Emperor compels Juriste to marry her and then be beheaded, she reveals "her natural kindness" and begs successfully for the life of her wronger. There are several important differences between this account and Shakespeare's play: Vico is actually killed, unlike Claudio, and Epitia sleeps with Juriste and then is married to him. No equivalent to Mariana appears, or to Lucio, Pompey, Mistress Overdone, Elbow, and other characters in the comic scenes of Shakespeare's play. No duke oversees the career of Juriste and ensures that no fatal wrong will occur.

Shakespeare may also have consulted Cinthio's play *Epitia*, but his chief sources were George Whetstone's two-part play *Promos and Cassandra* (1578) and a novella on the same subject. In the English play, the corrupt judge is Promos, administrator of the city of Julio under the King of Hungary. The law forbidding adultery has lain in abeyance for some years when a young gentleman named Andrugio is arrested and condemned for "incontinency." His sister Cassandra, like Epitia in Cinthio, lays down her precious chastity to Promos in response to her brother's piteous entreaties. Promos gives his assurance that he will marry her and save Andrugio's life. When Promos instead treacherously orders the execution of Andrugio, the jailer secretly substitutes the head of a felon, newly executed and so mutilated as to be unrecognizable even by Cassandra. (This rescue is seen as an intervention "by the providence of God.") The King sentences Promos just as the Emperor sentences Juriste in Cinthio, but in Whetstone's play the King refuses Cassandra's pleas for the life of her new husband until Andrugio reveals himself to be still alive and offers to die for Promos. The King forgives Andrugio on condition that he marry Polina, whom he wronged. The play also features a courtesan named Lamia and

her man, Rosko, who ingratiate themselves with the corrupt officer (Phallax) in charge of investigating their case. Phallax is
ultimately caught and dismissed from office while Lamia is publicly humiliated.

Whetstone wrote a prose novella of this same story in the
Heptameron of Civil Discourses (1582). Shakespeare appears to
have consulted it as well as the play, for the prose version mentions the names of Isabella (as the narrator of the story) and
Crassus (compare *Measure for Measure*, 4.5.8), and the King's
awarding of measure for measure in his sentencing of Promos—
"You shall be measured with the grace you bestowed on
Andrugio"—may have given Shakespeare an idea for the title
of his play. The prose version is given in the following pages,
since the two-part play is far too long for inclusion and since
the novella gives much of what Shakespeare used, other than
the important dramatic structure of *Promos and Cassandra*.
Shakespeare was also indebted for a few details to a version in
Thomas Lupton's *Too Good to Be True* (1581).

Even though Shakespeare's play is closely related to
Whetstone's play and novella, Shakespeare has changed much.
He adds the motif of the Duke's mysterious disguise. (A not very
compelling analogue to this motif occurs in Sir Thomas Elyot's
The Image of Governance, 1541.) Shakespeare introduces the use
of the bed trick, found also in his presumably earlier play *All's
Well That Ends Well*. Most important, Shakespeare stresses the
moral and legal complexity of his story. Isabella is about to renounce the world by entering a convent. By contrast, Lucio, a
Shakespearean addition, is an engaging cynic, hedonist, and
slanderer. Claudio, although guilty of fornication, is only technically in violation of the laws against sexual license. Isabella
does not surrender her chastity. Her breakdown in the scene
with Claudio intensifies her emotional crisis and renders all the
more triumphant her final ability to forgive Angelo. Angelo
himself is made puritanical in temperament, and is spared the
actual consequences of his worst intentions so that he can be
worthy of being forgiven. Isabella need not marry Angelo, since
he has not actually seduced her; she is thus free to marry the

Duke. No felon need be executed in Claudio's stead, for providence provides a natural death in the prison. In the subplot, going well beyond the merest hints in Whetstone, Pompey is a brilliantly original innovation, Elbow a characteristically Shakespearean clown modeled on the earlier Dogberry of *Much Ado About Nothing*, and Escalus a significant spokesman for a moderate and practical course of equity in the law.

AN HEPTAMERON[1] OF CIVIL DISCOURSES
By *George Whetstone*

THE RARE HISTORY OF PROMOS AND CASSANDRA

[*The story is narrated by a lady called Isabella at the court of Queen Aurelia.*]

At what time[2] Corvinus, the scourge of the Turks, reigned as King of Bohemia, for to[3] well govern the free cities of his realm he sent divers worthy magistrates. Among the rest he gave the Lord Promos the lieutenantship of Julio, who in the beginning of his government purged the city of many ancient vices and severely punished new offenders.

In this city there was an old custom, by the suffering[4] of some magistrates grown out of use,[5] that what man soever committed adultery should lose his head, and the woman offender should ever after be infamously noted by the wearing of some disguised apparel.[6] For the man was held to be the greatest offender and therefore had the severest punishment. Lord Promos, with a rough execution, revived this statute, and in the highest degree of injury brake it himself, as shall appear by the sequel of Andrugio's adventures.

---

1 **An Heptameron** a collection of stories, represented (on the pattern of Boccaccio's *Decameron*) as having been told on seven successive days 2 **At what time** When   3 **for to** in order to   4 **suffering** allowance 5 **grown out of use** fallen into disuse   6 **disguised apparel** i.e., distinctive costume appropriate to her shame.

This Andrugio, by the yielding favor[7] of fair Polina, trespassed against this ordinance, who through envy[8] was accused, and by Lord Promos condemned to suffer execution.

The woeful Cassandra, Andrugio's sister, prostrates herself at Lord Promos's feet, and with more tears than words thus pleaded for her brother's life:

"Most noble lord and worthy judge, vouchsafe me the favor to speak, whose case is so desperate as,[9] unless you behold me with the eyes of mercy, the frail trespass of condemned Andrugio, my brother, will be the death of sorrowful Cassandra, his innocent sister. I will not presume to excuse his offense or reproach the law of rigor.[10] For in the general construction[11] he hath done most evil, and the law hath judged but what is right. But, reverend judge, pardon that necessity maketh me here tell that[12] your wisdom already knoweth. The most sovereign Justice is crowned with laurel,[13] although she be girt with a sword; and this privilege she giveth unto her administrators, that they shall mitigate the severity of the law according to the quality of the offense. Then, that justice be not robbed of her gracious pity, listen, good Lord Promos, to the nature of my brother's offense and his able means to repair the injury. He hath defiled no nuptial bed, the stain whereof dishonoreth the guiltless husband. He hath committed no violent rape, in which act the injured maid can have no amends. But with yielding consent of his mistress Andrugio hath only sinned through love, and never meant but with marriage to make amends. I humbly beseech you to accept his satisfaction, and by this example you shall be as much beloved for your clemency as feared for your severity. Andrugio shall be well warned, and he, with his sister, woeful Cassandra, shall ever remain Your Lordship's true servants."

7 **by the yielding favor** through the compliant and unresisting indulgence   8 **envy** malice   9 **as** that   10 **reproach . . . rigor** accuse the law of being too rigorous.   11 **general construction** interpretation of people generally   12 **that** that which   13 **laurel** (Here symbolic of mercy, balanced against the sword of rigor.)

Promos's ears were not so attentive to hear Cassandra's ruthful[14] tale as his eyes were settled to regard her excellent beauty. And love, that was the appointed headsman[15] of Andrugio, became now the sovereign of his judge's thought. But because he would seem to bridle his passions, he answered:

"Fair damsel, have patience. You importune me with an impossibility. He is condemned by law. Then, without injury to law, he cannot be saved."

"Princes' and their deputies' prerogatives," quoth she, "are above the law. Besides, law, truly construed, is but the amends of[16] injury, and where the fault may be valued and amends had,[17] the breach of law is sufficiently repaired."

Quoth Lord Promos:

"Your passions moveth more than your proofs. And for your sake I will reprieve Andrugio and study how to do you ease without apparent breach of law."

Cassandra, recomforted,[18] with humble thanks received his favor, and in great haste goeth to participate[19] this hope with her dying brother. But, oh, that authority should have power to make the virtuous to do amiss, as well as through correction to enforce the vicious to fall unto goodness! Promos is a witness of this privilege,[20] who, not able to subdue his incontinent[21] love, and withal resolved[22] that Cassandra would never be overcome with fair words, large promises, or rich rewards, demanded the spoil of her virginity for ransom of her brother's liberty.

Cassandra imagined at the first that Lord Promos used this speech but to try her behavior; answered[23] him so wisely as, if he had not been the rival[24] of virtue, he could not but have suppressed his lewd affection and have subscribed to her just

14 ruthful pitiful   15 headsman executioner (with a play on *sovereign*)   16 amends of compensation for   17 where . . . had where a price tag may be put on the offense and paid accordingly   18 recomforted relieved   19 participate share   20 privilege i.e., abuse of authority   21 incontinent lacking in self-restraint   22 withal resolved in addition persuaded   23 answered i.e., and answered   24 rival opponent

petition. But to leave circumstances,[25] Promos was fired with a vicious desire which must be quenched with Cassandra's yielding love, or Andrugio must die.

Cassandra, moved with a chaste disdain, departed with the resolution rather to die herself than to stain her honor, and with this heavy news greeted her condemned brother. Poor man, alas! What should he do? Life was sweet. But to be redeemed with his sister's infamy could not but be always unsavory. To persuade her to consent was unnatural; to yield to death was more grievous. To choose the least of these evils was difficult; to study long was dangerous. Fain[26] would he live, but shame closed his mouth when he attempted to persuade his sister. But necessity, that mastereth both shame and fear, brake a passage[27] for his imprisoned intent.

"Sweet Cassandra," quoth he, "that men love is usual, but to subdue affection is impossible, and so thorny are the motions of incontinent desire as, to find ease, the tongue is only occupied to persuade, the purse is ever open to entice, and, where neither words nor gifts can corrupt—with the mighty—force shall constrain or despite[28] avenge. That Promos do love is but just; thy beauty commands him. That Promos be refused is more just, because consent is thy shame. Thou mayst refuse and live. But he being rejected, I die. For wanting his will[29] in thee, he will wreak his teen[30] on me. This is my hard estate: my life lieth in thy infamy, and thy honor in my death. Which of these evils be least I leave for thee to judge."

The woeful Cassandra answered that death was the least, whose dart we cannot shun, when[31] honor, in death's despite, outliveth time.

"It is true," quoth Andrugio, "but thy trespass will be in the least degree of blame. For, in forced faults, justice saith there is no intent of evil."

25 to leave circumstances to make a long story short   26 Fain Gladly, eagerly   27 brake a passage broke a way out of confinement   28 despite malice   29 wanting his will failing to achieve his desire   30 wreak his teen exercise his wrath   31 when whereas

"O Andrugio," quoth she, "intent is nowadays little considered. Thou art not condemned by the intent but by the strict word of the law. So shall my crime be reproached and the forced cause pass unexcused.[32] And, such is the venom of envy, one evil deed shall disgrace ten good turns; and in this yielding, so shall I be valued. Envy, disdain, spite, malice, slander, and many more furies will endeavor to shame me, and the meanest[33] virtue will blush to help to support my honor; so that I see no liberty for thee but death nor no ease for me but to hasten my end."

"Oh, yes," quoth Andrugio, "for if this offense be known, thy fame will be enlarged, because it will likewise be known that thou received'st dishonor to give thy brother life. If it be secret, thy conscience will be without scruple of guiltiness. Thus, known or unknown, thou shalt be deflowered but not dishonested;[34] and for amends[35] we both shall live. This further hope remaineth: that, as the gillyflower both pleaseth the eye and feedeth the sense, even so the virtue of thy chaste behavior may so grace thy beauty as Promos's filthy lust may be turned into faithful love and so move him to salve thy honor in making thee his wife, or for conscience forbear to do so heinous an injury."

Sovereign madam, and you fair gentlewomen (quoth Isabella),[36] I entreat you in Cassandra's behalf, these reasons well weighed, to judge her yielding a constraint and no consent, who, weary of her own life and tender over her brother's, with the tears of her lovely eyes bathed his cheeks with this comfortable sentence:

"Live, Andrugio, and make much of this kiss, which breatheth my honor into thy bowels and draweth the infamy of thy first trespass into my bosom."

The sharp encounters between life and death so occupied

---

32 and . . . unexcused i.e., and the fact that I was compelled to commit my crime of unchastity will not excuse it.   33 meanest least   34 dishonested proclaimed as unchaste   35 for amends by way of compensation   36 Isabella (The narrator of this story at the court of Queen Aurelia.)

Andrugio's senses that his tongue had not the virtue[37] to bid her farewell. To grieve you with the hearing of Cassandra's secret plaints were an injury, virtuous ladies, for they concluded with their good fortune and everlasting fame.[38] But for that[39] her offense grew neither of frailty, free will, or any motion of a woman, but by the mere[40] enforcement of a man, because she would not stain the modest weeds of her kind[41] she attired herself in the habit of a page, and with the bashful grace of a pure virgin she presented wicked Promos Andrugio's precious ransom.

This devil in human shape, more vicious than Heliogabalus of Rome[42] and withal as cruel as Denis of Sicily,[43] received this jewel with a thousand protestations of favor.[44] But what should I say? In the beginning of his love Promos was metamorphosed into Priapus.[45] And of a fiend what may we expect but vengeance heaped upon villainy? And therefore let it not seem strange that, after this hellhound had dishonored Cassandra, he sent his warrant to the jailer privily[46] to execute Andrugio, and, with his head, crowned with these two briefs, in Promos's name to present Cassandra:[47]

> Fair Cassandra, as Promos promised thee,
> From prison, lo, he sends thy brother free.

This was his charge,[48] whose cursed will had been executed had not God, by an especial providence, at the hour of his death possessed Andrugio with the virtues of the two brave Romans,

---

37 virtue strength   38 with . . . fame i.e., with prayers for good fortune and an everlasting reputation for virtue.   39 for that because   40 by the mere utterly by the   41 weeds of her kind i.e., feminine dress   42 Heliogabalus of Rome Elagabalus, notoriously licentious Roman emperor from 218 to 222   43 Denis of Sicily i.e., Dionysius, tyrant of Syracuse, who died in 367 B.C.   44 protestations of favor promises of showing favor.   45 Priapus god of lechery.   46 privily secretly   47 with . . . Cassandra i.e., and to present to Cassandra in Promos's name the head of Andrugio crowned with the following short lines   48 his charge his orders

Marcus Crassus and Marius,[49] one of which by the force of his tongue and the other by the motions of his eyes caused the ax to fall out of the headsman's hand and mollified his cruel mind. With like compassion the jailer, in hearing Andrugio's hard adventure, left his resolution, and upon a solemn oath to live unknown, yea, to his dear sister,[50] he gave him life, and in the dead of the night betook[51] him to God and to good fortune. Which done, this good jailer took the head of a young man new executed who somewhat resembled Andrugio, and according to lewd Promos's commandment made a present thereof to Cassandra.

How unwelcome this present was, the testimony of her former sorrows somewhat discover. But to give her present passion a true grace were the task of Prometheus,[52] or such a one as hath had experience of the anguishes of hell.

"O," quoth she, "sweet Andrugio, whether shall I first[53] lament thy death, exclaim of[54] Promos's injury, or bemoan my own estate, deprived of honor, and, which is worse, cannot die but by the violence of my own hands? Alas, the least of these griefs are too heavy a burden for a man! Then all, joined in one poor woman's heart, cannot be eased but by death, and to be avenged of injurious Fortune I will forthwith cut my fillet[55] of life. But so[56] shall Promos's lewdness escape unpunished. What remedy? I am not of power to revenge. To complain, I express my own infamy, but withal proclaim his villainy; and to hear his lewdness reproved would take away the bitterness of my death. I will go unto the King, who is just and merciful. He shall hear the ruthful events of Promos's tyranny, and to give him example of vengeance I will seal my complaints with my dearest blood."

49 Marcus Crassus (d. 53 B.C.) one of the first triumvirate   **Marius** (157–87 B.C.) Roman general and statesman   **50 to live . . . sister** i.e., that Andrugio would conceal himself and live unknown even to his sister   **51 betook** committed   **52 Prometheus** Greek hero who stole fire from heaven, in punishment for which he was chained to a rock where an eagle fed daily on his liver   **53 whether shall I first** which of these shall I do first   **54 of** on   **55 fillet** thread   **56 so** accordingly

Continuing this determination, Cassandra buried her imagined brother's head, and with speed journeyed unto King Corvinus's court, before whose presence when she arrived, her mourning attire, but especially her modest countenance, moved him to behold her with an especial regard. Cassandra, upon the grant of audience, with her eyes overcharged with tears, reported the already discoursed accidents[57] with such an appearance of grief as the King and his attendants were astonied to hear her; and sure, had she not been happily[58] prevented, she had concluded her determination with chaste Lucretia's[59] destiny. The King comforted her with many gracious words and promised to take such order that, although he[60] could not be revived, her brother's death should fully be revenged and her crazed[61] honor repaired without blemish of her former reputation.

Cassandra, upon these comfortable words, a little succored her afflicted heart and with patience attended the justice of the King, who with a chosen company made a progress to Julio and entered the town with a semblance of great favor towards Promos, by that color to learn what other corrupt magistrates ruled in the city. For well he knew that birds of a feather would fly together, and wicked men would join in affection to bolster each other's evil.

After this gracious king had by heedful intelligence understood the factions of the people, unlooked-for of the magistrates he caused a proclamation to be published in which was a clause that, if any person could charge any magistrate or officer with any notable or heinous offense, treason, murder, rape, sedition, or with any such notorious crime, where they were the judges of the multitude he would himself be the judge of them, and do justice unto the meanest.[62] Upon this proclamation it was a hell to hear the exclamations of the poor, and the festered

---

57 **accidents** happenings   58 **astonied . . . happily** astonished . . . luckily   59 **Lucretia** Roman matron who committed suicide rather than outlive the shame of having been raped by Tarquin   60 **he** i.e., Andrugio   61 **crazed** shattered   62 **meanest** least (citizen).

consciences of the rich appeared as loathsome as the River of Styx.[63]

Among many that complained and received judgment of comfort, Cassandra's process[64] was presented, who, led between sorrow and shame, accused Promos to his face. The evidence was so plain as[65] the horror of a guilty conscience reaved[66] Promos of all motions of excuse; so that, holding up his hand among the worst degree of thieves, the little hope that was left moved him to confess the crime and with repentance to sue for mercy.

"Oh," quoth the King, "such especial mercy were tyranny to a commonwealth. No, Promos, no. *Hoc facias alteri, quod tibi vis fieri.*[67] You shall be measured with the grace you bestowed on Andrugio. O God," quoth he, "if men durst bark as dogs, many a judge in the world would be bewrayed for[68] a thief. It behooveth a prince to know to whom he committeth authority, lest the sword of justice, appointed to chasten the lewd, wound the good, and where good subjects are wronged, evil officers receive the benefit and their sovereigns beareth the blame. Well, wicked Promos, to scourge thy impious offenses I here give sentence that thou forthwith marry Cassandra to repair her honor by thee violated, and that the next day thou lose thy head, to make satisfaction for her brother's death."

This just judgment of the good King in the first point was forthwith executed. But sacred is the authority[69] that the virtues of the good are a shield unto the lewd. So sweet Cassandra, who simply by virtue overcame the spite of Fortune, in this marriage was charged with a new assault of sorrow, and preferring the duty of a wife before the natural zeal of a sister, where she before prosecuted the revenge of her brother's death she now was an humble suitor to the King for her husband's life.

The gracious King sought to appease her with good words,

63 Styx river of the underworld.   64 process story   65 as that   66 reaved bereaved   67 Hoc . . . fieri (The King freely translates in his next sentence.)   68 bewrayed for revealed as   69 sacred is the authority i.e., we have scriptural authority for it

but he could not do her this private favor without injury unto the public weal. "For though," quoth he, "your suit be just and the bounden[70] duty of a wife, yet I in fulfilling the same should do unjustly and generally injure my subjects. And therefore, good gentlewoman, have patience, and no doubt virtue in the end will give you power over all your afflictions."

There was no remedy; Cassandra must depart out of hope to obtain her suit. But, as the experience is in daily use,[71] the doings of princes post through the world on Pegasus' back,[72] and as their actions are good or bad so is their fame. With the like speed the King's justice and Promos's execution was spread abroad, and by the tongue of a clown[73] was blown into Andrugio's ears, who till then lived like an outlaw in the desert woods. But upon these news, covertly in the habit[74] of an hermit, by the divine motion of the soul who directs us in things that be good and the flesh in actions of evil, Andrugio goes to see the death of his capital enemy. But on the other part,[75] regarding the sorrow of his sister, he wished him life as a friend.

To conclude, as well to give terror to the lewd as comfort to his good subjects, the King personally came to see the execution of Promos; who, guarded with officers and strengthened with the comfortable persuasions of his ghostly fathers[76] (among whom Andrugio was), meekly offered his life as a satisfaction for his offenses—which were many more than the law took knowledge of. And yet, to say the truth, such was his repentance as the multitude did both forgive and pity him. Yea, the King wondered that his life was governed with no more virtue, considering the grace he showed at his death.

Andrugio, beholding this ruthful spectacle, was so overcome with love towards his sister as, to give her comfort, he frankly consented anew to imperil his own life. And following this resolution, in his hermit's weed upon his knees he humbly desired

70 **bounden** bound, required   71 **as . . . daily use** as we see every day
72 **post . . . back** i.e., travel quickly far and near. (Pegasus is a winged horse of Greek mythology.)   73 **clown** rustic   74 **habit** garb, dress
75 **part** hand   76 **ghostly fathers** spiritual fathers, priests or monks

the King to give him leave to speak. The King graciously granted him audience. Whereupon quoth he: "Regarded[77] sovereign, if law may possibly be satisfied, Promos's true repentance meriteth pardon."

"Good father," quoth the King, "he cannot live and the law satisfied, unless by miracle Andrugio be revived."

"Then," quoth the hermit, "if Andrugio live, the law is satisfied and Promos discharged?"

"Ay," quoth the King, "if your prayer can revive the one, my mercy shall acquit the other."

"I humbly thank Your Majesty," quoth Andrugio, and discovering himself showed the providence of God and the means of his escape; and tendering his sister's comfort above his own safety, he prostrated himself at His Majesty's feet, humbly to obey the sentence of his pleasure.

The King, upon the report of this strange adventure, after good deliberation pardoned Promos, to keep his word and withal[78] holding an opinion that it was more beneficial for the citizens to be ruled by their old evil governor, new reformed, than to adventure upon a new whose behaviors were unknown. And to perfect Cassandra's joy, he pardoned her brother Andrugio, with condition that he should marry Polina. Thus, from between the teeth of danger every party was preserved and in the end established in their hearts' desire.

77 Regarded Highly respected   **78 withal** in addition

George Whetstone's *An Heptameron of Civil Discourses, Containing the Christmas Exercise of Sundry Well-Courted Gentlemen and Gentlewomen* was published in London in 1582. The present text is based on the original edition.

FURTHER READING

❧

Bennett, Josephine Waters. *"Measure for Measure" as Royal Entertainment.* New York: Columbia Univ. Press, 1966. Bennett argues that Shakespeare carefully designed the play for its performance at court in December of 1604. Accordingly, she sees the play as a comedy enacting the spirit of the Christmas season and reflecting and reinforcing the political views the King had expressed in his recently reissued *Basilicon Doron.* Bennett even suggests that Shakespeare may have played the role of the Duke himself as part of his effort to recommend himself and his company to King James.

Berry, Ralph. *"Measure for Measure." Changing Styles in Shakespeare.* London: George Allen and Unwin, 1981. Berry examines recent productions of the play in relation to changing social and sexual attitudes. In 1950 Peter Brook's production presented a dignified and benevolent Duke successfully united with Isabella. Contrastingly, in the 1960s the emerging feminism and distrust of authority figures required a shift to productions that portrayed the Duke as manipulative and Isabella as ambivalent (and sometimes horrified) at the prospect of marrying him. Since the late 1970s, however, productions seem to be moving toward a greater dramatic and political balance, responding fully to the ambiguities of the play text.

Coleridge, Samuel Taylor. *"Measure for Measure." Coleridge's Writings on Shakespeare,* ed. Terence Hawkes. New York: G. P. Putnam's Sons, 1959. Anticipating the modern emphasis upon the disturbing qualities of the comic action, Coleridge finds *Measure for Measure* "the most painful—say rather, the only painful" work of Shakespeare. He is troubled by the conjunction of its comic and tragic aspects, and he finds Angelo's pardon and marriage not merely baffling to "the strong indignant claim of justice" but "likewise degrading to the character of woman."

DiGangi, Mario. "Pleasure and Danger: Measuring Female Sexuality in *Measure for Measure.*" *ELH* 60 (1993): 589–609. Noting the gap between the promise of its title, as well as its

classification as a comedy, and *Measure for Measure*'s "skewed
and dismal account of female desire," DiGangi brilliantly focuses
on the play's definitions and manipulations of female sexuality as
a "graphic symptom of male anxiety about female agency."

Dollimore, Jonathan. "Transgression and Surveillance in *Measure
for Measure*." *Political Shakespeare: New Essays in Cultural
Materialism*, ed. Jonathan Dollimore and Alan Sinfield. Ithaca,
N.Y., and London: Cornell Univ. Press, 1985. Dollimore argues
that the play's concern with sexual transgression reflects political rather than ethical considerations. The effort to control
sexual license is revealed to be part of a deeper cultural anxiety
about control of the lower classes. The crisis in Vienna is attributed to unregulated desire, but the play discloses that this desire,
rather than undermining government control, in fact permits
the legitimation of its authority.

Frye, Northrop. "The Reversal of Action." *The Myth of Deliverance:
Reflections on Shakespeare's Problem Comedies*. Toronto: Univ. of
Toronto Press, 1983. In a stimulating analysis of dramatic form
and its relation to social experience in the so-called problem
comedies, Frye focuses on the remarkable shift midway through
Measure for Measure from a tragic to a comic action. In containing (instead of avoiding) tragic aspects of experience through
this reversal, the comedy satisfies our desire for a "myth of
deliverance"—a triumph of love over law, and the release of
energies that permit reconciliation and renewal.

Gless, Darryl J. *"Measure for Measure," the Law, and the Convent*.
Princeton, N.J.: Princeton Univ. Press, 1979. Gless explores the
intellectual contexts invoked by the play's language and action.
In his analysis of the play's legal and theological concerns,
Isabella and Claudio, no less than Angelo, appear as examples of
the necessary spiritual depravity of fallen humanity who are,
however, finally redeemed by the working of a benign
Providence through the agency of the Duke.

Hawkins, Harriett. " 'They That Have Power to Hurt and Will Do
None': Tragic Facts and Comic Fictions in *Measure for Measure*."
Likenesses of Truth in Elizabethan and Restoration Drama. Oxford:
Oxford Univ. Press, 1972. The play for Hawkins is a failure,
though a magnificent one. The conclusion never satisfies the
tragic expectations aroused by the powerful and emotionally

gripping first half of the play. When Shakespeare, through the omniscient Duke, initiates an artificial comic resolution, the audience, Hawkins argues, feels cheated and is left with the conviction that the yoking of tragic and comic action results in irreconcilable contradictions.

Hazlitt, William. "Measure for Measure." Characters of Shakespear's Plays. London, 1817. Hazlitt finds the play to be "as full of genius as it is of wisdom," but admits that it does not allow an audience to admire its characters: "our sympathies are repulsed and defeated in all directions." Even the Duke, Hazlitt finds (anticipating much recent criticism), is "more absorbed in his own plots and gravity than anxious for the welfare of the state."

Hunter, Robert Grams. "Measure for Measure." Shakespeare and the Comedy of Forgiveness. New York: Columbia Univ. Press, 1965. Measure for Measure, Hunter finds, offers a secular version of the pattern of moral regeneration in the medieval drama. Three times in the play someone stands caught between the conflicting claims of Mercy and Justice, and the comic action of the play, like that of its sacred prototypes, insists upon the rejection of self-righteousness in favor of a generous recognition of human weakness. In Measure for Measure only charity permits a solution to the complex problems of sexual morality explored in the play.

Kaplan, M. Lindsay. "Slander for Slander in Measure for Measure." The Culture of Slander in Early Modern England. Cambridge: Cambridge Univ. Press, 1997. In a book focusing on slander as a central social, literary, and legal concern in Shakespeare's England, Kaplan's chapter on Measure for Measure identifies slander as a central concern of the play, which shows that, although the state inevitably seeks to control slander by presenting it as a threat to civic order, in fact slander is a primary strategy of governmental control and punishment.

Kirsch, Arthur. "Measure for Measure." Shakespeare and the Experience of Love. Cambridge: Cambridge Univ. Press, 1981. Emphasizing the psychological and theological assumptions that Elizabethans would have brought to the theater, Kirsch argues that Measure for Measure explores the paradoxical conditions of Christian experience. Though the play emphasizes the sinfulness of fallen humanity, the grace offered at the play's conclusion appropriately completes the pattern of the fortunate fall that the play enacts; and for Kirsch, what the Duke's "play" becomes for the characters on stage—a process leading to self-knowledge and a recognition of what it means to be mortal—is mirrored in the audience's own experience of Shakespeare's tragicomic play.

Leavis, F. R. "The Greatness of *Measure for Measure*." *The Common Pursuit*. London: Chatto and Windus, 1952. Leavis challenges the critical view that the play is problematic and morbidly pessimistic. He proposes instead that in balancing the need for social order against the New Testament injunction "Judge not, that ye be not judged," Shakespeare achieves a delicate complexity of attitudes toward justice and sexuality that is the measure of the play's coherence, and not an indication, as many critics have maintained, of Shakespeare's own moral uncertainty.

MacDonald, Ronald R. "*Measure for Measure*: The Flesh Made Word." *Studies in English Literature* 30 (1990): 265–82. In an essay alert to the play's refusal to be genial about the usual comic pattern of arousing, shaping, and containing of sexual passion, MacDonald sensitively explores *Measure for Measure*'s resistance to the traditional form and promise of comedy. Shakespeare's play, which "looks like a comedy and yet feels at every step more like a tragedy," is finally an acknowledgment of his own "ebbing faith in the ability of comic scheming to produce real solutions for the social malaise."

Miles, Rosalind. *The Problem of "Measure for Measure."* New York: Barnes and Noble, 1976. In the first half of her book Miles provides a valuable overview of the play's fate at the hands of critics, actors, illustrators, and imitators; its critical history suggests how susceptible has been the interpretation of the play to shifts in taste and morality. Miles then locates Shakespeare's achievement within the context of the drama of his age, by focusing on the play's use of dramatic conventions, especially its use of disguisings, stock character types, and the bed trick. She concludes that Shakespeare never fully assimilates and transcends his models and that the result, though always intellectually provocative, is something less than a total dramatic success.

Schanzer, Ernest. "*Measure for Measure*." *The Problem Plays of Shakespeare: A Study of "Julius Caesar," "Measure for Measure," and "Antony and Cleopatra."* New York: Schocken, 1963. Like Shakespeare's other problem plays, *Measure for Measure* deals with moral issues (here, justice and mercy) that the dramatist presents in such a way as to make us unsure of our moral bearings. Schanzer's analysis focuses on how these ethical conflicts— both personal and political—are embodied in Shakespeare's complex characters, and how Shakespeare shapes our moral response to character and action in the play.

Shuger, Debora Kuller. *Political Theologies in Shakespeare's England: The Sacred and The State in "Measure for Measure."* Houndsmill, U.K.: Palgrave, 2001. Shuger sees the play as "a meditation on its political moment," and in response offers not an account of its formal achievement but a study of the political thought that underlies it. For Shuger the play is about the possibilities and problems of Christian rule as this was being debated in the years around the play's composition, particularly as this concerns the "relation of private morals and public authority."

Stevenson, David L. *The Achievement of Shakespeare's "Measure for Measure."* Ithaca, N.Y.: Cornell Univ. Press, 1966. Stevenson's book offers a careful reading of the play, concluding that *Measure for Measure* is Shakespeare's greatest and most ingeniously constructed comedy. Its ironies, reversals, and resolution lead Stevenson to liken its structure to that of a poem by John Donne. This surface structure, he argues, serves to "unlock" deeper levels of awareness of the human condition and of the inevitability of moral paradox. Stevenson includes in an appendix a revision of an earlier historical study of the impact on the play of King James I and his political doctrine.

Wheeler, Richard P. "Vincentio and the Sins of Others: The Expense of Spirit in *Measure for Measure*." *Shakespeare's Development and the Problem Comedies.* Berkeley, Los Angeles, and London: Univ. of California Press, 1981. For Wheeler, *Measure for Measure* possesses a disturbing power derived from the psychological complexity of the experience of its protagonists, something we are more accustomed to discovering in Shakespeare's tragedies. The providential and comic ending does not clarify or resolve the inner conflicts of the characters. The tension between sexuality and moral order remains unresolved, and the unsatisfying marriage of the Duke and Isabella "is the appropriate barren conclusion" to a problematic play that exposes the artificiality of the comic form.

ALL'S WELL
THAT ENDS WELL

INTRODUCTION

❧

All's Well That Ends Well belongs to that period of Shakespeare's creative life when he concentrated on his great tragedies and wrote little comedy.

The few apparent exceptions do not fit readily into conventional dramatic genres. *Measure for Measure* (1603–1604), usually called a problem play, is darkly preoccupied with human carnality and injustice. *Troilus and Cressida* (c. 1601–1602), printed between the histories and the tragedies in the Folio of 1623, is a disillusioning satire of love and war somewhat akin to the black comedy of our modern theater. *All's Well* shares, to an extent, the satiric and brooding spirit of these two plays. Its "bed trick," in which one woman is substituted for another in an assignation with the protagonist, Bertram, poses ethical problems for the audience (as does a similar trick in *Measure for Measure*). Helena, in arranging the substitution, may seem too much of a schemer. The relations between the sexes are problematic in this play, written, as it seemingly was, at a time when Shakespeare was preoccupied with tragedies that are haunted by images of destructive femaleness and of debasing sexuality. The action of *All's Well* is, to a large extent, controlled by an admirable and attractive woman, and yet the play dwells more than do earlier comedies on the potential hazards of sexuality. For these and other reasons, *All's Well* is often grouped with the problem plays.

At the same time, the play also looks forward to Shakespeare's late romances, *Pericles, Cymbeline, The Winter's Tale,* and *The Tempest.* Here the mode of comedy turns toward the miraculous and tragicomic, with journeys of separation ending in tearful reunion and sinful error ending in spiritual rebirth. This mode was not unknown in Shakespeare's comedies of the late 1590s: *As You Like It* ends with the sudden and implausible conversion of its villains, and *Much Ado About Nothing* offers forgiveness to the undeserving Claudio while restoring his traduced fiancée, Hero, to a new life. *Measure for Measure* follows a similar pattern of redemptive pardon for the corrupted Angelo and providential deliverance for Isabella. Both *All's Well* and *Measure for Measure* contain features of this comedy of forgiveness, even if admittedly the ironies surrounding the gesture of forgiving are far less controlled than in the late romances.

Certainly, in any case, *All's Well* occupies a central position in the line of development from the early comedies to the late romances. Helena points back to earlier comic women in her role as engineer of the love plot and points forward to women of the late romances in her role as daughter, victim, and savior (though early comedy and late romance are, to be sure, not as neatly distinguishable as this antithesis suggests). Bertram, who is virtually without precedent in earlier comedies, anticipates, to a degree, Posthumus in *Cymbeline*, Florizel in *The Winter's Tale*, and Ferdinand in *The Tempest* in that he takes part in a marriage sanctioned and defined largely by paternal intervention. *All's Well*, like the romances and unlike the earlier comedies, affords a remarkably prominent role to the older generation.

The probable date of *All's Well* is consistent with such a transitional function. Its dates are hard to fix by external evidence, for it was neither registered nor printed until 1623, and allusions to it are scarce. Some scholars think that it is the *Love's Labor's Won* intriguingly mentioned by Francis Meres in *Palladis Tamia* in 1598, which Shakespeare might then have revised sometime around 1601–1604. Portions of the play do feature the rhymed couplets, letters in sonnet form, and witty conceits that we normally associate with Shakespeare's early style. These old-fashioned effects may have been deliberate on Shakespeare's part, however, not unlike the anachronisms he later introduces in *Pericles* and *Cymbeline*. Certainly, a major portion of the play dates stylistically from 1601–1604 or even later. Here the language is elliptical and compact, the images complexly interwoven, the verse rhythms free.

In any event, with its two contrasting styles poised between romance and satire, *All's Well* juxtaposes the reassurances of comedy with the pessimistic ironies of Shakespeare's tragic period. It lacks many of the felicities we associate with the festive comedies of the 1590s: the love songs, the innocently hedonistic joy, and the well-mated young lovers escaping from stern parents or an envious court. *All's Well* has too often been judged negatively for its failure to achieve a festive mood that Shakespeare probably did not intend it to have. Both of its central figures are flawed, to the extent that they seem oddly cast in the roles normally demanded by romantic comedy of young men and women who fall in love and eventually marry. Bertram as nominal hero quickly loses our sympathy when he runs away from his marriage vows to pursue warmongering, male camaraderie, and the attempted seduction of a virgin; Helena as nominal heroine complicates our response by the ethically dubious ways in which she tricks Bertram into marrying her and then becoming her partner in bed when he has sworn he will never do so. As the undeserving hero, forgiven in spite of his waywardness, however, Bertram plays an essential role in the play's problematic resolution—or failure to achieve complete resolution. He is, in the common Renaissance view of all humanity, unworthy of the forgiveness he receives, whereas Helena's generosity in forgiving him suggests at least a capability in humanity for decency and compassion. We are left, as in *Measure for Measure*, with a sense of the perennially unbridgeable gap between human ideals and their achievement, and yet we view this dilemma in a comic context where second chances and hope are bestowed even on those who appear to deserve them least.

The satiric mode in *All's Well* is conveyed chiefly through Lavatch the clown and through Parolles, the boastful, cowardly knave who accompanies Bertram to the wars. Lavatch, with the bitter and riddling wit of the professional fool, gives expression to many of the satirical themes that are also illustrated by the exposure of Parolles. Lavatch jests about cuckoldry and the other marital difficulties that cause men to flee from women; he pokes fun at court manners and apes the prodigal disobedience of his master Bertram. He is, like Parolles, called a "foulmouthed and calumnious knave" (1.3.56–7), although the inversion of appearance and reality is evident here, as with all Shakespearean fools: Parolles is truly more fool and knave than his mocking counterpart. Parolles is all pretense. Full of sound, but hollow like the drum to which he is compared, he is a swaggerer and a fashionmonger whose clothes conceal his lack of inner substance. He is a recognizable satiric type that goes back to the Latin dramatists Plautus and Terence: the braggart soldier. He is, to be sure, endearing in his outrageousness; Shakespeare endows him with that vitality we find also in those earlier braggart soldiers, Falstaff and Pistol. He enlists sympathy and fellow-feeling from an audience when, having been exposed and humiliated by his military comrades for his cowardice, he rejoins, "Who cannot be crushed with a plot?", and goes on to insist in soliloquy that "Simply the thing I am / Shall make me live" (4.3.327–36). Ultimately, his ebullient vitality leads to his being forgiven even by old Lafew, who has long been on to Parolles's tricks but finds him irresistible nonetheless.

Because Parolles lacks the self-awareness of Falstaff, we merely laugh at him rather than with him. To the impressionable young Bertram, hungry for fame, Parolles represents smartness and military style. Bertram rejects the true worth of Helena because she lacks family position and, ironically, he embraces the false worth of a parvenu. Parolles and Helena are foils from their first encounter, when the braggart sardonically derides virginity as unnatural and out of fashion. Parolles stands opposite also to Lafew, the Countess, and the King—those dignified embodiments of a traditional chivalric order, whose generous teachings Bertram rejects for the company of Parolles and of women he hopes to seduce. By disguising his slick insolence in the guise of fashionable manliness, Parolles is able to win Bertram's friendship for a time. Parolles is not really a tempter, for we never see him bending Bertram from his true inclination; rather, Bertram is himself too much in love with sham reputation, too rebellious against the civilized decencies of his elders. He is the Prodigal

Son, or Youth in the old morality play, perversely eager to prove his own worst enemy.

Yet Bertram is not without a redeeming nobleness—he bears himself bravely in the Florentine wars—and cannot be fooled indefinitely by his roguish companion. The exposure of Parolles is one of satiric humiliation, even if he is eventually forgiven and reconciled in a way that Malvolio in *Twelfth Night* or many of Ben Jonson's humorous gulls are not. The engineers of Parolles's exposure use the language of Jonsonian satire in their devices to outwit him: their game is a "sport" done "for the love of laughter," employing a snare whereby the "fox" or the "woodcock" will entrap himself (3.6.34–102 and 4.1.92). The device of public humiliation is particularly appropriate, because Parolles is himself a railing slanderer, like Lucio in *Measure for Measure*, caustically brilliant in his invective but nonetheless a slayer of men's reputations. The punishment of ridicule fits his particular crime. His callous disregard for the good name of various French military commanders is parallel to Bertram's indifference to the public shame he has heaped upon his virtuous wife. Once Parolles's bluff has been called, Bertram is, in part, disabused of his folly; but other means are needed to convince him of the wrong he has done to Helena. Indeed, Bertram's very coldness in turning away from Parolles shows a lack of humility. Bertram must learn to know himself better by being tricked, exposed, and humiliated.

The fabulous romance-like aspect of *All's Well* is conveyed chiefly through its folktale plot and through the character of Helena. The story is derived from the third "day" of Giovanni Boccaccio's *Decameron*, a day devoted to tales of lovers obliged to overcome seemingly impossible obstacles in order to achieve love's happiness. The story was translated into English by William Painter in *The Palace of Pleasure* (1566). To win the nobly born Beltramo, Giletta of Narbona must cure the French king with her physician-father's secret remedy and then must perform the riddling tasks assigned her by Beltramo as his means of being rid of her. Both these motifs have ancient antecedents in folklore, and, as in his late romances, Shakespeare puts great stress on the wondrous and improbable nature of these events.

All common sense warns against the likelihood of Helena's success. She is vastly below Bertram in social station or in "blood," even though she excels in "virtue." (This low station is unique among Shakespeare's comic heroines, and it contributes to what is so unusual about this play.) Her only hope is a desperate gamble: to cure the ailing King and so win Bertram as her reward. No one supposes at first she will even be admitted to the King, who has given up all hope of living; his "congregated college" of learned doctors "have concluded / That laboring art can never ransom nature / From her inaidible estate" (2.1.119–21). Helena transcends these rational doubts through resourcefulness and, above all, through a faith in help from above. She is willing to "hazard" all for love. She senses that her father's legacy will "be sanctified / By th' luckiest stars in heaven" (1.3.243–4), and she manages to convince not only the Countess and Lafew (persons who do not appear in Boccaccio) but also the King himself. Believing, like George Bernard Shaw's Saint Joan, that God will perform his greatest works through the humblest of his creatures, Helena inspires her listeners with faith in the impossible. Lafew is so moved by her simple eloquence that he proclaims to the King, "I have seen a medicine / That's able to breathe life into a stone" (2.1.73–4). Soon the King, too, is persuaded that in Helena "some blessèd spirit doth speak / His powerful sound within an organ weak" (lines 177–8). Once the King's cure has been effected, even Parolles and Bertram must agree with Lafew that the age of miracles, long thought to have passed, is with them again. The King's cure by the "Very hand of heaven," through the agency of a "weak— / And debile minister," is matter for a pious ballad or an old tale (2.3.31–4). At the same time, Helena is very determined and is willing to use whatever means are necessary to get what she wants.

Helena's assuming the role of wooer is a problem for Bertram—as indeed it was for many a male reader in Victorian times, who found her worrisomely guilty of transgressing the boundaries between acceptable and unacceptable female behavior. Bertram nominally objects to her lower social station, but that is a matter the King can remedy. Evidently, Bertram is daunted by something else: by the very prospect of marriage with a virtuous and attractive young woman who unmistakably wants him. He reacts with subterfuge and flight, subscribing to Parolles's notion that it is better to be a soldier than to be one who "hugs his kicky-wicky here at home, / Spending his manly marrow in her arms" (2.3.281–2). War gives Bertram his excuse to evade the responsibilities of marriage. In Italy, to be sure, he finds the prospect of sexual encounter with Diana irresistible, since he thinks he can obtain and then discard her when the affair is done. He is prepared to cheapen "available" women this way but not to commit himself to the complex and mutual commitment that marriage requires. In these terms, Helena's task is to bring Bertram to the point of understanding that sexuality and deep friendship can and should exist in a single relationship, and that women must not be bifurcated by his imagination into those who are respectable but untouchable (like his mother) or cheap and violable. Bertram's unself-knowing friendship with Parolles is symptomatic of his immaturity, and hence the exposure of Parolles is a necessary part of Bertram's education, but Helena must also find a way to help Bertram get over his mistrust of her sexuality.

In so doing, she resembles other Shakespeare heroines, such as Desdemona in *Othello*, Rosalind in *As You Like It*, and Silvia in *The Two Gentlemen of Verona*, who take the initiative in wooing. Helena is fully aware that her intrepidity offends Bertram. Yet she is abundantly admired by the King, Lafew, the Countess, and other rightminded persons in the play, all of whom find Bertram's reluctance immature and virtually incomprehensible. Moreover, her enterprising spirit (see 1.1.216–29) finds its reward in marital success at the end. Throughout his romantic comedies, Shakespeare invites us to admire women who take the lead in wooing, even if he problematizes the issue in *All's Well* by emphasizing Bertram's hostility and Helena's consequent need for deceptive stratagems, and even if he also sees how such a story can end tragically in *Romeo and Juliet* and *Othello*.

The impossible tasks Helena must perform are stated as riddles, as is usual in a folktale, and must be solved by riddling or paradoxical means. Bertram writes that she must "get the ring upon my finger, which never shall come off, and show me a child begotten of thy body that I am father to" (3.2.57–9). Such a challenge invites ingenuity, as in Boccaccio, but in Shakespeare the solution also requires providential aid. Helena's first sad response is to set Bertram free and renounce her audacious pretentions. Her pilgrimage of grief takes her to Florence, where Bertram happens to be serving in the wars. This cannot be mere coincidence, and yet we do not accuse her of scheming in any opprobrious sense. Throughout, her motives are at once virtuous and deceitful, lawful and sinful, just as her very sexuality is wholesome and yet is seen by us in a context of debased human nature (as is generally not the case with Shakespeare's earlier heroines). Her acts are prompted at once by providence and by shrewd calculation. Even if providence must be credited with introducing her to Diana, the very lady whom Bertram is importuning in love, Helena makes the most of such opportunities afforded her, never doubting that "heaven" has "fated" her both to help Diana and simultaneously to serve her own turn (4.4.18–20). The bed trick is a "plot," but a virtuous one, a "deceit" that is "lawful," a deed that is "not sin, and yet a sinful fact" (3.7.38–47). Diana repeatedly plays upon these same riddles in accusing Bertram before the King: he is "guilty, and he is not guilty" (5.3.290).

These conundrums, although playful and entertaining in Shakespeare's highly complicated denouement (not found in Boccaccio), also hint at paradoxes in the nature of humanity. Bertram's typically human waywardness justifies a cunning response. "I think't no sin," argues Diana, "To cozen him that would unjustly win" (4.2.75–6). Justice on earth, as in *Measure for Measure*, must take forms only roughly approximating those of heavenly justice, for human depravity sometimes requires a harsh remedy in kind. Yet, by a providential paradox, humanity's thwarted and evil nature, seemingly so fatal, leads instead to re-generation: by being humbled, humanity is enabled to rise: "The web of our life is of a mingled yarn, good and ill together," says a sympathetic observer of Bertram. "Our virtues would be proud if our faults whipped them not, and our crimes would despair if they were not cherished by our virtues" (4.3.70–3). Human perversity accentuates the need for divine grace.

Helena is a romantic heroine, only metaphorically the "angel" who must "Bless this unworthy husband," reprieving him by her "prayers" from "the wrath / Of greatest justice" (3.4.25–9). Indeed, she is capable of being quite threatening to Bertram. If Bertram typifies the "Natural rebellion" of all youth and Helena the "herb of grace" whom he has willfully rejected (5.3.6 and 4.5.17), Helena is also an aggressive woman whose clever plans to win Bertram against his will produce an understandable reluctance in the young man. Still, the spiritual overtones are not extraneous to this bittersweet comedy. However much we may sympathize with his desire to choose in love for himself, Bertram's revolt is incomprehensible to every witness except Parolles. Bertram himself concedes, too late it seems, that he has recognized Helena's precious worth. This note of "love that comes too late," wherein the penitent sinner confesses "That's good that's gone," hovers over the play with its tragicomic mood (5.3.58–61). Helena is a "jewel" thrown away and seemingly forever lost (5.3.1). The semblance of her death is, in fact, only another one of her inventive schemes, along with the bewildering contretemps of the final scene. Yet, when she reappears, setting all to rights, she comes as "one that's dead" but is now "quick," alive again, merely a "shadow" of her former self (5.3.304–8). Bertram has not actually committed the evil he intended; by a providential sophistry, he is innocent, like Claudio in *Much Ado* or Angelo in *Measure for Measure*, and so is reconciled to the goodness he has failed to merit. Even Parolles is given a second chance by the magnanimous Lafew. As the play's title implies, all might have miscarried through humanity's "rash faults" that "Make trivial price of serious things we have" (5.3.61–2), were it not for a forgiving power that can make people's worst failings an instrument of their penitence and recovery. This resolution fleetingly comforts us in the final scene, even though it must do battle with such manifest imbalances as the prolonged shaming of Bertram and the scant attention paid to his reunion with Helena. The web of human life remains a mingled yarn.

The balance in this remarkable play between comedy and tragedy is very much subject to decisions made in performance; see stage and screen histories, below, for detailed history and analysis. This history demonstrates how fluid interpretation can be: there are many Helenas, many Bertrams, many Parolles.

ALL'S WELL THAT ENDS WELL
ON STAGE

No record exists of any performance of *All's Well That Ends Well* during Shakespeare's lifetime. The first of which we know, in fact, took place in 1741 at a theater in Goodman's Fields, London. The following year, the play was added to the repertory at the Theatre Royal, Drury Lane, with Theophilus Cibber as Parolles (to the great displeasure of Charles Macklin, who had to settle for the role of Lavatch). The fact that they fought over the role of Parolles and not Bertram suggests that eighteenth-century audiences, when they saw the play at all, saw a cut and revised version that concentrated on the play's satirical comedy. Playgoers and producers of that era evidently concurred in the judgment of Charles I, who had written "Monsieur Parolles" next to the play's title in his copy of the Second Folio. The actor and producer David Garrick continued this emphasis on the satiric and comic in his revival at Drury Lane in 1756, even assigning the epilogue to Parolles. John Bell's acting edition of 1775 made substantial cuts in order to focus on the bawdy of Parolles and Lavatch, the quarrel of Lafew and Parolles, and most of all the unmasking of the braggart soldier. Frederick Pilon's production at the Haymarket Theatre in 1785 so reshaped the play to accommodate the comic skills of John Bannister in the role of Parolles that the first three acts of Shakespeare's play were virtually eliminated. It was not until 1794 (at Drury Lane) that John Philip Kemble became the first leading actor to play Bertram, and even then his effort to refocus the play as the sentimental story of thwarted love was not a success.

In the nineteenth century, audiences generally found the

morality of the play distasteful. Even an operatic version by
Frederic Reynolds (the Theatre Royal, Covent Garden, 1832),
with generous borrowings from other Shakespeare plays, such as
a masque of Oberon and Robin Goodfellow (adapted out of *A
Midsummer Night's Dream*) and various arias, including "Love is
a smoke made with the fume of sighs" (*Romeo and Juliet*),
"Sometimes lurk I in a gossip's bowl" and "Trip away, make
no stay" (*A Midsummer Night's Dream*), and "If she be made
of white and red" (*Love's Labor's Lost*), failed to overcome
Victorian aversion for a tale of bed tricks and faithless husbands.
Actor-manager Samuel Phelps, at the Sadler's Wells Theatre in
1852, took out the bed trick and other offensive material, but to
no avail; the verdict seems to have been that the play was
morally irredeemable. Theater managers knew when they were
beaten and gave up entirely for over forty years. George Bernard
Shaw reviewed the next production negatively (at the Irving
Dramatic Club in 1895) and later concluded that the best parts
of the play were simply too good and too modern for public
taste.

The coming of the women's emancipation movement in the
early twentieth century provided an opportunity to consider the
play in modern terms as Shaw proposed. Directors Frank
Benson, at Stratford-upon-Avon in 1916, and William Poel, in
1920, took up the challenge of viewing Bertram as a callow
young man in need of redemption by a woman's means. It was
Benson who first restored Shakespeare's text to the stage.

Tyrone Guthrie deserves credit for what may have been the
play's first genuine theatrical success, in 1953 at Stratford,
Canada, and then in 1959 at Stratford-upon-Avon. Guthrie set
the play in Edwardian England, with the scenes of military action located in the North African desert. Helena (Irene Worth
in Canada, Zoe Caldwell in England) was serious and purpose-
ful, austerely dressed in black and with her hair set in a tight
bun. Parolles's inquisitors were guerrilla soldiers with automatic
weapons, while the officers sported jodhpurs and riding whips.
In the Canadian production Alec Guinness played the French
King in a wheelchair. Lavatch's role disappeared; Diana was a

cockney tart who worked in a wartime factory and flirted with the soldiers. To a disillusioned postwar world, the perfidies of Bertram no longer seemed inexplicable and shocking, as they had to many Victorians.

Other directors have found ways in which *All's Well* can speak to modern audiences. Michael Benthall, in the Old Vic company's production in 1953, produced a farcical fairy tale, with a beautiful Claire Bloom as Helena (by way of Cinderella) and John Neville's Bertram as a callow Prince Charming misled by Michael Hordern's Parolles (who dominated the performance not as a hapless boaster but, in the words of one reviewer, as a sort of "amateurish Mephistopheles"). Whereas this production used comic business to alleviate the play's bitterness, Noel Willman (Stratford-upon-Avon, 1955) chose to exploit it. In his version Lavatch was a hunchbacked dwarf; Helena, pertinacious and even aggressive, pursued Bertram with a thoroughness that gave new insight into the anxieties generated in this play about male unwillingness to cope with dominant women. In 1959, at Stratford, Connecticut, John Houseman directed the play as a moving tragicomedy, emphasizing the characters' unawareness of the implications of their willful behavior. John Barton's 1967 production for the Royal Shakespeare Company responded to the mood of the 1960s by accentuating the generational gap between youth and age and by taking an ironic view of war as a gentleman's game. The exposure of Parolles (Clive Swift) was remorseless, even cruel, that of Bertram (Ian Richardson) more understanding and comic. Trevor Nunn (Royal Shakespeare Company, 1981) explored the pre–World War era of Edwardian England from a later and disenchanted point of view; the military scenes suggested the Crimean War, while elder figures such as the Countess and Lafew were Victorian gentlefolk confronting an uncertain future of shifting social values. Bertram's ambivalent view of women was not sympathetically presented, and he was denied any final opportunity to redeem himself. David Jones's successful staging at Stratford, Canada, in 1977, with William Hutt (the French King), Margaret Tyzack (the Countess), Nicholas Pennell (Bertram), and Martha Henry (Helena), was movingly autumnal, opening with Lavatch sweeping dead leaves from the base of a sundial.

In 1989, Barry Kyle directed the play in Stratford-upon-Avon for the Royal Shakespeare Company, in a production that later moved to London's Barbican Theatre. This was clearly a story of maturation, less bitter than the company's previous effort with the play by Trevor Nunn in 1981. The opening scene was set in a playroom with a rocking horse and boxes of toys, and a tree-house set in one of the pillars on the stage; later these would reappear, but this time as an artificial war horse for soldiers to practice on, boxes of ammunition, and a military sentry box. Play gave way to reality; the transformation of the objects announced the transformation of the characters. Patricia Kerrigan's Helena moved from a socially awkward girl, uncomfortable with her own desires, to a young woman with an appealing if somewhat inexplicable resiliency; Paul Venables's Bertram grew from his arrogance and selfishness to a young man never wholly good but whose lies were so palpable that one felt his own self-loathing and eagerness to be exposed—and the audience finally was led to accept him as a worthy match for Helena. At the end the two of them exited comfortably hand-in-hand, the possibility of their happiness strong enough that the discordant notes often heard never unsettled the ending. If in this production Helena and Bertram were permitted less humiliation than is usually their fate, Kyle's version nonetheless reminded audiences of how interesting and theatrically effective this complex variation on the battle between the sexes can be.

Three years later, Sir Peter Hall directed the play more austerely, again for the RSC, at the intimate Swan Theatre in Stratford-upon-Avon. On a bare stage, with changing ornaments to denote the various geographical locales, actors in mid-seventeenth-century dress spoke the verse clearly, energetically, and, as Hall increasingly demands of his actors, with great emphasis upon the internal stresses of the line and the line endings. Yet the sacrifice of naturalistic speech patterns here seemed somehow appropriate for the social and emotional awkwardness of the play. Sophie Thompson's Helena was interestingly edgy, usually dressed in black and never comfortable in any of her social surroundings. She was a strange mixture of determination and timidity, certain about what she wanted and yet hesitant as she pursued it. Richard Johnson's King was impatient and often angry, clearly physically uncomfortable because of the fistula (decorously displaced to his heavily bandaged hand). Toby Stephens's Bertram was graceful and handsome, if always brittle in his pride. In the final scene, it was systematically undone, and he fell to his knees in shame as an obviously pregnant Helena entered. She then read out the conditions of his letter, but, before she finished, ripped it in half, refusing her victory and sparing both of them any greater embarrassment than both already obviously felt. Their reconciliation was appropriately muted, as the two hesitantly hugged, even as Barbara Jefford's Countess all too eagerly greeted the gesture as proof that all had indeed ended well.

In spite of the commercial and critical successes of both Kyle's and Hall's versions, eleven years would pass until the Royal Shakespeare Company would turn again to the play. In December 2003, Gregory Doran opened his production, again at Stratford-upon-Avon's Swan, and later transferred to London's Gielgud Theatre. This too offered eloquent testimony of how effective the play can be on stage. A simple grey arch and backdrop with bare trees etched into the steel defined the playing space. Doran's brilliant production was all restraint: Claudia Blakely's Helena in her high-necked dress and pleated hair, Jamie Glover's Bertram stiff and uncomfortable in his tight suit and sash, and Judi Dench's Countess periodically looking sadly down at the ring on her finger. Only Parolles was broad and expansive, and from the first this was revealed as empty posturing. Throughout the production the melancholy of the situation was unmistakable but subtly countered by a willingness to find a life-affirming spirit even in the most appalling circumstances. As the King at the end offered Diana the same option to choose a husband that started the problem of the play, the courtiers got a laugh with their obvious surprise and determination to ignore him. All then left the stage, with the Countess and the King looking back at Helena and Bertram, who stood apart gazing at each other as the lights went down. In the absence of the epilogue, the final tableaux offered a poignant image of the inescapable sadness of aging and the seemingly unavoidable folly of youth.

On its original stage the play made little effort to exploit the spatial resources of the theater; there are few large scenes, a minimum of ceremony, no battle sequences (even the military action in this play is drama of comic intrigue), no demand for the gallery or discovery space or trapdoor. What Shakespeare's audiences thought of *All's Well* we do not know. Shakespeare seems to have written an understated, disturbing play, far ahead of its time and only now gaining, through some of the productions here considered, the critical and theatrical recognition it richly deserves.

ALL'S WELL THAT ENDS WELL

ON SCREEN

❧

This play has not often been filmed. A Royal Shakespeare Company stage production directed by John Barton at Stratford-upon-Avon in 1967, with Ian Richardson as Bertram, Lynn Fairleigh as Helena, Clive Swift as Parolles, and Catherine Lacey as the Countess of Rossillion, was filmed for television and shown by the BBC in 1968, but copies appear to be lost. Similarly, the New York Shakespeare Festival version in the Delacorte Theatre, Central Park, in 1978, directed by Wilford Leach and produced by Joseph Papp, was recorded on film; it is available, but not widely so.

Most available and worth watching is the BBC production in its series the Shakespeare Plays, produced in this instance by Jonathan Miller and directed by Elijah Moshinsky in 1980. By general acclaim, this is one of the best in a very uneven series. The intimate use of the camera, along with the aesthetically tasteful landscapes and opulent interiors that are so inappropriate when applied by the BBC to the fantasy worlds of *As You Like It*, *A Midsummer Night's Dream*, and *The Tempest*, are here well suited to a bittersweet comedy of macho male anxiety that is painfully unwilling to make a commitment to marriage. In pictorial settings consciously modeled on the interiors of Rembrandt and Vermeer, the patrician gracefulness of Celia Johnson as the Countess of Rossillion is nicely matched by Michael Hordern's maturely self-aware Lafew. In the generation below them, Angela Down is a repressed though volcanically resourceful Helena, facing the dilemma of how to win the affection of the caddishly unresponsive Bertram (Ian Charleson). David Jeffrey's Parolles is a made-up thing, emblematic of all the self-inflating postures that Bertram must learn to eschew in himself. To be sure, the scene of Parolles's interrogation is not nearly as funny as it can be on stage; elsewhere, too, the quipping humor of Lavatch (Paul Brooke) is curtailed and maimed. On the other hand, the filming of the complex ending adroitly captures, through closeups, the sense of wonder among the characters as they finally see Helena and begin to understand the meaning of the riddle of the ring with which Diana (Pippa Guard) has puzzled the French King (Donald Sinden) and indeed everyone else on stage.

All's Well That Ends Well
Filmography

1. 1968
   BBC/Royal Shakespeare Company
   Ronald Travers, producer
   John Barton and Claude Whatham, directors

   Helena—Lynn Fairleigh
   Bertram—Ian Richardson
   Countess of Rosillion—Catherine Lacey

2. 1978
   New York Shakespeare Festival
   Joseph Papp, producer
   Wilford Leach, director

   Helena—Pamela Reed
   Bertram—Marc Linn Baker
   Countess of Rosillion—Elizabeth Wilson

3. 1980
   BBC/Time-Life Television
   Jonathan Miller, producer
   Elijah Moshinsky, director

Helena—Angela Down
Bertram—Ian Charleson
Countess of Rosillion—Celia Johnson
Lafew—Michael Hordern
King of France—Donald Sinden

ALL'S WELL
THAT ENDS WELL

[Dramatis Personae

COUNTESS OF ROSSILLION, *Bertram's mother and Helena's guardian*
BERTRAM, *Count of Rossillion*
HELENA (or HELEN), *orphaned daughter of the Countess's physician*
PAROLLES, *a follower of Bertram*
RINALDO, *a steward,*
LAVATCH, *a clown or fool,*   *servants of the Countess of Rossillion*
PAGE,

KING OF FRANCE
LAFEW, *an old lord*
Two FRENCH LORDS, *the brothers Dumain, later captains in the Florentine army*
Other LORDS
Two FRENCH SOLDIERS
A GENTLEMAN
A MESSENGER

DUKE OF FLORENCE
WIDOW CAPILET *of Florence*
DIANA, *her daughter*
MARIANA, *neighbor and friend of the Widow*

Lords, Attendants, Soldiers, Citizens

SCENE: *Rossillion; Paris; Florence; Marseilles*]

1.1 ❧ *Enter young Bertram, Count of Rossillion, his*
mother [the Countess], and Helena, [with] Lord
Lafew, all in black.

COUNTESS In delivering my son from me, I bury a 1
second husband.

BERTRAM And I in going, madam, weep o'er my
father's death anew. But I must attend His Majesty's 4
command, to whom I am now in ward, evermore in 5
subjection.

LAFEW You shall find of the King a husband, madam; 7
you, sir, a father. He that so generally is at all times 8
good must of necessity hold his virtue to you, whose 9
worthiness would stir it up where it wanted rather 10
than lack it where there is such abundance. 11

COUNTESS What hope is there of His Majesty's amend- 12
ment? 13

1.1 *Location: Rossillion, i.e., Roussillon, in southern France, on*
the Spanish border near the Mediterranean. The Count's
residence.
1 **delivering** sending. (With play on "giving birth to" and
"freeing.") 4 **attend** obey 5 **in ward** (According to a feudal
custom, the King became the guardian of orphaned heirs to
estates, who remained "in ward" so long as they were minors. The
King's jurisdiction extended even so far as the bestowal of his ward
in marriage, but only to someone of equal rank.) 7 **of** in the
person of. **husband** i.e., protector 8 **generally** to all people
9 **hold** continue to devote 9–11 **whose . . . abundance** you
whose virtue is such that it would inspire generosity even in those
who normally lack it, and who therefore cannot fail to find it in a
king who is so abundantly generous. 10 **wanted** is lacking
12–13 **amendment** recovery.

LAFEW   He hath abandoned his physicians, madam, under whose practices he hath persecuted time with 15
hope, and finds no other advantage in the process but 16
only the losing of hope by time.

COUNTESS   This young gentlewoman had a father—oh, that "had," how sad a passage 'tis!—whose skill was 19
almost as great as his honesty; had it stretched so far, 20
would have made nature immortal, and death should have play for lack of work. Would for the King's sake 22
he were living! I think it would be the death of the King's disease.

LAFEW   How called you the man you speak of, madam?

COUNTESS   He was famous, sir, in his profession, and it was his great right to be so: Gerard de Narbonne.

LAFEW   He was excellent indeed, madam. The King very lately spoke of him admiringly and mourningly. He was skillful enough to have lived still, if knowl- 30
edge could be set up against mortality.

BERTRAM   What is it, my good lord, the King languishes of?

LAFEW   A fistula, my lord. 34

BERTRAM   I heard not of it before.

LAFEW   I would it were not notorious.—Was this gentlewoman the daughter of Gerard de Narbonne?

15–16 **hath . . . hope** has tormented his time with painful treatments in vain hope of cure   19 **passage** (1) phrase, expression (2) passing away   20 **honesty** integrity of character   22 **Would** Would that   30 **still** (1) now as before (2) forever   34 **fistula** ulcerous sore

COUNTESS His sole child, my lord, and bequeathed to
my overlooking. I have those hopes of her good that 39
her education promises her dispositions she inherits, 40
which makes fair gifts fairer; for where an unclean 41
mind carries virtuous qualities, there commendations 42
go with pity—they are virtues and traitors too. In her 43
they are the better for their simpleness. She derives 44
her honesty and achieves her goodness. 45

LAFEW Your commendations, madam, get from her
tears.

COUNTESS 'Tis the best brine a maiden can season her 48
praise in. The remembrance of her father never
approaches her heart but the tyranny of her sorrows
takes all livelihood from her cheek.—No more of this, 51
Helena. Go to, no more, lest it be rather thought you 52
affect a sorrow than to have— 53

HELENA I do affect a sorrow indeed, but I have it too. 54

LAFEW Moderate lamentation is the right of the dead, 55
excessive grief the enemy to the living.

COUNTESS If the living be enemy to the grief, the excess 57
makes it soon mortal. 58

BERTRAM Madam, I desire your holy wishes.

---

39 overlooking supervision.   **39–45 I have . . . goodness** I
have those high hopes for her future well-being which her
education will further, nurturing the goodness which she was born
with, and enhancing her innate gifts; for where a corrupted mind
carries a veneer of learned goodness, praise is mingled with regret
for good qualities betrayed by their opposite. In her there is no
such division: she inherits a pure heart and nourishes it with good
deeds.   **48 season** (1) add flavor to (2) preserve (as with salt)
51 livelihood animation   **52 Go to** i.e., Come, come
53 affect are enamored of, make an exaggerated show of.   **than**
rather than   **54 I do . . . too** I do put on an outward show of
sorrow, but I feel it as well.   **55 right** rightful due   **57–8 If . . .
mortal** i.e., If grief is by its nature injurious to human happiness,
excess of it soon proves fatal.

LAFEW   How understand we that?   60

COUNTESS
    Be thou blest, Bertram, and succeed thy father
    In manners as in shape! Thy blood and virtue   62
    Contend for empire in thee, and thy goodness   63
    Share with thy birthright! Love all, trust a few,   64
    Do wrong to none. Be able for thine enemy   65
    Rather in power than use, and keep thy friend   66
    Under thy own life's key. Be checked for silence   67
    But never taxed for speech. What heaven more will,   68
    That thee may furnish and my prayers pluck down,   69
    Fall on thy head! Farewell. [To Lafew] My lord,   70
    'Tis an unseasoned courtier; good my lord,   • 71
    Advise him.

LAFEW   He cannot want the best   72
    That shall attend his love.   73

COUNTESS   Heaven bless him!—Farewell, Bertram.

BERTRAM   The best wishes that can be forged in your   75
    thoughts be servants to you!   [Exit Countess.] 76
    [To Helena]   Be comfortable to my mother, your   77
    mistress, and make much of her.   78

60 **How . . . that?** What do you mean? (Spoken perhaps in
response to the Countess in lines 57–8, simultaneously with
Bertram's speech in line 59.)   62 **manners** conduct.   **Thy
blood** May your noble birth   63–4 **thy goodness . . .
birthright** may the good qualities you achieve share with your
inherited qualities in ruling your life.   65–7 **Be able . . . key** Be
powerful enough to resist your enemy without having to use that
power, and hold your friend's life as dearly as your own.
67 **checked** reproved   68–70 **What . . . head!** May such
blessings heaven intends for you, such as will assist you and that
my prayers can draw down from heaven, bestow their goodness
upon you!   71 **unseasoned** inexperienced   72–3 **He . . . love**
He will not be without the best advice that my love can provide
him with.   75–6 **The best . . . you!** May the best wishes you
can imagine always assist you!   77 **comfortable** comforting,
serviceable   78 **make much of** be devoted to

LAFEW   Farewell, pretty lady. You must hold the credit   79
of your father.   [*Exeunt Bertram and Lafew.*]

HELENA   Oh, were that all! I think not on my father,
And these great tears grace his remembrance more   82
Than those I shed for him. What was he like?   83
I have forgot him. My imagination
Carries no favor in't but Bertram's.   85
I am undone. There is no living, none,
If Bertram be away. 'Twere all one   87
That I should love a bright particular star   88
And think to wed it, he is so above me.
In his bright radiance and collateral light   90
Must I be comforted, not in his sphere.
Th'ambition in my love thus plagues itself;
The hind that would be mated by the lion   93
Must die for love. 'Twas pretty, though a plague,   94
To see him every hour, to sit and draw
His archèd brows, his hawking eye, his curls,   96
In our heart's table—heart too capable   97
Of every line and trick of his sweet favor.   98
But now he's gone, and my idolatrous fancy   99
Must sanctify his relics. Who comes here?

    Enter Parolles.

[*Aside*] One that goes with him. I love him for his sake;   101
And yet I know him a notorious liar,

---

79 **hold the credit** uphold the reputation   82 **his** Bertram's
83 **for him** i.e., for my father when he died.   85 **favor** (1) image, face
(2) preference   87–8 **'Twere . . . That** It would be all the same if
90 **collateral** distant and parallel, shed from a different sphere. (The
different Ptolemaic spheres were said to move collaterally, the
implication here being that the distance cannot be closed.)
93 **hind** (1) female deer. (2) servant.   94 **pretty** pleasing
96 **hawking** keen   97 **table** drawing board or tablet
97–8 **capable Of** susceptible to   98 **trick** characteristic expression.
favor face.   99 **fancy** (1) imagination, fantasy (2) love   101 **his**
Bertram's

Think him a great way fool, solely a coward.   103
Yet these fixed evils sit so fit in him   104
That they take place when virtue's steely bones   105
Looks bleak i'th' cold wind. Withal, full oft we see   106
Cold wisdom waiting on superfluous folly.   107

PAROLLES   Save you, fair queen!   108

HELENA   And you, monarch!

PAROLLES   No.

HELENA   And no.

PAROLLES   Are you meditating on virginity?

HELENA   Ay. You have some stain of soldier in you; let   113
me ask you a question. Man is enemy to virginity;
how may we barricado it against him?   115

PAROLLES   Keep him out.

HELENA   But he assails, and our virginity, though
valiant, in the defense yet is weak. Unfold to us some   118
warlike resistance.

PAROLLES   There is none. Man setting down before you   120
will undermine you and blow you up.

HELENA   Bless our poor virginity from underminers and
blowers-up! Is there no military policy how virgins   123
might blow up men?

103 **a great way** in large measure a.   **solely** completely
104 **fixed** ineradicable, firmly established.   **sit so fit** are so natural
and plausible (in him)   105–6 **take . . . wind** find acceptance and
take precedence, while virtue, in its uncompromising severity, is left
out in the cold.   106 **Withal** Consequently   107 **Cold . . .
folly** wisdom lacking warmth obliged to dance attendance on a
useless display of comfortable foolishness.   108 **Save** i.e., God
save.   **queen** (A hyperbolical compliment, which Helena answers
in kind, whereupon they both deny their titles.)   113 **stain** tinge
115 **barricado** barricade   118 **Unfold** Reveal   120 **setting . . . you**
laying siege (as though to a town, but with bawdy quibbling that is
elaborated in the following lines. To *undermine* in 121 is to tunnel
under and into [in both a military and sexual sense]; to *blow up* is to
explode with mines and impregnate.)   123 **policy** stratagem

PAROLLES Virginity being blown down, man will 125
quicklier be blown up. Marry, in blowing him down 126
again, with the breach yourselves made you lose your 127
city. It is not politic in the commonwealth of nature to 128
preserve virginity. Loss of virginity is rational increase, 129
and there was never virgin got till virginity was 130
first lost. That you were made of is metal to make vir- 131
gins. Virginity by being once lost may be ten times 132
found; by being ever kept, it is ever lost. 'Tis too cold 133
a companion. Away with't!

HELENA I will stand for't a little, though therefore I die 135
a virgin.

PAROLLES There's little can be said in't; 'tis against the 137
rule of nature. To speak on the part of virginity is to 138
accuse your mothers, which is most infallible disobedience. He that hangs himself is a virgin; virginity 140
murders itself, and should be buried in highways out 141
of all sanctified limit, as a desperate offendress against 142

125–8 **Virginity . . . city** Continuing the metaphor of siege
warfare, Parolles argues that virginity's attempts to defend itself
against male assault are doomed to self-defeat, just as a defending
city, by digging countermines, opens up more breaches through
which the defenses can be undermined. Virginal resistance will
only sharpen a man's appetite and blow him up—i.e., make him
erect. (*Marry* is a mild oath derived from "by the Virgin Mary.")
128 **politic** expedient   129 **rational increase** (1) an increase by
the law of nature (2) an increase of rational beings   130 **got**
begotten   131 **That** That which.   **metal** substance, as in
minting of coins or compounding of interest. (With idea also of
mettle, "spirit," "temperament.")   132–3 **may . . . found** i.e.,
may reproduce itself tenfold   135 **stand** fight, stand up. (With a
sexual quibble.)   **die** (With probable quibble on "experience
orgasm.")   137 **in't** in its behalf   138 **on the part of** in behalf
of   140 **is a virgin** i.e., is like a virgin, since virginity is a kind of
suicide   141–2 **buried . . . limit** (Suicides were customarily
buried at crossroads of highways, not in consecrated ground.)

nature. Virginity breeds mites, much like a cheese,
consumes itself to the very paring, and so dies with   144
feeding his own stomach. Besides, virginity is peevish,   145
proud, idle, made of self-love, which is the most
inhibited sin in the canon. Keep it not; you cannot   147
choose but lose by't. Out with't! Within th'one year   148
it will make itself two, which is a goodly increase, and
the principal itself not much the worse. Away with't!   150

HELENA   How might one do, sir, to lose it to her own   151
liking?

PAROLLES   Let me see. Marry, ill, to like him that ne'er   153
it likes. 'Tis a commodity will lose the gloss with lying;   154
the longer kept, the less worth. Off with't while 'tis
vendible; answer the time of request. Virginity, like   156
an old courtier, wears her cap out of fashion, richly
suited, but unsuitable, just like the brooch and the   158
toothpick, which wear not now. Your date is better in   159
your pie and your porridge than in your cheek; and   160

---

144 **paring** covering rind   145 **his** its.   **stomach** (1) maw
(2) pride.   147 **inhibited** prohibited.   **canon** catalogue of
sins. (Pride is the first of the Deadly Sins.)   147–8 **Keep . . .
by't** (With a play on the idea of losing one's virginity.)   148 **Out
with't!** (1) Away with it! (2) Put it out at interest!   150 **the
principal** the original investment   151 **How** What
153–4 **ill . . . likes** i.e., one must do ill, by liking a man that
dislikes virginity.   154 **will . . . lying** that will lose the gloss of
newness with being unused. (With a quibble on "lying down.")
156 **vendible** marketable.   **the time of request** when there is
still demand.   158 **unsuitable** unfashionable   159 **wear not**
are not in fashion. (Brooches in hats and the affectation of using
toothpicks, once fashionable, are no longer so.)   159–60 **Your . . .
cheek** i.e., The date does better as an ingredient in cooking
than as an emblem of withering in your cheek. (*Date* also suggests
age.)

your virginity, your old virginity, is like one of our
French withered pears—it looks ill, it eats drily. Marry, 162
'tis a withered pear; it was formerly better; marry,
yet 'tis a withered pear. Will you anything with it?

HELENA
Not my virginity, yet . . .   165
There shall your master have a thousand loves,   166
A mother, and a mistress, and a friend,   167
A phoenix, captain, and an enemy,   168
A guide, a goddess, and a sovereign,   169
A counselor, a traitress, and a dear;   170
His humble ambition, proud humility   171
His jarring concord, and his discord dulcet,   172
His faith, his sweet disaster, with a world   173
Of pretty, fond, adoptious christendoms   174
That blinking Cupid gossips. Now shall he—   175
I know not what he shall. God send him well!
The court's a learning place, and he is one—

PAROLLES   What one, i'faith?

HELENA   That I wish well. 'Tis pity—

PAROLLES   What's pity?

162 **withered pears** poppering pears, a variety that are not edible
until partly decayed (and that physically resemble the aging female
genitalia, as does the *date,* line 159)   **eats drily** is dry to eat.
165 **Not . . . yet** The moment for surrendering my virginity has
not yet arrived (?) (There may be a textual omission here.)
166 **There** i.e., At court   167–73 **A mother . . . disaster**
(Helena here provides a catalogue of the various emotional
relationships and paradoxical emotional attitudes found in
Elizabethan courtly love poetry.)   168 **phoenix** i.e., nonpareil.
(Literally, a fabulous bird of which only one exists at any given
time.)   173 **disaster** unlucky star   174–5 **Of . . . gossips** of
pretty, foolish lovers who give pet names to their mistresses and at
whose love-christenings Cupid acts as godfather.

HELENA

That wishing well had not a body in't   181
Which might be felt, that we, the poorer born,   182
Whose baser stars do shut us up in wishes,   183
Might with effects of them follow our friends   184
And show what we alone must think, which never   185
Returns us thanks.   186

    Enter Page.

PAGE Monsieur Parolles, my lord calls for you.   [*Exit.*]

PAROLLES Little Helen, farewell. If I can remember thee, I will think of thee at court.

HELENA Monsieur Parolles, you were born under a charitable star.

PAROLLES Under Mars, I.

HELENA I especially think under Mars.

PAROLLES Why under Mars?

HELENA The wars hath so kept you under that you   195
must needs be born under Mars.

PAROLLES When he was predominant.   197

HELENA When he was retrograde, I think rather.   198

PAROLLES Why think you so?

HELENA You go so much backward when you fight.

181–6 **That . . . thanks** It is a pity that wishing good fortune to someone does not command a tangible reality enabling us of humble station, whose lesser fortune confines us to mere wishing, to be able instead to bestow positive effects of that wishing on those whom we love, thereby yielding a benefit which, as things now stand, we can only ponder in our private thoughts without receiving any thanks.   195 **under** down, in an inferior position. (Playing on Parolles's *Under,* line 192, in the sense of "governed by.")   197 **predominant** in the ascendant, ruling.
198 **retrograde** moving backward (i.e., in a direction from east to west relative to the fixed positions of the signs of the zodiac)

PAROLLES   That's for advantage.   201

HELENA   So is running away, when fear proposes the
safety. But the composition that your valor and fear   203
makes in you is a virtue of a good wing, and I like the   204
wear well.   205

PAROLLES   I am so full of businesses I cannot answer
thee acutely. I will return perfect courtier, in the which   207
my instruction shall serve to naturalize thee, so thou   208
wilt be capable of a courtier's counsel and understand   209
what advice shall thrust upon thee; else thou diest in
thine unthankfulness, and thine ignorance makes thee   211
away. Farewell. When thou hast leisure, say thy pray-   212
ers; when thou hast none, remember thy friends. Get   213
thee a good husband, and use him as he uses thee. So,
farewell.   [Exit.]

HELENA
Our remedies oft in ourselves do lie
Which we ascribe to heaven. The fated sky   217
Gives us free scope, only doth backward pull
Our slow designs when we ourselves are dull.   219
What power is it which mounts my love so high,   220

201 **for advantage** to gain tactical advantage. (But Helena
caustically interprets it as "craven self-protection.")
203 **composition** mixture   204 **of a good wing** strong in flight
(and hence useful in rapid retreat; with a quibble on a sartorial
sense of *wing*, meaning "an ornamental shoulder flap")
205 **wear** fashion   207 **perfect** complete.   **in the which** i.e.,
in which courtly behavior   208 **naturalize** familiarize; also,
deflower.   **so** provided that   209 **capable** receptive. (With
bawdy double meaning, continued in *understand, thrust,* and *diest.*)
211–12 **makes thee away** destroys, puts an end to you.
212–13 **When . . . friends** i.e., (patronizingly) Don't forget to say
your prayers, but remember you have friends who can help you out.
217 **fated** invested with the power of destiny   219 **dull** slow,
sluggish.   220 **so high** to so exalted an object, i.e., to Bertram

That makes me see and cannot feed mine eye?   221
The mightiest space in fortune nature brings   222
To join like likes and kiss like native things.   223
Impossible be strange attempts to those   224
That weigh their pains in sense and do suppose   225
What hath been cannot be. Who ever strove   226
To show her merit that did miss her love?   227
The King's disease—my project may deceive me,
But my intents are fixed and will not leave me.   *Exit.*

[1.2] ᕯᕲ *Flourish cornets. Enter the King of France, with
        letters, and [two Lords and] divers attendants.*

KING

The Florentines and Senoys are by th' ears,   1
Have fought with equal fortune and continue
A braving war.

FIRST LORD   So 'tis reported, sir.   3

KING

Nay, 'tis most credible. We here receive it
A certainty, vouched from our cousin Austria,   5

221 **That . . . eye?** that puts Bertram before me as an object of
desire but gives my gazing no fulfillment?   222–3 **The . . .
things** i.e., Natural affection can cause even those separated by the
widest diversity in social status to come together as if they
belonged together.   224–6 **Impossible . . . be** Extraordinary
attempts (at surmounting social barriers) seem impossible to those
who calculate too carefully the extent and cost of their difficulties
and suppose something to be impossible even though it has been
done before.   227 **miss** fail to achieve

1.2 Location: Paris. The royal court.
1 **Senoys** natives of Siena.   **by th' ears** at variance, quarreling.
(The King plans to deny Florence help [see 3.1], though allowing
his lords free choice in what they do.)   3 **braving war** war of
mutual defiance.   5 **our cousin** my fellow sovereign of

With caution that the Florentine will move us   6
For speedy aid, wherein our dearest friend   7
Prejudicates the business, and would seem   8
To have us make denial.

FIRST LORD   His love and wisdom,   9
Approved so to Your Majesty, may plead   10
For amplest credence.

KING   He hath armed our answer,   11
And Florence is denied before he comes.
Yet for our gentlemen that mean to see   13
The Tuscan service, freely have they leave
To stand on either part.

SECOND LORD   It well may serve   15
A nursery to our gentry who are sick   16
For breathing and exploit.

KING   What's he comes here?   17

  Enter Bertram, Lafew, and Parolles.

FIRST LORD
It is the Count Rossillion, my good lord,   18
Young Bertram.

KING [*to Bertram*]   Youth, thou bear'st thy father's face.
Frank nature, rather curious than in haste,   20
Hath well composed thee. Thy father's moral parts   21
Mayst thou inherit too! Welcome to Paris.

6 **move** petition   7 **friend** i.e., the Duke of Austria
8 **Prejudicates** prejudges   8–9 **would . . . denial** appears to
wish that we deny aid (to the Florentines).   10 **Approved**
demonstrated, proved   11 **credence** belief.   **armed** fortified
(against denial)   13 **for** as for.   **see** i.e., participate in
15 **stand** serve, fight.   **part** side.   **serve** serve as
16 **nursery** training school   16–17 **sick . . . exploit** longing for,
or sick for lack of, action.   18 **Rossillion** (The Folio *"Rosignoll"*
suggests a nightingale: French *rossignol*.)   20 **Frank** Generous,
bountiful.   **curious** careful, skillful   21 **parts** qualities

BERTRAM
My thanks and duty are Your Majesty's.

KING
I would I had that corporal soundness now   24
As when thy father and myself in friendship
First tried our soldiership! He did look far   26
Into the service of the time, and was   27
Discipled of the bravest. He lasted long,   28
But on us both did haggish age steal on,   29
And wore us out of act. It much repairs me   30
To talk of your good father. In his youth
He had the wit which I can well observe
Today in our young lords; but they may jest   33
Till their own scorn return to them unnoted   34
Ere they can hide their levity in honor.   35
So like a courtier, contempt nor bitterness   36
Were in his pride or sharpness; if they were,   37
His equal had awaked them, and his honor,   38

24 **corporal soundness** physical health   26 **tried** tested
26–7 **He did . . . time** He had a deep understanding of the affairs
of war   27–8 **was Discipled of** had as his pupils (or, perhaps,
"was taught by")   29 **haggish** like a hag, malevolent
30 **wore . . . act** wore us down into inactivity.   **repairs** restores
33–5 **but . . . honor** but the young men of today may jest until
their witty scorn goes scornfully unheeded sooner than they can
hide the effects of their frivolous jesting with truly honorable
action.   36–45 **So . . . humbled** True courtier that he was, he
allowed neither contempt nor asperity to darken his proper self-
esteem and sharpness of wit; if he ever showed contempt or
asperity, it was to a social equal who had done something to
deserve such a response; and his honor, self-governing, knew the
exact minute when unacceptable behavior (such as an insult) bade
him speak, at which time he did exactly what he said he would do
and no more. Those who were below him in social station he
treated as though they were not in fact his inferiors, bowing his
head graciously to their humbleness, making them proud that he
should humble his own eminence in acknowledgment of them.

Clock to itself, knew the true minute when   39
Exception bid him speak, and at this time   40
His tongue obeyed his hand. Who were below him   41
He used as creatures of another place   42
And bowed his eminent top to their low ranks,   43
Making them proud of his humility   44
In their poor praise he humbled. Such a man   45
Might be a copy to these younger times,   46
Which, followed well, would demonstrate them now   47
But goers backward.

BERTRAM   His good remembrance, sir,   48
Lies richer in your thoughts than on his tomb.
So in approof lives not his epitaph   50
As in your royal speech.

KING
Would I were with him! He would always say—
Methinks I hear him now; his plausive words   53
He scattered not in ears, but grafted them   54
To grow there and to bear—"Let me not live—"   55
This his good melancholy oft began
On the catastrophe and heel of pastime,   57
When it was out—"Let me not live," quoth he,   58
"After my flame lacks oil, to be the snuff   59
Of younger spirits, whose apprehensive senses   60
All but new things disdain, whose judgments are   61
Mere fathers of their garments, whose constancies   62

---

46 copy model   **47–8 demonstrate . . . backward** show today's
young men to be inferior to him.   **50 So . . . epitaph** The epitaph
on his tomb is nowhere so amply confirmed   **53 plausive**
praiseworthy   **54 scattered not** did not strew haphazardly
55 bear bear fruit   **57–8 On . . . out** at the drawing to a close of
some sport (such as hunting), when the sport was over   **59 snuff**
burned wick that interferes with proper burning of the candle,
hence, hindrance   **60 apprehensive** quick to perceive, keen but
impatient   **61–2 whose . . . garments** i.e., whose wisdom
produces nothing but new fashions   **62 constancies** loyalties

Expire before their fashions." This he wished.   63
I, after him, do after him wish too,   64
Since I nor wax nor honey can bring home,   65
I quickly were dissolvèd from my hive
To give some laborers room.

SECOND LORD   You're lovèd, sir.
They that least lend it you shall lack you first.   68

KING
I fill a place, I know't.—How long is't, Count,
Since the physician at your father's died?
He was much famed.

BERTRAM   Some six months since, my lord.

KING
If he were living, I would try him yet.—
Lend me an arm.—The rest have worn me out   73
With several applications. Nature and sickness   74
Debate it at their leisure. Welcome, Count;   75
My son's no dearer.

BERTRAM   Thank Your Majesty.

                                    Exeunt. Flourish.

[1.3] ᵒ⤳ *Enter Countess, Steward [Rinaldo], and Clown
[Lavatch].*

COUNTESS   I will now hear. What say you of this   1
    gentlewoman?   2

___

63 **before** even before   64 **I . . . too** I, surviving him, wish as he
did. (With a suggestion also of wishing to follow him in death.)
65 **nor wax** neither wax   68 **lend it you** give love to you.
lack miss   73 **The rest** i.e., My physicians   74 **several
applications** various medical treatments.   75 **Debate . . .
leisure** i.e., contend over my condition at length.

1.3 *Location: Rossillion.*
1–2 **this gentlewoman** Helena.

RINALDO   Madam, the care I have had to even your con-   3
tent I wish might be found in the calendar of my past   4
endeavors; for then we wound our modesty, and   5
make foul the clearness of our deservings, when of   6
ourselves we publish them.   7

COUNTESS   What does this knave here?—Get you
gone, sirrah. The complaints I have heard of you I do   9
not all believe. 'Tis my slowness that I do not, for I
know you lack not folly to commit them and have
ability enough to make such knaveries yours.

LAVATCH   'Tis not unknown to you, madam, I am a
poor fellow.

COUNTESS   Well, sir.

LAVATCH   No, madam, 'tis not so well that I am poor,   16
though many of the rich are damned; but if I may have
Your Ladyship's good will to go to the world, Isbel   18
the woman and I will do as we may.   19

COUNTESS   Wilt thou needs be a beggar?

LAVATCH   I do beg your good will in this case.

COUNTESS   In what case?

3–4 **to . . . content** to meet your expectations   4 **calendar**
record. (Rinaldo hopes that his blameless record will clear him of
blame in what he is about to say to the Countess about Helena.)
5–7 **and make . . . them** (Rinaldo expresses an unwillingness to
insist on his own deservings or reliability as a witness, for fear of
protesting too much.)   7 **publish** make known   9 **sirrah**
(Form of address to a social inferior.)   16 **well** (The Clown plays
on the Countess's "Well" in line 15, i.e., "Well, go ahead"; he
means "satisfactory." He also plays on *poor* in lines 14 and 16:
[1] wretched [2] impoverished.)   18 **go . . . world** i.e., marry
18–19 **Isbel the woman** Lavatch appears to be interested
amorously in Isbel or Isabel, a woman presumably serving in the
Countess's household. She does not appear on stage in the play.
19 **do** (1) get along (2) copulate

LAVATCH   In Isbel's case and mine own. Service is no   23
heritage, and I think I shall never have the blessing of   24
God till I have issue o' my body; for they say bairns are   25
blessings.

COUNTESS   Tell me thy reason why thou wilt marry.

LAVATCH   My poor body, madam, requires it. I am
driven on by the flesh, and he must needs go that the   29
devil drives.

COUNTESS   Is this all Your Worship's reason?   31

LAVATCH   Faith, madam, I have other holy reasons,   32
such as they are.

COUNTESS   May the world know them?

LAVATCH   I have been, madam, a wicked creature, as
you and all flesh and blood are, and indeed I do marry
that I may repent.   37

COUNTESS   Thy marriage, sooner than thy wickedness.   38

LAVATCH   I am out o' friends, madam, and I hope to
have friends for my wife's sake.   40

COUNTESS   Such friends are thine enemies, knave.

LAVATCH   You're shallow, madam, in great friends, for   42
the knaves come to do that for me which I am aweary

---

23 **case** (With a bawdy pun on "female pudenda.")   23–4 **Service is no heritage** i.e., Being a servant gives me little to bequeath to my posterity   25 **bairns** children   29 **needs** necessarily
31 **Your Worship's** (The Countess uses a mock title.)   32 **holy reasons** i.e., reasons sanctioned by the marriage service. (With obscene puns on "holey" and "raisings.")   37 **repent** i.e.,
(1) atone for my carnal ways by making them legitimate
(2) regret marrying.   38 **Thy marriage** i.e., You'll repent your marriage (since proverbially hasty marriage leads to regret)
40 **for . . . sake** to keep my wife company. (With a suggestion of sexual activity as a result.)   42 **shallow . . . in** a superficial judge of

of. He that ears my land spares my team and gives me   44
leave to in the crop. If I be his cuckold, he's my   45
drudge. He that comforts my wife is the cherisher of   46
my flesh and blood; he that cherishes my flesh and
blood loves my flesh and blood; he that loves my flesh
and blood is my friend. Ergo, he that kisses my wife
is my friend. If men could be contented to be what   50
they are, there were no fear in marriage; for young   51
Charbon the puritan and old Poysam the papist, how-   52
some'er their hearts are severed in religion, their heads
are both one—they may jowl horns together like any   54
deer i'th' herd.

COUNTESS   Wilt thou ever be a foulmouthed and calum-   56
nious knave?   57

LAVATCH   A prophet I, madam, and I speak the truth
the next way: 59
    For I the ballad will repeat
      Which men full true shall find:
    Your marriage comes by destiny,
      Your cuckoo sings by kind.   63

COUNTESS   Get you gone, sir. I'll talk with you more
anon.

RINALDO   May it please you, madam, that he bid Helen
come to you. Of her I am to speak.

44–5 **He . . . crop** i.e., He that plows (*ears*) my wife sexually takes
the load off my *team*, my sexual organs, and provides me with a
crop of children.   45 **in** bring in, harvest.   **cuckold** a man
whose wife is unfaithful   46 **drudge** menial laborer.
50–1 **what they are** i.e., cuckolds   52 **Charbon . . . papist** the
meat-eating Puritan and the fish-eating Catholic. (Corruptions of
chairbonne, good meat, and *poisson*, fish, the fast-day diets of
Puritans and Catholics, respectively.)   54 **both one** alike (in
having cuckolds' horns).   **jowl** dash, knock   56 **ever** always
56–7 **calumnious** slandering   59 **next** nearest, most direct
63 **kind** nature (since cuckoldry is natural).

COUNTESS [*to Lavatch*]   Sirrah, tell my gentlewoman I
     would speak with her—Helen, I mean.

LAVATCH [*sings*]

       "Was this fair face the cause," quoth she,   70
         "Why the Grecians sackèd Troy?
       Fond done, done fond.   72
         Was this King Priam's joy?"   73
       With that she sighèd as she stood,
       With that she sighèd as she stood,
         And gave this sentence then: 76
       "Among nine bad if one be good,   77
       Among nine bad if one be good,
         There's yet one good in ten."

COUNTESS   What, one good in ten? You corrupt the   80
     song, sirrah.   81

LAVATCH   One good woman in ten, madam, which is a   82
     purifying o'th' song. Would God would serve the   83
     world so all the year! We'd find no fault with the tithe-   84
     woman if I were the parson. One in ten, quoth 'a? An   85
     we might have a good woman born but ere every blaz-   86
     ing star, or at an earthquake, 'twould mend the lottery   87
     well. A man may draw his heart out ere 'a pluck one.   88

---

70 **fair face** i.e., Helen of Troy's face.   **she** i.e., Hecuba, wife of
Priam, or Helen, or the singer of the ballad   72 **Fond** Foolishly
73 **Was . . . joy?** i.e., Was the taking of Helen, that led to the Trojan
War and the eventual sacking of Priam's palace, his joy?
76 **sentence** maxim   77 **Among** along with   80–1 **You . . .
song** (The song must have had "nine good in ten," or "one bad in
ten.")   82–3 **which . . . song** which corrects the song's incorrect
statistics.   83–8 **Would . . . one** If only God would give us one
good woman in ten as a regular thing! I'd settle for that. (Literally, if
I were the parson, I'd settle for that tithing, or payment to the
church of one-tenth of one's income.) If only we could find one
good woman born on the occasion of rare events like comets or
earthquakes, it would improve the odds. A man might just as easily
pull his own heart out of his chest as draw one good woman by
lottery.

COUNTESS You'll be gone, sir knave, and do as I command you?

LAVATCH That man should be at woman's command,   91
and yet no hurt done! Though honesty be no Puritan,   92
yet it will do no hurt; it will wear the surplice of humil-   93
ity over the black gown of a big heart. I am going,   94
forsooth. The business is for Helen to come hither.

                                                            Exit.

COUNTESS Well, now.

RINALDO I know, madam, you love your gentlewoman entirely.

COUNTESS Faith, I do. Her father bequeathed her to me, and she herself, without other advantage, may   100
lawfully make title to as much love as she finds. There   101
is more owing her than is paid, and more shall be paid her than she'll demand.

RINALDO Madam, I was very late more near her than I   104
think she wished me. Alone she was, and did communicate to herself her own words to her own ears; she thought, I dare vow for her, they touched not

91–2 **That . . . done!** Lavatch sardonically professes to be horrified at the idea of a man being at a woman's command, in disregard of the Saint Paul's insistence that the man should be the head of the woman. (*That* means "To think that.")   92–4
Though . . . heart i.e., Though my outspokenness has no desire to be hypocritical, it will, like the Puritan, hide its proud spirit (*big heart*) beneath the guise of humble obedience. (Many Puritans who demurred at the rubrics and canons of the Established Church, in order to *do no hurt,* conformed outwardly by wearing the prescribed surplice while still wearing underneath that surplice the black gown customarily worn by Calvinists.)
100–1 **may . . . finds** i.e., may claim love of me, which she will find in abundance. (The Countess's metaphor is of the inheritance of a valuable property that is entitled to high regard in its own right.)   104 **late** recently

any stranger sense. Her matter was, she loved your 108
son. Fortune, she said, was no goddess, that had put 109
such difference betwixt their two estates; Love no god, 110
that would not extend his might only where qualities 111
were level; Dian no queen of virgins, that would suffer 112
her poor knight surprised without rescue in the first 113
assault or ransom afterward. This she delivered in the 114
most bitter touch of sorrow that e'er I heard virgin 115
exclaim in, which I held my duty speedily to acquaint
you withal, sithence, in the loss that may happen, it 117
concerns you something to know it. 118

COUNTESS   You have discharged this honestly. Keep it 119
to yourself. Many likelihoods informed me of this 120
before, which hung so tottering in the balance that I
could neither believe nor misdoubt. Pray you, leave 122
me. Stall this in your bosom, and I thank you for your 123
honest care. I will speak with you further anon.

> *Exit Steward* [*Rinaldo*].

Enter Helena.

Even so it was with me when I was young. 125
　　If ever we are nature's, these are ours. This thorn 126

---

108 **any stranger sense** any other person's sense of hearing.
matter theme   109 **was no goddess** i.e., was a thing of
accident only, not divine   110–14 **Love . . . afterward** Cupid,
she said, was capricious and unworthy of being worshiped as a
god, in that Cupid would give his blessing and assistance only to
couples who were socially equal; and Diana unworthy of being
called the patron goddess of virgins, in that she would allow her
hapless devotee, her *poor knight,* to be captured and left
unransomed in the war of the sexes.   114 **delivered** spoke
115 **touch** note, pang   117 **withal** with.   **sithence . . .
happen** since in view of the harm that may come of this
118 **something** somewhat   119 **discharged** performed
120 **likelihoods** indications   122 **misdoubt** doubt.   123 **Stall**
Lodge   125 **Even so** (The Countess speaks without being heard
by Helena, who has entered.)   126 **these** i.e., these pangs of love
(signs of which the Countess sees manifested in Helena)

Doth to our rose of youth rightly belong;
    Our blood to us, this to our blood is born.   128
It is the show and seal of nature's truth,   129
Where love's strong passion is impressed in youth.   130
By our remembrances of days forgone,
Such were our faults, or then we thought them
    none.   132
Her eye is sick on't. I observe her now.   133

HELENA   What is your pleasure, madam?

COUNTESS
You know, Helen, I am a mother to you.

HELENA
Mine honorable mistress.

COUNTESS   Nay, a mother.
Why not a mother? When I said "a mother,"
Methought you saw a serpent. What's in "mother"
That you start at it? I say I am your mother,
And put you in the catalogue of those
That were enwombèd mine. 'Tis often seen
Adoption strives with nature, and choice breeds   142
A native slip to us from foreign seeds.   143
You ne'er oppressed me with a mother's groan,   144
Yet I express to you a mother's care.
God's mercy, maiden, does it curd thy blood
To say I am thy mother? What's the matter,

128–9 **Our . . . truth** sexual passion is an inborn part of us, and
these pangs of love are born of that passion. It is the sign and
guarantee of nature's authority   130 **impressed** imprinted (as
by a seal in wax, or a thorn)   132 **or . . . none** or rather things
we didn't consider faults at the time.   133 **on't** with it.
142 **strives** vies (in strength of attachment)   142–3 **choice . . .
seeds** grafting from an unrelated stock makes wholly ours what
was originally foreign.   144 **with a mother's groan** i.e., in
childbirth

That this distempered messenger of wet,   148
The many-colored Iris, rounds thine eye?   149
Why? That you are my daughter?

HELENA   That I am not.   150

COUNTESS
I say I am your mother.

HELENA   Pardon, madam;
The Count Rossillion cannot be my brother.
I am from humble, he from honored name;
No note upon my parents, his all noble.   154
My master, my dear lord he is, and I
His servant live and will his vassal die.
He must not be my brother.

COUNTESS   Nor I your mother?

HELENA
You are my mother, madam. Would you were—
So that my lord your son were not my brother—   159
Indeed my mother! Or were you both our mothers,   160
I care no more for than I do for heaven,   161
So I were not his sister. Can't no other   162
But, I your daughter, he must be my brother?   163

COUNTESS
Yes, Helen, you might be my daughter-in-law.
God shield you mean it not! "Daughter" and
    "mother"   165

148-9 **That . . . eye?** that the many-colored rainbow, representing
Juno's messenger Iris as the bringer of sad news and rain, is
refracted in your tearful eyes?   150 **not** i.e., not daughter-in-law.
154 **note** mark of distinction. **parents** ancestors   159 **So**
provided   160 **both our mothers** mother of us both   161 **I . . .
heaven** (Helena ambiguously suggests [1] she wouldn't care much
for this [2] she would care for it as much as she longs for heaven.)
162 **So** so long as   162-3 **Can't . . . daughter** Must it be that if
I'm your daughter   165 **shield** forbid. (But the construction
with *not* is ambiguous.)

So strive upon your pulse. What, pale again?
My fear hath catched your fondness. Now I see   167
The mystery of your loneliness and find
Your salt tears' head. Now to all sense 'tis gross: 169
You love my son. Invention is ashamed,   170
Against the proclamation of thy passion,   171
To say thou dost not. Therefore tell me true,
But tell me then 'tis so, for look, thy cheeks
Confess it th'one to th'other, and thine eyes
See it so grossly shown in thy behaviors
That in their kind they speak it. Only sin   176
And hellish obstinacy tie thy tongue,
That truth should be suspected. Speak, is't so?   178
If it be so, you have wound a goodly clew;   179
If it be not, forswear't. Howe'er, I charge thee,   180
As heaven shall work in me for thine avail,   181
To tell me truly.

HELENA   Good madam, pardon me!

COUNTESS
Do you love my son?

HELENA   Your pardon, noble mistress!

COUNTESS
Love you my son?

HELENA   Do not you love him, madam?

167 **catched** caught.   **fondness** love (of Bertram); or
foolishness. (The Countess speaks ambiguously while she tests
Helena.)   169 **head** source.   **sense** perception.   **gross**
palpable, apparent   170 **Invention** i.e., Your ability to invent
excuses   171 **Against** in the face of   176 **in their kind**
according to their nature, i.e., by weeping   178 **suspected**
surmised (by me) rather than openly declared; or, rendered
suspect, brought into disrepute.   179 **wound . . . clew** wound
up a fine ball of twine, i.e., snarled things up beautifully
180 **forswear't** deny it under oath.   **Howe'er** In any case
181 **avail** benefit

COUNTESS
    Go not about. My love hath in't a bond   185
    Whereof the world takes note. Come, come, disclose   186
    The state of your affection, for your passions
    Have to the full appeached.

HELENA [kneeling]   Then I confess   188
    Here on my knee, before high heaven and you,
    That before you, and next unto high heaven,   190
    I love your son.
    My friends were poor but honest, so's my love.   192
    Be not offended, for it hurts not him
    That he is loved of me. I follow him not
    By any token of presumptuous suit,   195
    Nor would I have him till I do deserve him,
    Yet never know how that desert should be.
    I know I love in vain, strive against hope;
    Yet in this captious and intenible sieve   199
    I still pour in the waters of my love
    And lack not to lose still. Thus, Indian-like,   201
    Religious in mine error, I adore
    The sun, that looks upon his worshiper
    But knows of him no more. My dearest madam,   204
    Let not your hate encounter with my love   205
    For loving where you do; but if yourself,
    Whose agèd honor cites a virtuous youth,   207

185 **Go not about** Don't evade me.   **bond** i.e., maternal bond
186 **Whereof . . . note** which society acknowledges.
188 **appeached** informed against (you).   190 **before you** even
more than (I love) you: or, even more than you love him
192 **friends** kinfolk   195 **By . . . suit** with any indication of my
presumptuous love   199 **captious** deceptive; also, capacious.
intenible incapable of holding   201 **lack . . . still** still have
enough to keep pouring without diminishing my supply; also,
continually lose.   **Indian-like** idolatrously, like the savage (who
worships the sun)   204 **no more** nothing else.   205 **encounter
with** oppose   207 **agèd honor cites** honorable old age bespeaks,
gives evidence of

Did ever in so true a flame of liking   208
Wish chastely and love dearly, that your Dian   209
Was both herself and Love, oh, then, give pity   210
To her whose state is such that cannot choose
But lend and give where she is sure to lose;
That seeks not to find that her search implies,   213
But riddle-like lives sweetly where she dies.   214

COUNTESS
Had you not lately an intent—speak truly—
To go to Paris?

HELENA   Madam, I had.

COUNTESS   Wherefore?   216
Tell true.

HELENA
I will tell truth, by grace itself I swear.
You know my father left me some prescriptions
Of rare and proved effects, such as his reading
And manifest experience had collected   221
For general sovereignty; and that he willed me   222
In heedfull'st reservation to bestow them,   223
As notes whose faculties inclusive were   224
More than they were in note. Amongst the rest   225
There is a remedy, approved, set down,   226
To cure the desperate languishings whereof
The King is rendered lost.   228

208 **liking** love   209 **that** so that   210 **both . . . Love** i.e.,
both Diana and Venus, chaste and passionate   213 **that . . .
implies** what her search is for   214 **riddle-like** paradoxically,
with an unguessed mystery   216 **Wherefore?** Why?
221 **manifest experience** i.e., the practice, in antithesis to the
theory (*reading*)   222 **general sovereignty** universal efficacy
and use   222–5 **he . . . note** he exhorted me to take great care in
making use of them, as prescriptions whose comprehensive
powers were greater than recognized.   226 **approved** tested
228 **rendered lost** reckoned to be incurable.

COUNTESS
    This was your motive for Paris, was it? Speak.

HELENA
    My lord your son made me to think of this,
    Else Paris and the medicine and the King
    Had from the conversation of my thoughts   232
    Haply been absent then.

COUNTESS   But think you, Helen,   233
    If you should tender your supposèd aid,   234
    He would receive it? He and his physicians
    Are of a mind: he, that they cannot help him,
    They, that they cannot help. How shall they credit   237
    A poor unlearnèd virgin, when the schools,
    Emboweled of their doctrine, have left off   239
    The danger to itself?

HELENA   There's something in't
    More than my father's skill—which was the great'st
    Of his profession—that his good receipt   242
    Shall for my legacy be sanctified
    By th' luckiest stars in heaven; and would your honor   244
    But give me leave to try success, I'd venture   245
    The well-lost life of mine on His Grace's cure   246
    By such a day and hour.   247

COUNTESS   Dost thou believe't?

HELENA   Ay, madam, knowingly.   249

COUNTESS
    Why, Helen, thou shalt have my leave and love,
    Means and attendants, and my loving greetings

---

232 **conversation** movement, train   233 **Haply** perhaps
234 **tender** offer   237 **credit** trust   239 **Emboweled** emptied.
left off abandoned   242 **that** whereby.   **receipt** prescription
244 **th' luckiest** i.e., the most able to confer luck   245 **venture**
risk, wager   246 **well-lost** i.e., well lost in such a cause, worthless
otherwise   247 **such a** i.e., a specific   249 **knowingly** with
confidence.

To those of mine in court. I'll stay at home
And pray God's blessing into thy attempt.   253
Be gone tomorrow, and be sure of this:
What I can help thee to thou shalt not miss.   *Exeunt.*   255

2.1 ✤ *Enter the King [in his chair] with divers young*
Lords taking leave for the Florentine war,
[Bertram] Count Rossillion, and Parolles.
Flourish cornets.

KING
Farewell, young lords. These warlike principles   1
Do not throw from you. And you, my lords, farewell.   2
Share the advice betwixt you; if both gain all,   3
The gift doth stretch itself as 'tis received,   4
And is enough for both.

FIRST LORD   'Tis our hope, sir,
After well-entered soldiers, to return   6
And find Your Grace in health.

KING
No, no, it cannot be; and yet my heart
Will not confess he owes the malady   9
That doth my life besiege. Farewell, young lords.
Whether I live or die, be you the sons
Of worthy Frenchmen. Let higher Italy—   12

253 **into** upon   255 **miss** be lacking.

2.1 *Location: Paris. The royal court.*
1–2 **These . . . you** i.e., Remember this military advice.
3–4 **if . . . received** if both groups wish to profit fully from my
advice, it will stretch to the extent that it is accepted   6 **After . . .**
soldiers after having become seasoned soldiers; or, in the manner
of experienced soldiers   9 **he owes** it owns   12 **higher Italy**
(1) the knightly class of Italy, corresponding to *worthy Frenchmen,*
or (2) Tuscany, of which Florence and Siena are cities

Those bated that inherit but the fall   13
Of the last monarchy—see that you come   14
Not to woo honor, but to wed it. When   15
The bravest questant shrinks, find what you seek,   16
That fame may cry you loud. I say, farewell.   17

SECOND LORD
Health at your bidding serve Your Majesty!

KING
Those girls of Italy, take heed of them.
They say our French lack language to deny   20
If they demand. Beware of being captives   21
Before you serve.

BOTH   Our hearts receive your warnings.   22

KING
Farewell.—Come hither to me.   [*The King converses*
                   privately with various lords; Bertram, Parolles,
                              and their companions move apart.]

FIRST LORD [*to Bertram*]
Oh my sweet lord, that you will stay behind us!

PAROLLES
'Tis not his fault, the spark.

SECOND LORD   Oh, 'tis brave wars!   25

PAROLLES   Most admirable. I have seen those wars.

BERTRAM   I am commanded here and kept a coil with   27
"Too young" and "The next year" and " 'Tis too early."

13–14 **Those . . . monarchy** i.e., except those who inherit
unworthily the poor remains of the Holy Roman Empire. (Such
undeserving knights are not to be taken into account.)   15 **woo**
flirt with.   **wed** possess as your own   16 **questant** seeker
(after honor)   17 **cry you loud** proclaim you loudly.
20–2 **They . . . serve** People say we French have low resistance
to the sexual blandishments of women. Beware of being captive to
their charms even before you enter into military action.
25 **spark** elegant young man.   **brave** splendid   27 **here** i.e.,
to remain here.   **kept a coil** pestered, fussed over

PAROLLES   An thy mind stand to't, boy, steal away   29
   bravely.   30

BERTRAM
   I shall stay here the forehorse to a smock,   31
   Creaking my shoes on the plain masonry,   32
   Till honor be bought up, and no sword worn   33
   But one to dance with. By heaven, I'll steal away! 34

FIRST LORD
   There's honor in the theft.

PAROLLES   Commit it, Count.

SECOND LORD
   I am your accessory. And so, farewell.

BERTRAM   I grow to you, and our parting is a tortured 37
   body.   38

FIRST LORD   Farewell, Captain.

SECOND LORD   Sweet Monsieur Parolles!

PAROLLES   Noble heroes, my sword and yours are kin.
   Good sparks and lustrous, a word, good metals: you 42
   shall find in the regiment of the Spinii one Captain
   Spurio, with his cicatrice, an emblem of war, here on 44
   his sinister cheek; it was this very sword entrenched it. 45
   Say to him I live, and observe his reports for me. 46

---

29 **An** If   30 **bravely** (1) worthily (2) valiantly.   31 **the
forehorse . . . smock** the lead horse of a team driven by a woman
32 **plain masonry** smooth masonry floor (instead of a battlefield)
33 **Till . . . up** till opportunity for winning honor in the wars is
past, all consumed   34 **one . . . with** i.e., a light ornamental
weapon.   37 **grow to** grow deeply attached to, become as one
with   37–8 **a tortured body** i.e., as painful as a body being torn
apart by torture.   42 **metals** i.e., "blades"; spirits of mettle
44 **Spurio** (This name suggests "spurious," "counterfeit.")
cicatrice scar   45 **sinister** left.   **it was . . . entrenched it**
mine was the sword that dug that trench-like scar.   46 **reports**
reply

FIRST LORD   We shall, noble Captain.

PAROLLES   Mars dote on you for his novices!   48

                                        [*Exeunt Lords.*]

  [*To Bertram*] What will ye do?

BERTRAM   Stay the King.   50

PAROLLES   Use a more spacious ceremony to   51
the noble lords; you have restrained yourself within
the list of too cold an adieu. Be more expressive to   53
them, for they wear themselves in the cap of the time;   54
there do muster true gait, eat, speak, and move under   55
the influence of the most received star; and, though the   56
devil lead the measure, such are to be followed. After   57
them, and take a more dilated farewell.   58

BERTRAM   And I will do so.

PAROLLES   Worthy fellows, and like to prove most sin-   60
ewy swordmen.   *Exeunt [Bertram and Parolles].*   61

    Enter Lafew [and approaches the King].

LAFEW [*kneeling*]
  Pardon, my lord, for me and for my tidings.   62

KING   I'll fee thee to stand up.   63

---

48 **Mars** May Mars.   **novices** devotees.   50 **Stay the King**
Support or wait on the King. (But also interpreted, with different
punctuation, as "Stay; the King wills it" or "Stay; the King
approaches.")   51 **spacious ceremony** effusive courtesy
53 **list** boundary. (Literally, the selvage or finished edge of cloth.)
54 **wear . . . time** stand out as ornaments of the fashionable world
55 **muster true gait** set the right pace, move gracefully
56 **received** fashionable   57 **measure** dance   58 **dilated**
protracted; expansive   60 **like** likely   60–1 **sinewy** energetic,
forceful   62 **tidings** news, information.   63 **I'll . . . up** i.e., I
bid you rise; or, I will rather reward you for rising.

LAFEW [*rising*]

    Then here's a man stands that has brought his pardon.   64

    I would you had kneeled, my lord, to ask me mercy,   65

    And that at my bidding you could so stand up.   66

KING

    I would I had, so I had broke thy pate   67

    And asked thee mercy for't.

LAFEW   Good faith, across!   68

    But, my good lord, 'tis thus: will you be cured

    Of your infirmity?

KING   No.

LAFEW   Oh, will you eat   70

    No grapes, my royal fox? Yes, but you will   71

    My noble grapes, an if my royal fox   72

    Could reach them. I have seen a medicine   73

    That's able to breathe life into a stone,

    Quicken a rock, and make you dance canary   75

    With sprightly fire and motion, whose simple touch   76

    Is powerful to araise King Pepin, nay,   77

64 pardon i.e., something to win the King's indulgence.
65–8 I would . . . for't (Lafew hyperbolically suggests that he and the King really ought to change places, turning the King into the petitioner, since Lafew has brought something worth begging for. The King, not knowing what is in store, jests that he might be willing to beg forgiveness of Lafew if he could first give Lafew a sharp blow to the head for his seeming insolence, thus providing the King an occasion for begging pardon.)   **68 across** i.e., well parried.   **70–1 will . . . fox?** i.e., will you be like the fox in Aesop's fable and call the grapes sour because they are beyond your reach?   **72 an if** if   **73 medicine** i.e., physician
75 Quicken bring to life.   **canary** a lively Spanish dance
76 simple (1) mere (2) medicinal, making use of "simples" or herbs   **77 to araise . . . Pepin** to raise from the dead King Pepin, a French king of the eighth century and father of Charlemagne. (The name has a folklorish ring.)

To give great Charlemain a pen in's hand
And write to her a love line.

KING   What "her" is this?   79

LAFEW

Why, Doctor She! My lord, there's one arrived,
If you will see her. Now by my faith and honor,
If seriously I may convey my thoughts
In this my light deliverance, I have spoke   83
With one that in her sex, her years, profession,   84
Wisdom, and constancy hath amazed me more   85
Than I dare blame my weakness. Will you see her,   86
For that is her demand, and know her business?
That done, laugh well at me.

KING   Now, good Lafew,
Bring in the admiration, that we with thee   89
May spend our wonder too; or take off thine   90
By wondering how thou took'st it.

LAFEW   Nay, I'll fit you,   91
And not be all day neither.   [He goes to the door.]

KING

Thus he his special nothing ever prologues.   93

LAFEW [to Helena]   Nay, come your ways.   94

          Enter Helena.

KING   This haste hath wings indeed.

79 **love line** (Some of Lafew's terms, such as *stone, quicken, fire and
motion, touch, araise,* and *pen in's hand,* have possible erotic
undertones that link recovery to restored potency.)
83 **deliverance** manner of speaking   84 **profession** what she
professes to be able to do   85–6 **more . . . weakness** more than
I can attribute to my feebleness or susceptibility as an old man.
89 **admiration** wonder   90 **spend** expend.   **take off** dispel,
end   91 **took'st** conceived. (With a play on *take* in the previous
line.)   **fit** satisfy   93 **special nothing** particular trifles.
prologues introduces.   94 **come your ways** come along.

LAFEW Nay, come your ways.
 This is His Majesty. Say your mind to him.
 A traitor you do look like, but such traitors   98
 His Majesty seldom fears. I am Cressid's uncle,   99
 That dare leave two together. Fare you well.   *Exit.*

KING
 Now, fair one, does your business follow us?   101

HELENA Ay, my good lord.
 Gerard de Narbonne was my father;
 In what he did profess, well found.

KING   I knew him.   104

HELENA
 The rather will I spare my praises towards him;
 Knowing him is enough. On 's bed of death
 Many receipts he gave me, chiefly one   107
 Which, as the dearest issue of his practice,   108
 And of his old experience th'only darling,   109
 He bade me store up as a triple eye   110
 Safer than mine own two, more dear. I have so;   111
 And hearing Your High Majesty is touched
 With that malignant cause wherein the honor   113
 Of my dear father's gift stands chief in power,   114

---

98 traitor (Lafew's joke depends on the idea that it is dangerous to leave an unknown person alone with a king, for fear of a plot.) **99 Cressid's uncle** Pandarus, go-between for the lovers Troilus and Cressida **101 follow** concern **104 In . . . found** in his medical practice he was reputed to be skilled. **107 receipts** remedies **108–9 the dearest . . . darling** the favorite child or product of his many years of practice **110 triple** third **111 Safer** more safely **113–14 With . . . power** with that malignant disease over which my father's medical skill has chief power to effect a cure

I come to tender it and my appliance   115
With all bound humbleness.

KING   We thank you, maiden,   116
But may not be so credulous of cure   117
When our most learnèd doctors leave us and
The congregated college have concluded   119
That laboring art can never ransom nature   120
From her inaidible estate. I say we must not
So stain our judgment, or corrupt our hope,   122
To prostitute our past-cure malady   123
To empirics, or to dissever so   124
Our great self and our credit, to esteem   125
A senseless help when help past sense we deem.   126

HELENA
My duty then shall pay me for my pains.   127
I will no more enforce mine office on you,   128
Humbly entreating from your royal thoughts
A modest one to bear me back again.   130

KING
I cannot give thee less, to be called grateful.
Thou thought'st to help me, and such thanks I give
As one near death to those that wish him live.
But what at full I know, thou know'st no part,   134
I knowing all my peril, thou no art.   135

115 **tender** offer.   **appliance** treatment   116 **bound** dutiful
117 **credulous of** ready to believe in   119 **congregated college**
college of physicians   120 **art** skill, i.e., medicine   122 **stain**
sully   123–6 **To . . . deem** by basely submitting my past-cure
illness to quack doctors, or by divorcing my kingly greatness from
my reputation to such an extent as to put credulous faith in a cure
too improbable to be believed when the disease exceeds all
reasonable hope.   127 **My . . . pains** My thanks then must be that
I have dutifully offered my aid.   128 **office** dutiful service
130 **A modest . . . again** i.e., a favorable regard commensurate
with my humble station and with my maidenly modesty to take
back with me.   134 **no part** not at all   135 **thou no art**
i.e., you having no medical skill capable of saving my life.

HELENA

What I can do can do no hurt to try,
Since you set up your rest 'gainst remedy.   137
He that of greatest works is finisher   138
Oft does them by the weakest minister.
So holy writ in babes hath judgment shown,   140
When judges have been babes; great floods have
      flown   141
From simple sources; and great seas have dried   142
When miracles have by the great'st been denied.
Oft expectation fails, and most oft there
Where most it promises, and oft it hits   145
Where hope is coldest and despair most fits.

KING

I must not hear thee. Fare thee well, kind maid.
Thy pains, not used, must by thyself be paid;   148
Proffers not took reap thanks for their reward.   149

HELENA

Inspirèd merit so by breath is barred.   150
It is not so with Him that all things knows
As 'tis with us that square our guess by shows;   152
But most it is presumption in us when
The help of heaven we count the act of men.   154
Dear sir, to my endeavors give consent;

---

137 **set . . . rest** stake your all. (A figure from the gambling game
of primero.)   138 **He** God   140–1 **So . . . babes** (See, for
example, Matthew 11:25 and 1 Corinthians 1:27.)   141 **babes**
i.e., babyish, foolish. (The inversion of babes and wise men
appears often in the Bible.)   142 **simple** small, insignificant.
great seas (Probably the Red Sea; *the great'st* in line 143 is
presumably Pharaoh.)   145 **hits** succeeds, is confirmed
148 **by . . . paid** i.e., be their own reward   149 **Proffers . . .
thanks** offers not accepted reap thanks (and only thanks)
150 **Inspirèd . . . barred** Divinely inspired virtue is thus denied by
mere spoken words.   152 **square . . . shows** support our
conjectures on the basis of appearances   154 **count** account

Of heaven, not me, make an experiment.   156
I am not an impostor that proclaim   157
Myself against the level of mine aim;   158
But know I think, and think I know most sure,   159
My art is not past power, nor you past cure.   160

KING

Art thou so confident? Within what space   161
Hop'st thou my cure?

HELENA   The great'st grace lending grace,   162
Ere twice the horses of the sun shall bring
Their fiery torcher his diurnal ring,   164
Ere twice in murk and occidental damp   165
Moist Hesperus hath quenched her sleepy lamp,   166
Or four-and-twenty times the pilot's glass   167
Hath told the thievish minutes how they pass,
What is infirm from your sound parts shall fly,
Health shall live free, and sickness freely die.

KING

Upon thy certainty and confidence
What dar'st thou venture?

HELENA   Tax of impudence,   172
A strumpet's boldness, a divulgèd shame
Traduced by odious ballads; my maiden's name   · 174

---

156 **experiment** trial.   157–8 **that . . . aim** who claims to be
more of a marksman than my ability to aim would warrant
159–60 **But . . . power** but I have every confidence, given the
uncertainty of all human knowing, that what I claim to be able to
do is not beyond my power to perform   161 **space** period of
time   162 **Hop'st thou** do you hope for.   **The great'st . . .
grace** i.e., With God's help   164 **Their . . . ring** i.e., the fiery
sun-god on his daily round   165 **occidental** western, sunset
166 **Hesperus** evening star (actually Venus)   167 **glass** hour-
glass   172 **venture** risk, wager.   **Tax** Accusation
174 **Traduced** slandered

Seared otherwise; nay, worse of worst, extended   175
With vilest torture let my life be ended.

KING

Methinks in thee some blessèd spirit doth speak
His powerful sound within an organ weak;
And what impossibility would slay   179
In common sense, sense saves another way.   180
Thy life is dear, for all that life can rate   181
Worth name of life in thee hath estimate: 182
Youth, beauty, wisdom, courage, all
That happiness and prime can happy call.   184
Thou this to hazard needs must intimate   185
Skill infinite, or monstrous desperate.   186
Sweet practicer, thy physic I will try,   187
That ministers thine own death if I die.   188

HELENA

If I break time or flinch in property   189
Of what I spoke, unpitied let me die,
And well deserved. Not helping, death's my fee;   191
But, if I help, what do you promise me?

KING

Make thy demand.

HELENA   But will you make it even?   193

175 **Seared otherwise** branded in other ways as well.
extended stretched out on the rack; or, drawn out in time
179–80 **what . . . way** what common sense would regard as
impossible, a higher sense (faith) can regard as possible.
181–2 **for . . . estimate** for everything that life can consider
worthy the name of life is to be found and esteemed in you.
181 **rate** value   184 **That . . . call** that good fortune and the
"springtime" of youth can call happy.   185–6 **Thou . . .
desperate** The fact that you are prepared to hazard all this argues
infinite skill or desperation.   187 **physic** medicine
188 **ministers** administers   189 **If . . . property** If I fail to meet
my deadline or fall short in any respect   191 **Not helping** If I do
not help   193 **make it even** carry it out.

KING

Ay, by my scepter and my hopes of heaven.

HELENA

Then shalt thou give me with thy kingly hand
What husband in thy power I will command.
Exempted be from me the arrogance
To choose from forth the royal blood of France,
My low and humble name to propagate
With any branch or image of thy state;
But such a one, thy vassal, whom I know
Is free for me to ask, thee to bestow.

KING

Here is my hand. The premises observed,   203
Thy will by my performance shall be served.
So make the choice of thy own time, for I,
Thy resolved patient, on thee still rely.   206
More should I question thee, and more I must—
Though more to know could not be more to trust—
From whence thou cam'st, how tended on; but rest   209
Unquestioned welcome and undoubted blest.—   210
Give me some help here, ho!—If thou proceed
As high as word, my deed shall match thy meed.   212

                    Flourish. Exeunt, [the King carried in].

[2.2] ❧ *Enter Countess and Clown [Lavatch].*

COUNTESS   Come on, sir. I shall now put you to the   1
          height of your breeding.   2

203 **The premises observed** The conditions of the agreement
having been fulfilled   206 **still** continually   209 **tended on**
attended   210 **Unquestioned** (1) without being questioned
(2) unquestionably   212 **As high as word** as fully as you have
promised.   **meed** merit, worth.

2.2 *Location: Rossillion.*
1–2 **put . . . breeding** test your good manners.

LAVATCH I will show myself highly fed and lowly 3
taught. I know my business is but to the court. 4

COUNTESS "To the court"? Why, what place make you 5
special, when you put off that with such contempt? 6
"But to the court"!

LAVATCH Truly, madam, if God have lent a man any
manners, he may easily put it off at court. He that 9
cannot make a leg, put off's cap, kiss his hand, and 10
say nothing has neither leg, hands, lip, nor cap; and
indeed such a fellow, to say precisely, were not for the
court. But for me, I have an answer will serve all men.

COUNTESS Marry, that's a bountiful answer that fits all
questions.

LAVATCH It is like a barber's chair that fits all buttocks:
the pin-buttock, the quatch-buttock, the brawn-but- 17
tock, or any buttock.

COUNTESS Will your answer serve fit to all questions?

LAVATCH As fit as ten groats is for the hand of an 20
attorney, as your French crown for your taffety punk, 21
as Tib's rush for Tom's forefinger, as a pancake for 22
Shrove Tuesday, a morris for May Day, as the nail to 23
his hole, the cuckold to his horn, as a scolding quean 24

3–4 highly . . . taught overfed and underdisciplined. ("Better fed than taught" was proverbial for a spoiled child.)   **5–6 make you special** do you consider special   **6 put off** dismiss   **9 put it off** carry it off. (With a play on *put off* in line 6 and anticipating the meaning "doff" in line 10.)   **10 leg** respectful bow or curtsy   **17 pin** narrow, pointed.   **quatch** fat, wide.   **brawn** hefty, fleshy   **20 ten groats** forty pence   **21 French crown** (1) coin (2) *corona veneris,* a scab on the head symptomatic of syphilis, the "French disease."   **taffety punk** finely dressed prostitute   **22 Tib's rush** (Refers to a folk custom of exchanging rings made of reed in a marriage without benefit of clergy.)   **pancake** (Traditionally eaten as a last feast on the final day before Lent, Shrove Tuesday.)   **23 morris** morris dance, country dance common at May Day celebrations   **24 his hole** its hole.   **quean** wench

to a wrangling knave, as the nun's lip to the friar's
mouth, nay, as the pudding to his skin.   26

COUNTESS Have you, I say, an answer of such fitness
for all questions?

LAVATCH From below your duke to beneath your
constable, it will fit any question.

COUNTESS It must be an answer of most monstrous
size that must fit all demands.

LAVATCH But a trifle neither, in good faith, if the   33
learned should speak truth of it. Here it is, and all that
belongs to't. Ask me if I am a courtier. It shall do you
no harm to learn.

COUNTESS To be young again, if we could! I will be a
fool in question, hoping to be the wiser by your
answer. I pray you, sir, are you a courtier?

LAVATCH Oh, Lord, sir!—There's a simple putting off.   40
More, more, a hundred of them.

COUNTESS Sir, I am a poor friend of yours, that loves
you.

LAVATCH Oh, Lord, sir!—Thick, thick, spare not me.   44

COUNTESS I think, sir, you can eat none of this homely   45
meat.   46

LAVATCH Oh, Lord, sir!—Nay, put me to't, I warrant you.

COUNTESS You were lately whipped, sir, as I think.

LAVATCH Oh, Lord, sir!—Spare not me.

COUNTESS Do you cry, "Oh, Lord, sir!" at your whipping, and "spare not me"? Indeed your "Oh, Lord, sir!"

---

26 **pudding** sausage.   **his** its   33 **But . . . neither** On the
contrary, it's only a trifle   40 **Oh, Lord, sir** (A foppish phrase
currently in vogue at court. Here it suggests, "I do indeed presume
to be a courtier; isn't that plain enough from my appearance?")
putting off evasion.   44 **Thick** Quickly   45–6 **homely meat**
plain fare.

is very sequent to your whipping. You would answer 52
very well to a whipping, if you were but bound to't. 53

LAVATCH   I ne'er had worse luck in my life in my "Oh,
Lord, sir!" I see things may serve long, but not serve
ever.

COUNTESS
I play the noble huswife with the time,
To entertain it so merrily with a fool.

LAVATCH   Oh, Lord, sir!—Why, there't serves well again.

COUNTESS
An end, sir! To your business. Give Helen this,
                         [giving a letter]
And urge her to a present answer back.   61
Commend me to my kinsmen and my son.   62
This is not much.

LAVATCH   Not much commendation to them?

COUNTESS   Not much employment for you. You understand me?

LAVATCH   Most fruitfully. I am there before my legs. 67

COUNTESS   Haste you again.   Exeunt [separately]. 68

52 **is very sequent to** is a pertinent response to (because it would
be a plea for mercy)   52–3 **answer . . . to** (1) reply cleverly to
(2) serve as a suitable subject for   53 **bound to't** (1) obliged to
reply (2) tied up for it.   61 **present** immediate   62 **Commend
me** Give my greetings   67 **before my legs** (A comically absurd
hyperbole suggesting incredible speed.)   68 **again** back again.

[2.3] ⁓ *Enter Count [Bertram], Lafew, and Parolles.*

LAFEW   They say miracles are past, and we have our   1
philosophical persons to make modern and familiar   2
things supernatural and causeless. Hence is it that we   3
make trifles of terrors, ensconcing ourselves into seem-   4
ing knowledge when we should submit ourselves to
an unknown fear.   6

PAROLLES   Why, 'tis the rarest argument of wonder   7
that hath shot out in our latter times.   8

BERTRAM   And so 'tis.

LAFEW   To be relinquished of the artists—   10

PAROLLES   So I say, both of Galen and Paracelsus.   11

LAFEW   Of all the learned and authentic fellows—   12

PAROLLES   Right, so I say.

LAFEW   That gave him out incurable—   14

PAROLLES   Why, there 'tis; so say I too.

LAFEW   Not to be helped.

PAROLLES   Right! As 'twere a man assured of a—

2.3 Location: Paris. The royal court.
1 **They . . . past** (It was commonplace wisdom that the miracles
described in the Bible and other early religious writings were
somehow unique to an era long past.)   2–3 **philosophical . . .
causeless** scientists who can cause happenings that strike us as
supernatural and inexplicable seem commonplace and familiar.
(*Modern* means ordinary or commonplace.)   4 **ensconcing**
taking refuge, fortifying   6 **unknown fear** awe of the
unknown.   7–8 **'tis . . . times** it is the most remarkable
demonstration of the extraordinary that has suddenly appeared in
recent times.   10 **relinquished . . . artists** abandoned by the
physicians   11 **Galen** Greek physician of the second century;
the traditional authority.   **Paracelsus** Swiss physician of the
sixteenth century; the new and more radical authority.
12 **authentic fellows** those properly accredited   14 **gave him
out** proclaimed him

LAFEW   Uncertain life and sure death.

PAROLLES   Just, you say well; so would I have said.   19

LAFEW   I may truly say it is a novelty to the world.

PAROLLES   It is, indeed. If you will have it in showing,   21
you shall read it in—what-do-ye-call there?

> [*He points to a ballad in Lafew's hand.*]

LAFEW [*reading*]   "A showing of a heavenly effect in
an earthly actor."

PAROLLES   That's it, I would have said the very same.

LAFEW   Why, your dolphin is not lustier. 'Fore me, I   26
speak in respect—   27

PAROLLES   Nay, 'tis strange, 'tis very strange, that is the   28
brief and the tedious of it; and he's of a most faci-   29
norous spirit that will not acknowledge it to be the—   30

LAFEW   Very hand of heaven.

PAROLLES   Ay, so I say.

LAFEW   In a most weak—

PAROLLES   And debile minister, great power, great   34
transcendence, which should indeed give us a further
use to be made than alone the recovery of the King, as
to be—

LAFEW   Generally thankful.   38

> *Enter King, Helena, and attendants. [The King*
> *sits.*]

PAROLLES   I would have said it; you say well. Here
comes the King.

---

19 **Just** Exactly   21 **in showing** i.e., in print   26 **dolphin** (A
sportive and vigorous sea animal; with a pun perhaps on *dauphin*,
"French crown prince.")   **'Fore me** i.e., Upon my soul   27 **in
respect** intending no disrespect   28–9 **the brief . . . it** i.e., the
short and the long of it   29–30 **facinorous** infamous, wicked
34 **debile minister** weak agent   38 **Generally** universally

LAFEW   Lustig, as the Dutchman says. I'll like a maid   41
    the better whilst I have a tooth in my head. Why, he's   42
    able to lead her a coranto.   43

PAROLLES   *Mort du vinaigre!* Is not this Helen?   44

LAFEW   'Fore God, I think so.   45

KING
  Go, call before me all the lords in court.

                        [Exit one or more attendants.]
  Sit, my preserver, by thy patient's side,   *[She sits.]*
  And with this healthful hand, whose banished sense   48
  Thou hast repealed, a second time receive   49
  The confirmation of my promised gift,
  Which but attends thy naming.   51

     Enter four Lords.

  Fair maid, send forth thine eye. This youthful parcel   52
  Of noble bachelors stand at my bestowing,   53
  O'er whom both sovereign power and father's voice
  I have to use. Thy frank election make;   55
  Thou hast power to choose, and they none to forsake.   56

HELENA
  To each of you one fair and virtuous mistress
  Fall, when Love please! Marry, to each but one!   58

---

41 **Lustig** Lusty, sportive.   **Dutchman** i.e., from any Germanic country   42 **have a tooth** (With a play on the meaning "have a sweet tooth, a taste for the pleasures of the senses.")
43 **coranto** lively dance.   44 *Mort du vinaigre!* (An oath, perhaps referring to the vinegar offered by a bystander to Christ to drink as he hung dying on the cross; see Matthew 27:48, Mark 15:36, and John 19:29; literally, "death of vinegar.")   45 **I think so** i.e., I should say it is. (Lafew knows it is Helena.)   48 **banished sense** loss of feeling   49 **repealed** recalled (from death)   51 **attends** waits upon   52 **parcel** group   53 **stand . . . bestowing** i.e., are my wards, whom I may give in marriage   55 **frank election** free choice   56 **forsake** refuse.   58 **Love** Cupid

LAFEW [*aside*]
I'd give bay Curtal and his furniture   59
My mouth no more were broken than these boys',   60
And writ as little beard.

KING   Peruse them well.   61
Not one of those but had a noble father.

HELENA   Gentlemen,
Heaven hath through me restored the King to health.

ALL THE LORDS
We understand it, and thank heaven for you.

HELENA
I am a simple maid, and therein wealthiest
That I protest I simply am a maid.—   67
Please it Your Majesty, I have done already.
The blushes in my cheeks thus whisper me,
"We blush that thou shouldst choose; but, be refused,   70
Let the white death sit on thy cheek forever,   71
We'll ne'er come there again."

KING   Make choice and see.
Who shuns thy love shuns all his love in me.   73

HELENA
Now, Dian, from thy altar do I fly,   74
And to imperial Love, that god most high,   75
Do my sighs stream. (*She addresses her to a Lord.*) Sir,
will you hear my suit?

---

59 **bay Curtal** my bay horse, Curtal. (From the French *court*,
short- or docked-tail.)   **furniture** trappings   60 **My . . .
broken** i.e., (1) that I had lost no more teeth (2) that I, like a young
horse, were no more "broken to the bit"   61 **And writ** i.e., and
that I laid claim to. (Lafew wishes he were young enough to be a
suitor of Helena.)   67 **protest** avow   70 **be refused** i.e., if
you are refused   71 **the white death** i.e., death in its pallor
73 **Who** He who   74 **Dian** Diana, the goddess of chastity
75 **imperial Love** i.e., the god of love, Cupid

FIRST LORD
    And grant it.

HELENA   Thanks, sir. All the rest is mute.   77

LAFEW [*aside*] I had rather be in this choice than
    throw ambs-ace for my life.   79

HELENA [*to Second Lord*]
    The honor, sir, that flames in your fair eyes
    Before I speak too threateningly replies.
    Love make your fortunes twenty times above   82
    Her that so wishes, and her humble love!   83

SECOND LORD
    No better, if you please.

HELENA   My wish receive,   84
    Which great Love grant! And so I take my leave.

LAFEW [*aside*] Do all they deny her? An they were   86
    sons of mine, I'd have them whipped, or I would
    send them to the Turk to make eunuchs of.

HELENA [*to Third Lord*]
    Be not afraid that I your hand should take;
    I'll never do you wrong for your own sake.
    Blessing upon your vows, and in your bed
    Find fairer fortune, if you ever wed!

LAFEW [*aside*] These boys are boys of ice; they'll none
    have her. Sure they are bastards to the English; the   94
    French ne'er got 'em.   95

77 **All . . . mute** I have nothing more to say to you.   79 **ambs-
ace** two aces, the lowest possible throw in dice. (To throw ambs-ace
with one's life at stake is to risk all on a throw.)   82 **Love make**
May Love make   83 **Her . . . love** her that speaks this wish—i.e.,
myself—and the humble love I deserve or can give.   84 **No
better** i.e., I wish for nothing better than your humble love.   **My
wish receive** i.e., Take my *wish* for your fortunate marriage, rather
than me   86 **Do . . . her?** (Lafew, unable to hear, misinterprets
her passing from one to another.)   **An** If   94 **Sure** Certainly.
bastards to illegitimate children of   95 **got** begot

HELENA [to Fourth Lord]
> You are too young, too happy, and too good   96
> To make yourself a son out of my blood.

FOURTH LORD   Fair one, I think not so.

LAFEW [aside]   There's one grape yet; I am sure thy father   99
> drunk wine. But if thou be'st not an ass, I am a   100
> youth of fourteen; I have known thee already.   101

HELENA [to Bertram]
> I dare not say I take you, but I give
> Me and my service, ever whilst I live,
> Into your guiding power.—This is the man.

KING
> Why, then, young Bertram, take her; she's thy wife.

BERTRAM
> My wife, my liege? I shall beseech Your Highness,
> In such a business give me leave to use
> The help of mine own eyes.

KING   Know'st thou not, Bertram,
> What she has done for me?

BERTRAM   Yes, my good lord,
> But never hope to know why I should marry her.

KING
> Thou know'st she has raised me from my sickly bed.

BERTRAM
> But follows it, my lord, to bring me down   112
> Must answer for your raising? I know her well;
> She had her breeding at my father's charge.   114

---

96 **happy** fortunate   99 **grape** i.e., scion of a good family.
thy i.e., Bertram's   100 **drunk wine** i.e., was red-blooded.
101 **known** i.e., seen through   112 **bring me down** i.e., lower
me to a socially inferior wife, to the (marriage) bed. (With sexual
wordplay in *bring me down*, and *raising* in line 113.)   114 **charge**
cost.

A poor physician's daughter my wife? Disdain   115
Rather corrupt me ever!   116

KING

'Tis only title thou disdain'st in her, the which   117
I can build up. Strange is it that our bloods,
Of color, weight, and heat, poured all together,
Would quite confound distinction, yet stands off   120
In differences so mighty. If she be   121
All that is virtuous save what thou dislik'st—
A poor physician's daughter—thou dislik'st
Of virtue for the name. But do not so.   124
From lowest place when virtuous things proceed,   125
The place is dignified by th' doer's deed.
Where great additions swell's, and virtue none,   127
It is a dropsied honor. Good alone   128
Is good without a name; vileness is so;   129
The property by what it is should go,   130
Not by the title. She is young, wise, fair;
In these to nature she's immediate heir,   132
And these breed honor. That is honor's scorn   133
Which challenges itself as honor's born   134
And is not like the sire. Honors thrive   135
When rather from our acts we them derive

115–16 **Disdain . . . ever!** i.e., Rather let my disdain for her ruin me forever in your favor! (With unintentional irony; disdain does indeed corrupt Bertram.)   117 **title** i.e., her lack of title
120–1 **Would . . . mighty** (blood) is indistinguishable from one person to the next, yet is made the basis of such mighty differences in rank.   124 **name** i.e., lack of a name (title).   125 **proceed** emanate   127 **great . . . swell's** pompous titles puff us up
128 **dropsied** unhealthily swollen   128–9 **Good . . . so** What is in itself good is so without a title; the same is true of vileness
130 **property** quality.   **go** i.e., be judged, be valued
132 **In . . . heir** in these qualities she inherits directly from nature
133–5 **That . . . sire** True honor is scornful of any claim to honor based only on birth that is not validated by behavior worthy of one's heritage.

Than our foregoers. The mere word's a slave
Debauched on every tomb, on every grave   138
A lying trophy, and as oft is dumb   139
Where dust and damned oblivion is the tomb
Of honored bones indeed. What should be said?   141
If thou canst like this creature as a maid,
I can create the rest. Virtue and she   143
Is her own dower; honor and wealth from me.   144

BERTRAM

I cannot love her, nor will strive to do't.

KING

Thou wrong'st thyself, if thou shouldst strive to
    choose.   146

HELENA

That you are well restored, my lord, I'm glad.
Let the rest go.

KING

My honor's at the stake, which to defeat,   149
I must produce my power. Here, take her hand,
Proud, scornful boy, unworthy this good gift,
That dost in vile misprision shackle up   152
My love and her desert; that canst not dream,   153
We, poising us in her defective scale,   154
Shall weigh thee to the beam; that wilt not know 155
It is in us to plant thine honor where   156

---

138 **Debauched** corrupted   139 **trophy** memorial.   **dumb**
silent   141 **honored bones indeed** i.e., the remains of those
who were genuinely honorable.   143–4 **Virtue . . . dower** i.e.,
Her marriage gift to you will be her virtue and herself
146 **strive to choose** try to assert your own choice.   149 **which**
i.e., which threat to my honor   152–5 **That . . . beam** you who
with base mistaking fetter both my love and her worth; you who
cannot imagine how I, adding my royal weight to her deficiency in
order to counterbalance your wealth and position, will equalize
the cross-beam of the balance scales. (*We* is the royal plural,
continued in lines 157–8.)   156 **in us** within my royal power

We please to have it grow. Check thy contempt;   157
Obey our will, which travails in thy good;   158
Believe not thy disdain, but presently   159
Do thine own fortunes that obedient right   160
Which both thy duty owes and our power claims,
Or I will throw thee from my care forever
Into the staggers and the careless lapse   163
Of youth and ignorance, both my revenge and hate
Loosing upon thee in the name of justice   165
Without all terms of pity. Speak; thine answer.   166

BERTRAM
Pardon, my gracious lord, for I submit
My fancy to your eyes. When I consider   168
What great creation and what dole of honor   169
Flies where you bid it, I find that she, which late   170
Was in my nobler thoughts most base, is now
The praisèd of the King, who, so ennobled,
Is as 'twere born so.

KING   Take her by the hand,
And tell her she is thine, to whom I promise
A counterpoise, if not to thy estate,   175
A balance more replete.

BERTRAM   I take her hand.   176

---

157 **Check** Curb, restrain   158 **travails in** labors for
159 **Believe not** do not place faith in or obey.   **presently** at
once   160 **obedient right** right of obedience   163 **staggers**
giddy decline. (Literally, a horse disease.)   **careless lapse**
irresponsible fall   165 **Loosing** turning loose   166 **all . . .
pity** pity in any form.   168 **fancy** desires   169 **great creation**
creating of greatness.   **dole** share, doling out   170 **which
late** who lately   175–6 **A counterpoise . . . replete** i.e., an
equal weight of wealth as dowry, if not an amount even exceeding
your estate.

KING

    Good fortune and the favor of the King

    Smile upon this contract, whose ceremony   178

    Shall seem expedient on the now-born brief   179

    And be performed tonight. The solemn feast   180

    Shall more attend upon the coming space,   181

    Expecting absent friends. As thou lov'st her,   182

    Thy love's to me religious; else, does err.   183

                Exeunt. Parolles and Lafew stay behind,

                         commenting of this wedding.

LAFEW   Do you hear, monsieur? A word with you.

PAROLLES   Your pleasure, sir?

LAFEW   Your lord and master did well to make his recantation.

PAROLLES   Recantation? My lord? My master?

LAFEW   Ay. Is it not a language I speak?

PAROLLES   A most harsh one, and not to be understood without bloody succeeding. My master?   191

LAFEW   Are you companion to the Count Rossillion?   192

PAROLLES   To any count, to all counts, to what is man.   193

178–9 whose . . . brief whose performing ceremoniously will seem appropriate to the present contract. (*Brief* suggests both "short" and "expeditious." The King specifies a marriage contract rather than a full wedding ceremony.)   **180–2 The solemn . . . friends** The full festival of celebration must be delayed for a time until absent friends and relatives can arrive. (Following the formal betrothal just completed, there is to be a wedding tonight and a celebratory feast later on when all can gather.)   **182–3 As . . . err** So long as you love her truly, I will regard your love for me as holy and true; otherwise, regarding your obligations to me you are a heretic and a traitor.   **183.2 of** on   **191 bloody succeeding** outcome with bloodshed, attendant on change of faith. (Sustaining the language of religion and treachery from lines 182–3.)   **192 companion** (1) comrade (2) rascally knave   **193 what is man** i.e., any true man; or, what is manly.

LAFEW   To what is count's man. Count's master is of   194
  another style.   195

PAROLLES   You are too old, sir; let it satisfy you, you are   196
  too old.

LAFEW   I must tell thee, sirrah, I write man, to which   198
  title age cannot bring thee.

PAROLLES   What I dare too well do, I dare not do.   200

LAFEW   I did think thee, for two ordinaries, to be a   201
  pretty wise fellow; thou didst make tolerable vent of   202
  thy travel; it might pass. Yet the scarves and the   203
  bannerets about thee did manifoldly dissuade me   204
  from believing thee a vessel of too great a burden. I   205
  have now found thee. When I lose thee again, I care   206
  not; yet art thou good for nothing but taking up, and   207
  that thou'rt scarce worth.

PAROLLES   Hadst thou not the privilege of antiquity
  upon thee—

LAFEW   Do not plunge thyself too far in anger, lest thou
  hasten thy trial; which if—Lord have mercy on thee   212

194–5 **Count's . . . style** i.e., "Man" and "master" are worlds
apart, and you belong to the first.   196 **too old** i.e., for me to
duel with.   **let . . . you** i.e., take that as a satisfaction instead of
a duel   198 **write man** i.e., account myself a man, lay claim to
that title   200 **What . . . not do** i.e., What I could too easily
accomplish—thrash you—I must not do because of your age.
201 **for two ordinaries** during the space of two meals
202 **didst . . . of** discoursed tolerably upon   203–4 **scarves,
bannerets** i.e., soldiers' scarves, reminding Lafew of a ship's
pennants   205 **burden** cargo, capacity.   206 **found** found out.
lose thee lose your company. (With a play on the antithesis of
"find" and "lose.")   207 **yet . . . taking up** you are like a
commodity one *takes up* in the sense of taking a loan at exorbitant
rates of interest and being paid in shoddy goods not worth the
amount borrowed   212 **thy trial** i.e., the testing of your
supposed valor

for a hen! So, my good window of lattice, fare thee 213
well. Thy casement I need not open, for I look through 214
thee. Give me thy hand.

PAROLLES My lord, you give me most egregious indig- 216
nity.

LAFEW Ay, with all my heart, and thou art worthy of it.

PAROLLES I have not, my lord, deserved it.

LAFEW Yes, good faith, every dram of it, and I will not 220
bate thee a scruple. 221

PAROLLES Well, I shall be wiser. 222

LAFEW Even as soon as thou canst, for thou hast to pull 223
at a smack o'th' contrary. If ever thou be'st bound in 224
thy scarf and beaten, thou shall find what it is to be 225
proud of thy bondage. I have a desire to hold my ac- 226
quaintance with thee, or rather my knowledge, that I
may say in the default, "He is a man I know." 228

---

213 **hen** i.e., cackling, cowardly female.   **window of lattice**
wooden frame with cross-hatched slats (instead of glass), often
painted red and used as the sign of an alehouse; something easily
seen through and common, disreputable   214 **casement**
window sash   216 **give** offer. (But Lafew mockingly replies as
though he were indeed making a valuable gift. He plays with
deserved the same way in lines 220–1: "Oh, you *deserved* it, all
right.")   **egregious** outrageous, flagrant   220 **dram** bit.
(Literally, one-eighth of an ounce.)   221 **bate** abate, remit.
scruple smallest bit. (Literally, one-third of a dram.)   222 **wiser**
i.e., wiser than to deal with such dotards in the future. (But Lafew
jestingly answers that Parolles indeed has to learn to be wise, i.e.,
less foolish.)   223–4 **for . . . contrary** i.e., because it's necessary
for you to have a taste of your own folly before you can be called
self-knowing and wise.   224–5 **If . . . beaten** i.e., If even you are
subjected to one of the greatest indignities an officer can suffer, to
be tied up in the scarves you festoon yourself with and thrashed as
a poltroon. (See note 248–50 below.)   226 **bondage** i.e., the
scarf, in which you would be bound and of which you are now
vainly proud.   **hold** continue   228 **in the default** when you
default, i.e., show your emptiness on being brought to trial

PAROLLES   My lord, you do me most insupportable
   vexation.

LAFEW   I would it were hell-pains for thy sake, and my   231
   poor doing eternal; for doing I am past, as I will by   232
   thee, in what motion age will give me leave.   *Exit.*   233

PAROLLES   Well, thou hast a son shall take this disgrace   234
   off me—scurvy, old, filthy, scurvy lord! Well, I must   235
   be patient; there is no fettering of authority. I'll beat   236
   him, by my life, if I can meet him with any conve-   237
   nience, an he were double and double a lord. I'll have   238
   no more pity of his age than I would have of—I'll beat
   him, an if I could but meet him again.   240

      Enter Lafew.

LAFEW   Sirrah, your lord and master's married; there's
   news for you. You have a new mistress.

PAROLLES   I most unfeignedly beseech Your Lordship to
   make some reservation of your wrongs. He is my   244
   good lord; whom I serve above is my master.   245

LAFEW   Who? God?

PAROLLES   Ay, sir.

231–2 **my poor doing** i.e., my inadequate power to teach you a
lesson   232 **for doing** for energetic activity. (With a sexual
suggestion.)   232–3 **will by thee** i.e., will pass by you. (Punning
on *past*, "passed.")   233 **in . . . leave** with whatever speed age
will allow me.   234–5 **shall . . . me** i.e., on whom I will
vindicate myself for these insults. (Parolles, pretending to be
unwilling to fight Lafew because of the latter's older years, asserts
that only a son of Lafew would be a fit opponent for Parolles in a
duel.)   236 **there . . . authority** there's no use trying to bring a
figure of authority like Lafew to account.   237–8 **with any
convenience** on a suitable occasion   238 **an** even if   240 **an if**
if   244 **make . . . wrongs** put some restraint upon your insults,
qualify the insults you've given me.   245 **good lord** i.e., patron
(not master, as Lafew has insultingly said).   **whom** i.e., he
whom (God)

LAFEW   The devil it is that's thy master. Why dost thou   248
garter up thy arms o' this fashion? Dost make hose of   249
thy sleeves? Do other servants so? Thou wert best set   250
thy lower part where thy nose stands. By mine honor,   251
if I were but two hours younger, I'd beat thee.
Methink'st thou art a general offense, and every man
should beat thee. I think thou wast created for men to
breathe themselves upon thee.   255

PAROLLES   This is hard and undeserved measure, my
lord.

LAFEW   Go to, sir. You were beaten in Italy for picking   258
a kernel out of a pomegranate. You are a vagabond   259
and no true traveler. You are more saucy with lords   260
and honorable personages than the commission of   261
your birth and virtue gives you heraldry. You are not   262
worth another word, else I'd call you knave. I leave
you.   *Exit.*

PAROLLES   Good, very good! It is so, then. Good, very
good. Let it be concealed awhile.

Enter [Bertram] Count Rossillion.

BERTRAM   Undone, and forfeited to cares forever!

PAROLLES   What's the matter, sweetheart?

248–50 Why . . . sleeves? (Parolles apparently has decorative
scarves tied around the sleeves of his outfit. Lafew acidly points
out that the *hose* or breeches would be a fitter place for such
decorations in Parolles's case.)   **249 o'** of, in   **250–1 Thou . . .
stands** i.e., Mixing up sleeves and breeches is turning things upside
down, as if your ass were where your nose is. (With a scatological
suggestion of smelling one's own excrement.)   **255 breathe**
exercise   **258–9 for . . . pomegranate** i.e., for some petty
offense, or, on a slight pretext.   **259 vagabond** (A word used by
the authorities to describe actors—thus inviting sympathy for
Parolles, a play-actor to the core, whose business, like theirs, is
words.)   **260 saucy** unbecomingly familiar   **261 commission**
warrant   **262 gives you heraldry** entitles you to be.

BERTRAM Although before the solemn priest I have
sworn, I will not bed her.

PAROLLES What, what, sweetheart?

BERTRAM
Oh, my Parolles, they have married me!
I'll to the Tuscan wars, and never bed her.

PAROLLES France is a dog-hole, and it no more merits
the tread of a man's foot. To th' wars!

BERTRAM There's letters from my mother. What th'im-   276
port is I know not yet.

PAROLLES Ay, that would be known. To th' wars, my
boy, to th' wars!
He wears his honor in a box unseen
That hugs his kicky-wicky here at home,   281
Spending his manly marrow in her arms,   282
Which should sustain the bound and high curvet   283
Of Mars's fiery steed. To other regions!
France is a stable, we that dwell in't jades.   285
Therefore, to th' war!

BERTRAM
It shall be so. I'll send her to my house,
Acquaint my mother with my hate to her
And wherefore I am fled, write to the King
That which I durst not speak. His present gift
Shall furnish me to those Italian fields   291
Where noble fellows strike. Wars is no strife
To the dark house and the detested wife.   293

---

276 **letters** i.e., a letter   281 **kicky-wicky** woman. (With sexual
suggestion, as also in *box* in the previous line and *Spending* and
marrow in the following line.)   282 **manly marrow** masculine
essence, semen   283 **curvet** leap   285 **jades** worn-out horses.
291 **furnish me** (Knights customarily provided themselves with
trappings and armed retainers when enlisting in warlike
enterprises.)   293 **To . . . house** i.e., compared to the madhouse
(of marriage)

PAROLLES

 Will this capriccio hold in thee? Art sure?   294

BERTRAM

 Go with me to my chamber and advise me.

 I'll send her straight away. Tomorrow   296

 I'll to the wars, she to her single sorrow.

PAROLLES

 Why, these balls bound; there's noise in it. 'Tis hard! 298

 A young man married is a man that's marred.

 Therefore away, and leave her bravely. Go.

 The King has done you wrong, but hush, 'tis so.

              Exeunt.

[2.4]   ❧ *Enter Helena [with a letter], and Clown [Lavatch].*

HELENA

 My mother greets me kindly. Is she well?

LAVATCH She is not well, but yet she has her health. 2
She's very merry, but yet she is not well. But thanks
be given, she's very well and wants nothing i'th'
world; but yet she is not well.

HELENA If she be very well, what does she ail that she's
not very well?

LAVATCH Truly, she's very well indeed, but for two
things.

HELENA What two things?

294 **capriccio** caprice, whim 296 **straight** at once
298 **Why . . . hard!** i.e., Now you're talking; that's the way! (*Balls*
here are tennis balls.)

2.4 Location: Paris. The royal court.
2 **not well** (Referring to the Elizabethan euphemism by which the
dead were spoken of as "well," i.e., well rid of this life and well off
in heaven.)

LAVATCH   One, that she's not in heaven, whither God send her quickly. The other, that she's in earth, from whence God send her quickly.

Enter Parolles.

PAROLLES   Bless you, my fortunate lady!

HELENA   I hope, sir, I have your good will to have mine   15
own good fortunes.   16

PAROLLES   You had my prayers to lead them on, and to   17
keep them on have them still.—Oh, my knave, how   18
does my old lady?

LAVATCH   So that you had her wrinkles and I her   20
money, I would she did as you say.   21

PAROLLES   Why, I say nothing.

LAVATCH   Marry, you are the wiser man, for many a
man's tongue shakes out his master's undoing. To say   24
nothing, to do nothing, to know nothing, and to have
nothing is to be a great part of your title, which is   26
within a very little of nothing.

PAROLLES   Away! Thou'rt a knave.

LAVATCH   You should have said, sir, "Before a knave   29
thou'rt a knave"; that's, "Before me thou'rt a knave."   30
This had been truth, sir.

15–16 **I hope . . . fortunes** I hope my good fortunes need not depend on your good wishes, if you don't mind my saying so. 17 **them** i.e., your good fortunes. (A plural concept.) 17–18 **to . . . still** to maintain your good fortune, you have my prayers continually.   20–1 **So . . . say** Provided you were old (and wise), like her, and I had her wealth, I'd be happy to have her follow your advice.   24 **man's** servant's.   **shakes out** i.e., brings about by talking too freely   26 **your title** i.e., your reputation for being all bluster and no substance. (With wordplay on *title/tittle,* any tiny amount.)   29 **Before** In presence of 30 **Before me** i.e., Upon my soul. (But, by substituting *me* for *knave,* Lavatch suggests that Parolles call himself a knave.)

PAROLLES Go to, thou art a witty fool. I have found   32
thee.   33

LAVATCH Did you find me in yourself, sir? Or were   34
you taught to find me? The search, sir, was profitable;
and much fool may you find in you, even to the
world's pleasure and the increase of laughter.

PAROLLES
A good knave, i'faith, and well fed.—   38
Madam, my lord will go away tonight;
A very serious business calls on him.
The great prerogative and rite of love,
Which, as your due time claims, he does
    acknowledge,   42
But puts if off to a compelled restraint,   43
Whose want and whose delays is strewed with
    sweets,   44
Which they distill now in the curbèd time,   45
To make the coming hour o'erflow with joy
And pleasure drown the brim.

HELENA   What's his will else?   47

PAROLLES
That you will take your instant leave o'th' King
And make this haste as your own good proceeding,   49

32–3 **found thee** found you out, found you to be a fool.
34 **Did . . . sir?** i.e., Did you find folly in yourself, sir? (Since I,
Lavatch, am a fool.)   38 **well fed** (Referring to the proverb
"better fed than taught," as at 2.2.3.)   42 **Which . . .
acknowledge** he does acknowledge as your due, in the fullness of
time, the rite and privilege of sexual consummation   43 **to**
owing to   44 **Whose . . . sweets** the desire for which, being
delayed, is made all the sweeter by waiting, like perfume made
sweeter by distillation. (*Sweets* are sweet-smelling flowers.)
45 **Which . . . time** which sweet-smelling flowers of desire and
delay distill their essence into this period of restraint   47 **drown**
overflow.   **else** besides.   49 **make** represent.   **proceeding**
course of action

Strengthened with what apology you think
May make it probable need.

HELENA   What more commands he?   51

PAROLLES
That, having this obtained, you presently
Attend his further pleasure.   53

HELENA
In every thing I wait upon his will.

PAROLLES   I shall report it so.

HELENA   I pray you.   *Exit Parolles*.
[*To Lavatch*]   Come, sirrah.   *Exeunt*.

[2.5] ⤳ *Enter Lafew and Bertram*.

LAFEW   But I hope Your Lordship thinks not him a
    soldier.

BERTRAM   Yes, my lord, and of very valiant approof.   3

LAFEW   You have it from his own deliverance.   4

BERTRAM   And by other warranted testimony.

LAFEW   Then my dial goes not true. I took this lark for   6
    a bunting.   7

BERTRAM   I do assure you, my lord, he is very great in
    knowledge, and accordingly valiant.   9

---

51 **probable need** a plausible necessity.   53 **Attend** await.
pleasure command.

2.5 Location. Paris. The royal court.
3 **valiant approof** proven valor.   4 **deliverance** testimony,
word.   6 **dial** clock, compass, i.e., judgment   6–7 **I . . .
bunting** i.e., I underestimated him. (The bunting resembles the
lark but lacks the lark's beautiful song. Lafew suggests that Parolles
is all show and no substance. Compare 1.2.18, where, in the Folio,
Bertram is called Count *Rosignoll*, nightingale.)   9 **accordingly**
correspondingly

LAFEW   I have then sinned against his experience and
transgressed against his valor; and my state that way   11
is dangerous, since I cannot yet find in my heart to   12
repent. Here he comes. I pray you, make us friends; I
will pursue the amity.

   Enter Parolles.

PAROLLES [*to Bertram*]   These things shall be done, sir.

LAFEW [*to Bertram*]   Pray you, sir, who's his tailor?   16

PAROLLES   Sir?

LAFEW   Oh, I know him well. Ay, sir, he, sir, 's a good   18
workman, a very good tailor.   19

BERTRAM [*aside to Parolles*]   Is she gone to the King?

PAROLLES   She is.

BERTRAM   Will she away tonight?

PAROLLES   As you'll have her.

BERTRAM
I have writ my letters, casketed my treasure,
Given order for our horses; and tonight,
When I should take possession of the bride,
End ere I do begin.

LAFEW   A good traveler is something at the latter end of   28
a dinner; but one that lies three thirds, and uses a   29
known truth to pass a thousand nothings with, should

---

11 **my state** i.e., the state of my soul. (Lafew uses an elaborate
metaphor of religious penitence ironically.)   12 **find in** find it
in   16 **who's his tailor?** i.e., what tailor made this stuffed
(bombast) figure? (Lafew says this to Bertram but is taunting
Parolles, who replies indignantly.)   18–19 **Oh . . . tailor** (Lafew
mockingly takes Parolles's *Sir* in line 17 as the name of his tailor.)
28–9 **A good . . . dinner** i.e., A person with many traveling
experiences is an asset as a storyteller after dinner   29 **three
thirds** i.e., all the time

be once heard and thrice beaten. God save you, Captain.

BERTRAM [to Parolles] Is there any unkindness between 33
my lord and you, monsieur?

PAROLLES I know not how I have deserved to run into
my lord's displeasure.

LAFEW You have made shift to run into't, boots and 37
spurs and all, like him that leapt into the custard; and 38
out of it you'll run again, rather than suffer question 39
for your residence. 40

BERTRAM It may be you have mistaken him, my lord. 41

LAFEW And shall do so ever, though I took him at 's
prayers. Fare you well, my lord, and believe this of
me: there can be no kernel in this light nut. The soul
of this man is his clothes. Trust him not in matter of
heavy consequence. I have kept of them tame, and 46
know their natures.—Farewell, monsieur. I have
spoken better of you than you have or will to deserve 48
at my hand; but we must do good against evil.

[Exit.]

PAROLLES An idle lord, I swear. 50

BERTRAM I think so. 51

33 **unkindness** ill will   37 **made shift** contrived (at our
previous meeting)   38 **like . . . custard** i.e., like a clown at a city
entertainment jumping into a large, deep custard   39 **you'll run**
you will want to run   39–40 **suffer . . . residence** undergo
questioning about your being there, i.e., explain how your
cowardice displeased me.   41 **mistaken him** misjudged him.
(But Lafew deliberately takes the phrase in the sense of "taken
exception to his behavior.")   46 **heavy** serious.   **I . . . tame** I
have kept tame creatures of this kind (for the amusement they
provide)   48 **have . . . deserve** have deserved or are likely to
deserve   50 **idle** foolish   51 **I think so** i.e., I suppose you're
right. (Parolles emphasizes *know* in the next line to contrast with
think.)

PAROLLES   Why, do you not know him?

BERTRAM
Yes, I do know him well, and common speech
Gives him a worthy pass. Here comes my clog.   54

    Enter Helena.

HELENA
I have, sir, as I was commanded from you,
Spoke with the King, and have procured his leave
For present parting; only he desires
Some private speech with you.

BERTRAM   I shall obey his will.
You must not marvel, Helen, at my course,
Which holds not color with the time, nor does   60
The ministration and requirèd office   61
On my particular. Prepared I was not   62
For such a business; therefore am I found
So much unsettled. This drives me to entreat you
That presently you take your way for home;
And rather muse than ask why I entreat you,   66
For my respects are better than they seem,   67
And my appointments have in them a need   68
Greater than shows itself at the first view
To you that know them not. This to my mother.

                               [He gives a letter.]
'Twill be two days ere I shall see you, so
I leave you to your wisdom.

HELENA   Sir, I can nothing say   72
But that I am your most obedient servant.

---

54 **pass** reputation.   **clog** a heavy weight attached to the leg or
neck of a man or animal to prevent freedom of movement.
60–2 **Which . . . particular** which does not appear to suit with
the occasion (of our marriage), nor does it fulfill what is
incumbent upon me as a husband.   66 **muse** wonder   67 **my
respects** the circumstances prompting me   68 **appointments**
purposes   72 **to your wisdom** to do what you think best.

BERTRAM
Come, come, no more of that.

HELENA   And ever shall
With true observance seek to eke out that   75
Wherein toward me my homely stars have failed   76
To equal my great fortune.

BERTRAM   Let that go.
My haste is very great. Farewell. Hie home.   78

                              [*He starts to go.*]

HELENA
Pray, sir, your pardon.

BERTRAM   Well, what would you say?

HELENA
I am not worthy of the wealth I owe,   80
Nor dare I say 'tis mine, and yet it is;
But, like a timorous thief, most fain would steal   82
What law does vouch mine own.

BERTRAM   What would you have?   83

HELENA
Something, and scarce so much; nothing, indeed.
I would not tell you what I would, my lord. Faith,
    yes—
Strangers and foes do sunder, and not kiss.   86

BERTRAM
I pray you, stay not, but in haste to horse.   87

HELENA
I shall not break your bidding, good my lord.

75 **observance** dutiful and reverential service.   **eke out** add
to   76 **homely stars** i.e., lowly origin   78 **Hie** Hasten
80 **owe** own   82 **fain** gladly   83 **vouch** affirm to be
86 **Strangers . . . kiss** i.e., Only strangers and enemies depart
from one another without a farewell kiss.   87 **stay** delay

BERTRAM [to Parolles]

Where are my other men, monsieur?—Farewell.

Exit [Helena.]

Go thou toward home, where I will never come

Whilst I can shake my sword or hear the drum.

Away, and for our flight.

PAROLLES   Bravely, coraggio!   [Exeunt.]   92

3.1 ·S· *Flourish. Enter the Duke of Florence [attended];*
the two Frenchmen, with a troop of soldiers.

DUKE

So that from point to point now have you heard

The fundamental reasons of this war,

Whose great decision hath much blood let forth,   3

And more thirsts after.

FIRST LORD   Holy seems the quarrel   4

Upon Your Grace's part, black and fearful

On the opposer.   6

DUKE

Therefore we marvel much our cousin France   7

Would in so just a business shut his bosom

Against our borrowing prayers.

SECOND LORD   Good my lord,   9

92 *coraggio!* courage, bravo!

3.1 *Location: Florence.*
3–4 **Whose . . . after** the violent deciding of which has led to
much shedding of blood and a thirsting after still more.   6 **the**
opposer the opposer's part.   7 **cousin** i.e., fellow sovereign
9 **borrowing prayers** prayers for assistance.

The reasons of our state I cannot yield   10
But like a common and an outward man   11
That the great figure of a council frames   12
By self-unable motion, therefore dare not   13
Say what I think of it, since I have found
Myself in my incertain grounds to fail
As often as I guessed.

DUKE   Be it his pleasure.   16

FIRST LORD
But I am sure the younger of our nature,   17
That surfeit on their ease, will day by day   18
Come here for physic.

DUKE   Welcome shall they be,   19
And all the honors that can fly from us   20
Shall on them settle. You know your places well;
When better fall, for your avails they fell.   22
Tomorrow to the field.   *Flourish.* [*Exeunt.*]

[3.2] ✥ *Enter Countess and Clown* [*Lavatch*].

COUNTESS   It hath happened all as I would have had it,
save that he comes not along with her.

10–13 **The reasons . . . motion** I cannot explain to you the
rationale of our statecraft other than as an ordinary citizen, not
being privy to the workings of the state; I am one who constructs
in his own imagination an imperfect idea of whatever grand
schemes the King and his counsel may be devising   16 **Be . . .
pleasure** i.e., Be it as the King of France wishes.   17 **nature**
outlook, disposition   18 **surfeit** grow sick   19 **physic** i.e.,
cure of their surfeit (through bloodletting).   20 **can fly from us**
i.e., we can grant   22 **When . . . fell** whenever better places fall
vacant, they will have done so for you to fill.

3.2 Location: Rossillion.

LAVATCH   By my troth, I take my young lord to be a   3
very melancholy man.

COUNTESS   By what observance, I pray you?   5

LAVATCH   Why, he will look upon his boot and sing,
mend the ruff and sing, ask questions and sing, pick   7
his teeth and sing. I know a man that had this trick of   8
melancholy sold a goodly manor for a song.   9

COUNTESS   Let me see what he writes and when he
means to come.   [*Opening a letter.*]

LAVATCH   I have no mind to Isbel since I was at court.
Our old lings and our Isbels o'th' country are nothing   13
like your old ling and your Isbels o'th' court. The
brains of my Cupid's knocked out, and I begin to love
as an old man loves money, with no stomach.   16

COUNTESS   What have we here?

LAVATCH   E'en that you have there.   *Exit.*   18

COUNTESS [*reads*] *a letter.*   "I have sent you a daughter-
in-law. She hath recovered the King and undone me.   20
I have wedded her, not bedded her, and sworn to
make the 'not' eternal. You shall hear I am run away;   22
know it before the report come. If there be breadth
enough in the world, I will hold a long distance. My   24
duty to you.

Your unfortunate son,
Bertram."

---

3 **troth** faith   5 **observance** observation   7 **mend the ruff**
adjust the loose turned-over flap at the top of his boot or his frilled
collar   7–8 **pick his teeth** (An affected mannerism, as at 1.1.159.)
9 **sold** who sold   13 **lings** cunts. Lavatch is saying that all
women, both old ("old lings") and young ("Isbels"), are much
better at the court than in the country.   16 **stomach** appetite.
18 **E'en . . . there** (The Clown is playfully literal: to the Countess's
"What's this?" he replies, "It looks like a letter.")   20 **recovered**
cured   22 **not** (With a pun on "knot.")   24 **hold a long
distance** stay far away.

This is not well, rash and unbridled boy,
To fly the favors of so good a king,
To pluck his indignation on thy head   30
By the misprizing of a maid too virtuous   31
For the contempt of empire.   32

            Enter Clown [Lavatch].

LAVATCH   O madam, yonder is heavy news within   33
            between two soldiers and my young lady!

COUNTESS   What is the matter?

LAVATCH   Nay, there is some comfort in the news,
            some comfort. Your son will not be killed so soon as I
            thought he would.

COUNTESS   Why should he be killed?

LAVATCH   So say I, madam, if he run away, as I hear he
            does. The danger is in standing to't; that's the loss of   41
            men, though it be the getting of children. Here they   42
            come will tell you more. For my part, I only hear your
            son was run away.   [Exit.]   44

            *Enter Helena and [the] two [French] Gentlemen
            [or Lords].*

SECOND LORD   Save you, good madam.

HELENA
            Madam, my lord is gone, forever gone!

FIRST LORD   Do not say so.

COUNTESS
            Think upon patience.—Pray you, gentlemen,
            I have felt so many quirks of joy and grief

30 **pluck** bring down   31 **misprizing** scorning, failing to
appreciate   32 **of empire** of even an emperor.   33 **heavy** sad
41 **standing to't** standing one's ground. (With sexual pun. The
Clown jests on running from a battle and running from a woman;
in both cases, a soldier can avoid the *danger* of dying; with its
suggestion of sexual climax.)   42 **getting** begetting   44 **was** has

That the first face of neither, on the start,   50
Can woman me unto't. Where is my son, I pray you?   51

FIRST LORD
Madam, he's gone to serve the Duke of Florence.
We met him thitherward; for thence we came,   53
And, after some dispatch in hand at court,   54
Thither we bend again.   55

HELENA
Look on his letter, madam; here's my passport.   56
[*She reads.*] "When thou canst get the ring upon my
finger, which never shall come off, and show me a
child begotten of thy body that I am father to, then call
me husband; but in such a 'then' I write a 'never.' "
This is a dreadful sentence.   61

COUNTESS
Brought you this letter, gentlemen?

FIRST LORD   Ay, madam,
And for the contents' sake are sorry for our pains.

COUNTESS
I prithee, lady, have a better cheer.
If thou engrossest all the griefs are thine,   65
Thou robb'st me of a moi'ty. He was my son,   66
But I do wash his name out of my blood,
And thou art all my child.—Towards Florence is he?   68

50–1 **That . . . unto't** i.e., that neither joy nor grief, appearing
so suddenly, can make me weep as women are supposed to do.
53 **thitherward** on his way there   54 **dispatch in hand**
business to be taken care of   55 **Thither . . . again** to
Florence we will direct our steps.   56 **passport** license to
wander as a beggar.   61 **sentence** (1) sentence of punishment
(2) statement, utterance.   65–6 **If thou . . . moi'ty** If you
refuse to share your griefs, you rob me of my right to half of
them (in that Bertram is my son).   68 **all my** my only

FIRST LORD
  Ay, madam.

COUNTESS   And to be a soldier?

FIRST LORD
  Such is his noble purpose; and, believe't,
  The Duke will lay upon him all the honor
  That good convenience claims.

COUNTESS   Return you thither?   72

SECOND LORD
  Ay, madam, with the swiftest wing of speed.

HELENA [*reading*]
  "Till I have no wife, I have nothing in France."
  'Tis bitter.

COUNTESS   Find you that there?

HELENA   Ay, madam.

SECOND LORD
  'Tis but the boldness of his hand, haply,   76
  Which his heart was not consenting to.

COUNTESS
  Nothing in France, until he have no wife!
  There's nothing here that is too good for him
  But only she, and she deserves a lord
  That twenty such rude boys might tend upon
  And call her, hourly, mistress. Who was with him?

SECOND LORD
  A servant only, and a gentleman
  Which I have sometime known.

COUNTESS   Parolles, was it not?

SECOND LORD   Ay, my good lady, he.

72 **That . . . claims** that he can in propriety claim.   76 **haply**
perhaps

COUNTESS
A very tainted fellow, and full of wickedness.
My son corrupts a well-derivèd nature   88
With his inducement.

SECOND LORD   Indeed, good lady,   89
The fellow has a deal of that too much   90
Which holds him much to have.   91

COUNTESS   You're welcome, gentlemen.
I will entreat you, when you see my son,
To tell him that his sword can never win
The honor that he loses. More I'll entreat you
Written to bear along.

FIRST LORD   We serve you, madam,   96
In that and all your worthiest affairs.

COUNTESS
Not so, but as we change our courtesies.   98
Will you draw near?   *Exit [with Gentlemen].*   99

HELENA
"Till I have no wife, I have nothing in France."
Nothing in France, until he has no wife!
Thou shalt have none, Rossillion, none in France;   102
Then hast thou all again. Poor lord, is't I
That chase thee from thy country and expose
Those tender limbs of thine to the event   105
Of the none-sparing war? And is it I
That drive thee from the sportive court, where thou   107

88–9 **My . . . inducement** My son corrupts the fine qualities he
inherited from his ancestors, through Parolles's corrupt influence.
90–1 **The fellow . . . have** The fellow has a great supply of that
"excess" which it would suit him better to restrain or withhold.
96 **Written . . . along** to take with you in the form of a letter.
98 **but . . . courtesies** i.e., only if I can repay or exchange your
courtesy with my own.   99 **draw near** come with me.
102 **Rossillion** i.e., Bertram (whom Helena refers to by his title)
105 **event** hazard, outcome   107 **sportive** amorous

Wast shot at with fair eyes, to be the mark   108
Of smoky muskets? O you leaden messengers,   109
That ride upon the violent speed of fire,
Fly with false aim; move the still-piecing air,   111
That sings with piercing; do not touch my lord!   112
Whoever shoots at him, I set him there;
Whoever charges on his forward breast,   114
I am the caitiff that do hold him to't;   115
And, though I kill him not, I am the cause
His death was so effected. Better 'twere
I met the ravin lion when he roared   118
With sharp constraint of hunger; better 'twere
That all the miseries which nature owes   120
Were mine at once. No, come thou home, Rossillion,
Whence honor but of danger wins a scar,   122
As oft it loses all. I will be gone.   123
My being here it is that holds thee hence.
Shall I stay here to do't? No, no, although   125
The air of paradise did fan the house
And angels officed all. I will be gone,   127
That pitiful rumor may report my flight   128
To consolate thine ear. Come, night; end, day!   129
For with the dark, poor thief, I'll steal away.   *Exit.*   130

108 **mark** target   109 **leaden messengers** i.e., bullets
111–12 **move . . . piercing** part the always-parting air, which
appears to be still but which whistles musically when a bullet
passes through it. (The Folio reading, "still-peering," is here
emended to "still-piecing," always parting and then closing again.)
114 **forward** facing forward in battle, in the van   115 **caitiff**
base wretch   118 **ravin** ravenous   120 **nature owes** human
nature possesses, suffers   122–3 **Whence . . . all** i.e., from war,
in which honor is at best rewarded for danger with a scar, and
often loses life itself.   125 **do't** i.e., keep you hence.
although even if   127 **officed all** performed all domestic duties.
128 **pitiful** compassionate   129 **consolate** console   130 **poor
thief** (The night is thief of the light of day; Helen is an unwilling
thief in having "stolen" the title of wife and in having to steal away.)

[3.3] ❧ *Flourish. Enter the Duke of Florence, [Bertram, Count] Rossillion, drum and trumpets, soldiers, Parolles.*

DUKE
The General of our Horse thou art, and we,
Great in our hope, lay our best love and credence   2
Upon thy promising fortune.

BERTRAM   Sir, it is
A charge too heavy for my strength, but yet
We'll strive to bear it for your worthy sake
To th'extreme edge of hazard.

DUKE   Then go thou forth,   6
And Fortune play upon thy prosperous helm,   7
As thy auspicious mistress!

BERTRAM   This very day,
Great Mars, I put myself into thy file.   9
Make me but like my thoughts, and I shall prove   10
A lover of thy drum, hater of love.   *Exeunt omnes.*

[3.4] ❧ *Enter Countess and Steward [Rinaldo].*

COUNTESS
Alas! And would you take the letter of her?
Might you not know she would do as she has done,
By sending me a letter? Read it again.

3.3 *Location: Florence.*
2 **Great** pregnant, expectant.   **lay** wager.   **credence** trust
6 **edge of hazard** limit of peril.   7 **helm** helmet   9 **file** battle
line; ranks, catalogue.   10 **like my thoughts** i.e., as valiant as I
aspire to be

3.4 *Location. Rossillion.*

RINALDO [*reads the*] *letter*
  "I am Saint Jaques' pilgrim, thither gone.   4
  Ambitious love hath so in me offended
  That barefoot plod I the cold ground upon,
  With sainted vow my faults to have amended.   7
  Write, write, that from the bloody course of war
  My dearest master, your dear son, may hie.   9
  Bless him at home in peace, whilst I from far
  His name with zealous fervor sanctify.
  His taken labors bid him me forgive;   12
  I, his despiteful Juno, sent him forth   13
  From courtly friends, with camping foes to live   14
  Where death and danger dogs the heels of worth.
  He is too good and fair for death and me;
  Whom I myself embrace, to set him free."   17

COUNTESS
  Ah, what sharp stings are in her mildest words!
  Rinaldo, you did never lack advice so much   19
  As letting her pass so. Had I spoke with her,
  I could have well diverted her intents,
  Which thus she hath prevented.

RINALDO   Pardon me, madam.   22
  If I had given you this at overnight,   23

4–17 (The letter is in the form of a sonnet.)   **4 Saint Jaques'**
pilgrim i.e., a pilgrim to the shrine of Saint James, presumably the
famous shrine of Santiago de Compostella in Spain   **4 Jaques'**
(Pronounced in two syllables.)   7 **sainted** (1) holy (2) offered to
a saint   9 **hie** hasten.   12 **His taken labors** The labors he has
undertaken   13 **despiteful Juno** spitefully jealous queen of
Olympus, who imposed on Hercules his twelve labors because he
was the product of one of Jupiter's many amours. She was also
partisan in the Trojan War on the Greek side because of the
abduction of Helen.   14 **camping** encamped, contending.
(Playing on the antithesis of court and military camp.)
17 **Whom** i.e., death   19 **advice** judgment   22 **prevented**
forestalled.   23 **at overnight** last night

She might have been o'erta'en; and yet she writes
Pursuit would be but vain.

COUNTESS   What angel shall
Bless this unworthy husband? He cannot thrive,
Unless her prayers, whom heaven delights to hear   27
And loves to grant, reprieve him from the wrath
Of greatest justice. Write, write, Rinaldo,
To this unworthy husband of his wife.   30
Let every word weigh heavy of her worth   31
That he does weigh too light. My greatest grief,
Though little he do feel it, set down sharply.
Dispatch the most convenient messenger.
When haply he shall hear that she is gone,
He will return; and hope I may that she,
Hearing so much, will speed her foot again,
Led hither by pure love. Which of them both
Is dearest to me, I have no skill in sense   39
To make distinction. Provide this messenger.   40
My heart is heavy and mine age is weak;
Grief would have tears, and sorrow bids me speak.
                                        Exeunt.

[3.5] ᕉᕽ *A tucket afar off. Enter old Widow of Florence,
        her daughter [Diana], and Mariana, with other
        citizens.*

WIDOW   Nay, come, for if they do approach the city we
        shall lose all the sight.   2

27 **her** i.e., Helena's. (Helena is likened to saints who can intercede
with heaven on behalf of a sinner.)   30 **unworthy . . . wife**
husband unworthy of his wife.   31 **weigh heavy of** emphasize
39 **in sense** in perception   40 **this messenger** a messenger to
carry this letter.

3.5 *Location: Florence. Outside the walls.*
0.1 *tucket* a trumpet fanfare   2 **lose . . . sight** miss seeing them.

DIANA   They say the French count has done most honorable service.

WIDOW   It is reported that he has taken their great'st   5
commander, and that with his own hand he slew the
Duke's brother. [*Tucket.*] We have lost our labor; they
are gone a contrary way. Hark! You may know by
their trumpets.

MARIANA   Come, let's return again and suffice ourselves   10
with the report of it.—Well, Diana, take heed of
this French earl. The honor of a maid is her name, and   12
no legacy is so rich as honesty.   13

WIDOW [*to Diana*]   I have told my neighbor how you   14
have been solicited by a gentleman, his companion.

MARIANA   I know that knave, hang him! One Parolles,
a filthy officer he is in those suggestions for the young   17
earl. Beware of them, Diana; their promises, entice-
ments, oaths, tokens, and all these engines of lust are   19
not the things they go under. Many a maid hath been   20
seduced by them; and the misery is, example, that so   21
terrible shows in the wreck of maidenhood, cannot for   22
all that dissuade succession, but that they are limed   23
with the twigs that threatens them. I hope I need not   24
to advise you further, but I hope your own grace will   25

---

5 **their** i.e., the Sienese's   10 **suffice** content   ·   12 **earl** i.e.,
Count Bertram.   **her name** her reputation (for chastity)
13 **honesty** chastity.   14 **my neighbor** i.e., Mariana
17 **officer** agent.   **suggestions for** solicitings on behalf of, or,
temptations of   19 **engines** artifices, devices   20 **go under**
pretend to be.   21–3 **example . . . succession** the dreadful
example of what happens with the loss of virginity nonetheless
cannot dissuade another from a similar course   23–4 **they . . .
twigs** i.e., other maidens are caught in the same trap. (Birdlime
was smeared on twigs to ensnare birds.)   25 **grace** virtuous
strength of grace given by God to resist temptation

keep you where you are, though there were no further   26
danger known but the modesty which is so lost.   27

DIANA   You shall not need to fear me.   28

Enter Helena [disguised like a pilgrim].

WIDOW   I hope so.—Look, here comes a pilgrim. I
know she will lie at my house; thither they send one   30
another. I'll question her.—God save you, pilgrim!
Whither are bound?   32

HELENA   To Saint Jaques le Grand.
Where do the palmers lodge, I do beseech you?   34

WIDOW
At the Saint Francis here beside the port.   35

HELENA   Is this the way?   (*A march afar.*)

WIDOW
Ay, marry, is't. Hark you, they come this way.
If you will tarry, holy pilgrim,
But till the troops come by,
I will conduct you where you shall be lodged,
The rather for I think I know your hostess
As ample as myself.   42

HELENA   Is it yourself?

WIDOW   If you shall please so, pilgrim.

HELENA
I thank you, and will stay upon your leisure.   45

WIDOW
You came, I think, from France?

HELENA   I did so.

26 **though** even though   26–7 **further danger** i.e., pregnancy
27 **modesty** chastity and chaste reputation   28 **fear** worry
about   30 **lie** lodge   32 **are** are you   34 **palmers** pilgrims
35 **the Saint Francis** the inn with the sign of Saint Francis.
port city gate   42 **ample** fully, completely   45 **stay . . .
leisure** await your convenience.

WIDOW

Here you shall see a countryman of yours
That has done worthy service.

HELENA   His name, I pray you?

DIANA

The Count Rossillion. Know you such a one?

HELENA

But by the ear, that hears most nobly of him.
His face I know not.

DIANA   Whatsome'er he is,
He's bravely taken here. He stole from France,   52
As 'tis reported, for the King had married him   53
Against his liking. Think you it is so?

HELENA

Ay, surely, mere the truth. I know his lady.   55

DIANA

There is a gentleman that serves the Count
Reports but coarsely of her.

HELENA   What's his name?

DIANA

Monsieur Parolles.

HELENA   Oh, I believe with him.   58
In argument of praise, or to the worth   59
Of the great Count himself, she is too mean   60
To have her name repeated. All her deserving   61
Is a reservèd honesty, and that   62
I have not heard examined.

DIANA   Alas, poor lady!   63
'Tis a hard bondage to become the wife
Of a detesting lord.

---

52 **bravely taken** highly regarded   53 **for** because   55 **mere**
absolutely   58 **believe** agree   59 **In argument of** As a subject for.
to compared to   60 **mean** lowly   61–2 **All . . . honesty** Her only
merit is a well-guarded chastity   63 **examined** doubted, questioned.

WIDOW
> I warrant, good creature, wheresoe'er she is,
> Her heart weighs sadly. This young maid might do
>   her
> A shrewd turn, if she pleased.

HELENA   How do you mean?   68
> Maybe the amorous Count solicits her
> In the unlawful purpose?

WIDOW   He does indeed,
> And brokes with all that can in such a suit   71
> Corrupt the tender honor of a maid.
> But she is armed for him and keeps her guard
> In honestest defense.   74

> *Drum and colors. Enter [Bertram] Count*
> *Rossillion, Parolles, and the whole army.*

MARIANA   The gods forbid else!   75

WIDOW   So, now they come.
> That is Antonio, the Duke's eldest son;
> That, Escalus.

HELENA   Which is the Frenchman?

DIANA   He,
> That with the plume. 'Tis a most gallant fellow.
> I would he loved his wife. If he were honester   80
> He were much goodlier. Is't not a handsome
>   gentleman?

HELENA   I like him well.

> *[The warriors pass in file and exit in succession.*
> *Parolles comes last.]*

---

68 **shrewd** crafty, cunning   71 **brokes** bargains   74 **honestest**
most chaste   75 **else** that it should be otherwise.
80 **honester** more honorable (and more chaste)

DIANA   'Tis pity he is not honest. Yond's that same knave
That leads him to these places. Were I his lady
I would poison that vile rascal.

HELENA   Which is he?

DIANA
That jackanapes with scarves. Why is he melancholy?   86

HELENA   Perchance he's hurt i'th' battle.

PAROLLES   Lose our drum? Well.

MARIANA   He's shrewdly vexed at something. Look, he   89
has spied us.

WIDOW [to Parolles]   Marry, hang you!

MARIANA [to Parolles]   And your courtesy, for a ring-   92
carrier!   93

Exeunt [Bertram and the last of the army,
Parolles among them].

WIDOW
The troop is past. Come, pilgrim, I will bring you
Where you shall host. Of enjoined penitents   95
There's four or five, to great Saint Jaques bound,
Already at my house.

HELENA   I humbly thank you.
Please it this matron and this gentle maid   98
To eat with us tonight, the charge and thanking   99
Shall be for me; and, to requite you further,   100
I will bestow some precepts of this virgin   101
Worthy the note.

BOTH   We'll take your offer kindly.   102

Exeunt.

---

86 **jackanapes** monkey   89 **shrewdly** sorely   92 **courtesy**
ceremonious bow   92–3 **ring-carrier** go-between.   95 **host**
lodge.   **enjoined penitents** those bound by oath to undertake
a pilgrimage as penance for sin   98 **Please it** If it please
99–100 **the charge . . . me** i.e., I will bear the expense and be
grateful at the same time   101 **of** on   102 **kindly** gratefully.

[3.6] ⌇ *Enter [Bertram] Count Rossillion, and the [two] Frenchmen, as at first.*

FIRST LORD   Nay, good my lord, put him to't. Let him   1
have his way.

SECOND LORD   If Your Lordship find him not a hilding,   3
hold me no more in your respect.

FIRST LORD   On my life, my lord, a bubble.

BERTRAM   Do you think I am so far deceived in him?

FIRST LORD   Believe it, my lord, in mine own direct
knowledge, without any malice, but to speak of him   8
as my kinsman, he's a most notable coward, an infi-   9
nite and endless liar, an hourly promise-breaker, the
owner of no one good quality worthy Your Lordship's
entertainment.   12

SECOND LORD   It were fit you knew him, lest, reposing   13
too far in his virtue, which he hath not, he might at
some great and trusty business in a main danger fail   15
you.

BERTRAM   I would I knew in what particular action to
try him.   18

SECOND LORD   None better than to let him fetch off his   19
drum, which you hear him so confidently undertake
to do.

FIRST LORD   I, with a troop of Florentines, will suddenly
surprise him; such I will have whom I am sure   23
he knows not from the enemy. We will bind and

___

3.6 Location: The Florentine camp.
0.2 as at first (See 3.1.0.2.)   1 **to't** i.e., to the test.   3 **hilding**
good-for-nothing   8–9 **to speak . . . kinsman** to speak as
candidly and fairly as I would even if he were my own kinsman
12 **entertainment** patronage.   13 **reposing** trusting
15 **trusty** demanding trustworthiness   18 **try** test   19 **fetch
off** recapture   23 **surprise** capture

hoodwink him so that he shall suppose no other but   25
that he is carried into the leaguer of the adversary's,   26
when we bring him to our own tents. Be but Your
Lordship present at his examination. If he do not, for
the promise of his life and in the highest compulsion
of base fear, offer to betray you and deliver all the intel-   30
ligence in his power against you, and that with the   31
divine forfeit of his soul upon oath, never trust my
judgment in anything.

SECOND LORD   Oh, for the love of laughter, let him fetch
his drum. He says he has a stratagem for't. When Your
Lordship sees the bottom of his success in't, and to   36
what metal this counterfeit lump of ore will be melted,
if you give him not John Drum's entertainment, your   38
inclining cannot be removed. Here he comes.   39

Enter Parolles.

FIRST LORD   [*aside to Bertram*]   Oh, for the love of
laughter, hinder not the honor of his design. Let him
fetch off his drum in any hand.   42

BERTRAM   How now, monsieur? This drum sticks sorely   43
in your disposition.   44

SECOND LORD   A pox on't, let it go. 'Tis but a drum.   45

PAROLLES   But a drum! Is't but a drum? A drum so lost!
There was excellent command—to charge in with our
horse upon our own wings and to rend our own   48
soldiers!

---

25 **hoodwink** blindfold   26 **leaguer** camp
30–1 **intelligence in his power** information at his command
36 **bottom** extent   38 **John Drum's entertainment** (Slang
phrase for a thorough beating and unceremonious dismissal.)
39 **inclining** partiality (for Parolles)   42 **in any hand** in any
case.   43–4 **sticks . . . disposition** i.e., greatly troubles you.
45 **A pox on't** Plague take it   48 **wings** flanks.   **rend** cut up,
attack

SECOND LORD That was not to be blamed in the com- 50
mand of the service. It was a disaster of war that 51
Caesar himself could not have prevented, if he had
been there to command.

BERTRAM Well, we cannot greatly condemn our success. 54
Some dishonor we had in the loss of that drum,
but it is not to be recovered.

PAROLLES It might have been recovered.

BERTRAM It might, but it is not now.

PAROLLES It is to be recovered. But that the merit of 59
service is seldom attributed to the true and exact
performer, I would have that drum or another, or *hic* 61
jacet. 62

BERTRAM Why, if you have a stomach, to't, monsieur! 63
If you think your mystery in stratagem can bring this 64
instrument of honor again into his native quarter, be 65
magnanimous in the enterprise and go on. I will grace 66
the attempt for a worthy exploit. If you speed well in 67
it, the Duke shall both speak of it and extend to you
what further becomes his greatness, even to the 69
utmost syllable of your worthiness.

PAROLLES By the hand of a soldier, I will undertake it.

BERTRAM But you must not now slumber in it.

PAROLLES I'll about it this evening, and I will presently 73
pen down my dilemmas, encourage myself in my 74

50–1 **in . . . service** upon the orders given for the action.
54 **we . . . success** i.e., we were successful enough.   59 **But
that** Were it not that   61–2 *hic jacet* Latin for *here lies,* the
beginning phrase of tomb inscriptions. Hence, Parolles means "I
would die in the attempt."   63 **stomach** appetite
64 **mystery** skill   65 **again . . . quarter** back home again
66 **grace** honor   67 **speed** succeed   69 **becomes** does credit
to   73 **presently** immediately   74 **pen . . . dilemmas** make
note of my difficult choices

certainty, put myself into my mortal preparation; and   75
by midnight look to hear further from me.

BERTRAM   May I be bold to acquaint His Grace you are
gone about it?

PAROLLES   I know not what the success will be, my
lord, but the attempt I vow.

BERTRAM   I know thou'rt valiant, and to the possibility   81
of thy soldiership will subscribe for thee. Farewell.   82

PAROLLES   I love not many words.   *Exit.*

FIRST LORD   No more than a fish loves water. Is not this
a strange fellow, my lord, that so confidently seems to
undertake this business, which he knows is not to be
done, damns himself to do, and dares better be   87
damned than to do't?   88

SECOND LORD   You do not know him, my lord, as we
do. Certain it is that he will steal himself into a man's
favor and for a week escape a great deal of discover-   91
ies; but when you find him out, you have him ever   92
after.

BERTRAM   Why, do you think he will make no deed at   94
all of this that so seriously he does address himself
unto?

FIRST LORD   None in the world, but return with an
invention, and clap upon you two or three probable   98
lies. But we have almost embossed him. You shall see   99

---

75 **my mortal preparation** spiritual preparedness for my death;
or, death-dealing readiness   81 **possibility** capacity
82 **subscribe** vouch   87–8 **damns . . . do't** i.e., swears perjured
oaths to carry out the mission, but ends up damned if he does and
damned if he doesn't.   91–2 **escape . . . discoveries** i.e., almost
get away with it   92 **have him** have a true knowledge of him
94 **deed** attempt   98 **invention** fabrication.   **probable**
plausible   99 **embossed** driven to exhaustion, cornered. (A
hunting term.)

his fall tonight; for indeed he is not for Your Lordship's   100
respect.   101

SECOND LORD   We'll make you some sport with the fox
ere we case him. He was first smoked by the old lord   103
Lafew. When his disguise and he is parted, tell me   104
what a sprat you shall find him, which you shall see   105
this very night.

FIRST LORD
I must go look my twigs. He shall be caught.   107

BERTRAM
Your brother he shall go along with me.   108

FIRST LORD
As't please Your Lordship. I'll leave you.   [Exit.]

BERTRAM
Now will I lead you to the house and show you
The lass I spoke of.

SECOND LORD   But you say she's honest.   111

BERTRAM
That's all the fault. I spoke with her but once
And found her wondrous cold; but I sent to her,
By this same coxcomb that we have i'th' wind,   114
Tokens and letters, which she did re-send,   115
And this is all I have done. She's a fair creature.
Will you go see her?

SECOND LORD   With all my heart, my lord.

                                        Exeunt.

---

100 **not for** not worthy of   101 **respect** regard.   103 **case**
skin, strip, unmask.   **smoked** smelled out; smoked out into the
open   104 **is parted** are separated   105 **sprat** a small fish; a
contemptible creature   107 **look my twigs** i.e., see to my trap
(as in catching birds with birdlime on twigs).   108 **Your brother**
i.e., the Second Lord   111 **honest** chaste.   114 **coxcomb** fool.
have i'th' wind have to our downwind side, whom we are
tracking   115 **re-send** send back

[3.7] ✧ *Enter Helena and Widow.*

HELENA
    If you misdoubt me that I am not she,   1
    I know not how I shall assure you further
    But I shall lose the grounds I work upon.   3

WIDOW
    Though my estate be fall'n, I was well born,   4
    Nothing acquainted with these businesses,
    And would not put my reputation now
    In any staining act.

HELENA   Nor would I wish you.
    First give me trust the Count he is my husband,   8
    And what to your sworn counsel I have spoken   9
    Is so from word to word; and then you cannot,   10
    By the good aid that I of you shall borrow,   11
    Err in bestowing it.

WIDOW   I should believe you,
    For you have showed me that which well approves   13
    You're great in fortune.

HELENA [*giving money*]   Take this purse of gold,
    And let me buy your friendly help thus far,
    Which I will overpay and pay again
    When I have found it. The Count he woos your
        daughter,   17
    Lays down his wanton siege before her beauty,

3.7 Location: Florence. The Widow's house.
1 **misdoubt** doubt   3 **But . . . upon** i.e., without abandoning
my disguise and thus forfeiting the ground upon which my plans
are built.   4 **estate** worldly condition   8 **give me trust**
believe me (that)   9 **to . . . counsel** to your private
understanding, guarded by your oath of secrecy   10 **Is so . . . to
word** is true in every word   11 **By** with regard to
13 **approves** proves   17 **found it** i.e., received your help with
success.

Resolved to carry her. Let her in fine consent,   19
As we'll direct her how 'tis best to bear it.   20
Now his important blood will naught deny   21
That she'll demand. A ring the County wears,   22
That downward hath succeeded in his house
From son to son some four or five descents
Since the first father wore it. This ring he holds
In most rich choice, yet, in his idle fire,   26
To buy his will it would not seem too dear,   27
Howe'er repented after.

WIDOW
Now I see the bottom of your purpose.

HELENA
You see it lawful, then. It is no more
But that your daughter, ere she seems as won,
Desires this ring; appoints him an encounter;   32
In fine, delivers me to fill the time,
Herself most chastely absent. After,
To marry her, I'll add three thousand crowns   35
To what is passed already.

WIDOW   I have yielded.
Instruct my daughter how she shall persever,
That time and place with this deceit so lawful
May prove coherent. Every night he comes   39
With musics of all sorts, and songs composed   40
To her unworthiness. It nothing steads us   41

19 **carry** win.   **in fine** finally, or, to sum up. (As also in line 33.)
20 **bear** manage   21 **important blood** importunate passion
22 **That** whatever.   **County** Count   26 **choice** estimation,
regard.   **idle fire** foolish passion   27 **will** sexual desire
32 **appoints him an encounter** arranges a rendezvous   35 **To**
marry her as her dowry   39 **coherent** suitable.   40 **musics**
musicians   41 **To her unworthiness** to her, my humble
daughter; or, to the end of persuading her to do an unworthy
deed.   **nothing steads us** profits us not at all

To chide him from our eaves, for he persists   42
As if his life lay on't.

HELENA   Why then tonight   43
Let us essay our plot, which, if it speed,   44
Is wicked meaning in a lawful deed,   45
And lawful meaning in a wicked act,   46
Where both not sin, and yet a sinful fact.   47
But let's about it.   [*Exeunt.*]

4.1 ◆ *Enter one of the Frenchmen [the First Lord]*
     with five or six other Soldiers, in ambush.

FIRST LORD   He can come no other way but by this
hedge corner. When you sally upon him, speak what   2
terrible language you will. Though you understand it   3
not yourselves, no matter; for we must not seem to
understand him, unless someone among us whom   5
we must produce for an interpreter.

FIRST SOLDIER   Good Captain, let me be th'interpreter.

FIRST LORD   Art not acquainted with him? Knows he
not thy voice?

FIRST SOLDIER   No, sir, I warrant you.

FIRST LORD   But what linsey-woolsey hast thou to   11
speak to us again?   12

---

42 **chide . . . eaves** i.e., drive him away   43 **lay** depended
44 **essay** try.   **speed** succeed   45–6 **Is . . . act** i.e., is wicked
intention (on Bertram's part) converted into a lawful act of sex
between married partners, and lawful intent (on Helena's part)
carried out in an ethically dubious way   47 **fact** deed (which
would have been sinful as Bertram intended it).

4.1 *Location: Outside the Florentine camp.*
2 **sally** rush out   3 **terrible** terrifying   5 **unless** except for
11 **linsey-woolsey** a fabric woven from wool and flax; figuratively,
a hodge-podge   12 **again** in reply.

FIRST SOLDIER E'en such as you speak to me.

FIRST LORD He must think us some band of strangers 14
i'th'adversary's entertainment. Now he hath a smack 15
of all neighboring languages. Therefore we must every 16
one be a man of his own fancy, not to know what we 17
speak one to another; so we seem to know is to know 18
straight our purpose: choughs' language, gabble 19
enough and good enough. As for you, interpreter,
you must seem very politic. But couch, ho! Here he 21
comes, to beguile two hours in a sleep, and then to 22
return and swear the lies he forges.   [They hide.]

    Enter Parolles.

PAROLLES Ten o'clock. Within these three hours 'twill
be time enough to go home. What shall I say I have
done? It must be a very plausive invention that carries 26
it. They begin to smoke me, and disgraces have of late 27
knocked too often at my door. I find my tongue is too
foolhardy; but my heart hath the fear of Mars before it, 29
and of his creatures, not daring the reports of my 30
tongue. 31

FIRST LORD [aside] This is the first truth that e'er thine
own tongue was guilty of.

PAROLLES What the devil should move me to undertake the recovery of this drum, being not ignorant of

14 **strangers** foreigners   15 **entertainment** service.   **smack**
smattering   16–19 **we . . . purpose** each of us must make up
his own imaginative language, unintelligible to the others; so long
as we seem to know what is said, we'll accomplish our purpose
19 **choughs' language** the chattering of a small species of the
crow family, the jackdaw   21 **politic** shrewd, cunning.   **couch**
take concealment   22 **beguile** while away.   **sleep** nap
26 **plausive** plausible   26–7 **carries it** carries it off.
27 **smoke** suspect   29–31 **hath . . . tongue** is frightened by the
prospect of the god of war and his followers, and I dare not carry
out my boast.

the impossibility, and knowing I had no such purpose?
I must give myself some hurts, and say I got
them in exploit. Yet slight ones will not carry it—they
will say, "Came you off with so little?"—and great
ones I dare not give. Wherefore? What's the instance? 40
Tongue, I must put you into a butter-woman's mouth 41
and buy myself another of Bajazeth's mule, if you 42
prattle me into these perils.

FIRST LORD [*aside*] Is it possible he should know what
he is, and be that he is?

PAROLLES I would the cutting of my garments would
serve the turn, or the breaking of my Spanish sword. 47

FIRST LORD [*aside*] We cannot afford you so. 48

PAROLLES Or the baring of my beard, and to say it was 49
in stratagem. 50

FIRST LORD [*aside*] 'Twould not do.

PAROLLES Or to drown my clothes, and say I was
stripped.

FIRST LORD [*aside*] Hardly serve.

PAROLLES Though I swore I leapt from the window of
the citadel—

FIRST LORD [*aside*] How deep?

PAROLLES Thirty fathom. 58

FIRST LORD [*aside*] Three great oaths would scarce
make that be believed.

---

40 **Wherefore . . . instance?** (Parolles may be saying "Why did I
ever open my mouth?" or "Where's the evidence to be produced
from?")   41 **butter-woman** dairywoman, i.e., a proverbial scold
and garrulous talker   42 **of Bajazeth's mule** i.e., from a
Turkish mule, since mules are notoriously mute (?) (Many
emendations have been proposed, including *mute* for *mule*.)
47 **serve the turn** suffice   48 **afford you so** i.e., let you off so
lightly.   49 **baring** shaving   50 **in stratagem** an act of
cunning.   58 **fathom** (A fathom is a unit of measure equal to six
feet.)

PAROLLES   I would I had any drum of the enemy's. I
would swear I recovered it.

FIRST LORD [*aside*]   You shall hear one anon.   63

PAROLLES   A drum now of the enemy's—   64

                                                 Alarum within.

FIRST LORD [*coming forward*]   *Throca movousus, cargo,*
cargo, cargo.

ALL   *Cargo, cargo, cargo, villianda par corbo, cargo.*

                                   [*They seize and blindfold him.*]

PAROLLES
Oh, ransom, ransom! Do not hide mine eyes.

FIRST SOLDIER   *Boskos thromuldo boskos.*

PAROLLES
I know you are the Muskos' regiment,   70
And I shall lose my life for want of language.   71
If there be here German, or Dane, Low Dutch,
Italian, or French, let him speak to me,
I'll discover that which shall undo the Florentine.   74

FIRST SOLDIER   *Boskos vauvado.* I understand thee and
can speak thy tongue. *Kerelybonto.* Sir, betake thee to   76
thy faith, for seventeen poniards are at thy bosom.   77

PAROLLES   Oh!

FIRST SOLDIER   Oh, pray, pray, pray! *Manka revania*
dulche.

FIRST LORD   *Oscorbidulchos volivorco.*

FIRST SOLDIER
The General is content to spare thee yet,
And, hoodwinked as thou art, will lead thee on   83

---

63 **anon** immediately.   64.1 *Alarum* Call to arms
70 **Muskos'** Muscovites'   71 **want** lack   74 **discover** reveal
76–7 **betake . . . faith** i.e., say your prayers   77 **poniards**
daggers   83 **hoodwinked** blindfolded.   **on** onward,
elsewhere

To gather from thee. Haply thou mayst inform   84
Something to save thy life.

PAROLLES   Oh, let me live,
And all the secrets of our camp I'll show,
Their force, their purposes; nay, I'll speak that
Which you will wonder at.

FIRST SOLDIER   But wilt thou faithfully?

PAROLLES
If I do not, damn me.

FIRST SOLDIER   *Acordo linta.*
Come on; thou art granted space.   *Exit [with Parolles* 90
                          guarded]. A short alarum within.

FIRST LORD
Go tell the Count Rossillion and my brother
We have caught the woodcock and will keep him
    muffled   92
Till we do hear from them.

SECOND SOLDIER   Captain, I will.

FIRST LORD
'A will betray us all unto ourselves.   94
Inform on that.   95

SECOND SOLDIER   So I will, sir.

FIRST LORD
Till then I'll keep him dark and safely locked.   *Exeunt.*

---

84 **gather** get information.   **Haply** Perhaps   90 **space** time.
92 **woodcock** (A proverbially stupid bird.)   **muffled** blindfolded
94 **'A** He   95 **Inform on** Report

[4.2] ❧ *Enter Bertram and the maid called Diana.*

BERTRAM
　They told me that your name was Fontibell.

DIANA
　No, my good lord, Diana.

BERTRAM   Titled goddess,   2
　And worth it, with addition! But, fair soul,   3
　In your fine frame hath love no quality?   4
　If the quick fire of youth light not your mind,   5
　You are no maiden, but a monument.   6
　When you are dead, you should be such a one
　As you are now; for you are cold and stern,
　And now you should be as your mother was
　When your sweet self was got.   10

DIANA
　She then was honest.

BERTRAM   So should you be.

DIANA   No.   11
　My mother did but duty—such, my lord,
　As you owe to your wife.

BERTRAM   No more o' that.
　I prithee, do not strive against my vows.   14
　I was compelled to her, but I love thee

4.2 Location: Florence. The Widow's house.
2–3 **Titled . . . addition!** You who have the name of a goddess,
and who deserve that and more!　　4 **frame** makeup, being.
quality position, part.　　5 **quick** lively　　6 **monument** statue,
lifeless effigy.　　10 **got** begotten.　　11 **honest** chaste, true to
marriage vows. (But Bertram uses it to mean "frank.")　　14 **vows**
i.e., vows to live apart from Helena.

By love's own sweet constraint and will forever
Do thee all rights of service.

DIANA   Ay, so you serve us
Till we serve you; but when you have our roses,   18
You barely leave our thorns to prick ourselves   19
And mock us with our bareness.

BERTRAM   How have I sworn!   20

DIANA
'Tis not the many oaths that makes the truth,
But the plain single vow that is vowed true.
What is not holy, that we swear not by,   23
But take the High'st to witness. Then pray you, tell me, 24
If I should swear by Jove's great attributes
I loved you dearly, would you believe my oaths
When I did love you ill? This has no holding,   27
To swear by Him whom I protest to love   28
That I will work against Him. Therefore your oaths   29
Are words and poor conditions but unsealed,   30
At least in my opinion.

BERTRAM   Change it, change it!   31
Be not so holy-cruel. Love is holy,   32
And my integrity ne'er knew the crafts   33
That you do charge men with. Stand no more off,

---

18 **serve you** i.e., serve you sexually. (The sexual suggestion is
continued in *roses* and in *prick*, line 19.)   19 **You . . . thorns** you
leave us with only the bare thorns (of shame and guilt)   20 **our
bareness** i.e., the loss of our rose of virginity.   23–4 **What . . .
witness** When we swear an oath, we do so not in the name of
unholy things, but with God as our witness.   27 **ill** perfidiously
and hence contrary to the purport of an oath sworn to God.
holding power to bind; consistency   28 **protest** profess
29 **work against Him** oppose His will by my sinful action.
30 **Are words . . . unsealed** are mere words and invalid provisos,
unratified and hence lacking in legally binding force   31 **it** i.e.,
your opinion   32 **holy-cruel** i.e., cruel to me in your holiness.
33 **crafts** deceits

But give thyself unto my sick desires,   35
Who then recovers. Say thou art mine, and ever   36
My love as it begins shall so persever.

DIANA

I see that men may rope 's in such a snare   38
That we'll forsake ourselves. Give me that ring.

BERTRAM

I'll lend it thee, my dear, but have no power
To give it from me.

DIANA   Will you not, my lord?

BERTRAM

It is an honor 'longing to our house,
Bequeathèd down from many ancestors,
Which were the greatest obloquy i'th' world   44
In me to lose.

DIANA   Mine honor's such a ring.
My chastity's the jewel of our house,
Bequeathèd down from many ancestors,
Which were the greatest obloquy i'th' world
In me to lose. Thus your own proper wisdom   49
Brings in the champion Honor on my part   50
Against your vain assault.

BERTRAM   Here, take my ring!
My house, mine honor, yea, my life, be thine,
And I'll be bid by thee.   [He gives the ring.]   53

DIANA

When midnight comes, knock at my chamber
     window.
I'll order take my mother shall not hear.   55

35 **sick** i.e., unfulfilled and in need of your ministrations
36 **Who then recovers** I who will then recover.   38 **rope 's** rope
us, entrap us. (The Folio reads "make rope 's in such a scarre.")
44 **obloquy** disgrace. (As also in line 48.)   49 **proper** personal
50 **part** side   53 **bid** commanded   55 **order take** make
provision

Now will I charge you in the bond of truth,
When you have conquered my yet maiden bed,
Remain there but an hour, nor speak to me.
My reasons are most strong, and you shall know
    them   59
When back again this ring shall be delivered.   60
And on your finger in the night I'll put
Another ring, that what in time proceeds   62
May token to the future our past deeds.   63
Adieu till then; then, fail not. You have won
A wife of me, though there my hope be done.   65

BERTRAM
A heaven on earth I have won by wooing thee.

                                  [*Exit.*]

DIANA
For which live long to thank both heaven and me!
You may so in the end.
My mother told me just how he would woo,
As if she sat in 's heart. She says all men
Have the like oaths. He had sworn to marry me   71
When his wife's dead; therefore I'll lie with him   72
When I am buried. Since Frenchmen are so braid,   73
Marry that will, I live and die a maid.   74
Only in this disguise I think't no sin
To cozen him that would unjustly win.   *Exit.*   76

59–60 you . . . delivered (Diana hints obscurely at the eventual
return of Bertram's ring, when he will understand everything; see
5.3.192ff.)   **62 Another ring** i.e., the ring the King gave Helena;
see 5.3.77ff.)   **62–3 that . . . deeds** so that whatever happens
and whatever we do may be known in time.   **63 token** betoken,
indicate   **65 A wife . . . done** i.e., me as your love partner,
although all hope of marriage is thereby destroyed for me.
71–3 He . . . buried i.e., Divorce being impossible, Bertram has
promised under oath to marry me after Helen dies and then
remain true to me until we both die and are buried together.
71 had has (?) would have (?)   **73 braid** i.e., deceitful. (A *braid* is
a trick.)   **74 Marry** let those marry   **76 cozen** cheat

[4.3] ❧ *Enter the two French Captains and some two or three Soldiers.*

FIRST LORD   You have not given him his mother's letter?

SECOND LORD   I have delivered it an hour since. There   2
is something in't that stings his nature, for on the
reading it he changed almost into another man.

FIRST LORD   He has much worthy blame laid upon him   5
for shaking off so good a wife and so sweet a lady.

SECOND LORD   Especially he hath incurred the everlasting displeasure of the King, who had even tuned his   8
bounty to sing happiness to him. I will tell you a   9
thing, but you shall let it dwell darkly with you.   10

FIRST LORD   When you have spoken it, 'tis dead, and I
am the grave of it.

SECOND LORD   He hath perverted a young gentlewoman   13
here in Florence, of a most chaste renown, and this
night he fleshes his will in the spoil of her honor. He   15
hath given her his monumental ring and thinks him-   16
self made in the unchaste composition.   17

4.3 Location: The Florentine camp.
2 **since** ago.   5 **worthy** deserved   8–9 **who . . . to him** i.e., who
had especially tuned the instrument of his generosity in order to
make Bertram happy (by bestowing Helena on him).   10 **darkly**
secretly   13 **perverted** seduced   15 **he fleshes . . . honor** he
rewards and stimulates his lust, permitting his desires to triumph in
the (de)spoiling of her honor. (The image may also suggest a hunter
rewarding his hounds or hawks with some flesh from the animal they
have hunted down, the *spoil* or quarry of the hunt.)
16 **monumental** i.e., serving as a token of his identity. (With a
continuation of the genital imagery, with an interesting confusion of
gender identity; rings are commonly vaginal in connotation.)
17 **made** a made man. (With a painful suggestion that the deed has
"unmade" [un-maid] him by despoiling him of honor as much as it
has "un-maid" her. He has lost his ring, as she also has, in losing her
virginity.)   **composition** bargain.

FIRST LORD   Now, God delay our rebellion! As we are   18
ourselves, what things are we!   19

SECOND LORD   Merely our own traitors. And as in the   20
common course of all treasons we still see them reveal   21
themselves till they attain to their abhorred ends, so   22
he that in this action contrives against his own   23
nobility, in his proper stream o'erflows himself.   24

FIRST LORD   Is it not meant damnable in us to be   25
trumpeters of our unlawful intents? We shall not then   26
have his company tonight?

SECOND LORD   Not till after midnight, for he is dieted   28
to his hour.   29

FIRST LORD   That approaches apace. I would gladly have
him see his company anatomized, that he might take   31
a measure of his own judgments wherein so curiously   32
he had set this counterfeit.   33

SECOND LORD   We will not meddle with him till he   34
come, for his presence must be the whip of the other.   35

FIRST LORD   In the meantime, what hear you of these
wars?

SECOND LORD   I hear there is an overture of peace.

FIRST LORD   Nay, I assure you, a peace concluded.

18 **delay our rebellion** make us slow to rebel, assuage our lustful
appetites.   18–19 **As . . . ourselves** Being as we are
unregenerate and fallen   20 **Merely** Absolutely, entirely
21–2 **still . . . themselves** always see traitors express their true
natures   23–4 **he . . . himself** i.e., Bertram, who thus seduces a
woman, subverts his own nobility by abusing the qualities that
should channel and perpetuate it.   25–6 **Is it . . . intents?** Is it
not a sign of our fallen natures to be proud proclaimers of our
sinful intents?   28–9 **dieted to his hour** tied to his schedule.
31 **his company** the company he keeps, his companion.
anatomized dissected, exposed   32 **curiously** carefully,
elaborately   33 **counterfeit** false jewel, i.e., Parolles.
34 **him** Parolles.   **he** Bertram   35 **his . . . the other** i.e.,
Bertram's . . . Parolles.

SECOND LORD   What will Count Rossillion do then? Will he travel higher or return again into France?   41

FIRST LORD   I perceive, by this demand, you are not altogether of his council.   42 43

SECOND LORD   Let it be forbid, sir! So should I be a great deal of his act.   45

FIRST LORD   Sir, his wife some two months since fled from his house. Her pretense is a pilgrimage to Saint Jaques le Grand, which holy undertaking with most austere sanctimony she accomplished. And, there residing, the tenderness of her nature became as a prey to her grief; in fine, made a groan of her last breath, and now she sings in heaven.   47 49 51

SECOND LORD   How is this justified?   53

FIRST LORD   The stronger part of it by her own letters, which makes her story true even to the point of her death. Her death itself, which could not be her office to say is come, was faithfully confirmed by the rector of the place.   55

SECOND LORD   Hath the Count all this intelligence?

FIRST LORD   Ay, and the particular confirmations, point from point, to the full arming of the verity.   61

SECOND LORD   I am heartily sorry that he'll be glad of this.

FIRST LORD   How mightily sometimes we make us comforts of our losses!   64 65

SECOND LORD   And how mightily some other times we drown our gain in tears! The great dignity that his   66 67

---

41 **higher** farther   42 **demand** question   43 **of his council** in his confidence.   45 **of his act** an accessory to his misdeeds.
47 **pretense** intent   49 **sanctimony** holiness   51 **in fine** at last   53 **justified** made certain.   55 **point** time, moment
61 **arming** corroboration, strengthening.   **verity** truth.
64–7 **make . . . tears** perversely take comfort in misfortune and at other times weep when we are fortunate. (Bertram is glad to lose Helena, having previously grieved at gaining her.)

valor hath here acquired for him shall at home be
encountered with a shame as ample.

FIRST LORD   The web of our life is of a mingled yarn,
good and ill together. Our virtues would be proud if   71
our faults whipped them not, and our crimes would   72
despair if they were not cherished by our virtues.   73

    Enter a [Servant as] messenger.

How now? Where's your master?

SERVANT   He met the Duke in the street, sir, of whom
he hath taken a solemn leave. His Lordship will next   76
morning for France. The Duke hath offered him letters
of commendations to the King.

SECOND LORD   They shall be no more than needful   79
there, if they were more than they can commend.   80

    Enter [Bertram] Count Rossillion.

FIRST LORD   They cannot be too sweet for the King's
tartness. Here's His Lordship now.—How now, my
lord, is't not after midnight?

BERTRAM   I have tonight dispatched sixteen businesses,
a month's length apiece, by an abstract of success: I   85
have congeed with the Duke, done my adieu with his   86
nearest, buried a wife, mourned for her, writ to my   87

71–3 **Our virtues . . . virtues** Our virtues would become
arrogant if they were not chastized by our faults, and our
wickednesses would despair if the presence of our virtues did not
comfort them.   76 **will** i.e., intends to depart   79–80 **They . . .
commend** Even if they were stronger than any recommendation
could be, they would still be no more than what is needed (to calm
the King's anger at Bertram).   85 **by . . . success** by a series of
successful moves, as follows, or, by a series of moves that may be
summarized as follows   86 **congeed with** taken leave of
86–7 **his nearest** those persons nearest him

lady mother I am returning, entertained my convoy, 88
and between these main parcels of dispatch effected 89
many nicer needs. The last was the greatest, but that 90
I have not ended yet.

SECOND LORD   If the business be of any difficulty, and
this morning your departure hence, it requires haste
of Your Lordship.

BERTRAM   I mean, the business is not ended, as fearing 95
to hear of it hereafter. But shall we have this dialogue 96
between the fool and the soldier? Come, bring forth
this counterfeit module; he's deceived me like a 98
double-meaning prophesier. 99

SECOND LORD [to the Soldiers]   Bring him forth.

[Exit one or more.]

He's sat i'the stocks all night, poor gallant knave.

BERTRAM   No matter; his heels have deserved it, in
usurping his spurs so long. How does he carry
himself?

SECOND LORD   I have told Your Lordship already, the
stocks carry him. But to answer you as you would be
understood, he weeps like a wench that had shed her 107
milk. He hath confessed himself to Morgan, whom he
supposes to be a friar, from the time of his remem- 109
brance to this very instant disaster of his setting i'th' 110
stocks. And what think you he hath confessed?

BERTRAM   Nothing of me, has 'a?

88 **entertained my convoy** hired my transportation
89 **main . . . dispatch** major items to be settled   90 **nicer** more
delicate.   **The last** i.e., The affair with Diana   95–6 **the
business . . . hereafter** (Bertram fears that Diana may be
pregnant, with inevitable consequences.)   98 **module** mere
image   99 **double-meaning** ambiguous, equivocating
107 **shed** spilled. (With the implication of crying over spilt milk.)
109–10 **the time . . . remembrance** as far back as he can recall
110 **instant** present

SECOND LORD   His confession is taken, and it shall be
    read to his face. If Your Lordship be in't, as I believe
    you are, you must have the patience to hear it.

*Enter Parolles [guarded and blindfolded] with
[First Soldier as] his interpreter.*

BERTRAM   A plague upon him! Muffled! He can say   116
    nothing of me.

FIRST LORD   Hush, hush! Hoodman comes!—*Portotar-*   118
    tarosa.

FIRST SOLDIER *[to Parolles]* He calls for the tortures.
    What will you say without 'em?

PAROLLES   I will confess what I know without con-
    straint. If ye pinch me like a pasty, I can say no more.   123

FIRST SOLDIER   *Bosko chimurcho.*

FIRST LORD   *Boblibindo chicurmurco.*

FIRST SOLDIER   You are a merciful general.—Our gener-
    al bids you answer to what I shall ask you out of a note.   127

PAROLLES   And truly, as I hope to live.

FIRST SOLDIER *[as if reading]* "First demand of him how   129
    many horse the Duke is strong." What say you to that?   130

PAROLLES   Five or six thousand, but very weak and
    unserviceable. The troops are all scattered and the
    commanders very poor rogues, upon my reputation
    and credit and as I hope to live.

FIRST SOLDIER   Shall I set down your answer so?

                                [He makes as though to write.]

PAROLLES   Do. I'll take the sacrament on't, how and
    which way you will.

---

116 **Muffled!** Blindfolded!   118 **Hoodman comes** (Customary
call in the game of blindman's buff.)   123 **pasty** meat pie
127 **note** memorandum or list.   129 **demand** ask   130 **horse**
horsemen, cavalry troops

BERTRAM [*aside to the Lords*] All's one to him. What a
   past-saving slave is this!   139

FIRST LORD [*aside to Bertram*] You're deceived, my lord.
   This is Monsieur Parolles, the gallant militarist—that
   was his own phrase—that had the whole theoric of   142
   war in the knot of his scarf, and the practice in the
   chape of his dagger.   144

SECOND LORD [*aside*] I will never trust a man again
   for keeping his sword clean, nor believe he can have   146
   everything in him by wearing his apparel neatly.

FIRST SOLDIER [*to Parolles*] Well, that's set down.

PAROLLES "Five or six thousand horse," I said—I will
   say true—"or thereabouts," set down, for I'll speak
   truth.

FIRST LORD [*aside*] He's very near the truth in this.

BERTRAM [*aside*] But I con him no thanks for't, in the   153
   nature he delivers it.   154

PAROLLES "Poor rogues," I pray you, say.

FIRST SOLDIER Well, that's set down.

PAROLLES I humbly thank you, sir. A truth's a truth.
   The rogues are marvelous poor.

FIRST SOLDIER [*as if reading*] "Demand of him of what
   strength they are afoot." What say you to that?   160

PAROLLES By my troth, sir, if I were to live this present   161
   hour, I will tell true. Let me see: Spurio, a hundred and
   fifty; Sebastian, so many; Corambus, so many; Jaques,   163
   so many; Guiltian, Cosmo, Lodowick, and Gratii, two

---

139 **past-saving** beyond redemption. (Referring back to
"sacrament" in line 136.)   142 **theoric** theory   144 **chape**
scabbard tip   146 **clean** i.e., polished   153 **con** offer. (Literally,
"know.")   153–4 **in . . . it** considering what sort of truth
it is that he tells.   160 **afoot** in numbers of foot soldiers.
161 **live** i.e., live only   163 **so many** the same number

hundred fifty each; mine own company, Chitopher, Vaumond, Bentii, two hundred fifty each; so that the muster-file, rotten and sound, upon my life, amounts 167 not to fifteen thousand poll, half of the which dare not 168 shake the snow from off their cassocks, lest they shake 169 themselves to pieces.

BERTRAM [*aside to the Lords*] What shall be done to him?

FIRST LORD [*aside*]   Nothing, but let him have thanks.— Demand of him my condition and what credit I have with the Duke.

FIRST SOLDIER   Well, that's set down. [*As if reading*] "You shall demand of him whether one Captain Dumain be i'th' camp, a Frenchman; what his reputation is with the Duke; what his valor, honesty, and expertness in wars; or whether he thinks it were not possible, with well-weighing sums of gold, to 181 corrupt him to a revolt." What say you to this? What 182 do you know of it?

PAROLLES   I beseech you, let me answer to the particular of the inter'gatories. Demand them singly. 185

FIRST SOLDIER   Do you know this Captain Dumain?

PAROLLES   I know him. 'A was a botcher's prentice in 187 Paris, from whence he was whipped for getting the sheriff's fool with child—a dumb innocent that could 189 not say him nay.

BERTRAM [*aside to First Lord, who makes as if to strike Parolles*]   Nay, by your leave, hold your hands—

---

167 **file** roll   168 **poll** heads   169 **cassocks** cloaks
181 **well-weighing** heavy and persuasive   182 **revolt** desertion.
185 **inter'gatories** questions.   187 **botcher's** mender's,
especially a tailor or cobbler who makes "botch-job" repairs
189 **sheriff's fool** feeble-minded girl in the sheriff's custody

though I know his brains are forfeit to the next tile   193
that falls.   194

FIRST SOLDIER   Well, is this captain in the Duke of Florence's camp?

PAROLLES   Upon my knowledge, he is, and lousy.   197

FIRST LORD [*aside to Bertram*]   Nay, look not so upon
me. We shall hear of Your Lordship anon.

FIRST SOLDIER   What is his reputation with the Duke?

PAROLLES   The Duke knows him for no other but a
poor officer of mine, and writ to me this other day to
turn him out o'th' band. I think I have his letter in my   203
pocket.

FIRST SOLDIER   Marry, we'll search.

                    [*They search his pockets.*]

PAROLLES   In good sadness, I do not know; either it is   206
there, or it is upon a file with the Duke's other letters
in my tent.

FIRST SOLDIER   Here 'tis, here's a paper. Shall I read it
to you?

PAROLLES   I do not know if it be it or no.

BERTRAM [*aside*]   Our interpreter does it well.

FIRST LORD [*aside*]   Excellently.

FIRST SOLDIER [*reads*]
"Dian, the Count's a fool, and full of gold—"

PAROLLES   That is not the Duke's letter, sir. That is an
advertisement to a proper maid in Florence, one   216
Diana, to take heed of the allurement of one Count

193–4 **his . . . falls** i.e., such a liar is headed straight for sudden
and violent death.   197 **lousy** (1) contemptible (2) infested with
lice.   203 **band** company, army.   206 **sadness** seriousness
216 **advertisement** warning.   **proper** respectable

Rossillion, a foolish idle boy, but for all that very
ruttish. I pray you, sir, put it up again.   219

FIRST SOLDIER   Nay, I'll read it first, by your favor.

PAROLLES   My meaning in 't, I protest, was very honest
in the behalf of the maid, for I knew the young Count
to be a dangerous and lascivious boy, who is a whale
to virginity, and devours up all the fry it finds.   224

BERTRAM [*aside*]   Damnable both-sides rogue!

FIRST SOLDIER [*reads the*] *letter.*
"When he swears oaths, bid him drop gold, and
       take it;   226
    After he scores, he never pays the score.   227
Half won is match well made; match, and well make
       it.   228
    He ne'er pays after-debts; take it before.   229
And say a soldier, Dian, told thee this:
Men are to mell with, boys are not to kiss.   231
For count of this, the Count's a fool, I know it,   232
Who pays before, but not when he does owe it.   233
       Thine, as he vowed to thee in thine ear,
                                        Parolles."

BERTRAM [*aside*]   He shall be whipped through the
army with this rhyme in's forehead.

219 **ruttish** lecherous.   224 **fry** small fish   226 **drop** i.e.,
offer, pay.   **take it** i.e., you should take it   227 **scores**
(1) buys on credit (2) hits the mark, scores sexually.   **score** bill.
228 **Half . . . make it** i.e., One is halfway to success if the *match* or
bargain is well stated with dearly defined agreements, so be sure to
do this.   229 **after-debts** debts payable after the goods are
received.   **it** i.e., payment   231 **Men . . . kiss** i.e., Don't fool
around with mere boys (like Bertram), but with real men (like me).
(*Mell with* means "mingle with in intercourse.")   232 **For count
of** On account of, or, therefore take note of   233 **before** in
advance (when he is required to do so).   **does owe it** (1) owes
payment for something already received (2) possesses it, i.e., her
maidenhead.

SECOND LORD [aside] This is your devoted friend, sir,
the manifold linguist and the armipotent soldier.   239

BERTRAM [aside] I could endure anything before but a
cat, and now he's a cat to me.   241

FIRST SOLDIER I perceive, sir, by our general's looks,
we shall be fain to hang you.   243

PAROLLES My life, sir, in any case! Not that I am afraid
to die, but that, my offenses being many, I would
repent out the remainder of nature. Let me live, sir, in   246
a dungeon, i'th' stocks, or anywhere, so I may live.

FIRST SOLDIER We'll see what may be done, so you
confess freely. Therefore, once more to this Captain
Dumain. You have answered to his reputation with
the Duke, and to his valor. What is his honesty?

PAROLLES He will steal, sir, an egg out of a cloister. For
rapes and ravishments he parallels Nessus. He pro-   253
fesses not keeping of oaths; in breaking 'em he is   254
stronger than Hercules. He will lie, sir, with such
volubility that you would think truth were a fool.   256
Drunkenness is his best virtue, for he will be swine-
drunk, and in his sleep he does little harm, save to his
bedclothes about him; but they know his conditions,   259
and lay him in straw. I have but little more to say, sir,
of his honesty. He has everything that an honest man
should not have; what an honest man should have, he
has nothing.

FIRST LORD [aside] I begin to love him for this.

239 **manifold linguist** speaker of many languages.
armipotent powerful in arms   241 **cat** (A term of contempt.)
243 **fain** obliged   246 **the remainder of nature** what is left of
my natural life.   253 **Nessus** a centaur who attempted to rape
the wife of Hercules.   253–4 **professes** makes a practice of
256 **volubility** fluency, facility.   **truth were a fool** i.e., truth
here seems so easily put down and made to look foolish.
259 **they** i.e., his servants.   **conditions** habits

BERTRAM [*aside*]   For this description of thine honesty?
A pox upon him for me, he's more and more a cat.

FIRST SOLDIER   What say you to his expertness in war?

PAROLLES   Faith, sir, he's led the drum before the   268
English tragedians. To belie him I will not, and more   269
of his soldiership I know not, except in that country he
had the honor to be the officer at a place there called
Mile End, to instruct for the doubling of files. I would   272
do the man what honor I can, but of this I am not
certain.

FIRST LORD [*aside*]   He hath out-villained villainy so far   275
that the rarity redeems him.   276

BERTRAM [*aside*]   A pox on him, he's a cat still.

FIRST SOLDIER   His qualities being at this poor price, I
need not to ask you if gold will corrupt him to revolt.

PAROLLES   Sir, for a cardecu he will sell the fee simple of   280
his salvation, the inheritance of it, and cut th'entail   281
from all remainders, and a perpetual succession for it   282
perpetually.   283

FIRST SOLDIER   What's his brother, the other Captain
Dumain?

SECOND LORD [*aside*]   Why does he ask him of me?

FIRST SOLDIER   What's he?

268–9 **led . . . tragedians** (It was a custom of actors entering a
village or town to parade in the street before the performance of a
play.)   272 **Mile End** place near London where citizen
militiamen were regularly exercised. (A slur of amateurism.)
doubling of files simple drill maneuver in which the soldiers
stand in a row two deep.   275–6 **He . . . him** His villainy has so
surpassed ordinary villainy that its extraordinariness redeems him.
280 **cardecu** quart d'écu, one-quarter of a French crown.   **fee
simple** total and perpetual ownership   281–3 **cut . . .
perpetually** prevent it from being passed on successively to
subsequent heirs.

PAROLLES   E'en a crow o'th' same nest; not altogether
so great as the first in goodness, but greater a great
deal in evil. He excels his brother for a coward, yet his
brother is reputed one of the best that is. In a retreat he
outruns any lackey; marry, in coming on he has the   292
cramp.

FIRST SOLDIER   If your life be saved, will you undertake
to betray the Florentine?

PAROLLES   Ay, and the Captain of his Horse, Count   296
Rossillion.

FIRST SOLDIER   I'll whisper with the General and know
his pleasure.

PAROLLES [*to himself*]   I'll no more drumming. A plague
of all drums! Only to seem to deserve well, and to
beguile the supposition of that lascivious young boy,   302
the Count, have I run into this danger. Yet who would
have suspected an ambush where I was taken?

FIRST SOLDIER   There is no remedy, sir, but you must
die. The General says, you that have so traitorously
discovered the secrets of your army and made such   307
pestiferous reports of men very nobly held can serve   308
the world for no honest use; therefore you must
die.—Come, headsman, off with his head.

PAROLLES   Oh, Lord, sir, let me live, or let me see my   311
death!

FIRST SOLDIER   That shall you, and take your leave of
all your friends. [*Unblindfolding him.*] So, look about you.
Know you any here?

BERTRAM   Good morrow, noble Captain.

292 **lackey** running footman.   **coming on** moving forward
296 **Captain of his Horse** cavalry commander
302 **supposition** judgment   307 **discovered** revealed
308 **pestiferous** malicious, pernicious.   **held** regarded
311 **Oh, Lord, sir** (Unconsciously echoing Lavatch's parody of the
courtier at 2.2.49–59.)

SECOND LORD   God bless you, Captain Parolles.

FIRST LORD   God save you, noble Captain.

SECOND LORD   Captain, what greeting will you to my   319
  Lord Lafew? I am for France.   320

FIRST LORD   Good Captain, will you give me a copy of
  the sonnet you writ to Diana in behalf of the Count
  Rossillion? An I were not a very coward, I'd compel it   323
  of you; but fare you well.   *Exeunt [Bertram and Lords].*

FIRST SOLDIER   You are undone, Captain, all but your
  scarf; that has a knot on't yet.

PAROLLES   Who cannot be crushed with a plot?

FIRST SOLDIER   If you could find out a country where
  but women were that had received so much shame,
  you might begin an impudent nation. Fare ye well, sir.   330
  I am for France too. We shall speak of you there.

                              Exit [with Soldiers].

PAROLLES

Yet am I thankful. If my heart were great,   332
'Twould burst at this. Captain I'll be no more,
But I will eat and drink, and sleep as soft
As captain shall. Simply the thing I am
Shall make me live. Who knows himself a braggart,   336
Let him fear this, for it will come to pass
That every braggart shall be found an ass.
Rust, sword! Cool, blushes! And, Parolles, live
Safest in shame! Being fooled, by fool'ry thrive!   340
There's place and means for every man alive.
I'll after them.   *Exit.*

319 **will you** do you wish to send   320 **for** bound for, off to
323 **An** If   330 **impudent** shameless   332 **heart** (Thought to
be the seat of courage.)   336 **Who** He who   340 **Being . . .
thrive!** i.e., Since they have made a fool of me, I will now thrive by
being what I am, a fool!

[4.4] ❧ *Enter Helena, Widow, and Diana.*

HELENA
  That you may well perceive I have not wronged you,
  One of the greatest in the Christian world   2
  Shall be my surety; 'fore whose throne 'tis needful, 3
  Ere I can perfect mine intents, to kneel.
  Time was, I did him a desirèd office,
  Dear almost as his life, which gratitude   6
  Through flinty Tartar's bosom would peep forth 7
  And answer thanks. I duly am informed
  His Grace is at Marseilles, to which place
  We have convenient convoy. You must know   10
  I am supposèd dead. The army breaking,   11
  My husband hies him home, where, heaven aiding, 12
  And by the leave of my good lord the King,
  We'll be before our welcome.

WIDOW   Gentle madam,   14
  You never had a servant to whose trust
  Your business was more welcome.

HELENA   Nor you, mistress,
  Ever a friend whose thoughts more truly labor
  To recompense your love. Doubt not but heaven
  Hath brought me up to be your daughter's dower, 19
  As it hath fated her to be my motive   20
  And helper to a husband. But oh, strange men,
  That can such sweet use make of what they hate,

4.4 *Location: Florence. The Widow's house.*
2 **One . . . world** i.e., the French King   3 **surety** guarantee
6 **which gratitude** gratitude for which   7 **Through** even
through   10 **convenient convoy** suitable transport.
11 **breaking** disbanding   12 **hies him** hastens   14 **We'll be . . .
welcome** we will arrive before we are expected.   19 **Hath . . .
dower** i.e., has groomed me for the role of providing a dowry for
your daughter   20 **motive** means

When saucy trusting of the cozened thoughts   23
Defiles the pitchy night! So lust doth play   24
With what it loathes for that which is away.   25
But more of this hereafter. You, Diana,
Under my poor instructions yet must suffer   27
Something in my behalf.

DIANA   Let death and honesty   28
Go with your impositions, I am yours   29
Upon your will to suffer.

HELENA   Yet, I pray you;   30
But with the word the time will bring on summer,   31
When briers shall have leaves as well as thorns,   32
And be as sweet as sharp. We must away;
Our wagon is prepared, and time revives us.   34
All's well that ends well. Still the fine's the crown;   35
Whate'er the course, the end is the renown.   *Exeunt.*   36

23–4 **When . . . night** when lustful confidence in deceived fancies
sullies the darkness of night. (Recalling the proverbial idea that
"pitch doth defile"; here man's lust defiles pitch, i.e., night.)
24–5 **So . . . away** i.e., Thus Bertram's lust enjoys itself with
Helena, the loathed wife, supposing her to be Diana.   27 **yet** for
a time yet   28–30 **Let . . . suffer** Even if a chaste death were a
result of what you ask of me, I am yours, ready to accede to your
will.   30 **Yet** A little longer   31–2 **But . . . thorns** i.e., but
soon enough, time will bring on a happier state of affairs, with
rewards to compensate for our suffering   34 **revives** will revive
35 **the fine's the crown** the end is the crown of all
36 **Whate'er . . . renown** by whatever means we proceed, the
conclusion is what makes for worth (i.e., the end justifies the
means).

[4.5] ❧ *Enter Clown [Lavatch], Old Lady [Countess],*
and Lafew.

LAFEW No, no, no, your son was misled with a   1
snipped-taffeta fellow there, whose villainous saffron   2
would have made all the unbaked and doughy youth   3
of a nation in his color. Your daughter-in-law had
been alive at this hour, and your son here at home,
more advanced by the King than by that red-tailed
humble-bee I speak of.   7

COUNTESS I would I had not known him! It was the
death of the most virtuous gentlewoman that ever
nature had praise for creating. If she had partaken of
my flesh, and cost me the dearest groans of a mother,   11
I could not have owed her a more rooted love.   12

LAFEW 'Twas a good lady, 'twas a good lady. We may
pick a thousand salads ere we light on such another
herb.

LAVATCH Indeed, sir, she was the sweet marjoram of
the salad, or rather the herb of grace.   17

LAFEW They are not herbs, you knave, they are nose-   18
herbs.   19

4.5 Location: Rossillion.
1 **with** by   2 **snipped-taffeta** wearing taffeta silk garments with
slashes to allow the under material to be visible (suggestive of
Parolles's hollow flashiness).   **saffron** bright yellow spice used
in making pastry and also in dyeing starched ruffs and collars
3 **unbaked and doughy** raw and unformed   7 **humble-bee**
bumblebee (noisy and useless)   11 **dearest** (1) direst (2) most
loving.   **groans of a mother** pains of childbirth   12 **rooted**
firm   17 **herb of grace** rue for remembrance. (Also picking up
on the theological theme of "grace.")   18 **not herbs** i.e., not
edible salad herbs or greens   18–19 **nose-herbs** fragrant herbs
used for bouquets, not salads.

LAVATCH   I am no great Nebuchadnezzar, sir. I have   20
not much skill in grass.   21

LAFEW   Whether dost thou profess thyself, a knave or a   22
fool?

LAVATCH   A fool, sir, at a woman's service, and a knave
at a man's.

LAFEW   Your distinction?

LAVATCH   I would cozen the man of his wife and do his   27
service.   28

LAFEW   So you were a knave at his service, indeed.

LAVATCH   And I would give his wife my bauble, sir, to   30
do her service.

LAFEW   I will subscribe for thee, thou art both knave   32
and fool.

LAVATCH   At your service.

LAFEW   No, no, no!   35

LAVATCH   Why, sir, if I cannot serve you, I can serve as
great a prince as you are.

LAFEW   Who's that, a Frenchman?

LAVATCH   Faith, sir, 'a has an English name, but his   39
physnomy is more hotter in France than there.   40

LAFEW   What prince is that?

20–1 **Nebuchadnezzar . . . grass** In Daniel 4:28–37, King
Nebuchadnezzar is reported to have gone mad and eaten grass like
a grazing ox. (With a pun on *grass/grace* and also *graze;* the word in
the Folio is "grace.")   22 **Whether** Which of the two
27 **cozen** cheat   27–8 **do his service** i.e., usurp his sexual role.
30 **bauble** stick carried by a court fool. (With bawdy suggestion.)
32 **subscribe** vouch   35 **No, no, no!** i.e., Not under the terms of
service you have described!   39 **English name** i.e., the Black
Prince, a widely known name for the eldest son of Edward III who
defeated the French.   40 **physnomy** physiognomy.   **more
hotter** (1) more choleric in the fury of fighting (2) more
susceptible to the "French disease," syphilis

LAVATCH The black prince, sir, alias the prince of
    darkness, alias the devil.

LAFEW Hold thee, there's my purse. [*He gives money.*] I
    give thee not this to suggest thee from thy master thou   45
    talk'st of; serve him still.

LAVATCH I am a woodland fellow, sir, that always   47
    loved a great fire, and the master I speak of ever keeps
    a good fire. But sure he is the prince of the world; let   49
    his nobility remain in 's court. I am for the house with
    the narrow gate, which I take to be too little for pomp   51
    to enter. Some that humble themselves may, but the
    many will be too chill and tender, and they'll be for the   53
    flowery way that leads to the broad gate and the great   54
    fire.   55

LAFEW Go thy ways. I begin to be aweary of thee; and   56
    I tell thee so before, because I would not fall out with   57
    thee. Go thy ways. Let my horses be well looked to,
    without any tricks.

LAVATCH If I put tricks upon 'em, sir, they shall be
    jades' tricks, which are their own right by the law of   61
    nature.   *Exit.*

LAFEW A shrewd knave and an unhappy.   63

---

45 suggest tempt   **47 woodland** rustic   **49 a good fire** i.e.,
hellfire.   **51 narrow gate** (Compare with Matthew 7:14: "Strait
is the gate, and narrow is the way, which leadeth unto life.")
53 many multitude.   **chill and tender** sensitive to cold and
pampered. (Most people are so fond of a good fire that they are
not keeping in mind the great fire [lines 54–5] of hell.)   **53–5 the
flowery . . . fire** (Compare with Matthew 7:13: "Wide is the gate,
and broad is the way, that leadeth to destruction.")   **56 Go thy
ways** Get along with you.   **57 before** i.e., before I grow
thoroughly weary   **61 jades' tricks** (1) the vicious behavior of
jades or ill-tempered horses (2) malicious tricks that hostlers might
play on horses, such as greasing their teeth or their hay
63 shrewd sharp-tongued and witty.   **unhappy** discontented.

COUNTESS   So 'a is. My lord that's gone made himself   64
much sport out of him. By his authority he remains
here, which he thinks is a patent for his sauciness; and
indeed he has no pace, but runs where he will.   67

LAFEW   I like him well; 'tis not amiss. And I was about
to tell you, since I heard of the good lady's death, and   69
that my lord your son was upon his return home, I
moved the King my master to speak in the behalf of
my daughter, which, in the minority of them both, His   72
Majesty, out of a self-gracious remembrance, did first   73
propose. His Highness hath promised me to do it, and
to stop up the displeasure he hath conceived against
your son there is no fitter matter. How does Your
Ladyship like it?

COUNTESS   With very much content, my lord, and I
wish it happily effected.

LAFEW   His Highness comes post from Marseilles, of as   80
able body as when he numbered thirty. 'A will be here   81
tomorrow, or I am deceived by him that in such   82
intelligence hath seldom failed.   83

COUNTESS   It rejoices me that I hope I shall see him ere
I die. I have letters that my son will be here tonight. I
shall beseech Your Lordship to remain with me till they
meet together.

LAFEW   Madam, I was thinking with what manners I
might safely be admitted.   89

---

64 **gone** dead   67 **has no pace** observes no restraint. (A term
from horse training.)   69 **the good lady's** Helena's   72 **in . . .
both** i.e., since both my daughter and Bertram are legally minors
or wards   73 **self-gracious remembrance** thoughtful
recollection that came to him without prompting   80 **post**
posthaste   81 **numbered thirty** was thirty years old.   82 **him**
i.e., a messenger   83 **intelligence** news   89 **admitted** i.e.,
allowed to be present at that meeting.

COUNTESS   You need but plead your honorable privi-   90
lege.   91

LAFEW   Lady, of that I have made a bold charter, but I   92
thank my God it holds yet.

Enter Clown [Lavatch].

LAVATCH   Oh, madam, yonder's my lord your son with a
patch of velvet on 's face. Whether there be a scar
under't or no, the velvet knows, but 'tis a goodly
patch of velvet. His left cheek is a cheek of two pile   97
and a half, but his right cheek is worn bare.   98

LAFEW   A scar nobly got, or a noble scar, is a good livery   99
of honor; so belike is that.   100

LAVATCH   But it is your carbonadoed face.   101

LAFEW   Let us go see your son, I pray you. I long to talk
with the young noble soldier.

LAVATCH   Faith, there's a dozen of 'em, with delicate
fine hats, and most courteous feathers, which bow the
head and nod at every man.   *Exeunt.*

[5.1] ❧ *Enter Helena, Widow, and Diana, with two
attendants.*

HELENA

But this exceeding posting day and night   1
Must wear your spirits low. We cannot help it.

90–1 **honorable privilege** privilege due your honor.
92 **made . . . charter** asserted my claim as far as I dare
97–8 **two . . . half** i.e., a thick velvet   98 **worn bare** i.e.,
without a velvet patch.   99 **livery** uniform   100 **belike**
probably   101 **But** Unless.   **carbonadoed** slashed or scored
across with gashes, as to broil meat (here suggesting a cut made to
drain a venereal ulcer and covered with a velvet patch)

5.1 *Location: Marseilles. A street.*
1 **posting** riding in haste

But since you have made the days and nights as one
To wear your gentle limbs in my affairs,   4
Be bold you do so grow in my requital   5
As nothing can unroot you.

    Enter a Gentleman.

                        In happy time!   6
This man may help me to His Majesty's ear,
If he would spend his power.—God save you, sir.   8

GENTLEMAN   And you.

HELENA
Sir, I have seen you in the court of France.

GENTLEMAN   I have been sometimes there.

HELENA
I do presume, sir, that you are not fall'n
From the report that goes upon your goodness;
And therefore, goaded with most sharp occasions   14
Which lay nice manners by, I put you to   15
The use of your own virtues, for the which
I shall continue thankful.

GENTLEMAN   What's your will?

HELENA   That it will please you
To give this poor petition to the King

                        [showing a petition]
And aid me with that store of power you have
To come into his presence.

GENTLEMAN
The King's not here.

HELENA   Not here, sir?

GENTLEMAN   Not indeed.

---

4 **wear** wear out   5 **bold** confident.   **requital** i.e., debt,
thankfulness   6 **happy** opportune   8 **spend** expend
14 **sharp occasions** urgent circumstances   15 **nice** scrupulous.
put urge

He hence removed last night, and with more haste   23
Than is his use.

WIDOW   Lord, how we lose our pains!   24

HELENA   All's well that ends well yet,
Though time seem so adverse and means unfit.
I do beseech you, whither is he gone?

GENTLEMAN
Marry, as I take it, to Rossillion,
Whither I am going.

HELENA   I do beseech you, sir,
Since you are like to see the King before me,
Commend the paper to his gracious hand,   31

[*giving the petition*]

Which I presume shall render you no blame
But rather make you thank your pains for it.
I will come after you with what good speed
Our means will make us means.

GENTLEMAN   This I'll do for you.   35

HELENA   And you shall find yourself to be well
    thanked,
Whate'er falls more. We must to horse again.—   37
Go, go, provide.   [*Exeunt separately.*]

[5.2] ꜱ◆ *Enter Clown [Lavatch], and Parolles.*

PAROLLES   Good Monsieur Lavatch, give my Lord
Lafew this letter. [*He offers a letter.*] I have ere now, sir,

___

23 **removed** departed   24 **use** usual practice.   31 **Commend**
present as worthy of favorable consideration   35 **Our . . .**
means our resources will allow us.   37 **falls more** else may
happen.

5.2 Location: Rossillion.

been better known to you, when I have held familiarity with fresher clothes; but I am now, sir, muddied in Fortune's mood, and smell somewhat strong of her strong displeasure.

LAVATCH   Truly, Fortune's displeasure is but sluttish if it smell so strongly as thou speak'st of. I will henceforth eat no fish of Fortune's buttering. Prithee, allow   9
the wind.   10

PAROLLES   Nay, you need not to stop your nose, sir. I spake but by a metaphor.

LAVATCH   Indeed, sir, if your metaphor stink, I will stop my nose, or against any man's metaphor. Prithee, get thee further.

PAROLLES   Pray you, sir, deliver me this paper.   16

LAVATCH   Foh! Prithee, stand away. A paper from Fortune's close-stool to give to a nobleman! Look, here   18
he comes himself.

    Enter Lafew.

Here is a purr of Fortune's sir, or of Fortune's cat—but   20
not a musk cat—that has fallen into the unclean fish-   21
pond of her displeasure, and, as he says, is muddied

---

9 **of Fortune's buttering** i.e., prepared and served by Fortune.
9–10 **allow the wind** stand downwind of me. (The hunter stands downwind of the deer so that the prey won't smell him. Lavatch responds with jesting literalness to Parolles's lament that he has been befouled by evil-smelling Fortune.)   16 **me** for me
18 **close-stool** privy   20 **purr** (The multiple pun here may include "male child," "piece of dung," "the purr of a cat," and the name given to the jack or knave in the card game post and pair. Or perhaps the word should be *paw;* Parolles is a cat's paw; he has been fishing as a cat does in Fortune's pond and has fallen in himself. Fortune's paw has scratched.)   21 **musk cat** (Both the civet cat and musk deer were prized for their musk scent, used in perfumes.)

withal. Pray you, sir, use the carp as you may, for he   23
looks like a poor, decayed, ingenious, foolish, rascally   24
knave. I do pity his distress in my similes of comfort,   25
and leave him to Your Lordship.   [*Exit.*]

PAROLLES My lord, I am a man whom Fortune hath
cruelly scratched.

LAFEW And what would you have me to do? 'Tis too
late to pare her nails now. Wherein have you played
the knave with Fortune that she should scratch you,
who of herself is a good lady and would not have
knaves thrive long under her? There's a cardecu for   33
you. [*He gives money.*] Let the justices make you and   34
Fortune friends; I am for other business.

          [*He starts to leave.*]

PAROLLES I beseech Your Honor to hear me one single
word.

LAFEW You beg a single penny more. Come, you shall
ha't. Save your word.

PAROLLES My name, my good lord, is Parolles.

LAFEW You beg more than "word," then. Cox my   41
passion! Give me your hand. How does your drum?   42

PAROLLES O my good lord, you were the first that
found me.   44

LAFEW Was I, in sooth? And I was the first that lost   45
thee.

---

23 **carp** (1) a fish often bred in sewage-rich fish ponds or moats (2) a
chatterer   24 **ingenious** stupid, lacking in genius or intellect (?)
25 **similes of comfort** comforting or instructive similes
33 **cardecu** quart d'écu, one-quarter of a French crown   34 **justices**
i.e., Justices of the Peace, responsible in Elizabethan England for
beggars under the Elizabethan poor law   41 **more than "word"**
i.e., many words; *Parolles* suggests a plural of the French *parole,*
"word"   41–2 **Cox my passion!** i.e., By God's (Christ's) passion on
the cross!   44 **found me** found me out.   45 **lost** abandoned.
(Playing on *lost* and *found,* and recalling the parable of the lost sheep.)

PAROLLES   It lies in you, my lord, to bring me in some
grace, for you did bring me out.   48

LAFEW   Out upon thee, knave! Dost thou put upon me
at once both the office of God and the devil? One
brings thee in grace and the other brings thee out.
[*Trumpets sound.*] The King's coming; I know by his
trumpets. Sirrah, inquire further after me. I had talk of
you last night. Though you are a fool and a knave, you
shall eat. Go to, follow.

PAROLLES   I praise God for you.   [*Exeunt.*]

[5.3]   ❧ *Flourish. Enter King, Old Lady* [*Countess*],
       Lafew, the two French Lords, with attendants.

KING
   We lost a jewel of her, and our esteem   1
   Was made much poorer by it; but your son,
   As mad in folly, lacked the sense to know   3
   Her estimation home.

COUNTESS   'Tis past, my liege,   4
   And I beseech Your Majesty to make it   5
   Natural rebellion, done i'th' blade of youth,   6
   When oil and fire, too strong for reason's force,
   O'erbears it and burns on.

KING   My honored lady,
   I have forgiven and forgotten all,

48 **grace** favor. (With perhaps a suggesting of "graze.")   **out**
(1) out of favor, out of safe pasture (2) "out" in the theatrical sense
of having forgotten one's lines.

5.3 Location: Rossillion.
0.2 *Lafew* (Lafew may remain on stage from the end of the
previous scene.)   1 **of** in.   **our esteem** my own value
3–4 **know . . . home** appreciate her value fully.   5 **make**
account, consider   6 **Natural rebellion** rebellion by the
passions.   **blade** greenness, freshness

Though my revenges were high bent upon him   10
And watched the time to shoot.

LAFEW   This I must say—   11
But first I beg my pardon—the young lord   12
Did to His Majesty, his mother, and his lady
Offense of mighty note, but to himself
The greatest wrong of all. He lost a wife
Whose beauty did astonish the survey   16
Of richest eyes, whose words all ears took captive,   17
Whose dear perfection hearts that scorned to serve   18
Humbly called mistress.

KING   Praising what is lost   19
Makes the remembrance dear. Well, call him hither.
We are reconciled, and the first view shall kill
All repetition. Let him not ask our pardon.   22
The nature of his great offense is dead,   23
And deeper than oblivion we do bury
Th'incensing relics of it. Let him approach   25
A stranger, no offender; and inform him   26
So 'tis our will he should.

GENTLEMAN   I shall, my liege.   [Exit.]   27

KING [to Lafew]
What says he to your daughter? Have you spoke?

---

10 **high bent** i.e., as with a fully drawn bow   11 **watched**
waited for   12 **But . . . pardon** (Lafew ceremoniously begs
pardon for expressing an opinion that may seem critical.)
16 **astonish the survey** dazzle the sight   17 **richest** (1) richest
in experience (2) nobly born   18–19 **Whose . . . mistress**
whose dear perfection was such that gallants who scorned to owe
service to anyone humbly did so to her.   22 **repetition**
reviewing of past wrongs, with recurrence of my anger.
23 **dead** i.e., forgotten   25 **Th'incensing relics** reminders that
kindle anger   26 **A stranger** i.e., as one whose story is unknown
27 GENTLEMAN (This could be one of the two French lords or
some other person in attendance.)

LAFEW

   All that he is hath reference to Your Highness.   29

KING

   Then shall we have a match. I have letters sent me
   That sets him high in fame.

     Enter Count Bertram.

LAFEW   He looks well on't.

KING   I am not a day of season,   33
   For thou mayst see a sunshine and a hail
   In me at once. But to the brightest beams
   Distracted clouds give way; so stand thou forth.   36
   The time is fair again.

BERTRAM   My high-repented blames,   37
   Dear sovereign, pardon to me.

KING   All is whole;   38
   Not one word more of the consumèd time.   39
   Let's take the instant by the forward top;   40
   For we are old, and on our quick'st decrees   41
   Th'inaudible and noiseless foot of Time
   Steals ere we can effect them. You remember
   The daughter of this lord?

BERTRAM   Admiringly, my liege. At first
   I stuck my choice upon her, ere my heart   46
   Durst make too bold a herald of my tongue;

---

29 **hath reference to** defers to   33 **of season** i.e., of one
consistent kind of weather   36 **Distracted . . . way** clouds
disperse and give way   37 **high-repented blames** sorely
repented failings   38 **whole** mended, well   39 **consumèd**
past   40 **take . . . top** take time by the forelock   41 **quick'st**
most urgent   46 **stuck** fixed

Where the impression of mine eye infixing,   48
Contempt his scornful perspective did lend me,   49
Which warped the line of every other favor,   50
Scorned a fair color, or expressed it stolen,   51
Extended or contracted all proportions   52
To a most hideous object. Thence it came   53
That she whom all men praised and whom myself,   54
Since I have lost, have loved, was in mine eye
The dust that did offend it.

KING   Well excused.   56
That thou didst love her strikes some scores away
From the great compt. But love that comes too late,   58
Like a remorseful pardon slowly carried,   59
To the great sender turns a sour offense,   60
Crying, "That's good that's gone." Our rash faults
Make trivial price of serious things we have,   62
Not knowing them until we know their grave.   63
Oft our displeasures, to ourselves unjust,   64
Destroy our friends, and after weep their dust;   65

---

48 **Where . . . infixing** i.e., the image of her entering first at my eye and then fixing itself in my heart. (Bertram seems to say, in lines 45–56, that he loved Lafew's daughter some time ago but dared not speak of his love, and that, on her account, he came to scorn all women, especially Helena, who was like an offending speck in his eye, though since then he has learned to love the memory of the wife he lost.)   49 **perspective** an optical glass for producing distorted images   50 **favor** face   51 **expressed it stolen** declared it to be painted cosmetically   52–3 **Extended . . . object** elongated or compressed all other forms until they made a hideous sight.   54 **she** i.e., Helena   56 **offend it** (1) give it offense (2) blur its vision.   58 **compt** account, reckoning. (With a suggestion of the Day of Judgment.)   59 **remorseful** compassionate. **slowly carried** i.e., arriving too late   60 **turns . . . offense** i.e., turns sour on him   62 **Make trivial price of** greatly undervalue   63 **knowing** i.e., appreciating.   **know their grave** i.e., are aware of their irrevocable loss.   64 **displeasures** offenses   65 **weep their dust** mourn over their remains

Our own love waking cries to see what's done,
While shameful hate sleeps out the afternoon.   67
Be this sweet Helen's knell, and now forget her.
Send forth your amorous token for fair Maudlin.   69
The main consents are had; and here we'll stay
To see our widower's second marriage day.

COUNTESS
Which better than the first, O dear heaven, bless!
Or, ere they meet, in me, O nature, cesse!   73

LAFEW
Come on, my son, in whom my house's name
Must be digested: give a favor from you   75
To sparkle in the spirits of my daughter,   76
That she may quickly come. [*Bertram gives a ring.*]
    By my old beard,
And every hair that's on't, Helen that's dead
Was a sweet creature; such a ring as this,
The last that e'er I took her leave at court,   80
I saw upon her finger.

BERTRAM   Hers it was not.

KING
Now, pray you, let me see it, for mine eye,
While I was speaking, oft was fastened to't.
                    [*The ring is given to the King.*]
This ring was mine, and when I gave it Helen
I bade her, if her fortunes ever stood   85
Necessitied to help, that by this token   86

---

67 **sleeps . . . afternoon** i.e., sleeps at ease, having done its work.
69 **Maudlin** i.e., Magdalen, the daughter of Lafew.   73 **ere they
meet** i.e., before the two marriages come to resemble one another
in unhappiness.   **cesse** cease.   75 **digested** incorporated.
favor token   76 **To sparkle in** i.e., to cheer with its luster
80 **The last** the last time.   **took her leave** took leave of her
85 **bade her** i.e., bade her remember   86 **Necessitied to** in
need of

I would relieve her. Had you that craft to reave her   87
Of what should stead her most?

BERTRAM   My gracious sovereign,   88
Howe'er it pleases you to take it so,
The ring was never hers.

COUNTESS   Son, on my life,
I have seen her wear it, and she reckoned it
At her life's rate.

LAFEW   I am sure I saw her wear it.   92

BERTRAM   You are deceived, my lord; she never saw it.
In Florence was it from a casement thrown me,
Wrapped in a paper, which contained the name
Of her that threw it. Noble she was, and thought
I stood engaged; but when I had subscribed   97
To mine own fortune, and informed her fully   98
I could not answer in that course of honor   99
As she had made the overture, she ceased   100
In heavy satisfaction, and would never   101
Receive the ring again.

KING   Plutus himself,   102
That knows the tinct and multiplying med'cine,   103
Hath not in nature's mystery more science   104
Than I have in this ring. 'Twas mine, 'twas Helen's,
Whoever gave it you. Then, if you know   106
That you are well acquainted with yourself,   107

---

87 **reave** deprive, rob   88 **stead** help   92 **rate** value.
97 **engaged** i.e., pledged to her; or, possibly, not pledged to another.
(The Folio spelling, "ingag'd," may suggest a negative prefix.)
97–8 **subscribed . . . fortune** i.e., explained my true situation (of my
marriage)   99–100 **in that . . . overture** in the same honorable
way that she had followed when she proposed   101 **heavy
satisfaction** doleful resignation   102 **Plutus** the god of wealth
103 **the tinct . . . med'cine** the alchemical elixir for transmuting
base metals into gold   104 **science** knowledge   106–7 **if . . .
yourself** i.e., if you are willing to examine yourself and your motives
(something that Bertram has been notoriously unable to do)

Confess 'twas hers, and by what rough enforcement
You got it from her. She called the saints to surety   109
That she would never put it from her finger
Unless she gave it to yourself in bed,
Where you have never come, or sent it us
Upon her great disaster.

BERTRAM   She never saw it.   113

KING

Thou speak'st it falsely, as I love mine honor,
And mak'st conjectural fears to come into me   115
Which I would fain shut out. If it should prove   116
That thou art so inhuman—'twill not prove so,
And yet I know not. Thou didst hate her deadly,
And she is dead, which nothing but to close
Her eyes myself could win me to believe,
More than to see this ring.—Take him away.
My forepast proofs, howe'er the matter fall,   122
Shall tax my fears of little vanity,   123
Having vainly feared too little. Away with him!   124
We'll sift this matter further.

BERTRAM   If you shall prove
This ring was ever hers, you shall as easy
Prove that I husbanded her bed in Florence,
Where yet she never was.   [Exit, guarded.]

     Enter a Gentleman.

KING

I am wrapped in dismal thinkings.

GENTLEMAN   Gracious sovereign,

109 **to surety** to witness   113 **Upon . . . disaster** when a
catastrophe befell her.   115 **conjectural fears** fearful conjectures
116 **fain** willingly   122 **My forepast proofs** The evidence I
already have.   **fall** turn out   123–4 **Shall . . . too little** will
hardly censure my fears (concerning Helena) as inconsequential;
indeed, I have foolishly been too little apprehensive.

Whether I have been to blame or no, I know not.
Here's a petition from a Florentine,   [*giving petition*]
Who hath for four or five removes come short   132
To tender it herself. I undertook it,   133
Vanquished thereto by the fair grace and speech   134
Of the poor suppliant, who by this I know   135
Is here attending. Her business looks in her   136
With an importing visage, and she told me,   137
In a sweet verbal brief, it did concern   138
Your Highness with herself.

KING [*reads*] *a letter* "Upon his many protestations to
marry me when his wife was dead, I blush to say it,
he won me. Now is the Count Rossillion a widower,
his vows are forfeited to me, and my honor's paid to
him. He stole from Florence, taking no leave, and I   144
follow him to his country for justice. Grant it me, O
King! In you it best lies; otherwise a seducer flourishes and a poor maid is undone.   Diana Capilet"

LAFEW I will buy me a son-in-law in a fair, and toll for   148
this. I'll none of him.   149

KING
The heavens have thought well on thee, Lafew,
To bring forth this discovery.—Seek these suitors.   151
Go speedily and bring again the Count.

                  [*Exeunt one or more attendants.*]

132 **for . . . short** on account of four or five shifts of residence of
the court (as it moved from Marseilles to Rossillion) come too late
133 **tender** offer   134 **Vanquished** won   135 **by this** by this
time   136 **looks** manifests itself   137 **importing** urgent and
full of import   138 **brief** summary   144 **taking no leave** not
even saying goodbye   148 **in a fair** i.e., where stolen and
disreputable merchandise are common. (Lafew says he can do
better at such a place than with Bertram.)   148–9 **toll for this**
i.e., put Bertram up for sale. (Merchants wishing to sell at market
paid a toll or fee in order to enter their goods in a register.)
151 **suitors** petitioners.

I am afeard the life of Helen, lady,
Was foully snatched.

COUNTESS   Now, justice on the doers!

    Enter Bertram [guarded].

KING

I wonder, sir, since wives are monsters to you,
And that you fly them as you swear them lordship,   156
Yet you desire to marry.

    Enter Widow [and] Diana.

                   What woman's that?   157

DIANA

I am, my lord, a wretched Florentine,
Derivèd from the ancient Capilet.   159
My suit, as I do understand, you know,
And therefore know how far I may be pitied.

WIDOW

I am her mother, sir, whose age and honor
Both suffer under this complaint we bring,
And both shall cease, without your remedy.   164

KING

Come hither, Count. Do you know these women?

BERTRAM

My lord, I neither can nor will deny
But that I know them. Do they charge me further?

DIANA

Why do you look so strange upon your wife?

BERTRAM

She's none of mine, my lord.

DIANA   If you shall marry,

---

156 **as . . . lordship** as soon as you swear to be their lord and
husband   157 **Yet** still   159 **Derivèd** descended   164 **both**
i.e., both age and honor. (I will die dishonored.)

You give away this hand, and that is mine;   170
You give away heaven's vows, and those are mine;
You give away myself, which is known mine;
For I by vow am so embodied yours
That she which marries you must marry me,
Either both or none.

LAFEW [to Bertram] Your reputation comes too short
    for my daughter; you are no husband for her.

BERTRAM
    My lord, this is a fond and desp'rate creature,   178
    Whom sometime I have laughed with. Let Your
        Highness
    Lay a more noble thought upon mine honor
    Than for to think that I would sink it here.

KING
    Sir for my thoughts, you have them ill to friend   182
    Till your deeds gain them. Fairer prove your honor
    Than in my thought it lies!

DIANA   Good my lord,
    Ask him upon his oath if he does think
    He had not my virginity.

KING   What say'st thou to her?

BERTRAM   She's impudent, my lord,   188
    And was a common gamester to the camp.   189

DIANA   He does me wrong, my lord. If I were so,
    He might have bought me at a common price.
    Do not believe him. Oh, behold this ring,

                              [showing a ring]

    Whose high respect and rich validity   193
    Did lack a parallel; yet for all that

---

170 **this hand** i.e., Bertram's hand   178 **fond** foolish   182 **for**
as for.   **you . . . friend** they are not well disposed toward you
188 **impudent** shameless   189 **gamester** prostitute
193 **validity** value

He gave it to a commoner o'th' camp,
If I be one.

COUNTESS   He blushes, and 'tis hit.   196
Of six preceding ancestors, that gem,
Conferred by testament to th' sequent issue,   198
Hath it been owed and worn. This is his wife;   199
That ring's a thousand proofs.

KING [to Diana]   Methought you said
You saw one here in court could witness it.

DIANA
I did, my lord, but loath am to produce
So bad an instrument. His name's Parolles.

LAFEW
I saw the man today, if man he be.

KING
Find him, and bring him hither.   [Exit an Attendant.]

BERTRAM   What of him?
He's quoted for a most perfidious slave,   206
With all the spots o'th' world taxed and debauched,   207
Whose nature sickens but to speak a truth.
Am I or that or this for what he'll utter,   209
That will speak anything?

KING   She hath that ring of yours.

BERTRAM
I think she has. Certain it is I liked her,
And boarded her i'th' wanton way of youth.   212
She knew her distance and did angle for me,   213

196 **'tis hit** i.e., that point scored.   198 **sequent issue** next heir
199 **owed** owned   206 **quoted for** known as   207 **With . . .
debauched** accused of, and corrupted by, all the stains of the
world   209 **Am I . . . utter** Am I to be considered either one
thing or another on the evidence of what he will say
212 **boarded her** accosted her sexually   213 **knew her
distance** i.e., knew how to keep her distance, knew her value

Madding my eagerness with her restraint,   214
As all impediments in fancy's course   215
Are motives of more fancy; and, in fine,   216
Her infinite cunning, with her modern grace,   217
Subdued me to her rate. She got the ring,   218
And I had that which any inferior might
At market price have bought.

DIANA   I must be patient.
You that have turned off a first so noble wife
May justly diet me. I pray you yet—   222
Since you lack virtue, I will lose a husband—
Send for your ring, I will return it home,
And give me mine again.

BERTRAM   I have it not.

KING [to Diana]   What ring was yours, I pray you?

DIANA
Sir, much like the same upon your finger.

KING
Know you this ring? This ring was his of late.

DIANA
And this was it I gave him, being abed.

KING
The story then goes false you threw it him   231
Out of a casement?

DIANA   I have spoke the truth.

   Enter Parolles [attended].

BERTRAM
My lord, I do confess the ring was hers.

214 **Madding** making mad, exciting   215 **fancy's** love's
216 **motives** causes.   **in fine** in conclusion   217 **modern**
commonplace   218 **her rate** her terms.   222 **diet me** refuse
me as a part of your fare, as you did her. (Bertram has turned away
Helena as he would a dish, and thus does the same to Diana.)
231 **The story . . . false** The story then is not true that

KING
> You boggle shrewdly; every feather starts you.—   234
> Is this the man you speak of?

DIANA   Ay, my lord.

KING [to Parolles]
> Tell me, sirrah—but tell me true, I charge you,
> Not fearing the displeasure of your master,
> Which on your just proceeding I'll keep off—   238
> By him and by this woman here what know you?   239

PAROLLES   So please Your Majesty, my master hath been an honorable gentleman. Tricks he hath had in him, which gentlemen have.

KING   Come, come, to th' purpose. Did he love this woman?

PAROLLES   Faith, sir, he did love her; but how?

KING   How, I pray you?

PAROLLES   He did love her, sir, as a gentleman loves a woman.

KING   How is that?

PAROLLES   He loved her, sir, and loved her not.   250

KING   As thou art a knave and no knave. What an equivocal companion is this!   252

PAROLLES   I am a poor man, and at Your Majesty's command.

LAFEW   He's a good drum, my lord, but a naughty or-   255
ator.

DIANA   Do you know he promised me marriage?

PAROLLES   Faith, I know more than I'll speak.

---

234 **boggle shrewdly** shy away violently.   **starts** startles
238 **on . . . proceeding** if you speak honestly   239 **By**
concerning   250 **loved her not** i.e., desired her only sexually.
252 **equivocal companion** equivocating knave   255 **drum**
drummer (capable of mere noise).   **naughty** worthless

KING   But wilt thou not speak all thou know'st?

PAROLLES   Yes, so please Your Majesty. I did go between them, as I said; but more than that, he loved her, for indeed he was mad for her, and talked of Satan and of Limbo and of Furies and I know not what. Yet I was in that credit with them at that time that I knew of 264 their going to bed, and of other motions, as promising 265 her marriage, and things which would derive me ill 266 will to speak of. Therefore I will not speak what I know.

KING   Thou hast spoken all already, unless thou canst say they are married. But thou art too fine in thy 269 evidence; therefore stand aside.—
This ring, you say, was yours?

DIANA   Ay, my good lord.

KING
Where did you buy it? Or who gave it you?

DIANA
It was not given me, nor I did not buy it.

KING
Who lent it you?

DIANA   It was not lent me neither.

KING
Where did you find it, then?

DIANA   I found it not.

KING
If it were yours by none of all these ways,
How could you give it him?

DIANA   I never gave it him.

LAFEW   This woman's an easy glove, my lord; she goes off and on at pleasure.

264 **in . . . with them** so much in their confidence
265 **motions** proposals   266 **derive** gain   269 **fine** subtle

KING

    This ring was mine. I gave it his first wife.

DIANA

    It might be yours or hers, for aught I know.

KING

    Take her away; I do not like her now.
    To prison with her. And away with him.—
    Unless thou tell'st me where thou hadst this ring,
    Thou diest within this hour.

DIANA   I'll never tell you.

KING

    Take her away.

DIANA   I'll put in bail, my liege.   286

KING

    I think thee now some common customer.   287

DIANA

    By Jove, if ever I knew man, 'twas you.   288

KING

    Wherefore hast thou accused him all this while?   289

DIANA

    Because he's guilty, and he is not guilty.
    He knows I am no maid, and he'll swear to't;
    I'll swear I am a maid, and he knows not.
    Great King, I am no strumpet, by my life;
    I am either maid or else this old man's wife.

                              [*Pointing to Lafew.*]

KING

    She does abuse our ears. To prison with her!

DIANA   Good mother, fetch my bail.   [*Exit Widow.*]
                             Stay, royal sir.

---

286 **put in bail** make bail, i.e., produce evidence to assure my
liberty   287 **customer** i.e., prostitute.   288 **if . . . you** i.e., I
have known no man sexually any more than I have slept with Your
Majesty.   289 **Wherefore** Why

The jeweler that owes the ring is sent for,   297
And he shall surety me. But for this lord,   298
Who hath abused me, as he knows himself,
Though yet he never harmed me, here I quit him.   300
He knows himself my bed he hath defiled,
And at that time he got his wife with child.
Dead though she be, she feels her young one kick.
So there's my riddle: one that's dead is quick—   304
And now behold the meaning.

Enter Helena and Widow.

KING   Is there no exorcist   305
Beguiles the truer office of mine eyes?
Is't real that I see?

HELENA   No, my good lord,
'Tis but the shadow of a wife you see,
The name and not the thing.

BERTRAM   Both, both. Oh, pardon!

HELENA
Oh, my good lord, when I was like this maid,   310
I found you wondrous kind. There is your ring,   311
And, look you, here's your letter. [*She produces a
    letter.*] This it says:
"When from my finger you can get this ring
And are by me with child," et cetera. This is done.
Will you be mine, now you are doubly won?

BERTRAM
If she, my liege, can make me know this clearly,
I'll love her dearly, ever, ever dearly.

---

297 **owes** owns   298 **surety me** be my security.   300 **quit**
(1) acquit (2) repay   304 **quick** alive (and pregnant)
305 **exorcist** one who conjures up spirits   310 **like this maid**
i.e., disguised as Diana   311 **There** i.e., On Diana's finger
(unless Diana has returned the ring to Helena)

HELENA

If it appear not plain and prove untrue,
Deadly divorce step between me and you!—   319
O my dear mother, do I see you living?

LAFEW

Mine eyes smell onions; I shall weep anon.
[*To Parolles*] Good Tom Drum, lend me a handkerchief.
So, I thank thee. Wait on me home, I'll make sport
with thee. Let thy curtsies alone; they are scurvy ones.   324

KING

Let us from point to point this story know,
To make the even truth in pleasure flow.   326
[*To Diana*] If thou be'st yet a fresh uncroppèd flower,
Choose thou thy husband, and I'll pay thy dower;   328
For I can guess that by thy honest aid
Thou kept'st a wife herself, thyself a maid.
Of that and all the progress, more and less,
Resolvedly more leisure shall express.   332
All yet seems well, and if it end so meet,   333
The bitter past, more welcome is the sweet.   *Flourish.* 334

319 **Deadly divorce** may divorcing death   324 **curtsies**
courteous bows. (A word applied to men as well as women.)
326 **even** precise, plain   328 **Choose . . . dower** (The king
offers Diana what he offered earlier to Helena.)
332 **Resolvedly** in such a way that all doubts are removed
333 **meet** fittingly   334 **past** being past

[Epilogue] ❧

KING. [*advancing*]
> The king's a beggar, now the play is done.
> All is well ended, if this suit be won,
> That you express content; which we will pay,   3
> With strife to please you, day exceeding day.   4
> Ours be your patience then, and yours our parts;   5
> Your gentle hands lend us, and take our hearts.   6

> > > > > *Exeunt omnes.*

Epilogue
3 **express content** i.e., applaud   3–4 **which . . . day** which we
will repay by striving to please you, day after day.   5 **Ours . . .
parts** i.e., We will patiently attend, like an audience, while you
undertake the active role by applauding   6 **Your . . . us** i.e.,
please applaud.   **hearts** i.e., gratitude.

DATE AND TEXT

All's Well That Ends Well was first registered in the Stationers' Register, the official record book of the London Company of Stationers (booksellers and printers), in November 1623 and was published in the First Folio of that same year. The text contains numerous inconsistencies in speech headings, "ghost" characters, anomalies of punctuation, and vague or literary stage directions, indicating it was set from the author's working papers, but these errors are not as extensive as once thought and the text is basically sound. Shakespeare's manuscript may have been sporadically annotated by the bookkeeper. Its printing in the First Folio is unusually laden with errors.

Information on the date of the play is sparse. Francis Meres does not mention it in 1598 in his *Palladis Tamia*, unless it is the intriguing *"Loue labours wonne"* on his list. Its themes and style are more suggestive of the period of *Hamlet* and *Troilus and Cressida*. The common assumption today is that the play was written sometime around 1601–1605. It may be later than *Measure for Measure;* the two plays are closely related, but the order of composition is hard to determine. The role of Lavatch is clearly designed for the actor Robert Armin, who did not join Shakespeare's acting company until 1599 or 1600. Scholars once argued that *All's Well* is an early play later revised, but this means of explaining the inconsistencies in the text no longer seems necessary.

TEXTUAL NOTES

These textual notes are not a historical collation, either of the early folios or of more recent editions; they are simply a record of departures in this edition from the copy text. The reading adopted in this edition appears in boldface, followed by the rejected reading from the copy text, i.e., the First Folio. Only major alterations in punctuation are noted. Changes in lineation are not indicated, nor are some minor and obvious typographical errors.

Copy text: the First Folio. Act divisions are from the Folio; scene divisions are editorially provided.

1.1. 1 [and elsewhere] COUNTESS *Mother* **3** [and elsewhere] BERTRAM *Ros.* **17** [and elsewhere] **losing** loosing **52** [and elsewhere] **to** too **lest** least **70 Farewell. My** Farewell my **130 got** goe **148 th'one** ten **159 wear** were

1.2. 3 [and elsewhere] FIRST LORD *1. Lo.* G. **15** [and elsewhere] SECOND LORD *2. Lo.* E **18 Rossillion** *Rosignoll* **52 him! He** him he **76.1** *Exeunt Exit*

1.3. 3 [and elsewhere] RINALDO *Ste.* **13** [and elsewhere] LAVATCH *Clo.* **19 I** w **74–5** [F indicates the repetition of the line by printing a single line, followed by "*bis*"] **86 ere** or **112 Dian no queen** Queene **115 e'er** ere **124.2** [and elsewhere] *Helena Hellen* **125** [F has s.p. here, *Old. Cou.*, used subsequently in other s.p.] **127 rightly belong** righlie belong **168 loneliness** louelinesse **174 th'one to th'other** 'ton tooth to th'other **180 forswear't. Howe'er,** forswear't how ere **199 intenible sieve** intemible Siue **233 Haply** Happily **247 day and** day, an

2.1. 3–4 gain all, / The gaine, all / The **5** FIRST LORD *Lord.* G **15–16 it. When . . . shrinks, find** it, when . . . shrinkes: finde **18** SECOND LORD *L.G* **25** SECOND LORD *2 Lo.* E **44 with his cicatrice** his sicatrice, with **63 fee** see **94.1** [and elsewhere]

Helena Hellen   **111 two, more dear.** I two: more deare I   **146 fits**
shifts   **157 impostor** Impostrue   **175 nay** ne   **194 heaven** helpe
212 meed deed   **212.1 *Exeunt*** Exit

2.2. 1 [and elsewhere in scene] COUNTESS *Lady*   **60 An end, sir!**
To An end sir to

2.3. 1 [and elsewhere] LAFEW *Ol. Laf.*   **21 indeed. If** indeede if
34 minister, great minister great   **44 *Mort du vinaigre*** Mor du
vinager   **51.1 four** 3 *or* 4   **65 ALL THE LORDS** All   **70–1 choose;
but, be refused, /** Let choose, but be refused; / Let   **76 s.d.** [below
line 62 in F]   **94 her** heere   **96 HELENA** *La.*   **99 LAFEW** *Ol. Lord*
125 when whence   **129 name; vileness** name? Vilenesse   **130 it
is** is is   **137–8 word's a slave / Debauched** words, a slaue / Debosh'd
138–9 grave /A graue: / A   **140–1 tomb / Of** Tombe. / Of
168 eyes. When eies, when   **170 it, I** it: I   **213 lattice** Lettice
266.1 [at line 264 in F]   **293 detested** detected   **301.1 *Exeunt***
Exit

2.4. 11 [and elsewhere] **whither** whether   **16 fortunes** fortune
35 me? [F adds a s.d., *Clo.*]   **56 you.** you   **s.d. *Exit Parolles*** [at
line 55 in F]   **s.d. *Exeunt*** Exit

2.5. 16 who's whose   **27 End** And   **29 one** on   **31 heard** hard
89 BERTRAM [at line 90 in F]   **89 men, monsieur?** men? Monsieur,

3.1. 9 SECOND LORD *French* E   **17** FIRST LORD *Fren.* G   **23 to the**
to'th the

3.2. 9 sold hold   **18 E'en** In   **19 COUNTESS** [not in F]   **45** [and
throughout scene] SECOND LORD *French* E   **47** [and throughout
scene] FIRST LORD *French* G   **64** COUNTESS *Old La.*
65 engrossest all engrossest, all   **111 still-piecing** still-peering

3.4. 4 RINALDO [not in F]   **9–10 hie. / Bless** hie, / *Blesse*
10 peace, whilst *peace. Whilst*   **18 COUNTESS** [not in F]

3.5. 0.2 *daughter* daughter, *Violenta*   **10** [and elsewhere] MARIANA
Maria   **33 le** *la*   **66 warrant** write   **93.1 *Exeunt*** Exit

3.6. 1 [and throughout scene until line 109] FIRST LORD *Cap.* E
3 [and throughout scene until line 109] SECOND LORD *Cap.* G
36 his this   **37 metal** mettle   **ore** ours   **109** FIRST LORD *Cap.* G
111, 117 SECOND LORD *Cap.* E

3.7. 19 Resolved Resolue   **41 steads** steeds   **46 wicked** lawfull

4.1. 1 [and throughout scene] FIRST LORD 1. *Lord E* **69** [and throughout scene] FIRST SOLDIER *Inter.* **90 art** are **93** SECOND SOLDIER *Sol.* [and at line 96] **97** s.d. **Exeunt** *Exit*

4.2. 6 monument. monument **31 least** lest **38 may** make **snare** scarre **56 bond** band

4.3. 1 [and throughout scene] FIRST LORD *Cap. G* **2** [and throughout scene] SECOND LORD *Cap. E* **24 nobility, . . . stream** Nobility . . . streame, **81** FIRST LORD *Ber.* **89 effected** affected **98 he's** ha s [also at line 268] **118 Hush, hush** [assigned in F to Bertram] **125** FIRST LORD *Cap.* **138 All's one to him** [assigned in F to Parolles] **168 poll** pole **189 sheriff's** Shrieues **199 Lordship** Lord **242 our** your **316** BERTRAM *Count*

4.4. 16 you, your

4.5. 21 grass grace **39 name** maine **46 of** off **70 home, I** home. I **80 Marseilles** *Marcellus*

5.1. 6 s.d. **a Gentleman** *a gentle Astringer* [after line 6 in F]

5.2. 1 Monsieur Mr **25 similes** smiles **33 under her** vnder

5.3. 50 warped warpe **59–60 carried, / To** carried / To **60 sender turns** sender, turnes **72** COUNTESS [not in F] **102 Plutus** *Platus* **115 conjectural** connecturall **123 tax** taze **140** KING [not in F] **148 toll** toule **154.1** [after line 152 in F] **155 since** sir **157** s.d. *Diana* Diana, *and Parolles* [after line 157 in F] **183 them. Fairer prove** them fairer: proue **208 sickens but** sickens: but **217 infinite cunning** insuite comming **314 are** is

Epilogue 1 KING [not in F] **4 strife** strift

SHAKESPEARE'S SOURCES

❧

Shakespeare's only known source for *All's Well That Ends Well* is the tale of Giglietta of Nerbone from Boccaccio's *Decameron* (c. 1348–1358), as translated into English by William Painter in *The Palace of Pleasure* (1566, 1575). Painter may have based his translation on a French intermediary by Antoine le Maçon, and Shakespeare possibly knew the Italian and French versions although the English was the most available to him. All three are essentially the same except for the forms of the proper names. The Helena story is also widely dispersed in folktales.

Painter's version appears in the following pages with modernized spelling. From it we see that, except for Helena, many of the characters' names in Shakespeare's play are derived from this source: Helena is Giletta in Painter, but her father is Gerardo of Narbon or Narbona (compare Shakespeare's Gerard de Narbon or Narbonne), and the young man she vainly loves is Beltramo, Count of Rossiglione (i.e., Bertram, Count of Rossillion), who is left after his father's death "under the royal custody of the King" of France. Giletta is no ward and helpless dependent, however, as in Shakespeare; she is well-to-do, is cared for by her kinsfolk after her father's death, and refuses many favorable offers of marriage before journeying to Paris to cure the King of a fistula and claim her reward. Shakespeare's Helena on the other hand is not rich, and so can serve as an example of innate virtue or "gentleness" in contrast with Bertram's hereditary nobility. Shakespeare enhances the roles of the Countess and Lafew and makes the King more sympathetic than in Painter to Helena's (or Giletta's) cause: in Painter, the King is reluctant to give Giletta to Beltramo, whereas in Shakespeare the King becomes a spokesman for faith in the miraculous. Other courtiers in Shakespeare's play join the King in approving of Helena, so that, however much Bertram's resistance to an enforced marriage might seem understandable in most circumstances, his refusal of Helena is made to appear willful. Lavatch, the Countess's fool, quizzically expounds questions of moral consequence that are absent in Painter. Conversely, the added character Parolles highlights the callowness and insensitivity of Bertram and serves as a scapegoat when Bertram belatedly gains a better understanding of himself. At the same time, Shakespeare eschews Painter's easy romantic ending for one that is highly problematic: he does not offer Bertram much opportunity to show a real change of heart toward Helena, as Painter does, and thus places a greater strain on credibility in this comedy of forgiveness. Helena, because she is so far below Bertram in wealth and position, is obliged to be more aggressive than her counterpart in Painter, an aggressiveness which raises troublesome issues of female assertiveness. She does not enjoy Giletta's prerogative of governing Rossiglione in her husband's absence and winning such love from her advisers and subjects that they all lament her public resolution to go on a pilgrimage; Helena is thrown more on her own resources and so is at once more self-reliant and self-asserting.

Shakespeare also gives his play a unity of construction and an economy of time not found in the sources. Characters such as the King and Diana are not discarded once their primary roles have been discharged but are brought importantly into the denouement. As in his use of other Italianate fictional sources, Shakespeare compresses time: for example, Helena vows to cure the King in two days rather than eight (as in Painter), and Helena sleeps with Bertram once rather than often. No convincing source has been found for the comic exposure of Parolles.

THE PALACE OF PLEASURE

By William Painter

THE THIRTY-EIGHTH NOVEL: GILETTA OF NARBONNE

Giletta, a physician's daughter of Narbonne, healed the French King of a fistula, for reward whereof she demanded Beltramo, Count of Rossiglione, to husband.[1] The Count, being married against his will, for despite fled to Florence and loved another. Giletta, his wife, by policy found means to lie with her husband in place of his lover and was begotten with child of two sons, which known to her husband, he received her again, and afterwards she lived in great honor and felicity.

In France there was a gentleman called Isnardo, the Count of Rossiglione, who, because he was sickly and diseased, kept always in his house a physician named Master Gerardo of Narbonne. This Count had only one son, called Beltramo, a very young child, pleasant and fair, with whom there was nourished and brought up many other children of his age—amongst whom[2] one of the daughters of the said physician, named Giletta, who fervently fell in love with Beltramo, more than was meet for a maiden of her age.

This Beltramo, when his father was dead, and left[3] under the royal custody of the King, was sent to Paris, for whose departure the maiden was very pensive. A little while after, her father being likewise dead, she was desirous to go to Paris, only to see the young Count, if for that purpose she could get any good occasion.[4] But being diligently looked unto[5] by her kinsfolk, because

---

1 **to husband** as husband   2 **amongst whom** amongst whom was
3 **and left** i.e., and he, Beltramo, being left   4 **get any good occasion**
find any good excuse.   5 **looked unto** attended to. (Her relatives are
attentive to the question of her marriage because she is mistress of her
own considerable inheritance; they would not be happy to have her slip
away unattended.)

she was rich and fatherless, she could see no convenient way for her intended journey. And being now marriageable, the love she bare to the Count was never out of her remembrance, and refused[6] many husbands with whom her kinsfolk would have placed her without making them privy to the occasion of her refusal.[7]

Now it chanced that she burned more in love with Beltramo than ever she did before, because she heard tell that he was grown to the state of a goodly young gentleman. She heard by report that the French King had a swelling upon his breast which by reason of ill cure was grown to a fistula and did put him to marvelous[8] pain and grief, and that there was no physician to be found, although many were proved,[9] that could heal it, but rather did impair[10] the grief and made it worse and worse. Wherefore the King, like one that was in despair, would take no more counsel or help. Whereof the young maiden was wonderful glad, and thought to have by this means not only a lawful occasion to go to Paris but, if the disease were such as she supposed, easily to bring to pass that she might have the Count Beltramo to her husband.

Whereupon, with such knowledge as she had learned at her father's hands beforetime, she made a powder of certain herbs which she thought meet for that disease and rode to Paris. And the first thing she went about when she came thither was to see the Count Beltramo. And then she repaired to[11] the King, praying His Grace to vouchsafe to show her his disease.

The King, perceiving her to be a fair young maiden and a comely, would not hide it but opened the same unto her. So soon as she saw it, she put him in comfort that she was able to heal him, saying:

"Sire, if it shall please Your Grace, I trust in God, without any pain or grief unto Your Highness, within eight days I will make you whole of this disease."

6 and refused and she refused   **7 without . . . refusal** without letting them in on her secret reasons for refusing.   **8 marvelous** excruciating   **9 proved** tested   **10 impair** make worse   **11 repaired to** went to

The King, hearing her say so, began to mock her, saying: "How is it possible for thee, being a young woman, to do that which the best-renowned physicians in the world cannot?" He thanked her for her good will and made her a direct answer that he was determined no more to follow the counsel of any physician. Whereunto the maiden answered: "Sire, you despise my knowledge because I am young and a woman. But I assure you that I do not minister physic[12] by profession but by the aid and help of God and with the cunning of Master Gerardo of Narbonne, who was my father and a physician of great fame so long as he lived."

The King, hearing those words, said to himself: "This woman, peradventure, is sent unto me of God, and therefore why should I disdain to prove her cunning, sithence[13] she promiseth to heal me within a little space,[14] without any offense or grief unto me?" And being determined to prove[15] her, he said: "Damosel, if thou dost not heal me, but make me to break my determination,[16] what wilt thou shall follow thereof?"[17]

"Sire," said the maiden, "let me be kept in what guard and keeping you list. And if I do not heal you within these eight days, let me be burnt. But if I do heal Your Grace, what recompense shall I have then?"

To whom the King answered: "Because thou art a maiden and unmarried, if thou heal me according to thy promise I will bestow thee upon some gentleman that shall be of right good worship[18] and estimation."

To whom she answered: "Sire, I am very well content that you bestow me in marriage. But I will have such a husband as I myself shall demand, without presumption to any of your children or other of your blood." Which request the King incontinently[19] granted.

---

12 physic medicine   **13 sithence** seeing that   **14 space** space of time   **15 prove** test   **16 determination** i.e., to follow no more the advice of any physician   **17 what . . . thereof?** what do you wish to see happen as a consequence?   **18 worship** rank, distinction **19 incontinently** immediately

The young maiden began to minister her physic, and in short space, before her appointed time, she had thoroughly cured the King. And when the King perceived himself whole, he* said unto her: "Thou hast well deserved a husband, Giletta, even such a one as thyself shalt choose."

"I have, then, my lord," quod she, "deserved the County[20] Beltramo of Rossiglione, whom I have loved from my youth."

The King was very loath to grant him unto her. But because he had made a promise which he was loath to break, he caused him to be called forth and said unto him: "Sir Count, because you are a gentleman of great honor, our pleasure is that you return home to your own house to order your estate according to your degree,[21] and that you take with you a damosel which I have appointed to be your wife."

To whom the Count gave his humble thanks and demanded what[22] she was.

"It is she," quoth the King, "that with her medicines hath healed me."

The Count knew her well and had already seen her; although she was fair, yet, knowing her not to be of a stock convenable to[23] his nobility, disdainfully said unto the King: "Will you then, sire, give me a physician to wife? It is not the pleasure of God that ever I should in that wise bestow myself."

To whom the King said: "Wilt thou, then, that we should break our faith which we to recover health have given to the damosel, who for a reward thereof asked thee to husband?"

"Sire," quoth Beltramo, "you may take from me all that I have and give my person to whom you please, because I am your subject. But I assure you I shall never be contented with that marriage."

"Well, you shall have her," said the King, "for the maiden is fair and wise and loveth you most entirely, thinking[24] verily you shall lead a more joyful life with her than with a lady of a greater house."[25]

---

20 quod . . . County quoth, said . . . Count   21 degree rank, social position   22 demanded what asked who   23 convenable to consistent with   24 thinking i.e., I do this being of the opinion that   25 house family.

The Count therewithal held his peace, and the King made great preparation for the marriage. And when the appointed day was come, the Count, in the presence of the King, although it were against his will, married the maiden, who loved him better than her own self. Which done, the Count, determining before what he would do, prayed license to return to his country to consummate the marriage. And when he was on horseback he went not thither but took his journey into Tuscany, where, understanding that the Florentines and Senois were at wars, he determined to take the Florentines' part and was willingly received and honorably entertained, and made Captain of a certain number of men, continuing in their service a long time.

The new-married gentlewoman, scarce contented with that and hoping by her well-doing to cause him to return into his country, went to Rossiglione, where she was received of all his subjects for their lady. And perceiving that through the Count's absence all things were spoiled and out of order, she, like a sage lady, with great diligence and care disposed all things in order again, whereof the subjects rejoiced very much, bearing to her their hearty love and affection, greatly blaming the Count because he could not content himself with her.

This notable gentlewoman, having restored all the country again, sent word thereof to the Count her husband by two knights of the country, which she sent to signify unto him that, if it were for her sake that he had abandoned his country, he should send her word thereof and she, to do him pleasure, would depart from thence. To whom he churlishly said: "Let her do what she list. For I do purpose to dwell with her when she shall have this ring"—meaning a ring which he wore—"upon her finger and a son in her arms begotten by me." He greatly loved that ring, and kept it very carefully and never took it off from his finger, for a certain virtue that he knew it had.

The knights, hearing the hard condition of two things impossible and seeing that by them he could not be removed from his determination, they returned again to the lady, telling her his answer, who, very sorrowful, after she had a good while bethought herself,[26] purposed to find means to attain to those two things, to the intent that thereby she might recover her husband. And having advised with herself what to do, she assembled the noblest and chiefest of her country, declaring unto them in lamentable wise what she had already done to win the love of the Count, showing them also what followed thereof. And in the end said unto them that she was loath the Count for her sake should dwell in perpetual exile; therefore she determined to spend the rest of her time in pilgrimages and devotion, for preservation of her soul, praying them to take the charge and government of the country, and that they would let the Count understand that she had forsaken his house and was removed far from thence with purpose never to return to Rossiglione again.

Many tears were shed by the people as she was speaking these words, and divers supplications were made unto him to alter his opinion, but all in vain. Wherefore, commending them all unto God, she took her way with her maid and one of her kinsmen, in the habit[27] of a pilgrim, well furnished with silver and precious jewels, telling no man whither she went, and never rested till she came to Florence; where, arriving by fortune at a poor widow's house, she contented herself with the state of a poor pilgrim, desirous to hear news of her lord, whom by fortune she saw the next day passing by the house where she lay, on horseback with his company. And although she knew him well enough, yet she demanded of the goodwife of the house what he was, who answered that he was a strange[28] gentleman called the Count Beltramo of Rossiglione, a courteous knight and well-beloved in the city and that he was marvelously in love with a neighbor of hers that was a gentlewoman, very poor and of small substance, nevertheless of right honest life and report, and by reason of her poverty was yet unmarried and dwelt with her mother, that a wise and honest lady.

The Countess, well noting these words, and by little and little debating every particular point thereof, comprehending the

26 bethought herself thought to herself about this   **27 habit** dress, garb   **28 strange** foreign

effect of those news, concluded what to do; and, when she had well understanded which was the house and the name of the lady and of her daughter that was beloved of the Count, upon a day repaired to the house secretly in the habit of a pilgrim; where, finding the mother and daughter in poor estate amongst their family, after she had saluted them, told the mother that she had to say[29] unto her. The gentlewoman, rising up, courteously entertained her, and being entered alone into a chamber, they sat down, and the Countess began to say unto her in this wise:

"Madam, methink that ye be one upon whom Fortune doth frown so well as[30] upon me. But, if you please, you may both comfort me and yourself."

The lady answered that there was nothing in the world whereof she was more desirous than of honest comfort. The Countess, proceeding in her talk, said unto her: "I have need now of your fidelity and trust, whereupon, if I do stay[31] and you deceive me, you shall both undo me and yourself."

"Tell me then what it is, hardly,"[32] said the gentlewoman, "if it be your pleasure, for you shall never he deceived of[33] me."

Then the Countess began to recite her whole estate[34] of love, telling her what[35] she was and what had chanced to that present day in such perfect order that the gentlewoman, believing her words because she had partly heard report thereof before, began to have compassion upon her. And after that[36] the Countess had rehearsed all the whole circumstance, she continued her purpose,[37] saying: "Now you have heard, amongst other my troubles, what two things they be which behooveth me to have if I do[38] recover my husband, which I know none can help me to obtain but only you, if it be true that I hear: which is that the Count, my husband, is far in love with your daughter."

To whom the gentlewoman said: "Madam, if the Count love

---

29 to say something to say   **30 so well as** just as   **31 stay** stand firm   **32 hardly** hardily, boldly   **33 of** by   **34 estate** circumstance, condition   **35 what** who   **36 after that** after   **37 she continued her purpose** i.e., the Countess continued laying out her plan   **38 do** am to

my daughter, I know not, albeit the likelihood is great. But what am I able to do in that which you desire?"

"Madam," answered the Countess, "I will tell you. But first I will declare what I mean to do for you if my determination be brought to effect. I see your fair daughter of good age, ready to marry, but, as I understand, the cause why she is unmarried is the lack of substance to bestow upon her. Wherefore I purpose, for recompense of the pleasure which you shall do for me, to give so much ready money to marry her honorably as you shall think sufficient."

The Countess's offer was very well liked of the lady, because she was but poor. Yet, having a noble heart, she said unto her:

"Madam, tell me wherein I may do you service, and if it be a thing honest I will gladly perform it; and, the same being brought to pass, do as it shall please you."

Then said the Countess: "I think it requisite that, by someone whom you trust, that you give knowledge to the Count my husband that your daughter is and shall be at his commandment. And to the intent she may be well assured that he loveth her indeed above any other, that she prayeth him to send her a ring that he weareth upon his finger, which ring, she heard tell, he loved very dearly. And when he sendeth the ring, you shall give it unto me, and afterwards send him word that your daughter is ready to accomplish his pleasure. And then you shall cause him secretly to come hither, and place me by him instead of your daughter. Peradventure[39] God will give me the grace that I may be with child. And so, having this ring on my finger and the child in mine arms begotten by him, I shall recover him and by your means continue with him as a wife ought to do with her husband."

This thing seemed difficult unto the gentlewoman, fearing that there would follow reproach unto her daughter. Notwithstanding, considering what an honest part it were to be a means that the good lady should recover her husband and that she should do it for a good purpose, having affiance in her honest

39 **Peradventure** Perhaps

affection,[40] not only promised the Countess to bring this to pass, but in few days, with great subtlety, following the order wherein she was instructed, she had gotten the ring—although it was with the Count's ill will—and took order that the Countess instead of her daughter did lie with him. And at the first meeting, so affectuously[41] desired by the Count, God so disposed the matter that the Countess was begotten with child of two goodly sons, and her delivery chanced[42] at the due time. Whereupon the gentlewoman not only contented the Countess at that time with the company of her husband, but at many other times, so secretly that it was never known—the Count not thinking that he had lien with his wife but with her whom he loved. To whom at his uprising in the morning he used many courteous and amiable words and gave divers fair and precious jewels, which the Countess kept most carefully.

And when she perceived herself with child, she determined no more to trouble the gentlewoman, but said unto her: "Madam, thanks be to God and you, I have the thing that I desire; and even so[43] it is time to recompense your desert, that afterwards I may depart."

The gentlewoman said unto her that if she had done any pleasure agreeable to her mind she was right glad thereof, which she did not for hope of reward but because it appertained to her by well-doing so to do.[44] Whereunto the Countess said: "Your saying pleaseth me well, and likewise for my part I do not purpose to give unto you the thing you shall demand of me in reward, but for consideration of your well-doing, which duty forceth me so to do."[45]

The gentlewoman then, constrained with[46] necessity, demanded[47] of her with great bashfulness an hundred pounds to

---

40 having . . . affection i.e., the Countess thus able to have a marriage fulfilled in chaste affection   **41 affectuously** ardently   **42 chanced** occurred   **43 even so** accordingly   **44 appertained . . . to do** befitted her to do so in the name of virtue.   **45 I do not . . . to do** i.e., I do not intend to give you what you ask as a reward but prompted by my own sense of duty in consideration of your virtuous act.   **46 with** by   **47 demanded** asked

marry her daughter. The Countess, perceiving the shamefastness[48] of the gentlewoman and hearing her courteous demand,
gave her five hundred pounds and so many fair and costly jewels
which almost amounted to like valor.[49] For which the gentlewoman, more than contented, gave most hearty thanks to the
Countess, who departed from the gentlewoman and returned to
her lodging. The gentlewoman, to take occasion from the
Count of any farther repair[50] or sending to her house, took her
daughter with her and went into the country to her friends. The
Count Beltramo, within few days after, being revoked[51] home to
his own house by his subjects, hearing that the Countess was departed from thence, returned.

The Countess, knowing that her husband was gone from
Florence and returned into his country, was very glad and contented, and she continued in Florence till the time of her
childbed was come and was brought abed of two sons, which
were very like unto their father, and caused them carefully to be
nursed and brought up. And when she saw time, she took her
journey, unknown to any man, and arrived at Montpellier. And
resting herself there for certain days, hearing news of the Count
and where he was, and that upon the day of All Saints he purposed to make a great feast and assembly of ladies and knights,
in her pilgrim's weed she went thither. And knowing that they
were all assembled at the palace of the Count, ready to sit down
at the table, she passed through the people without change of
apparel with her two sons in her arms; and when she was come
up into the hall, even to the place where the Count was, falling
down prostrate at his feet, weeping, said unto him:

"My lord, I am thy poor infortunate wife who, to the intent
thou mightest return and dwell in thine own house, have been a
great while begging about the world. Therefore I now beseech
thee, for the honor of God, that thou wilt observe the conditions which the two knights that I sent unto thee did command
me to do. For behold here in mine arms not only one son begotten

48 shamefastness modesty, decency   **49 valor** worth.   **50 farther
repair** additional visit   **51 revoked** recalled

by thee but twain, and likewise thy ring. It is now time, then, if thou keep promise, that I should be received as thy wife."

The Count, hearing this, was greatly astonied,[52] and knew the ring, and the children also, they were so like him.

"But tell me," quoth he, "how is this come to pass?"

The Countess, to the great admiration[53] of the Count and of all those that were in presence, rehearsed unto them in order all that which had been done and the whole discourse thereof. For which cause the Count, knowing the things she had spoken to be true and perceiving her constant mind and good wit and the two fair young boys, to keep his promise made, and to please his subjects and the ladies that made suit unto him to accept her from that time forth as his lawful wife and to honor her, abjected[54] his obstinate rigor, causing her to rise up, and embraced and kissed her, acknowledging her again for his lawful wife. And after he had appareled her according to her estate, to the great pleasure and contentation of those that were there and of all his other friends, not only that day but many others he kept great cheer, and from that time forth he loved and honored her as his dear spouse and wife.

52 astonied astonished   **53 admiration** astonishment   **54 abjected** cast off

Text based on *The Palace of Pleasure, Beautified, Adorned, and Well Furnished with Pleasant Histories and Excellent Novels, Selected out of Divers Good and Commendable Authors. By William Painter . . . 1566. Imprinted at London by Henry Denham for Richard Tottell and William Jones.*

In the following, the departure from the original text appears in boldface; the original reading is in roman.

p. 358 *he [not in 1566]

FURTHER READING

❧

Cole, Howard C. *The All's Well Story from Boccaccio to Shakespeare*. Urbana, Chicago, and London: Univ. of Illinois Press, 1981. Cole traces the development of the story of Giletta di Narbona, on which Shakespeare based his play, from Giovanni Boccaccio's *Decameron* to its appearance in fifteenth- and sixteenth-century redactions and translations. Considering this literary tradition and several relevant nonliterary contexts, Cole offers an ironic reading of the play in which Helena appears essentially self-seeking and self-deceived.

Donaldson, Ian. "*All's Well That Ends Well:* Shakespeare's Play of Endings." *Essays in Criticism* 27 (1977): 34–55. Donaldson discovers the complexity and coherence of *All's Well* in its insistence upon the difficulties of ending. The play's refusal to end well in either formal or human terms becomes for Donaldson evidence of its recognition that problems of ending are problems of life as well as art.

Foakes, R. A. "Shakespeare and Satirical Comedy." *Shakespeare, the Dark Comedies to the Last Plays: From Satire to Celebration*, esp. pp. 7–16. Charlottesville: Univ. Press of Virginia, 1971. Arguing that Parolles and Lavatch control the tone of the play, Foakes sees *All's Well* as a modified version of romantic comedy, one that achieves the fulfillment of the comic form but never the festive comic tone. The play is marked by an insistence upon the intractability of human nature (revealed both by Bertram's unattractiveness and by Helena's obsession with him) that resists the idealizations of the world of romance.

Frye, Northrop. "The Reversal of Energy." *The Myth of Deliverance: Reflections on Shakespeare's Problem Comedies*. Toronto: Univ. of Toronto Press, 1983. For Frye, *All's Well* reveals the fundamental rhythm of comedy found in the natural cycles of renewal. The play dramatizes the transformation of self-destructive energies such as Bertram's lust or Parolles's cowardice into creative social and emotional patterns that rejuvenate the family, the state, and perhaps even Bertram's nature.

Hunt, Maurice. "Helena and the Reformation Problem of Merit in *All's Well That Ends Well.*" *Shakespeare and the Culture of Christianity in Early Modern England,* ed. Dennis Taylor and David Beauregard. New York: Fordham Univ. Press, 2003. Hunt shows how a complex theological discourse of "merit," familiar as the Reformation focused attention on both Catholic and Protestant beliefs, underlies Helena's agency in the comic action. Shakespeare, according to Hunt, develops the character of Helena "within the matrices of an early modern religious controversy," which in many ways accounts for the contradictory response that critics and audiences have had to the character.

Hunter, Robert Grams. "*All's Well That Ends Well.*" *Shakespeare and the Comedy of Forgiveness.* New York: Columbia Univ. Press, 1965. Examining the play in the context of medieval dramatic forebears that celebrate God's forgiveness of erring sinners, Hunter sees *All's Well That Ends Well* as a secular "comedy of forgiveness": Helena achieves her romantic goal in marrying Bertram, but the comic conclusion of the play depends not (as in romantic comedy) upon the marriage but upon Bertram's moral regeneration, accomplished through the agency of Helena's redemptive love.

Johnson, Samuel. "*All's Well That Ends Well.*" *Johnson on Shakespeare,* ed. Arthur Sherbo. *The Yale Edition of the Works of Samuel Johnson,* vol. 7. New Haven, Conn.: Yale Univ. Press, 1968. In a celebrated and influential essay, Johnson faults the play's ending for its violation of moral decorum: "I cannot reconcile my heart to Bertram," he writes, finding him cowardly and ungenerous yet inexplicably "dismissed to happiness."

Kastan, David Scott. "*All's Well That Ends Well* and the Limits of Comedy." *ELH* 52 (1985): 575–589. Kastan argues that *All's Well* is Shakespeare's most insistent exploration of the formal and moral implications of comedy. Resisting the desires of both the characters and the audience for neat solutions, the play, unlike romantic comedy, refuses to shape itself into comforting patterns of wish-fulfillment.

Kirsch, Arthur. "*All's Well That Ends Well.*" *Shakespeare and the Experience of Love.* Cambridge and New York: Cambridge Univ. Press, 1981. Provocatively mingling Pauline theology and twentieth-century psychology, Kirsch examines the disjunctions of tone and action that distinguish the play. He discusses the tensions and contradictions that emerge from its profound exploration of the paradoxes of flesh and spirit inherent in human sexuality.

Lawrence, W. W. "*All's Well That Ends Well.*" *Shakespeare's Problem Comedies*, 1931. Rpt. Harmondsworth, U.K.: Penguin, 1960. Lawrence discusses Helena's healing of the King and satisfaction of Bertram's apparently impossible conditions in the context of their origin in folktales exalting clever and devoted wives. Helena is thus to be understood as honorable, courageous, and resolute, and Bertram's repentance as both an appropriate and a believable response to his wife's virtue.

Leech, Clifford. "The Theme of Ambition in *All's Well That Ends Well.*" *ELH* 21(1954): 17–29. Rpt. in *Discussions of Shakespeare's Problem Comedies*, ed. Robert Ornstein. Boston: D. C. Heath, 1961. In the face of efforts by his contemporaries to explain away the problems of this so-called problem comedy (see, for example, Lawrence above), Leech focuses on the problematic element of ambition in Helena's love. Helena is not the wholly virtuous heroine of folk tradition or of romantic comedy, but a woman whose love is often willful and self-absorbed.

Leggatt, Alexander. "In the Shadow of *Hamlet:* Comedy and Death in *All's Well That Ends Well.*" *Re-Visions of Shakespeare: Essays in Honor of Robert Ornstein*, ed. Evelyn Gajowski. Newark: Univ. of Delaware Press, 2004. Leggatt shows in a characteristically supple reading of the play how a figurative language of death, "anchored by memories of real deaths," marks this play and accounts for its odd tone. Where comedy usually finds its conclusion in the reconciliation of lovers successfully freeing themselves from their pasts, this play demands that the past be acknowledged and accepted, and the comic community that forms at the end thus extends across generations and "includes the living and the dead."

McCandless, David. *Gender and Performance in Shakespeare's Problem Comedies*. Bloomington and Indianapolis: Univ. of Indiana Press, 1997. In a book that argues that the problem comedies as a group dramatize male anxieties about female authority, McCandless, by sensitively focusing on potential stagings of central scenes, sees *All's Well* as a play working to question and complicate the traditional understandings of gender roles as they are usually encoded in the conventions of comedy.

Miola, Robert S. "New Comedy in *All's Well That Ends Well*." *Renaissance Quarterly* 46 (1993): 23–43. Miola subtly traces the influence of Roman New Comedy upon *All's Well*, showing how the familiar conventions, characters, and themes of the classical drama are reworked by Shakespeare to produce this unsettling and provocative comedy.

Muir, Kenneth, and Stanley Wells, eds. *Aspects of Shakespeare's "Problem Plays": Articles Reprinted from "Shakespeare Survey."* Cambridge, Mass.: Cambridge Univ. Press, 1982. Muir and Wells have edited a collection of criticism on the play published originally in *Shakespeare Survey*, including the essay by Roger Warren (see below) and an interview with Royal Shakespeare Company director John Barton about the problems of directing the "problem plays."

Price, Joseph G. *The Unfortunate Comedy: A Study of "All's Well That Ends Well" and Its Critics*. Toronto: Univ. of Toronto Press, 1968. Price's work, the first book-length study of *All's Well*, begins with valuable surveys of the play's stage and critical history and ends with his own interpretation of its unity and coherence. Price argues that the play dramatizes the maturation of Bertram's understanding of honor, a process that is completed only when he and Helena stand together at the end, dramatically reconciling the nobility of birth and of virtue.

Rossiter, A. P. "*All's Well That Ends Well*." *Angel With Horns and Other Shakespeare Lectures*, ed. Graham Storey. London: Longmans, Green, 1961. Rossiter examines Shakespeare's additions to and alterations of his source (Painter's translation of Boccaccio) in tracing the play's deliberate reversal of comic expectations. The play, for Rossiter, is a "tragi-comedy" marked by disquieting ambiguities raised by the conflict between its fairy-tale plot and the psychological exposure of its characters.

Styan, J. L. *All's Well That Ends Well*. Dover, N.H., and Manchester, U.K.: Manchester Univ. Press, 1984. Focusing on a number of influential productions of the play, Styan discusses the range of interpretations discovered in performance and permitted by the text. After identifying some of the central issues the play raises, he offers a scene-by-scene analysis demonstrating how productions have responded to and revealed the play's complex tone.

Warren, Roger. "Why Does It End Well? Helena, Bertram, and the Sonnets." *Shakespeare Survey* 22 (1969): 79–92. Warren clarifies the complex emotional concerns of the play by a comparison with Shakespeare's sonnets, where similarly a focus on intensity of love despite rejection is central. This parallel enables Warren to understand Bertram's cruelty and Helena's devotion in the context of Shakespeare's belief in the power of love to survive and overcome humiliation.

Wheeler, Richard P. "Imperial Love and the Dark House: *All's Well That Ends Well*." *Shakespeare's Development and the Problem Comedies*. Berkeley, Los Angeles, and London: Univ. of California Press, 1981. Wheeler argues that the play brings to the foreground conflicts and contradictions latent in romantic comedy, where the claims of society yield comfortably to the claims of young love. In *All's Well* Wheeler finds this accommodation strained, and he exposes and explores the tensions provoked by the forced marriage between the play's comic design and its psychological content.

TROILUS
AND CRESSIDA

INTRODUCTION

◆◇◆

Shakespeare must have had some relative failures in the theater, as well as enormous successes. *Troilus and Cressida* seems to have been a relative failure, at least on stage in its original run. As we shall see, questions arise as to whether it was produced at all. It is a bitter play about an inconclusive war and a failed love affair, quite unlike anything Shakespeare had written before in his romantic comedies and English history plays. Its bleak satire of political stalemate seems directed, in part, at the unhappy story of the abortive rebellion of the Earl of Essex in 1601; like many of the warriors in *Troilus and Cressida*, Essex was a tarnished hero whose charisma fell victim to his own egomaniacal ambitions and to the mood of anxious helplessness that hovered over Queen Elizabeth's last years. The play is unusually elliptical in its language, as though Shakespeare deliberately adopted a new, contorted style to express the unresolvable paradoxes of the political and psychological no-man's-land he wanted to describe. A major topic of the play is fame, or rather notoriety, for most of Shakespeare's major characters came to him in the story with full-blown legendary identities as antiheroes: Cressida, the faithless woman; Troilus, the rejected male; Pandarus, the go-between; and Achilles, the butcherer of Hector. Shakespeare's language has to deal with shattered identities, with the unstable subjectivity of human willfulness, and with spiritual exhaustion and neurosis. Perhaps some members of Shakespeare's audience were not quite prepared for all of this.

Today, on the other hand, the play enjoys high critical esteem and has shown itself to be theatrically powerful. What we perceive is that its mordant wit, its satirical depiction of war, and its dispiriting portrayal of sexual infidelity call for a response very different from the one required for an appreciation of

A Midsummer Night's Dream and *As You Like It* or *1 Henry IV.*
Troilus and Cressida, written probably in late 1601, shortly before the Stationers' Register entry of 1603, is attuned to a new
and darker mood emerging during this period in Shakespeare's
work and in the work of his contemporaries.

In the early 1600s, dramatic satire enjoyed a sudden and
highly visible notoriety. Catering, in large part, to select and
courtly audiences, and given new impetus by the reopening of
the boys' acting companies at the indoor theaters in 1599, satirical drama quickly employed the talents of Ben Jonson, John
Marston, and George Chapman, as well as other sophisticated
dramatists. Jonson launched a series of plays he called comical
satires, in which he rebuked the London citizenry and presumed
to teach manners to the court as well. The so-called War of the
Theaters among Jonson, Marston, and Thomas Dekker, although partly a personality clash of no consequence, was also a
serious debate between public and more courtly or select stages
on the proper uses of satire. Public dramatists complained about
the libelous boldness of the new satire and were galled by the
preference of some audiences for this new theatrical phenomenon; even Shakespeare fretted in *Hamlet* (2.2.353–79) about
the rivalry. Yet, as an artist in search of new forms, he also responded with positive interest. He experimented with a Jonsonian
type of satirical plot in the exposure of Malvolio in *Twelfth Night*
(1600–1602). *Troilus and Cressida* seems to have been another
and more ambitious experiment, embracing a different kind of
satire, not of witty exposure, but of disillusionment.

This satiric genre is hard to classify according to the conventional definitions of tragedy, comedy, or history, even though it
does have its own clearly defined rationale that makes special
sense in terms of our modern theater. The play is partly tragic in
that it presents the fall of great Hector and adumbrates the fall
of Troy, yet its love story merely dwindles into frustrated es-
trangement without the death of either lover. The play is comic
only insofar as it is black comedy or comedy of the absurd. Its
leering sexual titillation and its mood of spiritual paralysis link
Troilus and Cressida to the problem comedies *All's Well That Ends*

Well (c. 1601–1604) and *Measure for Measure* (1603–1604). The play is called a "history" on both of its early title pages and assuredly deals with the great events of history's most famous war, but history has become essentially ironic. In this, *Troilus and Cressida* represents a culmination of Shakespeare's ironic exploration of history as begun in the impasses of *Richard II* or *Henry IV* and as portrayed more fully in the sustained ambiguities of *Julius Caesar* (1599). However much Shakespeare may have been influenced by the contemporary vogue of satire in the boys' theater, his own satire of disillusion is integral to his development as an artist. *Troilus and Cressida* is a fitting companion and contemporary for *Hamlet* (c. 1599–1601). Like that play, it evokes a universal disorder that may well reflect the loss of an assured sense of philosophical reliance on the medieval hierarchies of the old Ptolemaic earth-centered cosmos.

Troilus and Cressida achieves its disillusioning effect through repeated ironic juxtaposition of heroic ideals and tarnished realities. Although it deals with the greatest war in history and a renowned love affair, we as audience know that Troy and the lovers will be overthrown by cunning and infidelity. Shakespeare partly inherited from his sources this duality of epic grandness and dispiriting conclusion. To learn of the war itself, he must have known George Chapman's translation of Homer's *Iliad* (of which seven books were published in 1598) and, of course, Virgil's account of the destruction of Troy, but he relied more particularly on medieval romances: Raoul Lefevre's *Recueil des Histoires de Troyes*, as translated and published by William Caxton, and perhaps John Lydgate's *Troy Book*, derived in part from Guido delle Colonne's *Historia Trojana*. These romances were Trojan in point of view and hence concerned with the fall of that city. For the bitter love story, Shakespeare went to Geoffrey Chaucer's *Troilus and Criseyde* (c. 1385–1386), which had been derived from the twelfth-century medieval romance of Benôit de Sainte-Maure, *Le Roman de Troie*, as amplified and retold in Boccaccio's *Il Filostrato*. Chaucer's Criseyde is an admirably self-possessed young woman, and her love for Troilus captures the spirit of the courtly love tradition upon which the story was based. After the late fourteenth century, however, Chaucer's heroine suffered a drastic decline in esteem. In Robert Henryson's *Testament of Cresseid*, for example, Cressida becomes a leper and beggar, the "lazar kite of Cressid's kind" to whom Pistol alludes in *Henry V*. Her name has become synonymous with womanly infidelity, as Shakespeare wryly points out in *Troilus and Cressida*: "Let all constant men be Troiluses, all false women Cressids, and all brokers-between Pandars" (3.2.201–3). Shakespeare is fascinated by this phenomenon of declining reputations. Just as the illustrious warrior Achilles must learn that envious time detracts from our best achievements and stigmatizes us for our worst failings, Troilus, Cressida, and Pandarus all anticipate the lasting consequences to their reputations of a failed love relationship. The passion to which they commit themselves eternally becomes not only an emblem of lost hopes and promises but also a caricature to later generations of enervating and frustrated desire, promiscuity, and pandering. Thus, Shakespeare finds in his materials both chivalric splendor and a deflation of it.

Stylistically, Shakespeare exploits this juxtaposition. He employs epic conventions more than is his custom. The narrative commences, as the chorus informs us, *in medias res*, "beginning in the middle." Epic similes adorn the formal speeches of Ulysses, Agamemnon, and Nestor. The rhetoric of persuasion plays an important role, as in *Julius Caesar* and other Roman plays. The great names of antiquity are paraded past us in a roll call of heroes. Hector, above all, is an epic hero, although in the fashion of medieval romance he is also the prince of chivalry. He longs to resolve the war by a challenge to single combat, in tournament, with the breaking of lances and with each warrior defending the honor of his lady-fair (1.3.264–83). The Greeks respond for a time to this stirring call to arms. Yet, in the broader context of the war itself, with its unworthy causes, its frustrating irresolution, and its debilitating effect on the morale of both sides, Hector's idealism cannot prevail. On the Greek side, Ulysses's ennobling vision of "degree, priority, and place" (1.3.86), by which the heavens show to humanity the value of harmonious order, serves more to criticize and mock the present disorder of the Greek army than to offer guidance toward a restoration of that order. Epic convention becomes hollow travesty, as chivalric aspirations repeatedly dissolve into the sordid insinuations of Thersites or Pandarus. Despite the play's epic machinery, the gods are nowhere to be found.

A prevailing metaphor is that of disease (as also in *Hamlet*). Insubordinate conduct "infect[s]" (1.3.187) the body politic. The Greek commanders hope to "physic" (1.3.378) Achilles lest his virtues, "like fair fruit in an unwholesome dish," rot untasted (2.3.119). Hector deplores the way his fellow Trojans "infectiously" enslave themselves to willful appetite (2.2.59). Elsewhere, love is described as an open ulcer and as an itch that must be scratched; Helen is "contaminated carrion" (4.1.73). Thersites, most of all, invites us to regard both love and war as disease-ridden, afflicted by boils, plagues, scabs, the "Neapolitan bone-ache" (syphilis), "lethargies, cold palsies, raw eyes, dirt-rotten livers, wheezing lungs, bladders full of imposthume [abscesses], sciaticas," and still more (2.3.18 and 5.1.19–21). Pandarus ends the play on a similarly tawdry note by jesting about prostitutes (Winchester geese, he calls them) and the "sweating" or venereal diseases.

The war is both glorious and absurd. It calls forth brave deeds and heroic sacrifices. Yet it is correctly labeled by the choric Prologue as a "quarrel," begun over an "old aunt," whom the Greeks have held captive, and Helen, whom the Trojans abducted in reprisal. No one believes the original cause to justify the bloodletting that has ensued. Menelaus's cuckoldry is the subject of obscene mirth in the Greek camp. Among the Trojans, Troilus can argue only that one does not return soiled goods; since all Troy consented to Helen's abduction, Troy must continue the war to maintain its honor. The war thus assumes a grim momentum of its own. The combatants repeatedly discover that they are trapped in the ironies of a situation they helped make but can no longer unmake. Hector's challenge to single combat falls upon Ajax, his "father's sister's son." Achilles, too, has allegiances in the enemy's camp, since he is

enamored of Priam's daughter Polyxena. In the parleys between
the two sides, the warriors greet one another as long-lost brothers, though they vow to slaughter one another on the morrow.
With fitting oxymoron, Paris comments on the paradox of this
"most despiteful gentle greeting," this "noblest hateful love"
(4.1.34–5). Only a barbarian could be free of regret for a peace
that seems so near and is yet so far. The war offers insidious
temptations to potentially worthy men, perverting Achilles's
once-honorable quest for fame into maniacal ambition and an
irresistible impulse to murder Hector. History and tradition, we
know, will mock Achilles for this craven deed. It will put him
down as a bully rather than as a brave soldier, just as Troilus,
Cressida, and Pandarus will come to be regarded in time as
stereotypes of the cheated man, the whore, and the procurer.
Even before the murder of Hector, Achilles sees his reputation
for bravery tarnished by his inaction, while Ajax is hoisted into
prominence by the machinations of Ulysses and the other generals.

Hector's tragedy is, in its own way, no less ironic. Even
though he emerges as the most thoughtful and courageous man
on either side and advises his fellow Trojans to let Helen go
in response to the "moral laws / Of nature and of nations"
(2.2.184–5), he nonetheless ends the Trojan council of war by
resolving to fight on with them. This conclusion may represent,
in part, a realization that the others will fight on, in any case,
and that he must therefore be loyal to them, but the choice also
reflects hubris. Hector is not unlike Julius Caesar in his proud re-
pudiation of his wife Andromache's ominous dreams, his sister
Cassandra's mad but oracular prophecies, and his own conviction that Troy's pursuit of honor stems from a sickened appetite.
He goes to his death because "The gods have heard me swear"
(5.3.15). His character is his fate. Even his humane compunc-
tions, like Brutus's, are held against him; he spares the life of
Achilles and is murdered in reward. War is no place for men of
scruple, as Troilus reminds his older brother. Yet Hector, at least,
is the better man for refusing to be corrupted by the savagery of

war; we honor his memory, even if we also view him as sense-lessly victimized by a meaningless conflict.

The lovers, as well, are caught in war's trap—not only Troilus and Cressida, but also Paris and Helen, Achilles and Polyxena. Achilles vows to Polyxena not to fight and thereby misses his cherished opportunity for fame; ironically, he is aroused to vengeful action only by the death of a male friend, Patroclus, who is whispered to be his "male varlet" or "mascu-line whore" (5.1.15–17). Paris is obliged to ask his brother Troilus to return Cressida to the Greeks, so that Paris may con-tinue to enjoy Helen. What else can Paris do? "There is no help," he complains. "The bitter disposition of the time / Will have it so" (4.1.49–51). Troilus prepares his own undoing when he argues in the Trojan council of war that Helen must be kept at all cost; the cost, it turns out, is his own Cressida. He sees this irony at once: "How my achievements mock me!" (4.2.71); that is, he has no sooner achieved her sexually than he must give her up so that the war may go on with Trojan honor intact and Helen still in Paris's bed. The love of Troilus and Cressida is dwarfed by the war, which has no regard for their private con-cerns. Troilus wins Cressida after many months of wooing, only to lose her the next day. Yet how could Cressida's father Calchas know of her personal situation? He wishes only to have his daughter back. And, although the Trojan leaders do know of Troilus's affair, they must pay heed first to such matters of state as the exchange of prisoners.

So, too, must Troilus. Perhaps the greatest irony is that he must himself choose to send Cressida to the Greeks, placing duty above personal longing. He appears to have no real choice, but the result is surrounded by absurdities, and it is something that Cressida cannot comprehend. She has determined to stay no matter what the world may think; passionate love is more important to her. Although Cressida was first introduced to us as a sardonic and worldly young woman, urbane, mocking, self-possessed, witty, unsentimental, even scheming and opportunis-tic, and, above all, wary of emotional commitment, her brief involvement with Troilus does touch deep emotion. For a moment, she catches a glimpse of something precious to which she would cling, something genuine in her unstable world. Yet Troilus, caught between love and duty, consents to her departure to the Greek camp. There she reverts to her former disillusioned self, behaving as is expected of her. Who has deserted whom? Cressida gives up, hating herself for doing so. She knows she cannot be true because, like too many women in her experience, she is led by "The error of our eye" and is thus a prey to male importunity (5.2.113). Alone and friendless in the Greek camp except for her neglectful father, she turns to a self-assured and opportunistic man (Diomedes) who is perfectly cynical about women generally but who will at least protect her against the other sex-starved Greek officers. Sometimes she seems, to Ulysses at least, one of those "sluttish spoils of opportunity / And daughters of the game" (4.5.63–4). Still, this surrender to will and appetite in her is not unsympathetic, and does not happen without inner struggle. Her weakness is emblematic of a universal disorder and is partly caused by it. In the grim interplay of war and love, both men and women are powerless to assert their true selves. As the malcontent Thersites concludes, "Lechery, lechery, still wars and lechery; nothing else holds fashion."

The printing history of *Troilus and Cressida* is full of obscurities that may give some insight into the play's apparent lack of stage success. On February 7, 1603, the printer James Roberts entered his name on the Register of the Company of Stationers (i.e., publishers and booksellers) to print, "when he hath gotten sufficient authority for it, the book of Troilus and Cressida as it is acted by my Lord Chamberlain's Men." Evidently, the authority was not forthcoming, for in 1609 the play was reregistered to R. Bonian and H. Walley and published by them that year in quarto as *The History of Troilus and Cressida. As it was acted by the King's Majesty's servants at the Globe. Written by William Shakespeare*. Immediately afterward, and well before this first printing had sold out, a new title page was substituted as follows: *The Famous History of Troilus and Cresseid. Excellently expressing the beginning of their loves, with the conceited wooing of Pandarus Prince of Lycia. Written by William Shakespeare.* This second version had, moreover, a preface to the reader (something found in no other Shakespearean quarto) declaring *Troilus and Cressida* to be "a new play, never staled with the stage, never clapper-clawed with the palms of the vulgar," nor "sullied with the smoky breath of the multitude." The preface goes on to imply that the play's "grand possessors" (i.e., Shakespeare's acting company) had not wished to see the play released at all. What this substituted title page and added preface may suggest is that Bonian and Walley felt constrained to present their text as a new one—a literary rather than a theatrical text—and hence different from the version entered in the Stationers' Register "as it is acted by my Lord Chamberlain's Men." Because that version had been legally registered in the name of James Roberts, the new publishers made their case for legal possession by offering a "new" play.

Later, the editors of the First Folio edition of 1623 seemed to have had difficulty in obtaining permission to print *Troilus and Cressida.* Three pages of the play were actually printed to follow *Romeo and Juliet,* among the tragedies, but were then withdrawn to be replaced by *Timon of Athens.* Ultimately, the play appeared in the Folio almost without pagination, unlisted in the table of contents, and placed with fitting ambiguity between the histories and the tragedies.

This unusual printing history offers conflicting information about original stage performance. Against the evidence of the second version of the 1609 quarto, with its preface proclaiming a play "never staled with the stage," we have the evidence of the first title page mentioning the King's Majesty's servants at the Globe and of the Stationers' Register entry in 1603 referring to the play "as it is acted." Since the 1609 preface may be part of a legal maneuver designed to represent the play as new, the case in favor of actual performance has some weight. We cannot be sure, however, that the performance was successful or that it reached a very large audience. Some scholars have hypothesized that Shakespeare's company mounted a special production of the play for a private audience at the Inns of Court (where young men studied law) or a similar place. Probably this venue would not have served for the play's opening performance; Shakespeare's company often took its regular plays to court or other special audiences, but no instance is positively known in which Shakespeare wrote on commission for a private showing. More likely, *Troilus and Cressida* was first performed publicly without great success. A sequel, promised in the closing lines of the play by Pandarus to be presented "some two months hence," evidently did not materialize, perhaps because public demand was insufficient. The 1609 quarto, with its revised title page and added preface, may have attempted to capitalize on the play's public failure by touting it as sophisticated fare, to be appreciated only by discerning readers. Possibly, Shakespeare and his company took another look at *Troilus and Cressida* for indoor performances for select audiences, only to discover anew that the play was not a great success on the stage. Its subsequent stage history, in any case, is largely a blank until the twentieth century, except for a much changed Restoration adaptation by John Dryden (1679) in which Cressida remains true to Troilus and slays herself when accused of infidelity.

Since 1907, on the other hand, when the play was finally revived on the London stage, it has enjoyed a genuine and growing success. Its disillusionment about war seems admirably suited to an era of world conflict, superpower confrontations, and deepening cynicism about politics. Thersites and Pandarus sound positively choric today in their chortling and obscene reflections on the perversions of human sexuality. Helen as insipid sex goddess and Paris as her languid admirer strike us as boldly modern. Most of all, perhaps, Cressida as failed heroine has come into her own. Centuries of disparaging sexist dismissal of her as a typically faithless woman have given way to nuanced interpretations in which male importunity is at least as much to blame for her desertion of Troilus as her own admitted weakness. Once Troilus has possessed her sexually, he seems less obsessively interested in her and consents, even if unwillingly, to her return to the Greeks. Her awareness that something of this sort was bound to happen provides modern actresses with a potent indictment of the male species. Paradoxically, this searing play about the decay of "notorious identities" (Linda Charnes's phrase) has led to a resuscitation of reputation for the woman who was once the most notorious of them all. See stage and screen histories below, for detailed history and analysis.

The following is a complete text of the preface to the reader from the second "state" of the 1609 quarto.

A NEVER WRITER,
TO AN EVER READER. NEWS.

Eternal reader, you have here a new play, never staled with the stage, never clapper-clawed with the palms of the vulgar, and yet passing full of the palm comical; for it is a birth of your brain that never undertook anything comical vainly. And were but the vain names of comedies changed for the titles of commodities, or of plays for pleas, you should see all those grand censors, that now style them such vanities, flock to them for the main grace of their gravities, especially this author's comedies, that are so framed to the life that they serve for the most common commentaries of all the actions of our lives, showing such a dexterity and power of wit that the most displeased with plays are pleased with his comedies. And all such dull and heavy-witted worldlings as were never capable of the wit of a comedy, coming by report of them to his representations, have found that wit there that they never found in themselves and have parted better witted than they came, feeling an edge of wit set upon them more than ever they dreamed they had brain to grind it on. So much and such savored salt of wit is in his comedies that they seem, for their height of pleasure, to be born in that sea that brought forth Venus. Amongst all there is none more witty than this; and had I time I would comment upon it, though I know it needs not, for so much as will make you think your testern well bestowed, but for so much worth as even poor I know to be stuffed in it. It deserves such a labor as well as the best comedy in Terence or Plautus. And believe this, that when he is gone and his comedies out of sale, you will scramble for them and set up a new English Inquisition. Take this for a warning, and at the peril of your pleasure's loss, and judgment's, refuse not, nor like this the less for not being sullied with the smoky breath of the multitude; but thank fortune for the scape it hath made amongst you, since by the grand possessors' wills I believe you should have prayed for them rather than been prayed. And so I leave all such to be prayed for, for the states of their wits' healths, that will not praise it. *Vale*.

TROILUS AND CRESSIDA
ON STAGE

The stage history of *Troilus and Cressida* confirms our critical impression that Shakespeare never attempted a more puzzling, difficult, and uncompromisingly experimental play. With its mordant view of war and sexuality, it had to wait for the twentieth century to find its true audience. The play seems not to have prospered in Shakespeare's day (see the Introduction to the play, pp. 382–4); if performed publicly at all at the Globe Theatre, as the original quarto title page asserts, it evidently enjoyed so brief a run that the preface to a subsequent quarto printing could claim that the play had never been "staled with the stage" or "clapper-clawed with the palms of the vulgar."

This patrician sentiment of hostility toward popular taste and performance is the publisher's, not Shakespeare's; nonetheless, it raises questions about the play's intent. Did Shakespeare deliberately write a play that only sophisticated spectators or readers could appreciate? This elitist hypothesis has some appeal. Scholars have argued that *Troilus and Cressida* was performed at the Inns of Court (where lawyers were trained) for a select audience, and that it is full of topical references: to Ben Jonson's *Poetaster* (1601), to the vogue for satirical writing, and above all to the Earl of Essex. Since Shakespeare had already complimented Essex in his fifth chorus of *Henry V* (1599), and since Essex was a favorite of the actors as well as a close associate of Shakespeare's first patron, the Earl of Southampton, Shakespeare may have had reason to be concerned about the political fortunes of this talented but mercurial aristocrat in the waning months of Queen Elizabeth's reign. George Chapman, in his translation of Homer's *Iliad*, had already extolled Essex as "the

most honored now living instance of the Achilleian virtues," so
that politically savvy audiences or readers might well have been
expected to dwell on a possible analogy between the sulk-
ing Achilles of Shakespeare's play and England's unpredictable
military hero of 1601. The analogy is an uncertain one; if
Shakespeare had any such intention at all, he wisely did not
make clear any object lesson. His portrait of Achilles is both ad-
miring and critical, but mostly critical. Still, the play's experimental form and its satirical vein may have been prompted by a
mood of disillusionment and anxiety in 1601–1602 at the end of
Elizabeth's reign.

Whatever the immediate reason, *Troilus and Cressida* proved
to be a play far ahead of its time. Until the twentieth century,
the response to it was generally one of aversion, apathy, or be-
wilderment. It was either left unperformed or infrequently revived in a severely rewritten form. In fact, no performance of
Troilus and Cressida is recorded after 1601–1602 (other than one
of uncertain date but prior to the 1670s at Smock Alley, Dublin)
until 1679, when, at the theater in Dorset Garden, London,
John Dryden's *Troilus and Cressida, or Truth Found Too Late* undertook to remedy the play's presumed defects and make it
palatable for Restoration audiences. Dryden not only brings dramatic structure into line with the classical "rules," as he had
done in his more famous adaptation of Shakespeare's *Antony
and Cleopatra* called *All for Love* (1678), but sentimentalizes
Cressida into a heroine worthy of tragedy (as was his Cleopatra).
Cressida remains faithful to Troilus and reluctantly accepts the
attentions of Diomedes only as a ruse to make possible an escape
back to Troy. The wooing scene witnessed by Troilus is thus only
an illusion, and Cressida the victim of an ironic misunderstand-
ing; betrayed by Diomedes's treachery and no longer trusted by
Troilus, she commits suicide. Troilus, learning the truth too late,
kills Diomedes and is at last slain in battle by the Greeks. The
death of Hector is reported, not directly shown. Throughout, in
fact, Dryden cuts back the gritty war material of Shakespeare's
play, shortening the long council speeches and devising instead
a quarrel between Hector and Troilus about the exchange of

Cressida for Antenor—a conflict that relates to the love plot, not the war.

Dryden's adaptation enjoyed some success. Thomas Betterton played Troilus and also spoke the Prologue, "representing the ghost of Shakespeare." When the play was revived at the Theatre Royal, Drury Lane, in 1709, Betterton took the part of Thersites. Performances took place in five other seasons in the early eighteenth century, the last at the Theatre Royal, Covent Garden, in 1734. From that date on, however, *Troilus and Cressida* remained wholly unknown for nearly two centuries.

Significantly, if unexpectedly, the play belatedly surfaced in Europe rather than in England. As literary critic and editor Kenneth Muir has shown, Shakespeare's play was performed at Munich in 1898 as a travesty of Homer with an all-male cast (*Proceedings of the Leeds Philosophical and Literary Society*, 8 [1958], 233–8). Several other productions followed in Germany in the succeeding decades, evidently devised as commentaries on current political crises in that country. The play was produced in Hungary in 1900, Vienna in 1902, and Prague in 1921. *Troilus and Cressida* had at last found a world in which human experience could match the desolation of Shakespeare's script.

Revivals in England, beginning in 1907 with a production by Charles Fry at London's Great Queen Street Theatre, and one by William Poel and the Elizabethan Stage Society at the King's Hall, Covent Garden, in 1912, explored the play's experimental and theatrical dimensions as well as its anguish and disillusionment. Working on a bare stage, Poel attempted to reproduce the theatrical conventions and conditions of the Elizabethan theater. An as yet unknown actress, Edith Evans, played Cressida, Poel played Pandarus, and Hermione Gingold was Cassandra. In 1922, a Marlowe Society production (with the women's parts played by men) at Cambridge caught the mood of war-weariness in the aftermath of World War I. In 1923, celebrating the three-hundredth anniversary of the publication of the First Folio, the Old Vic completed a ten-year project of staging the entire canon with a production of *Troilus and Cressida*. Ion Swinley played Troilus in Robert Atkins's production. Nugent Monck, who had served as William Poel's stage manager, produced the play in 1928 at the intimate Maddermarket Theatre in Norwich. Iden Payne, at Stratford-upon-Avon in 1936, provided a respectful version of Shakespeare's play in Elizabethan dress. Michael Macowan, directing a production for London's Mask Theatre Company in 1938, employed modern dress and contemporary weapons and battle effects to underscore the play's relevance to Neville Chamberlain's appeasement of the Nazis at Munich (September 1938), and a Marlowe Society revival in 1940, produced by George Rylands, similarly found pertinent material in the anxious months leading up to and following Dunkirk (May 1940).

By mid-twentieth century, *Troilus and Cressida* had become a visible part of the Shakespearean repertory. Its timely bitterness seemed to invite a wide range of interpretations in the medium of modern theater, often in modern dress. In 1946, Robert Atkins again produced the play, this time in Regent's Park at the Open Air Theatre. Struggling against the difficulties of both the text and the weather, Atkins produced a thoughtful version whose evenhandedness is revealed in the program note identifying Thersites merely as "an independent-minded Grecian." Two years later, at Stratford-upon-Avon, Anthony Quayle directed Paul Scofield (as Troilus) in a production that emphasized the shabbiness of the Greek forces and the splendor of the Trojans. Quayle's production ended with Troilus's speech announcing Hector's death. In 1954, the play again was performed at Stratford-upon-Avon. Directed by Glen Byam Shaw, with Laurence Harvey as Troilus, the production eschewed any theatrical gimmickry to trace the emotional patterns of the play. Tyrone Guthrie's controversial production at the Old Vic in 1956 set the action in Edwardian England. With Pandarus in a gray top hat, Achilles in a chic dressing gown, Thersites as a war correspondent with sketchbook and camera, and Helen lounging decorously on a grand piano, Guthrie deftly exposed the affectation and folly that motivates the military action.

Troilus and Cressida's peculiarly modern fascination has been eloquently realized by director John Barton in a series of collaborations. The production by Barton and Peter Hall (Stratford-upon-Avon, 1960) played up the cynicism of Thersites (Peter O'Toole) as well as the alluring sensuality of Cressida (Dorothy Tutin) at a time of growing unease with the sexual revolution and a deteriorating international climate. Barton's Stratford-upon-Avon productions in 1968 and 1976 exploited even further a mood of nihilism in the wake of a bitter European response to the war in Vietnam and to Europe's own social and political tensions. All nobility disappeared in these versions of the play, both of which were dominated by Thersites's sneering cynicism. In the 1968 production, Achilles (Alan Howard) was a prancing homosexual with blond hair and shaved legs, Cressida (Helen Mirren) a coarse tease, and Troilus (Michael Williams) weak and confused. In 1976, Barton (with co-director Barry Kyle) saw the play as an unnecessary and ignoble conflict between aging, purposeless Greeks, dressed in gray wool and brown leather, and young, sensual Trojans in pastel silks and gold jewelry.

Today it is virtually impossible not to view the play as a bitter and timely commentary on war's dislocating effects, and recent productions have continued to find dramatic power in the dispiriting action. In 1985, Howard Davies's production for the Royal Shakespeare Company transposed the war to the late nineteenth century, successfully exposing the hypocrisy in the language of chivalry as it masks the tawdry and destructive reality of war. Juliet Stevenson's Cressida managed brilliantly to underline her vulnerability in this world of violent male assertion, never, however, becoming a passive victim but pragmatically finding her way between the unappetizing alternatives the world places before her. Ten years later, in New York's Central Park, Mark Wing-Davey similarly emphasized how war destroys cultures morally as well as physically, in an energetic production that universalized rather than merely modernized the action, with costumes ranging from medieval suits of armor to modern camouflage uniforms, weapons from lances to assault rifles, and a musical score with medieval chants, World War II popular music, and contemporary rock. In Stratford-upon-Avon the following year, Ian Judge returned the play to its classical setting in a production that emphasized the disturbing similarities of the warring camps, and made an undercurrent of a lurid sexuality the driving force of all actions in the play.

In 1990, at the Swan Theatre in Stratford-upon-Avon, the RSC again mounted the play. Directed by Sam Mendes, the production showed the tawdry reality behind the heroic surface. Amanda Root's Cressida was a confident coquette, Ralph Fiennes's Troilus was petulant and jealous, Norman Rodway's Pandarus was a creepy, if campy, voyeur. Perhaps most symptomatic of this production was Sally Dexter's crudely sexual, aging Helen, showing clearly the emptiness at the spoken values of the play. Late in 1998, the RSC again turned to the play, in a production directed by Michael Boyd, opening first at London's Pit Theatre and at the end of the year moving to Stratford-upon-Avon's Swan. Set in some twentieth-century war-torn country, the set showed the effects of the ongoing conflict with bullet-marked walls and broken windows. What marked this production was the openness of both William Houston's Troilus and Jayne Ashbourne's Cressida. Both were engaging, fresh-faced, and vulnerable, their hopes for the future cruelly shattered by the cynicism and selfishness of their elders. In London in early 1999, Trevor Nunn directed the play at the Olivier Theatre in the National Theatre complex. The stage was defined by a curved wall with six doors arranged around a circular acting space with red gravel suggesting nothing so much as blood-soaked ground. The Trojans were all played by black actors, with the exception of David Bamber's Pandarus, and all were dressed in white cotton robes. The Greeks were all white actors in dark leather. Yet for all the emphasis upon their physical differences, these were both ignorant armies clashing by night. What positive human value the play did find was focused on Sophie Okonedo's clever, sexy, spirited Cressida, who was betrayed by all the men around her. She was shocked at the decision to send her to the Greeks, but had the spirit and self-control mockingly to offer Ulysses her foot to kiss as the Greek generals disgustingly groped her, and, though she did give in to Diomedes, she did so in recognition that this was the only way to survive. Gradually, however, her spirit broke, and the play ended, through some substantial textual adjustment, with Cressida, in the dark, disoriented and alone, with gunfire barking behind her.

In Shakespeare's original staging conception, assuming that the play was staged at all, tents and eavesdropping dominate the dramatic action in the Greek camp, while courtly debate and indolent amorous encounters characterize the scene at Troy. We cannot be sure how many actual tents are intended to be visible on stage, but their presence is continually invoked in the dialogue: Agamemnon encounters Aeneas " 'fore our tent" (1.3.215), Troilus overhears Cressida's disloyal courtship with Diomedes outside of Calchas's tent (5.2), and Achilles is repeatedly seen *"at the opening of his tent"* (2.3.83). This last tent must be functional to the extent of providing entries and exits. The eavesdroppings are at times elaborately choreographed, as in 5.2: Troilus and his guide Ulysses form one party to witness the wooing of Cressida by Diomedes, while the entire scene is witnessed in turn by Thersites as a gloating and obscene omniscient presence. In Troy, the ardent wooing of Cressida by Troilus is deflated by an implicit comparison with the amorous dalliance of Paris and Helen (3.1). Pandarus officiates in both courtships, and we are made continually aware of the irony that Troilus will have to give up Cressida in order that Paris may continue to enjoy Helen. Juxtaposition is an essential technique throughout: a council of war in the Greek camp (1.3) is echoed by one in Troy (2.2), long, eloquent speech answering long, eloquent speech as though to emphasize that rhetoric can prove anything. The juxtapositions of public oratory and eavesdropping, war and love, Greek camp and Trojan citadel, reputation and individual worth, public morality and private cynicism, all demand on stage an evocation of contrasting worlds irreconcilably at odds, though perhaps disturbingly similar in the gap between their actions and their professed values.

TROILUS AND CRESSIDA
ON SCREEN

Not surprisingly, a play that may have been a stage failure in its own day, and that can claim virtually no performance history until the twentieth century, has seldom appeared on screen; even today, when the play has succeeded brilliantly in experimental theater, it has not been judged as promising material for movie or television viewing. Indeed, apart from a BBC televised version in 1954 that drew very small audiences and a verdict of having been both boring and difficult to follow, the only production of note is that of the BBC's the Shakespeare Plays series, which had dedicated itself to doing all the plays in the canon. This one came along in 1981 and was directed by Jonathan Miller.

The director and his Troilus, Anton Lesser, apparently did not see eye to eye with the actress playing Cressida, Suzanne Burden, as to the nature of the central love relationship in the play: they conceived of Cressida as sexually turned on by her discovery of the power she could exercise over men as a desired sex object, whereas Burden conceived of her character as a victimized woman forced to learn to become the plaything of powerful males. Despite this disagreement, or perhaps because of it, Burden's performance is powerfully perceptive, making use of her discovery (in the play itself, and evidently in the rehearsal process as well) that she must use her sex to get what she wants. The result is a performance in which men and women do not understand one another. Burden works her way along uncharted emotional paths: sardonic and bored at first, hiding her hesitancy beneath an exterior of witty badinage, then awkward and uncertain as she experiences what it is like for her to be the object of Troilus's fervent idealism, then going beyond her tongue-tied apprehensiveness to a confession of desire and an abandonment of the cautious restraints that her mind tells her she should heed.

Jack Birkett, a.k.a. the Incredible Orlando, a blind transvestite actor, is refreshingly cast as Thersites. The Renaissance costuming and sunlit stone corridors and archways of the various sets, though occasionally evocative of the dreariness of war (especially in the Greek camp with its tent city and camp prostitutes, and in an occasional visual homage to *M.A.S.H.*), are sufficiently committed to Miller's and the BBC's signature brand of handsome historical reconstruction (with indebtedness to woodcut artists and engravers of the northern European Renaissance like Dürer, Cranach, and Altdorfer, and architects like Jan Vredeman de Vries) that the production finds little opportunity for exploring the futility of war and the woeful decline of reputations among the great heroes of the Homeric past. Miller's idea of having Helen present when the Trojan leadership discusses whether or not to return her to the Greeks seems like a catchy idea at first, but it turns the assembly into a series of recriminations thrown against her rather than a reasoned if passionate debate on the meaning of the war. The result overall is a production that is occasionally quite perverse and yet somehow bland and unadventuresome, especially when compared with many far-out productions on stage in recent decades. Still, this version does boast the virtues of an essentially uncut text. Even at that, this version does do away with most of the battle sequences in act 5, since Miller wanted to focus on spoken language instead of what he regarded as a long and sporadic series of encounters.

Troilus and Cressida
Filmography

1. 1954
   BBC
   George Rylands and Douglas Allen, producers
   George Rylands, director

   Troilus—John Fraser
   Cressida—Mary Watson
   Pandarus—Frank Pettingell
   Thersites—Richard Wordsworth

2. 1966
   BBC
   Michael Bakewell and Paul Hill, producers
   Michael Croft, Bernard Hepton, and Paul Hill,
   directors

   Troilus—Andrew Murray
   Cressida—Charlotte Womersley
   Pandarus—David Stockton

3. 1981
   BBC/Time-Life Television
   Jonathan Miller, producer
   Jonathan Miller, director

   Troilus—Anton Lesser
   Cressida—Suzanne Burden
   Pandarus—Charles Gray
   Thersites—Jack Birkett (a.k.a. the Incredible
     Orlando)

TROILUS
AND CRESSIDA

[Dramatis Personae

PROLOGUE

PRIAM, *King of Troy*

HECTOR,
TROILUS,
PARIS,
DEIPHOBUS, } *his sons*
HELENUS, *a priest,*
MARGARETON, *a bastard,*

AENEAS,
ANTENOR, } *Trojan commanders*

CALCHAS, *a Trojan priest, Cressida's father, and defector to the Greeks*

PANDARUS, *Cressida's uncle*

SERVANT *to Troilus*

SERVANT *to Paris*

CASSANDRA, *Priam's daughter, a prophetess*

ANDROMACHE, *Hector's wife*

HELEN, *former wife of Menelaus, now Paris's mistress*

CRESSIDA, *Calchas's daughter, loved by Troilus*

ALEXANDER, *Cressida's servant*

AGAMEMNON, *the Greek General*

MENELAUS, *brother of Agamemnon*

ACHILLES,
AJAX,
ULYSSES, } *Greek commanders*
NESTOR,
DIOMEDES,

PATROCLUS, *Achilles's friend*

THERSITES, *a scurrilous fool*
SERVANT *to Diomedes*

Trojan and Greek Soldiers, and Attendants

SCENE: *Troy, and the Greek camp before it*]

❧

Prologue ❧ [Enter the Prologue, in armor.]

PROLOGUE

In Troy, there lies the scene. From isles of Greece
The princes orgulous, their high blood chafed,   2
Have to the port of Athens sent their ships,
Fraught with the ministers and instruments   4
Of cruel war. Sixty and nine, that wore
Their crownets regal, from th'Athenian bay   6
Put forth toward Phrygia, and their vow is made   7
To ransack Troy, within whose strong immures   8
The ravished Helen, Menelaus' queen,   9
With wanton Paris sleeps; and that's the quarrel.
To Tenedos they come,   11
And the deep-drawing barks do there disgorge   12

Prologue
2 **orgulous** proud.   **chafed** heated, angered   4 **Fraught**
laden.   **ministers** agents, i.e., soldiers   6 **crownets** coronets,
crowns worn by nobles   7 **Phrygia** district in western Asia
Minor, identified as Troy by the Roman poets, and hence in
Renaissance poetry   8 **immures** walls   9 **ravished** abducted
11 **Tenedos** small island in the Aegean Sea off the coast of Asia
Minor   12 **deep-drawing barks** ships lying low in the water
(with their heavy cargo)

Their warlike freightage. Now on Dardan plains   13
The fresh and yet unbruisèd Greeks do pitch
Their brave pavilions. Priam's six-gated city—   15
Dardan, and Timbria, Helias, Chetas, Troien,   16
And Antenorides—with massy staples   17
And corresponsive and fulfilling bolts,   18
Spar up the sons of Troy.   19
Now expectation, tickling skittish spirits   20
On one and other side, Trojan and Greek,
Sets all on hazard. And hither am I come,   22
A prologue armed, but not in confidence   23
Of author's pen or actor's voice, but suited   24
In like conditions as our argument,   25
To tell you, fair beholders, that our play
Leaps o'er the vaunt and firstlings of those broils,   27
Beginning in the middle, starting thence away   28
To what may be digested in a play.
Like or find fault; do as your pleasures are;
Now, good or bad, 'tis but the chance of war.

                                        [Exit.]

---

13 **Dardan** Trojan. (From *Dardanus,* son of Zeus and Electra,
daughter of Atlas. According to legend, Dardanus was the ancestor
of the Trojan race.)   15 **brave pavilions** splendid tents.
16–17 **Dardan . . . Antenorides** (The names of Troy's six gates.)
17–18 **massy . . . bolts** i.e., massive posts fitted with sockets to
receive matching and well-fitted bolts   19 **Spar** close
20 **skittish** lively   22 **Sets . . . hazard** puts all at risk.
23 **armed** in armor   23–4 **not . . . voice** i.e., not overconfident
in the value of the play or the acting   24–5 **suited . . .
argument** i.e., dressed in armor to match the character of the
military plot. (*Argument* means both "plot of the story" and
"quarrel.")   27 **vaunt and firstlings** beginnings
28 **Beginning in the middle** (Alluding to the tradition of
beginning epic poetry *in medias res.*)

[1.1] ❧ *Enter Pandarus and Troilus.*

TROILUS

    Call here my varlet; I'll unarm again.   1

    Why should I war without the walls of Troy,

    That find such cruel battle here within?

    Each Trojan that is master of his heart,

    Let him to field; Troilus, alas, hath none.   5

PANDARUS   Will this gear ne'er be mended?   6

TROILUS

    The Greeks are strong, and skillful to their strength,   7

    Fierce to their skill, and to their fierceness valiant;   8

    But I am weaker than a woman's tear,

    Tamer than sleep, fonder than ignorance,   10

    Less valiant than the virgin in the night,

    And skilless as unpracticed infancy.

PANDARUS   Well, I have told you enough of this. For

    my part, I'll not meddle nor make no farther. He that   14

    will have a cake out of the wheat must tarry the   15

    grinding.

TROILUS   Have I not tarried?

PANDARUS   Ay, the grinding, but you must tarry the

    bolting.   19

TROILUS   Have I not tarried?

PANDARUS   Ay, the bolting, but you must tarry the leav-

    ening.

TROILUS   Still have I tarried.

1.1 *Location: Troy.*
1 **varlet** page or servant of a knight   5 **none** i.e., no heart to
fight.   6 **gear** business   7, 8 **to** in addition to, in proportion to
10 **fonder** more foolish   14 **meddle nor make** have anything
more to do with it   15 **tarry** wait for   19 **bolting** sifting.

PANDARUS   Ay, to the leavening, but here's yet in the
word "hereafter" the kneading, the making of the
cake, the heating the oven, and the baking; nay, you
must stay the cooling too, or ye may chance burn   27
your lips.

TROILUS
Patience herself, what goddess e'er she be,   29
Doth lesser blench at suff'rance than I do.   30
At Priam's royal table do I sit,
And when fair Cressid comes into my thoughts—
So, traitor! When she comes? When is she thence?   33

PANDARUS   Well, she looked yesternight fairer than ever
I saw her look, or any woman else.

TROILUS
I was about to tell thee—when my heart,
As wedgèd with a sigh, would rive in twain,   37
Lest Hector or my father should perceive me,
I have, as when the sun doth light a-scorn,   39
Buried this sigh in wrinkle of a smile;
But sorrow that is couched in seeming gladness   41
Is like that mirth fate turns to sudden sadness.

PANDARUS   An her hair were not somewhat darker than   43
Helen's—well, go to—there were no more comparison   44
between the women. But, for my part, she is my
kinswoman; I would not, as they term it, praise her.

---

27 **stay** wait for   29 **what . . . be** however much a goddess; or, if
she is a goddess   30 **Doth . . . suff'rance** flinches under
suffering with less fortitude   33 **So, traitor . . . thence?** (Troilus
rebukes himself as a traitor to Love for implying that Cressida is
ever out of his thoughts, as she would have to be before she could
come into them.)   37 **As wedgèd** as if cleft by a wedge.   **rive**
split   39 **a-scorn** scornfully, mockingly. (Troilus compares his
face to that of the sun, putting on a false look of joviality.)
41 **couched** hidden   43 **An** If.   **darker** (A dark complexion
was considered less handsome; Helen is blonde.)   44 **go to** (An
exclamation of impatience or irritation.)   **were** would be

But I would somebody had heard her talk yesterday,
as I did. I will not dispraise your sister Cassandra's
wit, but—

TROILUS
Oh, Pandarus! I tell thee, Pandarus—
When I do tell thee there my hopes lie drowned,
Reply not in how many fathoms deep
They lie indrenched. I tell thee I am mad   53
In Cressid's love. Thou answer'st she is fair;
Pour'st in the open ulcer of my heart
Her eyes, her hair, her cheek, her gait, her voice;
Handlest in thy discourse—oh!—that her hand,   57
In whose comparison all whites are ink   58
Writing their own reproach, to whose soft seizure   59
The cygnet's down is harsh, and spirit of sense   60
Hard as the palm of plowman. This thou tell'st me,
As true thou tell'st me, when I say I love her;
But saying thus, instead of oil and balm   63
Thou lay'st in every gash that love hath given me
The knife that made it.

PANDARUS   I speak no more than truth.

TROILUS   Thou dost not speak so much.   67

PANDARUS   Faith, I'll not meddle in it. Let her be as she
is. If she be fair, 'tis the better for her; an she be not,
she has the mends in her own hands.   70

---

53 **indrenched** drowned.   57 **Handlest . . . hand** you
discourse on that wondrous hand of hers   58 **In whose
comparison** in comparison with which   59 **to . . . seizure** in
comparison with whose soft clasp   60 **cygnet's** young swan's.
spirit of sense the most delicate of all material substances.
(According to Renaissance physiology, spirits were the invisible
vapors that transmitted sense impressions to the soul.)   63 **oil
and balm** ointments, salves   67 **Thou . . . much** i.e., You
cannot possibly speak the whole truth about Cressida (since she is
indescribable).   70 **has . . . hands** i.e., can apply remedy, such as
cosmetics.

TROILUS   Good Pandarus, how now, Pandarus?

PANDARUS   I have had my labor for my travail; ill   72
thought on of her and ill thought on of you; gone be-   73
tween and between, but small thanks for my labor

TROILUS   What, art thou angry, Pandarus? What, with
me?

PANDARUS   Because she's kin to me, therefore she's not
so fair as Helen. An she were not kin to me, she would   78
be as fair o' Friday as Helen is on Sunday. But what   79
care I? I care not an she were a blackamoor. 'Tis all one   80
to me.

TROILUS   Say I she is not fair?

PANDARUS   I do not care whether you do or no. She's a
fool to stay behind her father. Let her to the Greeks,   84
and so I'll tell her the next time I see her. For my part,
I'll meddle nor make no more i'th' matter.

TROILUS   Pandarus—

PANDARUS   Not I.

TROILUS   Sweet Pandarus—

PANDARUS   Pray you, speak no more to me. I will leave
all as I found it, and there an end.   *Exit.*   91
                                    Sound alarum.

TROILUS
Peace, you ungracious clamors! Peace, rude sounds!
Fools on both sides! Helen must needs be fair,
When with your blood you daily paint her thus.   94

---

72 **had** had only   73 **of** by   78–9 **An . . . Sunday** i.e., If I were
free to praise her unreservedly, without appearing to be biased as her
kinsman, I would pronounce her to be as attractive in her plainest
attire as Helen in her Sunday best.   80 **blackamoor** dark-skinned
African.   84 **her father** i.e., Calchas, a Trojan priest, who, advised
by the oracle of Apollo that Troy would fall, fled to the Greeks.
91.1 *alarum* trumpet signal to arms.   94 **paint** (As though the
blood were cosmetic, reddening her complexion.)

I cannot fight upon this argument;   95
It is too starved a subject for my sword.   96
But Pandarus—O gods, how do you plague me!
I cannot come to Cressid but by Pandar,
And he's as tetchy to be wooed to woo   99
As she is stubborn-chaste against all suit.
Tell me, Apollo, for thy Daphne's love,   101
What Cressid is, what Pandar, and what we?   102
Her bed is India, there she lies, a pearl;
Between our Ilium and where she resides,   104
Let it be called the wild and wand'ring flood,   105
Ourself the merchant, and this sailing Pandar
Our doubtful hope, our convoy, and our bark.

Alarum. Enter Aeneas.

AENEAS
How now, Prince Troilus, wherefore not afield?

TROILUS
Because not there. This woman's answer sorts,   109
For womanish it is to be from thence.
What news, Aeneas, from the field today?

AENEAS
That Paris is returnèd home and hurt.

TROILUS
By whom, Aeneas?

AENEAS   Troilus, by Menelaus.

---

95 upon this argument for this cause, theme   **96 starved**
empty, trivial. (Troilus would have to fight on an empty stomach,
as it were.)   **99 tetchy to be** irritable at being   **101 Apollo**
(The ardent pursuer of the nymph Daphne who, coy like Cressida,
was changed into a bay tree to elude Apollo's pursuit.)   **102 we**
i.e., I.   **104 Ilium** i.e., Troy generally, but here Priam's palace
105 flood open sea   **109 sorts** is appropriate

TROILUS
    Let Paris bleed. 'Tis but a scar to scorn;   114
    Paris is gored with Menelaus' horn.   *Alarum.* 115

AENEAS
    Hark, what good sport is out of town today!   116

TROILUS
    Better at home, if "would I might" were "may."   117
    But to the sport abroad. Are you bound thither?

AENEAS
    In all swift haste.

TROILUS   Come, go we then together. *Exeunt.*

[1.2] ❦ *Enter Cressida and her man [Alexander].*

CRESSIDA
    Who were those went by?

ALEXANDER   Queen Hecuba and Helen.

CRESSIDA
    And whither go they?

ALEXANDER   Up to the eastern tower,
    Whose height commands as subject all the vale,
    To see the battle. Hector, whose patience
    Is as a virtue fixed, today was moved.   5
    He chid Andromache and struck his armorer,

---

114 **a scar to scorn** (1) a wound not sufficiently serious to be
regarded (2) a scar in return for Paris's scorn of Menelaus
115 **horn** i.e., cuckold's horn, since Paris had stolen Helen from
Menelaus.   116 **out of town** outside the walls   117 **Better . . .
"may"** If I had my wish, I'd have better entertainment at home in
amorous pursuit.

1.2 Location: Troy.
5 **fixed** steadfast.   **moved** angry. (With wordplay on the
antithesis between *fixed* and *moved*.)

And, like as there were husbandry in war,   7
Before the sun rose he was harnessed light,   8
And to the field goes he, where every flower
Did as a prophet weep what it foresaw   10
In Hector's wrath.

CRESSIDA   What was his cause of anger?

ALEXANDER
The noise goes, this: there is among the Greeks   12
A lord of Trojan blood, nephew to Hector;   13
They call him Ajax.

CRESSIDA   Good; and what of him?

ALEXANDER
They say he is a very man per se   15
And stands alone.   16

CRESSIDA   So do all men, unless they are drunk, sick, or
have no legs.

ALEXANDER   This man, lady, hath robbed many beasts
of their particular additions. He is as valiant as the   20
lion, churlish as the bear, slow as the elephant; a man
into whom nature hath so crowded humors that his   22
valor is crushed into folly, his folly sauced with discretion. There is no man hath a virtue that he hath not a
glimpse of, nor any man an attaint but he carries some   25
stain of it. He is melancholy without cause and merry

---

7 **like as** as if.   **husbandry** good management (by rising early
and getting to work. Hector is a stern "husband" in marriage and
in war.)   8 **harnessed light** dressed in light armor   10 **weep**
(The early morning dew on the flowers suggests tears and extends
the metaphor of a husbandman or farmer going into the field.)
12 **noise** rumor   13 **nephew** i.e., kinsman, first cousin
15 **per se** all to himself, without peer   16 **alone** without peer.
(But Cressida sardonically takes it to mean literally "all by himself,
without support.")   20 **additions** qualities bestowing special
distinction.   22 **humors** temperamental characteristics
25 **glimpse** trace.   **attaint** defect, stain.   **but** but that

against the hair. He hath the joints of everything, but   27
everything so out of joint that he is a gouty Briareus,   28
many hands and no use, or purblind Argus, all eyes   29
and no sight.

CRESSIDA   But how should this man, that makes me
smile, make Hector angry?

ALEXANDER   They say he yesterday coped Hector in the   33
battle and struck him down, the disdain and shame
whereof hath ever since kept Hector fasting and
waking.

   [*Enter Pandarus.*]

CRESSIDA   Who comes here?

ALEXANDER   Madam, your uncle Pandarus.

CRESSIDA   Hector's a gallant man.

ALEXANDER   As may be in the world, lady.

PANDARUS   What's that? What's that?

CRESSIDA   Good morrow, uncle Pandarus.

PANDARUS   Good morrow, cousin Cressid. What do you   43
talk of?—Good morrow, Alexander.—How do you,
cousin? When were you at Ilium?   45

CRESSIDA   This morning, uncle.

PANDARUS   What were you talking of when I came? Was
Hector armed and gone ere ye came to Ilium? Helen
was not up, was she?

CRESSIDA   Hector was gone, but Helen was not up?

PANDARUS   E'en so. Hector was stirring early.

---

27 **against the hair** contrary to natural tendency.   28 **Briareus**
Greek mythological monster with fifty heads and one hundred
hands; here, all those hands are gouty   29 **Argus** a monster with
one hundred eyes; here, all are blind (*purblind*)   33 **coped**
encountered, came to blows with   43 **cousin** kinswoman, i.e.,
niece   45 **Ilium** the palace.

CRESSIDA   That were we talking of, and of his anger.

PANDARUS   Was he angry?

CRESSIDA   So he says here.

PANDARUS   True, he was so. I know the cause too. He'll lay about him today, I can tell them that; and there's   56
Troilus will not come far behind him. Let them take heed of Troilus, I can tell them that too.

CRESSIDA   What, is he angry too?

PANDARUS   Who, Troilus? Troilus is the better man of the two.

CRESSIDA   O Jupiter! There's no comparison.

PANDARUS   What, not between Troilus and Hector? Do you know a man if you see him?   64

CRESSIDA   Ay, if I ever saw him before and knew him.

PANDARUS   Well, I say Troilus is Troilus.   66

CRESSIDA   Then you say as I say, for I am sure he is not Hector.

PANDARUS   No, nor Hector is not Troilus in some de-   69
grees.

CRESSIDA   'Tis just to each of them; he is himself.   71

PANDARUS   Himself? Alas, poor Troilus! I would he   72
were.

CRESSIDA   So he is.

PANDARUS   Condition, I had gone barefoot to India.   75

---

56 lay about him fight fiercely   **64 know a man** recognize a complete man. (But Cressida, pretending to misunderstand, takes it to mean simply "recognize.")   **66 is Troilus** is that extraordinary individual known far and wide as Troilus. (But, again, Cressida reduces it to the literal.)   **69 in some** by several   **71 he** each   **72 Himself** (Pandarus plays with the expression "not to be oneself," to be out of sorts.)   **75 Condition . . . India** i.e., Troilus is about as likely to be himself again as I am to have walked barefoot on pilgrimage to India, which of course I haven't.

CRESSIDA   He is not Hector.

PANDARUS   Himself? No, he's not himself. Would 'a   77
were himself! Well, the gods are above; time must
friend or end. Well, Troilus, well, I would my heart   79
were in her body. No, Hector is not a better man than
Troilus.

CRESSIDA   Excuse me.   82

PANDARUS   He is elder.

CRESSIDA   Pardon me, pardon me.

PANDARUS   Th'other's not come to't. You shall tell me   85
another tale, when th'other's come to't. Hector shall
not have his wit this year.   87

CRESSIDA   He shall not need it, if he have his own.

PANDARUS   Nor his qualities.

CRESSIDA   No matter.

PANDARUS   Nor his beauty.

CRESSIDA   'Twould not become him; his own's better.

PANDARUS   You have no judgment, niece. Helen herself
swore th'other day that Troilus, for a brown favor—   94
for so 'tis, I must confess—not brown neither—

CRESSIDA   No, but brown.   96

PANDARUS   Faith, to say truth, brown and not brown.

CRESSIDA   To say the truth, true and not true.

PANDARUS   She praised his complexion above Paris'.

CRESSIDA   Why, Paris hath color enough.

PANDARUS   So he has.

---

77 **'a** he   79 **friend** befriend   82 **Excuse me** i.e., I beg to
differ. (Line 84 means the same.)   85 **to't** i.e., to Hector's age, to
maturity.   87 **his wit** i.e., Troilus's intelligence   94 **for a
brown favor** considering he has a dark complexion   96 **No, but
brown** (Cressida mocks her uncle's hairsplitting: "It isn't brown,
but it's brown.")

CRESSIDA Then Troilus should have too much. If she 102
praised him above, his complexion is higher than his. 103
He having color enough, and the other higher, is too
flaming a praise for a good complexion. I had as lief 105
Helen's golden tongue had commended Troilus for a
copper nose. 107

PANDARUS I swear to you, I think Helen loves him
better than Paris.

CRESSIDA Then she's a merry Greek indeed. 110

PANDARUS Nay, I am sure she does. She came to him
th'other day into the compassed window—and, you 112
know, he has not past three or four hairs on his chin—

CRESSIDA Indeed, a tapster's arithmetic may soon bring 114
his particulars therein to a total.

PANDARUS Why, he is very young; and yet will he,
within three pound, lift as much as his brother Hector.

CRESSIDA Is he so young a man and so old a lifter? 118

PANDARUS But to prove to you that Helen loves him: she
came and puts me her white hand to his cloven chin— 120

CRESSIDA Juno have mercy! How came it cloven?

PANDARUS Why, you know, 'tis dimpled. I think his
smiling becomes him better than any man in all
Phrygia.

CRESSIDA Oh, he smiles valiantly.

PANDARUS Does he not?

102 **should** would of necessity   103 **higher than his** i.e.,
ruddier than Paris's.   105 **flaming** (1) flamboyant (2) inflamed
with pimples.   **lief** willingly   107 **copper** red (with drinking)
110 **merry Greek** (Slang for a frivolous person, loose in morals.)
112 **compassed** bay   114 **tapster** barkeep. (Proverbially slow at
simple addition.)   118 **old** experienced.   **lifter** (With a pun on
the meaning "thief.")   120 **puts me** i.e., puts. (*Me* is merely an
emphatic marker implying "listen to this.")

CRESSIDA   Oh, yes, an 'twere a cloud in autumn.   127

PANDARUS   Why, go to, then. But to prove to you that Helen loves Troilus—

CRESSIDA   Troilus will stand to the proof, if you'll prove   130
it so.

PANDARUS   Troilus? Why, he esteems her no more than I esteem an addle egg.   133

CRESSIDA   If you love an addle egg as well as you love an idle head, you would eat chickens i'th' shell.   135

PANDARUS   I cannot choose but laugh to think how she tickled his chin. Indeed, she has a marvelous white   137
hand, I must needs confess—

CRESSIDA   Without the rack.   139

PANDARUS   And she takes upon her to spy a white hair on his chin.

CRESSIDA   Alas, poor chin! Many a wart is richer.

PANDARUS   But there was such laughing! Queen Hecuba laughed that her eyes ran o'er.

CRESSIDA   With millstones.   145

PANDARUS   And Cassandra laughed.

CRESSIDA   But there was a more temperate fire under the   147
pot of her eyes. Did her eyes run o'er too?

---

127 **an** as if.   **an . . . autumn** i.e., his smile is like a dark and threatening rain cloud in autumn. (Cressida is teasing her uncle by dispraising Troilus.)   130 **stand . . . proof** i.e., not shrink from the test. (With bawdy pun on *stand,* be erect.)   133 **addle** spoiled 135 **idle** foolish. (With wordplay on *addle.*)   **you . . . shell** i.e., you would positively devour addled eggs (which are often spoiled in the sense of being several days old, so that the chick is starting to develop).   137 **marvelous** marvelously   139 **rack** torture device (used to elicit confessions).   145 **With millstones** i.e., Mirthlessly, since nothing has been said funny enough to make the eyes weep tears of laughter. (To *weep millstones* is to be cruel and heartless.)   147 **temperate** (since Cassandra was an unheeded prophetess who seldom laughed)

PANDARUS   And Hector laughed.

CRESSIDA   At what was all this laughing?

PANDARUS   Marry, at the white hair that Helen spied on Troilus' chin.

CRESSIDA   An't had been a green hair, I should have   153
laughed too.

PANDARUS   They laughed not so much at the hair as at his pretty answer.

CRESSIDA   What was his answer?

PANDARUS   Quoth she, "Here's but two-and-fifty hairs   158
on your chin, and one of them is white."

CRESSIDA   This is her question.

PANDARUS   That's true, make no question of that. "Two-and-fifty hairs," quoth he, "and one white. That white hair is my father, and all the rest are his sons." "Jupiter!" quoth she, "which of these hairs is Paris my husband?" "The forked one," quoth he, "pluck't out,   165
and give it him." But there was such laughing! And Helen so blushed, and Paris so chafed, and all the rest   167
so laughed, that it passed.   168

CRESSIDA   So let it now, for it has been a great while   169
going by.

PANDARUS   Well, cousin, I told you a thing yesterday. Think on't.

CRESSIDA   So I do.

---

153 **An't** If it   158 **two-and-fifty** (Priam had fifty sons. Perhaps the forked hair is to count for two.)   **hairs** (With a pun on "heirs"; the quarto spelling is "heires.")   165 **forked** (1) bifurcated (2) bearing a cuckold's horns. (The suggestion is that Helen will cheat Paris in love as she has done Menelaus.)   167 **so chafed** was so angry   168 **it passed** it exceeded all description. (But Cressida puns on the sense of "passed by.")   169 **it** i.e., Pandarus's story

PANDARUS   I'll be sworn 'tis true. He will weep you an   174
'twere a man born in April.   175

CRESSIDA   And I'll spring up in his tears an 'twere a   176
nettle against May.   *Sound a retreat.*   177

PANDARUS   Hark, they are coming from the field. Shall
we stand up here and see them as they pass toward
Ilium? Good niece, do, sweet niece Cressida.

CRESSIDA   At your pleasure.

PANDARUS   Here, here, here's an excellent place; here
we may see most bravely. I'll tell you them all by their   183
names as they pass by, but mark Troilus above the
rest.

Enter Aeneas [and passes across the stage].

CRESSIDA   Speak not so loud.

PANDARUS   That's Aeneas. Is not that a brave man? He's   187
one of the flowers of Troy, I can tell you. But mark
Troilus; you shall see anon.

Enter Antenor [and passes across the stage].

CRESSIDA   Who's that?

PANDARUS   That's Antenor. He has a shrewd wit, I can
tell you, and he's a man good enough. He's one o'th'
soundest judgments in Troy whosoever, and a proper   193
man of person. When comes Troilus? I'll show you
Troilus anon. If he see me, you shall see him nod
at me.

CRESSIDA   Will he give you the nod?   197

174–5 **an 'twere** as if he were   175 **April** i.e., the season of
showers.   176–7 **an 'twere . . . May** as if I were a nettle in
anticipation of May. (Cressida will "nettle" Troilus.)   177 s.d.
retreat trumpet signal for withdrawal.   183 **bravely** excellently.
187 **brave** excellent   193 **proper** handsome   197 **nod** nod of
recognition. (With a pun on *noddy*, fool, simpleton.)

PANDARUS   You shall see.

CRESSIDA   If he do, the rich shall have more.   199

    Enter Hector [and passes across the stage].

PANDARUS   That's Hector, that, that, look you, that.
There's a fellow! Go thy way, Hector! There's a brave
man, niece. O brave Hector! Look how he looks!
There's a countenance! Is't not a brave man?

CRESSIDA   Oh, a brave man!

PANDARUS   Is 'a not? It does a man's heart good. Look
you what hacks are on his helmet! Look you yonder,   206
do you see? Look you there. There's no jesting; there's
laying on, take't off who will, as they say. There be   208
hacks.

CRESSIDA   Be those with swords?

    Enter Paris [and passes across the stage].

PANDARUS   Swords, anything, he cares not; an the
devil come to him, it's all one. By God's lid, it does   212
one's heart good. Yonder comes Paris, yonder comes
Paris. Look ye yonder, niece. Is't not a gallant man,
too, is't not? Why, this is brave now. Who said he
came hurt home today? He's not hurt. Why, this will
do Helen's heart good now, ha! Would I could see
Troilus now! You shall see Troilus anon.

CRESSIDA   Who's that?

    Enter Helenus [and passes across the stage].

---

199 **the rich . . . more** i.e., the fool will become more foolish as
you are, will receive the *nod*, or noddy (line 197).   206 **hacks**
dents, gashes   208 **laying on** i.e., evidence of blows exchanged.
take't off who will whatever anyone may say to the contrary.
(With a pun on *taking off* as contrasted with *laying on*.)   212 **all
one** all the same to him.   **By God's lid** By God's eyelid. (An
oath.)

PANDARUS   That's Helenus. I marvel where Troilus is.
That's Helenus. I think he went not forth today. That's 221
Helenus.

CRESSIDA   Can Helenus fight, uncle?

PANDARUS   Helenus? No. Yes, he'll fight indifferent 224
well. I marvel where Troilus is. Hark, do you not hear 225
the people cry "Troilus"? Helenus is a priest.

CRESSIDA   What sneaking fellow comes yonder?

   Enter Troilus [and passes across the stage].

PANDARUS   Where? Yonder? That's Deiphobus. 'Tis
Troilus! There's a man, niece! Hem! Brave Troilus! The
prince of chivalry!

CRESSIDA   Peace, for shame, peace!

PANDARUS   Mark him, note him. O brave Troilus! Look
well upon him, niece. Look you how his sword is
bloodied and his helm more hacked than Hector's, 234
and how he looks, and how he goes! O admirable 235
youth! He ne'er saw three-and-twenty. Go thy way,
Troilus, go thy way! Had I a sister were a grace, or a 237
daughter a goddess, he should take his choice. O
admirable man! Paris? Paris is dirt to him; and
I warrant Helen, to change, would give an eye to 240
boot.   241

   [Enter common soldiers and pass across the stage.]

CRESSIDA   Here comes more.

PANDARUS   Asses, fools, dolts! Chaff and bran, chaff
and bran! Porridge after meat! I could live and die 244

---

221 **he** Troilus   224 **indifferent** moderately   225 **marvel**
wonder   234 **helm** helmet   235 **goes** walks.   237 **a grace**
one of the three Graces, the personifications of loveliness
240–1 **to change . . . boot** would give Paris plus one of her eyes
besides to have Troilus in exchange.   244 **Porridge** Soup (usually
eaten before the meat course; after, it would be an anticlimax)

i'th'eyes of Troilus. Ne'er look, ne'er look. The eagles
are gone; crows and daws, crows and daws! I had   246
rather be such a man as Troilus than Agamemnon and
all Greece.

CRESSIDA   There is among the Greeks Achilles, a better
man than Troilus.

PANDARUS   Achilles? A drayman, a porter, a very camel.   251

CRESSIDA   Well, well.

PANDARUS   "Well, well"! Why, have you any discretion?
Have you any eyes? Do you know what a man is? Is
not birth, beauty, good shape, discourse, manhood,
learning, gentleness, virtue, youth, liberality, and so
forth, the spice and salt that season a man?

CRESSIDA   Ay, a minced man; and then to be baked   258
with no date in the pie, for then the man's date is out.   259

PANDARUS   You are such another woman! One knows
not at what ward you lie.   261

CRESSIDA   Upon my back to defend my belly, upon my
wit to defend my wiles, upon my secrecy to defend   263
mine honesty, my mask to defend my beauty, and   264

---

246 **daws** jackdaws (glossy, black crowlike birds)   251 **drayman**
one who draws a cart   258 **minced** (1) chopped up fine
(2) affected, effeminate   259 **the man's date is out** (1) the man
is like a pie without any dates, a common ingredient used for
flavoring (2) the man is past his prime. (With a suggestion, too, of
his being a sexual failure.)   261 **at what . . . lie** what defensive
postures you adopt. (*Ward* and *lie* are technical terms from fencing.
Cressida picks up *lie* in a sexual sense.)   263 **my secrecy** (1) my
ability to keep a secret (2) my sexual anatomy   264 **honesty**
(1) chastity (2) reputation for chastity.   **mask** (Used to protect
fair skin from tanning, considered unhandsome, and also to ward
against public gaze.)

you to defend all these, and at all these wards I lie, at   265
a thousand watches.   266

PANDARUS   Say one of your watches.

CRESSIDA   Nay, I'll watch you for that; and that's one of
the chiefest of them too. If I cannot ward what I would   269
not have hit, I can watch you for telling how I took the
blow—unless it swell past hiding, and then it's past   271
watching.   272

PANDARUS   You are such another!   273

     Enter [Troilus's] Boy.

BOY   Sir, my lord would instantly speak with you.

PANDARUS   Where?

BOY   At your own house. There he unarms him.

PANDARUS   Good boy, tell him I come.   *[Exit Boy.]*
I doubt he be hurt. Fare ye well, good niece.   278

CRESSIDA   Adieu, uncle.

PANDARUS   I'll be with you, niece, by and by.

CRESSIDA   To bring, uncle?   281

PANDARUS   Ay, a token from Troilus.

CRESSIDA   By the same token, you are a bawd.

     [Exit Pandarus.]

Words, vows, gifts, tears, and love's full sacrifice
He offers in another's enterprise;
But more in Troilus thousandfold I see

265–6 at a thousand watches i.e., guarding myself in a thousand
ways. (Subsequently, in the wordplay, *watch* means "devotional
exercises" or "night watches," line 267, "keep under observation,"
line 268, and "watch out lest you tell," line 270.)   **269 ward**
shield   **271 swell** i.e., in pregnancy   **271–2 past watching**
too late to do anything about.   **273 You . . . another!** i.e., What
a woman you are!   **278 doubt** fear   **281 To bring** i.e., Are
you bringing someone or something? (But Cressida's phrase also
completes a colloquial expression, "be with you to bring," meaning
roughly, "I'll get even with you.")

Than in the glass of Pandar's praise may be.   287
Yet hold I off. Women are angels, wooing;   288
Things won are done; joy's soul lies in the doing.
That she beloved knows naught that knows not this: 290
Men prize the thing ungained more than it is.   291
That she was never yet that ever knew   292
Love got so sweet as when desire did sue.   293
Therefore this maxim out of love I teach: 294
Achievement is command; ungained, beseech.   295
Then though my heart's contents firm love doth
    bear,   296
Nothing of that shall from mine eyes appear.

                      Exit [*with Alexander*].

[1.3] ◦§◦ [*Sennet.*] *Enter Agamemnon, Nestor, Ulysses,
         Diomedes, Menelaus, with others.*

AGAMEMNON Princes,
    What grief hath set the jaundice on your cheeks?   2

287 **glass** mirror   288 **wooing** being wooed   290 **That she**
Any woman. (Also in line 292.)   291 **than it is** than its intrinsic
worth.   292–3 **That she . . . sue** No woman has ever lived who
experienced love so sweet as when the man still desires what he
has not yet obtained; the love once *got* or obtained by him is never
the same.   294 **out of love** as from love's book
295 **Achievement . . . beseech** To achieve and win a woman is to
command her; not yet won, she must be entreated.
296 **though . . . bear** though I carry firm love in my heart

1.3 *Location: The Greek camp. Before Agamemnon's tent.*
0.1 *Sennet* trumpet call signaling a processional entrance or exit
2 **jaundice** sallowness of complexion

The ample proposition that hope makes   3
In all designs begun on earth below   4
Fails in the promised largeness. Checks and disasters   5
Grow in the veins of actions highest reared,   6
As knots, by the conflux of meeting sap,   7
Infects the sound pine and diverts his grain   8
Tortive and errant from his course of growth.   9
Nor, princes, is it matter new to us
That we come short of our suppose so far   11
That after seven years' siege yet Troy walls stand,   12
Sith every action that hath gone before,   13
Whereof we have record, trial did draw   14
Bias and thwart, not answering the aim   15
And that unbodied figure of the thought   16
That gave't surmisèd shape. Why then, you princes,   17
Do you with cheeks abashed behold our works
And think them shames, which are indeed naught
    else
But the protractive trials of great Jove   20
To find persistive constancy in men?   21
The fineness of which metal is not found
In Fortune's love; for then the bold and coward,   23
The wise and fool, the artist and unread,   24
The hard and soft, seem all affined and kin.   25

3–5 **The ample . . . largeness** The ample hopes and desires that we
humans propose for ourselves fail to materialize fully as promised.
5–9 **Checks . . . growth** i.e., Hindrances and disasters attend great
enterprises, just as knots, at the points where a pine tree's sap should
fully flow, adversely affect the health of the tree by twisting and
diverting the proper course of its growth. (*Veins* are sap vessels in
plants.)   7 **conflux** flowing together   8, 9 **his** its   9 **Tortive
and errant** twisted and deviating   11 **suppose** expectation,
purpose   12 **yet** still   13–17 **Sith . . . shape** since every military
action on record has gone awry in the doing of it, not corresponding
to our aims and imaginings as to how it should go.   20 **protractive**
drawn out   21 **persistive** enduring   23 **In Fortune's love** i.e.,
when Fortune smiles   24 **artist** scholar   25 **affined** related

But in the wind and tempest of her frown,   26
Distinction, with a broad and powerful fan,   27
Puffing at all, winnows the light away,   28
And what hath mass or matter by itself
Lies rich in virtue and unminglèd.   30

NESTOR
With due observance of thy godly seat,   31
Great Agamemnon, Nestor shall apply   32
Thy latest words. In the reproof of chance   33
Lies the true proof of men. The sea being smooth,
How many shallow bauble boats dare sail   35
Upon her patient breast, making their way
With those of nobler bulk!
But let the ruffian Boreas once enrage   38
The gentle Thetis, and anon behold   39
The strong-ribbed bark through liquid mountains
      cut,
Bounding between the two moist elements   41
Like Perseus' horse. Where's then the saucy boat   42
Whose weak untimbered sides but even now   43
Corrivaled greatness? Either to harbor fled

---

26 **her** Fortune's   27–8 **Distinction . . . away** (Fortune is a
winnowing tool, blowing away like chaff those who do not
persevere and leaving behind like grain those who do.)
30 **virtue** excellence.   **unminglèd** unalloyed, uncontaminated.
31 **observance of** respect for.   **seat** throne, i.e., dignity of office
32 **apply** explore the implications of   33 **In . . . chance** In the
harsh test of misfortune   35 **bauble** toylike   38 **Boreas** north
wind   39 **Thetis** a sea deity, mother of Achilles; here, used for
the sea itself. (Probably confused with Tethys, the wife of
Oceanus.)   41 **moist elements** air and water   42 **Perseus'**
horse Pegasus, a winged horse that sprang from the blood of
Medusa when Perseus cut off her head. (The horse was given to
Bellerophon by the gods. It is associated, however, with Perseus,
probably because Ovid relates that the latter hero was mounted on
Pegasus when he rescued Andromeda from the sea monster.)
43 **but even now** only a moment ago

Or made a toast for Neptune. Even so   45
Doth valor's show and valor's worth divide   46
In storms of Fortune. For in her ray and brightness   47
The herd hath more annoyance by the breese   48
Than by the tiger; but when the splitting wind
Makes flexible the knees of knotted oaks,
And flies fled under shade, why, then the thing of
    courage,   51
As roused with rage, with rage doth sympathize,   52
And with an accent tuned in selfsame key
Retorts to chiding Fortune.

ULYSSES   Agamemnon,
Thou great commander, nerves and bone of Greece,   55
Heart of our numbers, soul and only sprite,   56
In whom the tempers and the minds of all   57
Should be shut up, hear what Ulysses speaks.   58
Besides th'applause and approbation   59
The which, [to Agamemnon] most mighty for thy
    place and sway,
[To Nestor] And thou most reverend for thy
    stretched-out life,
I give to both your speeches, which were such
As Agamemnon and the hand of Greece
Should hold up high in brass, and such again   64
As venerable Nestor, hatched in silver,   65

45 **toast** rich morsel to be swallowed, like toasted bread floating in liquor   46 **show** mere appearance   47 **storms of Fortune** trials and tests visited by misfortune.   **her** Fortune's   48 **breese** gadfly   51 **fled** are fled.   **the thing of courage** any brave heart   52 **As** being.   **sympathize** correspond   55 **nerves** sinews   56 **numbers** armies.   **sprite** spirit, animating principle   57 **tempers** dispositions   58 **shut up** gathered in, embodied   59 **approbation** approval   64 **Should . . . brass** should hold up for emulation, immortalized in brass inscription   65 **hatched in silver** (1) adorned with silver hair, a sign of age and wisdom (2) born wise

Should with a bond of air, strong as the axletree   66
On which the heavens ride, knit all Greeks' ears   67
To his experienced tongue, yet let it please both,
Thou great, and wise, to hear Ulysses speak.

AGAMEMNON

Speak, Prince of Ithaca, and be't of less expect   70
That matter needless, of importless burden,   71
Divide thy lips, than we are confident,   72
When rank Thersites opes his mastic jaws,   73
We shall hear music, wit, and oracle.

ULYSSES

Troy, yet upon his basis, had been down,   75
And the great Hector's sword had lacked a master,
But for these instances.
The specialty of rule hath been neglected;   78
And look how many Grecian tents do stand   79
Hollow upon this plain, so many hollow factions.   80
When that the general is not like the hive   81
To whom the foragers shall all repair,   82
What honey is expected? Degree being vizarded,   83
Th'unworthiest shows as fairly in the mask.   84

---

66 bond of air i.e., his breath or words as speech, powerful
oration   **66–7 axletree . . . ride** axis on which the heavens, in
the Ptolemaic cosmology, revolve around the earth
70–2 be't . . . than be it even less to be expected that matters of
unimportance pass through your lips than that   **73 rank**
disgusting, foul-smelling.   **mastic** gummy, abusive, scouring
75 yet . . . basis still standing on its foundations   **78 specialty
of rule** particular rights and responsibilities of supreme authority
79 look how many however many, just as many   **80 Hollow**
(1) empty, because of the present assembly (2) symbolizing faction
81 When . . . hive i.e., When General Agamemnon, and the
general state he embodies, fail to serve as the focus of activity, the
command center   **82 repair** return   **83 Degree being
vizarded** When the hierarchical function of authority is masked
84 shows as fairly appears as attractive (as the most noble)

The heavens themselves, the planets, and this center   85
Observe degree, priority, and place,
Insisture, course, proportion, season, form,   87
Office, and custom, in all line of order.
And therefore is the glorious planet Sol   89
In noble eminence enthroned and sphered   90
Amidst the other, whose med'cinable eye   91
Corrects the ill aspects of planets evil   92
And posts like the commandment of a king,   93
Sans check, to good and bad. But when the planets   94
In evil mixture to disorder wander,   95
What plagues and what portents, what mutiny,
What raging of the sea, shaking of earth,
Commotion in the winds, frights, changes, horrors,
Divert and crack, rend and deracinate   99
The unity and married calm of states
Quite from their fixure! Oh, when degree is shaked,   101
Which is the ladder to all high designs,
The enterprise is sick. How could communities,
Degrees in schools, and brotherhoods in cities,   104
Peaceful commerce from dividable shores,   105
The primogeneity and due of birth,   106
Prerogative of age, crowns, scepters, laurels,

---

85 **this center** the earth, center of the Ptolemaic universe
87 **Insisture** steady continuance in their path   89 **Sol** sun.
(Regarded as a planet because of its apparent movement around
the earth.)   90 **sphered** placed in its sphere   91 **other** others.
med'cinable healing   92 **aspects** relative positions of the
heavenly bodies as they appear to an observer on the earth's
surface at a given time, and the influence attributed thereto
93 **posts** speeds   94 **Sans . . . bad** without pause, to foster the
good and chastise the bad.   95 **mixture** conjunction
99 **deracinate** uproot   101 **fixure** stability.   104 **Degrees in
schools** academic rank.   **brotherhoods** corporations, guilds
105 **from . . . shores** between countries separated by the sea
106 **primogeneity** right of the eldest son to succeed to his father's
estate

But by degree stand in authentic place?
Take but degree away, untune that string,
And hark what discord follows. Each thing meets
In mere oppugnancy. The bounded waters   111
Should lift their bosoms higher than the shores
And make a sop of all this solid globe;   113
Strength should be lord of imbecility,   114
And the rude son should strike his father dead;   115
Force should be right; or rather, right and wrong,
Between whose endless jar justice resides,   117
Should lose their names, and so should justice too.
Then everything includes itself in power,   119
Power into will, will into appetite;
And appetite, an universal wolf,
So doubly seconded with will and power,
Must make perforce an universal prey   123
And last eat up himself. Great Agamemnon,
This chaos, when degree is suffocate,   125
Follows the choking.   126
And this neglection of degree it is   127
That by a pace goes backward in a purpose   128
It hath to climb. The general's disdained   129
By him one step below, he by the next,
That next by him beneath; so every step,
Exampled by the first pace that is sick   132
Of his superior, grows to an envious fever   133

---

111 **mere oppugnancy** total strife.   113 **sop** piece of bread or
cake floating in liquor; pulp   114 **imbecility** weakness
115 **rude** brutal   117 **Between . . . resides** i.e., justice is arrived
at only through an unceasing adjudication between right and
wrong. (*Jar* means "collision.")   119 **includes** subsumes
123 **Must . . . prey** must inevitably prey on everything
125 **suffocate** suffocated   126 **choking** act of suffocation.
127 **neglection** neglect   128 **by a pace** step by step
128–9 **in . . . climb** when it intends to climb.
132–3 **Exampled . . . superior** shown a precedent by the first
envious step that his superior takes

Of pale and bloodless emulation.
And 'tis this fever that keeps Troy on foot,
Not her own sinews. To end a tale of length,
Troy in our weakness lives, not in her strength.

NESTOR
Most wisely hath Ulysses here discovered   138
The fever whereof all our power is sick.   139

AGAMEMNON
The nature of the sickness found, Ulysses,
What is the remedy?

ULYSSES
The great Achilles, whom opinion crowns
The sinew and the forehand of our host,   143
Having his ear full of his airy fame,   144
Grows dainty of his worth and in his tent   145
Lies mocking our designs. With him Patroclus
Upon a lazy bed the livelong day
Breaks scurril jests,
And with ridiculous and awkward action,
Which, slanderer, he imitation calls,
He pageants us. Sometime, great Agamemnon,   151
Thy topless deputation he puts on,   152
And like a strutting player, whose conceit   153
Lies in his hamstring, and doth think it rich   154
To hear the wooden dialogue and sound   155
Twixt his stretched footing and the scaffoldage,   156
Such to-be-pitied and o'erwrested seeming   157

---

138 **discovered** revealed   139 **power** army   143 **forehand**
first in might.   **host** army   144 **airy fame** unsubstantial
reputation   145 **dainty** fastidious   151 **pageants** mimics
152 **topless deputation** supreme power   153–4 **whose . . .
hamstring** i.e., whose wits are in his thighs   154 **rich** admirable
155–6 **To hear . . . scaffoldage** i.e., to hear the echoing sound of
his marching to and fro on the stage or scaffolding   157 **to-be-
pitied . . . seeming** pitiful and exaggerated acting

He acts thy greatness in; and when he speaks,
'Tis like a chime a-mending, with terms unsquared,   159
Which, from the tongue of roaring Typhon dropped,   160
Would seem hyperboles. At this fusty stuff   161
The large Achilles, on his pressed bed lolling,   162
From his deep chest laughs out a loud applause,
Cries, "Excellent! 'Tis Agamemnon just.   164
Now play me Nestor; hem, and stroke thy beard,   165
As he being dressed to some oration."   166
That's done, as near as the extremest ends   167
Of parallels, as like as Vulcan and his wife,   168
Yet god Achilles still cries, "Excellent!
'Tis Nestor right. Now play him me, Patroclus,
Arming to answer in a night alarm."   171
And then, forsooth, the faint defects of age   172
Must be the scene of mirth; to cough and spit,
And with a palsy, fumbling on his gorget,   174
Shake in and out the rivet. And at this sport
Sir Valor dies; cries, "Oh, enough, Patroclus,
Or give me ribs of steel! I shall split all
In pleasure of my spleen." And in this fashion,   178
All our abilities, gifts, natures, shapes,

---

159 a-mending being repaired or retuned.   **terms unsquared**
expressions unadapted to their subject, ill-fitted (like unsquared
timbers or stones in architecture)   **160 from** even if from.
Typhon Greek mythological monster with a hundred heads that
breathed fire; he made war against the gods and was destroyed by
one of Zeus's thunderbolts   **161 fusty** stale. (And suggesting
fustian, bombastic.)   **162 pressed** weighed down (by its
occupant)   **164 just** exactly.   **165 me** for my benefit. (Also in
line 170.)   **166 dressed** addressed   **167–8 as near . . .
parallels** (Parallel lines never meet, no matter how far they are
extended.)   **168 Vulcan . . . wife** i.e., the ugliest god, and
Venus, the most beautiful goddess   **171 answer . . . alarm**
respond to a nighttime military alert.   **172 faint** weak
174 palsy tremor.   **gorget** piece of armor for the throat
178 spleen (Regarded as the seat of laughter.)

Severals and generals of grace exact,   180
Achievements, plots, orders, preventions,   181
Excitements to the field, or speech for truce,   182
Success or loss, what is or is not, serves
As stuff for these two to make paradoxes.   184

NESTOR
And in the imitation of these twain—
Who, as Ulysses says, opinion crowns   186
With an imperial voice—many are infect.   187
Ajax is grown self-willed and bears his head
In such a rein, in full as proud a place   189
As broad Achilles; keeps his tent like him;   190
Makes factious feasts; rails on our state of war,   191
Bold as an oracle; and sets Thersites,
A slave whose gall coins slanders like a mint,   193
To match us in comparisons with dirt,
To weaken and discredit our exposure,   195
How rank soever rounded in with danger.   196

ULYSSES
They tax our policy and call it cowardice,   197
Count wisdom as no member of the war,   198
Forestall prescience, and esteem no act   199
But that of hand. The still and mental parts   200
That do contrive how many hands shall strike

180 **Severals . . . exact** well-ordered gifts, individual and general
181 **preventions** defensive precautions   182 **Excitements**
exhortations   184 **paradoxes** absurdities.   186–7 **crowns . . .
voice** i.e., regards most highly, adulates   189 **In . . . rein** i.e., so
haughtily   190 **broad** hefty.   **keeps** keeps to   191 **factious**
for his faction; seditious.   **our state of war** our state of
preparedness for war; our soldiers in their readiness   193 **slave**
contemptible person.   **gall** the seat of bile and rancor
195 **exposure** vulnerable situation   196 **rank** thickly.   **rounded
in with** surrounded by   197 **tax our policy** censure our prudent
management   198 **no member** no fit guide or companion
199 **Forestall prescience** condemn beforehand any attempts at
foresight   200 **that of hand** any immediate physical response.

When fitness calls them on and know by measure   202
Of their observant toil the enemy's weight—   203
Why, this hath not a finger's dignity.   204
They call this bed-work, mapp'ry, closet war;   205
So that the ram that batters down the wall,   206
For the great swinge and rudeness of his poise,   207
They place before his hand that made the engine,   208
Or those that with the fineness of their souls   209
By reason guide his execution.   210

NESTOR
Let this be granted, and Achilles' horse   211
Makes many Thetis' sons.   [*Tucket.*]   212

AGAMEMNON   What trumpet? Look, Menelaus.

MENELAUS   From Troy.

          [*Enter Aeneas with a trumpeter.*]

AGAMEMNON   What would you 'fore our tent?

AENEAS
Is this great Agamemnon's tent, I pray you?

AGAMEMNON   Even this.

AENEAS
May one that is a herald and a prince
Do a fair message to his kingly ears?

202 **fitness** suitability of occasion   202–3 **know . . . weight**
figure out by laborious calculation the enemy's strength
204 **hath . . . dignity** is not worth a snap of the fingers.
205 **bed-work . . . war** i.e., armchair strategy, mere map-making,
war planned in the study   206–10 **So . . . execution** so that they
put more value on the great battering ram, because of its huge
impetus and roughness of impact, than they give to military
planners and generals who devised the weapon, or to those who,
with their superior insight, guide its operation.   211–12 **Let . . .**
sons If this is granted, then Achilles's horse in its brute strength
outvalues many an Achilles (the son of Thetis).   212 s.d. **Tucket**
signal given on a trumpet

AGAMEMNON

  With surety stronger than Achilles' arm   220
  'Fore all the Greekish host, which with one voice   221
  Call Agamemnon head and general.

AENEAS

  Fair leave and large security. How may   223
  A stranger to those most imperial looks
  Know them from eyes of other mortals?

AGAMEMNON   How?

AENEAS

  Ay. I ask, that I might waken reverence,
  And bid the cheek be ready with a blush
  Modest as morning when she coldly eyes   229
  The youthful Phoebus.   230
  Which is that god in office, guiding men?
  Which is the high and mighty Agamemnon?

AGAMEMNON

  This Trojan scorns us, or the men of Troy
  Are ceremonious courtiers.

AENEAS

  Courtiers as free, as debonair, unarmed,   235
  As bending angels—that's their fame in peace.   236
  But when they would seem soldiers, they have galls,   237
  Good arms, strong joints, true swords, and—Jove's
       accord—   238
  Nothing so full of heart. But peace, Aeneas,   239

---

220 **surety** security   221 **'Fore . . . voice** leading into battle the
entire Greek army, who with one voice   223 **Fair leave**
Courteous permission   229 **she** i.e., Aurora, the blushing dawn
goddess.   **coldly** demurely   230 **Phoebus** Apollo, here
referred to as the sun-god.   235 **free** generous.   **debonair**
gracious in manner   236 **bending** bowing.   **fame** reputation
237 **galls** i.e., spirit to resent injury. (See line 193.)   238 **Jove's
accord** Jove being in full accord, God willing   239 **Nothing . . .
heart** nothing is so full of unequaled courage as they.

Peace, Trojan; lay thy finger on thy lips!
The worthiness of praise distains his worth,   241
If that the praised himself bring the praise forth.   242
But what the repining enemy commends,   243
That breath fame blows; that praise, sole pure,
    transcends.   244

AGAMEMNON
Sir, you of Troy, call you yourself Aeneas?

AENEAS   Ay, Greek, that is my name.

AGAMEMNON   What's your affair, I pray you?

AENEAS
Sir, pardon. 'Tis for Agamemnon's ears.

AGAMEMNON
He hears naught privately that comes from Troy.

AENEAS
Nor I from Troy come not to whisper him.   250
I bring a trumpet to awake his ear,   251
To set his sense on the attentive bent,   252
And then to speak.

AGAMEMNON   Speak frankly as the wind;
It is not Agamemnon's sleeping hour.
That thou shalt know, Trojan, he is awake,
He tells thee so himself.

AENEAS   Trumpet, blow loud;
Send thy brass voice through all these lazy tents,

---

241 **distains his** sullies its own   242 **If . . . forth** if the person
being praised is the one who speaks this praise.   243–4 **But . . .
transcends** But whenever an enemy offers praise, being naturally
reluctant to do so, that praise is trumpeted by Fame herself; such
praise is transcendent because it is unmixed with unworthy
motives.   250 **whisper** whisper to   251 **trumpet** trumpeter
252 **set . . . bent** i.e., bend his sense of hearing attentively toward me

And every Greek of mettle, let him know
What Troy means fairly shall be spoke aloud.

Sound trumpet.

We have, great Agamemnon, here in Troy
A prince called Hector—Priam is his father—
Who in this dull and long-continued truce
Is resty grown. He bade me take a trumpet   263
And to this purpose speak: Kings, princes, lords!
If there be one among the fair'st of Greece
That holds his honor higher than his ease,
That seeks his praise more than he fears his peril,
That knows his valor and knows not his fear,
That loves his mistress more than in confession   269
With truant vows to her own lips he loves,   270
And dare avow her beauty and her worth
In other arms than hers—to him this challenge.   272
Hector, in view of Trojans and of Greeks,
Shall make it good, or do his best to do it,
He hath a lady, wiser, fairer, truer,
Than ever Greek did compass in his arms,   276
And will tomorrow with his trumpet call
Midway between your tents and walls of Troy
To rouse a Grecian that is true in love.
If any come, Hector shall honor him;
If none, he'll say in Troy when he retires,
The Grecian dames are sunburnt and not worth   282
The splinter of a lance. Even so much.   283

---

263 **resty** sluggish, inactive, restive   269–70 **That . . . loves** i.e.,
who shows his love for his beloved more in deeds of arms than in
sweet nothings promised lip to lip   272 **In . . . hers** i.e., in the
arms of warfare rather than those of his mistress   276 **compass**
encompass, embrace   282 **sunburnt** i.e., unattractive, according
to Elizabethan tastes in beauty   283 **Even so much** (A
formulaic conclusion to a delivered message, meaning, "that is the
totality of what I am bid to say.")

AGAMEMNON

    This shall be told our lovers, Lord Aeneas.

    If none of them have soul in such a kind,   285

    We left them all at home. But we are soldiers;

    And may that soldier a mere recreant prove   287

    That means not, hath not, or is not in love!   288

    If then one is, or hath, or means to be,

    That one meets Hector; if none else, I am he.

NESTOR

    Tell him of Nestor, one that was a man

    When Hector's grandsire sucked. He is old now,

    But if there be not in our Grecian host

    One noble man that hath one spark of fire

    To answer for his love, tell him from me

    I'll hide my silver beard in a gold beaver,   296

    And in my vambrace put this withered brawn,   297

    And meeting him will tell him that my lady

    Was fairer than his grandam and as chaste   299

    As may be in the world. His youth in flood,   300

    I'll prove this truth with my three drops of blood.

AENEAS

    Now heavens forbid such scarcity of youth!

ULYSSES   Amen.

AGAMEMNON

    Fair Lord Aeneas, let me touch your hand;

    To our pavilion shall I lead you first.

    Achilles shall have word of this intent;

    So shall each lord of Greece, from tent to tent.

---

285 **have . . . kind** i.e., have the spirit to undertake this challenge
287 **mere recreant** utter coward   288 **means not** intends not to
be   296 **beaver** face guard of a helmet   297 **vambrace** armor
for the front part of the arm.   **brawn** i.e., arm   299 **grandam**
grandmother   300 **His . . . flood** i.e., Though Hector's
manhood and vigor be at their height

Yourself shall feast with us before you go,
And find the welcome of a noble foe.   309

[Exeunt. Manent Ulysses and Nestor.]

ULYSSES   Nestor!

NESTOR   What says Ulysses?

ULYSSES

I have a young conception in my brain;
Be you my time to bring it to some shape.   313

NESTOR   What is't?

ULYSSES   This 'tis:

Blunt wedges rive hard knots; the seeded pride   316
That hath to this maturity blown up   317
In rank Achilles must or now be cropped   318
Or, shedding, breed a nursery of like evil   319
To overbulk us all.

NESTOR   Well, and how?   320

ULYSSES

This challenge that the gallant Hector sends,
However it is spread in general name,
Relates in purpose only to Achilles.

NESTOR

The purpose is perspicuous even as substance,   324
Whose grossness little characters sum up;   325
And, in the publication, make no strain   326
But that Achilles, were his brain as barren

309.1 *Manent* They remain   313 **Be . . . time** i.e., act as
midwife to my newly conceived plan   316 **rive** split, break apart.
seeded pride pride that has gone to seed, overblown
317 **blown up** sprouted, puffed up   318 **rank** overripe, swollen.
or either   319 **shedding** if it scatters its seeds.   **nursery**
(1) breeding ground (2) crop   320 **overbulk** overwhelm,
outgrow   324–5 **perspicuous . . . up** as perceivable as great
wealth or matter, the size of which can be rendered in little figures
326 **in . . . strain** when it is publicly announced, have no doubt

As banks of Libya—though, Apollo knows,   328
'Tis dry enough—will, with great speed of judgment,   329
Ay, with celerity, find Hector's purpose
Pointing on him.

ULYSSES   And wake him to the answer, think you?

NESTOR

Yes, 'tis most meet. Who may you else oppose   333
That can from Hector bring his honor off   334
If not Achilles? Though 't be a sportful combat,
Yet in this trial much opinion dwells,   336
For here the Trojans taste our dear'st repute   337
With their fin'st palate. And trust to me, Ulysses,   338
Our imputation shall be oddly poised   339
In this wild action. For the success,   340
Although particular, shall give a scantling   341
Of good or bad unto the general;   342
And in such indices, although small pricks   343
To their subsequent volumes, there is seen   344
The baby figure of the giant mass
Of things to come at large. It is supposed
He that meets Hector issues from our choice;
And choice, being mutual act of all our souls,
Makes merit her election and doth boil,   349
As 'twere from forth us all, a man distilled

---

328 **banks** sandbanks; shores   329 **dry** dull   333 **meet** fitting.
else oppose otherwise put forward as opponent   334 **That . . .
off** who can acquit himself honorably in doing battle with Hector
336 **opinion** reputation   337 **taste our dear'st repute** i.e., put
to the test Achilles, our warrior of greatest reputation   338 **their
fin'st palate** i.e., Hector.   339 **Our imputation** what is imputed
to us, our reputation.   **oddly poised** unequally balanced
340 **wild** rash.   **success** outcome   341 **particular** relating to
(two) particular men.   **scantling** specimen, sample
342 **general** army at large   343 **indices** indications, table of
contents   343–4 **small . . . volumes** small indicators in
comparison with the volumes that follow   349 **election** basis of
choice

Out of our virtues; who miscarrying,   351
What heart from hence receives the conquering part,   352
To steel a strong opinion to themselves?   353
Which entertained, limbs are his instruments,   354
In no less working than are swords and bows   355
Directive by the limbs.   356

ULYSSES   Give pardon to my speech:
Therefore 'tis meet Achilles meet not Hector.   358
Let us, like merchants, show our foulest wares,
And think perchance they'll sell; if not,
The luster of the better yet to show
Shall show the better. Do not consent
That ever Hector and Achilles meet;
For both our honor and our shame in this
Are dogged with two strange followers.

NESTOR
I see them not with my old eyes. What are they?

ULYSSES
What glory our Achilles shares from Hector,   367
Were he not proud, we all should wear with him.
But he already is too insolent,
And we were better parch in Afric sun
Than in the pride and salt scorn of his eyes,
Should he scape Hector fair. If he were foiled,   372

351 **miscarrying** i.e., if he should fail   352 **What . . . part** what
cheer will the conquering party, i.e., the Trojans, receive from this
353 **steel** strengthen   354–6 **Which . . . limbs** And in that
strengthening of opinion, the limbs that direct the use of weapons
are held no less effective than the weapons themselves. (The
implication is that those who choose a challenger to Hector will be
held as fully to account as the challenger himself.)   358 **meet**
fitting   367 **shares from** gains at the expense of   372 **scape
Hector fair** come off undefeated in fighting Hector. (Ulysses's
argument is that Achilles, already too proud, will be insufferable if
he wins, and that, if he loses, the Greeks will undergo the
humiliation of losing with their best-reputed warrior.)

Why then we did our main opinion crush   373
In taint of our best man. No, make a lottery,   374
And, by device, let blockish Ajax draw
The sort to fight with Hector. Among ourselves   376
Give him allowance as the worthier man;   377
For that will physic the great Myrmidon   378
Who broils in loud applause, and make him fall   379
His crest that prouder than blue Iris bends.   380
If the dull brainless Ajax come safe off,
We'll dress him up in voices; if he fail,   382
Yet go we under our opinion still
That we have better men. But, hit or miss,
Our project's life this shape of sense assumes: 385
Ajax employed plucks down Achilles' plumes.

NESTOR
Now, Ulysses, I begin to relish thy advice;
And I will give a taste of it forthwith
To Agamemnon. Go we to him straight.
Two curs shall tame each other; pride alone
Must tar the mastiffs on, as 'twere their bone.   391

                                        Exeunt.

373–4 **we . . . taint** we would destroy the mainstay of our
reputation in the dishonor   376 **sort** lot   377 **allowance as**
acknowledgment as   378 **physic** purge medically.
Myrmidon i.e., Achilles. (So called here because accompanied by
a band of Myrmidon warriors, from a tribe living in Thessaly.)
379 **broils in** basks in   379–80 **and make . . . bends** and cause
him to lower the plumes of his helmet that now arch and wave
more proudly than the rainbow. (Literally, Iris, the many-colored
messenger of Juno.)   382 **voices** applause   385 **life** success
391 **tar** provoke

[2.1] ⟩⟨ *Enter Ajax and Thersites.*

AJAX   Thersites!

THERSITES   Agamemnon—how if he had boils, full, all
over, generally?

AJAX   Thersites!

THERSITES   And those boils did run? Say so. Did not the
general run, then? Were not that a botchy core?   6

AJAX   Dog!

THERSITES   Then there would come some matter from   8
him. I see none now.

AJAX   Thou bitch-wolf's son, canst thou not hear?
[*Strikes him.*] Feel, then.

THERSITES   The plague of Greece upon thee, thou mon-   12
grel beef-witted lord!   13

AJAX   Speak then, thou vinewed'st leaven, speak. I will   14
beat thee into handsomeness.

THERSITES   I shall sooner rail thee into wit and holiness;
but I think thy horse will sooner con an oration than   17
thou learn a prayer without book. Thou canst strike,   18
canst thou? A red murrain o' thy jade's tricks!   19

AJAX   Toadstool, learn me the proclamation.   20

THERSITES   Dost thou think I have no sense, thou strik-   21
est me thus?

2.1 *Location: The Greek camp; Achilles's tent.*
6 **botchy core** central hard mass of a boil or tumor.   8 **matter**
(1) sense (2) pus   12–13 **mongrel** (Ajax's mother was a Trojan,
the sister of Priam; compare 2.2.77 [note], 4.5.84, and 4.5.121.)
13 **beef-witted** i.e., slow-witted. (Perhaps this refers to the belief
that eating beef made one dull, or Thersites may merely be calling
Ajax a "stupid ox.")   14 **vinewed'st leaven** moldiest dough
17 **con** memorize   18 **without book** by heart.   19 **murrain**
plague.   **jade's tricks** i.e., ill-tempered kicking and rearing, as of a
worthless horse.   20 **learn me** find out for me   21 **sense** feeling

AJAX   The proclamation!

THERSITES   Thou art proclaimed a fool, I think.

AJAX   Do not, porcupine, do not. My fingers itch.   25

THERSITES   I would thou didst itch from head to foot. An I had the scratching of thee, I would make thee the loathsomest scab in Greece. When thou art forth in the incursions, thou strikest as slow as another.   29

AJAX   I say, the proclamation!

THERSITES   Thou grumblest and railest every hour on Achilles, and thou art as full of envy at his greatness as Cerberus is at Proserpina's beauty, ay, that thou   33 bark'st at him.

AJAX   Mistress Thersites!

THERSITES   Thou shouldst strike him—   36

AJAX   Cobloaf!   37

THERSITES   He would pun thee into shivers with his   38 fist, as a sailor breaks a biscuit.

AJAX [*beating him*]   You whoreson cur!

THERSITES   Do, do.   41

AJAX   Thou stool for a witch!   42

THERSITES   Ay, do, do, thou sodden-witted lord! Thou   43 hast no more brain than I have in mine elbows; an asinego may tutor thee. Thou scurvy-valiant ass! Thou   45 art here but to thrash Trojans, and thou art bought   46 and sold among those of any wit, like a barbarian   47

---

25 porcupine (A term of abuse for one who is prickly and small.)
29 incursions i.e., attacks upon the Trojan forces   **33 Cerberus** three-headed dog that guarded the entrance to Hades.
Proserpina Queen of Hades   **36 Thou** If thou   **37 Cobloaf** Small round loaf; a bun.   **38 pun** pound.   **shivers** fragments
41 Do i.e., Go ahead, I dare you   **42 stool** privy   **43 sodden-witted** boiled-brained   **45 asinego** little ass   **46–7 bought and sold** i.e., treated like merchandise

slave. If thou use to beat me, I will begin at thy heel   48
and tell what thou art by inches, thou thing of no   49
bowels, thou!   50

AJAX   You dog!

THERSITES   You scurvy lord!

AJAX [*beating him*]   You cur!

THERSITES   Mars his idiot! Do, rudeness, do, camel,   54
do, do.

[*Enter Achilles and Patroclus.*]

ACHILLES   Why, how now, Ajax, wherefore do ye thus?   56
How now, Thersites, what's the matter, man?

THERSITES   You see him there, do you?

ACHILLES   Ay; what's the matter?

THERSITES   Nay, look upon him.

ACHILLES   So I do. What's the matter?

THERSITES   Nay, but regard him well.

ACHILLES   Well, why, I do so.

THERSITES   But yet you look not well upon him; for,
whomsomever you take him to be, he is Ajax.   65

ACHILLES   I know that, fool.

THERSITES   Ay, but that fool knows not himself.   67

AJAX   Therefore I beat thee.   68

THERSITES   Lo, lo, lo, lo, what modicums of wit he ut-   69
ters! His evasions have ears thus long. I have bobbed   70

---

48 **use** continue   49 **by inches** methodically, inch by inch
50 **bowels** sensitivity, human feeling   54 **Mars his** Mars's
56 **wherefore** why   65 **Ajax** (With probable pun on *a jakes,* a
latrine.)   67 **that fool . . . himself** (Thersites answers as though
Achilles had said, "I know that fool.")   68 **Therefore . . . thee**
i.e., I beat you because you are the real fool, not me. (This attempt
at wit draws Thersites's sarcasm in the next speech.)
69 **modicums** small amounts   70 **have . . . long** i.e., are those
of an ass, are asinine.   **bobbed** thumped

his brain more than he has beat my bones. I will buy   71
nine sparrows for a penny, and his pia mater is not   72
worth the ninth part of a sparrow. This lord, Achilles
—Ajax, who wears his wit in his belly and his guts
in his head—I'll tell you what I say of him.

ACHILLES What?

THERSITES I say, this Ajax—   [Ajax threatens him.]

ACHILLES Nay, good Ajax.

THERSITES Has not so much wit—

ACHILLES Nay, I must hold you.

THERSITES As will stop the eye of Helen's needle, for   81
whom he comes to fight.

ACHILLES Peace, fool!

THERSITES I would have peace and quietness, but the
fool will not—he there, that he. Look you there.

AJAX Oh, thou damned cur! I shall—

ACHILLES Will you set your wit to a fool's?   87

THERSITES No, I warrant you, for a fool's will shame it.   88

PATROCLUS Good words, Thersites.   89

ACHILLES What's the quarrel?

AJAX I bade the vile owl go learn me the tenor of the
proclamation, and he rails upon me.

THERSITES I serve thee not.

AJAX Well, go to, go to.

THERSITES I serve here voluntary.   95

71 **will** can   **pia mater** (Literally, membrane cover of the brain;
used here for the brain.)   81 **stop** stop up, fill. (Perhaps with a
bawdy sense.)   **Helen's needle** (Aristocratic women
customarily did needlework as an avocation.)   87 **set your wit
to** match wits with   88 **a fool's . . . shame it** i.e., Ajax's
intelligence is even less than a fool's.   89 **Good words** i.e.,
Speak gently   95 **voluntary** voluntarily.

ACHILLES   Your last service was suff'rance, 'twas not   96
    voluntary; no man is beaten voluntary. Ajax was here
    the voluntary, and you as under an impress.   98

THERSITES   E'en so. A great deal of your wit, too, lies in   99
    your sinews, or else there be liars. Hector shall have a 100
    great catch an 'a knock out either of your brains; 'a   101
    were as good crack a fusty nut with no kernel.   102

ACHILLES   What, with me too, Thersites?

THERSITES   There's Ulysses and old Nestor, whose wit
    was moldy ere your grandsires had nails on their toes,
    yoke you like draft-oxen and make you plow up the
    war.

ACHILLES   What? What?

THERSITES   Yes, good sooth. To, Achilles! To, Ajax! To!   109

AJAX   I shall cut out your tongue.

THERSITES   'Tis no matter. I shall speak as much wit as
    thou afterwards.   112

PATROCLUS   No more words, Thersites. Peace!

THERSITES   I will hold my peace when Achilles's brach   114
    bids me, shall I?

ACHILLES   There's for you, Patroclus.

THERSITES   I will see you hanged like clodpolls ere I   117
    come any more to your tents. I will keep where there
    is wit stirring and leave the faction of fools.   *Exit.*

---

96 **suff'rance** something imposed   98 **impress**
(1) impressment, military draft (2) imprint (of blows).   99 **E'en**
so Exactly.   100 **or . . . liars** unless Report is a liar.   101 **an 'a**
if he   101–2 **'a . . . good** he might as well   102 **fusty** moldy
109 **To . . . To!** (Thersites impersonates Nestor and Ulysses as
drivers of a team, urging Achilles and Ajax to plow.)
112 **afterwards** i.e., even after my tongue is cut out.   114 **brach**
bitch hound. (The quarto reading, "brooch," could mean "bauble,
plaything," referring to Patroclus.)   117 **clodpolls** blockheads

PATROCLUS   A good riddance.

ACHILLES
    Marry, this, sir, is proclaimed through all our host:
    That Hector, by the fifth hour of the sun,   122
    Will with a trumpet twixt our tents and Troy
    Tomorrow morning call some knight to arms
    That hath a stomach, and such a one that dare   125
    Maintain—I know not what, 'tis trash. Farewell.

AJAX   Farewell. Who shall answer him?

ACHILLES   I know not. 'Tis put to lottery. Otherwise
    He knew his man.   [*Exit with Patroclus.*]   129

AJAX   Oh, meaning you? I will go learn more of it.

                                                                Exit.

[2.2] ❧ *Enter Priam, Hector, Troilus, Paris, and*
              Helenus.

PRIAM
    After so many hours, lives, speeches spent,
    Thus once again says Nestor from the Greeks:
    "Deliver Helen, and all damage else—   3
    As honor, loss of time, travail, expense,   4
    Wounds, friends, and what else dear that is consumed
    In hot digestion of this cormorant war—   6
    Shall be struck off." Hector, what say you to't?   7

HECTOR
    Though no man lesser fears the Greeks than I
    As far as toucheth my particular,   9

122 **fifth hour** eleven o'clock   125 **stomach** appetite (for
fighting)   129 **knew** would know

2.2 Location: Troy. The palace.
3 **Deliver** Hand over   4 **travail** strenuous effort   6 **cormorant**
voracious (like the seabird)   7 **struck off** canceled.   9 **my**
particular me personally

Yet, dread Priam,
There is no lady of more softer bowels,   11
More spongy to suck in the sense of fear,
More ready to cry out, "Who knows what follows?"
Than Hector is. The wound of peace is surety,   14
Surety secure; but modest doubt is called   15
The beacon of the wise, the tent that searches   16
To th'bottom of the worst. Let Helen go.
Since the first sword was drawn about this question,
Every tithe soul, 'mongst many thousand dismes,   19
Hath been as dear as Helen; I mean, of ours.
If we have lost so many tenths of ours   21
To guard a thing not ours—nor worth to us,
Had it our name, the value of one ten—   23
What merit's in that reason which denies   24
The yielding of her up?

TROILUS   Fie, fie, my brother!
Weigh you the worth and honor of a king
So great as our dread father in a scale
Of common ounces? Will you with counters sum   28
The past-proportion of his infinite,   29
And buckle in a waist most fathomless   30
With spans and inches so diminutive   31
As fears and reasons? Fie, for godly shame!   32

---

11 **bowels** i.e., mercy, pity   14 **The . . . surety** The danger of
peace is in the sense of overconfidence and security it breeds
15 **secure** overconfident.   **modest doubt** a reasonable estimate of
danger   16 **beacon** warning signal.   **tent** surgical probe
19 **Every . . . dismes** every human life exacted by the war as a tithe
or tenth, amongst many thousand such exactions   21 **tenths** i.e.,
lives exacted by the war   23 **Had . . . name** i.e., even if Helen
were a Trojan.   **one ten** one tithe exacted by the war, one Trojan
life   24 **reason** reasoning   28–32 **Will . . . reasons?** Will you
employ the valueless disks used by shopkeepers in their commercial
bargaining to sum up Priam's infinite worth exceeding all calculation,
and attempt to confine his unfathomable greatness with fears and
pretexts that are as puny as the nine-inch span from hand to thumb?

HELENUS [*to Troilus*]

    No marvel, though you bite so sharp at reasons,   33
    You are so empty of them. Should not our father   34
    Bear the great sway of his affairs with reason,
    Because your speech hath none that tell him so?   36

TROILUS

    You are for dreams and slumbers, brother priest;
    You fur your gloves with reason. Here are your
       reasons: 38
    You know an enemy intends you harm;
    You know a sword employed is perilous,
    And reason flies the object of all harm.   41
    Who marvels then, when Helenus beholds
    A Grecian and his sword, if he do set
    The very wings of reason to his heels
    And fly like chidden Mercury from Jove   45
    Or like a star disorbed? Nay, if we talk of reason,   46
    Let's shut our gates and sleep. Manhood and honor
    Should have hare hearts, would they but fat their
       thoughts   48
    With this crammed reason. Reason and respect   49
    Make livers pale and lustihood deject.   50

33 **reasons** (Pronounced like "raisins," with pun.)   34 **not our father** our father not   36 **Because . . . so?** i.e., simply because you unreasonably urge him to govern unreasonably?   38 **fur** line with soft fur. (Troilus accuses Helenus of using reason as a justification for personal comfort, explaining cowardly flight as prudence.)   41 **And . . . harm** and such cowardly "reason" flees at the sight of anything threatening.   45 **chidden Mercury** (Mercury as Jove's errand boy was subject to his chiding or impatient bidding.)   46 **disorbed** removed from its sphere (like a shooting star).   48–9 **Should . . . reason** would have the craven hearts of hares if they would cram their thoughts with this "reason."   49 **respect** caution   50 **livers pale** (A bloodless liver was thought to be a sign of cowardice.)   **and . . . deject** and bodily vigor overthrown.

HECTOR [to Troilus]
 Brother, she is not worth what she doth cost
 The holding.

TROILUS   What's aught but as 'tis valued?

HECTOR
 But value dwells not in particular will;   53
 It holds his estimate and dignity   54
 As well wherein 'tis precious of itself   55
 As in the prizer. 'Tis mad idolatry   56
 To make the service greater than the god;
 And the will dotes that is inclinable   58
 To what infectiously itself affects   59
 Without some image of th'affected merit.   60

TROILUS
 I take today a wife, and my election   61
 Is led on in the conduct of my will—
 My will enkindled by mine eyes and ears,
 Two traded pilots twixt the dangerous shores 64
 Of will and judgment. How may I avoid,   65
 Although my will distaste what it elected,   66
 The wife I chose? There can be no evasion
 To blench from this and to stand firm by honor. 68
 We turn not back the silks upon the merchant
 When we have soiled them, nor the remainder viands 70

---

53 **particular will** i.e., one person's preference merely 54 **his**
its. **dignity** worth 55–6 **As well . . . prizer** as much in its
intrinsic worth as in the opinion of the person who prizes or
appraises it. 58–60 **the will . . . merit** any will is mere
willfulness that is derived from the will's own diseased affection
without some visible appearance of merit in the thing desired.
61 **I take today a wife** (Troilus, in setting up a hypothetical case
that applies to Paris, is also stating his own credo about love.)
election choice 64 **traded** skillful in their trade; trafficking
back and forth 65 **avoid** rid myself of 66 **distaste** dislike (in
time) 68 **blench** shrink. **and** and simultaneously
70 **remainder viands** leftover food

We do not throw in unrespective sieve   71
Because we now are full. It was thought meet
Paris should do some vengeance on the Greeks.   73
Your breath of full consent bellied his sails;   74
The seas and winds, old wranglers, took a truce   75
And did him service. He touched the ports desired,
And for an old aunt whom the Greeks held captive   77
He brought a Grecian queen, whose youth and
    freshness
Wrinkles Apollo's and makes stale the morning.   79
Why keep we her? The Grecians keep our aunt.
Is she worth keeping? Why, she is a pearl
Whose price hath launched above a thousand ships   82
And turned crowned kings to merchants.   83
If you'll avouch 'twas wisdom Paris went—
As you must needs, for you all cried, "Go, go"—
If you'll confess he brought home noble prize—
As you must needs, for you all clapped your hands
And cried, "Inestimable!"—why do you now
The issue of your proper wisdoms rate   89
And do a deed that never Fortune did,   90

---

71 **unrespective sieve** undiscriminating receptacle, i.e., garbage
can   73 **vengeance** i.e., in return for Hesione's abduction; see
line 77 and note   74 **bellied** swelled   75 **old wranglers**
traditional enemies   77 **an old aunt** i.e., Hesione, Priam's sister,
rescued from the wrath of Poseidon by Hercules and bestowed by
him on the Greek, Telamon, father of Ajax; we learn in 4.5.84 and
4.5.121 that she was Ajax's mother   79 **Wrinkles Apollo's**
makes Apollo's youthful countenance look old and ugly by
comparison   82 **Whose . . . ships** (Perhaps echoes the famous
line from Marlowe's *Doctor Faustus:* "Was this the face that
launched a thousand ships?")   83 **turned . . . merchants** i.e.,
has made kings behave like merchants seeking a rare pearl.
(Compare Matthew 13:45.)   89 **The issue . . . rate** condemn the
results of your own wise deliberation   90 **do . . . did** act more
capriciously than Fortune ever did

Beggar the estimation which you prized   91
Richer than sea and land? Oh, theft most base,
That we have stol'n what we do fear to keep!
But thieves unworthy of a thing so stol'n,   94
That in their country did them that disgrace   95
We fear to warrant in our native place!   96

Enter Cassandra, [raving,] with her hair about
her ears.

CASSANDRA
  Cry, Trojans, cry!
PRIAM   What noise? What shriek is this?
TROILUS
  'Tis our mad sister. I do know her voice.
CASSANDRA   Cry, Trojans!
HECTOR   It is Cassandra.
CASSANDRA
  Cry, Trojans, cry! Lend me ten thousand eyes,
  And I will fill them with prophetic tears.
HECTOR   Peace, sister, peace!
CASSANDRA
  Virgins and boys, mid-age and wrinkled old,   104
  Soft infancy, that nothing canst but cry,   105
  Add to my clamor! Let us pay betimes   106
  A moiety of that mass of moan to come.   107
  Cry, Trojans, cry! Practice your eyes with tears!   108

---

91 **Beggar . . . which** consider valueless the once-esteemed object
that   94 **But** i.e., We are but   95–6 **That . . . place** who
disgraced the Greeks in their own country through an act (the
abducting of Helen) that we are now too cowardly to justify right
here in our own native land.   96.1–2 *about her ears* (Betokening
unmarried status and also distraction. Perhaps Cassandra's wild
appearance helps explain why the Trojans do not recognize her at
first.)   104 **old** old persons   105 **nothing canst** can do
nothing   106 **betimes** before it is too late   107 **moiety** part
108 **Practice** Make use of

Troy must not be, nor goodly Ilium stand;
Our firebrand brother, Paris, burns us all.   110
Cry, Trojans, cry! A Helen and a woe!
Cry, cry! Troy burns, or else let Helen go.   *Exit.*

HECTOR
Now, youthful Troilus, do not these high strains
Of divination in our sister work
Some touches of remorse? Or is your blood
So madly hot that no discourse of reason,
Nor fear of bad success in a bad cause,
Can qualify the same?

TROILUS   Why, brother Hector,   118
We may not think the justness of each act   119
Such and no other than th'event doth form it,   120
Nor once deject the courage of our minds   121
Because Cassandra's mad. Her brainsick raptures   122
Cannot distaste the goodness of a quarrel   123
Which hath our several honors all engaged   124
To make it gracious. For my private part,   125
I am no more touched than all Priam's sons,   126
And Jove forbid there should be done amongst us   127
Such things as might offend the weakest spleen   128
To fight for and maintain!   129

---

110 **firebrand** (Paris's mother, Hecuba, dreamed when pregnant
with Paris that she would be delivered of a firebrand destined to
burn down Troy.)   118 **qualify** moderate   119–22 **We . . .
mad** we must not judge the justice of our proceedings on the
outcome, nor abate our courage solely because of Cassandra's
mad warnings.   123 **distaste** render distasteful   124 **our
several honors** the honor of each of us   125 **gracious**
righteous, dignified. (Because our honorable selves "grace" the
enterprise.)   126 **touched** affected   127–9 **Jove . . .
maintain!** Jove forbid that any act done by any of Priam's sons
(such as abducting Helen) should be such that even the least
courageous among us would not willingly fight to maintain!

PARIS

Else might the world convince of levity   130
As well my undertakings as your counsels.   131
But I attest the gods, your full consent   132
Gave wings to my propension and cut off   133
All fears attending on so dire a project.
For what, alas, can these my single arms?   135
What propugnation is in one man's valor   136
To stand the push and enmity of those
This quarrel would excite? Yet, I protest,
Were I alone to pass the difficulties,   139
And had as ample power as I have will,
Paris should ne'er retract what he hath done
Nor faint in the pursuit.   142

PRIAM   Paris, you speak
Like one besotted on your sweet delights.   143
You have the honey still, but these the gall.
So to be valiant is no praise at all.   145

PARIS

Sir, I propose not merely to myself
The pleasures such a beauty brings with it,
But I would have the soil of her fair rape   148
Wiped off in honorable keeping her.
What treason were it to the ransacked queen,   150
Disgrace to your great worths, and shame to me,
Now to deliver her possession up   152
On terms of base compulsion! Can it be

---

130 **convince** convict   131 **As well . . . as** both . . . and
132 **attest** call to witness   133 **propension** propensity,
inclination   135 **can . . . arms?** can my arms alone accomplish?
136 **propugnation** defense, might   139 **pass** experience,
undergo   142 **faint** lose heart   143 **besotted** drunk
145 **So** Thus, under these circumstances.   **praise** merit
148 **soil** stain.   **rape** abduction   150 **ransacked** carried off
152 **her possession** possession of her

That so degenerate a strain as this   154
Should once set footing in your generous bosoms?   155
There's not the meanest spirit on our party   156
Without a heart to dare or sword to draw   157
When Helen is defended, nor none so noble
Whose life were ill bestowed or death unfamed   159
Where Helen is the subject. Then I say,
Well may we fight for her whom we know well
The world's large spaces cannot parallel.   162

HECTOR

Paris and Troilus, you have both said well,
And on the cause and question now in hand
Have glozed—but superficially, not much   165
Unlike young men, whom Aristotle thought
Unfit to hear moral philosophy.   167
The reasons you allege do more conduce   168
To the hot passion of distempered blood
Than to make up a free determination   170
Twixt right and wrong, for pleasure and revenge
Have ears more deaf than adders to the voice   172
Of any true decision. Nature craves   173
All dues be rendered to their owners. Now,
What nearer debt in all humanity
Than wife is to the husband? If this law
Of nature be corrupted through affection,   177
And that great minds, of partial indulgence   178

---

154 **strain** muddied thought   155 **generous** noble
156–7 **There's . . . heart** Not even the most low-born Trojan would
lack the courage   159 **Whose . . . unfamed** whose life would be
unworthily given or whose death would be neglected by fame
162 **The world's . . . spaces** all the world   165 **glozed**
commented on   167 **moral philosophy** (Aristotle says this of
political philosophy in the *Nichomachean Ethics*.)   168 **conduce**
lead, tend   170 **free** unbiased   172 **adders** (Psalms 58:4–5 speaks
of adders as deaf.)   173 **craves** demands   177 **affection** erotic
passion   178 **that** if that, if.   **of partial** out of self-interested

To their benumbèd wills, resist the same,
There is a law in each well-ordered nation
To curb those raging appetites that are
Most disobedient and refractory.   182
If Helen then be wife to Sparta's king,
As it is known she is, these moral laws
Of nature and of nations speak aloud
To have her back returned. Thus to persist
In doing wrong extenuates not wrong
But makes it much more heavy. Hector's opinion
Is this in way of truth; yet ne'ertheless,   189
My sprightly brethren, I propend to you   190
In resolution to keep Helen still,
For 'tis a cause that hath no mean dependence   192
Upon our joint and several dignities.   193

TROILUS
Why, there you touched the life of our design!
Were it not glory that we more affected   195
Than the performance of our heaving spleens,   196
I would not wish a drop of Trojan blood
Spent more in her defense. But, worthy Hector,
She is a theme of honor and renown,
A spur to valiant and magnanimous deeds,
Whose present courage may beat down our foes,   201
And fame in time to come canonize us;   202
For I presume brave Hector would not lose
So rich advantage of a promised glory

182 **refractory** obstinate.   189 **truth** abstract principle
190 **sprightly** full of spirit.   **propend** incline   192–3 **'tis . . .
dignities** i.e., it is a cause upon which depends our collective and
individual honors, and they on it.   195 **more affected** desired
more   196 **heaving spleens** i.e., aroused anger
201 **Whose . . . foes** the ready and courageous spirit of which will
enable us to beat down our foes   202 **canonize** enroll among
famous persons

As smiles upon the forehead of this action   205
For the wide world's revenue.

HECTOR   I am yours,
   You valiant offspring of great Priamus.
   I have a roisting challenge sent amongst   208
   The dull and factious nobles of the Greeks
   Will strike amazement to their drowsy spirits.   210
   I was advertised their great general slept,   211
   Whilst emulation in the army crept.   212
   This, I presume, will wake him.   *Exeunt.*

[2.3] 🙠 *Enter Thersites, solus.*

THERSITES How now, Thersites? What, lost in the laby-
   rinth of thy fury? Shall the elephant Ajax carry it   2
   thus? He beats me, and I rail at him. Oh, worthy
   satisfaction! Would it were otherwise, that I could beat
   him whilst he railed at me. 'Sfoot, I'll learn to conjure   5
   and raise devils but I'll see some issue of my spiteful   6
   execrations. Then there's Achilles, a rare engineer! If   7
   Troy be not taken till these two undermine it, the walls
   will stand till they fall of themselves. O thou great
   thunder-darter of Olympus, forget that thou art Jove,

205 **forehead** i.e., prospect, beginning   208 **roisting** roistering,
clamorous   210 **Will** that will   211 **advertised** informed.
their great general i.e., Achilles; or possibly Agamemnon
212 **emulation** ambitious or jealous rivalry

2.3 *Location: The Greek camp. Before Achilles's tent.*
2 **carry it** carry off the honors   5 **'Sfoot** By His (God's) foot
6 **but . . . issue** i.e., if it takes that to see some result
7 **execrations** curses.   **engineer** one who digs countermines or
tunnels underneath the enemy's battlements, or devises plans for
such undertakings

the king of gods, and, Mercury, lose all the serpentine   11
craft of thy caduceus, if ye take not that little little less   12
than little wit from them that they have, which short-   13
armed ignorance itself knows is so abundant scarce it   14
will not in circumvention deliver a fly from a spider   15
without drawing their massy irons and cutting the   16
web! After this, the vengeance on the whole camp! Or
rather, the Neapolitan bone-ache! For that, methinks,   18
is the curse dependent on those that war for a placket.   19
I have said my prayers, and devil Envy say
"Amen."—What ho! My lord Achilles!

    [*Enter Patroclus at the door of the tent.*]

PATROCLUS   Who's there? Thersites? Good Thersites,
come in and rail.   [*Exit.*]

THERSITES   If I could ha' remembered a gilt counterfeit,   24
thou wouldst not have slipped out of my contemplation. But it is no matter; thyself upon thyself! The   26
common curse of mankind, folly and ignorance, be
thine in great revenue! Heaven bless thee from a tutor,   28

11–12 **serpentine . . . caduceus** (Alludes to Mercury's wand,
having two serpents twined round it.)   13–14 **short-armed**
inadequate in its reach, finding everything beyond its grasp
15 **circumvention** craft, stratagem   16 **massy irons** massive
swords. (Used with overkill on a mere spider's web.)
18 **Neapolitan bone-ache** i.e., venereal disease.   19 **dependent
on** hanging over.   **placket** slit in a petticoat; hence (indecently)
a woman.   24 **ha'** have.   **gilt counterfeit** counterfeit coin.
(Often called a "slip"; hence the quibble in line 25.)   26 **thyself
upon thyself** (Thersites, after alleging that he would have cursed
Patroclus along with Ajax and Achilles if he were not counterfeit
and hence so easily overlooked, now undertakes to curse Patroclus
with the most dire curse imaginable: may Patroclus simply be
himself, be plagued by himself.)   28 **great revenue** generous
amounts.   **bless thee from** bless you by protecting you from
(so as to preserve your native ignorance)

and discipline come not near thee! Let thy blood be　29
thy direction till thy death; then if she that lays thee　30
out says thou art a fair corpse, I'll be sworn and sworn　31
upon't she never shrouded any but lazars.　32

[Enter Patroclus.]

Amen.—Where's Achilles?

PATROCLUS　What, art thou devout? Wast thou in prayer?

THERSITES　Ay. The heavens hear me!

PATROCLUS　Amen.

Enter Achilles.

ACHILLES　Who's there?

PATROCLUS　Thersites, my lord.

ACHILLES　Where, where? Oh, where?—Art thou come? Why, my cheese, my digestion, why hast thou not　41
served thyself in to my table so many meals? Come, what's Agamemnon?

THERSITES　Thy commander, Achilles.—Then tell me, Patroclus, what's Achilles?

PATROCLUS　Thy lord, Thersites. Then tell me, I pray thee, what's thyself?

THERSITES　Thy knower, Patroclus. Then tell me, Patroclus, what art thou?

PATROCLUS　Thou mayst tell that knowest.

ACHILLES　Oh, tell, tell.

---

29 **discipline** instruction.　　**blood** violent passion
30–1 **she . . . out** the woman who prepares your body for burial
32 **lazars** lepers.　　41 **cheese** (Supposed, proverbially, to aid digestion.)

THERSITES   I'll decline the whole question. Agamemnon   52
commands Achilles, Achilles is my lord, I am Patroclus' knower, and Patroclus is a fool.

PATROCLUS   You rascal!

THERSITES   Peace, fool! I have not done.

ACHILLES   He is a privileged man.—Proceed, Thersites.   57

THERSITES   Agamemnon is a fool, Achilles is a fool,
Thersites is a fool, and, as aforesaid, Patroclus is a fool.

ACHILLES   Derive this. Come.   60

THERSITES   Agamemnon is a fool to offer to command   61
Achilles, Achilles is a fool to be commanded of
Agamemnon, Thersites is a fool to serve such a fool,
and Patroclus is a fool positive.   64

PATROCLUS   Why am I a fool?

THERSITES   Make that demand to the Creator. It suffices   66
me thou art. Look you, who comes here?

Enter [at a distance] Agamemnon, Ulysses,
Nestor, Diomedes, Ajax, and Calchas.

ACHILLES   Patroclus, I'll speak with nobody.—Come in
with me, Thersites.   [*Exit.*]

THERSITES   Here is such patchery, such juggling, and   70
such knavery! All the argument is a whore and a   71
cuckold, a good quarrel to draw emulous factions and   72
bleed to death upon. Now, the dry serpigo on the   73

---

52 **decline** go through in order from beginning to end (as when
declining a noun)   57 **privileged man** (Fools were permitted to
speak without restraint.)   60 **Derive** Explain, give the origin of.
(The grammatical metaphor is continued here and also in line 64.)
61 **offer** undertake   64 **positive** absolute.   66 **Make that
demand** Ask that question   70 **patchery** knavery   71–3 **All . . .
upon** i.e., This war is nothing but a quarrel about a whore and a
cuckold (Helen and Menelaus), a fine quarrelsome basis upon
which to draw rival factions into bloody and fatal conflict.
73 **serpigo** skin eruption

subject, and war and lechery confound all!   [*Exit.*]   74

AGAMEMNON   Where is Achilles?

PATROCLUS   Within his tent, but ill disposed, my lord.

AGAMEMNON   Let it be known to him that we are here.
He shent our messengers, and we lay by   78
Our appertainments, visiting of him.   79
Let him be told so, lest perchance he think
We dare not move the question of our place,   81
Or know not what we are.

PATROCLUS   I shall so say to him.   [*Exit.*]

ULYSSES   We saw him at the opening of his tent. He is
not sick.

AJAX   Yes, lion-sick, sick of proud heart. You may call it   85
melancholy if you will favor the man, but, by my
head, 'tis pride. But why, why? Let him show us the
cause.—A word, my lord. [*He takes Agamemnon aside.*]

NESTOR   What moves Ajax thus to bay at him?

ULYSSES   Achilles hath inveigled his fool from him.

NESTOR   Who, Thersites?

ULYSSES   He.

NESTOR   Then will Ajax lack matter, if he have lost his   93
argument.   94

ULYSSES   No, you see, he is his argument that has his   95
argument—Achilles.   96

74 **confound** destroy; throw into turmoil   78 **shent** sent back
insultingly   79 **appertainments** rights, prerogatives
81 **move the question** insist upon the prerogatives   85 **lion-
sick** i.e., sick with pride   93 **matter** subject matter (to rail upon)
93–4 **his argument** i.e., the subject of his railing, Thersites.
95–6 **No . . . Achilles** i.e., No, Ajax has not lost something to rail
on, since Achilles, who now has Thersites, has become Ajax's latest
object of quarreling.

NESTOR   All the better; their fraction is more our wish   97
than their faction. But it was a strong council that a   98
fool could disunite.   99

ULYSSES   The amity that wisdom knits not, folly may
easily untie.

     Enter Patroclus.

Here comes Patroclus.

NESTOR   No Achilles with him.

ULYSSES   The elephant hath joints, but none for courtesy.   104
His legs are legs for necessity, not for flexure.

PATROCLUS
Achilles bids me say he is much sorry
If anything more than your sport and pleasure
Did move your greatness and this noble state   108
To call upon him. He hopes it is no other
But for your health and your digestion sake,   110
An after-dinner's breath.

AGAMEMNON   Hear you, Patroclus: 111
We are too well acquainted with these answers;
But his evasion, winged thus swift with scorn,
Cannot outfly our apprehensions.   114
Much attribute he hath, and much the reason   115
Why we ascribe it to him. Yet all his virtues,
Not virtuously on his own part beheld,   117
Do in our eyes begin to lose their gloss,

97–9 **their fraction . . . disunite** i.e., this discord between
Achilles and Ajax better suits our wishes than their uniting in
faction against us. But the alliance between them cannot have been
strong in any case if a fool like Thersites was able to undo it.
104 **The elephant hath joints** (Refers to a common belief that
elephants' joints did not enable them to lie down.)   108 **state**
council of state   110 **digestion** digestion's   111 **breath** i.e.,
stroll for a breath of fresh air.   114 **apprehensions** (1) power of
arrest (2) understanding.   115 **attribute** credit, reputation
117 **Not . . . beheld** not being modestly observed or kept by him

Yea, like fair fruit in an unwholesome dish,
Are like to rot untasted. Go and tell him   120
We come to speak with him. And you shall not sin   121
If you do say we think him overproud
And underhonest, in self-assumption greater   123
Than in the note of judgment; and worthier than
   himself   124
Here tend the savage strangeness he puts on,   125
Disguise the holy strength of their command,
And underwrite in an observing kind   127
His humorous predominance—yea, watch   128
His pettish lunes, his ebbs, his flows, as if   129
The passage and whole carriage of this action   130
Rode on his tide. Go tell him this, and add
That if he overhold his price so much,   132
We'll none of him, but let him, like an engine   133
Not portable, lie under this report: 134
"Bring action hither; this cannot go to war."   135
A stirring dwarf we do allowance give   136
Before a sleeping giant. Tell him so.

PATROCLUS
I shall, and bring his answer presently.   138

119 **like** likely   121 **sin** err   123 **self-assumption** self-importance   124 **Than . . . judgment** than men of true judgment know him to be; or, than in qualities of wise judgment
124–5 **worthier . . . on** worthier persons than himself stand here in attendance while he assumes an uncivil aloofness
127–8 **underwrite . . . predominance** deferentially subscribe to the humor now dominant in him—i.e., arrogant pride
129 **pettish lunes** ill-humored tantrums   130 **this action** the Trojan War   132 **overhold** overvalue   133 **engine** military machine   134 **lie under** suffer under   135 **"Bring . . . war"** i.e., "Let the war come to me; I am too proud to accommodate myself to it."   136 **stirring** active.   **allowance** approbation, praise   138 **presently** right away.

AGAMEMNON

  In second voice we'll not be satisfied.   139

  We come to speak with him.—Ulysses, enter you.

                    [Exit Ulysses with Patroclus.]

AJAX What is he more than another?

AGAMEMNON No more than what he thinks he is.

AJAX Is he so much? Do you not think he thinks himself a better man than I am?

AGAMEMNON No question.

AJAX Will you subscribe his thought and say he is?   146

AGAMEMNON No, noble Ajax, you are as strong, as valiant, as wise, no less noble, much more gentle, and altogether more tractable.

AJAX Why should a man be proud? How doth pride grow? I know not what it is.

AGAMEMNON Your mind is the clearer, Ajax, and your virtues the fairer. He that is proud eats up himself. Pride is his own glass, his own trumpet, his own 154 chronicle; and whatever praises itself but in the deed 155 devours the deed in the praise.

    Enter Ulysses.

AJAX I do hate a proud man as I hate the engend'ring of toads.

NESTOR *[aside]* Yet he loves himself. Is't not strange?

ULYSSES

  Achilles will not to the field tomorrow.

AGAMEMNON

  What's his excuse?

---

139 **In second voice** i.e., With a mere messenger's report
146 **subscribe** concur in   154–5 **Pride . . . chronicle** Pride is its own mirror and proclaimer of its greatness   155 **but in the deed** in any way other than in doing (praiseworthy) deeds

ULYSSES   He doth rely on none,
But carries on the stream of his dispose   163
Without observance or respect of any,
In will peculiar and in self-admission.   165

AGAMEMNON
Why, will he not upon our fair request
Untent his person and share th' air with us?

ULYSSES
Things small as nothing, for request's sake only,   168
He makes important. Possessed he is with greatness,
And speaks not to himself but with a pride
That quarrels at self-breath. Imagined worth   171
Holds in his blood such swoll'n and hot discourse
That twixt his mental and his active parts
Kingdomed Achilles in commotion rages   174
And batters down himself. What should I say?
He is so plaguey proud that the death tokens of it   176
Cry "No recovery."

AGAMEMNON   Let Ajax go to him.—
Dear lord, go you and greet him in his tent.
'Tis said he holds you well and will be led,   179
At your request, a little from himself.   180

ULYSSES
Oh, Agamemnon, let it not be so!
We'll consecrate the steps that Ajax makes   182
When they go from Achilles. Shall the proud lord   183

---

163 **dispose** bent of mind   165 **will peculiar** his own
independent will.   **self-admission** self-approbation.
168 **for . . . only** only because they are requested   171 **quarrels
at self-breath** i.e., is almost too proud to speak to himself.
174 **Kingdomed** i.e., like a microcosm of a state   176 **death
tokens** fatal symptoms   179 **holds** regards   180 **from
himself** i.e., from his usual arrogant behavior.   182–3 **We'll . . .
Achilles** i.e., Let us instead venerate Ajax when he puts as much
distance between himself and Achilles as possible.

That bastes his arrogance with his own seam 184
And never suffers matter of the world 185
Enter his thoughts, save such as do revolve 186
And ruminate himself, shall he be worshiped 187
Of that we hold an idol more than he? 188
No, this thrice worthy and right valiant lord
Must not so stale his palm, nobly acquired, 190
Nor, by my will, assubjugate his merit, 191
As amply titled as Achilles' is, 192
By going to Achilles.
That were to enlard his fat-already pride
And add more coals to Cancer when he burns 195
With entertaining great Hyperion. 196
This lord go to him? Jupiter forbid,
And say in thunder, "Achilles, go to him."

NESTOR [aside to Diomedes]
    Oh, this is well. He rubs the vein of him. 199

DIOMEDES [aside to Nestor]
    And how his silence drinks up this applause!

AJAX
    If I go to him, with my armèd fist
    I'll pash him o'er the face. 202

AGAMEMNON   Oh, no, you shall not go.

---

184 **seam** fat, grease (by means of which Achilles feeds his own
pride)   185 **suffers** allows   186–7 **save . . . himself** other
than thoughts that serve for endless self-contemplation
188 **Of . . . idol** by one whom we venerate   190 **stale . . .
acquired** sully his nobly won honor. (*Palm* means "palm leaf.")
191 **assubjugate** debase, reduce to subjection   192 **As . . . is**
having as great a name as Achilles's. (Or, if *Achilles* is not a
possessive, this could mean, "granted that Achilles is also rich in
titles.")   195–6 **add . . . Hyperion** i.e., add a fire to the heat of
summer. (Cancer is the sign of the zodiac into which the sun
[Hyperion] enters at the beginning of summer.)   199 **vein**
humor, disposition   202 **pash** smash

AJAX
    An 'a be proud with me, I'll feeze his pride.   204
    Let me go to him.

ULYSSES
    Not for the worth that hangs upon our quarrel.   206

AJAX   A paltry, insolent fellow!

NESTOR [aside]   How he describes himself!

AJAX   Can he not be sociable?

ULYSSES [aside]   The raven chides blackness.

AJAX   I'll let his humor's blood.   211

AGAMEMNON [aside]   He will be the physician that
    should be the patient.

AJAX   An all men were o' my mind—

ULYSSES [aside]   Wit would be out of fashion.

AJAX   'A should not bear it so. 'A should eat swords first. 216
    Shall pride carry it?

NESTOR [aside]   An 'twould, you'd carry half.   218

ULYSSES [aside]   'A would have ten shares.   219

AJAX   I will knead him; I'll make him supple.

NESTOR [aside]   He's not yet through warm. Farce him   221
    with praises. Pour in, pour in; his ambition is dry.

ULYSSES [to Agamemnon]
    My lord, you feed too much on this dislike.   223

NESTOR
    Our noble general, do not do so.

---

204 **An . . . pride** i.e., If he puts on airs with me, I'll settle his
hash.   206 **our quarrel** i.e., with the Trojans.   211 **let . . .
blood** bleed him (as a physician would) to cure his excessive
humors.   216 **'A** He.   **eat swords** swallow my sword, i.e., be
beaten in fight   218 **An** If   219 **ten shares** i.e., the whole
without sharing.   221 **through** thoroughly.   **Farce** Stuff
223 **this dislike** i.e., Achilles's truculence.

DIOMEDES
You must prepare to fight without Achilles.

ULYSSES
Why, 'tis this naming of him does him harm.   226
Here is a man—but 'tis before his face;
I will be silent.

NESTOR   Wherefore should you so?
He is not emulous, as Achilles is.   229

ULYSSES
Know the whole world, he is as valiant—   230

AJAX A whoreson dog, that shall palter thus with us!   231
Would he were a Trojan!

NESTOR What a vice were it in Ajax now—

ULYSSES If he were proud—

DIOMEDES Or covetous of praise—

ULYSSES Ay, or surly borne—   236

DIOMEDES Or strange, or self-affected!   237

ULYSSES [*to Ajax*]
Thank the heavens, lord, thou art of sweet
     composure.   238
Praise him that got thee, she that gave thee suck;   239
Famed be thy tutor, and thy parts of nature   240
Thrice famed, beyond, beyond all erudition;   241
But he that disciplined thine arms to fight,   242

---

226 **this . . . harm** this continual citing of Achilles as our chief hero
that creates the difficulty.   229 **emulous** envious, eager for glory
230 **Know . . . world** Let the whole world know   231 **that shall
palter** who thinks he can trifle, dodge   236 **surly borne** bearing
himself in a surly fashion   237 **strange** distant. **self-affected**
in love with himself.   238 **composure** temperament,
constitution.   239 **got** begot   240–1 **thy parts . . . erudition**
i.e., your natural gifts thrice exceeding what erudition can add
thereto. (With an ironic double meaning, suggesting that erudition
can add little.)   242 **But he** but as for him

Let Mars divide eternity in twain
And give him half; and, for thy vigor,
Bull-bearing Milo his addition yield   245
To sinewy Ajax. I will not praise thy wisdom,   246
Which, like a bourn, a pale, a shore, confines   247
Thy spacious and dilated parts. Here's Nestor,   248
Instructed by the antiquary times;   249
He must, he is, he cannot but be wise.
But pardon, father Nestor, were your days
As green as Ajax' and your brain so tempered,   252
You should not have the eminence of him,   253
But be as Ajax.

AJAX   Shall I call you father?

ULYSSES
Ay, my good son.

DIOMEDES   Be ruled by him, Lord Ajax.

ULYSSES
There is no tarrying here; the hart Achilles
Keeps thicket. Please it our great general   257
To call together all his state of war.   258
Fresh kings are come to Troy; tomorrow
We must with all our main of power stand fast.   260
And here's a lord—come knights from east to west,
And cull their flower, Ajax shall cope the best.   262

---

245 **Bull-bearing . . . yield** let bull-bearing Milo yield up his title.
(Milo, a celebrated athlete of phenomenal strength, was able to
carry a bull on his shoulders.)   246 **I will not** (1) I will forbear
to (2) I won't   247 **bourn** boundary.   **pale** fence
248 **dilated parts** extensive and well-known qualities. (But also
hinting at Ajax's beefy build.)   249 **antiquary** ancient
252 **green** immature.   **tempered** composed   253 **have . . .
of** be reckoned superior to   257 **Keeps thicket** i.e., stays hidden.
(A *thicket* is a dense growth of shrubs or trees.)   258 **state**
council   260 **main** full force   262 **cull their flower** choose
their flower of chivalry.   **cope** prove a match for

AGAMEMNON
Go we to council. Let Achilles sleep.
Light boats sail swift, though greater hulks draw
  deep.   *Exeunt.* 264

[3.1] ❧ [*Music sounds within.*] *Enter Pandarus [and a
        Servant].*

PANDARUS Friend, you, pray you, a word. Do not you
  follow the young Lord Paris?   2

SERVANT Ay, sir, when he goes before me.   3

PANDARUS You depend upon him, I mean?   4

SERVANT Sir, I do depend upon the lord.   5

PANDARUS You depend upon a notable gentleman; I
  must needs praise him.   7

SERVANT The Lord be praised!

PANDARUS You know me, do you not?

SERVANT Faith, sir, superficially.   10

PANDARUS Friend, know me better. I am the Lord
  Pandarus.

SERVANT I hope I shall know Your Honor better.   13

PANDARUS I do desire it.

264 **hulks** big, unwieldy ships

3.1 *Location: Troy. The palace.*
2 **follow** serve. (But the servant takes it in the sense of "follow
after.")   3 **goes** walks   4 **depend upon** serve as dependent to.
(The servant mockingly uses a more spiritual sense.)   5 **lord**
(Quibbling on *lord,* referring to Paris, and "Lord" as "God.")
7 **needs** necessarily   10 **superficially** (1) slightly (2) as a
superficial person.   13 **know . . . better** (1) become better
acquainted with you (2) find something in you worthy of honor.
(*Your Honor* is a polite form of address to one of social
consequence.)

SERVANT   You are in the state of grace?   15

PANDARUS   Grace? Not so, friend. "Honor" and "lord-ship" are my titles. What music is this?

SERVANT   I do but partly know, sir. It is music in parts.   18

PANDARUS   Know you the musicians?

SERVANT   Wholly, sir.

PANDARUS   Who play they to?

SERVANT   To the hearers, sir.

PANDARUS   At whose pleasure, friend?

SERVANT   At mine, sir, and theirs that love music.

PANDARUS   Command, I mean, friend.

SERVANT   Who shall I command, sir?

PANDARUS   Friend, we understand not one another; I am too courtly and thou too cunning. At whose request do these men play?

SERVANT   That's to't indeed, sir. Marry, sir, at the   30 request of Paris my lord, who's there in person; with him, the mortal Venus, the heart-blood of beauty, love's visible soul—

PANDARUS   Who, my cousin Cressida?

SERVANT   No, sir, Helen. Could not you find out that by her attributes?

PANDARUS   It should seem, fellow, that thou hast not seen the Lady Cressida. I come to speak with Paris from the Prince Troilus. I will make a complimental   39 assault upon him, for my business seethes.   40

---

15 **in . . . grace** i.e., in the way of salvation because of desiring to be better. (Pandarus answers as though *grace* referred to the courtly title applicable to a duke or prince.)   18 **partly** (1) partially (2) in parts   30 **to't** to the point 39 **complimental** courteous   40 **seethes** boils, requires haste.

SERVANT Sodden business! There's a stewed phrase, 41
   indeed!

    Enter Paris and Helen [attended].

PANDARUS Fair be to you, my lord, and to all this fair 43
   company! Fair desires, in all fair measure, fairly guide 44
   them! Especially to you, fair queen, fair thoughts be
   your fair pillow!

HELEN Dear lord, you are full of fair words.

PANDARUS You speak your fair pleasure, sweet
   queen.—Fair prince, here is good broken music. 49

PARIS You have broke it, cousin, and, by my life, you 50
   shall make it whole again; you shall piece it out with 51
   a piece of your performance.—Nell, he is full of harmony.

PANDARUS Truly, lady, no.

HELEN Oh, sir—

PANDARUS Rude, in sooth; in good sooth, very rude. 56

PARIS Well said, my lord. Well, you say so in fits. 57

PANDARUS I have business to my lord, dear
   queen.—My lord, will you vouchsafe me a word? 59

HELEN Nay, this shall not hedge us out. We'll hear you 60
   sing, certainly.

---

41 **Sodden, stewed** (A play on *seethes* and with quibbling
reference to stews or brothels and to the sweating treatment for
venereal disease.)   43 **Fair** Fair wishes, good fortune. (With
wordplay in subsequent uses of *fair*: attractive, pleasing, just,
clean.)   44 **fairly** favorably   49 **broken music** music
arranged for different families of instruments.   50 **broke**
interrupted.   **cousin** (Often used at court in addressing a social
acquaintance.)   51 **piece it out** mend it   56 **Rude** (I am)
unpolished   57 **in fits** (1) by fits and starts (2) in divisions of a
song, in stanzas.   59 **vouchsafe** permit   60 **hedge** shut

PANDARUS Well, sweet queen, you are pleasant with   62
me.—But, marry, thus, my lord: my dear lord and
most esteemed friend, your brother Troilus—

HELEN My lord Pandarus, honey-sweet lord—

PANDARUS Go to, sweet queen, go to—commends   66
himself most affectionately to you—

HELEN You shall not bob us out of our melody. If you   68
do, our melancholy upon your head!

PANDARUS Sweet queen, sweet queen, that's a sweet
queen, i'faith.

HELEN And to make a sweet lady sad is a sour offense.

PANDARUS Nay, that shall not serve your turn, that shall
it not, in truth, la. Nay, I care not for such words, no,   74
no.—And, my lord, he desires you, that if the King
call for him at supper you will make his excuse.

HELEN My lord Pandarus—

PANDARUS What says my sweet queen, my very very
sweet queen?

PARIS What exploit's in hand? Where sups he tonight?

HELEN Nay, but, my lord—

PANDARUS What says my sweet queen? My cousin will   82
fall out with you.   83

HELEN [to Paris] You must not know where he sups.   84

PARIS I'll lay my life, with my disposer Cressida.   85

PANDARUS No, no, no such matter; you are wide.   86
Come, your disposer is sick.

---

62 **pleasant** jocular   66 **Go to** (An expression of mild protest.)
68 **bob** cheat   74 **la** (An exclamation accompanying a
conventional phrase.)   82–3 **My . . . you** i.e., my good friend
Paris will be angry with you for interrupting so.   84 **You must
not** i.e., Pandarus does not want you to.   **he** i.e., Troilus
85 **lay** wager.   **my disposer** i.e., one who may do what she likes
(with me or Troilus)   86 **wide** wide of the mark.

PARIS   Well, I'll make 's excuse.   88

PANDARUS   Ay, good my lord. Why should you say
Cressida? No, your poor disposer's sick.

PARIS   I spy.   91

PANDARUS   You spy! What do you spy?—Come, give
me an instrument.   [*He is handed a musical instrument.*]
Now, sweet queen.

HELEN   Why, this is kindly done.

PANDARUS   My niece is horribly in love with a thing
you have, sweet queen.

HELEN   She shall have it, my lord, if it be not my lord
Paris.

PANDARUS   He? No, she'll none of him. They two are
twain.   101

HELEN   Falling in, after falling out, may make them   102
three.   103

PANDARUS   Come, come, I'll hear no more of this. I'll
sing you a song now.

HELEN   Ay, ay, prithee. Now, by my troth, sweet lord,
thou hast a fine forehead.

PANDARUS   Ay, you may, you may.   108

HELEN   Let thy song be love. This love will undo us all.
Oh, Cupid, Cupid, Cupid!

PANDARUS   Love? Ay, that it shall, i'faith.

PARIS   Ay, good now, "Love, love, nothing but love."   112

---

88 **make 's excuse** make his (Troilus's) excuse (to Priam).
91 **I spy** I get it.   101 **twain** not in accord.   102–3 **Falling . . .
three** (Helen bawdily jokes that Cressida's game will result in the
birth of a child, a third person.)   108 **you may** go on, have your
joke.   112 **good now** please

PANDARUS   In good truth, it begins so: [*He sings.*]
      Love, love, nothing but love, still love, still more!
        For, oh, love's bow
        Shoots buck and doe.   116
        The shaft confounds   117
        Not that it wounds,   118
      But tickles still the sore.   119
      These lovers cry, "Oh! Oh!", they die!   120
        Yet that which seems the wound to kill   121
      Doth turn "Oh! Oh!" to "ha, ha, he!"
        So dying love lives still.   123
      "Oh! Oh!" awhile, but "ha, ha, ha!"
      "Oh! Oh!" groans out for "ha! ha! ha!"—
Heigh-ho!

HELEN   In love, i'faith, to the very tip of the nose.

PARIS   He eats nothing but doves, love, and that breeds
    hot blood, and hot blood begets hot thoughts, and hot
    thoughts beget hot deeds, and hot deeds is love.

PANDARUS   Is this the generation of love? Hot blood, hot   131
    thoughts, and hot deeds? Why, they are vipers. Is love
    a generation of vipers? Sweet lord, who's afield   133
    today?

PARIS   Hector, Deiphobus, Helenus, Antenor, and all
    the gallantry of Troy. I would fain have armed today,
    but my Nell would not have it so. How chance my
    brother Troilus went not?

---

116 **buck and doe** i.e., male and female.   117 **confounds**
overwhelms   118 **Not that** (1) not that which, or (2) not so
much that. (The erotic suggestion is that love does its harm by
penetrating and tickling.)   119 **sore** (1) wound (2) buck in its
fourth year.   120, 123 **die, dying** (Quibbling on the idea of
experiencing orgasm.)   121 **wound to kill** fatal wound
131 **generation** genealogy   133 **generation of vipers** (See
Matthew 3:7, 12:34, and 23:33.)

HELEN   He hangs the lip at something.—You know all,   139
Lord Pandarus.

PANDARUS   Not I, honey-sweet queen. I long to hear
how they sped today.—You'll remember your broth-   142
er's excuse?

PARIS   To a hair.   144

PANDARUS   Farewell, sweet queen.

HELEN   Commend me to your niece.

PANDARUS   I will, sweet queen.   [Exit.]

Sound a retreat.

PARIS
They're come from field. Let us to Priam's hall
To greet the warriors. Sweet Helen, I must woo you
To help unarm our Hector. His stubborn buckles,
With these your white enchanting fingers touched,
Shall more obey than to the edge of steel
Or force of Greekish sinews. You shall do more
Than all the island kings: disarm great Hector.   154

HELEN
'Twill make us proud to be his servant, Paris.
Yea, what he shall receive of us in duty
Gives us more palm in beauty than we have,   157
Yea, overshines ourself.

PARIS   Sweet, above thought I love thee.   *Exeunt.*

---

139 **He hangs the lip** Pandarus pouts, sulks   142 **sped**
succeeded   144 **To a hair** To the last detail.   154 **island kings**
i.e., Greek chieftains   157 **Gives . . . have** bestows more honor
on me than my own beauty does. (Helen uses the royal plural.)

[3.2] ∾ Enter *Pandarus* and *Troilus's Man*, [*meeting*].

PANDARUS   How now, where's thy master? At my cousin Cressida's?

MAN   No, sir, he stays for you to conduct him thither.

   [*Enter Troilus.*]

PANDARUS   Oh, here he comes.—How now, how now?

TROILUS   Sirrah, walk off.   [*Exit Man.*]

PANDARUS   Have you seen my cousin?

TROILUS
   No, Pandarus. I stalk about her door,
   Like a strange soul upon the Stygian banks   8
   Staying for waftage. Oh, be thou my Charon,   9
   And give me swift transportation to those fields   10
   Where I may wallow in the lily beds
   Proposed for the deserver! O gentle Pandar,   12
   From Cupid's shoulder pluck his painted wings,
   And fly with me to Cressid!

PANDARUS   Walk here i'th'orchard. I'll bring her   15
   straight.   [*Exit Pandarus.*]

TROILUS
   I am giddy; expectation whirls me round.
   Th'imaginary relish is so sweet
   That it enchants my sense. What will it be

3.2 *Location: The garden of Cressida's house (formerly her
father's house until he abandoned Troy).*
0.1 **Man** servant. (Probably the *varlet* referred to in 1.1.1.)
8–9 **a strange . . . Charon** (Refers to the Greek mythological
conception of the fate of departed souls who had to wait on the
banks of the Styx or Acheron until the boatman Charon ferried
them across to the infernal region.)   10 **fields** the Elysian fields
12 **Proposed for** promised to   15 **orchard** garden.

When that the wat'ry palates taste indeed   20
Love's thrice repurèd nectar? Death, I fear me,   21
Swooning destruction, or some joy too fine,
Too subtle-potent, tuned too sharp in sweetness
For the capacity of my ruder powers.
I fear it much; and I do fear besides
That I shall lose distinction in my joys,   26
As doth a battle, when they charge on heaps   27
The enemy flying.

    [Enter Pandarus.]

PANDARUS She's making her ready; she'll come
straight. You must be witty now. She does so blush,   30
and fetches her wind so short, as if she were frayed   31
with a spirit. I'll fetch her. It is the prettiest villain! She   32
fetches her breath as short as a new-ta'en sparrow.

                    Exit Pandarus.

TROILUS
Even such a passion doth embrace my bosom.
My heart beats thicker than a feverous pulse,   35
And all my powers do their bestowing lose,   36
Like vassalage at unawares encount'ring   37
The eye of majesty.

    Enter Pandarus, and Cressida, [veiled].

PANDARUS Come, come, what need you blush?
Shame's a baby.—Here she is now. Swear the oaths

---

20 **wat'ry palates** i.e., sense of taste watering with anticipation
21 **repurèd** refined, repurified   26 **lose . . . joys** be unable to
distinguish one delight from another   27 **battle** army
30 **witty** alert, resourceful in easy conversation   31 **fetches . . .
short** is short of breath   31–2 **frayed . . . spirit** frightened by a
ghost.   32 **villain** (Used endearingly.)   35 **thicker** faster
36 **bestowing** proper use   37 **vassalage at unawares** vassals
unexpectedly

now to her that you have sworn to me. [*Cressida draws
back.*] What, are you gone again? You must be watched   42
ere you be made tame, must you? Come your ways,
come your ways; an you draw backward, we'll put
you i'th' thills.—Why do you not speak to her?—   45
Come, draw this curtain, and let's see your picture.   46
[*She is unveiled.*] Alas the day, how loath you are
to offend daylight! An 'twere dark, you'd close sooner.   48
So, so, rub on, and kiss the mistress. [*They kiss.*] How   49
now, a kiss in fee-farm? Build there, carpenter, the air   50
is sweet. Nay, you shall fight your hearts out ere I part   51
you—the falcon as the tercel, for all the ducks i'th'   52
river. Go to, go to.   53

TROILUS   You have bereft me of all words, lady.

PANDARUS   Words pay no debts; give her deeds. But
she'll bereave you o'th' deeds too, if she call your ac-   56
tivity in question. What, billing again? Here's "In wit-   57
ness whereof the parties interchangeably"—Come in,   58
come in. I'll go get a fire.   [*Exit.*]   59

---

42 watched kept awake (like a hawk that is being tamed through
sleeplessness)   **45 thills** shafts of a cart or wagon. (An image of
domesticating the woman, as in hawking.)   **46 curtain** veil.
(Curtains were hung in front of pictures.)   **48 close**
(1) encounter (2) come to terms   **49 kiss the mistress** (In
bowls, to touch the central target; to *rub* is to maneuver obstacles
as the ball rolls; *mistress* is analogous to "master," short for "master
bowl," a small bowl placed as a mark for players to aim at.)
50 in fee-farm i.e., unending, as with land that is held in
perpetuity.   **50–1 Build . . . sweet** (1) Erect your house in this
fresh and unspoiled location (2) Place your love here where her
breath is sweet.   **52–3 the falcon . . . river** i.e., I'll bet all the
ducks in the river that the female hawk will be as eager as the
male.   **56–7 activity** virility. (Pandarus jests that Cressida will
wear Troilus down in lovemaking.)   **57 billing** kissing
57–8 "In . . . interchangeably" (A legal formula used for
contracts, ending "have set their hand and seals.")   **59 get a
fire** order a fire (for the bedroom).

CRESSIDA   Will you walk in, my lord?

TROILUS   Oh, Cressida, how often have I wished me thus!

CRESSIDA   Wished, my lord? The gods grant—Oh, my lord!

TROILUS   What should they grant? What makes this pretty abruption? What too curious dreg espies my   65 sweet lady in the fountain of our love?

CRESSIDA   More dregs than water, if my fears have eyes.

TROILUS   Fears make devils of cherubins; they never see   68 truly.

CRESSIDA   Blind fear that seeing reason leads finds   70 safer footing than blind reason stumbling without fear. To fear the worst oft cures the worse.   72

TROILUS   Oh, let my lady apprehend no fear. In all Cupid's pageant there is presented no monster.

CRESSIDA   Nor nothing monstrous neither?

TROILUS   Nothing but our undertakings, when we vow   76 to weep seas, live in fire, eat rocks, tame tigers, thinking it harder for our mistress to devise imposition   78 enough than for us to undergo any difficulty imposed. This is the monstrosity in love, lady, that the will is infinite and the execution confined, that the desire is boundless and the act a slave to limit.

CRESSIDA   They say all lovers swear more performance than they are able, and yet reserve an ability that they never perform, vowing more than the perfection of ten   85

---

65 **abruption** breaking off.   **curious dreg** finicky and anxiety-causing impurity   68 **make . . . cherubins** i.e., make things seem worst rather than best   70 **that . . . leads** that is led by clear-sighted reason   72 **oft . . . worse** enables us to avoid lesser dangers.   76 **undertakings** vows   78 **to devise imposition** to think up tasks to impose   85 **perfection of ten** accomplishment of ten perfect lovers

and discharging less than the tenth part of one. They
that have the voice of lions and the act of hares, are
they not monsters?

TROILUS   Are there such? Such are not we. Praise us as
we are tasted, allow us as we prove; our head shall go   90
bare till merit crown it. No perfection in reversion shall   91
have a praise in present; we will not name desert before his birth, and, being born, his addition shall be   93
humble. Few words to fair faith. Troilus shall be such   94
to Cressid as what envy can say worst shall be a mock   95
for his truth, and what truth can speak truest not truer   96
than Troilus.

CRESSIDA   Will you walk in, my lord?

        [Enter Pandarus.]

PANDARUS   What, blushing still? Have you not done
talking yet?

CRESSIDA   Well, uncle, what folly I commit, I dedicate   101
to you.

PANDARUS   I thank you for that. If my lord get a boy of
you, you'll give him me. Be true to my lord. If he
flinch, chide me for it.

TROILUS   You know now your hostages: your uncle's
word and my firm faith.

PANDARUS   Nay, I'll give my word for her too. Our
kindred, though they be long ere they are wooed,
they are constant being won. They are burrs, I can tell
you; they'll stick where they are thrown.   111

---

90 **tasted** tried, proved.   **allow** acknowledge, approve
91 **No . . . reversion** No promise of perfection to come
93 **addition** title   94 **Few . . . faith** (Compare the proverb:
"Where many words are, the truth goes by.")   95–6 **as what . . .
truth** that the worst that malice can do is to mock Troilus's loyalty
101 **folly** foolishness. (Pandarus understands it to mean "lechery.")
111 **thrown** (1) tossed (2) thrown down in the act of seduction.

CRESSIDA
    Boldness comes to me now and brings me heart.
    Prince Troilus, I have loved you night and day
    For many weary months.

TROILUS
    Why was my Cressid then so hard to win?

CRESSIDA
    Hard to seem won; but I was won, my lord,
    With the first glance that ever—pardon me;
    If I confess much, you will play the tyrant.
    I love you now, but till now not so much
    But I might master it. In faith, I lie;
    My thoughts were like unbridled children, grown   121
    Too headstrong for their mother. See, we fools!
    Why have I blabbed? Who shall be true to us,
    When we are so unsecret to ourselves?
    But, though I loved you well, I wooed you not;
    And yet, good faith, I wished myself a man,
    Or that we women had men's privilege
    Of speaking first. Sweet, bid me hold my tongue,
    For in this rapture I shall surely speak
    The thing I shall repent. See, see, your silence,
    Cunning in dumbness, in my weakness draws
    My soul of counsel from me! Stop my mouth.   132

TROILUS
    And shall, albeit sweet music issues thence.

                                         [He kisses her.]

PANDARUS   Pretty, i'faith.

CRESSIDA
    My lord, I do beseech you, pardon me;
    'Twas not my purpose thus to beg a kiss.

121 **unbridled** unrestrained   132 **My . . . counsel** my inmost
thoughts

I am ashamed. Oh, heavens, what have I done?
For this time will I take my leave, my lord.

TROILUS   Your leave, sweet Cressid?

PANDARUS   Leave? An you take leave till tomorrow   140
morning—

CRESSIDA   Pray you, content you.   142

TROILUS   What offends you, lady?

CRESSIDA   Sir, mine own company.

TROILUS   You cannot shun yourself.

CRESSIDA   Let me go and try.
I have a kind of self resides with you,
But an unkind self that itself will leave   148
To be another's fool. Where is my wit?   149
I would be gone. I speak I know not what.

TROILUS
Well know they what they speak that speak so wisely.   151

CRESSIDA
Perchance, my lord, I show more craft than love,   152
And fell so roundly to a large confession   153
To angle for your thoughts. But you are wise,   154
Or else you love not, for to be wise and love   155
Exceeds man's might; that dwells with gods above.   156

---

140 **An** If   142 **content you** don't be upset.   148 **unkind**
unnatural   148–9 **that . . . fool** that fears the loss of personal
autonomy in becoming the plaything of some other person like
yourself.   149 **Where . . . wit?** What am I saying?
151 **Well . . . wisely** Anyone who speaks as wisely as you do
knows what he or she is saying.   152 **Perchance** Perchance you
think that.   **craft** cunning   153 **roundly** outspokenly.
large free   154 **To . . . thoughts** to draw forth a confession
from you.   155–6 **Or . . . might** or, to put it another way, you
are too wise to be really in love, since to be wise and love at the
same time is beyond human capacity

TROILUS
    Oh, that I thought it could be in a woman—
    As, if it can, I will presume in you—   158
    To feed for aye her lamp and flames of love,
    To keep her constancy in plight and youth,   160
    Outliving beauty's outward, with a mind   161
    That doth renew swifter than blood decays!   162
    Or that persuasion could but thus convince me
    That my integrity and truth to you
    Might be affronted with the match and weight   165
    Of such a winnowed purity in love;   166
    How were I then uplifted! But, alas,
    I am as true as truth's simplicity,   168
    And simpler than the infancy of truth.   169

CRESSIDA
    In that I'll war with you.

TROILUS   Oh, virtuous fight,
    When right with right wars who shall be most right!
    True swains in love shall in the world to come
    Approve their truth by Troilus. When their rhymes,   173
    Full of protest, of oath and big compare,   174
    Wants similes, truth tired with iteration—   175
    "As true as steel, as plantage to the moon,   176
    As sun to day, as turtle to her mate,   177

158 **presume** presume that it is   160 **To . . . youth** to keep her
pledged constancy fresh   161 **outward** appearance
162 **blood decays** passions wane.   165–6 **affronted . . . love**
matched with an equal quantity of purified love (in you).
winnowed separated from the chaff   168 **truth's simplicity**
the simple truth   169 **the infancy of truth** i.e., pure, innocent
truth.   173 **Approve** attest.   **by Troilus** i.e., using Troilus as
an ideal comparison.   174 **protest** protestation (of love).   **big
compare** extravagant comparisons   175 **Wants . . . iteration**
are in need of new similes, having worn out their usual expressions
of love through too much repetition   176 **plantage** vegetation
(waxing in growth by the moon's influence)   177 **turtle**
turtledove

As iron to adamant, as earth to th' center"—   178
Yet, after all comparisons of truth,   179
As truth's authentic author to be cited,   180
"As true as Troilus" shall crown up the verse   181
And sanctify the numbers.

CRESSIDA   Prophet may you be!   182
If I be false or swerve a hair from truth,
When time is old and hath forgot itself,
When waterdrops have worn the stones of Troy,
And blind oblivion swallowed cities up,
And mighty states characterless are grated   187
To dusty nothing, yet let memory,
From false to false, among false maids in love,   189
Upbraid my falsehood! When they've said "as false
As air, as water, wind, or sandy earth,
As fox to lamb, or wolf to heifer's calf,
Pard to the hind, or stepdame to her son,"   193
Yea, let them say, to stick the heart of falsehood,   194
"As false as Cressid."

PANDARUS   Go to, a bargain made. Seal it, seal it; I'll be
the witness. Here I hold your hand, here my cousin's.
If ever you prove false one to another, since I have
taken such pains to bring you together, let all pitiful   199
goers-between be called to the world's end after my
name: call them all Pandars. Let all constant men be

---

178 **adamant** lodestone (magnetic).   **center** center of the earth,
axis   179 **comparisons** illustrative similes   180 **As . . . cited**
when we want to cite as our authority the very fountainhead of
truth   181 **crown up** give the finishing touches to
182 **numbers** verses.   187 **characterless** unrecorded, without a
mark left.   **grated** pulverized   189 **From . . . love**
remembering one false one after another among false-hearted
young women   193 **Pard** leopard or panther.   **hind** doe.
stepdame stepmother   194 **stick the heart** pierce the center
of the target   199 **pitiful** compassionate

Troiluses, all false women Cressids, and all brokers-
between Pandars! Say "Amen."

TROILUS   Amen.

CRESSIDA   Amen.

PANDARUS   Amen. Whereupon I will show you a chamber with a bed, which bed, because it shall not speak
of your pretty encounters, press it to death. Away!   208

                    Exeunt [*Troilus and Cressida*].

And Cupid grant all tongue-tied maidens here   209
Bed, chamber, pander to provide this gear!   *Exit.*   210

[3.3] ✑ *Flourish. Enter Ulysses, Diomedes, Nestor,*
        Agamemnon, [Ajax, Menelaus,] and Calchas.

CALCHAS
   Now, princes, for the service I have done you,
   Th'advantage of the time prompts me aloud   2
   To call for recompense. Appear it to your mind   3
   That, through the sight I bear in things to come,   4
   I have abandoned Troy, left my possessions,
   Incurred a traitor's name, exposed myself
   From certain and possessed conveniences   7
   To doubtful fortunes, sequest'ring from me all   8
   That time, acquaintance, custom, and condition
   Made tame and most familiar to my nature;   10
   And here, to do you service, am become   11

208 **press . . . death** (Alludes to the usual punishment by weights
for accused persons refusing to plead or "speak.")   209 **here** i.e.,
in the audience   210 **gear** equipment.

3.3 *Location: The Greek camp. Before Achilles's tent.*
2 **advantage of** favorable opportunity offered by   3 **Appear it**
Let it appear   4 **bear** am endowed with   7 **From** turning
from   8 **sequest'ring** separating, removing   10 **tame**
familiar, domestic   11 **am** have

As new into the world, strange, unacquainted.
I do beseech you, as in way of taste,   13
To give me now a little benefit
Out of those many registered in promise
Which, you say, live to come in my behalf.   16

AGAMEMNON
What wouldst thou of us, Trojan, make demand?

CALCHAS
You have a Trojan prisoner called Antenor
Yesterday took. Troy holds him very dear.
Oft have you—often have you thanks therefor—
Desired my Cressid in right great exchange,   21
Whom Troy hath still denied; but this Antenor,   22
I know, is such a wrest in their affairs   23
That their negotiations all must slack,
Wanting his manage, and they will almost   25
Give us a prince of blood, a son of Priam,
In change of him. Let him be sent, great princes,   27
And he shall buy my daughter; and her presence
Shall quite strike off all service I have done
In most accepted pain.

AGAMEMNON   Let Diomedes bear him,   30
And bring us Cressid hither. Calchas shall have
What he requests of us. Good Diomed,
Furnish you fairly for this interchange.
Withal bring word if Hector will tomorrow   34
Be answered in his challenge. Ajax is ready.   35

---

13 **taste** foretaste   16 **live to come** await fulfillment
21 **right great exchange** exchange for distinguished captives
22 **still** continually   23 **wrest** tuning key, i.e., one producing
harmony and order   25 **Wanting his manage** lacking his
management   27 **change of** exchange for   30 **In . . . pain** in
pains (troubles, hardships) which I have endured most willingly.
bear escort   34 **Withal** In addition   35 **Be answered in** meet
the answerer of

DIOMEDES
    This shall I undertake, and 'tis a burden
    Which I am proud to bear.   *Exit [with Calchas].*   37

    Achilles and Patroclus stand in their tent.

ULYSSES
    Achilles stands i'th'entrance of his tent.
    Please it our general pass strangely by him,   39
    As if he were forgot; and, princes all,
    Lay negligent and loose regard upon him.
    I will come last. 'Tis like he'll question me
    Why such unplausive eyes are bent, why turned, on
       him.   43
    If so, I have derision medicinable   44
    To use between your strangeness and his pride,   45
    Which his own will shall have desire to drink.   46
    It may do good. Pride hath no other glass   47
    To show itself but pride, for supple knees   48
    Feed arrogance and are the proud man's fees.   49

AGAMEMNON
    We'll execute your purpose and put on   50
    A form of strangeness as we pass along.
    So do each lord, and either greet him not
    Or else disdainfully, which shall shake him more
    Than if not looked on. I will lead the way.

        [They move in procession past Achilles's tent.]

37.1 **stand in** i.e., enter on stage and stand in the entrance of
39 **strangely** i.e., as one who pretends to be a stranger
43 **unplausive** disapproving   44 **derision medicinable** curative
scorn   45 **use** i.e., make connection.   **strangeness** aloofness
46 **Which . . . drink** which medicine his own pride will thirst for.
47 **glass** mirror   48 **To show . . . pride** in which to see its
image except the pride of others   48–9 **for supple . . . fees** i.e.,
since obsequiousness merely encourages arrogance by rewarding
pride with the adulation it expects.   50 **We'll** I will. (The royal
"we.")

ACHILLES
  What, comes the general to speak with me?
  You know my mind. I'll fight no more 'gainst Troy.

AGAMEMNON
  What says Achilles? Would he aught with us?   57

NESTOR
  Would you, my lord, aught with the general?

ACHILLES   No.

NESTOR   Nothing, my lord.

AGAMEMNON   The better.   61

                    [*Exeunt Agamemnon and Nestor.*]

ACHILLES [*to Menelaus*]   Good day, good day.

MENELAUS   How do you? How do you?   [*Exit.*]

ACHILLES   What, does the cuckold scorn me?

AJAX   How now, Patroclus!

ACHILLES   Good morrow, Ajax.

AJAX   Ha?

ACHILLES   Good morrow.

AJAX   Ay, and good next day too.

                    Exit. [*Ulysses remains behind, reading.*]

ACHILLES
  What mean these fellows? Know they not Achilles?

PATROCLUS
  They pass by strangely. They were used to bend,   71
  To send their smiles before them to Achilles,
  To come as humbly as they use to creep   73
  To holy altars.

ACHILLES   What, am I poor of late?
  'Tis certain, greatness, once fall'n out with fortune,

---

57 **Would he aught** Does he want anything   61 **The better** So
much the better.   71 **used** accustomed   73 **use** are
accustomed

Must fall out with men too. What the declined is   76
He shall as soon read in the eyes of others
As feel in his own fall; for men, like butterflies,
Show not their mealy wings but to the summer,   79
And not a man, for being simply man,   80
Hath any honor but honor for those honors   81
That are without him—as place, riches, and favor,   82
Prizes of accident as oft as merit;
Which, when they fall, as being slippery standers,   84
The love that leaned on them, as slippery too,
Doth one pluck down another and together
Die in the fall. But 'tis not so with me;
Fortune and I are friends. I do enjoy
At ample point all that I did possess,   89
Save these men's looks, who do, methinks, find out
Something not worth in me such rich beholding   91
As they have often given. Here is Ulysses;
I'll interrupt his reading.—How now, Ulysses?

ULYSSES   Now, great Thetis' son!

ACHILLES   What are you reading?

ULYSSES   A strange fellow here
Writes me that man, how dearly ever parted,   97
How much in having, or without or in,   98
Cannot make boast to have that which he hath,
Nor feels not what he owes, but by reflection;   100
As when his virtues, shining upon others,

76 **the declined** the man brought low   79 **mealy** powdery
80–2 **not . . . him** no one is honored for himself but, rather, for
those marks of distinction that are external to him   82 **as** such
as   84 **being . . . standers** standing on uncertain foundation
89 **At ample point** to the full   91 **Something . . . beholding**
something in me not worthy of such high respect
97–8 **Writes . . . or in** writes that any individual, however richly
endowed with natural good qualities both external and internal
100 **owes** owns.   **but by reflection** i.e., except as reflected in
others' opinions

Heat them, and they retort that heat again   102
To the first givers.

ACHILLES   This is not strange, Ulysses.
The beauty that is borne here in the face
The bearer knows not, but commends itself   105
To others' eyes; nor doth the eye itself,
That most pure spirit of sense, behold itself,   107
Not going from itself, but eye to eye opposed   108
Salutes each other with each other's form.   109
For speculation turns not to itself   110
Till it hath traveled and is mirrored there
Where it may see itself. This is not strange at all.

ULYSSES
I do not strain at the position—   113
It is familiar—but at the author's drift,   114
Who, in his circumstance, expressly proves   115
That no man is the lord of anything,
Though in and of him there be much consisting,   117
Till he communicate his parts to others;
Nor doth he of himself know them for aught   119
Till he behold them formed in the applause
Where they're extended; who, like an arch,
          reverb'rate   121
The voice again, or, like a gate of steel

102 **retort** reflect   105 **but** (1) unless it (2) but instead
107 **most . . . sense** most exquisite of the five senses. (Compare
1.1.60.)   108–9 **Not . . . form** since it cannot go out from itself;
instead, two persons' eyes gazing into each other must convey to
each of them a sense of what he or she looks like from the other's
point of view.   110 **speculation** power of sight   113 **strain . . .
position** find difficulty in the writer's general stance   114 **drift**
i.e., particular application   115 **circumstance** detailed
argument   117 **Though . . . consisting** though he enjoys many
fine qualities that cohere and harmonize   119 **aught** anything of
value   121 **Where they're extended** of those persons to
whom they are displayed.   **who** i.e., the applauders

Fronting the sun, receives and renders back   123
His figure and his heat. I was much rapt in this   124
And apprehended here immediately
Th'unknown Ajax. Heavens, what a man is there!   126
A very horse, that has he knows not what.   127
Nature, what things there are
Most abject in regard and dear in use!   129
What things again most dear in the esteem   130
And poor in worth! Now shall we see tomorrow—
An act that very chance doth throw upon him—
Ajax renowned. Oh, heavens, what some men do,
While some men leave to do!   134
How some men creep in skittish Fortune's hall,   135
Whiles others play the idiots in her eyes!   136
How one man eats into another's pride,   137
While pride is fasting in his wantonness!   138
To see these Grecian lords—why, even already
They clap the lubber Ajax on the shoulder,   140
As if his foot were on brave Hector's breast
And great Troy shrinking.

ACHILLES   I do believe it,
For they passed by me as misers do by beggars,
Neither gave to me good word nor look.
What, are my deeds forgot?

---

123 **Fronting** facing   124 **His** its, the sun's   126 **unknown** as
yet obscure in reputation   127 **has . . . what** does not know his
own strength.   129 **abject . . . use** lowly esteemed and yet
valuable, of practical value.   130 **again** on the other hand
134 **to do** undone.   135–6 **How . . . eyes!** How some men fawn
obsequiously upon the fickle goddess Fortune, while others make
perfect fools of themselves to gain her attention!   137–8 **How . . .
wantonness!** i.e., How one man, like Ajax, encroaches on another's
glory, while that other man, like Achilles, starves his own glory
through self-indulgence or caprice!   140 **lubber** clumsy lout

ULYSSES

Time hath, my lord, a wallet at his back,   146
Wherein he puts alms for oblivion,   147
A great-sized monster of ingratitudes.
Those scraps are good deeds past, which are
    devoured
As fast as they are made, forgot as soon
As done. Perseverance, dear my lord,
Keeps honor bright; to have done is to hang
Quite out of fashion, like a rusty mail   153
In monumental mock'ry. Take the instant way,   154
For honor travels in a strait so narrow
Where one but goes abreast. Keep then the path,   156
For emulation hath a thousand sons   157
That one by one pursue. If you give way,   158
Or hedge aside from the direct forthright,   159
Like to an entered tide they all rush by
And leave you hindmost;
Or, like a gallant horse fall'n in first rank,
Lie there for pavement to the abject rear,   163
O'errun and trampled on. Then what they do in
    present,   164
Though less than yours in past, must o'ertop yours;
For Time is like a fashionable host
That slightly shakes his parting guest by th' hand,   167

---

146 wallet knapsack   **147 alms for oblivion** i.e., noble deeds
destined to be forgotten   **153 mail** suit of armor   **154 In . . .
mock'ry** serving as a mocking trophy of forgotten noble deeds.
instant way way that lies immediately before you now
156 one but only one   **157 emulation** envious rivalry
158 one by one pursue crowd after one another in single file,
vying for supremacy.   **159 Or . . . forthright** or veer from the
straight path   **163–4 for pavement . . . on** as a pavement to be
trampled on by the cowardly and inferior troops who bring up the
rear.   **167 slightly** negligently

And with his arms outstretched, as he would fly,   168
Grasps in the comer. The welcome ever smiles,   169
And farewell goes out sighing. Let not virtue seek   170
Remuneration for the thing it was;   171
For beauty, wit,
High birth, vigor of bone, desert in service,
Love, friendship, charity, are subjects all
To envious and calumniating Time.   175
One touch of nature makes the whole world kin,   176
That all with one consent praise newborn gauds,
Though they are made and molded of things past,   178
And give to dust that is a little gilt   179
More laud than gilt o'erdusted.   180
The present eye praises the present object.
Then marvel not, thou great and complete man,   182
That all the Greeks begin to worship Ajax,
Since things in motion sooner catch the eye
Than what not stirs. The cry went once on thee,   185
And still it might, and yet it may again,
If thou wouldst not entomb thyself alive
And case thy reputation in thy tent,   188
Whose glorious deeds but in these fields of late   189

---

168 **as . . . fly** as if he were wearing wings   169 **Grasps in**
welcomes, embraces   170–1 **Let . . . was** Don't be so naive as to
expect reward for past achievements   175 **calumniating**
slandering   176 **nature** i.e., natural human weakness; here, the
propensity of men to praise frivolous novelty (*newborn gauds*)
178 **Though . . . past** i.e., even though their apparent novelty is all
derivative   179–80 **And . . . o'erdusted** i.e., and give more
praise to trivial things that have been made to look glittering than
to objects of true worth that have been covered by the dust of
oblivion.   182 **complete** accomplished   185 **cry** acclaim
188 **case** box up, enclose   189 **but . . . late** only recently on the
battlefield

Made emulous missions 'mongst the gods themselves   190
And drave great Mars to faction.

ACHILLES   Of this my privacy   191
I have strong reasons.

ULYSSES   But 'gainst your privacy
The reasons are more potent and heroical.   193
'Tis known, Achilles, that you are in love
With one of Priam's daughters.

ACHILLES   Ha! Known?   195

ULYSSES   Is that a wonder?
The providence that's in a watchful state   197
Knows almost every grain of Pluto's gold,   198
Finds bottom in th'uncomprehensive deeps,   199
Keeps place with thought and almost, like the gods,   200
Do thoughts unveil in their dumb cradles.   201
There is a mystery—with whom relation   202
Durst never meddle—in the soul of state,   203
Which hath an operation more divine
Than breath or pen can give expressure to.   205
All the commerce that you have had with Troy   206
As perfectly is ours as yours, my lord;   207
And better would it fit Achilles much
To throw down Hector than Polyxena.

190–1 **Made . . . faction** i.e., caused the gods themselves to join in
the fighting on opposing sides, emulously, and even drove the god
of war to be partisan.   193 **heroical** of heroic stature.
195 **one . . . daughters** i.e., Polyxena.   197 **providence**
foresight   198 **Pluto's** (Pluto, god of the underworld, was often
confused with Plutus, god of riches.)   199 **th'uncomprehensive**
the unfathomable   200 **Keeps . . . thought** keeps pace with
thought   201 **Do . . . cradles** uncover thoughts as they are
conceived in the mind and before they are spoken.
202–3 **with . . . meddle** that can never be talked about
205 **expressure** expression   206 **commerce** dealings (i.e., with
Polyxena)   207 **As perfectly . . . as yours** is known to us of the
Greek council as completely as to you

But it must grieve young Pyrrhus now at home,   210
When Fame shall in our islands sound her trump,   211
And all the Greekish girls shall tripping sing,
"Great Hector's sister did Achilles win,
But our great Ajax bravely beat down him."   214
Farewell, my lord. I as your lover speak.   215
The fool slides o'er the ice that you should break. 216

                                          [Exit.]

PATROCLUS
To this effect, Achilles, have I moved you.
A woman impudent and mannish grown   218
Is not more loathed than an effeminate man
In time of action. I stand condemned for this;
They think my little stomach to the war   221
And your great love to me restrains you thus.
Sweet, rouse yourself, and the weak wanton Cupid
Shall from your neck unloose his amorous fold   224
And, like a dewdrop from the lion's mane,
Be shook to air.

ACHILLES   Shall Ajax fight with Hector?

PATROCLUS
Ay, and perhaps receive much honor by him.

ACHILLES
I see my reputation is at stake;
My fame is shrewdly gored.

PATROCLUS   Oh, then, beware!   229
Those wounds heal ill that men do give themselves.
Omission to do what is necessary

---

210 **Pyrrhus** Achilles's son, also called Neoptolemus
211 **trump** trumpet   214 **him** i.e., Hector.   215 **lover** friend
216 **The fool . . . break** i.e., The fool easily escapes dangers that
to a man of your dignity would be fatal.   218 **impudent**
shameless   221 **little stomach to** lack of enthusiasm for
224 **fold** embrace   229 **shrewdly gored** severely wounded.

Seals a commission to a blank of danger;   232
And danger, like an ague, subtly taints   233
Even then when we sit idly in the sun.

ACHILLES
Go call Thersites hither, sweet Patroclus.
I'll send the fool to Ajax and desire him
T'invite the Trojan lords after the combat
To see us here unarmed. I have a woman's longing,
An appetite that I am sick withal,   239
To see great Hector in his weeds of peace,   240
To talk with him and to behold his visage,
Even to my full of view.

Enter Thersites.

              A labor saved.   242

THERSITES A wonder!

ACHILLES What?

THERSITES Ajax goes up and down the field, asking for
  himself.   246

ACHILLES How so?

THERSITES He must fight singly tomorrow with Hector
  and is so prophetically proud of an heroical cudgeling
  that he raves in saying nothing.

ACHILLES How can that be?

THERSITES Why, 'a stalks up and down like a peacock—
  a stride and a stand; ruminates like an hostess that   253
  hath no arithmetic but her brain to set down her reck- 254

---

232 **Seals . . . danger** i.e., gives danger unlimited license, a blank
check. (Literally, a warrant with blank spaces.) 233 **ague** fever.
taints infects. (Meat spoils when left lying in the sun.) 239 **withal**
with 240 **weeds** garments 242 **to . . . view** to the fullest
satisfaction of my eyes. 246 **himself** i.e., "Ajax." (With a quibble
on "a jakes" or latrine.) 253–4 **hostess . . . arithmetic** (Tavern
keepers were proverbially poor at addition; compare 1.2.114.)

oning; bites his lip with a politic regard, as who 255
should say, "There were wit in this head, an 'twould 256
out"—and so there is, but it lies as coldly in him as
fire in a flint, which will not show without knocking.
The man's undone forever, for if Hector break not his
neck i'th' combat, he'll break't himself in vainglory.
He knows not me. I said, "Good morrow, Ajax," and
he replies, "Thanks, Agamemnon." What think you of
this man, that takes me for the general? He's grown a
very land-fish, languageless, a monster. A plague of 264
opinion! A man may wear it on both sides, like a 265
leather jerkin. 266

ACHILLES Thou must be my ambassador to him, Thersites.

THERSITES Who, I? Why, he'll answer nobody; he
professes not answering. Speaking is for beggars; he 270
wears his tongue in 's arms. I will put on his presence. 271
Let Patroclus make demands to me; you shall see
the pageant of Ajax.

ACHILLES To him, Patroclus. Tell him I humbly desire
the valiant Ajax to invite the most valorous Hector to
come unarmed to my tent, and to procure safe-conduct
for his person of the magnanimous and most illustrious six-or-seven-times-honored Captain-General of
the Grecian army, Agamemnon, et cetera. Do this.

PATROCLUS Jove bless great Ajax!

THERSITES Hum!

PATROCLUS I come from the worthy Achilles—

255–6 **with a . . . say** with an assumption of a knowing manner,
as if one should say   264 **land-fish** i.e., monstrous creature
264–6 **A plague . . . jerkin** A curse on the way men flirt with
reputation! It can be turned inside out, like a man's close-fitting
jacket.   270 **professes** i.e., makes a point of   271 **arms**
weapons.   **put . . . presence** assume his demeanor.

THERSITES   Ha?

PATROCLUS   Who most humbly desires you to invite Hector to his tent—

THERSITES   Hum!

PATROCLUS   And to procure safe-conduct from Agamemnon.

THERSITES   Agamemnon?

PATROCLUS   Ay, my lord.

THERSITES   Ha!

PATROCLUS   What say you to't?

THERSITES   God b'wi'you, with all my heart.

PATROCLUS   Your answer, sir.

THERSITES   If tomorrow be a fair day, by eleven o'clock it will go one way or other. Howsoever, he shall 296 pay for me ere he has me.

PATROCLUS   Your answer, sir.

THERSITES   Fare ye well, with all my heart.

ACHILLES   Why, but he is not in this tune, is he?   300

THERSITES   No, but he's out o' tune thus. What music will be in him when Hector has knocked out his brains, I know not; but, I am sure, none, unless the 303 fiddler Apollo get his sinews to make catlings on.   304

ACHILLES

Come, thou shalt bear a letter to him straight.

THERSITES   Let me carry another to his horse, for that's the more capable creature.   307

---

296 **Howsoever** In either case   300 **tune** i.e., mood, disposition
303–4 **the fiddler Apollo** i.e., Apollo, as god of music
304 **catlings** catgut, of which strings for instruments were made
307 **capable** able to understand

ACHILLES
    My mind is troubled, like a fountain stirred,
    And I myself see not the bottom of it.

                                [*Exeunt Achilles and Patroclus.*]

THERSITES   Would the fountain of your mind were clear
    again, that I might water an ass at it! I had rather be a
    tick in a sheep than such a valiant ignorance.   [*Exit.*]   312

[4.1] ✤ *Enter, at one door, Aeneas, [with a torch;] at*
        another, Paris, Deïphobus, Antenor, Diomedes
        the Grecian [and others], with torches.

PARIS   See, ho! Who is that there?

DEIPHOBUS   It is the Lord Aeneas.

AENEAS   Is the prince there in person?
    Had I so good occasion to lie long
    As you, Prince Paris, nothing but heavenly business
    Should rob my bedmate of my company.

DIOMEDES
    That's my mind too. Good morrow, Lord Aeneas.   7

PARIS
    A valiant Greek, Aeneas; take his hand.
    Witness the process of your speech, wherein   9
    You told how Diomed, a whole week by days,   10
    Did haunt you in the field.

AENEAS   Health to you, valiant sir,
    During all question of the gentle truce;   13

---

312 **ignorance** ignoramus, fool.

4.1 *Location: Troy. A street, in an unspecified place.*
0.1, 3 *torch, torches* (These directions may indicate torchbearers.)
7 **mind** opinion   9 **process** drift   10 **a whole . . . days** every
day for a week   13 **question** discussion, parley (allowed by the
truce)

But when I meet you armed, as black defiance   14
As heart can think or courage execute.

DIOMEDES

The one and other Diomed embraces.   16
Our bloods are now in calm; and so long, health!   17
But when contention and occasion meet,   18
By Jove, I'll play the hunter for thy life
With all my force, pursuit, and policy.   20

AENEAS   And thou shalt hunt a lion that will fly
With his face backward. In humane gentleness,   22
Welcome to Troy! Now, by Anchises' life,   23
Welcome, indeed! By Venus' hand I swear,   24
No man alive can love in such a sort   25
The thing he means to kill more excellently.

DIOMEDES

We sympathize. Jove, let Aeneas live,   27
If to my sword his fate be not the glory,
A thousand complete courses of the sun!
But, in mine emulous honor, let him die   30
With every joint a wound, and that tomorrow!

AENEAS   We know each other well.

DIOMEDES

We do, and long to know each other worse.

PARIS

This is the most despiteful gentle greeting,   34
The noblest hateful love, that e'er I heard of.
What business, lord, so early?

---

14 as black defiance defiance as black   **16 The one and other**
i.e., Aeneas's promises of *health* and *defiance*   **17 so long** for as
long as this truce lasts   **18 when . . . meet** i.e., when the battle
gives us opportunity   **20 policy** cunning.   **22 face backward**
i.e., bravely facing the enemy.   **23, 24 Anchises, Venus**
(Aeneas's parents)   **25 in . . . sort** to such a degree
27 sympathize share your feeling.   **30 emulous** ambitious
34 despiteful contemptuous

AENEAS

    I was sent for to the King, but why, I know not.

PARIS

    His purpose meets you. 'Twas to bring this Greek   38
    To Calchas' house, and there to render him,   39
    For the enfreed Antenor, the fair Cressid.
    Let's have your company, or, if you please,
    Haste there before us. [*Aside to Aeneas*] I constantly
      do think—   42
    Or rather, call my thought a certain knowledge—
    My brother Troilus lodges there tonight.
    Rouse him and give him note of our approach,   45
    With the whole quality whereof. I fear   46
    We shall be much unwelcome.

AENEAS   That I assure you.

    Troilus had rather Troy were borne to Greece
    Than Cressid borne from Troy.

PARIS   There is no help.

    The bitter disposition of the time   50
    Will have it so. On, lord; we'll follow you.

AENEAS   Good morrow, all.   [*Exit Aeneas*.]

PARIS

    And tell me, noble Diomed, faith, tell me true,
    Even in the soul of sound good-fellowship: 54
    Who, in your thoughts, merits fair Helen most,
    Myself or Menelaus?

DIOMEDES   Both alike.

    He merits well to have her that doth seek her,   57

---

38 His . . . you i.e., I can tell you, since the matter is at hand.
39 render give   **42 constantly** confirmedly   **45 note** news,
notice   **46 the . . . whereof** all the causes thereof, reasons why.
50 disposition (1) temperament (2) arrangement, ordering
54 soul spirit   **57 He** Menelaus, or any cuckolded husband

Not making any scruple of her soilure,   58
With such a hell of pain and world of charge;   59
And you as well to keep her that defend her,
Not palating the taste of her dishonor,   61
With such a costly loss of wealth and friends.
He, like a puling cuckold, would drink up   63
The lees and dregs of a flat 'taměd piece;   64
You, like a lecher, out of whorish loins   65
Are pleased to breed out your inheritors.   66
Both merits poised, each weighs nor less nor more;   67
But he as he, the heavier for a whore.   68

PARIS
You are too bitter to your countrywoman.

DIOMEDES
She's bitter to her country. Hear me, Paris:
For every false drop in her bawdy veins
A Grecian's life hath sunk; for every scruple   72
Of her contaminated carrion weight   73
A Trojan hath been slain. Since she could speak,
She hath not given so many good words breath
As for her Greeks and Trojans suffered death.

PARIS
Fair Diomed, you do as chapmen do,   77
Dispraise the thing that you desire to buy.
But we in silence hold this virtue well: 79

---

58 Not . . . scruple not worrying about.   **soilure** dishonor,
stain   **59 charge** cost   **61 Not palating** not tasting, being
insensible of   **63 puling** complaining   **64 flat 'taměd piece**
wine so long opened that it is flat; hence, a used woman
65–6 out of . . . inheritors are content to breed your heirs out of
a whore's belly.   **67 poised** weighed, balanced.   **nor less**
neither less   **68 he as he** the one like the other   **72 scruple**
little bit. (Literally, one twenty-fourth of an ounce.)   **73 carrion**
putrified and rotten, like a carcass   **77 chapmen** traders,
merchants   **79 But . . . well** But we find this merit in the idea of
our keeping silent (and thus refusing to praise Helen)

We'll not commend what we intend to sell.   80
Here lies our way.   *Exeunt.*

[4.2] ❧ *Enter Troilus and Cressida.*

TROILUS
Dear, trouble not yourself. The morn is cold.

CRESSIDA
Then, sweet my lord, I'll call mine uncle down.
He shall unbolt the gates.

TROILUS   Trouble him not.
To bed, to bed! Sleep kill those pretty eyes,   4
And give as soft attachment to thy senses   5
As infants' empty of all thought!   6

CRESSIDA
Good morrow, then.

TROILUS   I prithee now, to bed.

CRESSIDA   Are you aweary of me?

TROILUS
Oh, Cressida! But that the busy day,
Waked by the lark, hath roused the ribald crows,   10
And dreaming night will hide our joys no longer,
I would not from thee.

CRESSIDA   Night hath been too brief.

TROILUS
Beshrew the witch! With venomous wights she stays   13
As tediously as hell, but flies the grasps of love.   14

---

80 **We'll . . . sell** i.e., we won't praise a thing that we would "sell"
to you only at the very dear price of bloodshed.

4.2 *Location: Troy. The courtyard of Calchas's house.*
4 **Sleep kill** Let sleep overpower, put to rest   5 **attachment** arrest,
confinement   6 **infants'** i.e., infants' eyes   10 **ribald** offensively
noisy, irreverent   13–14 **Beshrew . . . hell** i.e., Curse the night! She
lingers endlessly with malignant beings (since night and villainy accord)

With wings more momentary-swift than thought.
You will catch cold, and curse me.

CRESSIDA
Prithee, tarry. You men will never tarry.
O foolish Cressid! I might have still held off,
And then you would have tarried. Hark, there's one
    up.

PANDARUS [*within*]   What's all the doors open here?   20

TROILUS   It is your uncle.

        [*Enter Pandarus.*]

CRESSIDA
A pestilence on him! Now will he be mocking.
I shall have such a life!

PANDARUS   How now, how now, how go maiden-   24
    heads? Here, you maid! Where's my cousin Cressid?   25

CRESSIDA
Go hang yourself, you naughty mocking uncle!
You bring me to do—and then you flout me too.

PANDARUS   To do what, to do what?—Let her say
    what.—What have I brought you to do?

CRESSIDA
Come, come, beshrew your heart! You'll ne'er be
    good,   30
Nor suffer others.   31

PANDARUS   Ha, ha! Alas, poor wretch! Ah, poor *capoc-*   32
    chia! Has 't not slept tonight? Would he not—a   33
    naughty man—let it sleep? A bugbear take him!   34

20 **What's** Why are   24 **how go** what price   25 **Where's . . .
Cressid?** (Pandarus pretends not to recognize Cressida now that
she is no longer a virgin.)   30–1 **You'll . . . others** i.e., You think
such dirty thoughts that you can't imagine others to be otherwise.
32–3 *capocchia* dolt, simpleton. (Italian.)   33 **Has 't** Has it.
(Pandarus condescendingly uses the neuter pronoun, as one might
in referring to a baby. [Also in line 34.])   34 **bugbear** hobgoblin

CRESSIDA

    Did not I tell you? Would he were knocked i'th' head!

                                    One knocks.

    Who's that at door? Good uncle, go and see.—

    My lord, come you again into my chamber.

    You smile and mock me, as if I meant naughtily.

TROILUS   Ha, ha!

CRESSIDA

    Come, you are deceived. I think of no such thing.

                                    Knock.

    How earnestly they knock! Pray you, come in.

    I would not for half Troy have you seen here.

                        Exeunt [Troilus and Cressida].

PANDARUS   Who's there? What's the matter? Will you
    beat down the door? [*He opens the door.*] How now,
    what's the matter?

        [*Enter Aeneas.*]

AENEAS   Good morrow, lord, good morrow.

PANDARUS   Who's there? My lord Aeneas? By my troth,
    I knew you not. What news with you so early?

AENEAS   Is not Prince Troilus here?

PANDARUS   Here? What should he do here?   50

AENEAS

    Come, he is here, my lord. Do not deny him.

    It doth import him much to speak with me.   52

PANDARUS   Is he here, say you? It's more than I know,
    I'll be sworn. For my own part, I came in late. What
    should he do here?

50 **should he do** would he be doing   52 **import** concern

AENEAS   Hoo!—Nay, then. Come, come, you'll do him
   wrong ere you are ware. You'll be so true to him, to be   57
   false to him. Do not you know of him, but yet go fetch   58
   him hither. Go.

     [*Enter Troilus.*]

TROILUS   How now, what's the matter?

AENEAS
   My lord, I scarce have leisure to salute you,   61
   My matter is so rash. There is at hand   62
   Paris your brother and Deiphobus,
   The Grecian Diomed, and our Antenor
   Delivered to us; and for him forthwith,
   Ere the first sacrifice, within this hour,   66
   We must give up to Diomedes' hand
   The Lady Cressida.

TROILUS   Is it so concluded?

AENEAS
   By Priam and the general state of Troy.   69
   They are at hand and ready to effect it.

TROILUS
   How my achievements mock me!
   I will go meet them. And, my lord Aeneas,
   We met by chance; you did not find me here.   73

AENEAS
   Good, good, my lord, the secrets of nature
   Have not more gift in taciturnity.

                    Exeunt [*Troilus and Aeneas*].

57–8 **You'll . . . know of him** i.e., In seeking to guard Troilus's
secret, you'll protect him from knowing of a matter that concerns
him. Go ahead and pretend you don't know he is here
61 **salute** greet   62 **rash** urgent, pressing.   66 **Ere . . .**
sacrifice before the first religious ceremony of the day   69 **state**
council   73 **We met** i.e., Remember to say that we met. (This is
the fiction to which Aeneas agrees.)

PANDARUS   Is't possible? No sooner got but lost? The
    devil take Antenor! The young prince will go mad. A
    plague upon Antenor! I would they had broke's neck!

    Enter Cressida.

CRESSIDA
    How now? What's the matter? Who was here?

PANDARUS   Ah, ah!

CRESSIDA
    Why sigh you so profoundly? Where's my lord?
    Gone? Tell me, sweet uncle, what's the matter?

PANDARUS   Would I were as deep under the earth as I
    am above!

CRESSIDA   O the gods! What's the matter?

PANDARUS   Pray thee, get thee in. Would thou hadst
    ne'er been born! I knew thou wouldst be his death. Oh,
    poor gentleman! A plague upon Antenor!

CRESSIDA   Good uncle, I beseech you, on my knees I
    beseech you, what's the matter?

PANDARUS   Thou must be gone, wench, thou must be
    gone. Thou art changed for Antenor. Thou must to thy   92
    father and be gone from Troilus. 'Twill be his death,
    'twill be his bane; he cannot bear it.   94

CRESSIDA
    O you immortal gods! I will not go.

PANDARUS   Thou must.

CRESSIDA
    I will not, uncle. I have forgot my father.
    I know no touch of consanguinity;   98
    No kin, no love, no blood, no soul so near me
    As the sweet Troilus. O you gods divine!

92 **changed** exchanged   94 **bane** death   98 **touch of
consanguinity** sense or tiniest bit of kinship

Make Cressid's name the very crown of falsehood
If ever she leave Troilus! Time, force, and death,
Do to this body what extremes you can;
But the strong base and building of my love
Is as the very center of the earth,
Drawing all things to it. I'll go in and weep—

PANDARUS Do, do.

CRESSIDA
Tear my bright hair and scratch my praisèd cheeks,
Crack my clear voice with sobs and break my heart
With sounding "Troilus." I will not go from Troy.   110
                                        [Exeunt.]

[4.3] ᴥ Enter Paris, Troilus, Aeneas, Deiphobus,
        Antenor, [and] Diomedes.

PARIS
It is great morning, and the hour prefixed   1
For her delivery to this valiant Greek
Comes fast upon. Good my brother Troilus,
Tell you the lady what she is to do,
And haste her to the purpose.

TROILUS   Walk into her house.
I'll bring her to the Grecian presently;   6
And to his hand when I deliver her,
Think it an altar, and thy brother Troilus
A priest there off'ring to it his own heart.   [Exit.]

110 **sounding** uttering

4.3 Location: Troy. Before Cressida's house.
1 **great morning** broad day.   **prefixed** earlier agreed upon
6 **to . . . presently** to Diomedes immediately

PARIS   I know what 'tis to love;
    And would, as I shall pity, I could help!   11
    Please you walk in, my lords?   *Exeunt.*

[4.4] ✄ *Enter Pandarus and Cressida.*

PANDARUS   Be moderate, be moderate.
CRESSIDA
    Why tell you me of moderation?
    The grief is fine, full, perfect, that I taste,   3
    And violenteth in a sense as strong   4
    As that which causeth it. How can I moderate it?
    If I could temporize with my affection,   6
    Or brew it to a weak and colder palate,   7
    The like allayment could I give my grief.   8
    My love admits no qualifying dross;   9
    No more my grief, in such a precious loss.

       Enter Troilus.

PANDARUS   Here, here, here he comes. Ah, sweet
    ducks!
CRESSIDA   Oh, Troilus! Troilus!   [*Embracing him.*]
PANDARUS   What a pair of spectacles is here! Let me   14
    embrace, too. "O heart," as the goodly saying is,
       "O heart, heavy heart,
       Why sigh'st thou without breaking?"

11 **as** as much as

4.4 *Location: Troy. Cressida's house.*
3 **fine** refined, pure   4 **violenteth** is violent   6 **temporize**
compromise, come to terms   7 **brew** dilute.   **palate** taste
8 **allayment** dilution, mitigation   9 **qualifying dross** foreign
matter making it less pure   14 **spectacles** sights. (With
suggestion of "eyeglasses.")

where he answers again, 18
    "Because thou canst not ease thy smart
       By friendship nor by speaking." 20
There was never a truer rhyme. Let us cast away nothing, for we may live to have need of such a verse. We 22
see it, we see it. How now, lambs? 23

TROILUS
Cressid, I love thee in so strained a purity 24
That the blest gods, as angry with my fancy, 25
More bright in zeal than the devotion which 26
Cold lips blow to their deities, take thee from me. 27

CRESSIDA   Have the gods envy?

PANDARUS   Ay, ay, ay, ay; 'tis too plain a case.

CRESSIDA
And is it true that I must go from Troy?

TROILUS
A hateful truth.

CRESSIDA   What, and from Troilus too?

TROILUS
From Troy and Troilus.

CRESSIDA   Is't possible?

TROILUS
And suddenly, where injury of chance 33
Puts back leave-taking, jostles roughly by 34
All time of pause, rudely beguiles our lips
Of all rejoindure, forcibly prevents 36
Our locked embrasures, strangles our dear vows 37

---

18 **he** the heart   20 **By . . . speaking** by mere friendship or
words alone.   22–3 **We see it** i.e., We see how verses can
console   24 **strained** purified as by filtering   25 **as** as if.
fancy love   26–7 **More . . . deities** a love that is more zealous
than the devotion which the chaste lips of vestal virgins breathe to
the gods   33–4 **injury . . . leave-taking** injurious Fortune
prevents leisurely farewells   36 **rejoindure** reunion (in a
farewell kiss)   37 **embrasures** embraces

Even in the birth of our own laboring breath.
We two, that with so many thousand sighs
Did buy each other, must poorly sell ourselves
With the rude brevity and discharge of one.   41
Injurious Time now with a robber's haste
Crams his rich thiev'ry up, he knows not how.   43
As many farewells as be stars in heaven,
With distinct breath and consigned kisses to them,   45
He fumbles up into a loose adieu,   46
And scants us with a single famished kiss,   47
Distasted with the salt of broken tears.   48

AENEAS (*within*)   My lord, is the lady ready?

TROILUS
Hark! You are called. Some say the genius so   50
Cries "Come!" to him that instantly must die.—
Bid them have patience. She shall come anon.

PANDARUS   Where are my tears? Rain, to lay this wind,   53
or my heart will be blown up by the root.   [*Exit.*]   54

CRESSIDA
I must then to the Grecians?

TROILUS   No remedy.

CRESSIDA
A woeful Cressid 'mongst the merry Greeks!
When shall we see again?   57

---

41 discharge of one (1) exhalation of a single sigh (2) making of a single payment.   **43 thiev'ry** stolen property.   **he ... how** every which way, distractedly.   **45 With ... them** with the words of farewell and the kisses with which those words are confirmed, sealed   **46 He fumbles up** Time clumsily huddles together   **47 scants** inadequately supplies   **48 Distasted** rendered distasteful.   **broken** interrupted with sobs
50 genius attendant spirit supposed to be assigned to a person at birth   **53 Rain ... wind** i.e., Tears, to allay my sighs   **54 by the root** i.e., as though the heart were a tree in a storm of sighs. (Sighs were thought to deprive the heart of its blood.)   **57 see** see each other

TROILUS

    Hear me, my love. Be thou but true of heart—

CRESSIDA

    I true? How now? What wicked deem is this?   59

TROILUS

    Nay, we must use expostulation kindly,   60
    For it is parting from us.   61
    I speak not "Be thou true" as fearing thee,   62
    For I will throw my glove to Death himself   63
    That there's no maculation in thy heart;   64
    But "Be thou true," say I, to fashion in   65
    My sequent protestation: Be thou true,   66
    And I will see thee.

CRESSIDA

    Oh, you shall be exposed, my lord, to dangers
    As infinite as imminent! But I'll be true.

TROILUS

    And I'll grow friend with danger. Wear this sleeve.   70

                    [They exchange favors.]

CRESSIDA

    And you this glove. When shall I see you?

TROILUS

    I will corrupt the Grecian sentinels,   72
    To give thee nightly visitation.
    But yet, be true.

CRESSIDA   Oh, heavens, "Be true" again?

---

59 deem thought, surmise   **60–1 we must . . . from us** i.e., we must expostulate gently, for soon even this opportunity for speech will be lost to us.   **62 as fearing thee** i.e., as if not trusting your constancy   **63 throw . . . to** i.e., challenge   **64 maculation** stain of impurity   **65 fashion in** serve as introduction for **66 sequent** ensuing   **70 sleeve** (Sleeves were detachable and could be given as favors or tokens; *gloves* could be similarly given.) **72 corrupt** bribe

TROILUS   Hear why I speak it, love.
The Grecian youths are full of quality;   76
Their loving well composed with gifts of nature,   77
And flowing o'er with arts and exercise.   78
How novelty may move, and parts with person,   79
Alas, a kind of godly jealousy—   80
Which, I beseech you, call a virtuous sin—
Makes me afeard.

CRESSIDA   Oh, heavens! You love me not.

TROILUS   Die I a villain, then!
In this I do not call your faith in question
So mainly as my merit. I cannot sing,   85
Nor heel the high lavolt, nor sweeten talk,   86
Nor play at subtle games—fair virtues all,   87
To which the Grecians are most prompt and pregnant.   88
But I can tell that in each grace of these
There lurks a still and dumb-discoursive devil   90
That tempts most cunningly. But be not tempted.

CRESSIDA   Do you think I will?

TROILUS
No. But something may be done that we will not;   94
And sometimes we are devils to ourselves,
When we will tempt the frailty of our powers,   96
Presuming on their changeful potency.   97

---

76 **quality** flair, graceful manners   77 **Their . . . composed** i.e.,
their skill in wooing is well endowed   78 **arts and exercise**
skills sharpened by practice.   79 **parts with person** gifts and
accomplishments, combined with personal charm   80 **godly**
divinely sanctioned, as in a marriage   85 **mainly** strongly.
merit (Troilus plays on the Protestant insistence on salvation
through *faith*, line 84, not *merit*.)   86 **Nor heel . . . talk** nor
dance the lively dance called the lavolta, nor talk ingratiatingly
87 **subtle** (1) requiring skill (2) cunning, deceptive   88 **pregnant**
ready, alacritous.   90 **dumb-discoursive** eloquently silent
94 **will not** do not desire   96 **will tempt** deliberately tempt
97 **Presuming . . . potency** presuming fatuously on our ability to
control their unpredictable strength.

AENEAS (*within*)
Nay, good my lord—

TROILUS   Come, kiss, and let us part.

PARIS (*within*)
Brother Troilus!

TROILUS   Good brother, come you hither,
And bring Aeneas and the Grecian with you.

CRESSIDA   My lord, will you be true?

TROILUS
Who, I? Alas, it is my vice, my fault.
Whiles others fish with craft for great opinion,   103
I with great truth catch mere simplicity;   104
Whilst some with cunning gild their copper crowns,   105
With truth and plainness I do wear mine bare.

[*Enter Aeneas, Paris, Antenor, Deiphobus, and
Diomedes.*]

Fear not my truth. The moral of my wit   107
Is "plain and true"; there's all the reach of it.—   108
Welcome, Sir Diomed. Here is the lady
Which for Antenor we deliver you.
At the port, lord, I'll give her to thy hand,   111
And by the way possess thee what she is.   112
Entreat her fair, and by my soul, fair Greek,   113
If e'er thou stand at mercy of my sword,
Name Cressid, and thy life shall be as safe
As Priam is in Ilium.

DIOMEDES   Fair Lady Cressid,

103 **craft** cunning.   **opinion** reputation (for wisdom)
104 **I . . . simplicity** I, in my use of simple truth, earn a reputation
for being simple and plain   105 **crowns** (1) coins (2) royal
headdresses   107 **truth** fidelity.   **moral** maxim   108 **all the
reach** the full extent   111 **port** gate of the city   112 **possess**
inform   113 **Entreat her fair** Treat her with courtesy

So please you, save the thanks this prince expects.   117
The luster in your eye, heaven in your cheek,
Pleads your fair usage; and to Diomed
You shall be mistress, and command him wholly.

TROILUS
Grecian, thou dost not use me courteously,
To shame the zeal of my petition to thee
In praising her. I tell thee, lord of Greece,
She is as far high-soaring o'er thy praises
As thou unworthy to be called her servant.   125
I charge thee use her well, even for my charge;   126
For, by the dreadful Pluto, if thou dost not,
Though the great bulk Achilles be thy guard,   128
I'll cut thy throat.

DIOMEDES   Oh, be not moved, Prince Troilus.   129
Let me be privileged by my place and message
To be a speaker free. When I am hence,
I'll answer to my lust. And know you, lord,   132
I'll nothing do on charge. To her own worth   133
She shall be prized; but that you say "Be 't so,"   134
I'll speak it in my spirit and honor, "No."   135

TROILUS
Come, to the port.—I'll tell thee, Diomed,
This brave shall oft make thee to hide thy head.—   137
Lady, give me your hand, and, as we walk,
To our own selves bend we our needful talk.

---

117 **So . . . expects** i.e., please save yourself the trouble of
thanking Troilus for your good treatment at my hands; I'll do it for
your sake, not his.   125 **servant** male admirer.   126 **even . . .
charge** simply because I demand that you do so   128 **bulk** hulk
129 **moved** angry   132 **answer to my lust** do what I please—
with Cressida, and in responding to your challenge.   133 **on
charge** because you command it.   134–5 **but that . . . "No"**
but (I swear it by my honor) not because you tell me to.
137 **brave** boast, defiance

[*Exeunt Troilus, Cressida, and Diomedes.*] *Sound*
trumpet [*within*].

PARIS
  Hark! Hector's trumpet.

AENEAS   How have we spent this morning! 140
  The Prince must think me tardy and remiss,
  That swore to ride before him to the field.

PARIS
  'Tis Troilus' fault. Come, come, to field with him.

DEIPHOBUS Let us make ready straight.

AENEAS
  Yea, with a bridegroom's fresh alacrity,
  Let us address to tend on Hector's heels.   146
  The glory of our Troy doth this day lie
  On his fair worth and single chivalry.   *Exeunt.* 148

[**4.5**] ❧ *Enter Ajax, armed, Achilles, Patroclus,*
      Agamemnon, Menelaus, Ulysses, Nestor, etc.

AGAMEMNON
  Here art thou in appointment fresh and fair,   1
  Anticipating time with starting courage.   2
  Give with thy trumpet a loud note to Troy,
  Thou dreadful Ajax, that the appallèd air   4
  May pierce the head of the great combatant
  And hale him hither.

AJAX   Thou, trumpet, there's my purse. 6
                    [*He throws money to his trumpeter.*]

140 **spent** consumed wastefully   146 **address** get ready.
tend attend   148 **single chivalry** individual prowess.

4.5 *Location: Near the Greek camp. Lists set out as an arena for*
combat.
1 **appointment** equipment, accoutrement   2 **starting** bold, eager
to begin   4 **dreadful** inspiring dread   6 **trumpet** trumpeter

Now crack thy lungs and split thy brazen pipe.
Blow, villain, till thy spherèd bias cheek   8
Outswell the colic of puffed Aquilon.   9
Come, stretch thy chest, and let thy eyes spout blood;
Thou blowest for Hector.   [*Trumpet sounds.*]   11

ULYSSES   No trumpet answers.

ACHILLES   'Tis but early days.   13

> [*Enter Diomedes, with Cressida.*]

AGAMEMNON
Is not yond Diomed, with Calchas' daughter?

ULYSSES
'Tis he. I ken the manner of his gait;   15
He rises on the toe. That spirit of his
In aspiration lifts him from the earth.

AGAMEMNON
Is this the Lady Cressid?

DIOMEDES   Even she.

AGAMEMNON
Most dearly welcome to the Greeks, sweet lady.
                                          [*He kisses her.*]

NESTOR
Our general doth salute you with a kiss.

ULYSSES
Yet is the kindness but particular;   21
'Twere better she were kissed in general.   22

---

8 **bias** puffed out (and shaped like a weighted bowling ball used in
bowls)   9 **colic** i.e., swelling (like that caused by colic).
Aquilon the north wind (here personified as distended by colic).
11 **for Hector** to summon Hector.   13 **days** in the day.
15 **ken** recognize   21 **particular** single, limited to one   22 **in
general** by everyone. (With a play on "by the general.")

NESTOR

And very courtly counsel. I'll begin.   [*He kisses her.*]
So much for Nestor.

ACHILLES

I'll take that winter from your lips, fair lady.   25
Achilles bids you welcome.   [*He kisses her.*]

MENELAUS

I had good argument for kissing once.   27

PATROCLUS

But that's no argument for kissing now;
For thus popped Paris in his hardiment,   29
And parted thus you and your argument.

          [*He kisses her.*]

ULYSSES

Oh, deadly gall and theme of all our scorns,   31
For which we lose our heads to gild his horns!   32

PATROCLUS

The first was Menelaus' kiss; this, mine.
Patroclus kisses you.   [*He kisses her again.*]

MENELAUS   Oh, this is trim!   34

PATROCLUS

Paris and I kiss evermore for him.   35

MENELAUS

I'll have my kiss, sir.—Lady, by your leave.

CRESSIDA

In kissing, do you render or receive?

25 that winter (Alludes to Nestor's old age.)   **27 argument**
theme, i.e., Helen. (But Patroclus answers in the sense of
"supporting reason.")   **29 popped** came in suddenly. (With sexual
suggestion.)   **hardiment** bold exploits, boldness. (With bawdy
double meaning of "hardness.")   **31–2 Oh . . . horns!** Oh, fatal
bitterness and the theme that brings scorn on us all, in which we
lose our lives to gild over the fact of Menelaus's having been made a
cuckold!   **34 trim** fine. (Said ironically.)   **35 Paris . . . him** i.e., I
take the kiss Menelaus hoped for, just as Paris does in kissing Helen.

MENELAUS
  Both take and give.

CRESSIDA   I'll make my match to live,   38
  The kiss you take is better than you give;
  Therefore no kiss.

MENELAUS
  I'll give you boot; I'll give you three for one.   41

CRESSIDA
  You are an odd man; give even, or give none.   42

MENELAUS
  An odd man, lady? Every man is odd.

CRESSIDA
  No, Paris is not, for you know 'tis true
  That you are odd, and he is even with you.

MENELAUS
  You fillip me o'th' head.

CRESSIDA   No, I'll be sworn.   46

ULYSSES
  It were no match, your nail against his horn.   47
  May I, sweet lady, beg a kiss of you?

CRESSIDA
  You may.

ULYSSES   I do desire it.

CRESSIDA   Why, beg too.   49

---

38 **I'll . . . to live** I'll wager my life   41 **boot** odds, advantage
42 **odd** (The wordplay here and in lines 43–5 includes [1] strange
[2] single, no longer having a wife [3] unique, standing alone
[4] odd man out [5] the opposite of *even*.)   46 **fillip . . . head**
i.e., touch a sensitive spot, by alluding to my cuckold's horns.
47 **It . . . horn** i.e., Your fingernail is not nearly tough enough to
make any impression on his cuckold's horn.   49 **Why, beg too**
i.e., You must do more than merely *desire* a kiss; you must humble
yourself as a petitionary male.

ULYSSES

   Why then for Venus' sake, give me a kiss

   When Helen is a maid again, and his.   51

CRESSIDA

   I am your debtor; claim it when 'tis due.

ULYSSES

   Never's my day, and then a kiss of you.   53

DIOMEDES

   Lady, a word. I'll bring you to your father.

                        [They talk apart.]

NESTOR

   A woman of quick sense.

ULYSSES   Fie, fie upon her!   55

   There's language in her eye, her cheek, her lip,

   Nay, her foot speaks; her wanton spirits look out

   At every joint and motive of her body.   58

   Oh, these encounterers, so glib of tongue,   59

   That give accosting welcome ere it comes,   60

   And wide unclasp the tables of their thoughts   61

   To every ticklish reader! Set them down   62

   For sluttish spoils of opportunity   63

   And daughters of the game.   64

             Exeunt [Diomedes and Cressida].

---

51 When . . . his when Helen is once again the chaste wife of
Menelaus. (A virtually impossible condition.)   **53 Never's . . .
you** i.e., I'll never claim that kiss.   **55 of quick sense** of lively
wit and vibrant sensuality.   **58 motive** moving limb or organ
59 encounterers seductive women   **60–2 That . . . reader!**
who sidle up to men without waiting to be invited, and allow their
thoughts to be read avidly by every susceptible male! (With sexual
suggestiveness in the image of unclasping, though *tables* are
literally writing tablets, as in *Hamlet*, 1.5.108.)   **63 sluttish . . .
opportunity** "corrupt wenches, of whose chastity every
opportunity may make a prey" (Johnson)   **64 daughters of the
game** i.e., prostitutes.

Flourish. Enter all of Troy: [Hector, Paris,
Aeneas, Helenus, Troilus, and attendants].

ALL
  The Trojan's trumpet.

AGAMEMNON   Yonder comes the troop.   65

AENEAS
  Hail, all you state of Greece! What shall be done   66
  To him that victory commands? Or do you purpose   67
  A victor shall be known? Will you the knights   68
  Shall to the edge of all extremity   69
  Pursue each other, or shall they be divided   70
  By any voice or order of the field?   71
  Hector bade ask.

AGAMEMNON   Which way would Hector have it?

AENEAS
  He cares not; he'll obey conditions.   73

AGAMEMNON
  'Tis done like Hector.

ACHILLES   But securely done,   74
  A little proudly, and great deal disprising   75
  The knight opposed.

AENEAS   If not Achilles, sir,
  What is your name?

ACHILLES   If not Achilles, nothing.

65 **The Trojan's** Hector's   66 **state** noble lords.   **What . . .
done** i.e., What honors shall be afforded   67 **that . . .
commands** that wins the victory.   68 **known** adjudged and
declared.   68–71 **Will . . . field?** Do you desire that the
combatants fight to the death, or that they be required to separate
on order of the marshals, according to set regulations of the field
of honor?   73 **conditions** whatever conditions are agreed upon.
74 **securely** overconfidently   75 **disprising** disdaining,
underrating

AENEAS

    Therefore Achilles. But, whate'er, know this:

    In the extremity of great and little,   79

    Valor and pride excel themselves in Hector,   80

    The one almost as infinite as all,

    The other blank as nothing. Weigh him well,

    And that which looks like pride is courtesy.

    This Ajax is half made of Hector's blood,   84

    In love whereof half Hector stays at home;

    Half heart, half hand, half Hector comes to seek

    This blended knight, half Trojan and half Greek.

ACHILLES

    A maiden battle, then? Oh, I perceive you.   88

        [Enter Diomedes.]

AGAMEMNON

    Here is Sir Diomed. Go, gentle knight,

    Stand by our Ajax. As you and Lord Aeneas

    Consent upon the order of their fight,   91

    So be it, either to the uttermost,

    Or else a breath. The combatants being kin   93

    Half stints their strife before their strokes begin.

        [Ajax and Hector enter the lists.]

ULYSSES   They are opposed already.

AGAMEMNON *[to Ulysses]*

    What Trojan is that same that looks so heavy?   96

ULYSSES

    The youngest son of Priam, a true knight,

    Not yet mature, yet matchless firm of word,

79–80 In . . . Hector i.e., Hector's valor is extremely great; his pride, extremely little   **84 Ajax . . . blood** (Compare 2.2.77, note, and 4.5.121.)   **88 maiden battle** combat without bloodshed.   **perceive** understand   **91 Consent** agree. **order** procedure, rules   **93 a breath** a friendly bout for exercise. **96 heavy** sad.

Speaking in deeds and deedless in his tongue;   99
Not soon provoked, nor being provoked soon
   calmed;
His heart and hand both open and both free.   101
For what he has he gives; what thinks, he shows;
Yet gives he not till judgment guide his bounty,
Nor dignifies an impair thought with breath;   104
Manly as Hector, but more dangerous,
For Hector in his blaze of wrath subscribes   106
To tender objects, but he in heat of action   107
Is more vindicative than jealous love.   108
They call him Troilus, and on him erect
A second hope, as fairly built as Hector.
Thus says Aeneas, one that knows the youth
Even to his inches, and with private soul   112
Did in great Ilium thus translate him to me.   113

Alarum. [Hector and Ajax fight.]

AGAMEMNON   They are in action.

NESTOR   Now, Ajax, hold thine own!

TROILUS   Hector, thou sleep'st. Awake thee!

AGAMEMNON
His blows are well disposed. There, Ajax!   117

Trumpets cease.

DIOMEDES
You must no more.

AENEAS   Princes, enough, so please you.

AJAX
I am not warm yet. Let us fight again.

99 **Speaking . . . tongue** letting his deeds speak for him and never
boasting   101 **free** open, generous.   104 **impair**
unconsidered, unsuitable   106–7 **subscribes . . . objects** yields
mercy to the defenseless   108 **vindicative** vindictive
112 **Even . . . inches** i.e., every inch of him.   **with private**
soul in private confidence   113 **translate** interpret
117 **disposed** placed.

DIOMEDES
　　As Hector pleases.

HECTOR　　　　　　Why, then will I no more.
　　Thou art, great lord, my father's sister's son,
　　A cousin-german to great Priam's seed.　　　　　　122
　　The obligation of our blood forbids
　　A gory emulation twixt us twain.　　　　　　　　124
　　Were thy commixtion Greek and Trojan so　　　　125
　　That thou couldst say, "This hand is Grecian all,
　　And this is Trojan; the sinews of this leg
　　All Greek, and this all Troy; my mother's blood
　　Runs on the dexter cheek, and this sinister　　　129
　　Bounds in my father's," by Jove multipotent,
　　Thou shouldst not bear from me a Greekish member
　　Wherein my sword had not impressure made　　　132
　　Of our rank feud. But the just gods gainsay　　　133
　　That any drop thou borrow'dst from thy mother,
　　My sacred aunt, should by my mortal sword
　　Be drainèd! Let me embrace thee, Ajax.
　　By him that thunders, thou hast lusty arms!　　　137
　　Hector would have them fall upon him thus.
　　Cousin, all honor to thee!　　　　　　[They embrace.]

AJAX　　　　　　　　I thank thee, Hector.
　　Thou art too gentle and too free a man.
　　I came to kill thee, cousin, and bear hence
　　A great addition earnèd in thy death.　　　　　　142

---

122 **cousin-german** first cousin　　124 **gory emulation** bloody
rivalry　　125 **commixtion** mixture　　129 **dexter** right.
sinister left　　132 **impressure** impression　　133 **rank** hot,
intemperate.　　**gainsay** forbid　　137 **By . . . thunders** i.e., By
Jove　　142 **addition** honorable title

HECTOR

> Not Neoptolemus so mirable,   143
> On whose bright crest Fame with her loud'st "Oyez"   144
> Cries, "This is he," could promise to himself   145
> A thought of added honor torn from Hector.   146

AENEAS

> There is expectance here from both the sides   147
> What further you will do.

HECTOR   We'll answer it;
> The issue is embracement. Ajax, farewell.   149

> > > > > [They embrace.]

AJAX

> If I might in entreaties find success—
> As seld I have the chance—I would desire   151
> My famous cousin to our Grecian tents.

DIOMEDES

> 'Tis Agamemnon's wish, and great Achilles
> Doth long to see unarmed the valiant Hector.

HECTOR

> Aeneas, call my brother Troilus to me,
> And signify this loving interview   156
> To the expecters of our Trojan part;   157
> Desire them home. Give me thy hand, my cousin.   158
> I will go eat with thee and see your knights.

> > > [Agamemnon and the rest approach them.]

143–6 **Not . . . Hector** i.e., Not even the much-wondered-at
Achilles, on whose heraldic badge Fame herself in the role of the
public crier announces "This is the man," could assure himself of
added honor by defeating Hector. (*Neoptolemus* is actually the name
of Achilles's son.)   147 **expectance** eager desire to know
149 **issue** outcome   151 **seld** seldom.   **desire** invite
156 **signify** announce   157 **the expecters . . . part** those
awaiting the outcome on our Trojan side   158 **home** to go
home.

AJAX

    Great Agamemnon comes to meet us here.

HECTOR [*to Aeneas*]

    The worthiest of them tell me name by name;
    But for Achilles, mine own searching eyes
    Shall find him by his large and portly size.   163

AGAMEMNON

    Worthy of arms! As welcome as to one   164
    That would be rid of such an enemy—
    But that's no welcome. Understand more clear:
    What's past and what's to come is strewed with
        husks
    And formless ruin of oblivion;
    But in this extant moment, faith and troth,   169
    Strained purely from all hollow bias-drawing,   170
    Bids thee, with most divine integrity,
    From heart of very heart, great Hector, welcome.

HECTOR

    I thank thee, most imperious Agamemnon.   173

AGAMEMNON [*to Troilus*]

    My well-famed lord of Troy, no less to you.

MENELAUS

    Let me confirm my princely brother's greeting.
    You brace of warlike brothers, welcome hither.

HECTOR

    Who must we answer?

AENEAS   The noble Menelaus.

---

163 **portly** stately, dignified   164 **of arms** (1) to bear weapons
(2) to receive embracements.   **as to one** as it is possible to one
169 **extant** present   169–70 **faith . . . bias-drawing** faithfulness
and honesty, purified of all insincerities or obliquities (such as the
bias weight inserted in bowling balls in the game of bowls)
173 **imperious** imperial

HECTOR

    Oh, you, my lord? By Mars his gauntlet, thanks!   178

    Mock not that I affect th'untraded oath;   179

    Your quondam wife swears still by Venus' glove.   180

    She's well, but bade me not commend her to you.

MENELAUS

    Name her not now, sir. She's a deadly theme.   182

HECTOR   Oh, pardon! I offend.

NESTOR

    I have, thou gallant Trojan, seen thee oft,

    Laboring for destiny, make cruel way   185

    Through ranks of Greekish youth, and I have seen
       thee,

    As hot as Perseus, spur thy Phrygian steed,   187

    And seen thee scorning forfeits and subduements,   188

    When thou hast hung thy advancèd sword i'th'air,   189

    Not letting it decline on the declined,   190

    That I have said to some my standers-by,   191

    "Lo, Jupiter is yonder, dealing life!"   192

    And I have seen thee pause and take thy breath,

    When that a ring of Greeks have hemmed thee in,   194

---

178 **By . . . gauntlet** By Mars's armored leather glove
179 **th'untraded** the unhackneyed. (Hector insists that his newly
minted oath, "By Mars his gauntlet," is suited to a war fought over
a woman. In line 180 he contrasts this warlike oath with Helen's
favorite, "by Venus' glove.")   180 **quondam** former
182 **deadly theme** (1) subject for mortal strife (2) gloomy topic of
discourse.   185 **Laboring for destiny** employed in the service
of fate, putting people to death   187 **Perseus** (See the note for
1.3.42.)   188 **scorning . . . subduements** i.e., ignoring those
already vanquished, whose lives were forfeit; refusing easy prey
189 **advancèd** raised aloft   190 **the declined** those already
vanquished   191 **to . . . my standers-by** to some of my
followers   192 **dealing life** i.e., mercifully sparing the weak.
194 **When that** when

Like an Olympian, wrestling. This have I seen;   195
But this thy countenance, still locked in steel,   196
I never saw till now. I knew thy grandsire   197
And once fought with him. He was a soldier good,
But, by great Mars, the captain of us all,
Never like thee. Let an old man embrace thee;
And, worthy warrior, welcome to our tents.

                              [*They embrace.*]

AENEAS   'Tis the old Nestor.

HECTOR
Let me embrace thee, good old chronicle,   203
That hast so long walked hand in hand with Time.
Most reverend Nestor, I am glad to clasp thee.

NESTOR
I would my arms could match thee in contention
As they contend with thee in courtesy.

HECTOR   I would they could.

NESTOR   Ha!
By this white beard, I'd fight with thee tomorrow.
Well, welcome, welcome! I have seen the time!   211

ULYSSES
I wonder now how yonder city stands
When we have here her base and pillar by us.

HECTOR
I know your favor, Lord Ulysses, well.   214
Ah, sir, there's many a Greek and Trojan dead

---

195 **Olympian** Olympian god, or a wrestler in the Olympic games
196 **still** always   197 **grandsire** i.e., Laomedon, builder of the
walls of Troy and defender of the city against an earlier Greek
army under Hercules   203 **chronicle** i.e., storehouse of
memories   211 **I have . . . time!** i.e., There was a time when I
could have taken you on!   214 **favor** face

Since first I saw yourself and Diomed   216
In Ilium, on your Greekish embassy.   217

ULYSSES
Sir, I foretold you then what would ensue.
My prophecy is but half his journey yet,
For yonder walls, that pertly front your town,   220
Yon towers, whose wanton tops do buss the clouds,   221
Must kiss their own feet.

HECTOR   I must not believe you.
There they stand yet, and modestly I think   223
The fall of every Phrygian stone will cost
A drop of Grecian blood. The end crowns all,
And that old common arbitrator, Time,
Will one day end it.

ULYSSES   So to him we leave it.
Most gentle and most valiant Hector, welcome!
After the general, I beseech you next
To feast with me and see me at my tent.

ACHILLES
I shall forestall thee, Lord Ulysses, thou!—   231
Now, Hector, I have fed mine eyes on thee;
I have with exact view perused thee, Hector,
And quoted joint by joint.

HECTOR   Is this Achilles?   234

ACHILLES   I am Achilles.

HECTOR
Stand fair, I pray thee. Let me look on thee.   236

216–17 **Since . . . embassy** (Hector refers to a non-Homeric
episode, early in the war, when Ulysses and Diomedes visited Troy
to offer peace in return for Helen.)   220 **pertly front** boldly
stand before   221 **wanton** insolent, reckless. (With suggestion
of amorousness in the metaphor of kissing.)   **buss** kiss
223 **modestly** without exaggeration   231 **forestall** prevent
234 **quoted joint by joint** scrutinized limb by limb.   236 **fair** in
full view

ACHILLES
 Behold thy fill.

HECTOR   Nay, I have done already.

ACHILLES
 Thou art too brief. I will the second time,
 As I would buy thee, view thee limb by limb.

HECTOR
 Oh, like a book of sport thou'lt read me o'er;
 But there's more in me than thou understand'st.
 Why dost thou so oppress me with thine eye?

ACHILLES
 Tell me, you heavens, in which part of his body
 Shall I destroy him? Whether there, or there, or there?
 That I may give the local wound a name
 And make distinct the very breach whereout
 Hector's great spirit flew. Answer me, heavens!

HECTOR
 It would discredit the blest gods, proud man,
 To answer such a question. Stand again.
 Think'st thou to catch my life so pleasantly   250
 As to prenominate in nice conjecture   251
 Where thou wilt hit me dead?

ACHILLES   I tell thee, yea.

HECTOR
 Wert thou the oracle to tell me so,
 I'd not believe thee. Henceforth guard thee well;
 For I'll not kill thee there, nor there, nor there,
 But, by the forge that stithied Mars his helm,   256
 I'll kill thee everywhere, yea, o'er and o'er.—
 You wisest Grecians, pardon me this brag;

---

250 **pleasantly** jocosely, easily   251 **prenominate** name
beforehand.   **nice** precise   256 **stithied Mars his helm**
forged Mars's helmet

His insolence draws folly from my lips.
But I'll endeavor deeds to match these words,
Or may I never—

AJAX   Do not chafe thee, cousin.   261
And you, Achilles, let these threats alone,   262
Till accident or purpose bring you to't.   263
You may have every day enough of Hector,
If you have stomach. The general state, I fear,   265
Can scarce entreat you to be odd with him.   266

HECTOR [to Achilles]
I pray you, let us see you in the field.
We have had pelting wars since you refused   268
The Grecians' cause.

ACHILLES   Dost thou entreat me, Hector?
Tomorrow do I meet thee, fell as death;   270
Tonight all friends.

HECTOR   Thy hand upon that match.

                              [They grasp hands.]

AGAMEMNON
First, all you peers of Greece, go to my tent;
There in the full convive we. Afterwards,   273
As Hector's leisure and your bounties shall
Concur together, severally entreat him.   275
Beat loud the taborins, let the trumpets blow,   276
That this great soldier may his welcome know.

        [Flourish.] Exeunt [all except Troilus and Ulysses].

261 **chafe thee** anger yourself   262–3 **let . . . to't** stop making
such boastful threats until, by accident or on purpose, you come
face to face with Hector.   265 **stomach** appetite (for fighting).
general state i.e., Greek commanders in council   266 **be odd**
be at odds, undertake to fight   268 **pelting** paltry   270 **fell**
fierce   273 **convive we** let us feast together.   275 **severally**
entreat individually invite   276 **taborins** drums

TROILUS
    My lord Ulysses, tell me, I beseech you,
    In what place of the field doth Calchas keep?   279

ULYSSES
    At Menelaus' tent, most princely Troilus.
    There Diomed doth feast with him tonight,
    Who neither looks on heaven nor on earth
    But gives all gaze and bent of amorous view
    On the fair Cressid.

TROILUS
    Shall I, sweet lord, be bound to you so much,
    After we part from Agamemnon's tent,
    To bring me thither?

ULYSSES   You shall command me, sir.
    As gentle tell me, of what honor was   288
    This Cressida in Troy? Had she no lover there
    That wails her absence?

TROILUS
    Oh, sir, to such as boasting show their scars   291
    A mock is due. Will you walk on, my lord?
    She was beloved, she loved; she is, and doth.
    But still sweet love is food for fortune's tooth.   294

                             Exeunt.

---

279 **keep** dwell.   288 **As gentle** Be so courteous as to.
honor reputation   291 **such as** those who   294 **But . . .**
tooth i.e., Love will always prove to be the plaything (literally, the
sweet tooth) of fickle Fortune.

[5.1] ✒ *Enter Achilles and Patroclus.*

ACHILLES
   I'll heat his blood with Greekish wine tonight,
   Which with my scimitar I'll cool tomorrow.   2
   Patroclus, let us feast him to the height.

PATROCLUS
   Here comes Thersites.

     Enter Thersites.

ACHILLES   How now, thou core of envy!   4
   Thou crusty batch of nature, what's the news?   5

THERSITES   Why, thou picture of what thou seemest   6
   and idol of idiot-worshipers, here's a letter for thee.

ACHILLES   From whence, fragment?   8

THERSITES   Why, thou full dish of fool, from Troy.

             [*He gives a letter. Achilles reads it.*]

PATROCLUS   Who keeps the tent now?   10

THERSITES   The surgeon's box, or the patient's wound.   11

PATROCLUS   Well said, adversity! And what need these   12
   tricks?

THERSITES   Prithee, be silent, boy. I profit not by thy
   talk. Thou art thought to be Achilles's male varlet.

PATROCLUS   Male varlet, you rogue? What's that?

5.1 *Location: The Greek camp. Before Achilles's tent.*
2 **scimitar** sword. (Literally, a short, curved, single-bladed sword.)
4 **core** central hard mass of a boil or tumor   5 **batch of nature**
sample of humankind in its unimproved natural state   6 **picture**
mere image   8 **fragment** leftover, crust.   10 **Who . . . now?**
i.e., Who is looking after or occupying Achilles's tent these days?
(Patroclus implies that Achilles can no longer be taunted with
languishing here.)   11 **surgeon's box** (Thersites puns on *tent* in
the previous line, i.e., a probe for cleaning a wound.)
12 **adversity** perversity, contrariety.

THERSITES   Why, his masculine whore. Now, the rotten
diseases of the south, the guts-griping, ruptures, 18
catarrhs, loads o'gravel i'th' back, lethargies, cold 19
palsies, raw eyes, dirt-rotten livers, wheezing lungs, 20
bladders full of imposthume, sciaticas, limekilns 21
i'th' palm, incurable bone-ache, and the riveled fee sim- 22
ple of the tetter, take and take again such preposterous 23
discoveries!   24

PATROCLUS   Why, thou damnable box of envy, thou,
what mean'st thou to curse thus?

THERSITES   Do I curse thee?

PATROCLUS   Why, no, you ruinous butt, you whoreson 28
indistinguishable cur, no.   29

THERSITES   No? Why art thou then exasperate, thou idle 30
immaterial skein of sleave silk, thou green sarcenet 31
flap for a sore eye, thou tassel of a prodigal's purse, 32
thou? Ah, how the poor world is pestered with such
waterflies, diminutives of nature!

PATROCLUS   Out, gall!   35

THERSITES   Finch egg!   36

18–24 **guts-griping . . . discoveries!** may abdominal spasms,
hernias, respiratory infections, severe cases of kidney stones,
lethargy, paralysis, eye inflammations, liver diseases, asthma,
abscesses of the bladder, lower back pain, gout or psoriasis,
syphilitic bone-ache, and incurable wrinkling caused by skin
eruptions strike repeatedly with disease such unnatural perversions
as are discovered here!   28 **ruinous butt** dilapidated cask
29 **indistinguishable** misshapen   30 **exasperate** exasperated,
angry   30–2 **thou idle . . . purse** you useless, flimsy coil of
floss silk, you eye-patch of soft green silk, you fringed ornamental
pendant on a spendthrift's purse   31 **skein** coil.   **sleave silk**
floss silk, i.e., unwoven and hence worthless (*immaterial*).
sarcenet fine, soft silk   35 **gall** (1) bitter railer (2) blister.
36 **Finch egg** (The finch is a small bird.)

ACHILLES
My sweet Patroclus, I am thwarted quite
From my great purpose in tomorrow's battle.
Here is a letter from Queen Hecuba,
A token from her daughter, my fair love,
Both taxing me and gaging me to keep   41
An oath that I have sworn. I will not break it.
Fall, Greeks; fail, fame; honor, or go or stay.   43
My major vow lies here; this I'll obey.
Come, come, Thersites, help to trim my tent.   45
This night in banqueting must all be spent.
Away, Patroclus!   *Exit [with Patroclus].*

THERSITES   With too much blood and too little brain,   48
these two may run mad; but if with too much brain   49
and too little blood they do, I'll be a curer of madmen.   50
Here's Agamemnon, an honest fellow enough and   51
one that loves quails, but he has not so much brain as   52
earwax. And the goodly transformation of Jupiter   53
there, his brother, the bull—the primitive statue and   54
oblique memorial of cuckolds, a thrifty shoeing-horn   55
in a chain, hanging at his brother's leg—to what form   56

41 **taxing** urging.   **gaging** binding, pledging   43 **or go** either
go   45 **trim** prepare   48 **blood** passion, willfulness
49–50 **but . . . madmen** (Thersites considers it extremely unlikely
that Patroclus and Achilles should ever suffer from too much
intelligence or a lack of willful behavior; it's about as likely as if
he, Thersites, could cure mad folk.)   51 **honest . . . enough**
good enough chap   52 **quails** i.e., prostitutes. (Cant term.)
53–4 **transformation . . . bull** (Alludes ironically to the myth of
Jupiter's rape of Europa, whom he encountered in a meadow after
changing himself into a bull. Thersites has in mind the bull's
horns, which are like Menelaus's cuckold's horns.)   54–5 **the
primitive . . . cuckolds** i.e., the prototype and indirect reminder
of cuckolds in having horns   55–6 **a thrifty . . . leg** i.e., a
convenient tool, always available to do Agamemnon's will (the
shoeing-horn having been suggested in Thersites's mind by the
cuckold's horns)

but that he is should wit larded with malice and mal-   57
ice farced with wit turn him to? To an ass were noth-   58
ing, he is both ass and ox; to an ox were nothing, he's   59
both ox and ass. To be a dog, a mule, a cat, a fitchew,   60
a toad, a lizard, an owl, a puttock, or a herring   61
without a roe, I would not care; but to be Menelaus! I   62
would conspire against destiny. Ask me not what I
would be if I were not Thersites, for I care not to be   64
the louse of a lazar, so I were not Menelaus. Heyday!   65
Sprites and fires!   66

> *Enter [Hector, Troilus, Ajax,] Agamemnon,*
> *Ulysses, Nestor, [Menelaus,] and Diomed[es],*
> *with lights.*

AGAMEMNON
We go wrong, we go wrong.

AJAX   No, yonder 'tis,
There, where we see the light.

HECTOR   I trouble you.

AJAX
No, not a whit.

> *[Enter Achilles.]*

ULYSSES   Here comes himself to guide you.

ACHILLES
Welcome, brave Hector; welcome, princes all.

56–8 to what . . . him to? to what new shape other than his own
should my malicious wit and witty malice transform him? (*Farced*
means covered, adorned, stuffed, seasoned; or *faced*, trimmed.)
58–9 To . . . nothing To transform him into an ass would be to
accomplish nothing at all   **60 fitchew** polecat   **61 puttock**
bird of prey of the kite kind   **61–2 a herring . . . roe** i.e., a
sexually emaciated or "spent" herring   **64 I care not to be** I
wouldn't mind being   **65 lazar** leper.   **so** provided
66 Sprites and fires (Thersites sees those who are entering with
lights, reminding him of will-o'-the-wisps and other spirits.)

AGAMEMNON
    So now, fair Prince of Troy, I bid good night.
    Ajax commands the guard to tend on you.

HECTOR
    Thanks and good night to the Greeks' general.

MENELAUS   Good night, my lord.

HECTOR   Good night, sweet Lord Menelaus.

THERSITES [aside]   Sweet draft. "Sweet," quoth 'a?   76
    Sweet sink, sweet sewer.   77

ACHILLES
    Good night and welcome, both at once, to those
    That go or tarry.

AGAMEMNON   Good night.

                    Exeunt Agamemnon [and] Menelaus.

ACHILLES
    Old Nestor tarries; and you too, Diomed,
    Keep Hector company an hour or two.

DIOMEDES
    I cannot, lord. I have important business,
    The tide whereof is now. Good night, great Hector.   84

HECTOR   Give me your hand.

ULYSSES [aside to Troilus]
    Follow his torch; he goes to Calchas' tent.   86
    I'll keep you company.

TROILUS [aside to Ulysses]   Sweet sir, you honor me.

HECTOR
    And so, good night.

            [Exit Diomedes; Ulysses and Troilus following.]

76 **Sweet draft** Sweet cesspool. (An ironic echo of Hector's
"sweet Lord Menelaus," line 75.)   **'a** he   77 **sink** privy
84 **tide** time   86 **his** Diomedes's

ACHILLES   Come, come, enter my tent.

Exeunt [Achilles, Hector, Ajax, and Nestor].

THERSITES   That same Diomed's a false-hearted rogue, a
most unjust knave. I will no more trust him when he   90
leers than I will a serpent when he hisses. He will   91
spend his mouth and promise, like Brabbler the   92
hound, but when he performs, astronomers foretell it; 93
it is prodigious, there will come some change. The sun 94
borrows of the moon when Diomed keeps his word.   95
I will rather leave to see Hector than not to dog him. 96
They say he keeps a Trojan drab and uses the traitor   97
Calchas his tent. I'll after. Nothing but lechery! All incon- 98
tinent varlets!   *[Exit.]*   99

[5.2] ᏉᎦ *Enter Diomedes.*

DIOMEDES   What, are you up here, ho? Speak.

CALCHAS *[within]*   Who calls?

DIOMEDES
Diomed. Calchas, I think. Where's your daughter?

CALCHAS *[within]*   She comes to you.

*[Enter Troilus and Ulysses at a distance; after
them, Thersites.]*

90 **unjust** dishonest, perfidious   91–2 **He . . . promise** He will
bay loudly as though promising that he has caught the scent
92 **Brabbler** (An apt name for such a noisy hound.)
93–4 **astronomers . . . change** i.e., it is a rare and portentous
event.   95 **borrows of** borrows reflected light from (reversing
the natural superiority of the sun—something that will never
happen)   96 **leave to see** cease looking upon.   **him**
Diomedes.   97 **drab** whore.   **uses** frequents
98–9 **incontinent** (1) unchaste (2) incorrigible

*5.2 Location: The Greek camp. Before the tent where Calchas
stays with Menelaus. See 4.5.279–87.*

ULYSSES [*to Troilus*]
  Stand where the torch may not discover us.   5

          [*He and Troilus conceal themselves in one place,*
              Thersites in another. In the ensuing dialogue,
              Ulysses and Troilus continue to speak in asides
                  to each other; Thersites utters his asides in
                      commentary on the entire scene.]

      Enter Cressida.

TROILUS
  Cressid comes forth to him.

DIOMEDES [*to Cressida*]   How now, my charge?   6

CRESSIDA
  Now, my sweet guardian! Hark, a word with you.

                          [*She whispers.*]

TROILUS   Yea, so familiar?

ULYSSES   She will sing any man at first sight.   9

THERSITES [*aside*]   And any man may sing her, if he can
  take her clef. She's noted.   11

DIOMEDES   Will you remember?

CRESSIDA   Remember? Yes.

DIOMEDES   Nay, but do, then,
  And let your mind be coupled with your words.

TROILUS   What should she remember?

ULYSSES   List.   17

CRESSIDA
  Sweet honey Greek, tempt me no more to folly.

---

5 **discover** reveal   6 **charge** person entrusted to my care.
9 **sing** i.e., sing the Sirens' song to; play upon   11 **clef** key. (With
obscene pun on on "cleft," i.e., vulva.)   **noted** set to music.
(With pun on the meaning "known," i.e., notorious, or "used
sexually.")   17 **List** Listen.

THERSITES [*aside*] Roguery!

DIOMEDES Nay, then—

CRESSIDA I'll tell you what—

DIOMEDES
  Foh, foh! Come, tell a pin. You are forsworn.   22

CRESSIDA
  In faith, I cannot. What would you have me do?   23

THERSITES [*aside*] A juggling trick—to be secretly   24
open.   25

DIOMEDES
  What did you swear you would bestow on me?

CRESSIDA
  I prithee, do not hold me to mine oath.
  Bid me do anything but that, sweet Greek.

DIOMEDES Good night.   [*He starts to go.*]

TROILUS Hold, patience!

ULYSSES How now, Trojan?

CRESSIDA Diomed—

DIOMEDES
  No, no, good night. I'll be your fool no more.   33

TROILUS Thy better must.   34

CRESSIDA Hark, one word in your ear.

TROILUS Oh, plague and madness!

ULYSSES
  You are moved, Prince. Let us depart, I pray you,
  Lest your displeasure should enlarge itself

---

22 **tell a pin** i.e., don't trifle with me.   23 **I cannot** i.e., I cannot do what I promised.   24 **juggling trick** magic trick (since to be *secretly open* is an apparent contradiction in terms)   25 **open** (1) frank (2) sexually available.   33 **fool** dupe   34 **Thy better must** i.e., Better men than you (including myself) must play the fool to women like Cressida.

To wrathful terms. This place is dangerous,   39
The time right deadly. I beseech you, go.

                        [He tries to lead Troilus away.]

TROILUS
Behold, I pray you!

ULYSSES   Nay, good my lord, go off.
You flow to great distraction. Come, my lord.   42

TROILUS
I prithee, stay.

ULYSSES   You have not patience. Come.

TROILUS
I pray you, stay. By hell and all hell's torments,
I will not speak a word!

DIOMEDES
And so, good night.   *[He starts to go.]*

CRESSIDA   Nay, but you part in anger.

TROILUS
Doth that grieve thee? Oh, witherèd truth!

ULYSSES
Why, how now, lord?

TROILUS   By Jove, I will be patient.

CRESSIDA
Guardian!—Why, Greek!

DIOMEDES   Foh, foh! Adieu. You palter.   49

CRESSIDA
In faith, I do not. Come hither once again.

---

39 wrathful terms i.e., a fight.   **42 You . . . distraction** Your
overfull heart will vent itself in emotional turmoil.   **49 palter**
use trickery.

ULYSSES
    You shake, my lord, at something. Will you go?
    You will break out.

TROILUS   She strokes his cheek!

ULYSSES   Come, Come.

TROILUS
    Nay, stay. By Jove, I will not speak a word.
    There is between my will and all offenses   54
    A guard of patience. Stay a little while.   55

THERSITES [aside]   How the devil Luxury, with his fat   56
    rump and potato finger, tickles these together! Fry,   57
    lechery, fry!

DIOMEDES [to Cressida]   But will you, then?

CRESSIDA
    In faith, I will, la. Never trust me else.

DIOMEDES
    Give me some token for the surety of it.

CRESSIDA   I'll fetch you one.   Exit.

ULYSSES
    You have sworn patience.

TROILUS   Fear me not, sweet lord.
    I will not be myself, nor have cognition
    Of what I feel. I am all patience.

        Enter Cressida, [with Troilus's sleeve].

THERSITES [aside]   Now the pledge; now, now, now!

CRESSIDA   Here, Diomed, keep this sleeve.

                        [She gives it to him.]

54–5 **There . . . patience** I have patience to interpose between my
anger and the violence it would commit.   56 **Luxury** Lechery
57 **potato finger** (Potatoes were accounted stimulants to lechery.)
Fry Burn (with passion)

TROILUS
  O beauty, where is thy faith?

ULYSSES   My lord—

TROILUS
  I will be patient; outwardly I will.

CRESSIDA
  You look upon that sleeve. Behold it well.
  He loved me—O false wench!—Give 't me again.
                              [*She takes it back again.*]

DIOMEDES   Whose was 't?

CRESSIDA
  It is no matter, now I ha 't again.
  I will not meet with you tomorrow night.
  I prithee, Diomed, visit me no more.

THERSITES [*aside*]   Now she sharpens. Well said, whet-   76
  stone!

DIOMEDES
  I shall have it.

CRESSIDA   What, this?

DIOMEDES   Ay, that.

CRESSIDA
  O all you gods! O pretty, pretty pledge!
  Thy master now lies thinking on his bed
  Of thee and me, and sighs, and takes my glove,
  And gives memorial dainty kisses to it,   82
  As I kiss thee. Nay, do not snatch it from me;
  He that takes that doth take my heart withal.   84

DIOMEDES
  I had your heart before; this follows it.

76 **sharpens** whets his appetite.   82 **memorial** in loving
remembrance   84 **withal** with it.

TROILUS   I did swear patience.

CRESSIDA
You shall not have it, Diomed, faith, you shall not.   87
I'll give you something else.

DIOMEDES   I will have this. Whose was it?

                              [*He gets the sleeve from her.*]

CRESSIDA   It is no matter.

DIOMEDES   Come, tell me whose it was.

CRESSIDA
'Twas one's that loved me better than you will.
But, now you have it, take it.

DIOMEDES   Whose was it?

CRESSIDA
By all Diana's waiting-women yond,   94
And by herself, I will not tell you whose.

DIOMEDES
Tomorrow will I wear it on my helm
And grieve his spirit that dares not challenge it.   97

TROILUS
Wert thou the devil, and wor'st it on thy horn,   98
It should be challenged.

CRESSIDA
Well, well, 'tis done, 'tis past. And yet it is not;
I will not keep my word.

DIOMEDES   Why, then, farewell.
Thou never shalt mock Diomed again.

                              [*He starts to go.*]

---

87 **faith** in faith   94 **Diana's . . . yond** i.e., yonder stars. (Diana
is the moon goddess and, ironically, the goddess of chastity.)
97 **grieve his spirit** afflict the spirit of him   98 **wor'st** wore

CRESSIDA
   You shall not go. One cannot speak a word
   But it straight starts you.

DIOMEDES   I do not like this fooling.   104

THERSITES [*aside*]   Nor I, by Pluto; but that that likes not   105
   you pleases me best.

DIOMEDES   What, shall I come? The hour?

CRESSIDA
   Ay, come—O Jove!—do come—I shall be plagued.

DIOMEDES
   Farewell till then.   [*Exit Diomedes.*]

CRESSIDA   Good night. I prithee, come.—
   Troilus, farewell! One eye yet looks on thee,
   But with my heart the other eye doth see.   111
   Ah, poor our sex! This fault in us I find:
   The error of our eye directs our mind.
   What error leads must err. Oh, then conclude:
   Minds swayed by eyes are full of turpitude.   *Exit.*   115

THERSITES [*aside*]
   A proof of strength she could not publish more,   116
   Unless she said, "My mind is now turned whore."

ULYSSES
   All's done, my lord.

TROILUS   It is.

ULYSSES   Why stay we, then?

TROILUS
   To make a recordation to my soul   119
   Of every syllable that here was spoke.

---

104 **straight starts you** immediately starts you off on some
abrupt action.   105 **likes** pleases   111 **heart** i.e., sexual desire
and longing for security   115 **turpitude** wickedness.   116 **A
proof . . . more** She could not put the case in more forceful
terms. (*Publish* here means "announce," as in publishing printed
material.)   119 **recordation** record

But if I tell how these two did coact,
Shall I not lie in publishing a truth?
Sith yet there is a credence in my heart,   123
An esperance so obstinately strong,   124
That doth invert th'attest of eyes and ears,   125
As if those organs had deceptious functions   126
Created only to calumniate.   127
Was Cressid here?

ULYSSES   I cannot conjure, Trojan.

TROILUS
She was not, sure.

ULYSSES   Most sure she was.

TROILUS
Why, my negation hath no taste of madness.   130

ULYSSES
Nor mine, my lord. Cressid was here but now.

TROILUS
Let it not be believed, for womanhood!   132
Think, we had mothers. Do not give advantage
To stubborn critics, apt, without a theme   134
For depravation, to square the general sex   135
By Cressid's rule. Rather think this not Cressid.   136

ULYSSES
What hath she done, Prince, that can soil our
    mothers?

TROILUS
Nothing at all, unless that this were she.

123 **Sith** Since.   **credence** belief   124 **esperance** hope
125 **th'attest** the witness   126 **deceptious** deceiving
127 **calumniate** slander, defame.   130 **negation** denial
132 **for** for the sake of   134 **stubborn** hostile   134–6 **apt . . .
rule** apt enough, even when they lack grounds for negative
comment, to make Cressida the standard by which all womankind
is measured. (To *square* is to use a carpenter's square or measuring
tool.)

THERSITES [*aside*]   Will 'a swagger himself out on 's own   139
eyes?   140

TROILUS
This she? No, this is Diomed's Cressida.
If beauty have a soul, this is not she;
If souls guide vows, if vows be sanctimonies,   143
If sanctimony be the gods' delight,
If there be rule in unity itself,   145
This is not she. Oh, madness of discourse,   146
That cause sets up with and against itself!   147
Bifold authority, where reason can revolt   148
Without perdition, and loss assume all reason   149
Without revolt! This is and is not Cressid.   150
Within my soul there doth conduce a fight   151
Of this strange nature, that a thing inseparate   152
Divides more wider than the sky and earth,
And yet the spacious breadth of this division
Admits no orifex for a point as subtle   155
As Ariachne's broken woof to enter.   156
Instance, oh, instance, strong as Pluto's gates,   157
Cressid is mine, tied with the bonds of heaven;
Instance, oh, instance, strong as heaven itself,

139–40 **Will . . . eyes?** Will he succeed, with his blustering talk, in
denying the evidence of his own eyes?   143 **sanctimonies**
sacred things   145 **If . . . itself** i.e., if an entity (like Cressida)
can only be itself and not two entities   146–7 **Oh . . . itself!** Oh,
mad and paradoxical reasoning, that sets up an argument for and
against the very proposition being debated!   148–50 **Bifold . . .
revolt!** Inherent contradiction, when reason can revolt against
itself (by denying the testimony of the senses that this is indeed
Cressida) without actually seeming to contradict itself!
151 **conduce** take place   152 **a thing inseparate** i.e., Cressida,
an indivisible entity   155–6 **Admits . . . enter** provides
an orifice only as large as the tiny thickness of a spider's web.
(Arachne [the normal spelling] challenged Minerva to a weaving
contest; the goddess became angered, tore up Arachne's work, and
turned her into a spider.)   157 **Instance** Proof, evidence.
Pluto's gates the gates of hell

The bonds of heaven are slipped, dissolved, and
   loosed,
And with another knot, five-finger-tied,   161
The fractions of her faith, orts of her love,   162
The fragments, scraps, the bits and greasy relics
Of her o'ereaten faith, are bound to Diomed.   164

ULYSSES
May worthy Troilus be half attached   165
With that which here his passion doth express?

TROILUS
Ay, Greek; and that shall be divulgèd well
In characters as red as Mars his heart   168
Inflamed with Venus. Never did young man fancy   169
With so eternal and so fixed a soul.
Hark, Greek: as much as I do Cressid love,
So much by weight hate I her Diomed.   172
That sleeve is mine that he'll bear on his helm.
Were it a casque composed by Vulcan's skill,   174
My sword should bite it. Not the dreadful spout   175
Which shipmen do the hurricano call,
Constringèd in mass by the almighty sun,   177
Shall dizzy with more clamor Neptune's ear   178
In his descent than shall my prompted sword
Falling on Diomed.

THERSITES [aside]   He'll tickle it for his concupy.   181

---

161 **five-finger-tied** i.e., tied indissolubly by giving her hand to
Diomedes   162 **fractions** fragments.   **orts** leftovers, fragments
164 **o'ereaten** i.e., surfeiting through overfeeding, or begnawed,
eaten away   165 **half attached** half as much affected (as it
appears)   168 **red** bloody. (Troilus will manifest his passion now in
warlike deeds.)   **Mars his** Mars's   169 **fancy** love
172 **So . . . weight** to the same extent   174 **casque** headpiece,
helmet   175 **spout** waterspout   177 **Constringèd** compressed
178 **dizzy** make dizzy   181 **He'll . . . concupy** He'll rain ineffectual
blows on Diomed's helmet, fighting it out with Diomed for the sake
of his concubine (Cressida) and his concupiscence (his lust).

TROILUS

    O Cressid! O false Cressid! False, false, false!
    Let all untruths stand by thy stainèd name,
    And they'll seem glorious.

ULYSSES   Oh, contain yourself.
    Your passion draws ears hither.

    Enter Aeneas.

AENEAS

    I have been seeking you this hour, my lord.
    Hector, by this, is arming him in Troy;   187
    Ajax, your guard, stays to conduct you home.

TROILUS

    Have with you, Prince.—My courteous lord, adieu.   189
    Farewell, revolted fair! And, Diomed,
    Stand fast, and wear a castle on thy head!   191

ULYSSES   I'll bring you to the gates.

TROILUS   Accept distracted thanks.

                Exeunt Troilus, Aeneas, and Ulysses.

THERSITES   Would I could meet that rogue Diomed! I
    would croak like a raven; I would bode, I would bode.   195
    Patroclus will give me anything for the intelligence of   196
    this whore. The parrot will not do more for an almond
    than he for a commodious drab. Lechery, lechery, still   198
    wars and lechery; nothing else holds fashion. A burn-   199
    ing devil take them!   *Exit.*   200

---

187 **him** himself   189 **Have . . . Prince** I am ready to go with
you, Aeneas.   **lord** Ulysses   191 **castle** fortress, i.e., strong
helmet   195 **bode** warn, prognosticate   196 **intelligence of**
information about   198 **commodious drab** accommodating
harlot.   199–200 **A burning . . . them!** (1) May a devil take
them all to hell! (2) May venereal disease infect them!

[5.3] ∽ *Enter Hector, [armed,] and Andromache.*

ANDROMACHE
When was my lord so much ungently tempered
To stop his ears against admonishment?
Unarm, unarm, and do not fight today.

HECTOR
You train me to offend you. Get you in.   4
By all the everlasting gods, I'll go!

ANDROMACHE
My dreams will, sure, prove ominous to the day.   6

HECTOR
No more, I say.

    Enter Cassandra.

CASSANDRA   Where is my brother Hector?

ANDROMACHE
Here, sister, armed, and bloody in intent.
Consort with me in loud and dear petition;   9
Pursue we him on knees. For I have dreamt
Of bloody turbulence, and this whole night
Hath nothing been but shapes and forms of slaughter.

CASSANDRA
Oh, 'tis true.

HECTOR [*calling*]   Ho! Bid my trumpet sound.

CASSANDRA
No notes of sally, for the heavens, sweet brother.   14

HECTOR
Begone, I say. The gods have heard me swear.

5.3 Location: Troy. The palace.
4 **train** tempt, induce   6 **ominous to** prophetic regarding
9 **Consort** Join.   **dear** ardent   14 **sally** sallying, going forth to
battle.   **for the heavens** for heaven's sake

CASSANDRA
    The gods are deaf to hot and peevish vows.   16
    They are polluted off'rings, more abhorred
    Than spotted livers in the sacrifice.   18

ANDROMACHE
    Oh, be persuaded! Do not count it holy
    To hurt by being just. It is as lawful,
    For we would give much, to use violent thefts,   21
    And rob in the behalf of charity.

CASSANDRA
    It is the purpose that makes strong the vow,
    But vows to every purpose must not hold.   24
    Unarm, sweet Hector.

HECTOR   Hold you still, I say.
    Mine honor keeps the weather of my fate.   26
    Life every man holds dear, but the dear man   27
    Holds honor far more precious-dear than life.

    Enter Troilus.

    How now, young man, mean'st thou to fight today?

ANDROMACHE
    Cassandra, call my father to persuade.   30

                     Exit Cassandra.

HECTOR
    No, faith, young Troilus, doff thy harness, youth;   31
    I am today i'th' vein of chivalry.
    Let grow thy sinews till their knots be strong,

16 **peevish** headstrong   18 **spotted** tainted and hence ill-omened   21 **For . . . give** because we want to give 24 **vows . . . hold** not every vow must be held sacred (since not all purposes are valid).   26 **keeps the weather of** keeps to the windward side of (for tactical advantage), takes precedence over 27 **dear man** worthy man, man of nobility   30 **father** father-in-law, i.e., Priam   31 **doff thy harness** take off your armor

And tempt not yet the brushes of the war.   34
Unarm thee, go, and doubt thou not, brave boy,
I'll stand today for thee and me and Troy.

TROILUS
Brother, you have a vice of mercy in you,
Which better fits a lion than a man.   38

HECTOR
What vice is that? Good Troilus, chide me for it.

TROILUS
When many times the captive Grecian falls,   40
Even in the fan and wind of your fair sword,
You bid them rise and live.

HECTOR
Oh, 'tis fair play.

TROILUS   Fool's play, by heaven, Hector.

HECTOR
How now, how now?

TROILUS   For th' love of all the gods,
Let's leave the hermit Pity with our mothers,
And when we have our armors buckled on,
The venomed vengeance ride upon our swords,   47
Spur them to ruthful work, rein them from ruth.   48

HECTOR
Fie, savage, fie!

TROILUS   Hector, then 'tis wars.   49

HECTOR
Troilus, I would not have you fight today.

34 **tempt** attempt, assay.   **brushes** hostile encounters
38 **better fits a lion** (Lions were thought to be merciful to
submissive prey.)   40 **captive** overpowered in battle, wretched
47 **The venomed vengeance** may the envenomed spirit of
vengeance   48 **ruthful** lamentable, i.e., causing lamentation.
ruth pity, mercy.   49 **then 'tis wars** i.e., war is like that.

TROILUS   Who should withhold me?
   Not fate, obedience, nor the hand of Mars
   Beck'ning with fiery truncheon my retire,   53
   Not Priamus and Hecuba on knees,
   Their eyes o'ergallèd with recourse of tears,   55
   Nor you, my brother, with your true sword drawn
   Opposed to hinder me, should stop my way,
   But by my ruin.

    Enter Priam and Cassandra.

CASSANDRA
   Lay hold upon him, Priam, hold him fast;
   He is thy crutch. Now if thou loose thy stay,   60
   Thou on him leaning, and all Troy on thee,
   Fall all together.

PRIAM   Come, Hector, come. Go back.
   Thy wife hath dreamt, thy mother hath had visions,
   Cassandra doth foresee, and I myself
   Am like a prophet suddenly enrapt   65
   To tell thee that this day is ominous.
   Therefore, come back.

HECTOR   Aeneas is afield,
   And I do stand engaged to many Greeks,
   Even in the faith of valor, to appear   69
   This morning to them.

PRIAM   Ay, but thou shalt not go.

HECTOR   I must not break my faith.
   You know me dutiful; therefore, dear sir,
   Let me not shame respect, but give me leave   73

---

53 **Beck'ning . . . retire** beckoning me with a flaming baton to
withdraw   55 **o'ergallèd . . . tears** inflamed with the flow of
tears   60 **loose thy stay** let go your prop   65 **enrapt** carried
away, inspired   69 **the faith of valor** a warrior's honor
73 **shame respect** i.e., violate my filial duty

To take that course by your consent and voice
Which you do here forbid me, royal Priam.

CASSANDRA
O Priam, yield not to him!

ANDROMACHE   Do not, dear father.

HECTOR
Andromache, I am offended with you.
Upon the love you bear me, get you in.

                              Exit Andromache.

TROILUS
This foolish, dreaming, superstitious girl
Makes all these bodements.

CASSANDRA   Oh, farewell, dear Hector!   80
Look how thou diest! Look how thy eye turns pale!
Look how thy wounds do bleed at many vents!
Hark, how Troy roars, how Hecuba cries out,
How poor Andromache shrills her dolors forth!   84
Behold, distraction, frenzy, and amazement,
Like witless antics, one another meet,   86
And all cry, "Hector! Hector's dead! Oh, Hector!"

TROILUS   Away! away!

CASSANDRA
Farewell. Yet soft! Hector, I take my leave.   89
Thou dost thyself and all our Troy deceive.   [*Exit.*]

HECTOR
You are amazed, my liege, at her exclaim.   91
Go in and cheer the town. We'll forth and fight,
Do deeds of praise, and tell you them at night.

---

80 **Makes** causes.   **bodements** omens of ill fortune.
84 **shrills her dolors** wails her grief   86 **antics** fools   89 **soft**
i.e., gently; wait.   91 **amazed** dumbstruck.   **exclaim** outcry.

PRIAM

Farewell. The gods with safety stand about thee!

[*Exeunt Priam and Hector separately.*] *Alarum.*

TROILUS

They are at it, hark!—Proud Diomed, believe,
I come to lose my arm, or win my sleeve.

Enter Pandarus.

PANDARUS   Do you hear, my lord? Do you hear?

TROILUS   What now?

PANDARUS   Here's a letter come from yond poor girl.

[*He gives a letter.*]

TROILUS   Let me read.

PANDARUS   A whoreson phthisic, a whoreson rascally   101
phthisic so troubles me, and the foolish fortune of this
girl, and what one thing, what another, that I shall
leave you one o' these days. And I have a rheum in   104
mine eyes, too, and such an ache in my bones that,
unless a man were cursed, I cannot tell what to think
on't.—What says she there?

TROILUS

Words, words, mere words, no matter from the heart;
Th'effect doth operate another way.   109

[*He tears the letter and tosses it away.*]

Go, wind, to wind! There turn and change together.   110
My love with words and errors still she feeds,   111
But edifies another with her deeds.   *Exeunt.*   112

___

101 **phthisic** consumptive cough   104 **rheum** watery discharge
109 **Th'effect . . . way** i.e., her actions belie her words.
110 **Go, wind, to wind!** Go, empty words, to the air!
111 **errors** deceits   112 **edifies** i.e., elevates to the role of being
her lover   112 s.d. *Exeunt* (In the Folio version, Pandarus is
angrily dismissed at this point using the lines printed by the
quarto at 5.10.32–4.)

[5.4] ❧ *[Alarum.] Enter Thersites. Excursions.*

THERSITES   Now they are clapper-clawing one another.   1
I'll go look on. That dissembling abominable varlet,
Diomed, has got that same scurvy doting foolish
young knave's sleeve of Troy there in his helm. I
would fain see them meet, that that same young
Trojan ass that loves the whore there might send that
Greekish whoremasterly villain with the sleeve back to
the dissembling luxurious drab, of a sleeveless errand.   8
O'th'other side, the policy of those crafty swearing   9
rascals—that stale old mouse-eaten dry cheese,
Nestor, and that same dog-fox, Ulysses—is proved   11
not worth a blackberry. They set me up, in policy,   12
that mongrel cur, Ajax, against that dog of as bad a
kind, Achilles. And now is the cur Ajax prouder than
the cur Achilles, and will not arm today, whereupon
the Grecians began to proclaim barbarism, and policy   16
grows into an ill opinion.

    [Enter Diomedes, and Troilus following.]

Soft! Here comes Sleeve, and t'other.

**5.4 Location: *Between Troy and the Greek camp. The battlefield is
the setting for the rest of the play.***
0.1 *Excursions* sorties or issuings forth of soldiers   1 **clapper-
clawing** mauling, thrashing   8 **luxurious drab** lecherous slut.
sleeveless futile   9 **policy** craftiness   11 **dog-fox** male fox
12 **set me** set. (*Me* is used colloquially.)   16 **proclaim
barbarism** declare a state of anarchy; they will be governed by
policy or statecraft no longer

TROILUS

Fly not, for shouldst thou take the River Styx,   19
I would swim after.

DIOMEDES   Thou dost miscall retire.   20
I do not fly, but advantageous care   21
Withdrew me from the odds of multitude.   22
Have at thee!   [*They fight.*]

THERSITES   Hold thy whore, Grecian!—Now for thy   24
whore, Trojan!—Now the sleeve, now the sleeve!

          [*Exeunt Troilus and Diomedes, fighting.*]

     Enter Hector.

HECTOR

What art thou, Greek? Art thou for Hector's match?
Art thou of blood and honor?   27

THERSITES   No, no, I am a rascal, a scurvy railing knave,
a very filthy rogue.

HECTOR   I do believe thee. Live.   [*Exit.*]

THERSITES   God-a-mercy, that thou wilt believe me; but   31
a plague break thy neck for frighting me! What's be-
come of the wenching rogues? I think they have swallowed one another. I would laugh at that miracle—
yet, in a sort, lechery eats itself. I'll seek them.   *Exit.*   35

19 **take** enter (by way of escape).   **Styx** river of the underworld
20 **miscall retire** call my tactical withdrawal by the wrong name
of flight.   21–2 **advantageous . . . multitude** desire for better
military advantage prompted me to withdraw from the general
melee, where I faced heavy odds.   24 **Hold** Defend your right
to.   **for** fight for   27 **blood** noble blood   31 **God-a-mercy**
Thank God, thanks   35 **in a sort** in a way

[5.5] ❧ *Enter Diomedes and Servant.*

DIOMEDES
    Go, go, my servant, take thou Troilus' horse;
    Present the fair steed to my lady Cressid.
    Fellow, commend my service to her beauty;
    Tell her I have chastised the amorous Trojan
    And am her knight by proof.

SERVANT   I go, my lord.   [*Exit.*]   5

    Enter Agamemnon.

AGAMEMNON
    Renew, renew! The fierce Polydamas   6
    Hath beat down Menon; bastard Margareton
    Hath Doreus prisoner,
    And stands colossus-wise, waving his beam   9
    Upon the pashèd corpses of the kings   10
    Epistrophus and Cedius; Polyxenes is slain,
    Amphimachus and Thoas deadly hurt,
    Patroclus ta'en or slain, and Palamedes
    Sore hurt and bruised. The dreadful Sagittary   14
    Appals our numbers. Haste we, Diomed,   15
    To reinforcement, or we perish all.

    Enter Nestor [and soldiers].

5.5 Location: As before; the battle continues.
5 **by proof** by proof of arms.   6 **Renew** To it again
9 **colossus-wise** like the Colossus (the great bronze statue of
Apollo at Rhodes, one of the seven wonders of the ancient world).
beam lance   10 **pashèd** battered   14 **Sagittary** (Literally, the
archer; a centaur, i.e., a monster half man, half horse, who
according to medieval legends fought in the Trojan War against
the Greeks.)   15 **Appals our numbers** dismays our troops.

NESTOR

Go, bear Patroclus' body to Achilles,
And bid the snail-paced Ajax arm for shame.

                                        [*Exeunt some.*]

There is a thousand Hectors in the field.
Now here he fights on Galathe his horse,
And there lacks work; anon he's there afoot,
And there they fly or die, like scalèd schools   22
Before the belching whale; then is he yonder,
And there the strawy Greeks, ripe for his edge,   24
Fall down before him, like the mower's swath.   25
Here, there, and everywhere he leaves and takes,   26
Dexterity so obeying appetite
That what he will he does, and does so much
That proof is called impossibility.   29

        Enter Ulysses.

ULYSSES

Oh, courage, courage, princes! Great Achilles
Is arming, weeping, cursing, vowing vengeance.
Patroclus' wounds have roused his drowsy blood,
Together with his mangled Myrmidons,   33
That noseless, handless, hacked and chipped, come
     to him,
Crying on Hector. Ajax hath lost a friend   35
And foams at mouth, and he is armed and at it,
Roaring for Troilus, who hath done today

---

22 **scalèd schools** scattering schools of scaly fish   24 **strawy**
like straw ready for mowing.   **his edge** the edge of his sword
25 **swath** felled row of grain.   26 **he leaves and takes** like a
mower, he drops or *leaves* one cut of the grain and rhythmically
engages the next cut with his scythelike sword   29 **proof** fact,
accomplished deed   33 **Myrmidons** soldiers of Thessaly
(whom Achilles led to Troy)   35 **Crying on** exclaiming against

Mad and fantastic execution,   38
Engaging and redeeming of himself   39
With such a careless force and forceless care   40
As if that luck, in very spite of cunning,   41
Bade him win all.   42

Enter Ajax.

AJAX
Troilus! Thou coward Troilus!   *Exit.*
DIOMEDES   Ay, there, there.   *Exit.*
NESTOR
So, so, we draw together.

Enter Achilles.

ACHILLES   Where is this Hector?   44
Come, come, thou boy-queller, show thy face!   45
Know what it is to meet Achilles angry.
Hector! Where's Hector? I will none but Hector.

Exit [with others].

[5.6] ❧ *Enter Ajax.*

AJAX
Troilus, thou coward Troilus, show thy head!

Enter Diomedes.

38 execution deeds   **39–42 Engaging . . . all** committing
himself to battle and emerging unhurt with such nonchalant use
of strength and effortless self-defense as if Fortune herself cheered
him on to victory, in defiance of his enemies' skill in arms.
44 we draw together i.e., at last we Greeks are pulling together,
with Ajax and Achilles engaged to fight.   **45 boy-queller** boy
killer, i.e., slayer of Patroclus

5.6 Location: As before; the battle continues.

DIOMEDES
    Troilus, I say! Where's Troilus?

AJAX   What wouldst thou?

DIOMEDES   I would correct him.

AJAX
    Were I the general, thou shouldst have my office
    Ere that correction.—Troilus, I say! What, Troilus!   5

    Enter Troilus.

TROILUS
    O traitor Diomed! Turn thy false face, thou traitor,
    And pay the life thou owest me for my horse!

DIOMEDES   Ha, art thou there?

AJAX
    I'll fight with him alone. Stand, Diomed.   9

DIOMEDES
    He is my prize. I will not look upon.   10

TROILUS
    Come, both you cogging Greeks, have at you both!   11
        [Exit Troilus with Ajax and Diomedes, fighting.]

    [Enter Hector.]

HECTOR
    Yea, Troilus? Oh, well fought, my youngest brother!

    Enter Achilles.

ACHILLES
    Now do I see thee. Ha! Have at thee, Hector!
                      [They fight; Achilles tires.]

HECTOR   Pause, if thou wilt.

---

5 **Ere that correction** i.e., sooner than take from me the privilege
of chastising Troilus.   9 **Stand** i.e., Stand aside   10 **look
upon** remain an onlooker.   11 **cogging** deceitful

ACHILLES

  I do disdain thy courtesy, proud Trojan.

  Be happy that my arms are out of use.   16

  My rest and negligence befriends thee now,

  But thou anon shalt hear of me again;

  Till when, go seek thy fortune.   *Exit.*

HECTOR   Fare thee well.

  I would have been much more a fresher man,

  Had I expected thee.

    Enter Troilus.

             How now, my brother!

TROILUS

  Ajax hath ta'en Aeneas. Shall it be?

  No, by the flame of yonder glorious heaven,

  He shall not carry him. I'll be ta'en too,   24

  Or bring him off. Fate, hear me what I say!   25

  I reck not though thou end my life today.   *Exit.* 26

    Enter one in armor.

HECTOR

  Stand, stand, thou Greek! Thou art a goodly mark.   27

  No? Wilt thou not? I like thy armor well;

  I'll frush it and unlock the rivets all,   29

  But I'll be master of it.   *[Exit one in armor.]*

            Wilt thou not, beast, abide?   30

  Why then, fly on. I'll hunt thee for thy hide.   31

               Exit [in pursuit].

---

16 use practice.   **24 carry** prevail over   **25 bring him off**
rescue him.   **26 reck** care   **27 mark** target.   **29–30 I'll . . .
of it** I'll win it, if I have to smash it and pry open the rivets to do
so.   **31 hide** i.e., armor.

[5.7] <small>⌒</small> *Enter Achilles, with Myrmidons.*

ACHILLES
    Come here about me, you my Myrmidons;
    Mark what I say. Attend me where I wheel.   2
    Strike not a stroke, but keep yourselves in breath,
    And when I have the bloody Hector found,
    Empale him with your weapons round about;   5
    In fellest manner execute your arms.   6
    Follow me, sirs, and my proceedings eye.   7
    It is decreed Hector the great must die.   *Exeunt.*

     Enter Thersites; Menelaus [and] Paris [fighting].

THERSITES   The cuckold and the cuckold maker are at it.
    Now, bull! Now, dog! 'Loo, Paris, 'loo! Now my dou- 10
    ble-horned Spartan! 'Loo, Paris, 'loo! The bull has the 11
    game. Ware horns, ho!   *Exeunt Paris and Menelaus.* 12

     Enter Bastard [Margareton].

MARGARETON   Turn, slave, and fight.

THERSITES   What art thou?

MARGARETON   A bastard son of Priam's.

THERSITES   I am a bastard too; I love bastards. I am bas-
    tard begot, bastard instructed, bastard in mind, bas-
    tard in valor, in everything illegitimate. One bear will

5.7 Location: As before; the battle continues.
2 **wheel** execute a circling turning maneuver.   5 **Empale** fence
6 **fellest** fiercest.   **execute your arms** bring your weapons into
operation.   7 **my proceedings eye** watch what I do.   10 **bull**
i.e., Menelaus, a cuckold, a horned creature.   **'Loo** (A cry to
incite a dog against the bull in the sport of bullbaiting in
Shakespeare's England.)   11 **Spartan** i.e., Menelaus, King of
Sparta.   11–12 **has the game** wins.   12 **Ware** Beware

not bite another, and wherefore should one bastard?
Take heed, the quarrel's most ominous to us. If the
son of a whore fight for a whore, he tempts judgment.
Farewell, bastard.   [*Exit.*]

MARGARETON   The devil take thee, coward!   *Exit.*

[5.8]   ❧ *Enter Hector, [dragging the one in armor he has
          slain].*

HECTOR
Most putrefièd core, so fair without,   1
Thy goodly armor thus hath cost thy life.
Now is my day's work done. I'll take good breath.
Rest, sword; thou hast thy fill of blood and death.

                                        [*He disarms.*]

     Enter Achilles and [his] Myrmidons.

ACHILLES
Look, Hector, how the sun begins to set,
How ugly night comes breathing at his heels.
Even with the vail and dark'ning of the sun,   7
To close the day up, Hector's life is done.

HECTOR
I am unarmed. Forgo this vantage, Greek.

ACHILLES
Strike, fellows, strike! This is the man I seek.
                    [*They fall upon Hector and kill him.*]
So, Ilium, fall thou! Now, Troy, sink down!
Here lies thy heart, thy sinews, and thy bone.
On, Myrmidons, and cry you all amain,   13

5.8 Location: *As before; the battle continues.*
1 **core** i.e., the body of the Greek whom Hector has killed for his
armor   7 **vail** going down   13 **amain** with all your might

"Achilles hath the mighty Hector slain."

                               Retreat [sounded].

    Hark! A retire upon our Grecian part.   15

A MYRMIDON

    The Trojans trumpets sound the like, my lord.

ACHILLES

    The dragon wing of night o'erspreads the earth,

    And, stickler-like, the armies separates.   18

    My half-supped sword, that frankly would have fed,   19

    Pleased with this dainty bait, thus goes to bed.   20

                         [He sheathes his sword.]

    Come, tie his body to my horse's tail.   21

    Along the field I will the Trojan trail.

                   Exeunt [with Hector's body].

[5.9] ❧ *[Sound retreat.] Enter Agamemnon, Ajax,*
            Menelaus, Nestor, Diomedes, and the rest,
            marching. [Shout within.]

AGAMEMNON   Hark! Hark! What shout is that?

NESTOR   Peace, drums!

SOLDIERS (*within*)

    Achilles! Achilles! Hector's slain! Achilles!

DIOMEDES

    The bruit is, Hector's slain, and by Achilles.   4

AJAX

    If it be so, yet bragless let it be;   5

    Great Hector was a man as good as he.

15 **retire** call to cease fighting   18 **And . . . separates** and, like
a referee, separates the armies.   19 **frankly** abundantly; greedily
20 **dainty bait** tasty snack   21 **his** Hector's

5.9 *Location: The battlefield; the battle has concluded.*
4 **bruit** rumor, noise   5 **bragless** without boasting

AGAMEMNON

    March patiently along. Let one be sent
    To pray Achilles see us at our tent.
    If in his death the gods have us befriended,
    Great Troy is ours, and our sharp wars are ended.

                                   Exeunt.

[5.10] ❧ *Enter Aeneas, Paris, Antenor, [and] Deiphobus.*

AENEAS

    Stand, ho! Yet are we masters of the field.   1
    Never go home; here starve we out the night.   2

        Enter Troilus.

TROILUS

    Hector is slain.

ALL   Hector! The gods forbid!

TROILUS

    He's dead, and at the murderer's horse's tail,
    In beastly sort, dragged through the shameful field.
    Frown on, you heavens, effect your rage with speed!
    Sit, gods, upon your thrones and smite at Troy!
    I say, at once: let your brief plagues be mercy,   8
    And linger not our sure destructions on!   9

AENEAS

    My lord, you do discomfort all the host.   10

TROILUS

    You understand me not that tell me so.
    I do not speak of flight, of fear, of death,   12

5.10 *Location: The battlefield after the battle.*
1 **Yet** Still   2 **starve we out** let us endure, outlast   8 **let . . .
mercy** let your afflictions end us quickly, be mercifully brief
9 **linger** draw out, protract   10 **discomfort** discourage.
host army.   12 **of flight** merely of disordered retreat

But dare all imminence that gods and men   13
Address their dangers in. Hector is gone.   14
Who shall tell Priam so, or Hecuba?
Let him that will a screech owl aye be called
Go into Troy, and say their Hector's dead.
There is a word will Priam turn to stone,   18
Make wells and Niobes of the maids and wives,   19
Cold statues of the youth, and, in a word,
Scare Troy out of itself. But march away.
Hector is dead. There is no more to say.
Stay yet.—You vile abominable tents,
Thus proudly pitched upon our Phrygian plains,
Let Titan rise as early as he dare,   25
I'll through and through you! And, thou great-sized
    coward,   26
No space of earth shall sunder our two hates.   27
I'll haunt thee like a wicked conscience still,
That moldeth goblins swift as frenzy's thoughts.   29
Strike a free march! To Troy with comfort go.   30
Hope of revenge shall hide our inward woe.

                    [*They proceed to march away.*]

    Enter Pandarus.

PANDARUS [*to Troilus*]   But hear you, hear you!

13 **imminence** impending evils, threats of imminent disaster
14 **Address . . . in** prepare to endanger us with.   18 **will Priam
turn** that will turn Priam   19 **Niobes** (Niobe boasted that her
six sons and six daughters made her superior to Latona, mother of
Apollo and Diana, for which she was punished by seeing them put
to death by the arrows of these two deities. While weeping, she
was changed into a stone, but her tears continued to flow from the
rock. *Wells* are springs.)   25 **Titan** i.e., Helios, the sun-god, one
of the Titans   26 **coward** i.e., Achilles, cowardly slayer of
Hector   27 **sunder** keep apart   29 **moldeth** conjures up,
creates in the imagination   30 **free** unregimented, quick

TROILUS

Hence, broker-lackey! Ignomy and shame   33
Pursue thy life, and live aye with thy name!

Exeunt all but Pandarus.

PANDARUS   A goodly medicine for my aching bones! Oh,
world, world, world! Thus is the poor agent despised.
O traitors and bawds, how earnestly are you set
a-work, and how ill requited! Why should our endeavor be so desired and the performance so loathed?
What verse for it? What instance for it? Let me see: 40

Full merrily the humble-bee doth sing,   41
Till he hath lost his honey and his sting;
And being once subdued in armèd tail,   43
Sweet honey and sweet notes together fail.

Good traders in the flesh, set this in your painted   45
cloths: 46
As many as be here of Panders' hall,   47
Your eyes, half out, weep out at Pandar's fall;   48
Or if you cannot weep, yet give some groans,
Though not for me, yet for your aching bones.   50
Brethren and sisters of the hold-door trade,   51
Some two months hence my will shall here be made.

---

33 **broker-lackey** pander.   **Ignomy** Ignominy   40 **instance**
illustrative example   41 **humble-bee** bumblebee   43 **being . . .
tail** having lost its sting. (Much as a lover is emptied and perhaps
infected in the sexual act.)   45–6 **painted cloths** cheap wall
hangings worked or painted with scenes and mottoes   47 **of
Panders' hall** of the liveried company of panders   48 **half out**
i.e., already half destroyed by weeping and venereal disease
50 **aching bones** (A symptom of venereal disease, as in line 35.)
51 **hold-door trade** i.e., brothel keeping

It should be now, but that my fear is this:
Some gallèd goose of Winchester would hiss.   54
Till then I'll sweat and seek about for eases,   55
And at that time bequeath you my diseases.   [Exit.]

---

54 **gallèd . . . Winchester** i.e., a prostitute having venereal
disease; so called because the brothels of Southwark were under
the jurisdiction of the Bishop of Winchester   55 **sweat** (A
common treatment for venereal disease.)

DATE AND TEXT

❧

The textual history of *Troilus and Cressida* is complicated. On February 7, 1603, James Roberts entered in the Stationers' Register, the official record book of the London Company of Stationers (booksellers and printers), "when he hath gotten sufficient aucthority for yt, The booke of Troilus and Cresseda as yt is acted by my lord Chamberlens Men." On January 28, 1609, however, a new entry appeared in the Register, as though the first had never been made: "Richard Bonion Henry Walleys. Entred for their Copy vnder thandes of Master Segar deputy to Sir George Burke and master warden Lownes a booke called the history of Troylus and Cressida." Later that year appeared the first quarto, with the following title:

THE Historie of Troylus and Cresseida. *As it was acted by the Kings Maiesties seruants at the Globe. Written by* William Shakespeare. LONDON Imprinted by G. *Eld for R Bonian and H. Walley*, and are to be sold at the spred Eagle in Paules Church-yeard, ouer against the great North doore. 1609.

Before the first printing had sold out, still in 1609, the original title leaf was replaced by two new leaves containing a new title and an epistle. The title reads:

THE Famous Historie of Troylus *and* Cresseid. *Excellently expressing the beginning* of their loues, with the conceited wooing of *Pandarus* Prince of *Licia. Written by* William Shakespeare.

The epistle is addressed "A neuer writer, to an euer reader. Newes," and begins, "Eternall reader, you haue heere a new play, neuer stal'd with the Stage, neuer clapper-clawd with the palmes of the vulger, and yet passing full of the palme comicall."

The First Folio editors originally intended *Troilus and*

Cressida to follow *Romeo and Juliet*. After three pages and a title page had been set up in this position, however, the play was removed (perhaps owing to copyright difficulties) and *Timon of Athens* was inserted instead. Later, *Troilus* was placed between the Histories and the Tragedies, almost entirely without pagination. See the Introduction for some possible explanations of the unusual publishing history.

The quarto text was evidently set from a transcript of Shakespeare's working draft, made either by Shakespeare or by a scribe, or more probably from the working draft itself. The first three pages of the Folio text, those originally intended to follow *Romeo and Juliet*, were set from this first quarto. The remaining pages of the First Folio, however, seem to have been based on a copy of the quarto that had been collated with a manuscript, either Shakespeare's draft or more probably the playbook, which could itself have been a transcript of Shakespeare's fair copy of his original papers. As a result, both the quarto and Folio texts have independent textual authority. Recent editorial study has paid increasing attention to the Folio text on the theory that its readings, when not manifestly corrupt, may represent either Shakespeare's second thoughts as he fair copied or at least what the Folio collator found in Shakespeare's draft or the playbook. Hence, this edition, though using the first quarto as its copy text, introduces more Folio readings than are usually found in some previous editions; the Folio readings have been rejected only when there is some textual evidence against them.

The possibility that the play may not have been publicly performed and the failure of Shakespeare's company to provide the sequel promised at the end of *Troilus* suggest that the play was written not long before the first Stationers' Register entry of February 1603, probably in 1601. Certainly the play was not an old favorite in the company's repertoire. Failure as a stage play might have led to an attempt at quick publication, aimed at sophisticated readers. The current fad for satire would also have provided a motive for prompt publication. Stylistically, *Troilus* belongs to the period of *Hamlet* (c. 1599–1601). A seeming allusion in the Prologue of *Troilus* to the "armed" Prologue of Ben

Jonson's *Poetaster* (1601) helps set a probable early limit for date of composition; although the Prologue first appears in the First Folio of 1623 and may be an addition to the original play, it probably is not much later in date of composition. George Chapman's *The Seaven Bookes of Homers Illiads*, a source of information about the Trojan War, had appeared in 1598. The play is not mentioned by Francis Meres in 1598.

TEXTUAL NOTES

❧

These textual notes are not a historical collation, either of the early quartos and the early folios or of more recent editions; they are simply a record of departures in this edition from the copy text. The reading adopted in this edition appears in boldface, followed by the rejected reading from the copy text, i.e., the quarto of 1609. Only major alterations in punctuation are noted. Changes in lineation are not indicated, nor are some minor and obvious typographical errors.

Copy text: the quarto of 1609. As a text seemingly based on Shakespeare's own manuscript, with many unsupplied or imprecise stage directions, mislineation, authorial punctuation, and the like, Q is a suitable copy text, even though the work of the Q compositors (three in number) reduces the reliability of that text's authority even in incidental matters. Substantively, the First Folio text (F) often gives what may perhaps be Shakespeare's later decisions in a manuscript that may also have been put to use in the theater. Some such manuscript was used to annotate a copy of Q for the Folio printers. At the same time one needs to be careful not to include in an edited text those changes in F that appear likely to have been sophistications or compositorial errors. For these limited reasons only, Q serves as copy text for these collation notes, even though many readings that substantively vary between Q and F are decided in favor of F. All adopted readings are from [F] unless otherwise indicated; [eds.] means that the reading is that of some editor since the First Folio. [Fa] refers to the first setting of the Folio text, [Fb] to the second setting. Act and scene divisions are not provided in the quarto or the Folio. Some bracketed stage directions are from F.

Prologue [F; not in Q]   **8 immures** emures [F]   **12 barks** [eds.]
Barke [F]   **17 Antenorides** Antenonidus   **19 Spar** [eds.] Stirre [F]

1.1. 4 [and elsewhere] Trojan [eds.] Troyan   **26 the** [Q, Fa] of the
[Fb]   **27 [and elsewhere] ye** [eds.] yea   **33 When she** [eds.l then
she   **is she** she is   **38 [and elsewhere] Lest** [eds.] Least
55 Pour'st [eds.] Powrest   **55–7 heart / Her . . . voice; /
Handlest . . . discourse—oh!—** [eds.] heart: / Her . . . voice, /
Handlest . . . discourse: O   **63 instead** [eds.] in steed   **72 travail**
[eds.] trauell   **73 on of you** of you   **78 not kin** [Fb] kin [Q, Fa]
79–80 what care what   **85 her. For** her for   **99 woo** [eds.] woe
100 stubborn-chaste stubborne, chast   **104 resides** reides

1.2. 1 [and throughout] ALEXANDER *Man*   **17 they** the
34 struck [eds.] strooke   **36.1** [F; not in Q]   **48 ye** [eds.] yea
71 just . . . them; he [eds.] iust, . . . them he   **85 come** eome
87 wit [eds.] will   **117 lift** liste   **125 valiantly** valianty
130 the [eds.] thee   **148 pot** por   **177 s.d.** [at line 175 in Q]
180 Ilium Ilion   **189.1** [after line 190 in Q]   **192 a man** man
205 man's man   **219 [and elsewhere] Who's** [eds.] Whose
224–5 indifferent well [eds.] indifferent, well [Q, F]   **225 [and
elsewhere] hear** [eds.] here   **236 ne'er** neuer   **241.1 *Enter
common soldiers*** [F; not in Q]   **245 i'th'eyes** in the eyes
249 among amongst   **256–7 so forth** such like   **260 another** a
One a man   **269 too** two   **280 I'll** I wil   **281 bring, uncle?**
[eds.] bring vncle: [Q] bring Vnkle. [F]   **283.1** [F; not in Q]
291 prize price   **296 contents** content

1.3. 0.1 *Sennet* [F; not in Q]   **2 the jaundice on** these Iaundies ore
13 every euer   **19 think** call   **31 thy godly** the godlike
36 patient ancient   **48 herd** [eds.] heard   **breese** Bryze   **61 thy**
the   **67 On . . . ears** (On which heauen rides) knit all the Greekish
eares   **70–4** [F; not in Q]   **75 basis** bases   **92 ill . . . evil**
influence of euill Planets   **110 meets** melts   **118 [and elsewhere]
lose** [eds.] loose   **119 includes** include   **128 in** with   **137 lives**
stands   **143 sinew** sinnow   **149 awkward** sillie   **159 unsquared**
vnsquare   **164 just** right   **188 willed** wild   **195 and** our
209 fineness finesse   **212 s.d. *Tucket*** [F; not in Q]   **214.1 *Enter
Aeneas*** [F; not in Q]   **219 ears** eyes   **221 host** [eds.] heads
236 fame same   **238 Jove's** great *Ioues*   **247 affair** affaires
250 him with him   **252 sense** seat   **the** that   **256 loud** alowd
262 this his   **267 That seeks** And feeds   **276 compass** couple
289 or means a meanes   **294 One . . . one** A . . . no   **297 this**

withered brawn my withered braunes   **298 will** tell
302 forbid for-fend   **youth** men   **304 AGAMEMNON** [F; not in Q]
305 first sir   **309.1** [F; not in Q]   **315 This 'tis** [F; not in Q]
324 The True the   **even as** as   **327 were** weare   **333 Yes** Why
334 his honor those honours   **336 this** the   **340 wild** vilde
343 indices [eds.] *indexes* [Q, F]   **352 from hence receives the**
receiues from hence a   **354–6** [F; not in Q]   **354 his** [eds.] in his
[F]   **359 show our foulest wares** First shew foule wares
361–2 yet . . . better shall exceed, / By shewing the worst first
368 wear share   **370 we** it   **373 did** do   **377 as the worthier**
for the better   **388 of it** thereof   **391 tar** arre   **their** a

2.1. 8 there would would   **11 s.d.** [F; not in Q]   **14 vinewed'st**
[eds.] vnsalted [Q] whinid'st [F]   **17 oration** oration without booke
18 learn a learne   **19 o' thy** [eds.] ath thy [Q]   **24 a fool** foole
26–7 foot. An foot, and   **27 thee** the   **38, 40, 41 THERSITES,
AJAX, THERSITES** [F; not in Q]   **45 Thou scurvy** you scuruy
55.1 [F; not in Q]   **63 I do so** so do I   **71 I will** It will   **75 I'll** I
88 for a the   **101 an' a** and [Q] if the [F]   **out** at   **105 your**
[eds.] their   **nails on their toes** nailes   **107 war** wars   **111 wit**
as as   **114 brach** [eds.] brooch   **122 fifth** first   **130.1** [F; not in Q]

2.2. 3 damage domage   **4 travail** trauell   **7 struck** [eds.] stroke
14, 15 surety surely   **26 Weigh** Way   **27 father** fathers
30 waist [eds.] waste   **33 at** of   **34 them. Should . . . father** them
should . . . father;   **47 Let's** Sets   **52 holding** keeping
58 inclinable attributiue   **64 shores** shore   **67 chose** choose
70 spoiled soild   **71 sieve** siue   **74 of** with   **79 stale** pale
82 launched lansh't   **86 noble** worthy   **96.1 Enter . . . ears** *Enter
Cassandra rauing*   **97 shriek** shrike   **104 old** elders   **106 clamor**
clamours   **120 th'event** [eds.] euent   **149 off** of   **210 strike**
shrike

2.3. 1 THERSITES [not in Q]   **19 dependent** depending
21.1 Enter Patroclus [F; not in Q]   **24 ha'** a   **25 wouldst** couldst
31 art art not   **46 thyself** *Thersites*   **49 mayst** must   **54–9** [F;
not in Q]   **62–3 commanded of Agamemnon** commanded   **66 to
the creator** of the Prouer   **68 Patroclus** Come *Patroclus*   **69 s.d.**
[F; not in Q]   **73–4 Now . . . all** [F; not in Q]   **73 serpigo** [eds.]
Suppeago [F]   **78 shent** [eds.] sent [F] sate [Q]
79 appertainments appertainings   **82 so say** say so   **87 the** a

88 A word, my lord [F; not in Q]   98 council that composure
101.1 *Enter Patroclus* [F; not in Q]   111 Hear Heere
129 pettish lunes course, and time [Q] pettish lines [F]   his flows
and flowes   as and   130 carriage of this action streame of his
commencement   135 Bring [Q, Fb] ring [Fa]   140 enter you
entertaine   140.1 *Exit Ulysses* [F; not in Q]   151 it pride
152 clearer, Ajax cleerer   157 I hate I do hate   166 Why, will
Why will   179 led lead   186 do doth   190 Must Shall   stale
staule   192 titled liked   200 this his   202 pash push   204 'a
he   211 let tell   humors humorous   214 o' of   218 'twould
two'od   219 'A . . . shares [assigned in Q to Ajax]   221 He's . . .
warm [assigned in Q to Ajax]   Farce Force   222 praises praiers
in; his his   225 You Yon   231 thus with us with vs thus
241 beyond all all thy   247 bourn boord   248 Thy This
255 ULYSSES *Nest*.   262 cull call

3.1. 0.1–2 *Music . . . Servant* [F] *Enter Pandarus* [Q]   1 not you
you not   3 [and elsewhere] SERVANT Man   25 mean, friend mean
31 who's who is   33 visible [eds.] inuisible [Q, F]   37 that thou
thou   38 Cressida *Cressid*   41 There's theirs   52 Nell, he *Nel.*
he   76 supper you super. You   90 poor disposer's disposer's
106 lord lad   107 hast haste   113 [F; not in Q]   117 shaft
confounds *shafts confound*   120 Oh! Oh! *oh ho* [and similarly in
122–5]   148 They're Their   field the field   149 woo woe
151 these this   159 thee her

3.2. 3 he stays stayes   3.1 [F; not in Q]   8 a to a   10 those
these   16 s.d. [F; not in Q]   22 Swooning [eds.] Sounding [Q, F]
23 Too subtle-potent [eds.] To subtill, potent [Q, F]   28.1 [F; not in
Q]   33.1 [F; not in Q]   37 unawares vnwares   38.1 *Pandarus
and Cressida pandar and Cressid*   45 thills files   61 Cressida
Cressid   67 fears [eds.] teares   80 This is This   91 crown it.
No perfection louer part no affection   98.1 [F; not in Q]   109 are
be   117 glance that ever—pardon [eds.] glance; that euer pardon
[Q, F]   121 grown [eds.] grone [Q] grow [F]   131 Cunning
Comming   in [eds.] from [Q, F]   132 My . . . from me My very
soule of councell   149–50 Where . . . what I would be gone: /
Where is my wit? I know not what I speake   156 might; that might
that   159 aye age   175 similes, truth simele's truth   179 Yet,

after After   184 and or   197 witness. Here [eds.] witnes here
[Q, F]   199 pains paine   207 with a bed [eds.; not in Q, F]

3.3. 0.2 *Calchas* Chalcas   1 done you done   3 to your to
4 come [eds] loue   5 possessions [eds.] possession   29 off of
43 unplausive vnpaulsiue   55 What, comes [eds.] What comes
[Q, F]   69.1 *Exit* [eds.] *Exeunt* [Q, F]   73 use [eds.] us'd
101 shining ayming   111 mirrored [eds.] married   128 are are.
129 abject obiect   141 on one   142 shrinking shriking
153 mail [eds.] male [Q, F]   156 one on   159 hedge turne
161 hindmost him, most   162–4 Or . . . on [F; not in Q]
163 rear [eds.] neere [F]   165 past passe   179 give [eds.] goe
185 Than That   not stirs stirs not   198 grain . . . gold thing
199 th'uncomprehensive deeps the vncomprehensiue depth
225 like a like   234 we they   242 s.d. *Enter Thersites* [after line
242 in Q]   267 ambassador to him Ambassador   275 the most
the   279 Grecian [not in Q]   et cetera. Do Do   295–6 o'clock
of the clock   301 but he's but   o' of   306 carry beare

4.1. 0.1 *with a torch* [F; not in Q]   0.2 [and elsewhere] *Diomedes*
[eds.] *Diomed* [Q, F]   5 you your   18 But Lul'd   22–3
backward. In humane gentleness, back-ward, in humane gentlenesse:
39 Calchas' *Calcho's*   42 do think beleeue   46 whereof
wherefore   52 s.d. [F; not in Q]   54 the soul soule   55 merits
deserues   most best   58 soilure soyle   75 Hear Here   78 you
they

4.2. 15 gait [eds.] gate   18 off of   21.1 [F; not in Q]   32–3 Ah,
poor *capoccia!* [eds.] a poore *chipochia,*   35 s.d. *One knocks* [after
line 36 in Q, after 33 in F]   56 Hoo! [eds] Who   59.1 [F; not in
Q]   65 us; and for him him, and   74 nature neighbor *Pandar*
79 CRESSIDA [not in Q]   87 wouldst wouldest   89–90 knees I
beseech you knees   110.1 [F; not in Q]

4.3. 0.2 and [F; not in Q]

4.4. 6 affection affections   50 genius so *Genius*   51 "Come" so
54 the root my throate   58 my love loue   64 there's there is
70 Wear were   77 [F; not in Q]   gifts guift [F]   78 flowing
swelling   79 person portion   106 wear were   122 zeal [eds.]
seale   135 I'll I   139.1–2 *Sound trumpet* [F; not in Q]
144–8 [F; not in Q]   144 DEIPHOBUS [eds.] *Dio.* [F]
148 s.d. [after line 143 in Q, F]

4.5. 0.2 Nestor [eds.] *Nester, Calcas* [Q, F]   **2 time . . . courage.**
[eds.] time. With starting courage, [Q, F]   **16 toe** too
38 MENELAUS [eds.] *Patr.*   **44 not** nor   **49 too.** [eds.] then. [Q]
then? [F]   **60 accosting** [eds.] a coasting [Q, F]   **64.1 *Exeunt*** [F;
not in Q]   **66 you** the   **74 ACHILLES** [eds.; not in Q, F]
75 disprising misprising   **95** [F; not in Q]   **96 AGAMEMNON** *Vlises*
99 in deeds deeds   **133 Of our rank feud** [F; not in Q]   **134 drop**
day   **162 mine** my   **164 of all**   **166–71** [F; not in Q]
179 Mock . . . oath (Mock not thy affect, the vntraded earth)
188 And seen thee scorning Despising many   **189 thy** th'
194 hemmed shrupd   **200 Let** O let   **207** [F; not in Q]
253 the an   **256 stithied** stichied   **276 Beat . . . taborins** To taste
your bounties   **282 on heaven nor on** vpon the heauen nor
288 As But   **293 she loved** my Lord

5.1. 4 core curre   **12 need these** needs this   **14 boy** box
15 thought said   **19 catarrhs** [F; not in Q]   **i'** in   **20 wheezing**
whissing   **26 mean'st** meanes   **31 sarcenet** sacenet   **32 tassel**
toslell   **51 Here's** her's   **54 brother** be   **56 hanging . . . leg** at
his bare legge   **58 farced** [eds.] faced [Q] forced [F]   **59 he is** her's
60 dog day   **mule** Moyle   **60 fitchew** Fichooke   **63 not** [F; not
in Q]   **66.1–3 *Enter . . . lights*** *Enter Agam: Vlysses, Nest: and*
Diomed with lights   **68 light** lights   **68 s.d.** [F; not in Q]   **71 good**
God   **77 sewer** [eds.] sure   **78 both at once** both   **98 Calchas**
his *Calcas*

5.2. 4.1 *Enter . . . Ulysses* [F; not in Q]   **5 s.d. *Enter Cressida***
["*Enter Cressid*" after "to him" in line 6 in Q]   **11 clef** Cliff
13 CRESSIDA [eds.] *Cal.*   **16 should** shall   **35 one** a   **37 pray**
you pray   **41 Nay** Now   **42 distraction** distruction   **48 Why,**
how now, lord? How now my lord?   **49 Adieu, you** you
57 tickles these tickles   **59 But will** Will   **60 la** [eds.] lo
63 sweet my   **69** [F; not in Q]   **70 CRESSIDA** *Troy.*   **83 As I**
kiss thee [eds.; continued as Cressida's speech in Q, F]   **Nay . . . me**
[eds.; assigned to Diomedes in Q, F]   **87 CRESSIDA** [F; not in Q]
92 one's [eds.] on's [Q] one [F]   **94 By** And by   **109 s.d. *Exit*** [F;
not in Q]   **121 coact** Court   **126 had deceptious** were deceptions
137 soil spoile   **146 is** was   **156 Ariachne's** *Ariachna's* [Qb]
Ariathna's [Qa]   **161 five** finde   **164 bound** giuen   **171 much as**
[eds.] much

5.3. 14 CASSANDRA *Cres.*   **20–2** [F; not in Q]   **21 give** [eds.] count giue [F]   **use** [eds.] as [F]   **23** CASSANDRA [F; not in Q] **29 mean'st** meanest   **45 mothers** Mother   **58** [F; not in Q] **85 distraction** distruction   **90 s.d.** [F; not in Q]   **93 of worth 96.1** *Pandarus* [eds.] *Pandar* [Q, F]   **104 o' these** [eds.] ath's [Q] o'th's [F]   **112** [F follows with an alternate version, slightly varied, of 5.10.32–4]

5.4. 0.1 *Alarum* [F, at 5.2.112; not in Q]   **4 young knave's** knaues **17.1** *Enter . . . Troilus* [F; not in Q]   **26 art thou** art

5.5. 5 SERVANT *Man*   **5.1** *Enter Agamemnon* [after "proof" in line 5 in Q]   **7 Margareton** [eds.] *Margaleron* [Q, F]   **11 Epistrophus** [eds.] *Epostropus*   **Cedius** [eds.] *Cedus*   **12 Thoas** [eds.] *Thous* **22 scalèd** scaling   **schools** [eds.] sculls [Q] sculs [F]   **25 the** a **41 luck** lust   **43** AJAX [F; not in Q]

5.6. 1 AJAX [F; not in Q]   **2** DIOMEDES [F; not in Q]   **7 the** [eds.] thy [Q, F]   **11.1** *Exit Troilus* [F; not in Q]   **11.2** *Enter Hector* [F; not in Q]   **13** ACHILLES [F; not in Q]   **21 s.d.** *Enter Troilus* [eds.; after line 21 in Q, F]   **26 reck** [eds.] wreake   **thou end** I end

5.7. 1 ACHILLES [F; not in Q]   **8 s.d.** *Exeunt* [eds.] *Exit*   **and** [F; not in Q]   **10 'Loo** [eds.] lowe   **10–11 double-horned Spartan** [eds.] double hen'd spartan [Q] double hen'd sparrow [F]   **12 s.d.** *Exeunt* [eds.] *Exit*   **13** [and throughout scene] MARGARETON [eds.] *Bast.* [Q, F]

5.8. 3 good my   **4.2** *his* [F; not in Q]   **11 Now** next, come **15 part** prat   **16 A** MYRMIDON [eds.] *One.* [Q] *Gree.* [F]   **Trojan trumpets** Troyans trumpet

5.9. 0.1 *Sound retreat* [F; not in Q]   **0.3** *Shout* [F, at the end of scene 8; not in Q]   **1 shout is that** is this   **3 slain! Achilles!** [F subst.] slaine *Achilles,*   **6 a man as good** as good a man

5.10. 0.1 *and* [F; not in Q]   **2 Never** *Troy.* Neuer **2.1** [placement as in F; before line 2 in Q]   **3** TROILUS [F; not in Q] **7 smite** [eds.] smile [Q, F]   **20 Cold** Could [Q] Coole [F] **21 Scare** [eds.] Scarre [Q, F]   **21–2 But . . . dead** [F; not in Q] **23 yet. You vile abominable tents,** [F, subst.] yet you proud abhominable tents: [Q]   **33 broker-lacky!** broker, lacky,   **Ignomy and** ignomyny **36 world, world, world** world, world   **39 desired** lou'd   **50 your** my **51 hold-door** hold-ore   **56 s.d.** [*Exit*] *Exeunt* [F; not in Q]

SHAKESPEARE'S SOURCES

❧

Shakespeare had access to Homer for information about the Trojan War, since George Chapman's translation of *Seven Books of the Iliads of Homer* had appeared in 1598, and earlier translations of the entire *Iliad* were also available. Shakespeare ends his play with the death of Hector, as do Homer and some post-Homeric historians of the war, and portrays Achilles as a figure in tragic conflict with his sense of pride, as does Homer. Thersites and Nestor are based ultimately on the *Iliad*, as can be seen in the excerpt from Chapman's translation that follows. Ajax's ludicrous boastfulness may owe something to Homer's Ajax Telamon, as well as to Ovid's account of the quarrel between Ulysses and Ajax over Achilles's armor (*Metamorphoses*, 12–13). Yet for Shakespeare, and for most Englishmen of his time, the chief sources of information about the Trojan War were medieval romances. These were all pro-Trojan in their bias, since Englishmen traced their own mythic history to the lineage of Aeneas and tended to look on Homer as suspiciously pro-Greek. Medieval European culture generally was far more oriented to Roman than to Greek civilization; Greek texts went almost unread. In these circumstances, a pro-Trojan account of the war emerged and grew to considerable proportions, in which non-Homeric material became increasingly important.

The central work dealing with this expanded account of the war was Benoît de Sainte-Maure's *Roman de Troie* (c. 1160), a romance freely based on earlier accounts of two supposed eye-witnesses named Dictys the Cretan and Dares the Phrygian. Benoît not only narrates the war from Troy's point of view but introduces the love story of Troilus, "Breseida," and Diomedes. Benoît found a hint for this story in the *Iliad*, where two Trojan maidens named Chryseis and Briseis are captured and given to Agamemnon and Achilles respectively. When Chryseis's father calls down a plague on the Greeks for refusing to return

Chryseis, Agamemnon reluctantly gives her up but then seizes Briseis from Achilles, thereby precipitating Achilles's angry retirement to his tent and all that disastrously follows. Benoît freely transforms this situation into the rivalry of Troilus and Diomed, who appear in Homer but in entirely different roles.

Benoît's *Roman de Troie* became the inspiration for subsequent medieval accounts of the Trojan War. Guido delle Colonne translated Benoît in his *Historia Troiana* (completed 1287). Giovanni Boccaccio based his *Il Filostrato* (c. 1338) on Guido and Benoît but made significant alterations: the love story became the focus of attention, and Pandarus assumed the important role of go-between. (In Homer, Pandarus is a fierce warrior.) Geoffrey Chaucer based his *Troilus and Criseyde* (c. 1385–1386) on Boccaccio, giving still greater attention to the states of mind of the two lovers and endowing Pandarus with a humorous disposition, as is illustrated in the selection that follows. Shakespeare certainly knew Chaucer's masterpiece. He also consulted, however, at least two other medieval accounts of the war: John Lydgate's *The History, Siege, and Destruction of Troy* (first printed 1513), based on Guido and Chaucer and known also as the *Troy Book*, and William Caxton's *The Recuyell of the Histories of Troy* (printed 1474, the first book printed in English), a translation from the French of Raoul Lefevre, who had followed Guido rather closely. In Caxton, for example, Shakespeare found materials for the Trojan debate in act 2, scene 2 (see the selection from Caxton that follows) and for Hector's visit to the Greek camp (act 4, scene 5). In addition, Shakespeare was certainly familiar with the degeneration of Cressida's character since the time of Chaucer, as reflected for example in Robert Henryson's *The Testament of Cresseid* (published 1532), in which Cressida is punished for her faithlessness by leprosy and poverty.

Shakespeare pays a good deal more attention to the war than does Chaucer and portrays the lovers as caught in a conflict beyond their control. Shakespeare's Cressida is more sardonic and experienced in the ways of the world than is Chaucer's heroine, even though Chaucer's Criseyde is a widow and Shakespeare's

Cressida is unmarried. The subtle and elaborate code of courtly love evoked by Chaucer has almost completely disappeared in Shakespeare's work, leaving in its wake a more dispiriting and cynical impression. Shakespeare's Troilus is still a faithful and earnest lover, as in Chaucer, but betrayed by his own chauvinistic ideals about honor and patriotism in a way that Chaucer's Troilus is not. Pandarus is more leering, giddy, vapid, and coarse than his Chaucerian counterpart. Diomedes is also changed for the worse, being more hard and cynical.

Among the non-Chaucerian characters, Achilles is made to appear more guilty and brutal than in Shakespeare's sources: Achilles orders his Myrmidons (i.e., his soldiers) to murder the unarmed Hector, even though Hector had previously spared Achilles in battle. Lydgate and Caxton report that Achilles's Myrmidons kill Troilus, not Hector (in Caxton, Achilles cuts off Troilus's head and then drags Troilus's body behind his horse), whereas in Homer Achilles kills Hector in battle and only then do his Myrmidons desecrate the body. Shakespeare refuses to glamorize the war just as he refuses to glamorize the love story. He also compresses time, as he did with so many of his sources. The play begins only a short time before Cressida surrenders to Troilus; she is transferred to the Greeks immediately after she and Troilus become lovers; her surrender to Diomedes follows quickly after her transfer. This telescoping provides not only dramatic unity but a sense of sudden and violent change.

Other plays on Troilus and Cressida are known to have existed in Shakespeare's time, such as a "new" play acted by the Admiral's Men, an acting company, in 1596 and another by Thomas Dekker and Henry Chettle in 1599. Shakespeare may have known and even written in response to such productions by rival theatrical companies, but today nothing is known about these lost plays.

SEVEN BOOKS OF THE ILIADS OF HOMER
Translated by George Chapman

BOOK 2

[Morale is so low among the Greeks, after years of being in Troy with no victory yet in sight, that, when Agamemnon tests his army by inviting them to leave Troy, a mutiny nearly occurs. In the council meeting that ensues to discuss matters, the most disaffected and insubordinate troublemaker is Thersites.]

All sat and silent used their seats, Thersites sole except— 1
A man of tongue, whose ravenlike voice a tuneless jarring kept, 2
Who in his rank mind copy had of unregarded words 3
That rashly and beyond all rule used to oppugn the lords. 4
But whatsoever came from him was laughed at mightily—
The filthiest Greek that came to Troy. He had a goggle eye; 6
Stark lame he was of either foot; his shoulders were contract 7
Into his breast and crook'd withal; his head was sharp compact, 8
And here and there it had a hair. To mighty Thetides 9

1 **Thersites sole except** except only Thersites   2 **kept** kept up
3 **rank** haughty, rebellious; gross.   **unregarded** un-looked-after, disordered   4 **oppugn** assail, controvert   6 **goggle** protuberant; squinting
7 **Stark** severely.   **either foot** both feet.   **contract** contracted, shrunken   8 **withal** in addition.   **his . . . compact** i.e., his skull went up to a point   9–10 **To . . . disease** i.e., Thersites provoked much anger and annoyance in mighty Achilles and Ulysses. **Thetides** Achilles, son of Thetis

And wise Ulysses he retained much anger and
   disease,   10
For still he chid them eagerly, and then against the
   state   11
Of Agamemnon he would rail. The Greeks in
   vehement hate
And high disdain conceited him, yet he with violent
   throat   13
Would needs upbraid the General, and thus himself
   forgot: 14
   "Atrides, why complain'st thou now? What dost
   thou covet more?   15
Thy thrifty tents are full of coin, and thou hast
   women store,   16
Fair and well-favored, which we Greeks at every town
   we take   17
Resign to thee. Think'st thou, thou want'st some
   treasure thou might make   18
To be deduced thee out of Troy by one that comes to
   seek   19
His son for ransom, who myself or any other Greek   20
Should bring thee captive? Or a wench, filled with
   her sweets of youth,   21
Which thou mayst love and private keep for thy
   insatiate tooth?
But it becomes not kings to tempt by wicked
   precedent
Their subjects to dishonesty. O minds most impotent,

10 **disease** annoyance, grievance   11 **still** continually.   **eagerly**
keenly, violently.   **state** dignity, office   13 **conceited** regarded
14 **Would needs** felt compelled to.   **himself forgot** i.e., forgot his
manners   15 **Atrides** Agamemnon, son of Atreus   16 **store** in
great abundance   17 **well-favored** attractive   18–21 **Think'st . . .
captive?** i.e., Are you hankering after some huge sum you might get
from a Trojan father as ransom for his son whom I or another Greek
would capture and turn over to you?   19 **deduced thee** brought (from
Troy) to you

Not Argives but Achaean girls, come fall aboard and
     home!   25
Let him concoct his prey alone, alone Troy overcome,   26
To make him know if our free ears his proud
     commands would hear   27
In anything, or not disdain his longer yoke to bear   28
Who hath with contumely wronged a better man than
     he—   29
Achilles, from whose arms, in spite that all the world
     might see,
He took a prize won with his sword. But now it plain
     appears   31
Achilles hath no spleen in him, but most remissly
     bears   32
A female stomach; else, be sure, the robbery of his
     meed,   33
O Agamemnon, would have proved thy last injurious
     deed."
   Thus did Thersites chide the king to whom all
     Greece did bow;
When wise Ulysses straight stood up, and, with
     contracted brow   36
Beholding him, used this rebuke: "Prating Thersites,
     cease,
Though thou canst rail so cunningly, nor dare to
     tempt the peace   38

---

25 Argives i.e., Greeks, from Argos.   **Achaean** i.e., Greek, from
Achaea.   **come fall aboard and home** go aboard ship and head home.
26 Let him concoct Let Agamemnon digest or mull over   **27 free** i.e.,
free to hear what we wish   **28 or . . . bear** or rather disdain to bear his
yoke any longer   **29 contumely** insult, insolence   **31 prize** i.e., Briseis,
whom Agamemnon has taken away from Achilles when Agamemnon's
prize, Chryseis (compare Criseyde or Cressida), had to be returned to
the Trojans.   **his** i.e., Achilles's   **32 spleen** indignation; resolution
33 female stomach i.e., feminine lack of courage.   **meed** reward, i.e.,
the prize Briseis   **36 straight** straightaway, at once   **38–9 tempt . . .
kings** flout the general peace provided by the authority of kings

Of sacred kings; for well thou knowest I know well
    what thou art.   39
A baser wretch came not to Troy to take the Grecians'
    part.   40
Profane not kings, then, with thy lips. Examine our
    retreat,   41
Whereof ourselves are ignorant, nor are our states so
    great   42
That we dare urge upon the King what he will only
    know.   43
Sit then and cease thy barbarous taunts to him whom
    all we owe
So much observance, though from thee these insolent
    poisons flow.   45
But I protest, and will perform if I shall deprehend   46
Such frenzy in thy pride again as now doth all offend:
Then let Ulysses lose his head, and cease inglorious   48
To be the native father called of young Telemachus,   49
If from thee to thy nakedness thy garments be not
    stripped   50
And from the council to the fleet thou be not soundly
    whipped."   51
    This said, his back and shoulder blades he with his
        scepter smit;
Who then shrunk round, and down his cheeks the
    servile tears did flit.
The golden scepter in his flesh a bloody print did
    raise,
With which he, trembling, took his seat and, looking
    twenty ways,   55

40 take . . . part fight on the Grecian side.   **41 retreat** i.e., military option of retreating   **42 states** statures, ranks   **43 what . . . know** what only he can know.   **45 observance** deference   **46 protest** insist.   **deprehend** detect   **48–51 Then let . . . whipped** i.e., May I lose my very life and claims of paternity if I do not whip you and send you packing back to the ships if I catch you doing this again.   **48 inglorious** having lost all fame and glory   **55 looking twenty ways** i.e., his eyes shifting

Ill-favoredly he wiped the tears from his self-pitying
    eyes.
And then, though all the host were sad, they
    laughed to hear his cries.   57
When thus flew speeches intermixed: "O gods, what
    endless good
Ulysses still bestows on us, that to the field of blood   59
Instructs us, and in council doth for chief director
    serve!
Yet never action passed his hands that did more
    praise deserve   61
Than to disgrace this railing fool in all the army's
    sight,
Whose rudeness henceforth will take heed how he
    doth princes bite."

[Ulysses then speaks, casting more scorn on those discontents and cowards who would go home, and reminding them of Calchas's prophecy that the Greeks will win at the end of ten years.]

Ulysses having spoken thus, his words so likèd were
That of his praise the ships, the tents, the shore did
    witness bear,
Resounding with the people's noise, who gave his
    speech the prize.
Th' applause once ceased, from seat to speak old
    Nestor doth arise.
    "Fie, Greeks, what infamy is this? Ye play at
    children's game,
Your warlike actions thus far brought, now to neglect
    their fame.   69

---

57 sad serious   **59 still** always.   **field of blood** battlefield   **61 Yet . . . hands** Never yet did he do anything   **69 Your . . . fame** now to neglect to pursue the glory of the warlike action you have brought thus far.

Oh, whither from our lips profane shall oaths and
    compacts fly?
The councils and the cares of men now in the fire
    shall die   71
With those our sacred offerings made by pure
    unmixèd wine
And our right hands with which our faiths we freely
    did combine.   73
The cause is, since amongst ourselves we use
    discursive words,   74
And go not manlike to the field to manage it with
    swords,   75
Nor with the fineness of our wits by stratagems
    devise
In all this while against a world to work our
    enterprise.   77
But, great Atrides, as at first, thy counsel being
    sound,
Command to field! And be not led corruptly from the
    ground   79
Of our endeavors by the moods of one or two that
    use   80
Councils apart. They shall not go to Greece till Jove
    refuse   81
To ratify his promise made, or we may surely know
If those ostents were true or false that he from
    heaven did show. . . .   83
But if some be so mutinous, whom nothing may
    restrain,

71 in . . . die i.e., will not fly up to the gods and be heard. (The sacrificial fire will not be efficacious.)   **73 And** i.e., and by.   **faiths** pledges.   **combine** i.e., make mutually.   **74 since** i.e., that.   **discursive** unfocused, indecisive   **75 manage it** control the fighting successfully   **77 against a world** against great odds   **79 ground** arena   **80–1 use Councils apart** i.e., conspire separately and seek to divide authority.   **83 ostents** portents

Let him but touch his black-armed bark that he may
    first be slain.   85

Then, great Atrides, be advised, and other reasons
    see:

It shall not prove an abject speech that I will utter
    thee.

In tribes and nations let thy men be presently
    arrayed,   88

That still the tribes may second tribes, and nations
    nations aid.   89

Of every chief and soldier thus the proof shall rest in
    sight,

For both will thirst their country's fame and press
    for single fight.

What soldier, when he is allowed his countryman for
    guide,

Will not more closely stick to him than to a
    stranger's side?

Thus shalt thou know if gods detain thy hand from
    Ilion's harms   94

Or else the faintness of thy men and ignorance in
    arms."

[Agamemnon thanks Nestor for his inspiring address, says
he wishes he had ten such counselors, and urges an end to
the strife that has divided Greek against Greek, so that they
may turn their energies to leveling the Trojan citadel.]

85 him i.e., that traitorous person.   **black-armed bark** ship outfitted
and armed in black   **88 tribes and nations** political divisions.
presently at once   **89 still** always.   **second** support, assist   **94
from Ilion's harms** from inflicting harm on Troy

George Chapman's translation of *Seven Books of the Iliads of Homer*
was published in London in 1598. This modernized text is based on
that edition.

THE RECUYELL OF THE HISTORIES OF TROY

By William Caxton

BOOK 3

[King Priant (Priam) assembles a council of Trojans to consider what should be done about the fact that the Greeks hold captive his sister, Exione (Hesione). The debate resembles that in act 2, scene 2, of Shakespeare's play, where the capture of Hesione is talked about (ll. 77ff.); except that the present debate takes place years earlier, before the Trojans seize Helen in retaliation and thereby provide the immediate provocation for the Trojan War. Priant speaks first.]

My sons, ye have well in your memory the death of your grandfather[1] [and] the servitude of your Aunt Exione, that men holdeth by your living[2] in manner of a common woman. And ye be so puissant, meseemeth,[3] that reason should ensign you for to employ you[4] to avenge this great injury and shame. And if this move you not thereto, yet ye ought to do it to satisfy my will and pleasure, for I die for sorrow and anguish, to which[5] ye ought and been bound for to remedy to your power,[6] that have do you so well be[7] nourished and brought forth.

Title: **Recuyell** receuil, literary compilation
1 death of your grandfather (Laomedon, King of Troy, earned the wrath of Poseidon by refusing to pay him and Apollo for building the walls of Troy. When Poseidon sent a sea monster against Troy, Laomedon was told he could avert the danger only by sacrificing his daughter Hesione to it. Though assisted by Heracles in getting rid of the monster, Laomedon likewise defrauded Heracles of the famous horses he had promised as a reward. Heracles raised an army and captured Troy, slaying Laomedon and giving Hesione to Telamon.) **2 by your living** during your lifetime (?), from your possession (?) **3 puissant, meseemeth** powerful, it seems to me **4 ensign you for to employ you** instruct you to employ yourselves **5 to which** to whom **6 to your power** to the extent of your power **7 that have . . . be** I who have caused you to be so well

"And thou, Hector, my right dear son, that art the oldest of thy brethren, the most wise and the most strong: I pray thee first that thou emprise[8] to put in execution this my will, and that thou be duke and prince of thy brethren in this work, and all the other[9] shall obey gladly unto thee. And in like wise shall do all they[10] of this realm, for[11] the great prowess that they know in thee. And know that from this day forth I despoil me[12] of all this work and put it upon thee that art the most strong and asper[13] to maintain the battles. And I am ancient and old and may not forth on help[14] myself so well as I was wont to do," etc.

To these words answered Hector right soberly and sweetly, saying,

"My Father and my right dear and sovereign lord, there is none of all your sons but that it seemeth to him thing human[15] to desire vengeance of these injuries. And also to us that been of high noblesse[16] a little injury ought to be great.[17] As it is so that the quality of the person groweth and minisheth,[18] so ought the quality of the injury. And if we desire and have appetite to take vengeance of[19] our injuries, we forsake not ne[20] leave the nature human, for in like wise do and usen[21] the dumb beasts in the same manner, and nature ensigneth and giveth hem[22] thereto. My right dear lord and father, there is none of all your sons that ought more to desire the vengeance of the injury and death of our aiel[23] or grandfather than I, that am the oldest.

"But I will,[24] if it please you, that ye consider in this emprise[25] not only the beginning but also the middle and the end to what thing we may come hereafter, for otherwhile little profiten[26]

---

8 **emprise** undertake   9 **other** others   10 **all they** all those   11 **for** on account of   12 **despoil me** disrobe, divest myself   13 **asper** hardy, warlike   14 **on help** in way of assistance   15 **thing human** a human trait   16 **noblesse** nobility   17 **a little . . . great** even a little insult ought to be regarded as a great one.   18 **As . . . minisheth** i.e., And just as the rank of the person to whom the injury has been done is greater or lesser   19 **of** for   20 **ne** nor   21 **usen** practice, behave   22 **ensigneth and giveth hem** instructs and inclines them   23 **aiel** grandfather   24 **will** wish   25 **emprise** enterprise, undertaking   26 **little profiten** of little profit are

some things well begun that come unto an evil end. Then methinketh[27] that it is much more allowable to a man to abstain him for to begin things whereof the ends been dangerous and whereof may come more evil than good, for the thing is not said eurous[28] or happy unto[29] the time that it come unto a good end.

"I say not these things for any evil or cowardice, but only to the end that ye begin not a thing—and specially that thing that ye have on[30] your heart—to put it lightly in ure,[31] but that ye first be well counseled. . . . Exione is not of so high price that it behooveth all us to put us in peril and doubt[32] of death for her. She hath been now long time there where she is yet. It were better that she perform forth her time, that,[33] I trow, hath but little time to live, than we should put us all in such perils.

"And meekly I beseech you not to suppose in no manner that I say these things for cowardice, but I doubt[34] the turns of Fortune and that under the shadow of this thing she[35] not beat ne[36] destroy your great seigniory, and that we ne begin thing[37] that we ought to leave for to eschew[38] more great mischief," etc.

When Hector had made an end of his answer, Paris was nothing well content therewith. He stood up on his feet and said in this wise:

"My right dear lord, I beseech you to hear me say to what end ye may come if ye begin the war against the Greeks. How be not we garnished of[39] so many and noble chivalry as they been? Certes that be we which[40] in all the world is none that may discomfit.[41] And therefore begin ye hardily[42] that emprise[43] that ye have thought, and send of your ships and of your people to run[44]

---

27 **methinketh** it seems to me   28 **eurous** lucky, prosperous
29 **unto** until   30 **on** in   31 **ure** use, practice   32 **doubt** fear,
danger   33 **perform . . . time, that** live out her life, who   34 **doubt**
fear   35 **she** i.e., Fortune   36 **ne** nor   37 **ne begin thing** do not
begin something   38 **leave for to eschew** avoid in order to escape
39 **How . . . garnished of** In what way are we not provided with
40 **Certes . . . which** Certainly we are the ones who   41 **discomfit**
defeat.   42 **hardily** boldly   43 **emprise** enterprise   44 **run** move
about freely and quickly

in Greece and to take the people and damage the country. And
if it please you to send me, I shall do it with a good will and
heart, for I am certain that, if ye send me, that I shall do great
damage unto the Greeks. And I shall take some noble lady[45] of
Greece and bring her with me to this realm. And by the commutation[46] of her ye may recover your sister Exione. And if ye
will understand and know how I am certain of this thing, I shall
say it to you how the gods have promised it to me.

[Paris expounds to his father and the other Trojans a vision
he has had, and the promise made to him by the goddess Venus.
He is followed and seconded by Deiphoebus.]

After this spake Helenus, the fourth son of King Priant, that
said thus:

"Ha, ha, right puissant King and right sovereign dominator
upon[47] us your humble subjects and obedient sons! Beware that
coveteise of[48] vengeance put not you in such danger as lieth
herein. Ye know well how I know and can the science[49] to know
the things future and to come, as ye have proved[50] many times
without finding fault. The gods forbid that it never come that
Paris be sent into Greece! For know ye for certain that, if he go
to make any assault, ye shall see this noble and worshipful city
destroyed by the Greeks, the Trojans slain and we all that been
your children. . . ."

When the King heard Helenus thus speak he was all
abashed, and began to counterpoise[51] and think, and held his
peace and spake not of[52] a great while. And so did all the
other.[53]

Then arose upon his feet Troilus, the youngest son of King
Priant, and began to speak in this manner:

45 **some noble lady** (This lady of course turns out to be Helen.)
46 **commutation** exchanging   47 **dominator upon** lord over
48 **coveteise of** covetousness of, desire for   49 **can the science** am
master of the knowledge   50 **proved** discovered   51 **counterpoise**
weigh one possibility against another   52 **of** for   53 **other** others.

"O noble men and hardy, how be ye abashed for the words of this coward priest here? Is it not the custom of priests for to dread the battles by[54] pusillanimity, and for to love the delices[55] and to fat and increase hem[56] and fill their bellies with good wines and with good meats? Who is he that believeth that any man may know the things to come but if[57] the gods show it hem by revelation? It is but folly for to tarry upon this or to believe such things. If Helenus be afeard, let him go into the temple and sing the divine service. And let the other[58] take vengeance of their injuries by force of arms. O right dear father and lord, wherefore art thou so troubled for these words? Send thy ships into Greece, and thy knights wise and hardy, that may render to the Greeks their injuries that they have done to us."

All they that heard Troilus thus speak, they allowed[59] him, saying that he had well spoken. And thus they finished their parliament and went to dinner.

---

54 by by reason of   **55 delices** sensual pleasures   **56 hem** themselves   **57 but if** unless   **58 other** others   **59 allowed** praised

---

William Caxton translated *The Recuyell* from the French version by Raoul Lefevre in about 1474 and printed it in that same year. This modernized text is based on the 1474 edition.

TROILUS AND CRISEYDE
By *Geoffrey Chaucer*

BOOK 3

[With much ado, Criseyde's uncle Pandarus has managed to persuade her to take pity on the suffering of Troilus by allowing him to visit her at night in her chambers. An assignation is not mentioned; the pretense is that nothing short of seeing her immediately can save Troilus's life.]

"Then, em," quod she, "doth hereof as you list.	939
But ere he come, I will up first arise,	940
And, for the love of God, syn all my trist	941
Is on you two, and ye been bothe wise,	942
So werketh now in so discreet a wise	943
That I honor may have, and he pleasaunce;	944
For I am here all in your governaunce."	945
"That is well said," quod he, "my nece deere.	946
There good thrift on that wise gentle herte!	947
But liggeth still, and taketh him right here;	948
It needeth not no ferther for him sterte.	949
And each of you ease otheres sorwes smerte,	950
For love of God; and Venus, I thee herye;	951
For soon hope I we shull been alle merrye."	952

---

939 em uncle.   **quod** quoth, said.   **doth . . . list** do in this as you please.   **940 ere** before   **941 syn** since.   **trist** trust   **942 on** in. **been** be   **943 werketh** work, arrange matters   **944 pleasaunce** pleasure   **945 all** entirely   **946 nece deere** dear niece. **947 There good thrift on** May good success come to   **948 liggeth** lie. **taketh** take, receive   **949 It . . . sterte** there's no need to go anywhere else as far as he is concerned.   **950 sorwes smerte** painful sorrows **951 Venus, I thee herye** Venus, I praise you   **952 shull** shall

This Troilus full soon on knees him sette 953
Full soberly, right by her beddes head, 954
And in his beste wise his lady grette. 955
But, Lord, so she wex sodeynliche red! 956
Ne though men sholde smitten off her head 957
She couthe not a word aright out bringe 958
So sodeynly, for his sodeyn cominge. 959

But Pandarus, that so well coulde feele 960
In everything, to play anon began, 961
And saide, "Nece, see how this lord can kneele!
Now, for your trouthe, see this gentle man!" 963
And with that word he for a quysshen ran, 964
And saide, "Kneeleth now, while that you leste, 965
There God your hertes bringe soon at reste!" 966

Can I not seyn, for she bade him not rise, 967
If sorwe it put out of her remembraunce, 968
Or elles that she took it in the wise 969
Of dewete, as for his observaunce; 970
But well find I she did him this pleasaunce, 971
That she him kissed, although she siked sore, 972
And bade him sit adown withouten more. 973

953 him sette set himself   **954 soberly** gravely, demurely.   **by her beddes head** by the head of her bed   **955 grette** greeted.   **956 wex sodeynliche** waxed suddenly   **957 Ne . . . head** Even if men were to smite off her head   **958 couthe** could   **959 for** on account of   **960 so . . . feele** was so perceptive   **961 play** jest   **963 for your trouthe** i e., by your troth. (A mild oath.)   **964 quysshen** cushion   **965 Kneeleth** Kneel.   **while . . . leste** while you please   **966 There . . . bringe** may God bring your hearts   **967 Can . . . rise** I can't say, since she didn't bid him rise   **968 it put** put it   **969 that** if.   **wise** manner, way   **970 dewete** duty.   **as for his observaunce** as a part of his duty to her (in his capacity as her servant in the courtly love relationship)   **971 find I she did** I find (as I look into the history of this love story) that she did   **972 siked sore** sighed sorely   **973 more** more ado.

Quod Pandarus: "Now wol ye well beginne.   974
Now doth him sitte, goode nece deere,   975
Upon your beddes side all there withinne,   976
That each of you the bet may other heere."   977
And with that word he drow him to the feere,   978
And took a light, and fond his contenaunce   979
As for to look upon an old romaunce.   980

Criseyde, that was Troilus' lady right,   981
And clear stood on a ground of sikernesse,   982
All thoughte she her servant and her knight   983
Ne should of right none untruth in her guesse,   984
Yet natheless, considered his distresse,   985
And that love is in cause of swich follye,   986
Thus to him spake she of his jealousy:

"Lo, herte mine, as would the excellence   988
Of love, ageyns the which that no man may   989
Ne ought eke goodly make resistance;   990
And eke because I felte well and say   991
Youre grete truth and service every day,   992
And that your herte all mine was, soth to sayn,   993
This drof me for to rew upon your pain.   994

974 Now . . . beginne i.e., Now you can begin.   **975 doth him sitte**
have him sit   **976 there withinne** i.e., within the bed curtains
977 the bet . . . heere may hear the other better.   **978 drow him to**
drew himself to, approached.   **feere** i.e., fireplace   **979 fond his contenaunce** set his expression, made a show   **980 As . . . upon** as though
he were reading   **981 right** completely   **982 clear . . . sikernesse**
stood on a secure foundation   **983 All thoughte she her** was entirely of
the opinion that her   **984 Ne . . . guesse** by rights should not suspect
any lack of fidelity in her   **985 natheless, considered** nevertheless, having considered   **986 in cause** the cause.   **swich** such   **988–9 as . . .
love** i.e., as love in all its excellence wishes me to do   **989 ageyns the
which that** against which   **990 Ne . . . resistance** nor ought not indeed
to make strong resistance   **991 eke** also.   **felte well and say** was well
aware of and saw   **992 truth** troth, fidelity   **993 soth to sayn** to say
the truth   **994 drof** drove, induced.   **for to rew** to take pity

"And your goodness have I founden alway yit,   995
Of which, my deere herte and all my knight,   996
I thank it you, as fer as I have wit,   997
All can I not as much as it were right;   998
And I, emforth my cunning and my might,   999
Have and ay shall, how sore that me smerte,   1000
Been to you trew and whole with all mine herte;   1001

"And dredeless, that shall be found at preve.   1002
But, herte mine, what all this is to sayne   1003
Shall well be told, so that ye nought you greve,   1004
Though I to you right on yourself complaine.   1005
For therewith mean I finally the paine   1006
That halt your herte and mine in heaviness   1007
Fully to slain, and every wrong redress.   1008

"My goode mine, noot I forwhy ne how   1009
That jealousy, alas, that wicked wyvere,   1010
Thus causeless is croppen into you,   1011
The harm of which I woulde fain delivere.   1012
Alas, that he, all whole, or of him slivere,   1013
Should han his refut in so digne a place.   1014
There Jove him soon out of your herte arace!   1015

995 yit yet   996 all entirely   997 fer far   998 All . . . right albeit I can't thank you as much as I ought   999 emforth to the extent of   1000 ay always.   how . . . smerte how grievously soever it may cause me pain   1001 whole perfect, loyal   1002 dredeless without doubt.   at preve at proof, when tested.   1003 to sayne to say   1004 nought you greve do not grieve yourself at all   1005 right . . . complaine complain in downright fashion of your behavior.   1006–8 therewith . . . slain by that means I intend finally to slay fully the pain that holds your heart and mine in sorrow   1007 halt holds   1009 My goode mine i.e., My dear love   1009–10 noot . . . That I do not know why or how   1010 wyvere viper   1011 Thus . . . you has crept thus without cause into you   1012 woulde fain delivere would glady do away with.   1013 of him slivere even a sliver of him (Jealousy)   1014 han have.   refut refuge.   digne worthy   1015 There . . . arace! May Jove soon root him out of your heart!

"But O thou Jove, O auctour of nature,   1016
Is this an honor to thy deity
That folk unguiltif sufferen hire injure,   1018
And who that guiltif is, all quit goth he?   1019
Oh, were it leful for to plain on thee,   1020
That undeserved sufferest jealousy,   1021
Of that I would upon thee plain and cry!   1022

"Eke all my woe is this, that folk now usen   1023
To sayn right thus: 'Yea, jealousy is love!'   1024
And would a bushel venom all excusen,   1025
For that o grain of love is on it shove.   1026
But that wot heighe God that sit above,   1027
If it be liker love, or hate, or grame;   1028
And after that it oughte bear his name.   1029

"But certain is, some manner jealousy   1030
Is excusable more than some, iwis;   1031
As when cause is, and some swich fantasy   1032
With piety so well repressed is   1033

1016 auctour author, creator · **1018 folk . . . injure** innocent folk
suffer unjust wrongs inflicted on them. **hire** their **1019 who that**
he who. **quit** acquitted **1020 leful** allowable. **plain on thee**
complain against you (Jove) **1021 That . . . jealousy** who permit
undeserved jealousy **1022 upon thee plain** complain against you
1023 Eke Also. **usen** make it a practice **1024 sayn right thus** say
exactly as follows **1025 would . . . excusen** would excuse a bushel of
venom **1026 For that o** because one single. **shove** placed, contained. (People would excuse a whole bushel of jealousy for the one
grain of love in it.) **1027 But . . . above** But God who sits above on
high knows **1028 If it be liker** whether it (jealousy) is more like.
grame anger **1029 after . . . name** it ought to bear the name of what
it most resembles. **1030 some manner** some kinds of **1031 iwis**
to be sure **1032 As . . . is** as when there is genuine cause (for jealousy) **1032–5 and some . . . distresse** or when some jealousy based
in fantasy is so well and dutifully repressed that the sufferer scarcely does
or says anything to offend others, but instead drinks the cup of his own
private sorrow **1032 swich** such.

That it unnethe doth or saith amiss,   1034
But goodly drinketh up all his distresse;   1035
And that excuse I, for the gentilesse.   1036

"And some so full of fury is and despite
That it surmounteth his repressioun.   1038
But, herte mine, ye be not in that plight,
That thank I God; for which your passioun   1040
I woll nought call it but illusioun,
Of habundaunce of love and busy cure,   1042
That doth your herte this disease endure.   1043

"Of which I am right sorry, but nought wroth;   1044
But, for my devoir and your hertes reste,   1045
Whereso you list, by ordeal or by oath,   1046
By sort, or in what wise so you leste,   1047
For love of God, lat preve it for the beste;   1048
And if that I be guiltif, do me deye!   1049
Alas, what might I more done or saye?"   1050

With that a fewe brighte teris newe   1051
Out of her eyen fell, and thus she saide: 1052
"Now God, thou wost, in thought ne deed untrewe   1053
To Troilus was never yet Criseyde."   1054
With that her head down in the bed she laide,

1034 **unnethe** scarcely   1036 **for the gentilesse** for its courteous behavior.   1038 **surmounteth his repressioun** surmounts any attempt
at repression.   1040 **for which** because of which   1042 **Of habundaunce** generated by an oversupply.   **busy cure** attentive and anxious
caring   1043 **doth** causes.   **this disease endure** to endure this grief.
1044 **nought wroth** not at all angry   1045 **for my devoir** i.e., to satisfy the duty I owe   1046 **Whereso you list** wherever you wish.   **ordeal** trial by ordeal   1047 **sort** trial by drawing of lots.   **leste** list, wish
1048 **lat preve it** let it be proven, tested   1049 **do me deye** have me
put to death.   1050 **done** do   1051 **teris** tears   1052 **eyen** eyes
1053 **thou wost** thou knowest   1053–4 **in thought . . . Criseyde**
Criseyde was never yet untrue in thought or deed to Troilus.

And with the sheet it wreigh, and sighte sore,   1056
And held her peace; not o word spake she more.   1057

But now help God to quenchen all this sorwe!
So hope I that He shall, for He best may.
For I have seen, of a full misty morwe   1060
Followen full oft a merry summer's day;
And after winter followeth greene May.
Men seen all day, and readen eke in stories,   1063
That after sharpe showers been victories.   1064

This Troilus, when he her wordes herde,   1065
Have ye no care, him liste not to sleepe;   1066
For it thought him no strokes of a yerde   1067
To hear or seen Criseyde, his lady, weepe;   1068
But well he felt about his herte creepe,   1069
For every tear which that Criseyde asterte,   1070
The cramp of death to strain him by the herte.   1071

And in his mind he gan the time accurse
That he come there, and that he was born;   1073
For now is wikke turned into worse,   1074
And all that labor he hath done biforn   1075
He weened it lost; he thought he nas but lorn.   1076
"O Pandarus," thought he, "alas, thy wile   1077
Serveth of nought, so welaway the while!"   1078

1056 it wreigh covered it.   **sighte sore** sighed sorrowfully   **1057 o**
one.   **1060 of** i.e., after.   **morwe** morning   **1063 seen** see
1064 showers attacks   **1065 herde** heard   **1066 Have ye no care**
i.e., don't you worry, you can be sure.   **him . . . sleepe** he had no desire
to sleep   **1067 it . . . yerde** i.e., it seemed to him no mere blow of
a rod in comparison   **1068 seen** see   **1069 well** very much
1070 tear . . . asterte tear that Criseyde allowed to escape
1071 strain constrain   **1073 come** came   **1074 wikke** wicked,
evil   **1075 biforn** before, earlier   **1076 weened** thought.   **nas but
lorn** was utterly lost, as good as lost.   **1077 wile** guile   **1078 Serveth
of nought** serves for nothing.   **welaway** alas

And therewithal he heng adown the head,   1079
And fell on knees, and sorwfully he sighte.   1080
What might he sayn? He felt he nas but dead,   1081
For wroth was she that should his sorwes lighte.   1082
But natheless, when that he speken mighte,   1083
Then said he thus: "God wot that of this game,   1084
When all is wist, then am I not to blame."   1085

Therewith the sorwe so his herte shette   1086
That from his eyen fell there not a tere,   1087
And every spirit his vigor in knette,   1088
So they astoned or oppressed were.   1089
The feeling of his sorwe, or of his fere,   1090
Or of aught elles, fled was out of town,
And down he fell all sodeynly a-swoon.

This was no little sorwe for to see;
But all was hushed, and Pandar up as faste.   1094
"Oh, nece, peace, or we be lost!" quod he,   1095
"Beth naught aghast!" But certain, at the laste,   1096
For this or that, he into bed him caste,   1097
And said, "O thief, is this a mannes herte?"   1098
And off he rent all to his bare sherte;   1099

1079 **heng adown** hung down   1080 **sighte** sighed.   1081 **might he sayn** could he say.   **nas but dead** was utterly dead   1082 **For . . . lighte** since she who should lighten his sorrows was angry.   1083 **natheless . . . mighte** nevertheless, when he could speak   1084–5 **God . . . blame** God knows that, when all the truth of this business is known, I will be found blameless.   1086 **shette** shut down   1087 **eyen . . . tere** eyes not a tear fell   1088–9 **And . . . were** and every spirit contracted its vigor, so stunned and oppressed were they. (The three spirits that controlled bodily function were associated with the heart, liver, and brain; when they shut down, as here, the result was a swoon.)   1090 **fere** fear   1094 **up as faste** was on his feet as fast as possible.   1095 **nece** niece.   **peace** be calm   1096 **Beth** Be   1097 **For this or that** for one reason or another.   **into . . . caste** threw him into the bed   1098 **thief** i.e., villain, scoundrel. (Here a term of affectionate abuse.)   1099 **off he rent** off he tore (Troilus's clothes)

And saide, "Nece, but ye help us now,   1100
Alas, your owen Troilus is lorn!"   1101
"Iwis, so would I, an I wiste how,   1102
Full fain," quod she. "Alas, that I was born!"   1103
"Yea, nece, woll ye pullen out the thorn
That sticketh in his herte," quod Pandare,
"Say 'all foryeve,' and stint is all this fare."   1106

"Yea, that to me," quod she, "full levere were   1107
Than all the good the sun aboute goth."   1108
And therewithal she sware him in his ere,   1109
"Iwis, my deere herte, I am not wroth,
Have here my truth!" and many another oath;   1111
"Now speak to me, for it am I, Criseyde!"
But all for naught; yet might he not abreyde.   1113

Therewith his pous and palmes of his hondes   1114
They gan to frote, and eke his temples twain;   1115
And to deliveren him from bitter bondes,
She oft him kissed; and shortly for to sayn,   1117
Him to revoken she did all her pain.   1118
And at the last he gan his breath to drawe,
And of his swough soon after that adawe,   1120

And gan bet mind and reason to him take,   1121
But wonder sore he was abayst, iwis.   1122

1100 **but** unless   1101 **owen** own. **lorn** lost.   1102–3 **Iwis . . .
fain** Certainly I would if I knew how, most gladly   1106 **all foryeve**
all is forgiven.   **stint** stinted, ceased.   **fare** ado.   1107 **full levere
were** would be far more desirable   1108 **Than . . . goth** than all the
worldly wealth that the sun goes around.   1109 **him** i.e., Troilus.
ere ear   1111 **truth** troth, vow   1113 **abreyde** awake.
1114 **pous** pulse   1115 **frote** chafe.   **eke** also   1117 **shortly . . .
sayn** to put it briefly   1118 **revoken** recall (from his swoon)
1120 **swough** swoon.   **adawe** to awaken. (Literally, dawn.)
1121 **gan . . . take** began to gather his mind and reason to him better
1122 **wonder** wondrously.   **abayst** abashed

And with a sik, when he gan bet awake,   1123
He said, "O mercy, God, what thing is this?"
"Why do ye with yourselven thus amiss?"   1125
Quod tho Criseyde, "Is this a mannes game?   1126
What, Troilus, wol ye do thus for shame?"

And therewithal her arm over him she laide,
And all foryaf, and ofte time him keste.   1129
He thanked her, and to her spake, and saide
As fell to purpose for his hertes reste;
And she to that answerde him as her leste,   1132
And with her goodly wordes him disporte   1133
She gan, and oft his sorwes to comforte.

1123 sik sigh. **bet** better   **1125 Why . . . amiss?** Why do you
wrong yourself so, behave so wrongly?   **1126 Quod tho** said then
1129 all foryaf forgave all.   **keste** kissed.   **1132 as her leste** as
seemed pleasing to her   **1133 him disporte** to cheer him up

Chaucer wrote *Troilus and Criseyde* in about 1385–1386. Some sixteen
manuscripts are extant, and we appear to have two Chaucerian readings in some lines. This selection, based on Corpus Christi College,
Cambridge, ms. 61, has been lightly modernized in such a way as not to
interfere unduly with Chaucerian pronunciation and scansion: *him* for
hym, yea for *ye, thee* for *the, her* for *hire*, etc.

In the following, the departure from the original text appears in
boldface; the original reading is in roman.

940 up first first up   **941 for the** for   **942 been** beth   **944 honor
may have** may haue honour   **950 ease** eseth   **977 may other** may
980 an and   **1024–5** [partially defective in ms. 61]   **1073 that**
that that [the reading can be defended]   **1091 was** were
1106 stint is stynte   **1115 eke** wete   **1131 hertes** herte

FURTHER READING

❧

Adelman, Janet. " 'This Is and Is Not Cressid': The Characterization of Cressida." *The (M)other Tongue: Essays in Feminist Psychoanalytic Interpretation*, ed. Shirley Nelson Garner, Claire Kahane, and Madelon Sprengnether. Ithaca, N.Y., and London: Cornell Univ. Press, 1985. Finding Cressida's inconstancy paralleled by an inconsistency in characterization, Adelman contends that the play traps an audience in Troilus's psychological need to split Cressida into a betrayer and an idealized, unthreatening lover. The split Troilus requires becomes part of our experience of the play as Cressida's character, initially psychologically complete and available to us, becomes opaque in act 4, scene 4. Thus, our relationship with Cressida breaks down at the same point that Troilus's does, and the play itself enacts Troilus's fantasy.

Bayley, John. "Time and the Trojans." *Essays in Criticism* 25 (1975): 55–73. Rpt. in *Shakespeare, "Troilus and Cressida": A Casebook*, ed. Priscilla Martin. London: Macmillan, 1976. For Bayley, *Troilus and Cressida* strives for dramatic and intellectual effects different from those Shakespeare successfully achieves elsewhere; the play eschews the density of time and character that normally marks Shakespeare's art in favor of a disturbing insistence on present time detached from past and future. The play, according to Bayley, parodies traditional notions of representation and action as it presents a world in which all assurances of selfhood are dissolved.

Berry, Ralph. *"Troilus and Cressida." Changing Styles in Shakespeare*. London: George Allen and Unwin, 1981. In his study of how productions of Shakespearean plays have changed on the modern stage, Berry examines the post–World War II stage history of *Troilus and Cressida* as it reflects theatrical and intellectual movements of the last forty years. Until Peter Hall's 1960 production, Ulysses was usually taken as the moral center of the play; beginning with Hall, however, Ulysses has been seen as an example of the collapse of values, and his speech on "degree" as a self-serving strategy rather than a cultural norm.

Bevington, David. "Editing Informed by Performance History: The Double Ending of *Troilus and Cressida.*" *Shakespeare, Text and Theater: Essays in Honor of Jay Halio.* Newark and London: Univ. of Delaware Press, 1999. Bevington sensitively focuses on the "two dismissals of Pandarus in the Folio text" as evidence of the text perhaps having being adapted for different audiences and different "conditions of performance." If Pandarus leaves the play at the end of 5.3, the play ends on the "bitterly tragic note of Troilus' lament for the death of Hector"; if Pandarus is present at the end, the play is inescapably more satirical, "with Pandarus as the final dispiriting spokesman." Bevington then shows how twentieth-century performance, though in different styles, has tended to find "in Pandarus' sleazy farewell a key to the dispiriting play as a whole," thus adding theatrical support to the bibliographic argument that insists on retaining Pandarus's soliloquy at the end.

Bowen, Barbara. *Gender in the Theater of War: Shakespeare's Troilus and Cressida.* Garland: New York and London, 1993. Bowen's book is a collection of five provocative essays, each providing a different angle on the play. She considers various ways in which the play exists in history, both its own and that of succeeding generations, focusing particularly on issues of war and gender.

Campbell, Oscar James. *Comicall Satyre and Shakepeare's "Troilus and Cressida."* Los Angeles: Huntington Library, 1938. Seeing *Troilus and Cressida* as Shakespeare's single experiment with the genre of "comical satire" invented by Ben Jonson and John Marston, Campbell first traces the development of the new literary form and then focuses on Shakespeare's adaptation of its themes and techniques. Once seen in its proper dramatic context, Campbell claims, *Troilus and Cressida* reveals its ethical dimension, emerging as a satire on the irrational and impassioned codes of love and war that threatened to disrupt the social order of the last years of Elizabeth's reign.

Coghill, Neville. *Shakespeare's Professional Skills*, pp. 78–127. Cambridge, Mass.: Cambridge Univ. Press, 1964. Coghill devotes two chapters of his book to *Troilus and Cressida:* chapter four considers its early performances and texts as they cast light on its nature and meaning, and chapter five offers an analysis of the play's structure. For Coghill, the play is a tragedy of the fall of a great tradition of honor and faith before a new world of force and fraud, and it organizes the conflict between materialism and idealism so that our sympathies rest with the values and fate of Troy.

Foakes, R. A. "Shakespeare and Satirical Comedy." *Shakespeare, the Dark Comedies to the Last Plays: From Satire to Celebration.* Charlottesville: Univ. Press of Virginia, 1971. Attending to the dramatic context and shape of *Troilus and Cressida*, Foakes argues that the play reflects Shakespeare's use of satiric techniques learned from Ben Jonson and John Marston to explore and expand the satiric mode. The play, he finds, is the most balanced of the problem plays, exposing the inadequacies of the heroic and romantic action but preserving the ideals that are betrayed in the play.

Frye, Northrop. "The Reverse Side of Reality." *The Myth of Deliverance: Reflections on Shakespeare's Problem Comedies.* Toronto: Univ. of Toronto Press, 1983. In his study of the problem comedies as enactments of the "myth of deliverance" in which redemptive forces are released by forgiveness and reunification, Frye treats *Troilus and Cressida* as a play in which the ironic emphasis is too powerful to be redeemed by the comic drive. It is a play, Frye contends, that reveals, in its presentation of a disillusioning world of egotism and brutality, not the triumph of deliverance but the need for it.

Jensen, Phoebe. "The Textual Politics of *Troilus and Cressida.*" *Shakespeare Quarterly* 46 (1995): 414–23. Jensen focuses on internal evidence in the text and external information relating to its early printing and performance to consider what kind of play *Troilus and Cressida* in fact is. Focusing especially upon the bibliographic question about the status of the epilogue, she concludes that it should indeed be printed in any edition of the play and that the textual instability it defines, in addition to its tone, makes it "an appropriate ending" for a play that insists on the instability of almost every value that is considered.

Kermode, Frank. " 'Opinion' in *Troilus and Cressida.*" *Teaching the Text,* ed. Susanne Kappeler and Norman Bryson. London: Routledge and Kegan Paul, 1983. Arguing that the play explores the gap between opinion and truth, Kermode first traces the development and semantic range of the word "opinion" and then examines how the term emerges as a preoccupation of the play. *Troilus and Cressida*, Kermode finds, organizes the tensions between opinion and truth into a complex structure that neither yields a simple ethical sense nor fits a particular genre.

Kernan, Alvin B. *The Cankered Muse: Satire of the English Renaissance*, pp. 194–8. New Haven, Conn.: Yale Univ. Press, 1959. Excerpt rpt. in *Shakespeare, "Troilus and Cressida": A Casebook*, ed. Priscilla Martin. London: Macmillan, 1976. In Kernan's seminal study of Renaissance satire, *Troilus and Cressida* appears as a play that explores and criticizes the satiric vision itself. Thersites's perspective represents an extreme, if typical, satiric view of a turbulent world, one that is discovered to be inadequate in the face of the play's dark power. Hector, Troilus, and Ulysses are no better able than Thersites to reform the world of the play, but their efforts, Kernan finds, are at least serious engagements with the world rather than projections of a diseased mind.

Kimbrough, Robert. *Shakespeare's "Troilus and Cressida" and Its Setting.* Cambridge, Mass.: Harvard Univ. Press, 1964. Kimbrough locates *Troilus and Cressida* in its theatrical and literary contexts and finds that the play embraces often contradictory conventions and concerns of both Shakespeare's own public theater and the private stage. The result is not always successful as drama, but the play's formal experimentation, Kimbrough finds, permitted Shakespeare to develop techniques necessary for the great tragedies and final romances and produced a play that, by requiring its audience to view it in a detached, intellectual manner, seems peculiarly and powerfully modern.

Long, Michael. "The Comedy of *Troilus and Cressida*." *The Unnatural Scene: A Study in Shakespearean Tragedy.* London: Methuen, 1976. Provocatively assessing the tone of the play, Long maintains that *Troilus and Cressida* joins the tragic and the absurd, not as a "problem" play, but as a play demanding a derisive laughter that is itself a human value. The play, according to Long, forces an audience to laugh at the images of heroic and romantic pretension even when it is clear that real suffering will be the price of the human ineptness that has been revealed.

Maguire, Laurie E. "Performing Anger: The Anatomy of Abuse(s)." *Renaissance Drama* 31 (2002): 153–83. Noting the long history of critical focus on Cressida's faithlessness, Maguire offers a new answer to the question, "Why does Cressida give Diomedes the love token from Troilus?" Combining modern psychological insights with a careful reading of the text, she finds her answer in Diomedes's abusive manipulation of Cressida, as Shakespeare explores the disturbing dynamics in the scene of power, anger, and abuse.

Ornstein, Robert. *The Moral Vision of Jacobean Tragedy,* pp. 240–9. Madison and Milwaukee: Univ. of Wisconsin Press, 1960. Ornstein treats the play not as comical satire but as a serious if disillusioned study of heroic and romantic aspiration. The play presents ironically and analytically the traditional concerns of tragedy, probing the conflict between the human desire for ideal values and the ego's willingness to accept decadent substitutes.

Presson, Robert K. *Shakespeare's "Troilus and Cressida" and the Legends of Troy.* Madison: Univ. of Wisconsin Press, 1953. Presson's account of Shakespeare's use of his sources in *Troilus and Cressida* centers mainly on his debts to Homer, William Caxton, and Thomas Heywood. Presson argues that Chapman's 1598 translation of seven books of the *Iliad* (and a portion of an eighth) was of central importance in shaping the theme, structure, and characterization of Shakespeare's play, and that study of the sources reveals the play's relationship to the concerns and dramaturgy of Shakespeare's tragedies.

Rabkin, Norman. "*Troilus and Cressida:* The Uses of the Double Plot." *Shakespeare Studies* 1 (1965): 265–82. Rpt. and rev. in *Shakespeare and the Common Understanding.* New York: The Free Press, 1967. Rpt. also in *Essays in Shakespearean Criticism,* ed. James L. Calderwood and Harold E. Toliver. Englewood Cliffs, N.J.: Prentice-Hall, 1970. Focusing on Shakespeare's use of the convention of the double plot in *Troilus and Cressida* to organize the play's complex theme, Rabkin examines the presentation of the love story and the military action as independent but parallel explorations of the subjectivity of value. The two plots are juxtaposed to reveal that value is not what is willed but what is winnowed by the flux of time.

Rossiter, A. P. *"Troilus and Cressida." Angel with Horns and Other Shakespearean Lectures*, ed. Graham Storey. London: Longmans, Green, 1961. Rpt. as "*Troilus* as 'Inquisition' " in *Shakespeare, "Troilus and Cressida": A Casebook*, ed. Priscilla Martin. London: Macmillan, 1976. Rossiter locates the play in the skeptical, Jacobean intellectual environment, engaged by the contradictions rather than the achievements of Renaissance individualism. We see the play as a subtle comedy of deflation; values are debased, as in each of the play's three actions characters consistently act without faith or honor, blinded to their own motives by egotism and impassioned will.

Shaw, George Bernard. *"Troilus and Cressida." Shaw on Shakespeare*, ed. Edwin Wilson. New York: E. P. Dutton, 1961. In a paper presented in 1884 Shaw holds that Shakespeare treats the play's Homeric material "as an iconoclast treats an idol," undermining the claims of heroic virtue that Shakespeare had endorsed in *Henry V* ("It was to expose and avenge his mistake and failure in writing *Henry V* that he wrote *Troilus and Cressida*"). Elsewhere, Shaw notes the modernity of Shakespeare's play: "We find him ready and willing to start at the twentieth century if the seventeenth would only let him."

Taylor, Gary. *"Troilus and Cressida*: Bibliography, Performance, and Interpretation." *Shakespeare Studies* 15 (1982): 99–136. Taylor's analysis of the two substantive texts of *Troilus and Cressida* (the 1609 quarto and the First Folio of 1623) reveals that the Folio version represents a more authoritative version, based on a prompt book of the original productions. Our interpretation of the play's tone and meaning, Taylor argues, is affected by the choice of text: the quarto's epilogue and placement of Troilus's rejection of Pandarus at the end produces a play more alienating and distanced than the Folio's experimental but clearly tragic drama.

MEMORABLE LINES

❧

Measure for Measure

Good counselors lack no clients. (POMPEY 1.2.106–7)

And liberty plucks justice by the nose. (DUKE 1.3.29)

Hence shall we see,
If power change purpose, what our seemers be.

(DUKE 1.3.53–4)

Our doubts are traitors,
And makes us lose the good we oft might win,
By fearing to attempt. (LUCIO 1.4.77–9)

Some rise by sin, and some by virtue fall. (ESCALUS 2.1.38)

My name is Elbow. I do lean upon justice, sir, and do bring in
here before Your good Honor two notorious benefactors.

(ELBOW 2.1.48–50)

ESCALUS   What do you think of the trade, Pompey? Is it a
   lawful trade?
POMPEY   If the law would allow it, sir. (2.1.224–6)

. . . all the souls that were were forfeit once,
And He that might the vantage best have took
Found out the remedy. (ISABELLA 2.2.78–80)

Oh, it is excellent
To have a giant's strength, but it is tyrannous
To use it like a giant. (ISABELLA 2.2.112–14)

But man, proud man,
Dressed in a little brief authority,
Most ignorant of what he's most assured,
His glassy essence, like an angry ape
Plays such fantastic tricks before high heaven
As makes the angels weep. (ISABELLA 2.2.122–7)

Having waste ground enough,
Shall we desire to raze the sanctuary
And pitch our evils there? (ANGELO 2.2.177–9)

Then, Isabel, live chaste, and, brother, die.

(ISABELLA 2.4.185)

Be absolute for death. (DUKE 3.1.5)

Thou hast nor youth nor age,
But as it were an after-dinner's sleep
Dreaming on both. (DUKE 3.1.32–4)

The sense of death is most in apprehension.

(ISABELLA 3.1.77)

Ay, but to die, and go we know not where,
To lie in cold obstruction and to rot . . .

(CLAUDIO 3.1.119–20)

Do not satisfy your resolution with hopes that are fallible.

(DUKE 3.1.170–1)

The hand that hath made you fair hath made you good.

(DUKE 3.1.182–3)

Oh, what may man within him hide,
Though angel on the outward side! (DUKE 3.2.264–5)

Craft against vice I must apply. (DUKE 3.2.270)

[Song]   Take, oh, take those lips away,
     That so sweetly were forsworn . . . (BOY 4.1.1–2)

I am a kind of burr; I shall stick. (LUCIO 4.3.177)

My business in this state
Made me a looker-on here in Vienna. (DUKE 5.1.324–5)

Haste still pays haste, and leisure answers leisure;
Like doth quit like, and measure still for measure.

(DUKE 5.1.418–19)

They say best men are molded out of faults,
And, for the most, become much more the better
For being a little bad. (MARIANA 5.1.447–9)

What's mine is yours, and what is yours is mine.

(DUKE 5.1.548)

MEMORABLE LINES

❧

All's Well That Ends Well

Love all, trust a few,
Do wrong to none. Be able for thine enemy
Rather in power than use, and keep thy friend
Under thy own life's key. Be checked for silence
But never taxed for speech. (COUNTESS 1.1.64–8)

Our remedies oft in ourselves do lie
Which we ascribe to heaven. (HELENA 1.1.216–217)

"Was this fair face the cause," quoth she,
   "Why the Grecians sackèd Troy?" (LAVATCH 1.3.70–1)

My friends were poor but honest. (HELENA 1.3.192)

Oft expectation fails, and most oft there
Where most it promises. (HELENA 2.1.144–5)

Methinks in thee some blessèd spirit doth speak
His powerful sound within an organ weak.

(KING 2.1.177–8)

Oh, Lord, sir! (LAVATCH 2.2.40)

They say miracles are past. (LAFEW 2.3.1)

"When thou canst get the ring upon my finger, which never
shall come off, and show me a child begotten of thy body that
I am father to, then call me husband." (LETTER 3.2.57–60)

Oh, for the love of laughter, let him fetch his drum.

(SECOND LORD 3.6.34–5)

Let us essay our plot, which, if it speed,
Is wicked meaning in a lawful deed,
And lawful meaning in a lawful act. (HELENA 3.7.44–6)

The web of our life is of a mingled yarn, good and ill together.

(FIRST LORD 4.3.70–1)

Who cannot be crushed with a plot?   (PAROLLES 4.3.327)

There's place and means for every man alive.

(PAROLLES 4.3.341)

All's well that ends well. Still the fine's the crown;
Whate'er the course, the end is the renown.

(HELENA 4.4.35–6)

I am a man whom Fortune hath cruelly scratched.

(PAROLLES 5.2.27–8)

                    Praising what is lost
Makes the remembrance dear.   (KING 5.3.19–20)

Th' inaudible and noiseless foot of Time . . .   (KING 5.3.42)

Because he's guilty, and he is not guilty.
He knows I am no maid, and he'll swear to't;
I'll swear I am a maid, and he knows not.

(DIANA 5.3.290–2)

MEMORABLE LINES

❧

Troilus and Cressida

I cannot come to Cressid but by Pandar.   (TROILUS 1.1.98)

Upon my back to defend my belly, upon my wit to defend my
wiles, upon my secrecy to defend mine honesty, my mask to
defend my beauty, and you to defend all these.

(CRESSIDA 1.2.262–5)

Men prize the thing ungained more than it is.

(CRESSIDA 1.2.291)

Therefore this maxim out of love I teach:
Achievement is command; ungained, beseech.

(CRESSIDA 1.2.294–5)

The specialty of rule hath been neglected.   (ULYSSES 1.3.78)

The heavens themselves, the planets, and this center
Observe degree, priority, and place.   (ULYSSES 1.3.85–6)

        Oh, when degree is shaked,
Which is the ladder of all high designs,
The enterprise is sick.   (ULYSSES 1.3.101–3)

Take but degree away, untune that string,
And hark what discord follows. Each thing meets
In mere oppugnancy.   (ULYSSES 1.3.109–11)

Then everything includes itself in power,
Power into will, will into appetite;
And appetite, an universal wolf,
So doubly seconded with will and power,
Must make perforce an universal prey
And last eat up himself.   (ULYSSES 1.3.119–24)

. . . who wears his wit in his belly and his guts in his head . . .

(THERSITES 2.1.74–5)

There is a law in each well-ordered nation
To curb those raging appetites that are
Most disobedient and refractory.   (HECTOR 2.2.180–2)

If Helen then be wife to Sparta's king,
As it is known she is, these moral laws
Of nature and of nations speak aloud
To have her back returned.   (HECTOR 2.2.183–6)

Why, there you touched the life of our design!
    (TROILUS 2.2.194)

He that is proud eats up himself. Pride is his own glass, his
own trumpet, his own chronicle.
    (AGAMEMNON 2.3.153–5)

I am giddy; expectation whirls me round.   (TROILUS 3.2.17)

        for to be wise and love
Exceeds man's might; that dwells with gods above.
    (CRESSIDA 3.2.155–6)

Let all constant men be Troiluses, all false women Cressids,
and all brokers-between Pandars!   (PANDARUS 3.2.201–3)

Time hath, my lord, a wallet at his back,
Wherein he puts alms for oblivion,
A great-sized monster of ingratitudes.
    (ULYSSES 3.3.146–8)

        Perseverance, dear my lord,
Keeps honor bright.   (ULYSSES 3.3.151–2)

For beauty, wit,
High birth, vigor of bone, desert in service,
Love, friendship, charity, are subjects all
To envious and calumniating Time.
One touch of nature makes the whole world kin.
    (ULYSSES 3.3.172–6)

This is the most despiteful gentle greeting,
The noblest hateful love, that e'er I heard of.
    (PARIS 4.1.34–5)

There is no help.
The bitter disposition of the time
Will have it so.   (PARIS 4.1.49–51)

For every false drop in her bawdy veins
A Grecian's life hath sunk; for every scruple
Of her contaminated carrion weight
A Trojan hath been slain.   (DIOMEDES 4.1.71–4)

How my achievements mock me!   (TROILUS 4.2.71)

The kiss you take is better than you give.   (CRESSIDA 4.5.39)

Set them down
For sluttish spoils of opportunity
And daughters of the game.   (ULYSSES 4.5.62–4)

Now, the rotten diseases of the south, the guts-griping, ruptures, catarrhs, loads o' gravel i' th' back, lethargies, cold
palsies, raw eyes, dirt-rotten livers, wheezing lungs . . . take
and take again such preposterous discoveries!

(THERSITES 5.1.17–24)

This fault in us I find:
The error of our eye directs our mind.

(CRESSIDA 5.2.112–13)

Lechery, lechery, still wars and lechery; nothing else holds
fashion.   (THERSITES 5.2.198–9)

SEE YOUR BOOKSELLER FOR THESE
BANTAM CLASSICS

EARLY AFRICAN-AMERICAN CLASSICS, 0-553-21379-2
FIFTY GREAT SHORT STORIES, 0-553-27745-6
FIFTY GREAT AMERICAN SHORT STORIES, 0-553-27294-2
SHORT SHORTS, 0-553-27440-6
GREAT AMERICAN SHORT STORIES, 0-440-33060-2
SHORT STORY MASTERPIECES, 0-440-37864-8
THE VOICE THAT IS GREAT WITHIN US, 0-553-26263-7
THE BLACK POETS, 0-553-27563-1
THREE CENTURIES OF AMERICAN POETRY, (Trade) 0-553-37518-0,
   (Hardcover) 0-553-10250-8

THE BARD FOR A NEW GENERATION

The New Bantam Classic
Shakespeare Editions

Available 1/25/2005:

Hamlet
0-553-21292-3 • $4.99

Henry IV, Part One
0-553-21293-1 • $4.99

King Lear
0-553-21297-4 • $4.99

Merchant of Venice
0-553-21299-0 • $4.99

Available 3/1/2005:

As You Like It
0-553-21290-7 • $4.99

Julius Caesar
0-553-21296-6 • $4.99

Macbeth
0-553-21298-2 • $4.99

A Midsummer Night's Dream
0-553-21300-8 • $4.99

Much Ado About Nothing
0-553-21301-6 • $4.99

Othello
0-553-21302-4 • $4.99

Available 3/29/2005:

Four Comedies
0-553-21281-8 • $6.99

Four Tragedies
0-553-21283-4 • $6.99

Henry V
0-553-21295-8 • $4.99

The Taming of the Shrew
0-553-21306-7 • $4.99

Twelfth Night
0-553-21308-3 • $4.99

Available 1/31/2006:

A Comedy of Errors
0-553-21291-5 • $4.99

Richard II
0-553-21303-2 • $6.99

Richard III
0-553-21304-0 • $6.99

The Tempest
0-553-21307-5 • $4.99

Available 2/28/2006:

Three Plays: Measure for Measure, All's Well That Ends Well, Troilus and Cressida
0-553-21287-7 • $6.99

Ask for these titles wherever books are sold.

www.bantamshakespeare.com